For Carolyn & Muriel:

By the time you
finish reading this
one you will be
grateful that ours
is one of the
smaller faiths.

Sincerely,
DWF

THE RIVERS OF PARADISE

THE RIVERS OF PARADISE

Moses, Buddha, Confucius, Jesus, and Muhammad
as Religious Founders

Edited by

David Noel Freedman _and_ Michael J. McClymond

Foreword by

Hans Küng

WILLIAM B. EERDMANS PUBLISHING COMPANY
GRAND RAPIDS, MICHIGAN / CAMBRIDGE, U.K.

Wm. B. Eerdmans Publishing Company
255 Jefferson Ave. S.E., Grand Rapids, Michigan 49503 /
P.O. Box 163, Cambridge CB3 9PU U.K.

Printed in the United States of America

05 04 03 02 01   5 4 3 2 1

Library of Congress Cataloging-in-Publication Data

The rivers of paradise: Moses, Buddha, Confucius, Jesus, and Muhammad
as religious founders / edited by David Noel Freedman and Michael J. McClymond.
p.   cm.
Includes bibliographical references.
ISBN 0-8028-4540-1 (alk. paper)
1. Religious biography. 2. Religions.   I. Freedman, David Noel, 1922–   .
II. McClymond, Michael James, 1958–   .

BL72.R58 2001
291.6′3 — dc21
00-063665

www.eerdmans.com

Contents

CONTENTS

Foreword

HANS KÜNG

"Paradise lost," yes, but now "Paradise rediscovered" through this volume. I am grateful to my long-time friend and former colleague at Ann Arbor for his creative and inspiring approach to the history of religions. It is indeed suggestive how David Noel Freedman relates the symbolism of the five rivers of Paradise to the major religious systems. I am fascinated by his approach, the more so as I also have analyzed the history of religions according to three major "currents" or, better, "river systems": the prophetic Semitic religions, Judaism, Christianity, and Islam; the mystical Indian religions, Buddhism and Hinduism; and the Chinese wisdom religions, Confucianism and Daoism.

Over the millennia these great religious systems have shaped the cultural landscape of the globe in a way that is older, stronger, and more constant than many dynasties and empires. And just as, in an incessant rhythm of change, new mountain massifs and high plateaus sporadically rise on the various continents while great rivers, older, stronger, and more constant, continually cut their way through the rising landscape, so again and again, while new social systems erect states and ruling houses, the old great rivers of the religions constantly find a way through — despite all the rises and falls — and shape the features of the landscape of culture in a new way.

What is new today is the need for these religious river systems to flow in harmony with each other in order to irrigate our earth with peace.

After forty years of study and experience, I am fully aware of the weaknesses and dark sides of all religions. Yet, I still do not think that it is useful to propagate, in the style of Samuel Huntington, the "clash of civilizations" and cultures, simply because we no longer have the old East-West confrontation.

Nor is it useful to present Islam as a force against which we should pit ourselves in a confrontational way:

- The "clash theory" is too simplistic. It fails to notice that antagonisms within one religion or civilization tend in many cases to be stronger than those between religions. Tensions within Islam are often greater than tensions between Islam and the West. The most recent wars were fought between rivals belonging to the same culture: Iran-Iraq, Somalia, Rwanda, Ireland, Ethiopia-Eritrea.
- The "clash theory" promotes thinking in blocs. It delimits the seven or eight "civilizations" from each other as if they were monoliths and did not in most situations overlap, interact, and even intermingle, as is the case in British, continental European, and North American cities. Islam is erroneously taken to be a bloc, anti-Western, a replacement for the old Eastern bloc as a natural enemy.
- The "clash theory" takes no notice of commonalities. Everywhere it emphasizes the antagonisms of cultures without even considering basic commonalities, including those among Christianity, Judaism, and Islam.

I therefore disagree with Huntington's main conclusion that there is an unavoidable "clash of civilizations or religions." I strongly argue and passionately work for an alternative: a dialogue among cultures on the basis of the project of a global ethic ("Projekt Weltethos") for which I laid the foundation almost two decades ago in the book *Christianity and the World Religions* (1984) under the slogan "No world peace without religious peace." This project pursues a strategy that aims at preventing a "clash of civilizations." Along these lines, the United Nations has taken the timely initiative to proclaim the year 2001 the "International Year of Dialogue among Civilizations."

It is of course depressing to realize that the world religions often do not function as the great midwives of a new world era as they could, but rather as the great hinderers and disturbers of world peace. Yet, despite this, we must never abandon the hope that peace among the religions is possible. It is the prerequisite for peace among the nations of the world. I do not mean the unity of the world religions. Unity among the Christian churches is possible on the basis of their common belief in Jesus Christ. But as for example the basis of Judaism is the Torah, and of Islam the Koran, each of the world religions has a very different basis; they cannot build a unity. The world would however be much improved if the world religions would live in peace together, in dialogue and solidarity with one another. The new constructive relationship between Christians and Jews can be exemplary for other religions. For *there will be no peace among the nations and civilizations without peace among the religions.*

To be sure, we live in a world and a time in which peace is threatened in many countries by every possible kind of religious fundamentalism, whether Christian, Muslim, Jewish, Buddhist, or Hindu. Such fundamentalism is often less rooted in religion than in social misery, in reaction to Western secularization, and in the need for a basic orientation in life.

My response to this challenge is this: *there will be no peace between the religions without a dialogue between the religions.* Peace *(shalom, salaam, eirene, pax)* is a central feature in the system of most religions. Their first task in our age should be to make peace with one another. By every means, including those now offered by the media in cases like the former Yugoslavia, the religions must give priority to implementing those measures that create trust, specifically:

- clearing up misunderstandings
- healing traumatic memories
- dissolving hostile stereotypes
- coming to terms with conflicts caused by guilt in societies and individuals
- breaking down hatred and destructiveness
- reflecting on what is held in common
- offering positive models

Only if they implement this demanding program can the rivers of the religions become rivers of paradise. This new book is a step on the journey, and I wish this volume many readers.

HANS KÜNG
Tübingen, July 2000

Introduction: The Rivers of Paradise

DAVID NOEL FREEDMAN

*And a river goes forth from Eden to water the Garden. And from there
it divides itself and becomes four headwaters. The name of the first is
PISHON. It is the one that surrounds the whole land of the Havilah,
where the gold is. And the gold of that land is [very] fine. There is
bdellium and the Shoham stone. The name of the second river is
GIHON. It is the one that surrounds the whole land of Cush. And the
name of the third river is HIDDEKEL (TIGRIS); it is the one that
runs East of Asshur. And the fourth river is the PERAT (EUPHRA-
TES).*

(GENESIS 2:10-14)

The idea for this book is derived from the passage in the book of Genesis
that describes the Rivers of Paradise. Actually, according to the account, a
single unnamed river flows out of Eden to irrigate the Garden, and from there it
branches into four "heads" or tributaries, which are also called "rivers." This
original source-river is situated in Eden itself, where it waters the Garden. Only
after flowing through the Garden does it subdivide into four tributaries. These
rivers, in turn, run to different parts of the world, in some cases at least forming
territorial boundaries around whole lands.

Of these four subsidiary rivers, the latter two are well known major waterways of Mesopotamia (the name of which is derived from its location between them), while the identification of the first two remains doubtful and subject to considerable debate. Thus the Tigris and Euphrates dominate the
landscape of the Near East, the Land in the midst of the Two Rivers. The first

1

two rivers, the Pishon and the Gihon, are described in the text in similar fashion; and since they go around whole countries, they should be regarded as comparable in size and importance to the well-known pair. The Land of Cush is often identified with Ethiopia in the Bible, although this identification is not accepted by many scholars, who point out that the name Cush may also be applied to a region of Mesopotamia. A number of scholars accept the identification of the Pishon with the Nile, or one of its major branches. And there is even less agreement about the Pishon's presumed association with the land of the Havilah, often located on the Arabian peninsula. For the purposes of our parable or allegory, however, there is no need to solve any of these puzzles, as both clarity, as represented by the third and fourth rivers, and obscurity, as represented by the first and second rivers, are integral parts of the proposed schema.

We wish to use the *five* rivers of Paradise — the source or fountainhead and its four branches — as a model or pattern for the great personality religions of the world: their origins, development, history, and destiny. We could use the word "prophetic" as well, if we extended the scope and range of the term beyond the biblical definitions and categories to include the variety of features or qualities we associate with religious leaders: charismatic personality, authoritative teaching, organizational genius. Other requirements for our analogy or extended metaphor would include the tenacity or persistence of the religion associated with the founder, its size in numbers and geographic spread in the world, and its weight or importance in human affairs. Only those religions qualifying in all or most of these categories will be considered. Since we are operating in literary or metaphoric terms, we allow ourselves considerable freedom in adaptation and accommodation. No pretense is made of an organic or intrinsic connection between the model and geographic and historical reality.

In my judgment, only five major religions or religious communities, corresponding to the five rivers of Paradise in our picture, qualify for consideration in this exercise, religions that meet the requisite criteria: originating in and centering around the person, the life and experience, of a single individual — as it happens all of them men. We can connect each of these religious leaders and their communities with a corresponding River of Paradise, using the order in which the latter are listed in Genesis to conform to the chronological order of appearance in history of the religious leaders:

The first river, although unnamed, is nevertheless the source of all the others, and hence of prime importance. The earliest of the great world religions with which we wish to deal is represented by the figure of Moses, whose life story and teaching are enshrined in the Hebrew Bible, and whose religious community is embodied in the historic people of Israel and the ongoing Jewish community. The criteria mentioned earlier are met by the imposing figure of Moses himself, whose authoritative teaching is preserved in the Hebrew Bible, and successful survival of the religious community deriving from the Exodus from Egypt and the Wilderness Wandering. If a question is raised about the limited size of the existing Jewish community worldwide (the geographic spread easily meets the standard), the actual numbers, while small in comparison with the other religious communities to be discussed, is nevertheless substantial (perhaps 20,000,000 worldwide). More important, the power and influence of Mosaic religion are to be recognized in the offshoots or tributaries, the daughter religions which flow from the mainstream: Christianity and Islam, whose connections with the Hebrew Bible are transparent.

Now that we have mentioned these offshoot religions, let us proceed directly and diachronically to known quantities and connections, namely Jesus of Nazareth and Muhammad (Mohammed) and the major religious communities associated with their names and teachings — Christianity and Islam. These are great worldwide communions with hundreds of millions of adherents, powerful, persistent. Since both of these religions began in the Near East, where their founders were born and lived out their lives, and since they are also the most recent religions conforming to our criteria, we may appropriately connect them with the last two rivers in our list, the two great rivers of Mesopotamia, namely, the Tigris for Christianity and the Euphrates for Islam. We don't wish to press the geographic affinities or affiliations, since neither religion originated in the immediate neighborhood of either river, but both pairs, of rivers and religions, are rooted in the same geographic area, and both sets seem assured of permanence and persistence.

That leaves us with two rivers and two religions for which to give an account. Just as the remaining rivers so far defy clear location and identification, the religions we are about to list, while prominent and presumably permanent parts of the world scene, do not show the clear lines of linkage and filiation that are demonstrable for the three already mentioned. As for the religions, we can hardly avoid naming the major prophetic personality religions of India and China, founded independently but almost simultaneously in the late 6th century B.C.E. by Siddhartha Gautama (Buddhism) and Kung-Fu-tzu (Confucianism) respectively.

While any possible links between these religions and the Mosaic source are remote and matters of some speculation and contention, that circumstance of uncertainty shrouded in mystery is comparable to the murkiness surrounding the first two tributary rivers in the Genesis account (the Pishon and the Gihon) in regard to their identification and location. We might easily find great rivers in both India and China to associate with the founding and spread of Buddhism and Confucianism respectively, and then identify one or another of them with the mysterious rivers of Genesis 2:11, 13, but there is no need to pursue the matter further. The association remains metaphoric and parabolic.

3

We may summarize and correlate our findings on the rivers and the religions as follows:

1. The Source River: The Founding Father: Moses
   (ca. 1200 B.C.E.)
   The Sacred Writing: The Hebrew Bible
   The Religion: Judaism

2. The First Tributary: THE PISHON
   The Founding Father: Buddha
   (563-483 B.C.E.)
   The Sacred Writing: Buddhist Scriptures
   The Religion: Buddhism

3. The Second Tributary: THE GIHON
   The Founding Father: Confucius
   (551-479 B.C.E.)
   The Sacred Writing: Analects, etc.
   The Religion: Confucianism

4. The Third Tributary: THE TIGRIS
   The Founding Father: Jesus Christ
   (6 B.C.E.–30 C.E.)
   The Sacred Writing: New Testament
   The Religion: Christianity

5. The Fourth Tributary: THE EUPHRATES
   The Founding Father: Muhammad
   (570-632 C.E.)
   The Sacred Writing: The Koran (Qur'an)
   The Religion: Islam

The chronological pattern is curious and impressive. Without pressing the matter for precision, and by citing it more for mnemonic reasons and purposes rather than regarding it as somehow predetermined or predestined, we nevertheless point to a certain regularity or periodicity in the appearance of the founding fathers on the world-scene and the emergence of the religions associated with them. We can speak in round terms of a 600-year cycle that begins with Moses around 1200 B.C.E. (the outer limits for his life would be 1260 to 1140 B.C.E., based upon the tradition in the Bible that he lived for 120 years, unlikely perhaps, but not impossible as we know from both ancient records of the

4

Egyptian pharaohs and modern experience with long-lived people in Japan and France, both of whom reached that age). On the basis of the biblical and archaeological evidence, I think we can place Moses' activity in the first half of the 12th century, in all likelihood during the reign of the great Pharaoh of the Twentieth Dynasty, Rameses III.

Approximately 600 years later, the two founders of world religions, Buddha and Confucius, appeared on the world-scene in India and China respectively. Buddha was born around 563 B.C.E., and Confucius was born a dozen years later. Both died in the first quarter of the 5th century B.C.E. (Buddha in 483 and Confucius just four years later in 479 B.C.E.), their lives and active careers overlapping chronologically in large measure, although there is no evidence that either was aware of the other. It is even less likely that they ever met.

As many have noted, in the era in which they flourished, there was an extraordinary burst of intellectual activity in the arts, sciences, philosophy, and religion across the whole known world. Especially in Israel and Greece, outstanding personalities appeared on the scene: e.g., the great biblical prophets of the 7th-6th century — Jeremiah, Ezekiel, and Exilic Isaiah among others in Judah and Babylon, while Greece and Ionia produced major pre-Socratic philosophers such as Heraclitus, Anaxagoras, Democritus, etc., but especially a man like Pythagoras, mathematician and mystic, who founded a long-enduring religious fellowship.

Jesus Christ was born approximately 1,200 years after Moses (or when Moses' career as religious leader began) and somewhat less than 600 years after the births of Buddha and Confucius. Muhammad came along nearly 600 years after the birth of Jesus, and his death occurred almost exactly 600 years after that of Jesus (632 C.E., while Jesus probably died in 30 C.E.). We may diagram the data as follows:

MOSES (ca. 1200)

6th cent.: BUDDHA   PROPHETS   CONFUCIUS

1st cent.:   JESUS

MUHAMMAD (ca. 600)

The periodic pattern in which religious leaders appear on the scene every 600 years or so is very impressive. Equally impressive to this observer is that the cycle had a beginning with Moses and an apparent end with Muhammad. While a cycle extending over 1,800 years is extraordinary, the lapse since then, the failure of a world-class religious leader to come and found a new religious community, is equally impressive. What I am driving at is that the labors and achievements of these five men (and their followers) have defined not only for the times in which they lived and thereafter, but to the present and perhaps for the foreseeable future the framework and parameters of the religious situation in the world. Just as no previous religious leader or founding father (or mother) is known to us today through the existence and vital presence and activity of a religious community (Abraham, as the spiritual ancestor of the three great monotheistic faiths mentioned earlier, might be considered as a worthy candidate, especially if we could fix his dates around 1800 B.C.E., or conceivably around 2400 B.C.E., but there is no Abrahamic community as such, apart from the three religious communities mentioned), in the same way, no one subsequent to Muhammad has achieved in the religious sphere anything comparable to the five men we have identified as founding fathers. There is no shortage of possible candidates, and many significant and important religious innovators, initiators, and inaugurators have come and gone, made their impact, and left their imprint on communities and societies related to them. But none has succeeded in entering the elect and elite group we have identified, much less in replacing any of them.

We may consider a few failed candidates: (1) Certainly Zoroaster qualifies as a founding father, a prophet who had a powerful impact on his hearers. He left behind a Sacred Writing of great importance, and a community that grew and prospered over the centuries, being ascendant in the Persian Empire for a long time. His teachings exerted a profound influence on other mainstream religions, as we know, but in the end, the community he founded has foundered and today has few adherents. There seems to be no serious prospect of a revival in our world. So we reluctantly rule out Zoroaster and his movement. (2) Another possibility would be Mani, the reputed founder of Manichaeism. Much the same can be said of him and his movement. For a time, even a long time, it exerted a powerful influence in the world and among its religious communities, but as a movement it has all but disappeared. (3) If we turn to the modern world and recent times, we find a plethora of religious communities scattered across the continents, and it is always possible that one or another of them will emerge as a distinctive separate component in the spectrum of religions of the world. In my judgment, at least, none has yet qualified, although several have made an important impact and will bear watching for future developments. What about Bahai or several other religious movements that began in the 19th century (the era of 1800 in our cycle). Probably it is still too early to tell whether any one or more of them will emerge as separate powerful and permanent movements in the religious landscape. From this perspective, it doesn't look as though any will, chiefly because the founding figure (whether father or mother) hasn't captured the interest and recognition of that wider public, beyond the confines of the movement itself. There is also the question whether any of these many movements that have emerged within the bounds of established groups, especially in Christianity or Islam, for example, no matter how active and dynamic they become, will also be able to separate themselves or become separate entities in their own right, rather than being part of one of the larger movements. Separate identity or identification is also a requirement for listing among the great religions of the world.

If we look in particular at the period around 1200 c.e. and 1800 c.e. for signs of such a leader and such a movement, we find a sizable number of worthy candidates that are worthy of consideration and evaluation. Among the biblical religions, there was an extraordinary flowering of theological formulation and synthesis associated with figures such as Maimonides (Rambam) in Judaism and Thomas Aquinas in Christianity. I am sure that before and during the same period, there were Muslim scholars and thinkers of equal rank, who blazed the trail, combining Greek philosophy and revealed religion, and setting new high standards for philosophical theology. At the same time, a person like St. Francis of Assisi embodied in his life and teachings the ideals of Christian virtue in a way rarely matched and probably never exceeded. But in the end, we do not find the necessary qualifications for inclusion in our privileged circle: the outstanding individual innovator, founder of a separate movement, or which becomes separate, and which gains its distinct population, independent power, and becomes a permanent part of the religious landscape.

The same may be said of the era around 1800. We find innovative religious movements all over the world, including among others, Mormonism, Seventh-Day Adventism, and Christian Science in our own country, as well as others elsewhere, including Bahai. So far, at least, none has succeeded either in throwing off the yoke of the parent community or in establishing a dominant position comparable to the established members of the guild. While it may still be premature to make a pronouncement on any or all of them, it is true of the established handful that they made their move and their mark within a hundred or two hundred years of their founding. Therefore time is running out for the 1800 c.e. entries.

Under the circumstances, we think that for the world today and perhaps for the foreseeable future, we have these five, no more and no less, to reckon with. While the possible variations and combinations within and between and among the established units are almost infinite in number, especially in this age of interactive global and instantaneous communication, the outer framework will remain the same, as will the most important ingredients in and contributed by each of these movements.

What we propose in this book is to study and present each of the great prophetic personality religions in terms of its founder, the governing principles

7

and beliefs, and in brief compass, its history from the founding until now. Regarding the last component, only the major actors and actions can be presented, and as much as the material will allow, on a 600-year cycle, the latter offering a synchronic synthesis along with the normal diachronic treatment of each religion. Thus the effort will be made to present Moses, Buddha, Confucius, Jesus, and Muhammad and their movements in 600-year sequences from the beginning of each movement until the present time, with a synthesis in the form of a Summary of the present world situation. Apart from recording and presenting an interesting human phenomenon, namely, religion in the human experience, what is the purpose of the exercise? Taking a slogan from Hans Küng, we start with the affirmation that "Unless there is peace among the religions of the world, there will be no peace among the nations." Or: "There can be no peace among the nations unless there is peace among the religions." When we look around the hot spots of the world today, we see deeply embedded in the severe political and military conflicts a deeply entrenched religious component: e.g., in Ireland where Catholics and Protestants have been at odds for centuries; in Kashmir, where the conflict between Muslims and Hindus has deep religious roots; Bosnia and other parts of former Yugoslavia, where Muslims and Christians, Catholic and Orthodox, are often engaged in a three-cornered battle; the Near East, where Muslims and Jews have been warring for years, with Christians often involved in the conflict on one side or the other, not to speak of the divisions between Orthodox and Catholic, and others.

The religions of the world, in spite of ample protestations concerning their peaceful virtues, have shown a propensity for battling to the limit within their own communities, as well as across religious lines. In view of actual history, and the evident verdict of divine providence, these five religions, at least, having been with us for between 1,400 and 3,200 years, are going to be with us for a long time to come. So the first lesson is to learn to accept that model, one of diversity and plurality, and therefore to try to live in harmony with that scheme, and to be at peace with one another. So each must accept the permanent existence of the others, and that could lead to a civilized and intelligent discourse and interaction, which would no doubt produce positive results for everyone concerned, including saving lives, fortunes, and enormous resources of energy and enthusiasm. We can all learn much from the wisdom and experience of the others. No one knows what the future will bring, but it cannot fail to be better than the past or present if the forces of religion are used to make peace and promote good will, rather than in exacerbating and prolonging hostilities.

Going back to the picture of the Rivers of Paradise, we started with the somewhat anomalous circumstance of a source river dividing itself into four tributaries, each of which then goes its own way. The real situation in the geography of the world is more or less the opposite. In the great riverine systems, tributaries flow into rather than out of main streams, which proceed on to their destinations in the great seas of the world. Thus the Mississippi River in our country drains a vast basin from north to south, being fed by tributary rivers on both sides, e.g., the Ohio, itself the product of a vast tributary system flowing into the Mississippi from the East, while the mighty Missouri joins the Mississippi from the West. If we try to impose a real picture on the imagined one in the book of Genesis, we might come out in the following fashion: It may be that the flow of the biblical rivers from one source into many streams will be reversed and they will flow back into the main stream from which they came. Or more likely the rivers will continue on their courses and finally empty into the same ocean, in the direction of which they are all moving. Beginning from the same original source and moving inexorably to the same ultimate destination, they will end where they started, from the original source to the ultimate goal: the ground of being and the director of destiny. By whatever stream or path we go our way, we share a common origin and we will meet at a common endpoint.

The Rivers of Paradise came from Eden, which is also where the journey will end.

Moses, Torah, and Judaism

CARL S. EHRLICH

Introduction

Moses

Among the religious traditions discussed in this book, indeed among the so-called "world religions," Judaism is both historically the oldest and numerically the smallest. These two circumstances, combined with the influence Judaism has had on the development of Christianity and Islam, have lent to Judaism a significance on the world stage that is much greater than a simple reckoning of adherents would seem to indicate.

Although it traces its lineage back to a common ancestor, Abraham, who, according to the biblical chronologies, lived some four thousand years ago and was the first to enter into a personal relationship with the one universal God worshiped by Jews,[1] Judaism views Moses, who is said to have lived over half a millennium later, led his enslaved people out of Egypt, and gave them the divine laws that serve as the basis of Jewish life and practice, as its founding fig-

---

1. See Gen. 12–25.

The following abbreviations will be used in this chapter: *ABD* = David Noel Freedman, ed., *The Anchor Bible Dictionary*, 6 vols. (New York, London, Toronto, Sydney, Auckland: Doubleday, 1992); *ANET* = James B. Pritchard, ed., *Ancient Near Eastern Texts Relating to the Old Testament*, 3rd ed. with supplement (Princeton: Princeton University Press, 1969). In addition, the names of tractates from the Babylonian Talmud will be preceded by the letters *BT.*

ure. While the Jewish religion has, in analogy with Christianity, occasionally been referred to as the Mosaic faith, this is a misnomer that apotheosizes Moses in a manner out of keeping with Jewish tradition. In spite of the fact that Judaism is a complex phenomenon about which it is difficult to make generalizations, since one is almost always sure to find in the wealth of Jewish writings proof texts to support diametrically opposed contentions, it can be claimed that the Jewish Moses does not attain the divine status accorded Jesus in the Christian tradition. Although the figure of Jesus is in part based on that of Moses,[2] and although later Jewish tradition has often conceived of Moses in terms that may have been borrowed from Christianity,[3] Judaism has maintained the distinction between the object of worship, namely, God, and the major source of the revelation concerning the divine. Hence, Judaism is not a religion based on the adulation of Moses, but on the worship of God. Moses may have been the first and greatest mediator of divine revelation, but Jewish tradition is quite clear concerning his humanity, perfect in its imperfection.[4]

The unique status of Moses in the development of Judaism is encapsulated at the beginning of the talmudic tractate *Avot*:[5] "Moses received the Torah at Sinai and transmitted it to Joshua, Joshua to the Elders, and the Elders to the Prophets, and the Prophets to the men of the Great Synagogue."[6] In this passage the compiler of this beloved collection of pithy rabbinic sayings is attempting to establish an unbroken line of authority from Moses, the beginning of the unbroken chain of Jewish tradition, down to the time of his[7] own spiritual pro-

2. See, e.g., David M. Hay, "Moses through New Testament Spectacles," *Interpretation* 44 (1990): 240-52, who argues against a facile depiction of Jesus as a second Moses while conceding nonetheless that there are some clear points of contact and influence.

3. See, e.g., Avigdor Shinan, *The World of the Aggadah,* translated from the Hebrew by John Glucker (Tel Aviv: MOD Books, 1990), pp. 130-31, who argues for the influence of midrashic literature on the New Testament.

4. Contra Ira Sharkansky, *Israel and Its Bible: A Political Analysis* (New York and London: Garland, 1996), pp. 91, 93.

5. The Talmud is the great work of postbiblical rabbinic Judaism. It will be discussed in more detail below. The tractate *BT Avot* is also known as *Pirqê Avôt,* "Sayings/Ethics of the Fathers/Ancestors."

6. *BT Avot* 1:1a. Unless otherwise indicated, quotations from rabbinic literature are taken from Davka Corporation's *Judaic Classics Library, Version IIc4: The Soncino Classics Collection,* consisting of *The Soncino Talmud, The Soncino Midrash Rabbah,* and *The Soncino Zohar* on CD-ROM. Although this edition follows the convention of capitalizing selections from the Mishnah (codified ca. 200 C.E.), such as the present passage, for the sake of convenience the texts will be presented as normal text.

7. It is highly unlikely that the compiler of *Pirqê Avôt* could have been a woman. In addition to the predominantly patriarchal profile of rabbinic ideology and society, one may mention as evidence for this contention passages such as the arguably misogynist *BT Avot* 1:5.

genitors. The figure of Moses serves, hence, as the ultimate authority to whom recourse is made in establishing one's own Jewish credentials. Not only was Moses the instrument through whom the divine laws were revealed, and not only did he liberate his people from bondage, but as his biblical epitaph makes clear, "Never again did there arise in Israel a prophet like Moses — whom YHWH[8] singled out, face to face" (Deut. 34:10).[9] Moses enjoys a unique status even among those who have served as the mediators of divine revelation. Only he was the beneficiary of direct contact with God. His singular closeness to God in Jewish tradition has helped to foster an aura of divine authority for whatever has been derived from Moses. Which image of Moses has predominated at what time and who has the authority to claim to speak in the name of Moses are the questions that have driven the development of Jewish theology and fostered inner-Jewish tensions throughout the ages.

Torah

The Jews have often been characterized as the "people of the book." Although this term was originally borrowed from Islam, it has become a common self-description used by Jews throughout the world. The book to which reference is made is most often understood to be the Torah, the "teaching" of Moses.[10] Al-

---

8. These are the consonants that spell the personal name of God in the Hebrew Bible and Jewish tradition. While the name was presumably pronounced in biblical times, by the later Second Temple period (515 B.C.E.–70 C.E.) it had become taboo, i.e., too sacred to be uttered by anyone other than the high priest on the Day of Atonement (Yom Kippur). With the destruction of the temple by the Romans, the pronunciation of the name was forgotten. Jews generally substitute the word *Adonai*, "my Lord," for occurrences of YHWH in the text, although for some the circumlocution itself has become taboo, and hence other circumlocutions such as *ha-Shem*, "the Name," are substituted. The Tetragrammaton, or four-letter name of God, has been vocalized incorrectly as Jehovah by premodern scholars and more convincingly as Yahweh by modern scholars.

9. Unless otherwise indicated, biblical quotations are taken from *Tanakh: A New Translation of the Holy Scriptures according to the Traditional Hebrew Text* (Philadelphia and New York: Jewish Publication Society, 1985). The only standard variation that I have made to this text is the substitution of the English transcription of the consonants of the ineffable name of God in place of its common translation as "the Lord." The latter translation is generally avoided in our more-or-less egalitarian age. The interested reader is also referred to Everett Fox's excellent Hebraicizing translation of the Torah: *The Five Books of Moses*, The Schocken Bible I (New York: Schocken Books, 1995).

10. See Josh. 8:31-32; 23:6; 1 Kings 2:3; 2 Kings 14:6; 23:25; Mal. 3:22; Dan. 9:11, 13; Ezra 3:2; 7:6; Neh. 8:1; 2 Chron. 23:18; 30:16 for the term "teaching (Torah) of Moses." This is not to imply that what the biblical authors had in mind was necessarily what has become the traditional Torah or Pentateuch.

though the word "Torah" is often translated "law," this translation limits its semantic range. The Hebrew language has many other words for laws or ordinances, such as *mishpāt, ḥôq,* and *miṣwâ.* Torah more correctly means "teaching" or "instruction." These concepts more closely mirror the place of Torah within Jewish life. The infelicitous translation of Torah as "law" is derived, ironically, from the Septuagint, the ancient Jewish translation of the Hebrew Bible into Greek, in which "Torah" was translated as *nomos,* "law." Needless to say, this originally Jewish translation has led in part to the stereotyping of Judaism as a legalistic religion. While it cannot be gainsaid that the concept of "commandments," or *miṣwôt,* plays a central role in Judaism, in theory at least the commandments are meant to serve the interests of both the human and the divine, in spite of the oftentimes ambivalent relationship that Judaism has had with the "yoke of the kingdom of heaven."[11]

In its narrow sense Torah encompasses the Pentateuch, the five books of Moses, which together form the first division of the tripartite Hebrew Bible, or Tanakh.[12] The word "Bible" is derived from the Greek *ta biblia,* "the books," which was the Hellenistic Jewish way of referring to sacred scripture in antiquity. Once the Septuagint had become the official version of the Old Testament for the Christian church, the Jewish community abandoned it for a somewhat later Aramaic translation known as the Targum.[13] Eventually "the books" of Hellenistic Judaism became part of the "book" or Bible of Christianity, encompassing both the Old and New Testaments. Confusion reigns, however, when discussion of the Bible is pursued in interfaith settings. For Jews the Bible consists solely of the books that constitute the Tanakh. In a Jewish context there is no "Old Testament." That term is anathema, since it implies a supersession by the "new" and an impossible theological relegation of Judaism's central sacred text to the past. Nor is there a Jewish "New Testament," since that is a book that is not held sacred by Jews. Thus the term "Bible" has a restricted definition in Judaism. It is for this reason that the somewhat unwieldy but theologically neutral term "Hebrew Bible" has come into use in both an interfaith and a scholarly setting. Unfortunately it is a bit of a misnomer, since there are a number of pas-

---

11. This is a popular rabbinic expression (cf. *BT Berakhot* 13a, 13b, 14b). It is also found in the variants "yoke of heaven" (*BT Sotah* 47b; *BT Sanhedrin* 111b), "yoke of the commandments" (*BT Berakhot* 12b, 13a, 14b; *BT Yevamot* 47b), and "yoke of Torah" (*BT Sanhedrin* 94b).

12. The latter is an acronym derived from the three divisions of the Hebrew Bible, namely, the Torah, "Teaching," the Nebi'im, "Prophets," and the Ketubim, "Writings."

13. The literary history of both the Septuagint and the Targum is quite complex, both translations having been done in a piecemeal fashion over the course of a number of centuries, with various revisions and differing translations of individual books and sections. Hence, to speak of the Septuagint or the Targum is somewhat misleading.

sages in the so-called Hebrew Bible that are in fact written in the Aramaic language.[14]

Although Judaism and Christianity have the books of the Hebrew Bible in common, what the respective adherents actually end up reading are two separate works. The order of books in the Christian Old Testament is based ultimately on the Septuagint by way of the Latin Vulgate translation of Jerome. It is divided into four parts: the Pentateuch, which serves as the prehistory of salvation history; the Historical Books, which tell of the past; the Wisdom Books, which provide information for the here and now; and the Prophetic Books, which look to the future and to God's ultimate redemptive act, the life and passion of Jesus. Thus, it could be argued, the theological importance of the subdivisions ascends as one moves from beginning to end.

Jewish Bibles, on the other hand, are based on the Masoretic Text, the traditional Hebrew text that assumed canonical form by the first couple of centuries C.E. The subdivisions of the Hebrew Bible are arranged roughly in the order in which they were canonized. The Torah comes first, followed by the Prophetic Books (Nebi'im) and the Writings (Ketubim). There is definitely an aura of descending levels of holiness associated with these three subdivisions. The Torah most assuredly has pride of place, as is made graphically obvious in the context of the synagogue, in which the handwritten Torah scroll is housed in a special niche or ark at the front of the sanctuary, whence it is removed to be carried around in festive procession and to serve as the source for weekly and festival readings.

One basic definition of "Torah" is, therefore, a scroll that includes the books of Genesis, Exodus, Leviticus, Numbers, and Deuteronomy. Yet "Torah" is a fluid term within the context of Judaism. On the one hand it can refer to these five books in their totality; on the other hand it can be restricted to the teachings found within them. By extension the term "Torah" can refer to the totality of the twenty-four books of the Hebrew Bible.[15] Rabbinic Judaism, the progenitor of most modern Judaisms, would distinguish between the written

---

14. Gen. 31:47 (2 words); Jer. 10:11; Dan. 2:4b–7:28; Ezra 4:8–6:18; 7:12-26.

15. According to the Protestant Christian tradition, the Old Testament consists of thirty-nine books. The differences between it and Judaism on this point are to be found not in a different canonical collection of books, although their order is different, but in a difference in the system of numeration. The books of Samuel, Kings, and Chronicles, which are reckoned as two books each in the Christian tradition, count as only one each within the context of Judaism. In addition, the twelve minor prophets count as one book in Judaism, while being reckoned as twelve individual books in the Christian context. Finally Judaism does not count the books of Ezra and Nehemiah as separate books. It should be noted that both the Catholic Church and the Eastern Orthodox traditions include varying additional books, known as the Apocrypha or deuterocanonical books, in their Old Testament canons.

Torah *(Torah she-biktav)* and the oral Torah *(Torah she-be'al peh).* The written Torah is the Pentateuch as given to the people of Israel at Mount Sinai through the mediation of Moses. The oral Torah is the complete compendium of rabbinic law and custom as codified in the Talmud and its commentaries and in their interpretative traditions. According to the rabbis, the oral Torah is a revelation equivalent to that of the written Torah. Both were supposedly given by God to Moses at Mount Sinai. Hence, once again by extension, "Torah" can refer to the totality of Jewish law and custom. The fluidity of the term makes it oftentimes difficult to distinguish the one from the other.

The common denominator in all uses of the term is the sense that the Torah, however defined, is divinely inspired and mediated to Israel through the person of Moses. While fundamentalist Orthodoxy would understand Moses' mediatory activity literally, there is also a very strong tendency within Judaism to acknowledge Moses' role as a symbol of authority. By appealing to Moses and the revelation at Sinai, one lends a stamp of approval to a tradition or interpretation, whether or not the historical Moses, if there ever was such a person, had anything to do with the object of discussion or would have been able to comprehend the subject matter. There is a famous midrash ("homiletic tale") that expresses this concept very nicely:

When Moses ascended to heaven, he saw God writing the Torah and putting crowns on certain letters. When Moses asked God what he was doing, God replied that in future times Rabbi Akiva (d. ca. 135 C.E.) would infer many laws from these embellishments to the text. Moses asked to see the great Akiva at work and was transported to Akiva's academy. There Moses became perturbed, because he could not follow the discussion. It appeared completely foreign to him until he heard Akiva say, in answer to a student's query regarding the source of his learning, that it was to be found in the Torah given to Moses at Sinai. Reassured of his legacy, Moses returned to God.[16]

This midrash expresses an understanding of the place of the figure of Moses within the development of Judaism, yet includes an allusion to an underlying comprehension that his place is both ever-changing and a function of time and space. Hence it can quite legitimately be argued that Moses does indeed function in Judaism as the founder figure par excellence. It is to his time and mediatory role that the institution of most of what became Israelite and Jewish practice is attributed. Nonetheless, there exists a certain tension in some textual traditions regarding his exact and direct contribution to the effort.

---

16. *BT Menahot* 29b. This midrash continues by pointing to the inscrutable nature of God. Moses is allowed a glimpse of what the future holds for Akiva, namely, brutal martyrdom during the Hadrianic persecutions, which stands in seeming contrast to his stature as an interpreter of divine law.

Judaism

Defining Judaism is as difficult as defining who is a Jew.[17] Among the various components that make up Judaism are religion, culture, society, ethnic identity, and a common historical memory.

It has become a truism to say that Judaism rests on three pillars: God, Israel, and Torah. According to the founding myth[18] of Judaism, the one universal *God* of history, the creator of heaven and earth, rescued *Israel* from bondage in Egypt. At Mount Sinai God and Israel entered into a covenant with each other. As a debt of gratitude for God's great act of salvation, the people of Israel willingly accepted the "yoke of the kingdom of heaven" as laid out in the *Torah*. In other words, Israel undertook the obligation to fulfill God's ethical and moral injunctions in order to become a "kingdom of priests and a holy nation" (Exod. 19:6) and, hence, to be a "light of nations" (Isa. 49:6).[19]

The origins of Judaism are to be found in the state religion of the kingdom of Judah (ca. 925-586 B.C.E.). According to most modern scholars, the proto-Judaism of Judah evolved slowly from a polytheistic to a henotheistic and finally to a monotheistic religion by the early to mid–sixth century B.C.E. The official version of biblical Judaism's history, however, is recounted in the Hebrew Bible. The familiar story relates how the Israelites, namely, the descendants of Abraham through his grandson Jacob/Israel, were led forth from slavery in Egypt under the leadership of Moses and brought to Mount Sinai, where they entered into an everlasting covenant with God. After forty years of wandering in the desert, the Israelites were finally able to enter and conquer the land that God had promised them. After a "golden age" under the rule of David and Solomon, the kingdom of Israel split in two, with the larger kingdom of Israel to the north and the smaller kingdom of Judah to the south. Since Israel was the first to disappear from the stage (722 B.C.E.), and Judah possessed both

17. See Carl S. Ehrlich, "Jew," in *The Oxford Companion to the Bible*, ed. Bruce M. Metzger and Michael D. Coogan (New York and Oxford: Oxford University Press, 1993), p. 399.

18. Although many would attach a negative connotation to the term "myth," it is used here in its primary meaning as "a usu. traditional story of ostensibly historical events that serves to unfold part of the world view of a people or explain a practice, belief, or natural phenomenon" (*Merriam-Webster's Collegiate Dictionary*, 10th ed., on Infopedia 2.0 CD-ROM).

19. This latter quote from the anonymous sixth century B.C.E. prophet to whom scholars give the name Deutero- or Second Isaiah is generally interpreted as one of the great universalistic statements of the Hebrew Bible. For a decidedly contrary interpretation of what it means to be a "light to the nations," see Harry M. Orlinsky, "The So-Called 'Servant of the Lord' and 'Suffering Servant' in Second Isaiah," *Vetus Testamentum, Supplements* 14 (1967): 1-133.

Jerusalem and the Temple of Solomon (or First Temple), it was Judah that played the leading role in the transmission of Israelite traditions. Both Judaism and the Jews derive their name from Judah. After the destruction of Jerusalem and the temple in 586 B.C.E., a new chapter began in the history of Judaism. At this time Judaism became a diaspora community, i.e., an ethnic/social group with a national religion that was divided into communities that were to be found both in the homeland and in exile.

The Jews were allowed to build a second temple in Jerusalem under the benevolent despotism of the Persian Empire (515 B.C.E.), but with the exception of the Hasmonean period (164-63 B.C.E.), the land of Israel was under constant foreign domination. The never-ending struggle to emerge from this abject state led to the destruction of the Second Temple and the loss of national independence until the middle of the twentieth century.

The Jews of the land of Israel lost their central sanctuary and their nominal self-government as a consequence of two revolts against Roman rule (66-70 and 132-35 C.E.). As happened after the destruction of the First Temple, Judaism was able to survive these disasters thanks to its ability to adapt itself to changing circumstances. This process is embodied in the person of the Pharisee and rabbi Yohanan ben Zakkai. During the final siege of Jerusalem, he had himself smuggled out of the city and, with the blessing of the Romans, founded an academy in which he and his students studied and adapted the ancient traditions of Judaism.[20] Out of their studies was born rabbinic Judaism, the precursor of all modern Judaisms. The twin pillars of rabbinic Judaism were the synagogue and the home, to which the rabbis transferred and altered the rituals of the temple. The earliest rabbinic interpretations of their traditions were compiled in the Mishnah (ca. 200 C.E.). Later rabbinic discussions about the Mishnah were summarized in the Gemara. Together the Mishnah and the Gemara make up the Talmud, which is known in both a Jerusalem/Palestinian version (ca. 400) and a Babylonian one (ca. 500). The latter is without doubt the most important and influential postbiblical work of Jewish literature. The scholastic tradition that was embodied in rabbinic Judaism was determinative for the later evolution of the religion and its traditions.

The Jewish middle ages lasted from about the third to the eighteenth century. The development of Judaism during this time was determined to a great extent by the status of the Jews as a minority under either Christian or Muslim domination. Once Christianity, which had begun as a Jewish sect, had developed into an independent religion and become the official religion of the Roman Empire in the late fourth century, the situation of the Jews took a down-

---

20. See Lawrence H. Schiffman, *From Text to Tradition: A History of Second Temple and Rabbinic Judaism* (Hoboken, N.J.: KTAV, 1991), pp. 168-69.

turn. The triumph of the church was set in stark relief by the abject state of the synagogue. At best the Jewish community was legally tolerated under Christian domination. Oftentimes, however, the Jewish community became the victim of Christian violence, as happened at the time of the Crusades when the Jewish communities of the Rhineland were decimated (1096). The harshness of life in western Europe drove many Jews to seek greener pastures in eastern Europe over the course of time. Their unhappy lot led many to seek refuge in mystical and messianic movements, such as that of Shabbetai Zvi (Tzevi), which convulsed the whole Jewish world in the late seventeenth century. The situation of Jews in the Muslim world was also precarious, although at times of religious tolerance they were able to flourish there in a manner that would have been unthinkable in the Christian world. The most famous example of this is the so-called Golden Age of Spain (tenth to twelfth century). Among the major factors ensuring Jewish survival during this long period of persecution were the Jews' strong communal structures and their role as the mediators between the Christian and Muslim worlds. The division in the Jewish community between Sephardim, whose roots are in Muslim Spain, and Ashkenazim, who trace their roots to medieval Germany, is to be dated to this period of time.

As of the Enlightenment, the situation of the Jews in western Europe began to improve. For the first time Jews began to be accepted as equal under the law, particularly in the New World. However, more often than not the price of social acceptance was the abrogation of Jewish identity, since full acceptance could only be achieved through baptism. Some of those who were not willing to trade their Jewish identity for social acceptance were the driving forces behind the Jewish reform movement, which sought to make Judaism relevant in the modern world through radical changes to the religion, its practice and theology. Since others viewed the radical reforms as an escape from true Judaism, there developed over the course of the nineteenth century the three major religious movements that can be identified in modern Judaism, namely, Reform, Orthodox, and Conservative Judaism. The ancient antipathy toward Judaism in Christian society also underwent a radical change from a religiously motivated hatred to a racial one.[21] The ideology of anti-Semitism claimed that not even baptism could erase the stain of belonging to the Jewish race. The systematic murder of two-thirds of European Jewry during the Nazi period was the frightful legacy of anti-Semitism.[22] In light of the horrors of the Holocaust, the Zion-

---

21. Recently Peter Schäfer has argued that the roots of later anti-Semitism are to be found in Hellenistic and pre-Hellenistic Egypt. See his *Judeophobia: Attitudes toward the Jews in the Ancient World* (Cambridge, Mass., and London: Harvard University Press, 1997). Of particular interest in the present context is his discussion of the negative treatment of the exodus theme and of Moses in classical and Egyptian sources (pp. 15-33).

22. See, e.g., Leni Yahil, *The Holocaust: The Fate of European Jewry,* trans. Ina Fried-

ist movement offered a new hope for the future. This originally secular movement that came into being as a reaction against French anti-Semitism at the end of the nineteenth century promised a solution to the long and hopeless history of the Jews as a minority in the lands of their dispersion through the nationalist endeavor to rebuild a Jewish homeland in Palestine, the ancient Holy Land. The declaration of Israel's independence a mere three years after the end of the Holocaust presented Judaism with a new beginning and renewed hope for the future.

Throughout this whole history, spanning some three thousand years, the figure of Moses has been employed time and time again as the paragon of Jewish behavior, and his authority has constantly been appealed to in order to justify both innovation and tradition. While it could be argued that Abraham is traditionally regarded as the first Jew, it is Moses who plays the role of the founder figure within Judaism. As such he has become the exemplar of both Jewish life and practice. Whether Moses is depicted as a judge, a prophet, a lawgiver, a liberator, an intercessor, a mediator between God and humanity,[23] a philosopher, or a shepherd, his person is paradigmatic for future generations, each of which has read and interpreted Moses in light of its own needs. There is certainly an aura of charisma that surrounds him in Jewish readings of his person. Yet, from the narrow and unromantic historical perspective, can he truly be regarded as the founder of Judaism?

The Search for the "Historical" Moses

The biblical story of Moses and the exodus is extremely vague in its historical details. While it is most explicit in regard to issues such as the number of adult Israelite males who left Egypt, the stations of the desert wanderings, and the specifications for the construction of the ark of the covenant and the tabernacle in the desert, the narrative is silent in regard to the identities of the rulers of Egypt or any events known from other ancient Near Eastern texts. While this could be attributed to the arbitrary luck of the archaeological draw, the problem is compounded by the sheer weight of the extrabiblical materials that have been uncovered over the course of the last century and a half. In addition, the histories of Egypt and other contem-

---

man and Haya Galai from the Hebrew version of 1987 (New York and Oxford: Oxford University Press, 1990).

23. On Moses as a mediator, see John Macquarrie, *Mediators between Human and Divine: From Moses to Muhammad* (New York: Continuum, 1996), pp. 13-25. While Macquarrie's presentation of the life of Moses is not on the cutting edge of scholarship, his conclusions comparing various mediator figures (pp. 129-50) are useful in placing Moses within the larger framework of human religious experience.

poraneous and roughly contiguous countries were an object of intense study in ancient times. Included among these ancient histories were a number of attempts to place Moses and the Israelites within the context of Egyptian history. As the ensuing discussion of the first-century Jewish historian Flavius Josephus will indicate, these analyses played an important role in formulating pro- and anti-Jewish attitudes in the classical world. Basic to both sides of the issue was the assumption that both Moses and the exodus were historical. The scholarly endeavor lay in distilling truth from legend and ideological interpretation. The differences among the various accounts were a function of the specific "truths" that the historians were attempting to convey. The search for an objective truth would have been as foreign to the ancients as our high-tech society would be.

Even some twenty-five years ago when I first began to study the Hebrew Bible, the historicity of both Moses and the exodus was a given, at least in the eyes of the positivistic North American tradition of William Foxwell Albright and his school.[24] Although one was not sure exactly who Moses was and what he did, most scholars were reasonably certain that he lived during the latter part of the thirteenth century B.C.E. and that he led a band of Israelites out of Egyptian bondage to freedom.[25] He also appeared to have been the one who introduced the possibly monotheistic worship of YHWH into the Israelite consciousness. The attitude of one of the preeminent biblical historians of his generation, John Bright, a member of the positivistic Albright school, essentially summarizes that prevailing view: "Though we know nothing of his career save what the Bible tells us, the details of which we have no means of testing, there can be no doubt that he was, as the Bible portrays him, the great founder of Israel's faith. . . . [A] faith as unique as Israel's demands a founder just as surely as does Christianity — or Islam for that matter. To deny that role to Moses would force us to posit another person of the same name!"[26] In claiming this, Bright was to some extent echoing the opinion of his teacher, Albright, who stated that "Moses is the first great individual in history whose life and personality we can sketch with any degree of clarity. . . . To Moses we owe the emergence of higher religious life and moral culture in Western civilization."[27]

---

24. Albright (1891-1971) was arguably the most important and influential American Hebrew biblicist of the twentieth century. See Leona G. Running and David Noel Freedman, *William Foxwell Albright: A Twentieth Century Genius* (New York: Two Continents Publishing Group, 1975); Gus W. Van Beek, ed., *The Scholarship of William Foxwell Albright: An Appraisal,* Harvard Semitic Studies 33 (Atlanta: Scholars Press, 1989).

25. See, e.g., the account of the story of Moses in Harry M. Orlinsky, *Essays in Biblical Culture and Biblical Translation* (New York: KTAV, 1974), pp. 5-38.

26. John Bright, *A History of Israel,* 3rd ed. (Philadelphia: Westminster, 1981), pp. 126-27.

27. William Foxwell Albright, "Moses in Historical and Theological Perspective," in

Even though Albright conceded that the specific traditions associated with Moses in the Bible and by later interpreters were exaggerated, the underlying achievement of the man must have been formidable.[28]

Scholars in Germany, the birthplace of modern critical approaches to biblical study, were on the whole somewhat more cautious concerning the legacy of Moses. While they acknowledged that the vast corpus of legal materials that accrued to the person of Moses was most likely a later addition to the legend of the man,[29] the essential facts of an exodus from Egypt and of a man named Moses were not in doubt, although Gerhard von Rad viewed Moses as the literary glue that held disparate ancient traditions together[30] and Martin Noth deduced that the only reliable historical datum concerning Moses that can be gleaned from the biblical narrative is the account of his death and burial in Transjordan.[31]

Since the 1970s, however, the field of biblical studies has been in a state of turmoil. Many of the assumptions that had served as the basis of generations of biblical study have been called into question. One of the ironies of the current anarchic scholarly situation is that it has been engendered in part by those very scholars whose conservative religious dispositions did not allow them to apply the skeptical methodologies of the historical-critical school to supposedly sacred scripture. Hence these scholars turned to the literary analysis of the biblical text, perhaps naively believing such analysis would not lead to a questioning of the essential accuracy of its narrative framework. The end result is that the

---

Magnalia Dei — The Mighty Acts of God: Essays on the Bible and Archaeology in Memory of G. Ernest Wright, ed. Frank Moore Cross, Werner E. Lemke, and Patrick D. Miller, Jr. (Garden City, N.Y.: Doubleday, 1976), pp. 120-31, quoting 131.

28. Albright, p. 123.

29. While this assumption is one of the underpinnings of modern study of the Hebrew Bible, its initial proposal and acceptance were motivated in part by anti-Judaism. By dating the "Law" after the Prophets, Julius Wellhausen was able to reject it as a late and degenerate phenomenon in the development of biblical religion. This enabled him to accept the theological validity of the prelegal sections of the Hebrew Bible while rejecting all that he viewed as "Judaizing." See Lou H. Silberman, "Wellhausen and Judaism," in *Julius Wellhausen and His "Prolegomena to the History of Israel,"* ed. Douglas A. Knight, Semeia 25 (Chico, Calif.: Scholars Press, 1983), pp. 75-82; Jon D. Levenson, *The Hebrew Bible, The Old Testament, and Historical Criticism: Jews and Christians in Biblical Studies* (Louisville: Westminster/John Knox, 1993), pp. 10-15, 41-42; as well as John H. Hayes and Frederick Prussner, *Old Testament Theology: Its History and Development* (Atlanta: John Knox, 1985), esp. pp. 276-79.

30. Gerhard von Rad, *Theologie des Alten Testaments. Band I. Die Theologie der geschichtlichen Überlieferungen Israels* (Munich: Christian Kaiser, 1958), pp. 23-24, 288-94.

31. Martin Noth, *A History of Pentateuchal Traditions,* translated from the German of 1948 by Bernhard W. Anderson (Chico, Calif.: Scholars Press, 1981), pp. 156-75.

currently popular literary analyses of the biblical text have removed the text from the historical sphere and placed it squarely within the literary. Indicative of this trend is to some extent the work of Robert Polzin, who, although firmly grounded in the historical-critical school of biblical study, has argued that the analysis of a text as literature must be the framework into which the historical-critical analysis of the text must then be placed.[32] An appreciation of the story-teller's art has led in turn to a sophisticated understanding of the artifice of the text. Hence the text is no longer looked to primarily as a source of factual information, but as a reflection of competing ideologies and theologies presenting an idealized version of what they wished the past had been.[33]

To a certain extent this trend had been foreseen by the essayist Ahad Ha'am (Asher Ginsberg), who in a 1904 essay on Moses and prophecy derided the efforts of those who sought the historical facts behind his person.[34] As far as he was concerned, this search for the historical was an archaeological investigation of no interest to anyone but members of the small coterie of dusty-headed academics. In his opinion the realm of history was what took place in the here and now. Therefore the only image of Moses that had any hope of being relevant was the Moses of tradition, since that is the image that inspires the human heart. Ahad Ha'am argued further that it is completely irrelevant whether historians determine if there actually was a Moses or not, since that would not at all change the Moses that tradition has created and that has inspired untold generations. He even conceded that whoever and whatever Moses was, the legends that have accrued to him can never be separated from the historical kernel, if there is any. According to Ahad Ha'am, this is the fate of all famous people.

Despite being written at the turn of the twentieth century, his essay has a very postmodern ring to it that mirrors in some important aspects the basic assumptions of the present author. Thus, when treating the figure of Moses, the current inquiry will revolve more around what the individual texts, both biblical and postbiblical, are trying to convey about Moses than what Moses did or did not do, in spite of the fact that the latter cannot be completely ignored.

While Bright would have been the first to concede that there is no direct extrabiblical evidence for the existence of Moses or for the story of the exodus, generations of scholars such as Bright searched for circumstantial evidence confirming the Bible's underlying historical truth. Hence, if the Bible said there indeed was a Moses who led the Israelites out of Egypt and entered into a spe-

---

32. Robert Polzin, *Moses and the Deuteronomist: A Literary Study of the Deuteronomic History* (New York: Seabury Press, 1980).

33. An essay indicative of this new trend is S. Dean McBride, Jr., "Transcendent Authority: The Role of Moses in Old Testament Traditions," *Interpretation* 44 (1990): 229-39.

34. Ahad Ha'am, "Moses," in *Selected Essays of Ahad Ha-'Am*, ed. Leon Simon (New York: Atheneum, 1970), pp. 306-29.

cial relationship with the deity YHWH, it could be posited that there really was such a man, a man whose origins are to be sought in Egypt, who led the group that later became Israel and introduced the worship of YHWH into Israel, but who died shortly before the entry into and conquest of the land.

Among the various pieces of circumstantial evidence used to date Moses and place him within a historical context, one may mention the presence in Egypt of Semitic settlers throughout the Middle and Late Bronze Ages (ca. 1800-1200 B.C.E.), the "monotheism" of Pharaoh Akhenaten (fourteenth century B.C.E.), the upheavals associated with the transition from the Late Bronze Age to the Iron Age (ca. 1200 B.C.E.), and the supposed mention of Israel in a Victory Hymn of the Pharaoh Merneptah (ca. 1223-1214 B.C.E.).[35] This latter inscription, dubbed the Israel Stele by bibliocentric scholars, is an interesting case study regarding the interpretation of ancient inscriptional evidence. The other alleged pieces of evidence adduced, while including some textual witnesses, serve as illustrations of the subjective nature of archaeological interpretation.

The origins of the scientific archaeological investigation of the ancient Near East are to be sought in the desire of the European colonial powers to raid the past in order to stock the museums of the present.[36] In addition, an intense preoccupation with the Holy Land's past was intended not only to find objects with which to illustrate studies about the Bible, but also to prove the veracity of the biblical account. The underlying logic of the enterprise was that, by finding evidence for the historical framework of the biblical narrative, one was also adducing proofs for the theological truths of the biblical account. However, this line of argumentation has, in the opinion of the majority of scholars, proven itself to be logically inconsistent. Hence the whole enterprise of "biblical" archaeology has fallen into disrepute among those who consider themselves scientific and objective archaeologists.[37]

An analogy may help illustrate this contention. The Scottish author Sir Walter Scott is generally viewed as the father of the historical novel. Among his many works in this genre, his novel *Ivanhoe* arguably has pride of place. This romance spins a tale of medieval England during the time King Richard the Lion-Hearted was away fighting the Crusades and his brother, John, was his regent. An

35. See *ANET,* pp. 376-78.

36. See Neal Asher Silberman, *Digging for God and Country: Exploration, Archeology, and the Secret Struggle for the Holy Land, 1799-1917* (New York: Knopf, 1982).

37. William G. Dever has been a leading critic of biblical archaeology, although he himself has recently toned down his criticism of the term. Among Dever's many publications on the subject, see his *Recent Archaeological Discoveries and Biblical Research,* The Samuel and Althea Stroum Lectures in Jewish Studies (Seattle and London: University of Washington Press, 1990), pp. 12-36; and his "Archaeology, Syro-Palestinian and Biblical," *ABD,* 1:354-67.

underlying dynamic of the action is the tension between the older Saxon inhabitants of the land and their Norman overlords. In spite of these historical background details, all of which are well known from medieval sources, the figures and the adventures of Ivanhoe; his love interest, Rowena; as well as the Jew Isaac of York and his daughter Rebecca, among many others in this book with a "cast of thousands," are figments of the storyteller's imagination. In the same manner, just because certain aspects of the historical framework into which the biblical narrative fits can be corroborated externally, it does not mean that the aspects of the biblical account that are in essence theological interpretations of history are thereby empirically proven. One would not make this "leap of faith" with any other body of literature, and hence, in the seemingly cold world of academic scholarship, "just because the Bible says it's so" is not enough of an argument to clinch the case for theology's claims to truth. Even if it were, the problem of whose theological understanding of the text to view as the "truth" would preclude any unanimity concerning what the Bible allegedly claims as truth.

The dominant tendency in modern biblical studies is to question the historicity of the biblical narrative in matters pertaining to the exodus and the conquest, while investigating the theological and ideological assumptions underlying the narrative.[38] Thus the focus of research has moved quite radically from an attempt to "prove" the Bible to an attempt to understand the Bible's embedded ideologies. The impossibility of assuming the historicity of Israel's foundational narratives has focused attention on the recovery of ancient Israel's politicized theology.[39] The effect of these shifts in emphasis and focus has also influenced approaches to understanding Moses, the account of whose life and teachings is not historical in the sense of the great nineteenth-century historian Leopold von Ranke, who understood the task of the historian as the recovery of the past "as it actually was,"[40] but is rather a reflection of the various authors

---

38. As William A. Ward has written, "This is one of the hallmarks of ancient historical writing: the folk memories, with all their elaboration, have become real history and are ultimately written down as real history" ("Summary and Conclusions," in *Exodus: The Egyptian Evidence,* ed. Ernest S. Frerichs and Leonard H. Lesko [Winona Lake, Ind.: Eisenbrauns, 1997], pp. 105-12, quoting 108). On the subject of history and historiography in ancient Israel, see Marc Zvi Brettler, *The Creation of History in Ancient Israel* (London and New York: Routledge, 1995); Baruch Halpern, *The First Historians: The Hebrew Bible and History* (San Francisco: Harper & Row, 1988); John Van Seters, *In Search of History: Historiography in the Ancient World and the Origins of Biblical History* (New Haven and London: Yale University Press, 1983).

39. A recent and readable book that illustrates this point is S. David Sperling, *The Original Torah: The Political Intent of the Bible's Writers* (New York and London: New York University Press, 1998).

40. "wie es eigentlich gewesen [ist]." See R. G. Collingwood, *The Idea of History* (New York: Oxford University Press, 1956), p. 130.

throughout the centuries who have had an interest in claiming him for their own posterity.

Turning back to the "proofs" adduced for the dating and historicity of the exodus and, hence, of Moses, the earliest attempts to date the Israelite sojourn in Egypt are found in various Hellenistic and Roman authors,[41] many of whom are cited by Josephus in the course of his efforts to refute their anti-Jewish arguments and to present both a pro-Jewish and a pro-Roman account of Jewish history. One aspect that Josephus had in common with a number of classical and modern historians is that he dated the descent to Egypt and the biblical story of Joseph to the Hyksos period of Egyptian history.

Another piece of evidence adduced is the supposed influence on Moses of the "monotheism" of the heretic Pharaoh Akhenaten.[42] In the contextualization of Israel's biblical heritage within the ancient Near East, the search for possible parallels to the literature and theology of the Hebrew Bible has led to a recognition that Israel was a product of its times and not necessarily a unique phenomenon. This has led in turn to two oftentimes diametrically opposed academic enterprises, one which seeks to identify the ways in which Israel was indeed unique, and one which attempts to demonstrate how derivative Israelite thought and culture actually were. Both tendencies can be identified in the discussions that have revolved around the life and times of Akhenaten.

In 1887 a bedouin woman discovered the first of what eventually would become a cache of close to four hundred cuneiform tablets[43] at the desolate site

41. References to Jews in classical sources are conveniently anthologized in Menahem Stern, *Greek and Latin Authors on Jews and Judaism I-III* (Jerusalem: Israel Academy of Sciences and Humanities, 1974, 1980, 1984). See also John G. Gager, *Moses in Greco-Roman Paganism* (Nashville and New York: Abingdon, 1972).

42. See Donald B. Redford, *Akhenaten: The Heretic King* (Princeton: Princeton University Press, 1984); Redford, "The Monotheism of the Heretic Pharaoh: Precursor of Mosaic Monotheism or Egyptian Anomaly?" *Biblical Archaeology Review* 13, no. 3 (1987): 16-32.

43. Cuneiform writing refers to wedge-shaped writing impressed on clay tablets. This style of writing was characteristic of a number of ancient Near Eastern cultures at home in Mesopotamia, Anatolia, and Syria. In addition, the Akkadian language of Mesopotamia served as the international language of the Near East in the second and first millennia B.C.E. until the rise of the Persian Empire in the sixth century B.C.E., when it was supplanted by the alphabetically written Aramaic language. Akkadian cuneiform was a syllabic script employing hundreds of signs. Hence, knowledge of reading and writing was confined to a specially trained scribal class, as was the case for the contemporaneous hieroglyphic and hieratic styles of ancient Egypt. See *Reading the Past* (New York: Barnes & Noble, 1998), esp. pp. 15-73 (cuneiform) and 75-135 (Egyptian hieroglyphs); and concerning the origins of the alphabet, see Joseph Naveh, *Early History of the Alphabet: An Introduction to West Semitic Epigraphy and Paleography* (Jerusalem: Magnes Press; Leiden: Brill, 1982).

of Tell el ʿAmarna, about 190 miles south of Cairo.[44] These tablets constituted an archive of international correspondence that the pharaoh of ancient Egypt received from other major kings and from his own vassals in Syria and Canaan in the mid–fourteenth century B.C.E. The letters detail the breakdown of Egyptian authority over a stretch of years centering on the reign of Amenophis (Amenhotep) IV, who is better known by the name he later adopted, Akhenaten.

Within the first few years of his seventeen-year reign, Akhenaten (1377-1361 or 1350-1334 B.C.E.) instituted a religious and political revolution which broke the power of the entrenched priesthood of Thebes and Memphis by declaring sole allegiance to the deified sun disk, the Aten; founding a new capital city, Akhetaten (modern Tell el-ʿAmarna), in the desert; and instituting a revolutionary new hyperrealism in Egyptian art.[45] The failure of his revolution is indicated by the fate of his successor Tutankhaten, whose capitulation to the old priesthood is embodied in his change of name to Tutankhamun, the minor ruler whose claim to fame lies in the spectacular discovery of his pristine tomb by Howard Carter in 1927.[46]

In his function as son of the only god worshiped, Akhenaten was the conduit through which Aten made known his will. Over the years the argument has gone back and forth about whether Akhenaten was the world's first monotheist. In the sense that he denied the existence of gods other than the Aten, this would certainly apply. On the other hand, Akhenaten's own status within the theological structure may indicate at least a dualistic understanding of divinity. Be that as it may, the identification of Akhenaten as a monotheist has served a number of purposes. First, for some it has contextualized Moses' monotheism by indicating its source. After all, Moses is supposed to have been brought up at the Egyptian court, and if one dates Moses to the early thirteenth century, it would in theory have been possible for him to have learned about Akhenaten's revolutionary concept of divinity from primary witnesses to it or from their children. Second, it has provided those who would deny any originality to ancient Israel with another proof of Israel's derivative nature. What a damning indictment it would be if that which we consider most distinctive about ancient Israel, namely, its supposed invention of the concept of a unitary and unique god, was in fact borrowed from another culture. And third, it has satisfied the

---

44. On the ʿAmarna tablets and their discovery, see William L. Moran, *The Amarna Letters* (Baltimore and London: Johns Hopkins University Press, 1992), esp. pp. xiii-xxxix; Nadav Naʾaman, "Amarna Letters," *ABD*, 1:174-81.

45. For a slightly different account of the significance of Akhenaten's "revolution," see Kent R. Weeks, *The Lost Tomb* (New York: Morrow, 1998), pp. 233-37.

46. For an account of the whole King Tut affair that reads like a thriller, see Thomas Hoving, *Tutankhamun: The Untold Story* (New York: Simon & Schuster, 1978).

need of Egyptologists to prove to the world that the civilization that they study is indeed the oldest and greatest of the ancient world.[47]

In 1939 Sigmund Freud used the assumption that Moses obtained his view of God from Akhenaten as the basis of his theory that Moses was an Egyptian follower of Akhenaten's religion who, after its suppression, found some more-or-less willing adherents among the Hebrews enslaved in Egypt. Their murder of him in a primal Oedipal rage in the desert led to the formation of Judaism as Atenism's guilt-ridden successor.[48] More recently Jan Assmann, in a work of singular erudition, has sought to trace the lingering thread of Atenism as mediated by Mosaic faith throughout European religious thought.[49]

Nonetheless, Donald Redford has argued quite strongly against any direct influence of Atenism on biblical religion.[50] As he has indicated, the thesis of Akhenaten's direct influence on Moses rests on a number of very shaky presuppositions. First are the dates that are assigned to Moses in order to support such a proposition. According to the Hebrew Bible, the exodus took place 480 years before Solomon began to build the temple in the fourth year of his reign (1 Kings 6:1). If that latter event can be dated to circa 960 B.C.E., then the exodus took place circa 1440, which is impossible in light of what is known of Egyptian power and might in Canaan at that time.[51] Hence it has been argued that the figure 480 years is to be understood as twelve times forty, i.e., as twelve generations. If one then assigns a more reasonable number of years per generation, such as twenty-five, one arrives at a more "reasonable" number of years, namely, 300. In this manner scholars such as Bright were able to date the exodus to the mid–thirteenth century B.C.E., during the lengthy reign of Pharaoh Ramses II and shortly after the time of Akhenaten.[52] However, this dating on the basis of a desire to preserve the

47. Lest the reader think this is a nonissue, it should be pointed out that among those who study the ancient world there is a friendly (?) rivalry in trying to establish the originality of the civilization and culture in question. As an example of this the reader is referred to works such as Samuel Noah Kramer's *History Begins at Sumer: Twenty-seven "Firsts" in Man's Recorded History* (Garden City, N.Y.: Anchor Books, 1959), which stakes out the claim for the originality of the Sumerian civilization of Mesopotamia. In addition, one of the hottest topics currently being discussed is the origin of writing. Was it invented in Sumer (the leading contender), Egypt, or the Indus Valley (as some recent evidence may suggest)? On such discussions are based many a scholarly career.

48. See Sigmund Freud, *Moses and Monotheism,* translated from the German of 1939 by Katherine Jones (New York: Vintage Books, 1967).

49. Jan Assmann, *Moses the Egyptian: The Memory of Egypt in Western Monotheism* (Cambridge, Mass., and London: Harvard University Press, 1997).

50. Donald B. Redford, *Egypt, Canaan, and Israel in Ancient Times* (Princeton: Princeton University Press, 1992), pp. 377-82.

51. Redford, *Egypt, Canaan, and Israel,* pp. 260-63.

52. Bright, pp. 123-24.

Bible as a historical document, while negating a central aspect of its historical framework, has justly been criticized.[53] Even the increasingly fewer adherents of this theory, such as Bright, are compelled to admit that there is nothing in any Egyptian sources that would support the exodus narrative in any of its details.[54] In this manner the direct influence of Akhenaten on Moses cannot necessarily be assumed on the basis of their chronological sequence.

In addition, Redford has criticized the facile assumption that Mosaic monotheism is derived from Atenism on theological grounds. Leaving aside the increasingly clear evidence that Israelite religion was not initially monotheistic but underwent a long development until a true monotheism was first propounded by Jeremiah and Deutero-Isaiah[55] in the early to mid–sixth century B.C.E.,[56] Redford identifies, among others, the following difficulties in assuming a relationship between Atenism and Yahwism:

1. The act of comparing and assuming a direct relationship between a phenomenon of the fourteenth century B.C.E. and one of the sixth;
2. The difference in nature between the divine belief system of Yahwism and the royal ideology of Atenism;
3. The difference in nature between the invisible yet anthropomorphic YHWH and the visible yet lacking-in-personality Aten;
4. The iconography of Aten versus the aniconic nature of the worship of YHWH; and
5. The personal nature of Israelite worship, in which every worshiper could approach the deity through the cult, contrasted with the distant nature of Aten, who can only be approached through his son, Akhenaten.[57]

Hence, following Redford, it would appear unlikely that Mosaic faith was in any way derived from Atenism.

Another piece of circumstantial evidence that has been employed in the attempt to date the exodus relates to the unstable political situation in Canaan

---

53. E.g., by Redford, *Egypt, Canaan, and Israel,* pp. 408-29.

54. Bright, pp. 123-24.

55. I.e., the anonymous exilic prophet(s) whose prophecies (Isa. 40–55/66) are appended to those of the eighth-century prophet Isaiah of Jerusalem.

56. On the history of the religion of Israel, see Rainer Albertz, *A History of Israelite Religion in the Old Testament Period,* trans. John Bowden from the German of 1992, 2 vols. (Louisville: Westminster/John Knox, 1994); Tikvah Frymer-Kensky, *In the Wake of the Goddesses: Women, Culture, and the Biblical Transformation of Pagan Myth* (New York: Free Press, 1992); and Mark S. Smith, *The Early History of God: Yahweh and the Other Deities in Ancient Israel* (New York: Harper Collins, 1990).

57. Redford, *Egypt, Canaan, and Israel,* pp. 378-82.

during the waning years of the Late Bronze Age (ca. 1550-1200 B.C.E.) as it eventually led into the Iron Age (1200-586 B.C.E.). The assumption of an exodus under the leadership of Moses naturally implies as its correlation a conquest of Canaan under the leadership of Joshua. If the latter can be located in history, then the date of the former can be placed just before it.

The ʿAmarna letters give a snapshot of the contentious political life of Canaanite culture as it was in decline during the Late Bronze Age. Egyptian control over its vassal city-states was loosening as a consequence of Akhenaten's laissez-faire policies. This in turn led to a constant struggle between the petty kinglets of Canaan to extend their territory at the expense of their neighbors. In addition, there was a large class of people living at the fringes of society whose presence often was a source of worry to the rulers unless they could employ them for their own advantage as mercenaries against their foes. This class was known as ḫapiru/ḫabiru. While it was once thought that the term was related to the Hebrews (Heb. ʿibrî), and that the group gave birth to them, the term is not an ethnic designation, as it is in isolated passages in the Hebrew Bible, but a social designation. Although it has become common usage to refer to the Hebrews when one means the ancient Israelites, this designation only appears in isolated biblical passages and mainly when non-Israelites are referring to Israelites.[58] While it is certainly not outside the realm of possibility that the term gave rise to the later designation "Hebrew" and that some ancestors of the Israelites may have belonged to the social class known as ḫapiru/ḫabiru, a direct correlation between the two cannot be demonstrated.[59] As a consequence, the ʿAmarna letters cannot be taken as evidence for an Israelite presence in the land in the fourteenth century.

As indicated, the discipline of "biblical" archaeology arose from a desire to illustrate the truth or at any rate the historical accuracy of the Hebrew Bible. Therefore, archaeological finds were often correlated with the biblical narrative in a manner that attempted to harmonize and suppress conflicts between these two bodies of evidence. A case in point would relate to the putative period of the Israelite "conquest." According to the well-known account in the book of Joshua, the Israelites invaded the Holy Land promised to their ancestors in a well-organized series of campaigns, beginning with the miraculous conquest of Jericho and continuing until they had obliterated the Canaanites. Ignoring the inner-biblical conflicts regarding the extent and nature of an Israelite conquest,[60] a number of scholars took their lead from the narrative of Joshua in

---

58. The one exception is when Jonah refers to himself in a non-Israelite context as a Hebrew (Jon. 1:9). See Niels Peter Lemche, "Hebrew," *ABD*, 3:95.

59. See Niels Peter Lemche, "Ḫapiru/Ḫabiru," *ABD*, 3:6-10.

60. Compare the account of Josh. 1–12 with that of Judg. 1:1–2:5. For an in-depth

their interpretation of the archaeological sources for the transitional period between the Late Bronze and Iron Ages.

This was a time of change. In Canaan the city-states that had dominated the hierarchical social structure during both the Middle and Late Bronze Ages (ca. 1800-1200 B.C.E.) were in a state of decline that was mirrored along the whole eastern Mediterranean coast. Greece witnessed the collapse of Mycenaean civilization, a reflection of which is probably to be found in Homer's *Iliad* and *Odyssey*. In Asia Minor the Hittite empire collapsed. The Syrian coast witnessed the downfall of Ugarit. And in Egypt the New Kingdom came to an end. A number of theories have been proposed to account for this general collapse of urban and cosmopolitan civilization as it had existed for centuries in the eastern Mediterranean.[61] Pirates and "sea peoples" plied the Mediterranean and interrupted the flow of trade. Later traditions spoke of invasions in Greece (the Dorians) and Canaan (the Israelites). Ultimately there was probably no one cause of collapse, but rather a number of factors, including political, social, and environmental ones, that together brought about the end of the Bronze Age.

The major controversies in the interpretation of the finds relating to ancient Israel have raged around the dates of the destruction levels at archaeological sites throughout Canaan and the question of identifying ethnicity on the basis of material remains. Over the course of the years four major models for interpreting the "conquest" tradition and its relationship to the archaeological sources have been proposed.[62]

The first has been identified with Albright and his student G. Ernest Wright. In Israel the scholar, warrior, and statesman Yigael Yadin in particular was a proponent of this school of thought. This school, which propounded a "conquest" model based on the account of the book of Joshua, attempted to interpret the archaeological remains according to the biblical model. The proponents of this school postulated that the Israelites were invaders from outside the land and that various destruction levels at sites throughout Canaan were to be

---

discussion of the theological differences between these two accounts and their possible relationship to each other, see Moshe Weinfeld, *The Promise of the Land: The Inheritance of the Land of Canaan by the Israelites*, The Taubman Lectures (Berkeley, Los Angeles, and Oxford: University of California Press, 1993), esp. pp. 121-55.

61. Concerning the transition from the Bronze Age to the Iron Age in the eastern Mediterranean world, see the excellent collection of essays in Seymour Gitin, Amihai Mazar, and Ephraim Stern, eds., *Mediterranean Peoples in Transition: Thirteenth to Early Tenth Centuries BCE*, Trude Dothan Festschrift (Jerusalem: Israel Exploration Society, 1998).

62. On the issues involved see Niels Peter Lemche, "Israel, History of (Premonarchic Period)," *ABD*, 3:526-45; and William G. Dever, "Israel, History of (Archaeology and the 'Conquest')," *ABD*, 3:545-58.

attributed to the invaders. In cases in which the archaeological remains did not appear to support the biblical evidence, the archaeology was interpreted in such a way as to accord with the Bible. When it was found that Late Bronze Age Jericho was an unwalled village, hardly the great city with mighty walls conquered by Joshua (Josh. 6), the adherents of the conquest model speculated that the Middle Bronze Age walls of Jericho remained in use and that it is to these that the biblical tale is alluding, or that Jericho's walls had been subject to massive erosion. When it was discovered that Ai, the second major conquest of the invading Israelites (Josh. 7–8), was uninhabited during the second millennium B.C.E., the conquest of Ai, whose name in Hebrew means "the ruin," was transferred to nearby Bethel.[63] In the case of Yadin's excavation of Hazor, the destruction that brought an end to the Late Bronze city was attributed to Joshua. In positing this, Yadin was seeking an ancient model for his very modern attempt to reconquer the land by military means.[64]

The weaknesses of this approach are evident. First, rather than evaluating and drawing conclusions from the archaeological record in its own right, the archaeology has not been allowed to present its case unencumbered by presuppositions. This has led, secondly, to a manipulation of the archaeological record to serve the textual one, whose own witness is not as clear as has been supposed. Third, the assumption that any destruction level dating to 1200 B.C.E. ± 100 years must be attributed to the Israelites oversimplifies the historical record. There could be many causes for the destruction of a city, among which one can number natural causes, such as fires and earthquakes, and human agency, such as conflict with other Canaanite cities, with "sea peoples" such as the Philistines, or with Egyptian forces. Nothing in the archaeological record indicates that the Israelites were the ultimate cause of a global Canaanite destruction. And finally, in order to posit a unified invasion theory, the proponents of the conquest model must conflate an archaeological record that is much more expansive chronologically than they are able to allow.

---

63. See James L. Kelso et al., *The Excavation of Bethel (1934-1960),* Annual of the American Schools of Oriental Research 39 (Cambridge, Mass.: American Schools of Oriental Research, 1968), pp. 47-49.

64. According to Neal Asher Silberman (*A Prophet from amongst You: The Life of Yigael Yadin: Soldier, Scholar, and Mythmaker of Modern Israel* [New York: Addison-Wesley, 1993], pp. 370-71), Yadin wanted to show (a) that the wars he fought were reflective of those of the time of Joshua, and (b) that his ancestors were also warriors. For an example of a modern Israeli military analysis of the campaigns of Joshua, see Chaim Herzog and Mordechai Gichon, *Battles of the Bible: A Modern Military Evaluation of the Old Testament* (New York: Random House, 1978), pp. 25-45. Yadin's interpretation of his finds from Hazor can be found in Yigael Yadin, *Hazor: The Rediscovery of a Great Citadel of the Bible* (London and Jerusalem: Weidenfeld & Nicolson, 1975).

The second school of thought has become associated with the German scholars Albrecht Alt and Martin Noth. While retaining the notion that the Israelites entered Canaan from outside, Alt and Noth viewed this process as a mainly peaceful infiltration that later tradition expanded into a war of conquest. Assuming that the ancestors of the Israelites were seminomads, Alt and Noth postulated that they entered Canaan slowly but surely over a long stretch of time as shepherds in search of pasturage who occasionally came into conflict with the local population and eventually supplanted them. The agrarian settlements that arose in the central highlands of Canaan in the course of Iron Age I (1200-1000 B.C.E.) were thought to bear witness to this process, as did the eventual collapse of the urban culture of the Bronze Age. The weakness of this "infiltration" model lies in its lack of evidence for an external movement into Canaan.

This lack is addressed in the third model, which can be associated with the names of George Mendenhall and Norman Gottwald. Mendenhall proposed that the origin of the Israelites is not to be sought outside of Canaan, but in Canaan itself. According to him, the urban culture of the Bronze Age was toppled by an internal revolt of the peasant classes, who rose against their overlords, destroyed most of their cities over the course of time, and settled in the sparsely populated hill country. Gottwald combined Mendenhall's "peasant revolt" model with the liberation theology of the 1970s to provide a distinctly Marxist understanding of the origin of the Israelites in a liberating revolution of the underclasses against the tyranny of the exploitative and decadent rulers of the Canaanite city-states. The new religion of Yahwism was the liberation theology that inspired and united the oppressed. Although Gottwald acknowledged his debt to Mendenhall, the latter attempted to distance himself most vociferously from the Marxist elements of the former's modification of the peasant revolt model. The major weakness of this theory is the speculative nature of the retrojection into the past of a specific "liberation" theology.

The latest attempt to provide a model for the rise of the Israelites has been advanced by the Israeli archaeologist Israel Finkelstein, who includes elements of both the peaceful infiltration and the peasant revolt models in his new synthesis. In his examination of the archaeological record, Finkelstein has noticed a gradual increase and spread of population in the central hill country from east to west over the course of Iron Age I. In addition, he claims to be able to link the material culture of these highland settlements with Canaanite traditions, specifically in the realm of pottery styles. This would indicate that the new population was Canaanite in origin and not originally from elsewhere. However, the Canaanite culture that Finkelstein speculates is closest to that of the highland culture in Iron Age I is not the culture of the Late Bronze Age but that of the Middle Bronze Age. As a consequence, he argues that the nature of the Late Bronze Age must be rethought. In his opinion the Late Bronze Age was not the heyday of Canaanite civilization, but represented a Canaan already in decline. The basis for his contention is a general diminution in city sizes as one moves from the Middle to the Late Bronze Ages. The "golden age" of Canaan is, hence, to be sought in the Middle Bronze Age. Owing to environmental factors, the cities were no longer able to support their enormous populations, which led the surplus population to abandon their homes for a life on the fringes of society, specifically as transhumants or "seminomads" in Transjordan. After a few centuries on the fringes of the "civilized" world, these seminomads turned back west and began to resettle the hill country, far from the decaying urban centers of Canaanite life. This would explain the conservative nature of their material culture and would locate the origin of the Israelites in an originally Canaanite setting. It would also allow for the development of legends detailing a movement back into the country, as in the biblical account, which was later magnified into a series of legends about the violent conquest of the land and its Canaanite inhabitants, whom they used as the "other" in order to foster a sense of group solidarity and ethnic identity.

While what actually happened is shrouded in mystery, the Finkelstein model explains the origins both of the biblical traditions and of the basic identity of Israelite material culture with Canaanite culture. In essence they cannot be distinguished. In spite of the efforts of generations of biblical archaeologists, a distinctly Israelite material culture cannot be identified in Iron Age I. Nor can any evidence be found of the settlement of a group of exiles from Egypt. After all, it is inconceivable that a population would have spent generations in Egypt without absorbing noticeable features of Egyptian fashion in their material cultural remains. While one may assume that over the course of this period there developed an Israelite identity in the central highlands of Canaan, there is nothing in the archaeological record to distinguish an Israelite site from a Canaanite one. The ethnicity of the inhabitants of the highland settlements cannot be determined on the basis of archaeology. As has been demonstrated, the differences in Iron Age I Canaan were not between Canaanite and Israelite sites, but between urban and village settlements, both of them belonging to the continuum of the archaeological record in Canaan.[65]

At the beginning of the fifth year of his reign, Pharaoh Merneptah, the elderly successor of the long-lived Ramses II, fought against a Libyan coalition that included sea peoples. He memorialized his victory in a lengthy hymn, at the end of which is appended a section dealing with the supposed annihilation

---

65. See Gloria Anne London, "A Comparison of Two Contemporaneous Lifestyles of the Late Second Millennium BC," *Bulletin of the American Schools of Oriental Research* 273 (1989): 37-55.

of various Canaanite peoples. This coda is significant for biblical studies because of its mention of a people named Israel. This inscription has been taken as evidence for the date of the exodus and conquest:[66]

> The princes are prostrate, saying: "Mercy!"
>> Not one raises his head among the Nine Bows.
> Desolation is for Tehenu; Hatti is pacified;
>> Plundered is the Canaan with every evil;
> Carried off is Ashkelon; seized upon is Gezer;
>> Yanoam is made as that which does not exist;
> Israel is laid waste, his seed is not;
>> Hurru is become a widow for Egypt!
> All lands together, they are pacified;
>> Everyone who was restless, he has been bound
> by the King of Upper and Lower Egypt.[67]

Assuming for the sake of argument that the reference in the inscription is to a proto-form of the entity that later tradition knows as Israel, for a long time it was held that the Merneptah stele provided a *terminus ante quem* for the exodus from Egypt under Moses and for the conquest of the land of Canaan by his handpicked successor Joshua. Since the basic historicity of the biblical text was taken for granted, the evidence provided by the stele was fit into a preconceived historical pattern. In this manner the Merneptah stele was used as evidence for the date of the exodus, since Israel could not have been mentioned in the land before it had actually entered it. In other words, the exodus must have taken place before Israel was mentioned in the Merneptah stele. In this manner the stele was used to provide a date before which the exodus must have occurred. Yet the stele makes no mention of an exodus from Egypt, nor of a conquest of the land by Israel. Neither does it mention either Moses' or Joshua's contribution to a presumed conquest. A more cautious approach to the witness of the text would claim no more than that, by the late thirteenth century B.C.E., there existed in the highlands of Canaan an entity known as Israel. This would not conflict with, although neither would it be proven by, the archaeological record, which knows of no massive influx of foreigners into the land during the transitional Late Bronze/Early Iron Age.

66. See, e.g., Kenneth A. Kitchen, "Exodus, The," *ABD*, 2:702. While acknowledging that Israel is mentioned in the Merneptah stele, Abraham Malamat ("The Exodus: Egyptian Analogies," in *Exodus: The Egyptian Evidence*, pp. 15-26) admitted "that this stele has little or nothing to do with the Exodus" (p. 19). On the other hand, Bright (p. 123) expressed some reservations about identifying the Israel of the Merneptah inscription with the group that supposedly left Egypt.

67. Translated by John A. Wilson, *ANET*, p. 378.

There are scholars who find that the evidence for a literal reading of the biblical accounts of the exodus and the conquest is difficult to support on the basis of extrabiblical archaeological and textual evidence. They have, therefore, searched for other possibilities for understanding the stories in a symbolic or metaphorical manner. The concentration of references to the exodus tradition outside the Torah in the prophetic traditions about Elijah and in the book of Hosea has led some to posit that this tradition originated as a northern Israelite metaphor for the throwing off of the oppressive shackles of the southern kingdom of Judah at the time of Solomon. It could be argued that Moses himself, the great liberator from oppression, is a thinly veiled metaphor for Jeroboam I, the king who led the secession of Israel from Judah in the late tenth century B.C.E. following the death of Solomon (1 Kings 12). One could then argue that Solomon was the pharaoh of the oppression who did not know Joseph, itself a metaphor for the southern kingdom in any number of biblical texts. During the approximately two centuries of their mutual existence, Israel and Judah were constant rivals. A tale possibly based on their rivalry, namely, that of the Golden Calf, will be discussed below. Suffice it to note that both states claimed both political and cultic legitimacy on any number of different levels. However, it is true that "winners write history." What we know about Israel is filtered through the eyes of the authors of the Bible, who were for the most part Judeans loyal to the Davidic ruling house of Judah and to its central sanctuary in Jerusalem. No wonder then that everything associated with Israel in the biblical account is condemned on theological grounds. And yet, at times one can deduce a more balanced account of Israel's story by reading between the lines of the Bible.

David Sperling has recently argued that Moses, whom he regards as a wholly fictitious creation, does indeed stand for Israel, but not in the guise of Jeroboam.[68] In his opinion Moses stands for Saul, the first king of united Israel and the indirect progenitor of the claims of the north to legitimacy against the claims of the Davidic dynasty of Judah. Sperling has drawn attention to the fact that in the pro-Davidic textual tradition of Judah, Moses and the exodus play a minimal role at best. Nonetheless, the anti-Davidic Moses traditions had to be incorporated into the compromise document that has come down to us as the Hebrew Bible in order to lay claim to the inclusion of both north and south in a new entity that reread the antisouthern traditions in a pro-Judean light.

Others have highlighted the importance of the exodus tradition in the exilic writings of Deutero-Isaiah and have conjectured that it was only in the mid–sixth century that these traditions assumed or perhaps reassumed an importance in Israelite tradition. Contrary perhaps to the image that the literature

68. Sperling, pp. 121-34.

of the Hebrew Bible is attempting to convey, Judah was always a small and insignificant country, oftentimes consisting of not much more than the city of Jerusalem and its immediate environs. As the prophetic books of the eighth to sixth centuries B.C.E. indicate, Judah was confronted by the existential need to play coalition politics with the superpowers in Egypt and Mesopotamia in order to ensure its survival. For various reasons, including in part its relatively greater insignificance on the world stage than its larger cousin to the north, Judah was able to survive the threat posed by the neo-Assyrian empire that wiped Israel from the map circa 722 B.C.E. However, Judah eventually succumbed to the vindictive might of the neo-Babylonian empire in 586 B.C.E. after a series of serious political miscalculations. In addition to the decimation of the land, the loss of its political independence, and the destruction of its central sanctuary, its leaders in the fields of politics, learning, religion, the trades and crafts were exiled to Babylon. The land was left to be inherited by the underclass that survived the general calamity. This could have signaled the end of both the national identity and religion of Judah. After all, it could have been argued that the god of the Judeans had been defeated by the gods of Babylon. As Jeremiah 44 indicates, there were people who used the national disaster as an excuse for apostasy and a change in religious orientation. And yet the religion of Judah was able to survive owing to a theology that reinterpreted the destruction not as the defeat of YHWH by Marduk and the other Babylonian gods, but as the punishment of God against his people for their sins.[69]

In addition, while it could be expected that those Jews taken into Babylonian captivity would assimilate into their environment and disappear from the historical record, as did their cousins the "ten lost tribes of Israel" under Assyrian rule (notwithstanding persistent legendary claims to the contrary), a substantial core of exiled Jews were able to retain a strong sense of identity and entitlement to the homeland. The leading figures among the exiled Jews were Ezekiel, who, following in the footsteps of Jeremiah, fostered a sense that the true Judeans were the ones in exile,[70] and Deutero-Isaiah, who preached an imminent return to the homeland, effectively intermingling creation and exodus language to prepare the people for that triumphant return. Deutero-Isaiah's prophecies can be appreciated only on the background of a theology that presents the history of Israel in modern terms as a dysfunctional family relation-

---

69. That this type of theology was not unique to ancient Israel is indicated, e.g., by the stele of King Mesha of Moab from the second half of the ninth century B.C.E., in which Mesha attributes Moab's previous subservience to Israel to the anger of Moab's chief deity, Chemosh. See *ANET*, pp. 320-21.

70. See Carl S. Ehrlich, "'Anti-Judäismus' in der hebräischen Bibel. Der Fall: Ezechiel," *Vetus Testamentum* 46 (1996): 169-78; "Ezekiel: The Prophet, His Times, His Message," *European Judaism* 99, no. 1 (1999): 116-31, esp. pp. 125-28.

ship. In spite of all that God does for Israel, the latter always betrays God's trust and succumbs to the temptation of following other gods. This pattern is established already during the exodus narrative, specifically in the story of the Golden Calf (Exod. 32) and in the wilderness wanderings; is reiterated in the book of Judges (2:10b-23); and is the pattern into which the Deuteronomistic history (Joshua, Judges, Samuel, and Kings) places the story of biblical Israel. Deutero-Isaiah, however, envisioned a future redemption in terms of the past, but one in which all the mistakes of the past would be gloriously corrected. At the time of their new exodus the people would march in festive procession directly to Jerusalem, encountering no hindrances on the way (e.g., Isa. 43:16-21; 48:20-21).[71] God would level every mountain and fill in every valley in order to make a clear path for the redeemed. No enemy would attack Israel on the way, and Israel would not rebel against God's authority. The greatness of God would become manifest for all the earth to see; Jerusalem would become the center of the world; and Israel would live in peace. In this manner Deutero-Isaiah was attempting to fit his expectations for the future into the patterns of the past, but on a transcendental level. Granted, the new exodus would be from the east (Babylon) and not from the west (Egypt), but the basic idea was the same. With hindsight we know that the glorious future envisioned by Deutero-Isaiah did not come to pass as such on the historical plane, but the compilers of the Bible did not view that as a problem, as long as the theological import of his message accorded with their own vision.[72]

In essence, what both Ezekiel and Deutero-Isaiah were trying to do was to foster a sense of identity and common purpose among the exiles, who were accused by their cousins in the land of having fallen from God's graces by virtue of their being exiled (Ezek. 11:14-21). On the contrary, they argued that the true Israel was to be found in exile and would return to the land to repopulate it once again. Ezekiel and Deutero-Isaiah, in other words, were denying the legitimacy of those who remained in the land. Indeed, once some of the exiles returned and came into conflict with those who remained in the land, an attempt was made to identify those in the land as Canaanites (Ezra-Nehemiah). The exodus tradition served their purposes well. It set a pattern whereby all of true Israel was exiled, only to return home after a long absence to reclaim the land that was rightfully theirs from a population that had no theological claim to it. On the one hand this claim that all true Judeans had been exiled set up artificial

71. On the exodus theme in Deutero-Isaiah see Hans M. Barstad, *A Way in the Wilderness: The "Second Exodus" in the Message of Second Isaiah,* Journal of Semitic Studies Monograph 12 (Manchester: University of Manchester Press, 1989).

72. See the quotation of an unfulfilled prophecy of Micah as proof of the true nature of Jeremiah's status as a prophet in Jer. 26:17-19.

boundaries between the closely related in-group and out-group; on the other it fostered a sense of solidarity and community among those in the in-group, who characterized the out-group as the "other." This certainly applies to the exodus tradition, no matter when one dates it.

Archaeological and extrabiblical evidence would suggest that there never was a large-scale exodus of slaves from ancient Egypt, no matter how one twists and turns the outrageously high biblical numbers, nor was there a large-scale invasion of Canaan by a foreign population at the end of the Bronze Age. As Helga Weippert has written, "Kings come and go, but the cooking pots stay the same."[73] The population of Canaan did not change at the time the rise of the Israelites is dated. Hence the conclusion seems inescapable that the Israelites were in fact Canaanites, who at some point in time assumed a new religious and social identity that led them to reject their past and those who reminded them of their past in the strongest possible terms. In this forging of a new identity, the exodus played an important role. We will probably never know whether the exodus tradition bases itself on the historical memory of some individual or small group that did indeed leave Egyptian servitude.[74] However, in ancient times it served the purpose of guaranteeing a common Israelite identity, separate from that of the indigenous Canaanites. In the exodus tradition, Israel found a common heritage that served to unite a people made up of different tribal and ethnic elements. By means of the creative fiction that they shared a common experience of slavery, that they were all rescued from Egypt by their national God, that they all entered into a covenant with God at Mount Sinai, and that they conquered the land together, no one could claim any preferential status based in being there first. Israel came into existence at one moment in time as one unit under the leadership of one prophet. Moses thus serves as the ultimate authority figure and conduit of divine will.

The situation has been no different for Jews throughout the ages. Passover is the holiday that celebrates the redemption from Egypt, as biblically mandated (Exod. 12:1-28; Lev. 23:5-8; Num. 28:16-25; Deut. 16:1-8). Throughout history Jews all over the world have gathered on the evening of the fourteenth day of the first month, Nisan, to celebrate the Passover in a ritual meal known as the seder ("order"). The table is set with symbolic foods, and the story of the Passover and exodus is related according to a script laid

---

73. "Könige kommen, Könige gehen, aber die Kochtöpfe bleiben." Helge Weippert, *Palästina in vorhellenistischer Zeit* (Munich: Beck, 1988), p. 352.

74. It should be noted that the Egyptian slavery as depicted in the Bible is not chattel slavery but state-enforced labor. Redford (*Egypt, Canaan, and Israel*, p. 412) has conjectured that the exodus tradition is the Canaanite remnant of a dim historical memory of the Hyksos period in Egypt, with the expulsion of the Hyksos circa 1550 serving as the basis for the development of the mythology of the exodus.

out in a book known as the Haggadah ("Story" or "Retelling"). Every Jew is enjoined to regard himself or herself as if personally redeemed from Egypt. Indeed, there is a tradition according to which the souls of all Jews born and unborn were present to hear the revelation at Mount Sinai.[75] While not literally true, this does contain within it a theological truth that has helped sustain the Jewish people over the course of the millennia; that is, that there is a common experience and heritage that all share. Every Jew was there, every Jew was a witness to God's great act of salvation, and every Jew was a participant in the covenant at Mount Sinai. It does not matter if one is able to trace one's ancestry back a thousand generations or if one has just converted to Judaism. The story of the exodus plays the same role for modern Jews as it did for their ancestors. It is a foundational narrative that provides them with a shared common identity and a sense of equality. It is surely significant that Moses is not mentioned once in the context of the seder ritual. It is as if his memory is deliberately suppressed in order to emphasize God's central action, without the need for human agency. Introducing Moses into the narrative would perhaps lead to the veneration or even apotheosis of a mere mortal, which is not exactly a democratic concept.

To some extent, Ahad Ha'am was correct. Historicity is often a matter of perception, not fact. The power of the symbol generally outweighs any conclusions that dusty historians may draw about the past. Unlike Ahad Ha'am, those who explore the past as an avocation oftentimes live in two worlds. There is the world as they perceive it and the world as they reconstruct it. The one shelters them, the other provides them with an endless source of fascination.

In the view of many historians of the ancient world, Moses belongs firmly in the realm of legend. There is no external evidence for his life and deeds. Whoever he was, if indeed he was, all that remains of him is the legacy that future generations have attached to his name. And it is precisely this image of Moses, as Ahad Ha'am recognized, which has been most active and influential in the realm of history for Judaism, Christianity, and Islam.

De Vita Mosis

The life of Moses is not as straightforward a story as a cursory reading of the Hebrew Bible would have us suppose, although for the sake of convenience it is useful to adhere to the rough canonical sequence of events. As the past few centuries of biblical scholarship have shown, the Hebrew Bible is a composite

---

75. *Exodus Rabbah* 28:6.

document in which a variety of voices speak in oftentimes contradictory ways.

Jewish tradition views Moses as the author of, or at any rate the one who wrote down, the Torah.[76] As a matter of fact, this belief in the literal reception of the Torah by Moses on Mount Sinai has been used as a litmus test in orthodox Jewish circles to distinguish "Torah-true" Jews from supposedly heretical ones influenced by the skepticism of the modern world. This has led on the one hand to the sanctification of the text of the Torah, and on the other to the fiction that the text is perfect in every way. Generations of scribes are supposed to have handed it down with no mistakes over the course of the millennia, ever since the original version was received by Moses seven weeks after the night of the original Passover. Ironically, the tenability of this theology is gainsaid by editions of the Hebrew Bible printed by the very people who defend its perfection. At the back of every Bible printed, for example, by the Koren Publishing Company, one will find a list of manuscript variants, which stands in sharp contrast to the doctrine of the text's immutability. Nonetheless, the perfection of the text of the Bible and its antiquity continue to be defended in "fundamentalist" Jewish circles, a position whose lack of tenability has been clear for centuries to those versed in the Hebrew manuscript tradition. This was graphically illustrated in the middle of the last century by the find of the famous Dead Sea Scrolls, in which variant versions of the same biblical book were found in use within the context of one traditional community.[77]

Already in medieval times the unitary Mosaic nature of Torah was tentatively called into question. How could someone who really "was a very humble man, more so than any other man on earth" (Num. 12:3) refer to himself as such? In addition, would this very humble man have eulogized himself by claiming about himself in the third person that "Never again did there arise in Israel a prophet like Moses" (Deut. 34:10a)? This passage is difficult on a number of levels if one assumes Mosaic authorship. First there is the question of the contrast between the traditional meekness of the man and the seemingly immodest statement about his prophetic inspiration. Second is the perspective of the passage, which seems to indicate a familiarity with a long line of prophetic

---

76. Such arguments have also been adduced in Christianity and Islam. See S. A. Nigosian, "Moses as They Saw Him," *Vetus Testamentum* 43 (1993): 342.

77. On the Dead Sea Scrolls see Lawrence H. Schiffman, *Reclaiming the Dead Sea Scrolls: The History of Judaism, the Background of Christianity, the Lost Library of Qumran* (Philadelphia and Jerusalem: Jewish Publication Society, 1994); Neil Asher Silberman, *The Hidden Scrolls: Christianity, Judaism, and the War for the Dead Sea Scrolls* (New York: Riverhead Books, 1994); Hartmut Stegemann, *The Library of Qumran: On the Essenes, Qumran, John the Baptist, and Jesus*, translated from the German of 1993 (Grand Rapids and Cambridge, U.K.: Eerdmans; Leiden, New York, and Cologne: Brill, 1998).

tradition. After all, how could one refer to the greatest of the prophets without knowledge of who came later? And third is the question of how someone could be writing about his own life and legacy in the past tense.

The medieval period was the heyday of European Jewish biblical commentary. Major figures in both southern and northern Europe wrote verse-by-verse commentaries on biblical books, a tradition that continues until today. The most famous of these commentaries circulated widely among the disparate Jewish communities. Eventually a number of the most significant commentaries were anthologized in collections known as *miqrā'ôt gĕdôlôt,* or rabbinic Bibles. In the juxtaposition of the biblical text with its translation into Aramaic, the Targum, along with a number of commentaries from different centuries and countries, the reader is invited to become a part of an ongoing dialogue and debate that reach back into antiquity.

Among the many commentators, none is more beloved than Rabbi Shlomo ben Yitzhaq (1040-1105), known by his acronym as Rashi, who lived in northern France. Not surprisingly, the question of Mosaic authorship of the passage under consideration is one that he addressed. However, as is oftentimes typical of the methods of Jewish biblical interpretation, Rashi advances more than one interpretative possibility without, however, identifying *the* correct one. On the one hand Rashi comments on Deuteronomy 34:5, "And Moses died there,"[78] by asking how it could be possible that Moses continued writing. Thus he concludes that Moses wrote the whole Torah until the end of Deuteronomy 34:4. The final verses must have been penned by Moses' successor Joshua, the putative author of the book bearing his name according to Jewish tradition. On the other hand Rashi cites Rabbi Meir, an earlier authority who, when faced with the seeming paradox of Moses writing about his own death, asked whether it is conceivable that the Torah could have been left incomplete by Moses. He then cites a midrash according to which Moses was dutifully taking dictation from God until he reached the passage about his own death, at which point he objected to having to continue writing. However, when God reminded him that he had always been a faithful servant of the divine, Moses continued writing, but with a tear in his eye.[79] By juxtaposing these two interpretations, Rashi seems to give primacy to his own view, but perhaps modestly gives the last word to the tradition he inherited.

Another great commentator, Rabbi Abraham ibn Ezra, who lived in Spain (1089-1164), agreed with Rashi that Moses could not have written the last few verses of Deuteronomy. Indeed, he went beyond Rashi in attributing the whole of Deuteronomy 34 to another hand. According to tradition, Moses ascended

---

78. Author's translation.
79. *BT Bava Batra* 15a and *Menahot* 30a.

42

Mount Nebo, where he was to die alone, by himself. How then could Moses have written the passage about his death and have it delivered to the Israelites in the plains of Moab? Moses must have laid down his pen at the end of chapter 33, and the whole of chapter 34 must have been written by Joshua, who as a prophet was moved by the divine spirit to write about events that he had himself not witnessed.

In his skepticism regarding the overarching claim of Mosaic authorship of the Torah, ibn Ezra was giving voice to a decidedly rationalist streak in his interpretative method, the most famous example of which is his comment to Genesis 12:6b: "The Canaanites were then in the land." Ibn Ezra rightly deduced that the passage must have been written from the perspective of a much later author than Moses, since this parenthetical comment makes sense only in the context of hindsight. However, it is one thing to speculate that the final verses of the Torah were added by Moses' successor. It is quite another to question the attribution of a verse in the middle of the Torah, one that presents the perspective of an author who lived well after the time not only of Moses but also of Joshua. Hence ibn Ezra raises the possibility that the verse in question is to be understood along the lines of "at that time the Canaanites were *already* in the land," assuming that there was some lost tradition that the Canaanites themselves, like the Israelites, had invaded the land at some point in time. In the event that this is not the case, ibn Ezra hints that there may be a hidden meaning in the text, one that is better kept to oneself if one has indeed understood it. Ibn Ezra understood quite well that once one begins to question the traditional understanding of the nature of the text, one begins to descend a slippery slope that could end with the questioning of the religious truths that the interpreters of the text are attempting to convey.

While ibn Ezra would have been horrified to be considered anything but a paragon of the faithful and observant Jew, he was quite correct in identifying the paths down which it is difficult to travel and at the same time retain one's simple faith in the divine nature of the text — hence his cautionary note. However, slowly but surely over the course of the centuries rationalist and skeptical thought began to erode the notion that the text of the Torah was a divinely perfect creation.

In his *Tractatus Theologico-Politicus* (1670) Baruch (Benedict) Spinoza was one of the first to propose that the Torah is a human rather than a divine creation.[80] His basic hermeneutic insight was to read the Bible as he would any other work of literature. While he accepted the divine nature of the ethics of the Bible, he viewed the book itself as a human work. In this manner he attempted

---

80. See Brayton Polka, "Spinoza and Biblical Interpretation: The Paradox of Modernity," *European Legacy* 1 (1996): 1673-82.

to read the Bible on its own terms, without the presuppositions of what he viewed as later religious tradition. In this he was anticipating later approaches to the text. Needless to say, however, the Jewish community of his native Amsterdam did not take kindly to his humanizing of the Bible and excommunicated him.

It is ironic that the foundation of the critical theory that toppled the presumption of Mosaic authorship and dominated the field of biblical studies during the nineteenth and twentieth centuries was laid by someone who was trying to prove the exact opposite, namely, that Moses did indeed write the Pentateuch. In 1753 Jean Astruc, physician to Louis XIV of France, published an anonymous work in which he undertook an analysis of the methods that Moses employed in writing the Torah. On the basis of the variation between divine names that is particularly noticeable in Genesis, Astruc isolated two major literary documents and a number of minor ones that served Moses as his sources. Thus, although Astruc was conceding human agency in the writing of sacred scripture, he remained convinced that Moses was the one who did the compiling and editing of the Torah. In the end, Astruc's analysis came to be the progenitor of all later literary analyses of the Pentateuch that eventually came to deny the Mosaic authorship of the text, as well as in some cases its divine origin or inspiration.

The classic reconstruction of the literary composition of the Torah follows Julius Wellhausen's division of the Pentateuch into four sources, known by their initials as "J" (the Yahwistic or "Jehovist" source), "E" (the Elohistic source), "D" (the Deuteronomistic source), and "P" (the Priestly source).[81] According to the Wellhausenian reconstruction, the J source was the oldest (tenth/ninth century B.C.E.) and could be associated with the kingdom of Judah, the more southerly of the two Israelite countries in antiquity. It received its name on account of its early narrative use of YHWH, the Tetragrammaton. The E source, the most fragmentary of the Pentateuchal sources, was about a century younger and stemmed from the northern kingdom of Israel. It was so designated on account of its overwhelming use of the generic term *'ĕlōhîm*, "God," until the revelation of the Tetragrammaton to Moses. The D source, dated to the late seventh century B.C.E., was associated with the cultic reforms and centralization of King Josiah of Judah. The P source stemmed from circles of priests working to preserve their heritage during the time of the Babylonian exile in the mid–sixth century B.C.E. Hence, ascrib-

81. See Julius Wellhausen, *Prolegomena to the History of Ancient Israel* (1878; reprint, Gloucester, Mass.: Peter Smith, 1973). Although little is original to Wellhausen in his source division, it was he who formulated it in a manner that transformed the documentary hypothesis into the basis of most subsequent work on the Pentateuch. For an eminently readable recapitulation of a modified four-source theory, see Richard Elliot Friedman, *Who Wrote the Bible?* (New York: Summit Books, 1987).

ing a text to a specific source would also help in identifying the particular historical ideology motivating its composition.

The traditional source division as envisioned by Wellhausen has dominated
the field of biblical studies for more than a century, but it has come under attack
in recent years. New models have been proposed that in their own way are much
more complex than Wellhausen's scissors-and-paste model of the Bible's origin.
A number of scholars have called into question the existence of independent literary documents. Although none would dispute the existence of a D source that
was to serve as the basis of the book of Deuteronomy and was affiliated with the
Deuteronomistic school that produced the so-called Deuteronomistic history in
Joshua, Judges, Samuel, and Kings, the existence of E as well as J has been called
into question. Some scholars now advocate the division of the sources in the first
four books of the Hebrew Bible into P and non-P materials, with P being both the
creator and editor of the continuous narrative structure of Israel's ancient story.[82]
Nonetheless, one of the most radical aspects of the attack on Wellhausen's documentary hypothesis has come from those who would question his early dating of
the J and E sources, arguing instead that whatever the date of the possible oral traditions underlying these later texts, the texts themselves were not written down in
the form in which we have inherited them until the time of the Babylonian exile
or probably later. Hence, in the view of this very vocal group of scholars, nothing
in the biblical record preserves any historical memory that approaches the alleged
time of Moses, Joshua, the Judges, David, or Solomon. Needless to say, the date a
scholar assigns a text will to a great extent determine the meaning she or he derives from it. Thus dating is not simply an empty intellectual enterprise, but more
often than not governs the text's interpretation.

Birth and Infancy (Exodus 1:1–2:10)

Moses dominates the biblical books of Exodus, Leviticus, Numbers, and Deuteronomy. If Genesis can be considered the introduction or overture to the
main action, these latter four books form the central narrative around which
the Bible and Judaism revolve. And in this narrative, Moses is the predominant
human figure. In spite of the great importance attached to Moses in the Bible
and in later tradition, God remains the main actor.[83] The contrast between the

82. See, e.g., David M. Carr, *Reading the Fractures of Genesis: Historical and Literary
Approaches* (Louisville: Westminster/John Knox, 1996).

83. This is one of the factors that have led Daniel Jeremy Silver (*Images of Moses*
[New York: Basic Books, 1982], pp. 1-43) to refer to Moses as a "diminished hero." See also
Frederick Herzog, "Moses in Contemporary Theology," *Interpretation* 44 (1990): 258-59.

two is underlined by the differences in the manner in which they are introduced to the reader. God, who presumably preexists the creation of the world, appears in the first verse of the Bible as the main protagonist, setting the whole history of redemption into motion by his creative act. This stands in stark contrast to polytheistic notions of deity, in which creation is set in motion by the birth of the gods, who, although not mortal, can and do die. In spite of the fact that Moses' birth has aspects of the miraculous, he is a person born of the natural union between a man and a woman, who suckles and is weaned. Hence he is a human in every sense of the term.

The story of Moses' birth and infancy sets the scene for the lengthy narrative of redemption and covenant that is to follow. The book of Genesis has left the reader hanging. In order to escape a famine in Canaan, the family of Jacob/Israel has descended en masse to Egypt and settled there at the urging of Jacob's beloved son Joseph, who had risen to high esteem as Pharaoh's right-hand man. God's ancient promises to the ancestors — to Abraham and Sarah, to Isaac and Rebecca, to Jacob, Leah, and Rachel — namely, the assurances of numerous progeny and a land of their own, have yet to come to fulfillment. Indeed, according to the often-employed device of the cliff-hanger, the narrative seems to be moving in the opposite direction. While never great in number, at least the ancestors were able to roam in the land that had been promised them and even to purchase a parcel of it in Hebron as a burial cave (Gen. 23).[84] The descent of the Israelites into Egypt has physically removed them from what little concrete evidence they had of the eventual fulfillment of God's promise. However, what God takes with one hand he gives with the other. Ironically, the first verses of Exodus narrate the fulfillment of the first promise by telling how numerous the Israelites came to be in Egypt,[85] where, however, they became enslaved and subject to a policy of what anachronistically could be called genocide, when "[a] new king arose over Egypt who did not know Joseph" (Exod. 1:8).

In response to the perceived threat implied by the fecundity of the Israelites, Pharaoh determined to reduce their numbers through hard labor. However, all his efforts were in vain as the slaves continued to increase in number seemingly in direct proportion to the level of oppression (1:12). Finally Pharaoh tried a new tactic. He ordered the midwives of the Hebrews,[86]

84. The traditional location of the cave of Machpelah is a locus of tension between Jews and Muslims in the modern world.

85. Umberto Cassuto points out that seven terms are employed for the multiplication of the Israelites in Egypt, surely not a coincidental number but an indication of the craft of the author of the passage. See U. Cassuto, *A Commentary on the Book of Exodus,* translated from the Hebrew of 1961 by Israel Abrahams (Jerusalem: Magnes Press, 1967), p. 9.

86. The consonantal text is unclear whether the reference here should be to "He-

Shiphrah and Puah, to kill all baby boys at birth. However, being God-fearing women (whether Egyptian or Israelite), they subverted his command with a clever excuse that stereotyped the Israelite women as the "other" and different from "normal" Egyptian women. According to the midwives, the Hebrew women gave birth so quickly that by the time they arrived on the scene, the babies were long gone and hidden. The narrator makes sure to draw attention to the reward for good deeds by noting that God established their "households" (1:21). Frustrated in this strategy, Pharaoh now commanded his people to throw all Israelite boys into the Nile River, but to let the girls live.

This story encompasses many of the elements of a folktale, with all the lack of attention to narrative logic that such an ascription would imply. Who was the pharaoh who didn't know Joseph? How could only two midwives service a population consisting of 600,000 men (12:37) and their wives at a time when polygamy was presumably the norm? What was the logic behind killing the Israelites' baby boys rather than the girls? After all, if the Israelites were indeed engaged in heavy manual labor that included construction, wouldn't the Egyptians want as large a reserve as possible of strong male physical laborers available? Also, the number of children born to any population group is dependent on the number of women of childbearing age and not on the number of men, since one man can, in theory at least, impregnate a large number of women. On the other hand, since ethnicity in the Hebrew Bible was determined by patrilineal descent, in distinction from the matrilineal determination of Jewish identity established by later rabbinic Judaism, killing the Israelite males would destroy the people. The surviving women would then be absorbed into the general Egyptian population.

One of the literary devices the storyteller may be using here is irony. Pharaoh, who wanted to outsmart the Israelites ("Let us deal shrewdly with them," 1:10a), is himself outsmarted at every turn. Indeed, every one of his attempts to outsmart the Israelites is thwarted, in the first instance by God through their fecundity and in the development of the tale by all manner of women. This narrative detail must be read against the background of the patriarchal culture for which it was intended. Not only is Pharaoh, the god-king of Egypt, outsmarted by the God of the Israelites, but he is also the not-so-innocent victim of the weakest of the weak in patriarchal society, the women. In addition to the midwives, the women who play a significant role in defeating him in this narrative include the totality of the fertile Israelite women, as well as Moses' mother and sister and even Pharaoh's own daughter. His ultimate fate is in many ways similar to Saul's, namely, to stand alone, abandoned by all.

---

brew midwives" or to the "midwives of the Hebrew women." Thus their specific ethnicity is in question. See Brevard S. Childs, *The Book of Exodus: A Critical, Theological Commentary*, Old Testament Library (Philadelphia: Westminster, 1974), p. 16.

The (literally) high-born daughter of Pharaoh is carried back to the palace by her slaves. She gazes tenderly at the baby, who has been rescued from the Nile.
(An orientalizing scene by Sir Lawrence Alma-Tadema, *The Finding of Moses;* private collection)

The Hebrew Bible is a work that constantly subverts convention, in part because it is the legacy of a people that was itself a Johnny-come-lately on the world stage, and a very insignificant one at that. Thus there are any number of tales that end with the triumph of the one we would least expect. Isaac inherits the promise as his father's true heir, and not Ishmael. Jacob receives his father's blessing, and not Esau. David becomes king of Israel, and not one of his older brothers. Indeed, Moses becomes the leader of Israel, and not his older siblings Aaron or Miriam. In line with this narrative tendency are a number of stories in which women triumph over men. It is Tamar who outwits Judah (Gen. 38). It is Yael who triumphs over Sisera, and not Barak (Judg. 4–5). It is Delilah who vanquishes Samson (Judg. 16). And in the book of Esther it is the eponymous heroine who defeats the evil Haman. There is an additional passage that manages to convey the patriarchal horror of a man being defeated by a woman, namely, the story of Abimelech's failed attempt at kingship in Judges 9. After a woman has dropped a millstone on his head at the siege of Thebez, Abimelech begs his attendant to deliver the coup de grace so "that they may not say of me, 'A woman killed him!'" (Judg. 9:54). The frustration of Pharaoh's plans at the hands of the midwives can be viewed as his implicit emasculation. But from his perspective, there was worse yet to come.

Students of comparative religion and literature have often drawn attention to the cross-cultural phenomenon of the heralding of the birth of a significant figure by recounting the miraculous nature of his/her birth or of her/his miraculous rescue from some imminent and ominous threat. So too in the case of Moses, who is rescued from certain death both by divine providence and by the machinations of a number of women, all of whom ultimately work together to thwart the purpose of the supreme ruler of Egypt, the pharaoh.[87]

Once again a number of women band together in order to thwart Pharaoh's cruel intentions. The participation of Moses' mother and sister in his rescue was a brave but not unexpected act. The crucial role played by the very daughter of Pharaoh is the surprise twist in the story, and recalls Michal's betrayal of her father Saul by becoming the instrument of David's salvation (1 Sam. 19:11-17).

For the birth of Moses, the scene shifts focus once again to the Israelites, specifically to two Levites who marry and have a son.[88] When his mother could no longer hide him from the Egyptians, she placed him in a "wicker basket" (Exod. 2:3, 5)[89] and set it afloat on the Nile. In this manner the letter of Pharaoh's decree but not its spirit was fulfilled. Observing the scene was the baby's sister. As luck, providence, or motherly intention would have it, the basket came to rest in the reeds where it was found by Pharaoh's own daughter when she came down to the water to bathe. Recognizing immediately that the baby was a Hebrew, she nonetheless took pity on it and adopted it as her own. When the anonymous sister appeared and suggested that the princess give the baby to a Hebrew wet nurse, the child came into its own mother's possession until it was weaned. This birth narrative ends with an etiology of the name Moses. Pharaoh's daughter declares that she shall name him Moses (Heb. Mosheh) because "I drew him out of the water" (2:10).

The naming of Moses is one of the many small details that highlight the folktale nature of this account. In the context of the narrative, it would appear that the daughter of Pharaoh knew enough Hebrew to make a clever play on words in naming the child *mōsheh* on the basis of *mĕshîtîhû*, "I drew him out." Other than the unlikelihood of her knowing any Hebrew, let alone enough for

---

87. Pharaoh is a general designation for the ruler of Egypt. The word itself originally meant the palace, i.e., the "big house," and its usage as referring to the ruler of Egypt is akin to the personification of the "White House" or of "Buckingham Palace."

88. Members of the tribe of Levi. In Second Temple days (515 B.C.E.–70 C.E.) the Levites functioned as priests of second rank. Their origin may be sought among the priests of the north who fled to Judah after the Assyrian conquest.

89. The word that is used here for "basket," *tēbâ*, appears in one other narrative in the Hebrew Bible. It is also used in reference to Noah's "ark" (Gen. 6–9, passim).

such a clever pun, the name *mōsheh* in Hebrew would mean "the one who draws out" and not "the one who is drawn out." The latter meaning would more properly be attached to a hypothetical name such as *māshûy*. Hence, a Hebrew derivation of the name seems unlikely.[90] Much more likely is that the archetypal Jew had an Egyptian name.[91] On the level of the narrative, it would be much more logical for Pharaoh's daughter to want to hide the ethnic origin of her son by giving him an Egyptian name. And indeed, the root *msy* is a common element in Egyptian names such as Thutmoses and Ramses and means "child" or "son of." The name of Moses is, therefore, most likely an abbreviated Egyptian name which is missing the divine element that usually complements it, although whether this was done for theological or practical reasons is open to discussion. While Moses' Egyptian name could be taken as proof of the general historicity of the Exodus account[92] — and indeed, Freud used this as an important piece of evidence in arguing that Moses was in point of fact an Egyptian and not a Hebrew[93] — it could also be argued that the use of such a common element represents the attempt of the narrator to imbue the story with a putative but unconvincing Egyptian flavor.

Other than the names of Moses and the midwives, only one more element in this narrative evidences any specificity, namely, the names of the garrison or store cities upon which the Israelites had to labor. Pithom and Raamses (1:11) are identifiably Egyptian names, the former for a temple estate of the god Atum and the latter a city associated with Ramses II, both presumably located in the eastern Nile delta. Therefore, many would use this reference as evidence that the Israelites were enslaved during the reign of Ramses II, under whose rule the exodus would have presumably taken place.[94] Others would date it to the time of his successor Merneptah.[95] The iconoclastic Redford, however, has argued that the names entered the biblical account solely because of their geographic location in the part of Egypt nearest Canaan and their familiarity to a scribe writing long after the supposed time of the events narrated. In his opinion the mention of these names in this passage is a very weak hook upon which to hang

---

90. Nahum M. Sarna (*Exodus,* The JPS Torah Commentary [Philadelphia and New York: Jewish Publication Society, 1991], p. 10) argues that the active voice in Moses' name prefigures his later activity in drawing Israel out of the waters of the Reed Sea.

91. See, e.g., J. Gwyn Griffiths, "The Egyptian Derivation of the Name Moses," *Journal of Near Eastern Studies* 12 (1953): 225-31.

92. E.g., Nahum M. Sarna, *Exploring Exodus: The Heritage of Biblical Israel* (New York: Schocken Books, 1987), pp. 32-33.

93. Freud, pp. 4-6, 73-74.

94. E.g., Frank J. Yurco, "Merneptah's Canaanite Campaign and Israel's Origins," in *Exodus: The Egyptian Evidence,* p. 45.

95. On the issue of dating the exodus see Kitchen, 2:700-708, esp. pp. 702-3.

a chronology, particularly in light of the less than supportive archaeological evidence for the biblical account.[96]

Apart from these names, the story has a timeless quality about it. There is nothing about it that would indicate any sort of specific historical framework. The pharaoh is unnamed, as indeed are all the rulers of Egypt in the Pentateuch; nor, with the exception of Moses and the midwives, are any of the major actors of the birth narrative named. As has been pointed out innumerable times, the story of Moses' birth has all the elements of the typical "birth of the hero" legend.[97] This is a story type in which the important stature of the hero is emphasized through the device of placing him in mortal danger at birth. Only through the intervention of God, the gods, or fate does the hero survive to fulfill his mission in life. In addition to Moses, similar accounts are known from the ancient Mediterranean world concerning Sargon of Akkad, Oedipus of Thebes,[98] Cyrus the Great of Persia, and Jesus of Nazareth.[99] The major innovation of the Moses account is that after going from rags to riches by leaving behind the life of an Israelite slave and becoming a prince of Egypt, the Moses story continues by having Moses go from riches back to rags.[100]

The lack of specificity in the Moses birth narrative has provided the opening for the development of a rich interpretative literature whose function is to fill in the gaps in the story. Within the Jewish tradition this literature is known as midrash. Midrash is both a type of literature and a method of interpretation. The word itself is derived from the Hebrew verbal root *d.r.sh*, whose basic meaning is "to ask, seek, or interpret." It has given its name to a method of interpretation that seeks to elicit the meaning of a text by paying attention to every detail in it. Gaps in the text are filled in by the development of traditions that the interpreters feel are in the spirit of the basic text. In addition to this definition, midrash refers to the literature that is developed on the basis of the midrashic method. There are two basic forms of midrash. The first is termed "midrash halakah." This is a type of literature that concerns itself with the exposition of Jewish law and practice. By far the more beloved form of midrash is the "midrash aggada," which comprises the Jewish homiletic and legendary lit-

96. See Donald B. Redford, "Exodus 1:11," *Vetus Testamentum* 13 (1963): 401-18.

97. See, e.g., Brevard S. Childs, "The Birth of Moses," *Journal of Biblical Literature* 84 (1965): 109-22.

98. See Robert C. Marshall, "Moses, Oedipus, Structuralism, and History," *History of Religions* 28 (1989): 245-66.

99. The influence of the Moses story on the birth narratives of Jesus is particularly strong, although the latter seem to have influenced some later midrashic additions to the Moses cycle (see Allan Kensky, "Moses and Jesus: The Birth of the Savior," *Judaism* 42, no. 1 [1993]: 43-49).

100. See, e.g., Childs, *The Book of Exodus*, p. 12.

erature. As a rule of thumb, when midrash is referred to without any more explanation, there can be little doubt that the reference is to midrash aggada. Although it is common to refer to "the midrash," it should be borne in mind that
the reference is generally to "a midrash." The midrashic literature is a vast compendium spanning close to two millennia, in which stories and legends that are
mutually exclusive in their narrative development are able to exist comfortably
in close proximity to one another.[101]

Just as nature abhors a vacuum, so too does midrash. Therefore,
postbiblical midrashic literature fills in many of the details missing from the
story of Moses' birth, such as the names of the parents and the sister, which
can be deduced from later passages in the Bible; of the princess;[102] and of
Pharaoh's counselors,[103] as well as offering longer accounts devoted to the
midwives.[104] It is on the basis of later biblical passages that Moses' family
members are identified, although the names do not seem to be integral to his
birth narrative. According to the genealogy of Exodus 6:20, Moses' parents

101. On midrash as a literary genre see, e.g., Geoffrey H. Hartman and Sanford
Budick, eds., *Midrash and Literature* (New Haven and London: Yale University Press,
1986); Barry W. Holtz, "Midrash," in *Back to the Sources: Reading the Classic Jewish Texts,*
ed. Barry W. Holtz (New York: Summit Books, 1984), pp. 177-211; Jacob Neusner, *A Midrash Reader* (Minneapolis: Fortress, 1990); Neusner, *What Is Midrash?* (Philadelphia: Fortress, 1987); Gary G. Porton, *Understanding Rabbinic Midrash: Text and Commentary*
(Hoboken, N.J.: KTAV, 1985); Shinan, *The World of the Aggadah.* Excellent compilations of
midrashim can be found in Hayim Nahman Bialik and Yehoshua Hana Ravnitzky, eds.,
The Book of Legends (Sefer Ha-Aggadah): Legends from the Talmud and Midrash, translated
from the Hebrew of 1952 by William G. Braude (New York: Schocken Books, 1992); Louis
Ginzberg, ed., *Legends of the Jews,* 7 vols. (Philadelphia: Jewish Publication Society, 1928,
1956) (an eclectic text that presents the midrashim as a running parallel text to the Bible);
James L. Kugel, *The Bible as It Was* (Cambridge, Mass., and London: Harvard University
Press, 1997); Kugel, *Traditions of the Bible: A Guide to the Bible as It Was at the Start of the
Common Era* (Cambridge, Mass., and London: Harvard University Press, 1998). Quite a
number of midrashic collections have been translated directly from the Hebrew into En-
glish, among which one may mention — in addition to the Soncino Classics edition avail-
able on CD-ROM that was mentioned above and contains a translation of the *Midrash
Rabbah* — Jacob Z. Lauterbach, trans., *Mekilta de-Rabbi Ishmael,* 3 vols. (Philadelphia:
Jewish Publication Society, 1933, 1961).

102. Bithiah according to *Exodus Rabbah* 1:26; Thermoutis according to Flavius
Josephus, *Jewish (Judean) Antiquities* 2.224.

103. According to *Exodus Rabbah* 1:9 and *BT Sotah* 11a, they were Balaam, who advised Pharaoh to kill the males and hence was killed in turn (Num. 31:8); Job, who was silent and hence afflicted with personal misery; and Jethro, who left and was rewarded by
becoming Moses' father-in-law. Other ancient traditions identify them as Jannes and
Jambres. See Kugel, *Bible as It Was,* pp. 290-92.

104. See Jonathan Cohen, *The Origins and Evolution of the Moses Nativity Story*
(Leiden: Brill, 1993).

were named Amram and Yocheved. Significantly, when his sister is first intro-duced, it is as the sister of Aaron (15:20), who has already been introduced as Moses' brother (4:13). However, all this information is missing from the birth narrative. In this passage the parents are introduced simply as Levites, al-though the introduction of his mother literally as a "daughter of Levi" has been read in one midrashic tradition as implying that she was quite old[105] and that Moses' birth was miraculous also in the manner that the birth of Isaac was to Sarah at a very advanced age.

When the pregnancy of Moses' mother is related, it appears right after the notice about her wedding (2:1-2). This makes it appear as if her pregnancy with Moses is her first. However, when her baby is three months old and she sets him in a basket in the Nile, an older daughter suddenly appears on the scene (2:4). This tension in the text, which could lead a critical scholar to conclude that the daughter is a secondary motif, is harmonized by a midrash in the following manner:[106] When Amram, Moses' father and one of the leaders of the Israelites according to the midrashic tradition, heard about Pharaoh's decree, he imme-diately divorced his wife and urged all other Israelites to do the same, in order that no babies be born to them only to be slaughtered at birth. Miriam, for that is the name of the only sister of Moses known to tradition, castigated her father by claiming that he was worse than Pharaoh. Whereas Pharaoh only con-demned the males to death, Amram through his actions was ensuring that no Israelites at all would be born. Severely chastened, Amram returned to his wife and remarried her. In this manner the midrash is claiming that there is no ten-sion in the text. Moses' parents were both newlyweds and the parents of two older children.

The biblical text does not inform the reader how the princess knew that the baby in the basket was a Hebrew. Cecil B. DeMille solved this problem in his movie *The Ten Commandments* by having the baby wrapped in a cloth as worn by the Hebrew slaves. *Exodus Rabbah* 1:24 claims the princess knew because the baby was circumcised.[107] The authors of the midrash, living in a post-Hellenis-tic world, were not aware that circumcision was also practiced by the ancient Egyptians.[108]

---

105. According to *Exodus Rabbah* 1:19, Yocheved was 130 years old at the time of Moses' birth. This is based on a rabbinic tradition that there were 210 years between the descent to Egypt and the exodus. Since Moses was 80 years old at the time of the exodus, it was deduced that his mother, who must have been born after the descent since she is not listed among those who went down to Egypt, must have been 130 years old.

106. *Exodus Rabbah* 1:13.

107. There is also a tradition that Moses was born circumcised, as if to accentuate his holiness and later mission in life. See *Exodus Rabbah* 1:20.

108. On the question of the origin of the Israelite practice of circumcision and the

Turning back to the midwives, a commonsense approach to whether they were Israelite or Egyptian might dictate that they were Egyptian. As Pharaoh's decree was harsh and against the nature of a midwife dedicated to bringing life into the world and not snuffing it out, how much more absurd would it be to assume that he would ask Israelite midwives to murder their own children? Nonetheless, the majority of midrashim conclude that the midwives were Israelite, since non-Israelite women could not minister to the needs of Israelites according to later tradition.[109] Here one can identify another characteristic trend of rabbinic midrash, namely, to read the past in light of the midrashic author's present. Be that as it may, the midrash then continued to ask which Israelite women the midwives were, since it would be inconceivable that such important women should be part of the anonymous rabble. Although the Bible names them Shiphrah and Puah, the midrashic tradition attempted to find more significant figures behind these presumed aliases. Not surprisingly, the midwives were taken to be Yocheved and either her mother-in-law, Elisheva, or more probably her daughter, Miriam.[110] In this manner the women who in tandem watched over and protected Moses were transformed in the midrashic tradition into the figurative mothers and caretakers of the nation as a whole, which served to elevate their already heightened profiles in the same manner as other midrashim elevated Moses, the major object of their solicitous care.

In Pharaoh's Court (Exodus 2:11-15)

The biblical story of Moses' infancy ends with his naming by his adoptive mother once he has been weaned. The narrative is resumed with Moses a grown man. The intervening years are of no interest to the biblical narrator. In essence the stage has been set. The identity of Moses has been established. Through the story of his close brush with death and subsequent salvation, his importance in the divine scheme has been underlined. Since he is ostensibly being raised as an Egyptian, Moses has apparently left the Israelite fold. All of which serves to heighten the narrative tension.

Moses' lacking childhood and youth is one of those blatant gaps in the biblical account that cry out for the filling in of detail by postbiblical sources. Thus the years of Moses' life as a child and as an Egyptian prince are the subject of a number of midrashic traditions. These are stories that try to fill in the

---

differences between Egyptian and Israelite methods of circumcising, see Jack M. Sasson, "Circumcision in the Ancient Near East," *Journal of Biblical Literature* 85 (1966): 473-76.

109. Cohen, pp. 92-95.

110. *Exodus Rabbah* 1:13.

blanks concerning his upbringing and education, as well as the development of his character. If there is any unifying thread to these narratives, it is that they postulate the formation of all of Moses' positive and exemplary character traits at an early age. In addition, a number of midrashim lay stress on the divine guidance and protection of Moses.

One such tradition is preserved in the midrash according to which only the intervention of the angel Gabriel saved the baby Moses from a life-threatening ordeal organized by Pharaoh's magicians.[111] According to this midrash, Moses' mother used to bring her much-admired child along to the palace. Once when he was sitting on his adoptive grandfather's lap, he grabbed the crown from his head. Pharaoh's magicians were incensed by the act, and ominously warned that this was an omen that Moses would eventually threaten his kingship. Therefore they counseled a radical course of action, namely, putting the infant Moses to death. Jethro, who is identified in this midrash as one of Pharaoh's counselors, suggested putting Moses to the test by placing a golden object and a glowing coal before the child. If he reached for the gold, it would prove his pretensions to the throne. Moses was about to reach for the glittering gold when the angel Gabriel directed his hand to the coal. When Moses burned his hand, he instinctively moved his hand to his mouth and burned his tongue, thus giving rise to the speech impediment that would occasion his plea to God later in life to release him from presenting the Israelites' case in the public forum (4:10).

A version of this tale also appears in Josephus.[112] However, Josephus changed some details in order not to imply that Moses both figuratively and literally made a grab for Pharaoh's authority. In the Josephean version, Moses did not place the crown on his own head, but had it placed there by the playful pharaoh. The offense that so upset the court was Moses' innocent grabbing of the crown that was already on his head and hurling it to the ground. The supersessionist symbolism of this act would have been apparent to Josephus's first-century audience, without implying that Moses was a power-hungry potential usurper.[113] The supernatural is also missing from this version of the tale. It is not Gabriel who rescues Moses from an ordeal, but his mother who snatches him away to safety.

The question of Moses' education at the Egyptian court has also concerned Jewish interpreters. Although Josephus is relatively reticent on the subject, his older contemporary Philo of Alexandria waxed poetic about the subjects in

111. *Exodus Rabbah* 1:26.

112. Josephus, *Antiquities* 2.232-36.

113. Louis H. Feldman, *Jew and Gentile in the Ancient World* (Princeton: Princeton University Press, 1993), pp. 247-48. But see Shinan, pp. 54-57, for whom the tale in Josephus is primary and possibly based on an earlier Greek tale.

An enraged Moses leaps to the rescue and strikes the Egyptian taskmaster, while
two Israelite slaves cower in the background (see Exod. 2:12).

(Arthur Szyk, The Haggadah; Massada Press, Tel Aviv)

which Moses was instructed in the best schools of Egypt.[114] This is echoed in the New Testament's statement that "Moses was instructed in all the wisdom of the Egyptians and was powerful in his words and deeds" (Acts 7:22 NRSV).

When the biblical tale resumes, we are simply informed that, at some later time, Moses "went out to his kinsfolk and witnessed their labors" (Exod. 2:11). Is this the omniscient narrator ironically informing us that Moses, the prince of Egypt, happened to go out to observe the Hebrew slaves, his real kinsfolk (lit. "brothers"), working? Or are we to understand this as the point of view of Moses? Did he lead a double life while being raised at the Egyptian court? To what extent, if any, was he aware of a connection to the enslaved?[115] The text is silent on this point. And yet the same verse reiterates the family connection when it reports that Moses observed an Egyptian beating "one of his kinsmen." Moses' wrath was enflamed, and after ascertaining that no one was around, he struck the Egyptian down and buried his body in the sand. Once again the question arises, why did Moses kill the Egyptian? Was it because he was beating a fellow Hebrew? Or did Moses have a heightened and universal sense of justice that allowed him to play judge, jury, and executioner on the spot? Why else would an ostensible Egyptian step in and take the side of a mere slave?

Whatever the answers to these questions, the story serves a number of purposes. It establishes Moses' connection with his people at the same time it highlights his strong sense of justice. Moses is not afraid to risk all in order to fight for the underdog, which certainly has been a useful paradigm for the oppressed throughout the ages. Nonetheless, both ancient and modern interpreters have been disturbed by the violence and hotheadedness exhibited by Moses. Taken on its own merits, there is nothing in the biblical text that would justify Moses' act of what must be termed murder.[116] Along these lines, the recent film *Prince of Egypt* attempted to sanitize the tale by presenting the death of the Egyptian as an accident.

In some rabbinic traditions this moral conundrum was solved by fleshing out the story in a manner that would suggest that Moses was more than justified in murdering the Egyptian taskmaster.[117] First, Moses' constant concern

114. Philo Alexandrinus, *De Vita Mosis* 1.5.23. See also Feldman, *Jew and Gentile*, pp. 248-49.

115. Regarding these questions see Ernest Neufeld, "The Redemption of Moses," *Judaism* 42, no. 1 (1993): 50.

116. See Feldman, *Jew and Gentile*, p. 267. On the ambivalent attitudes in traditional Jewish sources regarding the (im)morality of Moses' act of murder, see Avi Sagi, "'He Slew the Egyptian and Hid Him in the Sand': Jewish Tradition and the Moral Element," *Hebrew Union College Annual* 67 (1996): 55-76.

117. For a positive evaluation of Moses' actions in this account, see Ari L. Zivotofsky, "The Leadership Qualities of Moses," *Judaism* 43 (1994): 258-69.

for the burden of his actual people is accentuated. According to the midrash, Moses would go out regularly to commiserate with and help the enslaved Israelites. Indeed, with Pharaoh's permission he instituted the Sabbath day as a day of rest for the overworked Hebrews.[118] This serves to place Moses' anger against the Egyptian within the broader framework of his great concern for his people. The midrash then justifies Moses' murderous rage by recounting a tale casting additional aspersions on the taskmaster. Once he saw the beautiful wife of an Israelite foreman. The next day, after her husband went to work, the Egyptian returned and ravished the woman. When her husband caught him *in flagrante delicto*, the Egyptian determined to kill her husband through hard labor and beating. Moses, having the gift of prophecy, was apprised of the situation, and when he saw that no one else was coming to the aid of the Israelite — for this is how this midrash interprets Moses' glancing around — he killed the taskmaster.[119] This midrash very nicely removes the moral ambiguity of Moses' actions and once again places emphasis on his passion for justice and for defending the weak and downtrodden.

Be that as it may, the biblical account continues with the betrayal of Moses by the very people he attempted to protect (2:13-14). The following day Moses attempted to intervene in an argument between two Israelites by confronting the one who had unjustly attacked his fellow. However, rather than shamefacedly backing off, the attacker brazenly confronted Moses and asked him on whose authority he was playing the role of judge over them. When he sarcastically continued by asking Moses whether he intended to kill him as he had killed the Egyptian, Moses knew that his deed was common knowledge and feared for his life. After a brief notice that Pharaoh learned about the matter and sought to kill him, Moses fled to Midian, where he rested by a well (2:15).

Once again the biblical account is terse and vague. In its great economy it is trying to get Moses to Midian as quickly as possible, in order to recount his first experience of the divine. But the midrashic tradition attempts to answer the questions that a careful reader of the story would raise: Who were the Israelites who were fighting? How did Pharaoh find out about Moses' deed?

As is to be expected, the midrash answers these questions and more.[120] The fighting Hebrews are identified with Dathan and Aviram, who in Numbers 16 are among the ringleaders of a major revolt against Moses' authority. Their challenge in that later narrative, "You have gone too far! . . . Why then do you raise yourselves [i.e., Moses and Aaron] above YHWH's congregation?" (Num. 16:3), is thus viewed as a distant echo of the challenge to Mosaic authority in this passage.

---

118. *Exodus Rabbah* 1:27-28.
119. *Exodus Rabbah* 1:28.
120. *Exodus Rabbah* 1:28-31.

In both instances, then, they imply that Moses was one who raised himself above other human beings and above the law itself. The unfairness of this accusation is underlined by the identification of Dathan with the aggressor in this case, as well as the victim of the evil Egyptian taskmaster. This then would explain in the eyes of the midrash how Moses' deed was known by at least one of the Hebrews. At the same time, it adds weight to the moral argument against Moses' adversary, for Dathan, who was the beneficiary of Moses' incisive action on the previous day, now turned ingrate and traitor. Indeed, it was Dathan according to the midrash who betrayed Moses to Pharaoh and caused his flight to Midian.

Although Moses' killing of a cruel Egyptian taskmaster and his subsequent exposure would seem to belie the contention that "Moses was a humble [or: meek] man, more so than any other man on earth" (Num. 12:3), this brief incident serves at least a dual purpose. First, it establishes Moses' passion for justice and for defending the rights of the weak and downtrodden. Second, it provides the impetus for Moses to leave his life as an Egyptian prince and flee from the only home he had ever known.

A Wanderer in Search of God (Exodus 2:16–4:31)

According to the biblical narrative, Moses headed east across the Sinai Peninsula to the land of Midian in southern Transjordan, where he once again evidenced his passion for justice by rescuing the daughters of Jethro, the priest of Midian, from shepherds who were molesting them. As a reward for his effort, Moses became the son-in-law of Jethro through his marriage to Zipporah.[121] Their union quickly, at least in terms of the biblical text's narrative economy, produced a son, whom Moses named Gershom, because he was a "stranger there" (Heb. *gēr shām*).

The locus of Moses' meeting with the daughters of Jethro is significant. Wells seem to have played a major role in ancient Israelite courtship rituals. A number of important biblical unions were first formed at wells. This was where Abraham's servant tested Rebekah as a potential mate for Isaac (Gen. 24), and where Jacob and Rachel first fell in love with each other (Gen. 29). The depiction of this scene in DeMille's *Ten Commandments,* which has the daughters of Jethro excitedly eyeing the exhausted Moses and crying out "a man," is Hollywood kitsch at its worst.

Although the biblical text would seem to imply that Moses led a bucolic

121. Coats views the relationship between Moses and his father-in-law as the essential datum of the traditions associating Moses with Midian. See George W. Coats, "Moses in Midian," *Journal of Biblical Literature* 92 (1973): 3-10.

existence until God revealed himself to him in the burning bush, extrabiblical literature adds extensive details concerning his years of wandering; he went to Ethiopia,[122] where he became a mighty king, before he headed off to Midian. Be that as it may, a number of crucial narrative details are added to the biblical account of Moses during his sojourn in Midian.

First, Moses was a shepherd. This is not an incidental detail. On the contrary, in the context of both biblical and ancient Near Eastern metaphor, a human being's status as shepherd presages his qualifications to rule over people in a just and wise manner.[123] It is surely not coincidental that David is also presented to us in the guise of a shepherd (1 Sam. 16–17). Any number of ancient Near Eastern rulers legitimate their claim to rule by employing shepherd imagery in describing their relationship to their people.[124] And in biblical poetry, God is also compared to a shepherd, the most famous instance of which is arguably the Twenty-third Psalm, which begins "YHWH is my shepherd; I lack nothing." Needless to say, the midrashic tradition expands on this theme in order to emphasize its importance.

In a midrash that is reminiscent of the apocryphal story about Abraham Lincoln in which the future president walked an enormous distance to return a book, Moses' care and concern for a small lamb that had run away from the rest of the flock confirmed God's judgment of Moses' qualifications to lead the Israelites. While tending his father-in-law's flocks, Moses noticed that one lamb had run away. He pursued it until it came to some shade near a pool of water, where it rested and drank. When Moses saw this sight, he understood that the lamb must be tired, so he lifted it upon his shoulders and carried it back to the rest of the flock. "Thereupon God said: 'Because thou hast mercy in leading the flock of a mortal, thou wilt assuredly tend my flock Israel.'"[125]

Second, Moses came into intimate contact with the priest of Midian. This is a detail that is basically disturbing to Jewish tradition. Not only did Moses, the exemplary Jew, intermarry, but he married into the family of a pagan priest!

122. These traditions presumably base themselves on the opaque reference to Moses' "Cushite" wife in Num. 12:1.

123. See, e.g., Mordecai Roshwald, "Moses: The Ideal of a Leader," *Diogenes* 146 (1989): 51-75, who, in his discussion of shepherd imagery as applied to Moses, has termed it "a veritable motto of the Welfare State" (pp. 59-60).

124. See Jack W. Vancil, "Sheep, Shepherd," *ABD*, 5:1187-90. Compare also the Code of Hammurabi (Hammurapi), in which the author, a king of Babylon in the early second millennium b.c.e., refers to himself as "Hammurabi, the shepherd, called by Enlil, am I" (col. i); "the shepherd of the people, whose deeds are pleasing to Ishtar" (col. iii); and "I, Hammurabi, the perfect king, was not careless (or) neglectful of the black-headed (people) whom Enlil had presented to me, (and) whose shepherding Marduk had committed to me" (col. rev. xxiv). Translated by Theophile J. Meek, *ANET*, pp. 163-80.

125. *Exodus Rabbah* 2:2.

How is one to reconcile this information with the Bible's standard abhorrence of both idolatry and idolaters? As expected, the answer lies in an addition to the terse biblical text. According to the midrash, Jethro had seen the evil of his ways and rejected the vanity of idolatry even before Moses arrived on the scene.[126] The midrash is silent, however, concerning what filled the spiritual void in Jethro's life until Moses had his revelation at the burning bush.

Many view Moses' sojourn in Midian and his relationship with the priest of Midian as the single most important detail of the Moses story from the perspective of the history of religions.[127] There has been a very strong movement in biblical studies since the nineteenth century advocating what is known as the Kenite or Midianite hypothesis, which claims that YHWH was a god originally at home in the southern reaches of Transjordan, an area inhabited by the Kenites and the Midianites, who seem to be related to each other according to some biblical traditions.[128] Since Moses first came into contact with YHWH while he was under the care of the priest of Midian, it is conjectured that the Midianites may be the source of the worship of YHWH, and that YHWH may have originated as a local god of that desert region.[129] Unfortunately, the chances of finding any texts or other remains that could shed light on the issue are very slim, although there are a few tantalizing but circumstantial hints at some sort of connection with Israelite worship.[130] Hence, this detail concerning Moses' sojourn among the Midianites may provide a clue concerning the origin of the worship of a deity upon whose worship three of the religious traditions examined in this book are based.

This assumption is bolstered by, third, the location of the primary revelation of YHWH to Moses in the Midianite desert, and not in Canaan or Egypt. There are also a number of biblical allusions to YHWH as a god of the southern reaches of the Holy Land, among which one may mention Judges 5:4 ("YHWH, when you came forth from Seir, / Advanced from the country of Edom") and

126. *Exodus Rabbah* 1:32.
127. See, e.g., George E. Mendenhall, "Midian," *ABD*, 4:815-18.
128. For a fuller discussion see Baruch Halpern, "Kenites," *ABD*, 4:17-22.
129. For a recent statement in favor of the Midianite origin of the worship of YHWH, see Niels Peter Lemche, *Prelude to Israel's Past: Background and Beginnings of the Israelite History and Identity,* translated from the German of 1996 by E. F. Maniscalco (Peabody, Mass.: Hendrickson, 1998), pp. 59-60.
130. See, e.g., the serpent, Nehushtan, which was a cultic object associated with Moses (Num. 21:6-9; 2 Kings 18:4). Coincidentally a copper snake was found in a sanctuary at Timnah within an area associated with the Midianites in ancient times. See Beno Rothenberg, *Were These King Solomon's Mines? Excavations in the Timna Valley* (New York: Stein & Day, 1972), pp. 183-84 and pl. xix. Yet, as Lowell K. Handy ("Serpent, Bronze," *ABD*, 5:1117) has pointed out, serpent imagery was quite at home in both Canaan and the rest of the ancient Near East.

Isaiah 63:1 ("Who is this coming from Edom, / In crimsoned garments from Bozrah?").

After a brief notice that the groans of the Israelites were finally heard by God (Exod. 2:23-25), the biblical story continues with the famous story of the burning bush, in which Moses is suddenly confronted by a divine revelation while tending his father-in-law's sheep at the mountain of God (3:1–4:17). While the mountain of God is called Horeb in this passage, in others it is called Sinai. The connection between the two traditions is encapsulated in the word employed for the bush, *sĕneh,* which is related to and a wordplay on Sinai, *sînay.*[131] As in so many other passages associated with the J and E sources of the Pentateuch, it is unclear whether it is God who is appearing to Moses or an angel.

At any rate, Moses saw a seemingly supernatural sight, a bush that was burning but was not consumed. Many have tried to rationalize the many miracles in the story of Moses and the exodus. The burning bush, the ten plagues, the parting of the Reed Sea, the provision of manna and quail in the wilderness — all have been explained as natural occurrences. And yet, such a literal reading of the narrative, besides straining the limits of our understanding of the natural world, actually destroys what it is trying to preserve. The miracles in the Hebrew Bible are supposed to be outside the boundaries of the natural world. Otherwise they would not be miraculous. The texts are not trying to preserve accurate observations of the natural world, but are attempting to express the grandeur of the events in terms that go beyond the natural and observable. Hence, within the context of the narrative, the burning bush at which God first reveals himself to Moses is meant to be outside the boundaries of nature. Otherwise it would not be worthy of God's presence.

When Moses turned aside to investigate, God's voice addressed him and commanded him to remove his sandals, since the ground upon which he was standing was holy. YHWH then identified himself as the God of Abraham, Isaac, and Jacob. This lent a historical context to his actions and to his relationship with the Israelites, which is one of the driving forces in the development of a Jewish sense of religious identity. He next informed Moses that the time of the redemption of the Israelites was at hand. Under Moses' guidance, God would lead them to a "land flowing with milk and honey" (3:8).

One would expect Moses to have been overjoyed at the prospect of serving the divine. However, a paradigmatic character trait of Moses now made itself manifest: his humility and sense of unworthiness. He pleaded with God to

---

131. See John Van Seters, *The Life of Moses: The Yahwist as Historian in Exodus-Numbers* (Kampen: Kok Pharos Publishing House, 1994), pp. 286-89, who has argued that it was only at a very late stage of the development of tradition that the word for "bush" was employed to give a name to a previously unknown mountain.

be released from this mission. In doing this he set a pattern that would be repeated among the prophets of Israel, whose reluctance to undertake their difficult missions is frequently an integral part of their call narratives.[132] Moses made a number of attempts to wrangle his way out of the mission; after all, who was he to confront Pharaoh or to lead the Israelites? God countered all of his objections with more-or-less convincing arguments.

It could be argued that God's response to Moses' plea of insignificance would have been less than comforting to Moses (3:11-12). While God did assure Moses that he would be by his side, the only sign he gave is that Moses and the Israelites would worship God at the same site, presumably equating Horeb with Sinai, upon their release from bondage.

Moses then questioned the wisdom of basing his authority on a vague reference to the "God of your fathers" (3:13), without any specific name to invoke on his behalf. God's answer, "Ehyeh-Asher-Ehyeh . . . Thus you shall say to the Israelites, 'Ehyeh has sent me to you'" (3:14), has been the object of much speculation over the course of the ages. Literally, the phrase *'ehyeh 'asher 'ehyeh* means something along the lines of "I am who I am" or "I will be who I will be." The Septuagint, the ancient Greek translation of the Hebrew Bible, paraphrases it "I am the one who is."[133] It is understood in the midrashic tradition both as a reference to God's penchant for using various appellations depending on the circumstances and the attribute of God involved, and as a reference to his eternal nature.[134] Whatever its exact implications, it appears clear that God's self-designation in this passage contains within it at least a play on words on the actual divine name, YHWH. As was already observed in antiquity, the verbal roots of YHWH and *'ehyeh* are identical, namely, *h.y.h < *h.w.y*. The midrash solved the similarity by positing that *'ehyeh* is the first-person form of the divine name, since God would not refer to himself in the third person.[135] This verbal understanding of YHWH is reflected in most of modern scholarship on the Tetragrammaton. One of the most influential theories in this regard is one espoused by, among others, Frank Moore Cross, who, in keeping with the dominant scholarly trend to vocalize the Tetragrammaton as *yahweh*, has parsed the name as a causative or hiphil form of the verb "to be."[136] The meaning of the Tetragrammaton

132. See, e.g., Jeremiah (Jer. 1:4-8) and Jonah (Jon. 1:1-3). Contrast this with Isaiah's eagerness to undertake his task (Isa. 6).

133. *Egō eimi ho ōn.*

134. *Exodus Rabbah* 3:6.

135. Compare the comments of Rabbi Samuel ben Meir (Rashbam, ca. 1085-1174) on this passage. See Martin I. Lockshin, *Rashbam's Commentary on Exodus: An Annotated Translation*, Brown Judaic Studies 310 (Atlanta: Scholars Press, 1997), pp. 36-38.

136. Frank Moore Cross, *Canaanite Myth and Hebrew Epic: Essays in the History of*

would then be related to YHWH's powers as creator, "the one who brings into being." Although Cross would elaborate on this by conjecturing that *'ehyeh 'asher 'ehyeh* is also to be read as a causative *'ahyeh 'asher 'ahyeh*[137] and the abbreviation of a longer cultic appellative of YHWH as "He who creates the heavenly armies," his theory has not found universal acceptance.[138]

'Ehyeh, the common imperfect first-person singular form of the verb *h.y.h,* "to be," appears one additional time in the biblical text in the context of divine speech. In Hosea God declares to the eponymous prophet that he will no longer be "your *'Ehyeh*" (Hos. 1:9). While many would see here a second instance of the self-referential use of the first-person form of the divine name,[139] others would emend the text to "your God" *('ĕlōhêkem).*[140]

The introduction of the apparently previously unknown name of God to Moses in this passage is one of the cornerstones upon which the documentary hypothesis is built. It appears to contradict both the witness of Genesis 4:26, according to which humanity began to call upon the name YHWH during the days of the second generation after Adam and Eve, and of Exodus 6:2-3, in which the divine name is seemingly introduced to Moses once again, albeit with a different nuance in argument.

Although the name of God was presumably pronounced during the First Temple period, over the course of time its pronunciation became taboo on account of its holiness in the Jewish community. By late Second Temple times, only the high priest was allowed to speak God's ineffable name on the Day of Atonement (Yom Kippur). Judaism has developed a number of circumlocutions designed to avoid taking the name of God in vain. The standard one is to substitute the plural of majesty Adonai, "my Lord," for the Tetragrammaton. As a matter of fact, this pronunciation is reflected in the vowel markers added to the biblical text in most occurrences of the consonants *yhwh.* The combination of the vowel markers or pointing for Adonai along with the Germanic transcription of the consonants *yhwh* as *jhvh* gave rise to the hybrid form Jehovah

---

the *Religion of Israel* (Cambridge, Mass., and London: Harvard University Press, 1973), pp. 68-70. See also David Noel Freedman et al., "יהוה *YHWH,*" in *Theological Dictionary of the Old Testament,* vol. 5, ed. G. Johannes Botterweck and Helmer Ringgren, translated from the German of 1977-80 (Grand Rapids: Eerdmans, 1986), pp. 500-521, esp. 513-17.

137. In the system of transcription employed by Cross, this would be written: *'ahyê 'aser 'ahyê (Canaanite Myth,* p. 68 n. 94). See also Freedman, "יהוה *YHWH,*" pp. 515-16.

138. See, e.g., Childs, *The Book of Exodus,* pp. 60-70.

139. See, e.g., Charles David Isbell, "The Divine Name אהיה as a Symbol of Presence in Israelite Tradition," *Hebrew Annual Review* 2 (1978): 101-18; Francis I. Andersen and David Noel Freedman, *Hosea,* Anchor Bible 24 (Garden City, N.Y.: Doubleday, 1980), pp. 198-99.

140. See, e.g., Carl S. Ehrlich, "The Text of Hosea 1:9," *Journal of Biblical Literature* 104 (1985): 13-19.

in Western languages. This was certainly never the pronunciation of the name of Israel's God. Although Adonai is commonly used for YHWH in Jewish prayer and blessing, outside of a prayer setting this circumlocution itself has in certain Jewish circles become viewed as too sacred to be pronounced. Therefore additional circumlocutions have been developed to avoid saying Adonai, such as ha-Shem, "the Name," and the hybrid Ado-Shem. Even the generic term "god" has, both in Hebrew (*'ēl* or *'ĕlōhîm*) and in English, become placed on the same level of holiness among some Jews, and hence it is deliberately mispronounced or miswritten in order, once again, not to take the name of God in vain, in spite of the fact that "god" is not, technically speaking, God's name in Jewish tradition.

One of the basic hermeneutic principles of Jewish biblical interpretation is that there is no extraneous information in the Torah. Every letter, no matter how insignificant, carries within it information of cosmic implications, if only one can unlock the key to its understanding. While this principle has led in modern times to the thoroughly repudiated hypothesis of hidden codes in the Bible,[141] its application in premodern times has revealed much about the interpreters and their search for meaning in this world on the basis of their textual traditions. One of the subsidiary methods developed within the Jewish mystical traditions is a sacred numerology known as *Gematria*. It bases itself on the fact that before the adoption of Arabic numerals a system of numeration using the individual letters in the Hebrew alphabet was developed. Thus the first letter, *aleph*, was one, the second letter, *bet*, was two, etc. By investigating the numerical value of the letters in a word or by adding them together, it was felt that a deeper truth might be revealed. Among other words to be analyzed in this manner was *'ehyeh* (consonantal: *'hyh*). Consisting of the letters *aleph* (one), *heh* (five), *yod* (ten), and *heh* (five), the word has been parsed as referring to *one* God, *five* books of the Torah, *ten* commandments, and *five* patriarchs (a bit of a stretch: Abraham, Isaac, Jacob, Moses, and Aaron). Another related tradition would view the name *'ehyeh* as an abbreviation for the three patriarchs of Israel. *Aleph* is the first letter of the name Abraham, while *yod* is the first letter of both Isaac and Jacob/Israel. The astute observer will, however, notice that there is only one *yod* in *'hyh*. The problem is solved by adding the two *heh*s, or fives, together to make a second *yod*, or ten, in the word.

A more serious attempt to find meaning in the peculiarities of the text, and one that has had a much greater influence on the development of Jewish practice as outlined above, has been to question why the word "forever" in Exodus 3:15, "This shall be My name forever, / and My appellation for all eternity,"

---

141. See, e.g., Ronald S. Hendel and Shlomo Sternberg, "The Bible Code — Cracked and Crumbling," *Bible Review* 13, no. 4 (1997): 22-25.

is written defectively.[142] In common with most Semitic languages, Hebrew is written as a consonantal language. Over the course of time, various consonants have come to be employed as vowel markers. A number of early stages in this evolution can be seen in the text of the Hebrew Bible as a whole. Overall, vowel markers are used inconsistently in the Hebrew Bible. In the case under consideration, the word "forever" (*lĕʿōlām*) is written defectively as *lʿlm* instead of the expected and common *lʿwlm*. While its meaning is clear from the parallel "all eternity" in the following poetic line, the rabbis were convinced that there was a deeper meaning hidden in the text, since their basic premise was that every letter, even a missing one, encoded a theological message. And indeed, the consonantal text can be vocalized either as "forever" *(lĕʿōlām)* or as "to hide" *(lĕʿallēm),* in which case it could be interpreted along the lines of "this is My name, make sure to hide it," i.e., do not pronounce the sacred name of God. The rabbis felt that such ambiguity in the text was not coincidental but deliberate, in order to assure that both meanings would be inherent in the word.

Even though God proceeded to predict the outcome of Moses' mission, Moses remained less than convinced of his chances of success. In this series of assurances (Exod. 3:16-22), God made the first of a number of statements that would prove disturbing to later commentators. God advised Moses to tell the pharaoh that he just wanted to take the Israelites on a three-day journey into the desert in order to sacrifice to him. This was a blatant lie, which the midrash attempted to mollify by rationalizing God's obfuscation. Rather than lying, God was protecting his charges by giving them three-days' head start before the Egyptians would pursue them.[143]

Yet, Moses' series of attempts to be relieved of his mission continued with the question: What if the knowledge of God's name would not be enough to convince the Israelite elders that he did indeed speak in God's name? God's reply this time was to teach Moses a number of magic tricks: turning a rod into a snake, making his hand scaly, and turning water into blood (4:1-9). Still Moses tried to back out of his mission. This time his excuse was that he was not "a man of words" since he was "slow of speech and slow of tongue" (4:10). Once again God assured him that he would be with him and instruct him in what to say (4:11-12).

Finally Moses had run out of excuses and blurted out what was really on his mind: "Please, YHWH, make someone else Your agent" (4:13). Exasperated with Moses, God became angry and told him that his brother Aaron the Levite would serve as his mouthpiece. Together they would confront the pharaoh and lead the people to freedom. The introduction of Aaron in this context is some-

142. *Exodus Rabbah* 3:7.
143. *Exodus Rabbah* 3:8.

what disconcerting. Where has he come from? How does Moses know him or of him, if he was raised as a prince of Egypt? The text is silent on this point.

The language used of the professional relationship between Moses and Aaron conveys an insight into the relationship between God and a prophet. It could be argued that the major function of the prophet in ancient Israel was to serve as the mouthpiece of God. This is probably what is being alluded to when God tells Moses that Aaron will be his mouthpiece and Moses will be Aaron's god. In light of the claim of some historians of religion that there existed a rivalry between competing priestly houses in ancient Israel, one may be able to read this passage on the background of arguments in favor of the primacy of the Mosaic or Mushite house against the claims of the Aaronide one.[144]

After receiving his father-in-law's blessing for his return to Egypt, Moses set out on the way. God had assured him that all who sought his life had died. However, once again making a morally ambivalent statement, God informed Moses that he would harden the pharaoh's heart and, in a case of tit for tat, that, just as the Egyptians had oppressed God's firstborn Israel, so too would God punish the firstborn of Egypt (4:18-23).

At God's command Aaron went forth to meet Moses at the mountain of God, and together they journeyed on to Egypt. There Aaron presented his case to the Israelites, Moses performed his magical tricks, and the elders believed them. What an irony that the sign that Moses presented was magical, since magic was associated with Egypt and its practice was expressly condemned and outlawed by biblical law.

However, just before Moses met up with Aaron, a rather bizarre incident is narrated in the biblical text. At an encampment on the journey back to Egypt, God attacked and threatened to kill him. Luckily, Zipporah had the presence of mind to circumcise her son, touch his legs or perhaps his genitals with the foreskin, and thereby save his life. Thus he became a "bridegroom of blood" to her (4:24-26). In interpreting the actions of this narrative, the task is made difficult by the lack of male personal names. Whom did God attack and threaten to kill, and why? Whose legs were touched with the foreskin?

The most logical assumption, and one made both by ancient and modern interpreters, is that it was Moses who was attacked by God.[145] Following Genesis 17:14, ancient Jewish interpreters conjectured that Moses was attacked because he had failed to circumcise his son. However, nowhere are the Israelites

---

144. On the priestly houses in ancient Israel, see Cross, *Canaanite Myth*, pp. 195-215.

145. See *Exodus Rabbah* 5:8. On the passage and the history of its interpretation, see Bernard P. Robinson, "Zipporah to the Rescue: A Contextual Study of Exodus IV 24-6," *Vetus Testamentum* 36 (1986): 447-61.

castigated for not circumcising their children during their forty years of wandering in the desert. Nonetheless, the mass circumcision of the Israelite males is an act preparatory to the conquest of the land (Josh. 5:2-9).

The story could also be a fragment of an ordeal tale, along the lines of Jacob's confrontation with a divine being on the eve of his return home after a lengthy absence (Gen. 32:23-33). Or it could mark Moses' return to civilization after the desert incubation of the hero in a story mixing motifs from ritual rites of passage and the threat to the hero at the undertaking of a mission. In an intriguing article, William Propp has proposed that the blood that is spilled here is the symbolic redemption of Moses and Zipporah's firstborn and related to the motif of the paschal sacrifice, which is to play such an important role in the Passover story.[146] Be that as it may, Zipporah's quick action saved both her husband, Moses, and possibly also her son, Gershom. The agent of Israel's redemption had survived his ordeal and was now qualified and able to undertake his mission.[147]

The similarities between the story of Moses and that of Joshua have often been remarked upon.[148] Until recently, the logical direction of influence of the one on the other has been assumed to be from the Moses narrative to the Joshua narrative, in a case of "anything you can do, I can do better." One such case is that of a divine revelation at which the object of the narrative is told to remove his sandals, since the ground on which he is standing is holy (Exod. 3:5; Josh. 5:15); another is the parallels between the parting of the Reed Sea and that of the Jordan River (Exod. 14–15; Josh. 3).[149] Recently John Van Seters has argued that the influence may have moved in the opposite direction.[150] If Van Seters is correct, then the primary status of the Moses traditions and their early dating may have to be rethought.

146. William H. Propp, "That Bloody Bridegroom (Exodus IV 24-6)," *Vetus Testamentum* 43 (1993): 495-518.

147. See also Robinson, "Zipporah to the Rescue." In a somewhat idiosyncratic article, Pamela Tamarkin Reiss ("The Bridegroom of Blood: A New Reading," *Judaism* 40 [1991]: 324-31) has argued that the threat to Moses' life was depression, since he had been living a lie in Midian and would now have to reveal his true identity as a slave to his wife. Furiously, Zipporah then circumcises their son.

148. See, e.g., George W. Ramsey, "Joshua (Person)," *ABD*, 3:999-1000; and James Nohrnberg, *Like unto Moses: The Constituting of an Interruption*, Indiana Studies in Biblical Literature (Bloomington and Indianapolis: Indiana University Press, 1995), pp. 147-49. Marsha White has drawn attention to the influence of the depiction of Moses (and Joshua) on the shaping of the Elijah (and Elisha) traditions. See Marsha C. White, *The Elijah Legends and Jehu's Coup*, Brown Judaic Studies 311 (Atlanta: Scholars Press, 1997), pp. 3-11.

149. Other similarities include the sending out of spies (Num. 12; Josh. 2) and the celebration of the Passover (Exod. 11–12; Josh. 5:10-12). For other references see the previous note.

150. Van Seters, *The Life of Moses*, esp. pp. 36-41.

Moses and Monotheism

At the burning bush God revealed himself to Moses and commissioned him to confront the pharaoh in order to lead the Israelites out of Egypt. The seemingly first revelation of the divine name to Moses in both Exodus 3:15 and 6:3 would appear to stand in contradiction to the tradition that humanity knew the name as of the second generation after Adam and Eve (Gen. 4:26). This is one of the basic proof texts in a discussion of the different religious and textual streams that went into the composition of the Hebrew Bible. The basic argument revolving around the division of the Pentateuch[151] into sources is based on the contention that no one author or "source," whether literary or oral, would be so inconsistent as to present variant and contradictory accounts of the same stories or factual claims.

Although religious tradition is divided on whether Abraham or Moses is to be considered the first monotheist, it has become axiomatic to view Moses as the one who introduced monotheism, which according to a simple reading of the biblical narrative had been the esoteric knowledge of one family, to a whole people.[152] Going under the assumption that Moses was a monotheist, or at worst a henotheist or monolatrist, many scholars have attempted to find a source for his monotheism. The Kenite or Midianite hypothesis was mentioned above. Another popular candidate for Moses' teacher in things monotheistic has been the apostate Pharaoh Akhenaten, who lived a century or more before the presumed time of Moses.[153] However, this rests on a few tenuous assumptions: (1) that Akhenaten was indeed a monotheist; (2) that Atenism lived on after Akhenaten's death; (3) that Moses received instruction in the now outlawed and discredited cult during his upbringing at the Egyptian court; and (4) that the religion Moses introduced to Israel was monotheistic. Recent scholarship on the history of the religion of ancient Israel has overwhelmingly come to the conclusion that the concept of monotheism was not introduced into a polytheistic world at one fell swoop. On the contrary, monotheism stood at the

151. Most scholars trace the sources of the documentary hypothesis through the books of the Pentateuch. Recently Richard Elliot Friedman (*The Hidden Book in the Bible* [San Francisco: Harper, 1998]) proposed reviving an older theory that claimed that the Pentateuchal sources could be traced into the books of the former prophets.

152. According to Yehezkel Kaufmann, "patriarchal monotheism" is a retrojection into the past of a later phenomenon. See Yehezkel Kaufmann, *The Religion of Israel: From Its Beginnings to the Babylonian Exile*, translated and abridged from the Hebrew of 1937-56 by Moshe Greenberg (New York: Schocken Books, 1972, 1960), pp. 221-23. On the other hand, Kaufmann followed inherited tradition in regarding Moses as "the initiator of a religious revolution, . . . the creator of an original idea" (p. 227).

153. For a provocative refutation of a putative influence, see Redford, *Egypt, Canaan, and Israel*, pp. 377-82.

end of a long line of development from polytheism through henotheism and monolatry.[154] The earliest texts from the Hebrew Bible that are unequivocally monotheistic stem from only the sixth century B.C.E., close to seven hundred years after monotheism was supposedly introduced by Moses. While it is not inconceivable that someone named Moses introduced the worship of a deity named YHWH into Israel, perhaps under the influence of Midianite or Kenite practice, later tradition attributed much more to him than he could ever have done himself. Indeed, just about every major religious innovation in Israelite tradition was attributed to him. The only major exception to this rule would be in the book of Chronicles, which is written from the Levitical perspective of the Second Temple period and claims primacy for Davidic innovation in the sphere of temple ritual, probably to counter the claims of the dominant priesthood that derived its authority from Moses. While acknowledging the place of Moses as the foundational figure in terms of the religious identity of the people as a whole, this approach allowed the Levites to nonetheless base their claims on another figure, namely, David, who was also viewed in many ways as foundational.[155] In later Judaism an appeal to Moses' authority was supposed to seal the argument for a ritual practice's legitimacy or for the binding interpretation of a point of Jewish legal innovation. In this manner he developed into the religious founder par excellence, albeit ex post facto.

The Rescuer of His People (Exodus 5:1–18:27)

This lengthy pericope details the struggles of Moses and his older brother Aaron, who materializes seemingly out of thin air in the narrative, to convince Pharaoh to let the people of Israel go, and culminates with their miraculous rescue from oppressive bondage. In order to accomplish their aim, Moses and Aaron engaged in various types of magical displays, among which the ten plagues have pride of place.

With no particular fanfare the biblical narrative continues with Moses and Aaron approaching the pharaoh and pleading with him to let their people

154. On the development of monotheism in ancient Israel, see among many others the essays in Diana Vikander Edelman, ed., *The Triumph of Elohim: From Yahwisms to Judaisms* (Grand Rapids: Eerdmans, 1996); Smith, *The Early History of God;* and Manfred Weippert, "Synkretismus und Monotheismus: Religionsinterne Konfliktbewältigung im alten Israel," in Manfred Weippert, *Jahwe und die anderen Götter: Studien zur Religionsgeschichte des antiken Israel in ihrem syrisch-palästinischen Kontext,* Forschungen zum Alten Testament 18 (Tübingen: Mohr Siebeck, 1997), pp. 1-24.

155. See Simon J. de Vries, "Moses and David as Cult Founders in Chronicles," *Journal of Biblical Literature* 107 (1988): 619-39.

go on a three-days' journey into the wilderness to celebrate a festival to their God. Pharaoh, however, refused to acknowledge the validity of their request and took no note of their God. On the contrary, he accused them and their fellow Hebrews of being shirkers and commanded that their daily burden of work be increased. Henceforth the Israelites were to gather their own straw for the making of bricks while maintaining the same daily output of bricks. When confronted with their added burden, the Israelites turned on Moses and attacked him for being the cause of their added suffering (Exod. 5). In light of the incident that occasioned Moses' flight to Midian, this was not the first time he would be subjected to the criticism of his compatriots, and it was certainly not the last.

Political theorists have drawn attention to the fact that the methods Pharaoh applied in countering the threat to his authority posed by Moses and Aaron's appeal are characteristic of those used by totalitarian regimes throughout history, namely, to drive a wedge between the oppressed and their leaders or the ones working to better their conditions.[156] A known source of oppression is oftentimes more palatable than an unknown and unsure future. The text seems to be implying that the Israelites were only able to think in terms of the short-term effects that Moses and Aaron's strategies had on them. On a simplistic level, they were only able to see that since the two of them had arrived on the scene, their burden had become greater. They were unable to anticipate the long-term results of their quest for freedom, thinking only of the here and now. Therefore they turned on their own leaders rather than on the oppressive might of Egypt. This theme, questioning the mental readiness of the Israelites to be truly free, can be traced throughout the story of the exodus.

Frustrated in his desire to solve his people's problems, Moses could well understand their castigation of his efforts. Nonetheless, God reiterated his assurances to Moses, this time clearly stating his ineffable name to Moses, a privilege that had not been granted the ancestors according to Exodus 6:3. "But when Moses told this to the Israelites, they would not listen to Moses, their spirits crushed by cruel bondage" (6:9). No wonder Moses despaired of the success of his mission. Not only was Pharaoh opposed to him, but his own people, the ones on whose behalf he was supposedly working, had rejected him. In light of this turn of events, it is understandable that Moses asked God how it would ever be possi-

---

156. See J. Severino Croatto, *Exodus: A Hermeneutics of Freedom*, translated from the Spanish of 1978 by Salvator Attanasio (Maryknoll, N.Y.: Orbis, 1981), pp. 21-22. See also Michael Walzer, *Exodus and Revolution* (New York: Basic Books, 1985), pp. 21-70, who, while not dealing directly with the passage in question, does offer a number of insights regarding the complex relationships between the oppressor, the oppressed, and those who would free them. See, however, Levenson, *Hebrew Bible*, pp. 127-59, who has argued against the applicability of the exodus story for liberation theology.

ble for him to convince Pharaoh when he could not even convince his own people to listen to him (6:12, 30). Once again God had to reassure Moses of the success of his mission by describing the great punishments that awaited the Egyptians, all of which would go to make YHWH known to those who refused to acknowledge his existence (5:2; 7:1-5). In order to magnify his "signs and marvels in the land of Egypt," God assured Moses that he would harden Pharaoh's heart (7:3).

Ethicists have long been disturbed by the motif of God hardening Pharaoh's heart in order to magnify the latter's obstinacy.[157] If God was truly in control of the situation, why did he have to compel the Egyptians to participate in their own destruction? It should, however, be noted that what was hardened was not Pharaoh's capacity for empathy or emotion, characteristics that we in the Western world associate with the heart, but rather his capacity for making sound judgments. In the ancient Near East the heart was not considered the seat of emotion; that function was fulfilled by the liver and the kidneys. The heart was the seat of the intellect, a function more correctly associated with the brain in Western culture.

The first few times the text relates the hardening appear to occur mainly through the agency of Pharaoh himself (7:22; 8:11, 15, 28; 9:7). Only during the last few times the motif is mentioned, in a narrative and not a predictive context, is it stated that God hardened Pharaoh's heart (9:12; 10:1, 20, 27; 11:10; 14:8).[158] This could be the narrator's attempt to convey the message that the initial evil impulse came from Pharaoh himself, and that YHWH was simply reinforcing a preexisting and previously evidenced predilection.[159]

Be that as it may, the midrashic literature also deals with this troubling question, in essence agreeing that God was simply reinforcing a preexisting tendency on Pharaoh's part. First, in an effort to justify the deserved punishment of the Egyptians for their cruelty toward the Hebrews, the midrash told many tales amplifying on the biblical narratives about the burden of the slaves in Egypt. Among them may be mentioned the tale in which an expectant mother in labor was not allowed to take a break from work in order to bear her child. She had to give birth while treading the clay for bricks. When her child was born, it fell into the mud and was drowned. The angel Michael took the child in the clay and brought it before the divine throne. It was then that the punishment of Egypt was ordained.[160] Second, the hardening of Pharaoh's heart was

---

157. See Sarna, *Exploring Exodus*, pp. 63-65.

158. The only exception to this pattern would appear to be Exod. 9:35, which is followed immediately by the clear comment in 10:1. See Moshe Greenberg, *Understanding Exodus*, The Heritage of Biblical Israel 2/1 (New York: Behrman House, 1969), pp. 138-40; Sarna, *Exploring Exodus*, pp. 63-65.

159. See also *Exodus Rabbah* 13:3.

160. *Pirqe de-Rabbi Eliezer* 48.

justified in the midrashic tradition through recourse to fables such as the one in which God is compared to a lion and the pharaoh to an uppity ass. The punch line of the tale was that if the ass had had a heart, i.e., what we would call a brain, it would never have defied the lion.[161] Through tales such as these, the midrashic tradition indicated its own discomfort with the justifications presented in the biblical text for the disasters that befell the Egyptians and felt compelled to add to the received text in order to justify God's actions against Egypt.

Once again Moses and Aaron appeared before Pharaoh at the command of God. This time they did not appeal to him to let their people go, but tried to demonstrate the divine power behind their mission by having Aaron cast his staff before Pharaoh, whereupon it turned into a snake. However, this display of hocus-pocus did not impress the Egyptians, since Pharaoh's magicians were able to duplicate this feat. Not even when Aaron's serpent ate those of his magicians did the pharaoh's attitude change, but he was strengthened in his obduracy (7:8-13). In an amplification of this story, the midrash concludes that Aaron's serpent swallowing up those of Pharaoh's magicians was no great miracle. After all, snakes eat each other every day. The miracle lay in Aaron's staff resuming its original form and then swallowing up the other snakes.[162]

Persuasion and demonstration not having the desired effect, God brought on the infamous series of ten plagues that was calculated to break the willpower of both Pharaoh and the Egyptians in resisting the divine desires. Although there have been a number of attempts to argue that the plagues could have taken place within the natural world of Egypt,[163] such attempts ultimately must fail. In order to preserve the Bible as written, the proponents of this view must strip it of its underlying theology, which is that the plagues were not natural but supernatural. Thus they both prove and disprove the Bible at the same time. In addition, their arguments rest on the positing of an extraordinary concatenation of events that were then interpreted as something other than what they were. And in a number of cases they have to rely on reinterpretations of the biblical account to make the evidence fit the theory. Finally, attempts to understand the ten plagues in a logical sequence are further weakened by recourse to inner-biblical parallels. The plagues of Egypt appear two other times in the Hebrew Bible, both in the book of Psalms (78:42-51; 105:28-36), in which the number of the plagues, their order, and their descriptions differ significantly enough from the account in Exodus to raise questions concerning the nature of

161. *Yalqut Shimoni*, Va-era 148.

162. *Exodus Rabbah* 9:7.

163. See, e.g., Greta Hort, "The Plagues of Egypt," *Zeitschrift für die Alttestamentliche Wissenschaft* 69 (1957): 84-103 and 70 (1958): 48-59.

the plague traditions.[164] It would appear that there was a fluid literary tradition in ancient Israel, according to which God punished the Egyptians through a series of plagues. Their exact number and what they were was not set in stone. In this manner different literary traditions were able to construct them in various ways. The two poetic Psalm traditions used as their basic organizing principle the sacred number seven, while the narrative of Exodus built its account up around the number ten.[165]

It is this latter and presumably later tradition in particular that evidences a most careful literary structure. An examination of the account of the ten plagues reveals three structurally parallel sequences of three each, with a culminating and unique tenth plague.[166] The forewarning to Pharaoh, the instructions to Moses and Aaron, and the time of the introduction of the plague all are composed in sets of three, with the last plague standing alone.

In their presentation the plagues represent a steadily increasing burden on the Egyptians. At first, Pharaoh's magicians could keep pace with the signs and wonders introduced on God's behalf by the Israelite brothers, but it became increasingly clear that the disasters striking Egypt were not of this world. Nonetheless, Pharaoh refused to yield until he himself was affected by the death of his firstborn son.

Moses' role as intermediary between the human and divine is striking already at the very beginning of the sequence of plagues. God commanded Moses to order Aaron to lift his staff over the waters of the Nile and turn those life-giving waters to blood (Exod 7:14-24). It was not for nothing that the ancient Greek historian Herodotus referred to Egypt as the "gift of the Nile." The Nile was the very lifeblood of the land, and one of its deities, Hapi, was the deified Nile inundation. As John Currid has argued, there is a strong element of anti-Egyptian polemic in the account of the plagues, which hits home at the very essence of Egypt and to some extent represents an undoing of the creative process.[167]

The next plague was an overabundance of frogs throughout the land. In return for agreeing to let the Israelites go into the desert to worship their God,

---

164. See John D. Currid, *Ancient Egypt and the Old Testament* (Grand Rapids: Baker, 1997), pp. 104-20; Sarna, *Exploring Exodus,* pp. 73-80.

165. See Samuel E. Lowenstamm, *The Evolution of the Exodus Tradition,* translated from the Hebrew of 1987 by Baruch J. Schwartz (Jerusalem: Magnes Press, 1992), pp. 69-111, 184-88.

166. The chart in Sarna, *Exploring Exodus,* p. 76, is most helpful in visualizing the literary structure.

167. Currid, pp. 108-20. See also Sarna, *Exploring Exodus,* pp. 78-80, and Terence E. Fretheim, "The Plagues as Ecological Signs of Historical Disaster," *Journal of Biblical Literature* 110 (1991): 385-96.

the pharaoh pleaded with Moses to end the plague. But afterward he hardened his heart and broke his word (7:25–8:11 [15]).[168] The first sequence of plagues ended unannounced with a plague of lice. Even though the magicians could not duplicate the feat and informed Pharaoh that this was the "finger of God" (8:15 [19]), the king of Egypt remained resolute (8:12-15 [16-19]).

The second set of plagues consisted of insects (8:16-28 [20-32]), animal pestilence (9:1-7), and boils affecting both people and animals (9:8-12). Again the pharaoh promised to let the Israelites go, but reneged as soon as the plagues subsided. These plagues were followed by hail (9:13-35), locusts (10:1-20), and darkness throughout the land (10:21-29). After the plague of hail, Pharaoh promised to let the Israelites go, as long as they left their wives and children behind. After the plague of darkness, he begged Moses to leave, but to leave the Israelites' flocks and herds behind. In these cases and others, Moses refused to accept a partial settlement. All the Israelites would have to leave unconditionally, with all of their possessions in addition to what the Egyptians would give them to get rid of them. After the ninth plague Pharaoh warned Moses never to come into his presence again at the risk of his life. Ominously, Moses concurred. This was indeed to be the last time they would see each other (10:28-29). However, contrary to Pharaoh's expectation, the king of Egypt was reduced to mouthing harmless threats against the leader of his slaves. If ever there was a passage subversive of worldly power, this is it.

God then informed Moses of what was to come. He would bring one last plague on the Egyptians, the death of all firstborn in the land, with the exception of those of the Israelites. In addition, the slaves would leave Egypt with much of the personal treasure of the Egyptians, who would "lend" the Israelites their gold and silver implements (Exod. 11). Thus would the Israelites leave with wealth, in spite of their abject status as slaves. However, before implementing the final plague, God instructed Moses in the observance of the holiday that would celebrate his great redemption of Israel from Egyptian bondage (Exod. 12–13).

The name of the holiday in English preserves the pun of the Hebrew. It is called *pesah*, "Passover," because on that night the Angel of Death *pissēah*, "passed over," the houses of the Israelites on his way to smite the firstborn of Egypt. Scholars seek the origins of the Passover in two originally separate and distinct pre-Israelite holidays.[169] One was celebrated by the sacrifice of the

---

168. Scripture citations in this chapter follow the versification of the Hebrew Bible. Where this differs from the versification used in Christian translations of the Hebrew Bible into English, that verse number is given in brackets.

169. See Baruch M. Bokser, "Unleavened Bread and Passover, Feasts of," *ABD*, 6:755-65.

firstborn of the flock, the other was observed by the eating of unleavened bread *(maṣṣâ)*. In essence, Passover can be viewed as the holiday that reconciles the antipodes represented by Cain the farmer and Abel the shepherd (Gen. 4:1-16). However, as is the case with the other ancient holidays that Israelite religion adapted from its predecessors, Passover was imbued with a new meaning, one that reflected traditional Israelite experience.

There are three ancient pilgrimage festivals that are still celebrated in Judaism: Passover; the Feast of Weeks, which is also known as Pentecost or Shavuot *(shābū'ôt);* and the Feast of Booths, which is also known as Tabernacles or Sukkot *(sukkôt).* All three have had their original cause for celebration assimilated to the story of the exodus. In this manner Passover became associated with the rescue of the Israelites from Egypt. Shavuot, whose origins are to be sought in the festival of the barley harvest, was reinterpreted to commemorate the giving of the commandments on Mount Sinai. Sukkot, named after the huts in which the Canaanite farmers would sleep during the frenzied last harvest before the onset of the winter rains, became a commemoration of the desert wanderings of the Israelites. The agricultural huts were reinterpreted as symbolic of the temporary shelters in which the Israelites are supposed to have slept during their forty years in the desert. The implausibility of this latter reinterpretation is made manifest in the symbolism of the holiday, which is more appropriate to a settled agrarian society than to desert wanderers.

The Passover itself is to be celebrated for one week beginning on the fourteenth day of the first month. According to the Gregorian calendar, this takes place in March/April. The new year, however, is not celebrated at this time according to the Jewish calendar. In ancient times there were a number of possibilities for ushering in the new year, and some of the complexities of biblical chronology have been occasioned by inconsistency in the dating system used.[170] In spite of the acknowledgment in the Hebrew Bible that the first month of the year is in the spring, Judaism has followed the biblical injunction to celebrate the new year (Rosh Hashanah) in the autumn at the beginning of the seventh month. Talmudic tradition records other new year celebrations, including one for trees at the end of the winter rainy season (Tu Bishevat).[171]

Central to the biblical celebration of the Passover is the eating of the paschal sacrifice, unleavened bread, and bitter herbs. This tradition of a festive meal on the first night of Passover has been amplified by later Jewish tradition into a set

170. On biblical chronology see Mordecai Cogan, "Chronology (Hebrew Bible)," *ABD,* 1:1002-11; John H. Hayes and Paul K. Hooker, *A New Chronology for the Kings of Israel and Judah and Its Implications for Biblical History and Literature* (Atlanta: John Knox, 1988).

171. See the extended discussion of the various new year celebrations in *BT Rosh ha-Shanah* 2a-15b.

ritual meal or seder ("order") at which these symbolic foods as well as others are consumed. Crucial to the observance of Passover is the injunction to recount the reasons for the celebration throughout the generations (Exod. 12:24-27). Significantly, during this retelling the name of Moses is conspicuous by its absence. While the overwhelming mood is festive and celebratory, Judaism has ritualized an ambivalence about the celebration in one important area. Freedom for the Israelites is joined with the suffering and defeat of the Egyptians in the biblical account. While God is praised for delivering Israel from captivity, the suffering of the Egyptians is symbolically noted by the ritualized spilling of drops of wine in commemoration of the plagues of Egypt. In this way the unrestrained joy of the holiday is diminished in order to take note of the suffering of others.

The passage detailing the observance of Passover is central to the exodus story from both a biblical and a later Jewish perspective. The importance of this story for the development of a common Israelite and Jewish identity is underscored by the injunction, read at the Passover seder on a yearly basis, to view oneself throughout the generations as personally redeemed from bondage in Egypt. People who live in immigrant societies are able to understand the power of such symbolism in the forging of a corporate identity. In Canada and the United States, it is technically irrelevant whether one's ancestors fought at the Plains of Abraham[172] or came over on the *Mayflower*. Once one becomes a member of the group through the assumption of citizenship, one also assumes the group's mythology and foundational narratives. So also in the case of the Israelites and later Judaism.

Another theme associated with the Passover concerns the redemption of the firstborn. As a number of biblical passages, including Exodus 13, indicate, the firstborn male of any living creature belonging to the Israelites was to be consecrated or sacrificed to God. While the Israelites were able to redeem their firstborn in a ceremony that is still observed in Judaism,[173] firstborn animals were to be slaughtered. It could be argued that the slaughter of the firstborn Egyptians, both human and animal, was an ex post facto sacrifice to YHWH. Those who had been unwilling to listen to him were condemned to adhere to his rituals in a most brutal manner.[174]

---

172. The Plains of Abraham in Quebec City is the site of a major battle between British and French forces in 1759. The battle, during which both commanders were mortally wounded, resulted in a decisive victory for the British and was eventually to lead to the incorporation of Quebec into Canada.

173. See "Redemption of the Firstborn," *Encyclopaedia Judaica*, 6:1308-10.

174. A similar argument directed against the Israelites has been proposed in the interpretation of Ezek. 20:25-26. For a discussion of this latter passage, see Moshe Greenberg, *Ezekiel 1–20*, Anchor Bible 22 (Garden City, N.Y.: Doubleday, 1983), pp. 368-70.

Finally, after God had struck the firstborn of Egypt, the Israelites were given permission to leave at once. They carried all their possessions, and in addition, the Egyptians were so happy to see them go that they let the Israelites strip them of their own valuable belongings. In their great haste to leave, the Israelites were not able to allow their bread to rise. In this manner the biblical narrative provides a distinctly inner-Israelite reason for the eating of unleavened bread at Passover. In addition to themselves and their livestock, the Israelites were accompanied by a "mixed multitude," which doubtless added a few people to their already prodigious numbers (12:29-39).

According to biblical tradition, 600,000 armed men, in addition to their wives and children and the mixed multitude, left Egypt (12:37). Estimates of how many people would be encompassed in a population totaling so many grown men range between 2 and 3 million souls in all. The implausibility of such a large contingent leaving Egypt without leaving a trace in the archaeological or inscriptional record, particularly in light of what is known concerning the total population of Egypt in antiquity, in addition to their leaving no remains in the Sinai Peninsula or their finding enough room there to get lost for forty years, has often been commented on. For the biblical literalist, that is part of the miracle of the exodus event. Attempts to rationalize the number down by claiming that the 600,000 should be understood as 600 military units or 600 families ring no more convincing in light of the historical and archaeological record.[175] It is surely no coincidence that these 600,000 were pursued by 600 choice Egyptian troops and more (14:7). These are large symbolic numbers that may perhaps be traced to the influence of the sexagesimal mathematical system of Mesopotamia and may, therefore, be regarded as late additions to the exodus traditions. Conversely, these numbers may be more indicators of the exilic dating of the exodus traditions as a whole alluded to above.

After the Israelites left Egypt, God took them on a circuitous route toward the Promised Land, avoiding the land of the Philistines and leading them toward the Reed Sea (13:17-18). The reference to the land of the Philistines is one of those blatant anachronisms that reveal the perspective of a later editor. In spite of past attempts to argue that there already was a region of Philistine settlement on the southwestern coastal strip of Canaan by the time to which the exodus is dated,[176] recent research has shown quite conclusively that the Philistines, a people of Aegean or Anatolian origin, did not settle in Canaan until the beginning of the twelfth century B.C.E., during the

175. Sarna (*Exploring Exodus*, pp. 94-102) has argued that the number represents the muster at the time of David and Solomon.
176. See, e.g., Cyrus H. Gordon, "The Role of the Philistines," *Antiquity* 30 (1956): 22-26.

reign of Ramses III.[177] Of course, if one were to argue that the exodus took place during the early twelfth century, the chronological problem associated with the textual reference to the Philistines would disappear. However, one would then be forced to explain the mention of Israel in the somewhat earlier Merneptah stele.

As for the identification of the Reed Sea, its location remains unknown. In Roman times the Hebrew *yām sûp*, "sea of reeds," was translated as Red Sea. Although many would argue that this is a faulty translation of the Hebrew but a correct identification of the sea in question, others would argue that the Reed Sea is to be located in the marshland between Egypt proper and the Sinai Peninsula.[178] Wherever it was, it was to be the location of one of the most spectacular scenes of rescue in literature, one well enacted by some Jell-O in Hollywood's *Ten Commandments*.

Led to the spot by God manifest as a pillar of cloud by day and a pillar of fire by night, the Israelites were wedged between the sea and the advancing Egyptian army. Pharaoh had had a change of heart about letting his erstwhile slaves go. Once again the biblical text is at pains to indicate that it was YHWH who was pulling the strings, in order to have an even greater victory over the Egyptians and their evil leader (13:20–14:9).

At the very moment God was setting the scene to make one of the most spectacular demonstrations of his great might and care for his people, the people who were being saved were in the process of complaining to Moses once again. Rather than rely on the divine assurances of rescue as mediated by Moses, the people were once again castigating their leadership. As usual, the object of their opprobrium was not the divinity who ordained their whole course of action but the one through whom this authority was transmitted. Why did Moses have to bring them out of Egypt to face certain death in the desert? Wouldn't it have been better to remain enslaved but alive (14:10-12)? Moses, however, assured them that God would battle for them against the Egyptians.

There are many texts in the Hebrew Bible that depict God as a divine warrior marching off to battle and overcoming Israel's foes.[179] There are also many studies about the divine warrior imagery and its theological import in the biblical text. One of the basic functions of both ancient and modern divinities has been to protect and to fight on the side of the divinity's adherents. YHWH was

177. See Carl S. Ehrlich, "'How the Mighty Are Fallen': The Philistines in Their Tenth Century Context," in *The Age of Solomon: Scholarship at the Turn of the Millennium*, ed. Lowell K. Handy, Studies in the History and Culture of the Ancient Near East 11 (Leiden: Brill, 1997), pp. 179-201, and literature there.

178. See the broad overview of the subject in John R. Huddlestun, "Red Sea," *ABD*, 5:633-42.

179. See Theodore Hiebert, "Warrior, Divine," *ABD*, 6:876-80, and literature there.

no exception to this general principle. Two broad categories of divine participation in war include YHWH's supporting the human combatants and his personal involvement in the battle. In the case of the latter, the fighting is done on a cosmic scale. God is the one who fights for his people; they do not need to participate, other than as witnesses to the divine victory. It is this latter situation that obtains in the account of the victory at the Reed Sea.

There are at least two versions of what transpired at the Reed Sea, one prose narrative (14:15-31) and one poetic account (15:1-21). According to the prose account, which itself is a complex interweaving of the J, E, and P sources of the Pentateuch according to source critics,[180] God told Moses to command the Israelites to advance to the shores of the sea. There Moses was to stretch out his arm while holding his staff in his hand (14:15-18). Protected from the Egyptians by either an angel or the pillar of cloud, the Israelites watched as a divine wind drove back the waters during the course of the night until they were heaped on either side of a dry path to the other side. While the midrash emphasized the faith of the first person to take a step between the walls of water,[181] the biblical account continues with the Israelites walking across the sea with the Egyptians in hot pursuit (14:19-23). God threw the Egyptians into a panic, and the wheels of their chariots became stuck in the mud. At daybreak Moses extended his arm over the waters once again and the sea returned to its original state, covering the mired Egyptians. The whole Egyptian army had been destroyed.

There is a tension in this narrative concerning the exact fate of the Egyptians. Exodus 14:27 claims that YHWH "hurled the Egyptians into the sea," while the following verse implies that the waters covered the Egyptians as they were traversing the sea in pursuit of the Israelites. The poetic account presents a somewhat different picture.

Exodus 15:1-22 is arguably one of the oldest passages in the Hebrew Bible,[182] although that ascription has been disputed by some.[183] Verses 1b-18 are a hymn of victory ascribed to Moses and the Israelites. Verses 20-21 attribute at least the first two lines of the poem to "Miriam the prophetess, Aaron's sister," who led the Israelite women in celebratory song and dance with a timbrel in her hand. Looking at this last aspect first, the type-scene of women welcoming victorious men home from battle occurs a few times in the Hebrew Bible, among which one may mention Jephthah's daughter tragically greeting her father

---

180. Friedman, *Who Wrote the Bible?* p. 251; Martin Noth, *Exodus: A Commentary,* trans. John S. Bowden (Philadelphia: Westminster, 1962), pp. 113-20.

181. *Mekhilta,* Beshallah 6.

182. Cross, *Canaanite Myth,* pp. 121-25.

183. See Albertz, p. 226 and n. 202.

upon his defeat of the Ammonites (Judg. 11:34) and the Israelite women welcoming Saul and David back after the defeat of Goliath (1 Sam. 18:6-7). However, in the Song of the Sea, they were not welcoming home a hero of flesh and blood, but God upon his defeat of the Egyptians.

The long version of the song is an elaborate paean to the victorious God. Although some of the elements of the representation of God's victory are similar to the prose account in the previous chapter — for instance, there is a divine wind and the Egyptians are drowned in the sea — the role played by these similar elements is different. In the prose account the wind drove back the waters and cleared a path for the redeemed. In the poem the wind of God is what apparently capsizes the Egyptians and hurls them into the water. Whereas it appears that the Egyptians' chariots became stuck in the mud in the prose account, in the poem the Egyptians appear to have been attempting to cross on the surface of the water when a divine storm put an end to their design. The popular picture of the waters parting is missing from the song.

One interesting detail of the song is a reference to gods other than YHWH in verse 11a. While some translations attempt to hide this fact,[184] the conclusion appears reasonable that the poem is to be dated to a time before the mid–sixth century B.C.E., when Judaism first developed a form of monotheism negating the existence of other gods. The declaration "Who is like You, O YHWH, among the [gods]; / Who is like You, majestic in holiness, / Awesome in splendor, working wonders" (15:11) is a clear henotheistic statement, one that promotes sole allegiance to YHWH while not negating the existence of other gods. While later Jewish tradition would understand this as an expression of Mosaic monotheism, the reality from the perspective of the history of Israel's religion appears a bit different.

A similar argument can be made regarding a verse from Deuteronomy that has come to be understood as the central Jewish declaration of belief in one God. This is a statement that is known simply as the Shema after its initial word: "Hear, O Israel! YHWH is our God, YHWH alone" (Deut. 6:4). While a traditional Jewish understanding of the significance of the last phrase would be "YHWH is one," this interpretation probably fits best into the context of an environment in which divinity is conceived of in either dualistic (Zoroastrianism) or trinitarian (Christianity) terms. It would also make sense in the context of the Josianic religious reforms of the late seventh century B.C.E., when the worship of YHWH at cultic centers outside of Jerusalem was outlawed, and to which time the core of Deuteronomy and its theology is dated. Thus the Shema could be a statement declaring that YHWH is to be worshiped at only one sanc-

---

184. See, e.g., the NJPS, which translates the word *'ēlîm* as "celestials" or "mighty," rather than as "gods."

tuary, and that local manifestations of YHWH were no longer acknowledged as legitimate forms of worship. Such local manifestations of YHWH as the YHWH of Samaria or the YHWH of Teman are now known from eighth century B.C.E. inscriptions found at a way station in the eastern Sinai known as Kuntillet ʿAjrud.[185] On a simple level, however, the Shema is a declaration that Israel is to worship only one God. Nowhere does it state that there exists only one god, only that Israel is to worship one alone. The same holds true for the commandment "You shall have no other gods besides me" (Exod. 20:3).[186] Similar declarations would not have been out of place among Israel's immediate neighbors in antiquity, most of whom appear to have had a national god to whom they owed primary allegiance. This allegiance, however, did not negate the possibility that other peoples had their own gods with whom they stood in a special relationship or that there were other gods in the pantheon, even if one was inclined to view one's national god as the first among equals.

The ambivalence of Jewish tradition regarding the suffering of the Egyptians necessary for the Israelites' redemption has already been alluded to. There is a dramatic painting by the Pre-Raphaelite Lawrence Alma-Tadema in which he depicts the death of the firstborn. A stone-faced and surprisingly youthful Pharaoh sits on a chair, dominating the center of the scene. On his lap is the limp body of his firstborn son, already a teenager. On her knees, throwing herself over her child in the agony of grief, is the child's mother. The sinister figures of Moses and Aaron lurk like vultures in the background, for all intents and purposes relishing the destruction and suffering of their foes. This is a scene that would probably not have been painted by an artist schooled in Jewish interpretations of the suffering of the Egyptians. At the same time as it attempts to justify the suffering inflicted upon the Egyptians, the midrashic tradition preserves stories that highlight God's, Moses', and the Israelites' empathy for their foes.

The destruction of the Egyptians at the Reed Sea was also addressed in the midrashic literature. One of the famous midrashim relates that the angels wanted to join the Israelites in the Song of the Sea. However, God castigated the angels for wanting to sing hymns of praise while God's creatures, the Egyptians, were dying.[187] The Israelites were allowed to sing because they had just been redeemed, but God's rebuke to the angels highlighted the universal understanding of divinity in Judaism. "The earth is YHWH's and all that it holds, / the world and all its inhabitants" (Ps. 24:1). While God had entered into a special relationship with Israel, some of the biblical authors tended toward a con-

185. See Zeev Meshel, "Kuntillet ʿAjrud," *ABD*, 4:103-9.
186. According to the traditional Jewish enumeration of the Ten Commandments, this one is the beginning of the second. In the Christian traditions this is the first.
187. *BT Sanhedrin* 39b.

sciousness that YHWH also cared for other peoples (cf. Amos 9:7). This consciousness eventually developed into a monotheistic universalism that has characterized Judaism and had an influence on the development of both Christian and Islamic theology.

As indicated above, the song of the Israelites at the Reed Sea (Exod. 15:1-18) has engendered much discussion, with some considering it one of the earliest texts in the Hebrew Bible[188] and others considering it an archaizing late poem. The latter would attribute the short two-line fragment supposedly uttered by Miriam (15:21), who in her first appearance is significantly identified as the sister of Aaron, to a much earlier period. This is based to some extent on a time-honored tradition in biblical studies to view shorter texts as primary. This attitude goes back at least as far as the time of Hermann Gunkel, one of the nineteenth-century founders of modern critical approaches to the biblical text, although the basic assumption that shorter texts are to be preferred was taken by biblical studies from the field of Homeric scholarship. While the automatic nature of this line of argumentation has been under attack in recent years, the assumption of the primacy of the shorter fragment has bolstered the arguments of feminist scholars, many of whom posit that Miriam and the contribution of women in general have been edited out of the patriarchal biblical tradition. Hence, a strong movement to take the Song of the Sea away from Moses and to attribute it to Miriam has made itself felt in biblical studies in recent years.[189] It has now become commonplace in some circles to refer to the "Song of Miriam" when referring to the lengthy poem of Exodus 15, although calling it the "Song of the Sea" may still be the safest neutral designation.

As so often happens in the presentation of the dysfunctional relationship between the Israelites and their God in the Hebrew Bible, supreme triumph is juxtaposed with abject apostasy and doubt. From the Reed Sea Moses led the Israelites into the wilderness of Shur. For three days they wandered without water, until they came to a place named Marah, after the bitter and unpotable water they found there. Once again they expressed their dissatisfaction with Moses. After he presented their case to God, God showed him a piece of wood, which Moses threw into the water, turning it sweet (15:22-25).[190]

188. See, e.g., Cross, *Canaanite Myth*, pp. 121-44.

189. See, e.g., Phyllis Trible, "Bringing Miriam out of the Shadows," *Bible Review* 5, no. 1 (1989): 170-90; reprinted in Athalya Brenner, ed., *A Feminist Companion to Exodus to Deuteronomy*, The Feminist Companion to the Bible 6 (Sheffield: Sheffield Academic Press, 1994), pp. 166-86, esp. 169-73.

190. On the biblical motif of water in the desert, see William Henry Propp, *Water in the Wilderness: A Biblical Motif and Its Mythological Background*, Harvard Semitic Monographs 40 (Atlanta: Scholars Press, 1987).

When they continued their wanderings and came to the wilderness of Sin, the Israelites once again commenced grumbling. This time it was the "fleshpots" of Egypt that they missed (16:3). At least when they were slaves in Egypt they had enough to eat. Now they could only look back longingly on their days of plenty along the Nile. Once again they blamed Moses for bringing them into the desert to starve them to death.

In response to the people's grumbling, God assured Moses that an abundance of food would rain down from the sky. Astutely, when Moses and Aaron conveyed this information to the people, they added that they knew that the people's complaints were not actually directed at them personally, but at God. This only served to place the people's complaining in an even more unfavorable light. What they were engaged in was not simply a difference of opinion regarding policy, but a thinly disguised rebellion against the God to whom they owed their salvation from bondage (16:4-8).

In the evening the Israelite camp was covered by quail. On the morrow a flaky white substance covered the ground. Since they asked each other *mān hû'*, "what is it?" the substance was known as *mān*, or manna in English (16:15, 31). Miraculously, this was to be their major source of sustenance during the upcoming forty years. Each morning, with the exception of the Sabbath day, the Israelites gathered just as much as each person needed. There was never any left over, since any that remained became maggot infested. On the sixth day, however, they were able to gather double portions to last them over the Sabbath, on which work was not allowed. On the day the Israelites finally entered the Promised Land, the daily supply of manna ceased (16:35; Josh. 5:12).

At their next way station, Rephidim, the Israelites once again did not have enough water to drink and turned on Moses. In a fit of pique, Moses told them to take their quarrel to the top, namely, to God. They, however, continued reproaching Moses and wondered, once again, why he had brought them out of Egypt only to have them, their children, and their livestock die of thirst. Presumably in fear for his life, Moses approached God and asked him what to do, since the people were certain to stone him in their great anger and frustration. God instructed him to take the staff with which he had struck the Nile and to strike a certain rock at Horeb, from which water would then gush. Moses did so, and another crisis was averted. In commemoration of the "trial and strife" that had taken place there, the place was named Massah ("trial") and Meribah ("strife") (Exod. 17:1-7).

Another crisis then arose. This time, however, the threat to Israel was not internal but external. They were attacked by the Amalekites, a people who were to be a bitter thorn in Israel's side for generations. The counterattack was led by Joshua, who would play an increasingly important role in the biblical story, first as Moses' deputy and finally as his successor. Moses watched the battle from a hilly vantage point. As long as he kept his arms raised according to the tenets of sympathetic magic, the Israelites prevailed. However, whenever his arms drooped on account of fatigue, the Amalekites had the upper hand. The eventual Israelite victory was assured when Aaron and Hur gave Moses a rock to sit on and supported his arms themselves (17:8-13).

This episode ends with a brutal declaration concerning the eternal enmity between YHWH and the Amalekites, and with God's oath to blot out even their memory from the earth (17:14-16). A later passage amplifies the reasons for the unusually strong negative attitude toward the Amalekites. Supposedly they did not attack the main Israelite columns, but the weakened stragglers bringing up the rear (Deut. 25:17-19). Eventually Saul's show of mercy to the Amalekite king, Agag, would lead to his rejection by God (1 Sam. 15). According to a notice in 1 Chronicles 4:42-43, members of the tribe of Simeon finally succeeded in wiping out the Amalekites. In later Jewish tradition the memory of the Amalekites has been kept alive as a symbol of evil in the world against which one has a moral obligation to fight.[191]

News about the great deeds of God in caring for the Israelites and bringing them out of slavery reached the ears of Jethro, the Midianite priest and father-in-law of Moses. So he brought his daughter Zipporah and her children to the Israelite encampment to meet Moses. After all, the Israelites were nearing the mountain of revelation, where Moses had first encountered God while tending Jethro's flocks. The last time Moses' wife and children were mentioned, they were accompanying him on his way to Egypt to undertake his mission to free his people. Nowhere does the biblical narrative mention how or why they should have returned to Midian, but these gaps are more than amply filled in by the midrash.[192]

When Moses had recounted to Jethro the whole marvelous story of what had befallen him since they had last seen each other, Jethro blessed YHWH and acknowledged that he was indeed greater than all other gods. After giving Moses a lesson in how to delegate authority in order to lessen his immense burden, Jethro departed for home (Exod. 18).

The Covenant at Mount Sinai
(Exodus 19–Numbers 10; Leviticus; Deuteronomy)

If the exodus is the central event in the *historical* consciousness of both ancient Israel and subsequent Judaism, then the covenant at Mount Sinai is the crown-

191. See Maimonides, *Mishneh Torah*, Hilkot Melakim (Laws of Kingship) 5.
192. *Mekhilta*, Beshallah, Amalek 3.

Moses, with rays of light emanating from his head, receives the tablets of the covenant from God. The enslaved and brutalized Israelites begin their march from slavery toward freedom. Nonetheless, to the left of the tablets, one can see the sin of the Golden Calf. In this multi-textured painting by Marc Chagall, who draws upon his origin in the Russian shtetl of Vitebsk, the exodus from Egypt becomes a metaphor for the exodus from Europe, after the time of pogroms and the Holocaust, to a new life in the land of Israel.

(Moses Tapestry, Knesset, Jerusalem; Lauros-Giraudon/Art Resource, N.Y.)

ing event in the *religious* consciousness of Israel and Judaism. It was at Mount Sinai that the Israelites and God entered into a formal relationship with each other, predicated on God's care for Israel and Israel's assumption of religious and cultic obligations vis-à-vis God. This relationship and these command-ments have been the central building blocks in the development of distinctly Jewish lifestyles through the ages.

At long last the Israelites arrived at Mount Sinai. There they pitched camp at the foot of the mountain, whereupon Moses ascended to God.[193] YHWH in-formed him that he was ready to enter into a covenant with the Israelites. If they would agree to obey him, the Israelites would be his treasured possession from among the nations. Even though God was the sovereign of the whole earth, he would make of Israel a "kingdom of priests and a holy nation" (19:1-6). This passage is one of the sources for the notion of the Jews as God's chosen people, although it should be noted that it does not posit God's sole relation-

---

193. On the confusing movements of Moses up and down the mountain and their implications for source criticism, see Baruch Schwartz, "What Really Happened at Mount Sinai?" *Bible Review* 13, no. 5 (1997): 20-30, 46.

ship with the Jews. As a number of scholars have pointed out, the notion of chosenness is a two-way street. In return for God's care, the Jews must assume what later tradition terms the "yoke of the kingdom of heaven," namely, the performance of the divine commandments. That Judaism has been ambivalent about the assumption of such responsibilities is indicated by two mutually contradictory midrashim. According to the first, God offered the Torah, meaning the commandments, to many more important nations before he approached the Jews. All of them turned God down because in each case there was a commandment in the Torah that they found inhibited their lifestyle. Finally God approached the Jews, who answered God by saying, "We will do and we will listen" (24:7),[194] which is understood in a Jewish context as implying that the Israelites entered into their covenant with God of their own free will.[195] According to the second midrash, the reference to Israel standing "at the foot of *(bĕtaḥtît)* the mountain" actually means that they were *under (taḥat)* the mountain when God gave them the Torah. It was only because of God's threat to drop the mountain on them that they agreed to submit themselves to the "yoke of the kingdom of heaven."[196]

When Moses informed the people of the proposition that God had put forward, they answered as one and accepted their coming obligations. One cannot escape the observation that Moses must have been in remarkable physical condition for a man of eighty, since he spent a good part of his time running up and down the mountain conveying messages to and from God. Now Moses had to inform the people that it was time to get ready for God's great revelation. God would descend in a cloud onto the mountain. Confronted with such great holiness, the Israelites were cautioned to take extraordinary measures in preparation for his revelation on the third day. They were to wash their clothes and stay "pure." In addition, if any of them ventured to touch the mountain of God, they were to be put to death.

Holiness is an interesting concept. It is not simply a positive force, but can be dangerous when improperly treated. The verbal root of "holy" *(q.d.sh)* in Hebrew includes the presumption of separation. That which is holy is different from the mundane. Improperly treated, it can wreak immense havoc.[197] Therefore, precautions in the form of ritual must be developed in order to harness the holy for the good of the community. Much of the book of Leviticus in par-

194. Author's translation.
195. *Pesiqta Rabbati* 21.
196. *BT Shabbat* 88a.
197. That great biblical commentator Steven Spielberg conveyed this concept quite nicely in *Raiders of the Lost Ark,* at the end of which the bad guys are destroyed by the power they unleash from the biblical ark of the covenant while attempting to re-create ancient ritual in order to harness that selfsame power.

ticular is concerned with defining levels of holiness and establishing the rituals to deal with it.

When Moses conveyed God's instructions to the people, he offered an interpretation of what was meant by staying "pure": "Be ready for the third day: do not go near a woman" (19:15).

This is one of the most disturbing passages in the Hebrew Bible for Jewish women and feminists. Whereas the whole of the people would appear to be addressed in the previous verses, this verse implies that "all the people" (19:8) does not include the women. While many other such antifemale passages could be cited from the Hebrew Bible — after all, the Tanakh is a product of a prefeminist patriarchal culture and speaks in the language of its time — this passage is so disturbing because it makes brutally clear that at the central revelation of the divine to the Jews, women were not counted among the congregation. This was a revelation directed solely to the Israelite men, at least in a simple reading of this biblical pericope. Indeed, the only consolation available to the reader troubled by this text is to point out that the exclusion of women from the revelation and, hence, the covenant was not contained in the words spoken by God to Moses, but only in those conveyed by Moses to the Israelites. This observation serves to make Moses the villain in at least one line of feminist thinking, but it rescues the integrity of God and the inclusiveness of the divine revelation.[198]

Finally the third day arrived, and God descended on the mountain accompanied by some impressive pyrotechnics. Mount Sinai was engulfed in smoke; God appeared in the flame; there was an earthquake; trumpets were blaring; and the voice of God sounded like thunder. Once again God warned Moses to make sure that the people respected the boundaries set around the mountain. Even the priests, purified and accustomed to higher levels of holiness than others, were warned to exercise caution (19:18-25). The stage was set for the greatest revelation in Jewish history.

As a whole slew of studies has shown, Israel's entry into a covenantal relationship with God is based on the model of ancient Near Eastern treaty texts. What this implies is that the relationship between God and Israel was conceived of in legally binding terms taken from the world of ancient Israel. Earlier studies of biblical covenant tended to emphasize the similarities between the structures of the Israelite *běrît*, "covenant," and Hittite suzerain/vassal treaties from

198. See, e.g., Miriam Frankel, *The Five Books of Miriam: A Woman's Commentary on the Torah* (New York: Putnam, 1996), pp. 117-18. Significantly, Frankel's section on this passage is entitled "Moses' Fateful Misquotation." The title of Judith Plaskow's *Standing Again at Sinai: Judaism from a Feminist Perspective* (San Francisco: Harper & Row, 1990) indicates the author's eloquent desire to re-create the Sinaitic revelation from an inclusive perspective.

the Late Bronze Age (1550-1200 B.C.E.).[199] On the one hand, this was due to the chance find of the Hittite treaties prior to other examples from the ancient Near East. On the other hand, the conjectured dependence of the biblical covenant on Hittite models seemed to be another brick in the structure supporting the early dating of the biblical traditions. More recent work, particularly on the book of Deuteronomy, has argued for a much later dependence of the biblical covenantal structure specifically on the vassal treaties of the Assyrian king Esarhaddon (681-669 B.C.E.).[200]

There were two types of treaties in the ancient Near East: those between equals, known as parity treaties, and those between unequals, known as suzerain or vassal treaties. Each type had its distinctive terminology to represent the relationship between the partners to the treaty. Parity treaties used the language of brotherhood in discussing the relationship between the partners. They also established a more-or-less reciprocal relationship between the equal partners. Suzerain/vassal treaties also used familial language to express the unequal relationship between the partners to the treaty. The overlord or great king was addressed as the father, while the vassal was the son. Just as one father can have many children, so too could the suzerain have many vassals. Conversely, just as every child has only one father, so too the vassal owed allegiance to only one suzerain. This type of treaty tended to emphasize the obligations of the vassal to the suzerain.

One can see how this covenant form proved appropriate in formulating the relationship between God and the Israelites in the biblical period. God was both king and father, Israel the servant[201] and son. Just as a human king could have many subjects, so too could God. On the other hand, just as a human vassal was restricted to serving one ruler, so too could Israel serve God and God alone. The biblical notion of covenant fits very comfortably into the henotheistic theology of biblical Israel. There may have been other gods, but Israel served YHWH alone on the basis of the covenant into which it had entered.

---

199. See, e.g., Dennis J. McCarthy, *Treaty and Covenant: A Study in Form in the Ancient Oriental Documents and in the Old Testament*, 2nd ed., Analecta Biblica 21a (Rome: Biblical Institute Press, 1987).

200. See Hans Ulrich Steymanns, *Deuteronomium 28 und die* adê *zur Thronfolgeregelung Asarhaddons: Segen und Fluch im Alten Orient und in Israel*, Orbis Biblicus et Orientalis 145 (Göttingen: Vandenhoeck & Ruprecht; Freiburg, CH: Universitätsverlag, 1996).

201. It should be noted that the freedom the Israelites won was, paradoxically, to serve their God. See Charles D. Isbell, "Exodus 1–2 in the Context of Exodus 1–14: Story Lines and Key Words," in *Art and Meaning: Rhetoric in Biblical Literature*, ed. David J. A. Clines, David M. Gunn, and Alan J. Hauser (Sheffield: JSOT Press, 1982), pp. 37-61, here 45.

The following six elements have been isolated by form critics as basic components of the treaty form: (1) a preamble identifying the partners to the treaty; (2) a historical prologue, in which the reason for the treaty is given; (3) the stipulations, i.e., the obligations, of the treaty; (4) the deposit of the treaty in a public place and arrangements for its periodic reading; (5) witnesses to the treaty; and (6) blessings and curses. All these elements have been identified within the biblical text, although not all in one place.

Indeed, three of them can be identified within the first two verses of the Ten Commandments, which usher in the account of God's covenant with Israel. "I YHWH am your God" (20:2a) identifies God as the suzerain in a passage paralleling the preamble of the treaty form. "[W]ho brought you out of the land of Egypt, the house of bondage" (20:2b) continues this literary genre with the historical prologue. Israel owes God allegiance because God led them out of Egypt. This is God's great act in history, on whose account God has earned Israel's eternal loyalty. "You shall have no other gods besides Me" (20:3) is the first of the list of stipulations that set forth what Israel's obligations to God are.

Although no single text in the Torah, with the possible exception of the core of the book of Deuteronomy, includes all the elements of the treaty form in close proximity to one another, all of them can be identified in the course of the Pentateuch. In addition to the examples mentioned above from the Ten Commandments, one can identify the deposit clause in Exodus 25:16, in which the deposit of the tablets of the pact, presumably the Ten Commandments, in the ark of the covenant is commanded. A witness clause is found in Exodus 24:7, in which Moses reads the covenant to the people and they assume its obligations.[202] A provision for the periodic reading of the laws is provided in Deuteronomy 31:10-13. Finally, the blessings that would accrue to those who kept the stipulations of the covenant and the curses that would befall those who broke them are listed in Leviticus 26 and Deuteronomy 28.

The study of law is a major subfield within Hebrew biblical studies. Two major areas of investigation have been the comparative aspects of biblical law and the form-critical investigation of these laws. Archaeological excavations over the last century and a half have uncovered much legal material from throughout the ancient Near East, the bulk of which is written on clay tablets in cuneiform scripts. Among the materials that have been found are treaty texts, collections of laws, and thousands of documents recording actual legal proceedings from the daily practice of law. The contribution of treaty texts to the understanding of biblical notions of covenant and the relationship between the human and the divine were discussed above. Legal collections, erroneously

202. See also Josh. 24:22.

known as "codes," were a widely disseminated form of royal literature. The most famous among these, both in modern research and as a much-copied text in the ancient world, is the "Code" or Laws of Hammurabi, a Babylonian ruler of the eighteenth century B.C.E. These collections of laws were not codes in the sense of Roman law, since they were not systematizations of legal rulings to be referred to in the actual practice of law. On the contrary, they were literary compositions whose purpose was to establish the authority of the king to rule in his function as the source of law in the land. Although the ruler backed up his claims by recourse to divine choice, the ruler himself was the source of law in the land. This can be contrasted with the ultimate authority of law in ancient Israel, which was not Moses per se but God. Moses and other authorities, such as David, were not considered the sources of the laws associated with their names, but as the ones who conveyed divine law to the people. On the basis of the divine origin of the laws in Israel, the law was viewed as eternally binding. In other ancient Near Eastern cultures, the laws promulgated by various kings were binding only as long as the kings themselves were sovereign. It is significant that among the tens of thousands of documents found that detail the daily practice of law in the ancient Near East, not one bases a decision on the precedent of a law supposedly promulgated in one of the royal legal codes. These literally tens of thousands of documents, with more being discovered all the time, are a major source for reconstructing ancient society and for placing ancient Israel within a broader social and economic context.

Basic to any discussion of Israelite law is the work of Albrecht Alt, who established the form-critical basis upon which later scholarship has based itself.[203] Although his theories regarding the origins of the different types of biblical law have not withstood the test of time, his distinction between two forms of law in the Hebrew Bible has. The first Alt termed "casuistic" law. This is case law, taken from the sphere of daily practice and codified in various places in the Pentateuch. Characteristic of casuistic law is its formulation in "if . . . then . . ." terms. The first clause sets out the case to be determined, the second prescribes the judgment in the case in question. The second type of law was called "apodictic" or "apodeictic" law by Alt. This type of law does not respond to cases, but states general principles. "You shall not murder" (Exod. 20:13) is an example of an apodictic law. Alt's attempt to posit that casuistic law is by definition secular law and that apodictic law is moral or ethical divine law has been shown to be overstated. The divisions between the two in the Hebrew Bible are not always as clear-cut as Alt had implied: a number of crossover cases do not fit into his neat categories. While

---

203. Albrecht Alt, "The Origins of Israelite Law," in Alt, *Essays on Old Testament History and Religion,* translated from the German of 1953, 1959, and 1964 by R. A. Wilson (Garden City, N.Y.: Anchor Books, 1968), pp. 101-71.

in general terms apodictic formulations lent themselves well to divine pronouncements, the distinction between divine and secular law is basically foreign
to biblical thought. In addition, Alt's claim that secular ancient Near Eastern law
did not employ apodictic formulations is simply false.

Among the attempts to seek aspects of biblical law that distinguish it
from its neighbors, one of the most successful was that of Moshe Greenberg.[204]
The issue he focused on was the seemingly paradoxical situation concerning the
relative valuation of human life and property obtaining in biblical and ancient
Near Eastern law. In general ancient Near Eastern law, capital punishment was
more often than not reserved not for crimes against humanity but for crimes
against property. Although murder could be punished by death in ancient Near
Eastern law, this was generally the case only when a member of the upper class
had been murdered. Crimes against people of lower classes were not punished
as harshly. This can be contrasted with the situation in the Hebrew Bible, in
which crimes against property were not capital offenses, with the exception of
cultic property and objects under the ban.[205] The latter category encompassed
cultic violations and crimes against humanity. The great paradox in biblical
legislation is that, since inviolate humanity was conceived of as created in the
image of God (see Gen. 1:26-27), crimes against human beings were punishable
by the death of the perpetrator.

No case illustrates this better than that of the goring ox.[206] Many ancient
Near Eastern legal collections had provisions governing the penalties to be applied in the case of an ox that injures or kills a human being. The penalties varied
according to the ox's previous history, whether the owner had been warned about
his property, and the social status of the injured party. However, in no case was
the ox destroyed. After all, the ox represented a major individual and communal
economic investment. One simply did not go about destroying property. In the
biblical law of the goring ox (Exod. 21:28-32), the penalties for the owner of the
ox varied depending on whether this was an isolated occurrence or whether the
owner had been forewarned and had not taken precautions. However, the ox that
gored someone to death was itself to be put to death by stoning. Killing a human
being was an act of murder punishable by death, no matter whether the murderer
was another human being or an animal. In addition, the meat of the ox was not to

204. See Moshe Greenberg, "Some Aspects of Biblical Criminal Law," in *Yehezkel
Kaufmann Jubilee Volume*, ed. Menahem Haran (Jerusalem: Magnes Press, 1960), pp. 5-28,
reprinted in Moshe Greenberg, *Studies in the Bible and Jewish Thought* (Philadelphia and
Jerusalem: Jewish Publication Society, 1995), pp. 25-41.

205. See the story of Achan, who was executed for stealing property from Jericho
that had been placed under the ban (Josh. 7).

206. See Jacob J. Finkelstein, *The Ox That Gored*, Transactions of the American
Philosophical Society 71/2 (Philadelphia: American Philosophical Society, 1981).

be consumed, for that would have been anathema. The community in this case would have had to absorb a major economic loss. Such was the importance attached to human life in the Hebrew Bible that only the death of the responsible party could make amends for a murder.[207]

Scholars have identified a number of major collections of laws in the Pentateuch, which presumably existed as independent sources until incorporated into the Torah. The first is the Ten Commandments, which exist in two versions (Exod. 20:2-14 [17]; Deut. 5:6-18 [21]).[208] These are followed by the "Book of the Covenant" (Exod 21:1–23:19), which is considered by some the oldest collection of laws in the Pentateuch.[209] It includes both casuistic (mainly 21:1–22:16) and apodictic (mainly 22:17–23:19) materials. The "Holiness Code" (Lev. 17–26) forms the core of the priestly legislation. It is concerned with preserving Israel's and particularly its priests' purity and holiness. Elaborate rules and safeguards to preserve the varying levels of holiness in Israel are laid out in great detail. Although it has often been viewed as an earlier source that was incorporated into the P source, some recent studies have argued that the Holiness Code represents a later insertion into a preexisting P.[210] Finally there are the Deuteronomic laws (Deut. 12–28), which form the core of the book of Deuteronomy. Although these are framed as a speech of Moses on the eastern side of the Jordan shortly before his death, for about two hundred years they have been considered in some way associated with the cultic reforms of the Judean king Josiah (640-609 B.C.E.), in whose days a scroll was "discovered" in the temple and used as the programmatic literature in a short-lived overhaul of cult and society (2 Kings 22:1–23:30; 2 Chron. 34–35).[211] The laws of Deuteronomy,

207. It should be noted that in the biblical law ransom could be laid upon the owner of the ox in lieu of capital punishment. In the case of slaves, punishment was set at thirty shekels of silver.

208. On the Ten Commandments see Raymond F. Collins, "Ten Commandments," *ABD*, 6:383-87; as well as the essays collected in Ben-Zion Segal and Gershon Levi, eds., *The Ten Commandments in History and Tradition,* translated from the Hebrew of 1985, Perry Foundation for Biblical Research (Jerusalem: Magnes Press, 1990).

209. See, e.g., Dale Patrick, *Old Testament Law* (Atlanta: John Knox, 1985), pp. 63-65, who dates this collection to the period of the judges (1200-1000 B.C.E.). On the other hand, Albertz, pp. 180-86, associates the Book of the Covenant with the reforms of Hezekiah in the late eighth century B.C.E.

210. See Jacob Milgrom, *Leviticus 1–16,* Anchor Bible 3 (New York: Doubleday, 1991), pp. 1-42; and Israel Knohl, *The Sanctuary of Silence: The Priestly Torah and the Holiness School* (Minneapolis: Fortress, 1995).

211. This theory was first proposed by Wilhelm Martin Leberecht De Wette in 1805. See Otto Eissfeldt, *The Old Testament: An Introduction,* translated from the 3rd German edition by Peter R. Ackroyd (New York, Hagerstown, Md., San Francisco, and London: Harper & Row, 1976), p. 171. On De Wette and his place in biblical studies, see Hans-

while in many ways parallel to the legislation known from the P source, also differ from the latter in many respects.[212] The major thrust of the Deuteronomistic laws lies in the centralization of all aspects of the cult in Jerusalem. Whereas previously there were both a central sanctuary in Jerusalem and local cult sites, the Deuteronomistic laws banned the latter and strengthened the power of the former. This necessitated some reinterpretation of practice, one example of which is in the area of diet.[213] According to the priestly legislation, animals to be eaten had to be brought to a priest and slaughtered.[214] Since there were sanctuaries throughout the land, finding a priest to slaughter the animal was no problem. Every slaughtered animal was hence also a sacrifice to God, thus literally killing two birds with one stone![215] Deuteronomic legislation, however, outlawed all cultic activity outside of Jerusalem. That meant that in order to sacrifice animals, they had to be brought to Jerusalem. While this ensured a steady supply of pilgrims traveling to the temple, it proved to be impractical to travel to Jerusalem from outlying districts every time one wanted to eat a meat meal. Hence Deuteronomy was forced to allow profane slaughter outside of Jerusalem, while reserving the practice of the sacrificial cult for the Jerusalem temple.

As indicated above, the Ten Commandments have the pride of place among the commandments uttered at Mount Sinai. Although they are viewed in Western Christian society as a form of universal moral code, within the context of Judaism they are viewed as an integral part of God's covenant specifically with Israel.[216] There is no sense of their universal applicability. Even

---

Joachim Kraus, *Geschichte der historisch-kritischen Erforschung des Alten Testaments*, 4th ed. (Neukirchen-Vluyn: Neukirchener Verlag, 1988), pp. 174-89.

212. See Bernard M. Levinson, *Deuteronomy and the Hermeneutics of Legal Innovation* (New York: Oxford University Press, 1997).

213. See Gary A. Anderson, "Sacrifice and Sacrificial Offerings (OT)," *ABD*, 5:870-86; and Jeffrey H. Tigay, *Deuteronomy*, The JPS Torah Commentary (Philadelphia and Jerusalem: Jewish Publication Society, 1996), pp. 120-27, 459-64.

214. Milgrom argues that this pertains solely to the Holiness Code, and that the original P source advocated a practice similar to that of Deuteronomy. See Milgrom, *Leviticus 1–16*, p. 29.

215. See Baruch J. Schwartz, "'Profane' Slaughter and the Integrity of the Priestly Code," *Hebrew Union College Annual* 67 (1996): 15-42.

216. On the place of the Ten Commandments within Judaism, see Carl S. Ehrlich, "'Du sollst dir kein Gottesbildnis machen.' Das zweite Wort vom Sinai im Rahmen der jüdischen Auslegung des Dekalogs," in *Im Anfang war das Wort: Interdisziplinäre theologische Perspektiven*, ed. Albrecht Grözinger and Johannes von Lüpke, Veröffentlichungen der Kirchlichen Hochschule Wuppertal, Neue Folge 1 (Neukirchen-Vluyn: Neukirchener Verlag/Wuppertal: Foedus Verlag, 1998), pp. 40-55, and bibliography there.

though the Ten Commandments are not regarded as a universal moral code in Judaism, the rabbis did develop a system of universal ethics. However, it is based not on the covenant at Sinai, but on the directives supposedly given to Noah, the second Adam, after the legendary flood. Hence they are termed the seven Noahide commandments.[217]

In their systematization of biblical and hence Mosaic law, the rabbis of the talmudic age distilled a grand total of 613 laws from the Torah. These were further subdivided into 365 negative commandments, listing things that one should not do, the most well-known formulation of which is "thou shalt not . . . ," and into 248 positively formulated commandments, as in the phrase "thou shalt. . . ." Because, according to the principles of rabbinic interpretation, nothing in the text is happenstance, these two numbers are linked in the first instance with the days of the solar year, in spite of the fact that the lunar calendar is the operative one in Judaism, and in the second with the supposed number of bones in the human body.[218] In this manner they were symbolically spread out across the year and hence became a part of daily life, and as parts of the body they were to be internalized as necessary for existence itself.

Of this rabbinic collection of 613 commandments to be found in the Torah, 10 stand out: the Ten Commandments, or as they are known in Hebrew: the Ten Words (*'ăśeret haddĕbārîm*, Exod. 34:28; Deut. 4:13; 10:4), from which the term "Decalogue" is derived. Although these are not the first commandments according to a Jewish systematization — that distinction belongs to "[b]e fertile and increase, fill the earth and master it" (Gen. 1:28) — they are the beginning of God's entering into an eternal covenant with the Jewish people. Nonetheless, it could be argued that Judaism has had an ambivalent relationship to these commandments. At the same time as there exists an understanding that the Ten Commandments represent a special moment in the relationship of God and Israel, there is also a tendency to view all Pentateuchal commandments as equal in importance. Although the recitation of the Ten Commandments belonged to the daily liturgy of the Second Temple in Jerusalem, the rabbis removed them from the daily liturgy, ostensibly to counter the claims of "sectarians"[219] that only these ten were important. They are therefore read only three times during the course of the Jewish year: twice when their recitation forms part of the cyclical weekly readings from the Torah and once on

217. See Klaus Müller, *Tora für die Völker. Die noachidischen Gebote und Ansätze zu ihrer Rezeption im Christentum,* Studien zu Kirche und Israel 15 (Berlin: Institut für Kirche und Judentum, 1994).

218. *Midrash Tehillim (Psalms)* 104:2.

219. There are many who consider this term a thinly veiled reference to the early Christian community and its Pauline rejection of the eternally binding nature of Pentateuchal legislation.

the holiday of Shavuot, which celebrates the giving of the commandments on Mount Sinai. The ambivalent relationship of Judaism toward the Decalogue is reflected in the difference in custom between Sephardi and Ashkenazi Jews when the Ten Commandments are read. Ashkenazi Jews stand in their honor, while Sephardi Jews remain seated, as both they and Ashkenazim do for all other readings from the Torah.

In light of attempts particularly in the United States to establish the Ten Commandments as a universal moral code, it bears repeating that within the context of Judaism they are no more and no less than an essential part of God's covenant specifically with the Jewish people. In addition, were one to establish the Ten Commandments as a universal moral code, the question would arise: Whose version of the Ten Commandments would be authoritative? There are differences among the various Christian denominations regarding the enumeration of the commandments, just as the various Christian enumerations differ from the system that has established itself as normative in Judaism.[220] It would appear logical that the enumeration begin with the first imperative phrase: "You shall have no other gods besides Me" (Exod. 20:3). Indeed, that is the first commandment according to Philo, Josephus, and at least one midrashic tradition,[221] and is regarded as such by leading modern biblical scholars.[222] Nonetheless, a different system of numeration has established itself as the normative one in Judaism, one that understands what is actually the introduction to the Decalogue, "I YHWH am your God who brought you out of the land of Egypt, the house of bondage" (20:2), as the first commandment. The second commandment then consists of the prohibitions of worshiping other gods (20:3) and of idolatry (20:4-6). The other commandments would be as follows: (3) the prohibition of swearing falsely or taking the name of God in vain (20:7), (4) hallowing the Sabbath (20:8-11), (5) honoring one's parents (20:12), (6) not murdering (20:13a),[223] (7) not committing adultery (20:13b [14]), (8) not stealing (20:13c [15]), (9) not bearing false witness (20:13d [16]), and finally (10) not coveting (20:14 [17]).

Particularly in the case of the tenth commandment, the male referent is blatantly obvious. The reference to "your neighbor's wife," coming between *his* house and *his* slaves, marks even the Ten Commandments as a document origi-

---

220. See Ronald Youngblood, "Counting the Ten Commandments," *Biblical Archaeology Review* 10, no. 6 (1994): 30-35, 50-52.

221. *Sifre Numbers* 15:31.

222. E.g., Moshe Greenberg, "The Decalogue Tradition Critically Examined," and Moshe Weinfeld, "The Uniqueness of the Decalogue," in *The Ten Commandments in History and Tradition,* pp. 83-119, esp. 99, and pp. 1-44, esp. 6-7 and n. 20, respectively.

223. It should be noted that what the text prohibits is murder, not capital punishment or warfare.

nally addressed to men in a patriarchal society.[224] In order to make these commandments relevant, the modern feminist is challenged either to rewrite the text in the manner of the midrash or to understand the text in a universal manner.

Among the Ten Commandments, the first two occupy a special niche in traditional Jewish thought. Turning once again to *Gematria,* the numerical value of the word "Torah" is 611. Why, the mystics asked, would two commandments be missing from the perfection of the word "Torah"? The answer was found in the first two commandments, the only ones in which God speaks to all of Israel in the first person. Hence, according to one line of thought, two commandments were spoken directly by God to Israel, and the rest were given to Moses and conveyed by him to the Israelites.

Challenges to Authority (Exodus 32–34; Numbers 11–36)

One of the recurrent themes running throughout the story of Moses and the Israelites is that of challenges to Moses' authority. Not only were the people constantly complaining, but there were some outright challenges to his leadership and mediator roles on the part not only of other community leaders, such as Korah, Dathan, and Abiram (Num. 16), but also of his own brother and sister, Aaron and Miriam (Num. 12). These stories are all worthy of closer investigation, on account of the information they contain concerning the Israelite ambivalence regarding worldly authority as well as the ambivalence they express regarding the ultimate authority of Moses within the tradition. Ultimately the theme of revolt would lead to the condemnation of the generation of the exodus, encumbered as it was by its slave mentality, to die in the wilderness.

Of all the revolts against Mosaic (and hence divine) authority, none has captured the imagination of subsequent commentators as has the "sin" of the Golden Calf (Exod. 32). As a matter of fact, the Golden Calf itself has become a readily understood cultural symbol with extremely negative connotations. Countless works of art attest to the hold the story has had on the lurid imagination of Western culture. In the dramatic arts one has only to think of Mephistopheles' aria of the Golden Calf ("Le veau d'or") from Charles Gounod's *Faust* or Arnold Schoenberg's stage directions for the orgy of the Golden Calf in the libretto to his opera *Moses und Aron* to witness the prurient fascination this tale has exerted on the Western mind. The symbolism of the Golden Calf was also

---

224. See the pained reflections on this fact in Athalya Brenner, "An Afterword: The Decalogue — Am I an Addressee?" in *A Feminist Companion to Exodus to Deuteronomy,* pp. 255-58.

used to great effect as the "idolatrous" logo for a hamburger chain in the movie *Dogma.* If it is employed by Hollywood, one can probably assume that the iconic symbolism of the Golden Calf is part and parcel of contemporary cultural consciousness.

In many respects the story of the Golden Calf is a paradigmatic story in the biblical narrative. Many contemporary commentators have alluded to the relationship between God and Israel as being dysfunctional.[225] The story of the Golden Calf is the ultimate proof text for such a contention. The juxtaposition of the zenith of Israelite history at Mount Sinai with the concurrent nadir of its relationship with God is quite evident in the biblical text. And yet, this is not a onetime occurrence. This sets a sorry pattern that will continue throughout the First Temple period (ca. 960-586 B.C.E.). It is the hope of the anonymous prophet of the exile, to whom scholarship has given the name Deutero-Isaiah (Isa. 40–55[66]), that the history of the exodus will be repeated, but this time with a happy ending.

While Moses was meeting with God on top of the mountain, the people began to entertain doubts about his eventual return. So they turned to Aaron and asked him to make them a tangible god, ironically in direct contravention of the second commandment, given but a short time before. Taking their gold from them, Aaron fashioned it into a "molten calf. And they exclaimed, 'This is your god,[226] O Israel, who brought you out of the land of Egypt!'" (Exod. 32:4). Subsequently Aaron proclaimed a festival of YHWH for the following day, at which the people brought sacrifices, ate, drank, and danced (32:1-6).

When God took note of what was happening in the valley, he informed Moses of it and of his intent to wipe the Israelites from the face of the earth and to establish a new nation descended from Moses. The latter, however, demurred. Such glory was not for him. On the contrary, Moses reminded God of his promises to the ancestors and played on God's ego by intimating that if God were to destroy the Israelites, the Egyptians, from whom God had rescued the Israelites, would have the last laugh. In light of such counterarguments, God repented. Moses had played the role of humble intermediary and intercessor to perfection (32:7-14). When Moses came down the mountain with the tablets of the covenant in his arms, he and Joshua heard a sound of tumult coming from the Israelite camp. Although Joshua thought it was a sound of war, Moses correctly identified it as the sound of celebration. When they arrived at the camp,

---

225. See, e.g., Athalya Brenner, "The Hebrew God and His Female Complements," in *Reading Bibles, Writing Bodies: Identity and the Book,* ed. Timothy K. Beal and David M. Gunn (London and New York: Routledge, 1997), pp. 56-71, esp. 58-59.

226. Or "These are your gods. . . ."

In the foreground, the Israelites dance with abandon around the Golden Calf. In the background, Moses descends from the Mountain bearing the two tablets of the covenant, which he is about to smash. The horns sprouting from Moses' head are a frequent motif in European Christian art.

(Master of St. Severin, *The Golden Calf*; Victoria and Albert Museum; photo by Carl S. Ehrlich)

Moses, who a short time before had interceded with God on behalf of this sinning people, grew enraged and shattered the divinely incised tablets that he held. In a fit of overkill, he burned the calf, ground it up, scattered it on water, and made the people drink it up (32:15-20).

Turning now to Aaron, Moses confronted his older sibling and demanded to know what had happened. In what must rank as one of the flimsiest excuses of all time, Aaron tried to absolve himself of blame by reminding Moses of how evil the people were and by trying to cover up his own active participation in the making of this supposed object of worship: "They gave [the gold] to me and I hurled it into the fire and out came this calf!" (32:24).

Mild and meek Moses, who had pleaded for the lives of his people but a short time before, now called for help from the Levites, whom he commanded to go through the camp and kill the sinners, "brother, neighbor, and kin" (32:27). Three thousand people are said to have died in that bloodbath. As if that were not enough, God followed that up with a plague (32:35).

As indicated above, contrasting the abject sin of the Golden Calf with the literal and figurative heights of the revelation at Mount Sinai sets a paradigm for the consistently dysfunctional relationship between God and Israel in the Hebrew Bible. As the story of the calf is framed in its narrative context, it is the low point of Israelite history, ironically for all intents and purposes coterminous with that history's high point. And yet there is another way of approaching the story of the Golden Calf, namely, as a political-religious allegory attacking the cult of the northern kingdom of Israel.

It is axiomatic to claim that "winners write history." In essence, the Hebrew Bible is a religious interpretation of the worldview of ancient Judah, which constantly had to defend itself against the claims of political and religious legitimacy of its more significant sister state Israel. There are a plethora of texts in the Hebrew Bible that engage in polemical attacks on the legitimacy of Israel from the perspective of the religious leadership of the Jerusalem priesthood and from that of the Judean ruling house of David. The story of the Golden Calf is arguably one of these texts. First it should be stated that the translation "calf" is somewhat unfortunate. When one thinks of a calf, one thinks of a weak and defenseless baby animal with big brown and languid eyes. However, the reference in the text is more properly to a young bull in the full bloom of its youthful power and energy.[227] Although some would argue that the bull imagery in this text is an allusion to the Apis bull of Egypt,[228] there is no need to go so far afield in seeking the roots of the symbolism in this passage. Bull imagery was quite common in Canaan both as an epithet for the ancient head of the Canaanite pantheon, El, and as the animal upon which the divinity sat enthroned.[229]

Although the second commandment has often been interpreted to indicate that ancient Israelite religion and Judaism have no iconographic tradition,

227. Unless the "calf" is to be understood as a deliberate denigration of the mighty image.

228. See, e.g., Childs, *The Book of Exodus*, p. 565, who views this opinion as characteristic of an older generation.

229. See the references in John R. Spencer, "Golden Calf," *ABD*, 2:1065-69, esp. 1068-69.

images and various artistic representations have at times played a decorative function in both temple and synagogue, in spite of the fact that YHWH himself has not been depicted visually.[230] When Solomon erected his temple and palace in Jerusalem, he called on artisans from Phoenicia to supply the decorative motifs. Among other aspects of Phoenician iconography imported into Israel was the cherub throne that served both the divine king in the Holy of Holies and the human king in his throne room. Contrary to representations in Western Christian art, cherubs were not plump little babies with wings, but fantastic hybrid creatures, similar to what are known from Greek mythology as sphinxes, although the closest artistic parallels are to be found in Mesopotamia and Phoenicia. These were regal beasts, fit for the throne of a king, whether human or divine.

When Israel seceded from Judah following the death of Solomon, its new king, Jeroboam, was faced with a dilemma. The central sanctuary of the Israelites was in Jerusalem, which was ruled by his rival Rehoboam. Since he couldn't have his subjects traveling to Judah to fulfill their religious obligations, he revived two sanctuaries at opposite ends of his country, Bethel in the south and Dan in the north. Since Solomon had already employed the cherub imagery, Jeroboam placed images in his temples based on the ancient Canaanite bull imagery (1 Kings 12:25-33a). It has been argued that Jeroboam was a religious conservative and Solomon was a religious innovator.[231] Be that as it may, the literary parallels between the story of the Golden Calf and that of Jeroboam are striking.[232]

Both narratives relate a supposedly sordid tale involving worship of an object that has the form of a bull. In both cases the presiding authority intones, "This is your god, O Israel, who brought you out of the land of Egypt" (Exod. 32:4; 1 Kings 12:28). In reality, the text reads literally "These are your gods," thus implying that some sort of idolatrous or unclean act is taking

230. On the second commandment and its interpretation, see Ehrlich, "'Du sollst dir kein Gottesbildnis machen,'" and literature there. For a provocative Freudian analysis concerning the evolution of the notion of an unseen deity, see Howard Eilberg-Schwartz, *God's Phallus and Other Problems for Men and Monotheism* (Boston: Beacon Press, 1994).

231. See, e.g., Gary N. Knoppers, *Two Nations under God: The Deuteronomistic History of Solomon and the Dual Monarchies*, vol. 2, *The Reign of Jeroboam, the Fall of Israel, and the Reign of Josiah*, Harvard Semitic Museum Monographs 53 (Atlanta: Scholars Press, 1994), pp. 35-44. For a critique of this position see Levenson, *Hebrew Bible*, pp. 84-88; and Levenson, *Sinai and Zion: An Entry into the Jewish Bible* (San Francisco: Harper & Row, 1985), pp. 203-4 n. 21. Levenson has identified a certain romantic idealization of Israel vis-à-vis Judah within critical biblical scholarship, whose origin he, following Kugel, attributes to the Protestant rejection of hierarchic Catholicism.

232. See Moses Aberbach and Levy Smolar, "Aaron, Jeroboam, and the Golden Calves," *Journal of Biblical Literature* 86 (1967): 129-40.

place, even though there is only one image in each location.[233] Significantly, when the tale of the Golden Calf is alluded to in the later book of Nehemiah, the language used is clearly in the singular (Neh. 9:18), which indicates that this may be how the passage was understood already in biblical times. It could be argued that both stories imply that a god other than YHWH was being worshiped. But Aaron clearly declares a feast of YHWH, and there is no hint even in the biblical text that Jeroboam was anything but a loyal Yahwist. Against the argument that the second commandment was being contravened by the erection of the calf, one could argue that according to what we know about Canaanite religion and iconography, not to mention the use of the images of cherubs in the temple, the calves/bulls were nothing other than the pedestals or thrones upon which the unseen deity was to perch. What then was the sin of the Golden Calf?

An answer may be found in a passage a few chapters later in the biblical account. Aaron, like Jeroboam after him, was not directly punished for his misdeed. As a matter of fact, Aaron, who is the object of a fair amount of criticism in the biblical text, never bore the consequences of his misdeed personally.[234] After all, it would be unseemly to punish the archetypal high priest. Nonetheless, a certain ambivalence concerning the figure of Aaron in the text has led many to posit the reflection here of an ancient power struggle between competing priestly houses and clans in Israel. At the same time, in a bizarre incident later in the narrative, Aaron's sons Avihu and Nadav are burnt to a crisp for offering "alien fire" (Lev. 10:1). Whatever was meant by "alien fire," and the midrash certainly speculates about what they did wrong, it would appear that whatever they did was not according to prescribed ritual. Significantly, the text later narrates the fate of the sons of Jeroboam, Aviyah and Nadav. After the former died (1 Kings 14:1-20), the latter became king and was assassinated after a short reign (15:25-31). In this way both pairs of siblings bore the brunt of their fathers' sins. The similarity of names would indicate that in its received version the tale of the Golden Calf and of Aaron's involvement in it is an inner-biblical midrash or allegory on the story of Jeroboam and his sons. The pro-Judean and pro–Jerusalem temple narrator was attempting to equate the cult of the north with the worst religious sin and transgression possible. Ultimately the sin of the Golden Calf and of Jeroboam was that the forms of worship specified were not according to the norms acceptable to the Judean transmitter of the tales. Significantly, a late "correction" to the biblical text attempted to cover up the tradi-

---

233. The reference in Exodus is to only one image. Kings clearly refers to two, one of which was erected at Dan in the north of Israel and one at Bethel in the south.

234. According to Deut. 9:20, it was only through the intercession of Moses that Aaron was preserved from the fatal wrath of God.

tion that the priestly house of Dan claimed descent from Moses (Judg. 18:30).[235]

After the episode of the Golden Calf, Moses prepared to take part in a second encounter with God on the mountain. Although the text informs us that when Moses would commune with God in the tent of meeting, which was outside the camp, God would descend in a cloud and speak with Moses face-to-face (Exod. 33:7-11), God turned down Moses' request to behold his presence with the explanation that no mere mortal could gaze on God and live. Nevertheless, God would station Moses in a cleft in the rock from which Moses could view God's backside, but not his face (33:23).[236]

Once again Moses ascended the mountain carrying two blank tablets upon which God would inscribe the terms of the covenant. When God passed before him, he intoned "YHWH! YHWH! A God compassionate and gracious, slow to anger, abounding in kindness and faithfulness, extending kindness to the thousandth generation, forgiving iniquity, transgression and sin; yet He does not remit all punishment, but visits the iniquity of parents upon children and children's children, upon the third and fourth generations" (34:6-7). The first part of this biblical passage is recited as part of the holiday Torah service in the synagogue. The second part is accorded embarrassed silence by later Judaism, which from the time of Ezekiel or perhaps earlier rejected the notion of vicarious punishment.[237] On the other hand, within the context of the patriarchal society of the Bible, family members were viewed as appendages of the patriarch. When the notion that only those who were alive at the time would suffer their deserved punishment is compared with the eternal reward of those who are faithful to God, the conclusion is inescapable that an astoundingly progressive statement is being made by this passage.

Although the text claims that Moses' second set of tablets repeated verbatim what was written down on the first set (34:1), the list of ten commandments given at the time of Moses' second ascent up the mountain differs markedly from the first set. Although religious tradition ignores this inconvenient fact, according to Exodus 34:12-26 the ten commandments that were placed within the ark of the covenant on the second set of tablets were not the ones so familiar to later generations. Because of this discrepancy, scholars tend to speak of two sets of ten commandments, the "ethical" ones that are so well known

235. In the Masoretic Text, an original reading of *m.sh.h,* "Moses," has been changed to read *m.n.sh.h,* "Manasseh," through the addition of a superscript nun. In this manner the name of the ancestor of the priestly house of Dan was "corrected" from Moses to Manasseh.

236. This cave appears again in the Elijah cycle, in which the thunder-and-lightning storm-god theophany of God is deconstructed and negated (1 Kings 19:8-14).

237. See Ehrlich, "Ezechiel," pp. 123-24.

and so often honored in their breach and the "cultic" ones that appear just in this pericope. This latter set of cultic commandments includes:

1. not making a covenant with the inhabitants of the land (34:12-16);
2. not making molten gods (34:17);
3. observing the Feast of Unleavened Bread (34:18);
4. redemption of the firstborn (34:19-20a);
5. not appearing before God empty-handed (34:20b);
6. resting on the Sabbath (34:21);
7. observing the Feast of Weeks and the Feast of Ingathering (34:22-24);
8. not preparing the Passover sacrifice with anything leavened, nor leaving any of it until morning (34:25);
9. bringing the firstfruits to the temple (34:26a); and
10. not boiling a kid in its mother's milk (34:26b).

Apparently it took Moses forty days and forty nights to write down these Ten Commandments. During that time he neither ate nor drank. When he came down from communing with God, his face was radiant and no one dared to look at him. Hence he started wearing a veil, unless he was in the presence of God. Most scholars assume that Moses' face glowed with rays of light that would represent the reflection of the divine nimbus in whose presence he had spent so much time. However, the Hebrew text claims that the skin of Moses' face "qāran," which is the term translated by most as "glowed" or "shone." Recently William Propp suggested translating the text along the lines of "the skin of Moses' face was disfigured."[238] Although ingenious, this suggestion has, however, not met with universal acceptance. Another possibility would be to relate qāran to qeren, "horn," and to conjecture that Moses wore here the horns associated with divinity in the iconography of the ancient Near East.[239] Mitigating against this assumption is the lack of a Mosaic apotheosis in any biblical text.[240]

238. William H. Propp, "The Skin of Moses' Face — Transfigured or Disfigured?" *Catholic Biblical Quarterly* 49 (1987): 375-86.
239. See, e.g., Benjamin Edidin Scolnic, "Moses and the Horns of Power," *Judaism* 40 (1991): 569-79.
240. See, however, Claire Gottlieb ("Will the Real Moses Please Step Forward [An Interpretation of the Exodus Story]," in *Jewish Studies at the Turn of the Twentieth Century. Proceedings of the Sixth EAJS Congress, Toledo 1998*, vol. 1, *Biblical, Rabbinical, and Medieval Studies*, ed. J. Targarona Borras and A. Sáenz-Badillos [Leiden, Boston, and Cologne: Brill, 1999], pp. 125-30), who has claimed that one of the miracles that God performed was to raise Moses to the level of a god on the basis of Exod. 7:1. Thus she would understand the text in question as signifying that Moses' head was adorned with the horns of divinity.

However, the Vulgate translation of Jerome into Latin employed a somewhat homophonic term for *qāran,* namely, *cornuus,* "horn." This latter translation has influenced the depiction of Moses as horned in European Christian art, the most famous example being Michelangelo's statue of Moses in Rome, and has also unfortunately fostered the development of the anti-Semitic caricature of Jews as horned and allied to the devil and the demonic.[241]

Moses next oversaw the building of the tabernacle in the desert, a portable sanctuary that in its traditional form mirrors in many respects the later temple and, hence, can perhaps be viewed as a retrojection of the temple and its cult into the past by appeal to the authority of Moses (Exod. 35–40).[242] Interestingly, the priestly line of Aaron also drew its authority from Moses, who is said to have been the one to anoint the first priest and his sons to serve as the eternal priestly line before YHWH in his shrine (40:9-16). The book of Leviticus continues the narration of the giving of the commandments to Moses. In effect, all of sacred Israelite custom and ritual is attributed to the mediation of God's word by Moses, who was thus transformed into the ultimate authority in all areas of Israelite life.

After somewhat over a year at Sinai, the divine cloud lifted from the tabernacle and the Israelites continued on their way (Num. 10:11). The complaints that had accompanied their journey to Sinai started once again. As punishment, God let a fire rage against them until Moses pleaded with him to relent. Once again Moses' selfless devotion to his undeserving people and his intercession with God saved their lives (11:1-3).

Never ones to count their blessings, the "riffraff" among the Israelites now began to pine for meat and "the fish that we used to eat free in Egypt, the cucumbers, the melons, the leeks, the onions, and the garlic. . . . There is nothing at all! Nothing but this manna to look to!" (11:5-6). While some would see here an allusion to typical foods of Egypt,[243] the ever practical eleventh-century exegete Rashi asked himself why these particular foods were listed and not others. His solution was to posit that the manna tasted like and thus satisfied the

241. See, e.g., Julius Trachtenberg, *The Devil and the Jews: The Medieval Conception of the Jew and Its Relation to Modern Anti-Semitism* (Philadelphia: Jewish Publication Society, 1983, 1943), esp. pp. 44-53. On the iconography of Moses see Elisabeth L. Flynn, "Moses in the Visual Arts," *Interpretation* 44 (1990): 265-76, esp. 266, as it relates to the horns of Moses.

242. See, e.g., Albertz (pp. 56-57, 131-32, 483), who understands the tabernacle description as an exilic Priestly retrojection, while not denying that there may have been some sort of simple tent shrine in Israel's past. Against this view see Frank Moore Cross, "The Priestly Tabernacle," *Biblical Archaeologist* 10, no. 3 (1947): 45-68 (reprinted several times); followed by Richard Elliot Friedman, "Tabernacle," *ABD*, 6:292-300.

243. Currid, pp. 145-46.

cravings for all other foods. However, the listed foods cause discomfort in babies, and hence are the ones that nursing mothers should avoid eating. Thus the manna could not taste like these foods or else the Israelite babies would suffer undue gaseous pain. In any case, Moses finally had enough. But this time the object of his frustration was God and not the Israelites. Rather than bear the burden of continuing to care for this people on his own, Moses begged God to take his life (11:15). As he so rightly reminded God, Moses neither conceived the people nor chose to lead them. They were God's chosen responsibility, not Moses'. This passage is eloquent in its use of female imagery to describe both Moses' and God's relationship to the people (11:12).[244]

God's response to Moses was twofold. First, he told Moses to bring seventy elders with him to the tent of meeting, where God would bestow some of his spirit on them, in this manner releasing Moses from sole responsibility for the people. Second, God ominously warned Moses that the people would get their wish for meat, "until it comes out of [their] nostrils" (11:20), on account of their rejection of God by longing to return to Egyptian bondage.

When Moses brought seventy elders with him to the tent of meeting, the spirit of God descended on them and they began to prophesy. Even Eldad and Medad, two elders left behind in the camp, were imbued with the spirit of prophecy. When the straitlaced Joshua asked Moses to restrain them, he replied that he wished that all of YHWH's people were prophets (11:24-30). A divine wind then brought an enormous number of quail to the Israelite camp. Barely had they sated their hunger when, with meat still between their teeth, God loosed a plague on them that killed the complainers (11:31-34).

When they arrived at their next way station, a new challenge was mounted against Moses, this time from those closest to him in blood. In a tantalizingly vague reference, the text informs the reader that Miriam and Aaron spoke out against Moses on account of the Cushite woman he had married (12:1). The question is, who was this Cushite wife? Other than this one passage, the Hebrew Bible knows of only one woman whom Moses married, Zipporah, the daughter of Jethro the Midianite. Thus the midrashic tradition equates the Cushite woman with Zipporah. Some modern scholars concur by arguing that the Cushites were a seminomadic tribe in the southern reaches of Transjordan.[245] Hence referring to Zipporah as a Cushite would be synonymous with calling her a Midianite. The problem with this interpretation arises from the

244. See Aaron Wildavsky, *The Nursing Father: Moses as a Political Leader* (Tuscaloosa: University of Alabama Press, 1984), pp. 57-59.

245. See Jacob Milgrom, *Numbers,* The JPS Torah Commentary (Philadelphia and New York: Jewish Publication Society, 1990), p. 93, for a variety of attempts to understand the meaning of "Cushite" in this passage.

more common meaning of Cushite as Ethiopian. Although one could argue that Miriam and Aaron were guilty of expressing racist antiblack sentiments, this interpretation is most unlikely. It would entail a retrojection into the past of racist European thought, something that is otherwise not attested in the Hebrew Bible nor in the ancient Near East.[246]

The midrashic tradition, as reflected for instance in the writings of Josephus, has, however, understood the reference to a Cushite in this text as a reference to Ethiopia, which was the great southern rival of Egypt in antiquity.[247] A number of legends were crafted to explain how Moses could have found a wife in Ethiopia, most of them connected with a supposed Ethiopian interlude in the life of Moses, not related in the biblical text. According to Josephus, Moses fought the Ethiopians as an Egyptian general before he reconnected with his Israelite roots. All the same, the reference to Moses' Ethiopian wife assumes ironic implications in the latter course of this narrative.

In the continuation of Miriam and Aaron's complaint against Moses, this woman was not mentioned again. What Miriam and Aaron apparently were attacking was Moses' claim of ultimate authority to serve as the mouthpiece of God: "Has YHWH spoken only through Moses? Has He not spoken through us as well?" (12:2). When God was apprised of their rebellion, he called all three of them to the tent of meeting and confronted the malefactors. The upshot of God's comments was that while there could be many prophets, as the story of Eldad, Medad, and the other elders had already indicated, there was only one Moses.

246. An example of the injection of European racialist thought into the biblical text can be identified in the standard translation into English of Song of Songs 1:5, which runs along the lines of "I am black but beautiful." This type of translation would imply an understanding of the text as "in spite of the fact that I am black, I am beautiful." However, the text can also and perhaps more correctly should be translated "I am black/dark *and* beautiful." This latter translation sees no contradiction between being dark and being beautiful and is probably more in keeping with the spirit of the text. The pivotal word is the Hebrew prefix *we-*, which is usually translated "and" but can sometimes also be translated "but." See also the discussion of this passage in Marvin H. Pope, *Song of Songs,* Anchor Bible 7C (Garden City, N.Y.: Doubleday, 1977), pp. 307-18.

247. Josephus, *Antiquities* 2.238-56. See also the discussion of this passage and its Ethiopian motif in Louis H. Feldman, *Judean Antiquities 1-4: Translation and Commentary,* Flavius Josephus: Translation and Commentary 3 (Leiden, Boston, and Cologne: Brill, 2000), pp. 200-202 nn. 663-64. The source of Josephus's story may have been Artapanus, a Hellenistic Jewish author of the second century B.C.E. See also Shinan, pp. 41-43, 52-54, and Arthur J. Droge, *Homer or Moses? Early Christian Interpretations of the History of Culture,* Hermeneutische Untersuchungen zur Theologie 26 (Tübingen: J. C. B. Mohr [Paul Siebeck], 1989), pp. 25-35. For an analysis of Josephus's presentation of the Moses story, see Paul Spilbury, *The Image of the Jew in Flavius Josephus' Paraphrase of the Bible,* Texte und Studien zum Antiken Judentum 69 (Tübingen: Mohr Siebeck, 1998), pp. 94-146.

There was only one human being with whom God communicated face-to-face, directly and not in dreams or riddles. Miriam and Aaron may have had the gift of prophecy, but they were clearly not of the same rank as Moses (12:4-9).

Once again Aaron, the archetypal priest, got off with only a slap on the wrist. And in a passage most disturbing to the feminist interpreter, Miriam bore the brunt of the punishment.[248] In a case of the punishment fitting the crime, her skin was turned sickly white with "leprosy" and she was banned from the camp for a week. Now the power of Moses became evident. Aaron in his weakness had to beg Moses to intercede with God to heal Miriam, which he did. The special and unassailable relationship that the humble man Moses had with God was reaffirmed in most dramatic fashion.

Nearing the goal of the journey, Moses sent out twelve spies to scout the Promised Land, one from each tribe. Although they brought back a glowing report of the bounty and beauty of the land, they were intimidated by the fortified cities and the supposed giants they encountered there. They were convinced they would never be able to conquer the land, and in spite of the protestations of two of them, Caleb and Joshua, they spread despair through the ranks of the Israelites. Once again they railed against God and Moses for bringing them out of the safety of Egypt only to let them die by the sword. Once again they urged a return to the security of Egyptian bondage. And this time they even threatened to kill those who counseled continuing.

Once more God reacted as he had after the sin of the Golden Calf, by threatening to wipe out the people and make a great nation of Moses, and once again Moses pleaded with God to relent. This God did, but he swore that as a consequence of their lack of faith, he would cause them to wander in the desert for forty years, until the whole generation that had come out of Egypt had died, with the exception of Caleb and Joshua. The former slaves had proven themselves unworthy to inherit the land. Only a new generation, born and raised in freedom, would be deserving of God's grace. Overcome by remorse, the people repented and tried unsuccessfully to take the land by force, only to be repulsed by their foes. The time of fulfillment had not yet arrived (Num. 13–14).

Soon thereafter another rebellion took place against the leadership of Moses. This time the ringleader was Korah, a Levite, assisted by Dathan and Aviram,[249] whom the midrash had identified as the Israelites whose quarrel Mo-

248. Indeed, Trible has termed Miriam the victim of a "vendetta" (see Trible, pp. 176-79).

249. Biblical source critics have identified two traditions that have been interwoven in this passage: (1) a revolt led by Dathan and Aviram belonging to the JE source (Num. 16:1-2, 12-15, 25-34), and (2) a revolt led by Korah belonging to the P source (Num. 16:3-11, 16-24, 35; 17). See Baruch A. Levine, *Numbers 1–20*, Anchor Bible 4 (New York: Doubleday, 1993), pp. 405-32.

ses had tried to break up so long ago. Like that of Miriam and Aaron, their attack on Moses was occasioned by their feeling that all Israel was equally holy. Why, then, did Moses raise himself up above all others? From a critical perspective, it would appear that one of the aims of this story is to justify the secondary status of the Levitical priesthood. In any event, the following day the rebels, their families, and their supporters gathered with their paraphernalia at the tent of meeting. Warned by Moses, the other Israelites drew away from them. The earth opened and they, their families, and their possessions were swallowed up. To drive home his point, God then sent a fire to annihilate their supporters (Num. 16).

One would think that such a dramatic display would put to rest any attempts to question Mosaic authority. But acquiescence would not have been the way of the Israelites! This time Moses and Aaron were accused of bringing death and destruction to their people. Yet, ironically, it was only Aaron's ritual intercession as ordered by Moses that once again spared the people from God's great wrath. Thanks to their quick action, "only" 14,700 died of a divine plague (Num. 17:14). The Israelites were never to understand that Moses had only their best interests at heart. No matter how much they railed against him for exalting himself, the biblical narrator is always concerned with bringing attention to Moses' reluctance to lead and to be exalted. After all, "Moses was a very humble man, more so than any other man on earth" (12:3).

On the Threshold of the Promised Land
(Numbers 20; Deuteronomy)

Although according to the biblical narrative Moses lived to the ripe old age of 120, with vigor undimmed (Deut. 34:7), his death has been viewed as a tragedy, inasmuch as he did not get to finish the journey that had occupied all his attention and being for forty years. For shortly before entering the promised land of Canaan and while within sight of his ultimate goal, Moses died. Although Sigmund Freud speculated that Moses was an Egyptian prince whose murder in an act of collective Oedipal rage imposed such a feeling of guilt on his followers that they elevated him in their subsequent traditions,[250] biblical and Jewish tradition have sought other answers to why Moses died before his time. The pivotal passage in

---

250. Freud, pp. 42-43, 57-59, 113-14. It should be noted that the theory of Moses' murder was not original to Freud. On Freud's study of Moses and its significance, see Yosef Hayim Yerushalmi, *Freud's Moses: Judaism Terminable and Interminable* (New Haven and London: Yale University Press, 1991); Robert A. Paul, *Moses and Civilization: The Meaning behind Freud's Myth* (New Haven and London: Yale University Press, 1996); Richard J. Bernstein, *Freud and the Legacy of Moses* (Cambridge: Cambridge University Press, 1998); as well as Eilberg-Schwartz, pp. 30-56.

understanding the tragedy of Moses' death while within sight of the goal of his travails is Numbers 20. Although it is attributed to the people's sins according to Deuteronomy 3:26, in Numbers Moses was condemned to an early death on account of his incorrect actions while fulfilling a divine directive. The nature of the sin of Moses has engendered much speculation and argument throughout the ages, all of which has conveniently been summarized by Jacob Milgrom.[251]

It could be argued that Numbers 20 is the most tragic chapter in the Pentateuch. The chapter begins with a brief notice regarding the death and burial of Miriam (v. 1) and ends with an account of the death of and mourning for Aaron (vv. 22-29). It is made quite clear that Aaron's presumably premature death, like Moses', is to be attributed to the sin of Meribah earlier in the chapter. The passage also includes a stately and formal description of how the mantle of priestly authority passed from Aaron to his eldest surviving son, Eleazar. The death of Aaron is preceded by an account of Israel's failure to enter the Promised Land through Edomite territory (vv. 14-21). Nonetheless, it is the account that immediately follows the death of Miriam that holds the key to the tragedy of the chapter, namely, the story of what happened at the waters of Meribah (vv. 2-13).

In many respects the story of the sin of Moses and Aaron at the waters of Meribah is a retelling of an earlier story about what happened at a place called Massah and Meribah (Exod. 17:1-7). Both accounts are concerned with the desire of the people for water; in both accounts water is provided from a rock; and in both cases the place is named Meribah on account of the "strife" that took place there. However, the function of the story within the overall narrative structure of the Exodus account is completely different. The Exodus account serves to highlight God's and Moses' authority vis-à-vis the recalcitrant Israelites; the Numbers narrative serves to condemn both Moses and Aaron to an early grave.

The juxtaposition of the death of Miriam with the sin of Moses and Aaron was already remarked on in midrashic literature. A causal relationship was sought in the notice of Miriam's death (Num. 20:1) and the immediately following observation that the Israelites were without water (20:2). Thus was born the legend of Miriam's well, which accompanied the Israelites during their desert wanderings but deserted them as soon as Miriam died.[252] A more modern feminist interpretation of the narrative juxtaposition would emphasize that trouble entered the brothers' lives as soon as their sister died.[253] But what was the sin that brought divine retribution upon their heads?

---

251. Milgrom, *Numbers,* pp. 448-56. Milgrom presents an excellent discussion of the various theories advanced to understand this text.

252. See *BT Pesahim* 54a and *Taanit* 9a, as well as *Leviticus Rabbah* 22:4; 27:6; *Numbers Rabbah* 13:20; *Song of Songs Rabbah* 4:14, 27.

253. See, e.g., Trible, pp. 180-81.

Moses strikes the rock before the thirsty and recalcitrant Israelites. Abundant water gushes out to quench their thirst, but clouds hover ominously overhead.
(Jacobo Tintoretto, *Moses Hitting the Rock;* Städelsches Kunstinstitut, Frankfurt)

Once again the people were hungry and thirsty. They castigated Moses and Aaron for bringing them into the barren wilderness and expressed their longing for the grain and figs, vines and pomegranates of Egypt. When Moses and Aaron approached God, he told them to take the staff and command the rock to yield its water. Moses took the staff and, with Aaron, assembled the people before the rock. Moses said to them, "Listen, you rebels, shall we get water for you out of this rock?" (20:10b). Thereupon Moses raised his arm and struck the rock twice. Water gushed forth from the rock, and the people and their animals drank their fill. God, however, turned on Moses and Aaron and castigated them for not affirming his sanctity before the people. Hence, they were not to lead the Israelites into the Promised Land, but to die beforehand.

Many theories have been put forward to explain what the sin of Moses and Aaron was. According to Milgrom's analysis,[254] medieval Jewish commentators came up with ten possible explanations, which fall into three overarching categories: (1) Moses' action in striking the rock was sinful, either because he struck it twice rather than once, or because he struck it instead of speaking to

254. Milgrom, *Numbers,* p. 448.

111

it,[255] or because of his choice of rock; (2) Moses' character was at fault, either because he showed anger,[256] or cowardice, or callousness; and (3) Moses' words were sinful, either because they expressed actual or implied doubt in God, or because they insulted the Israelites by calling them rebels, or because they focused attention on Moses and Aaron rather than on God. Because they base themselves on postbiblical midrashic traditions and cannot be supported on the bases of internal biblical criteria, a number of these explanations are rejected by Milgrom out of hand. However, a number of them can be supported by appeal to the biblical text. Milgrom mentions one additional approach to the textual conundrum. This is a modern critical resignation, which assumes that the text is so hopelessly corrupt that the explanation for the rejection of Moses has disappeared from the Bible. Since he believes he is able to demonstrate the reason for the rejection of Moses on the basis of the text, Milgrom dismisses the corrupt-text approach.

When all is said and done, Milgrom finds a solution to the conundrum in what Moses said ("shall we get water for you out of this rock?" 20:10) and in God's answer to him ("Because you did not trust Me enough to affirm my sanctity in the sight of the Israelite people," 20:12). According to God's address to him, Moses failed to act in a manner that would sanctify God in the eyes of the people. Instead, Moses' words, "shall we get water for you out of this rock?" arrogated unto himself and Aaron the miracle of producing water from a rock. It was this critical oversight, in which Moses took on God's role, which led to his rejection according to Milgrom. Severely chastised, Moses nonetheless continued serving God faithfully until the end of his life.

Having arrived at the plains of Moab overlooking the Jordan Valley near the end of the fortieth year after leaving Egypt, Moses prepared for death. His lengthy preparations are narrated in the book of Deuteronomy, mainly in the form of a series of valedictory addresses and poems.[257] First Moses recapitulated the story of the desert wanderings and urged the people to obey God's commandments (Deut. 1:6–4:43). This passage serves as a general introduction to the Deuteronomistic history, containing as it does a view of Israel's story that implies that faithfulness to God and his commandments is rewarded and un-

---

255. This explanation is favored, e.g., by William H. Propp, "The Rod of Aaron and the Sin of Moses," *Journal of Biblical Literature* 107 (1988): 19-26. According to Propp, the aim of this mainly P text is to accuse Moses of a sin, while presenting Aaron as nothing more than guilty by association.

256. As recently argued, e.g., by Alan M. Cooper and Bernard R. Goldstein, "At the Entrance to the Tent: More Cultic Resonances in Biblical Narrative," *Journal of Biblical Literature* 116 (1997): 214 n. 43.

257. There are three major speeches (Deut. 1:6–4:43; 4:44–26:19; 28; and 29–30) and a couple of poems (Deut. 32:1-43; 33) attributed to Moses in Deuteronomy.

faithfulness is punished in the historical sphere. Next Moses gave the Israelites a set of laws (4:44–26:19; 28) that was in many ways similar to the Sinaitic set. Nonetheless, there are important differences between the two sets of laws. These are so prominent that it has become a truism within the critical study of the Bible as of the early nineteenth century that the core of the Deuteronomic legislation is to be attributed not to the time of Moses but to that of King Josiah of Judah in the latter half of the seventh century B.C.E. Among the elements indicative of this conclusion are those that accord with Josiah's political and religious reforms, centralizing the cult and the power over it in Jerusalem.[258] Disloyalty to the laws of Moses and to the divine covenant is presented as the worst transgression imaginable. Loyalty to God is expressed through the language of love (e.g., 6:5; 30:16-20). The book of Deuteronomy also places great emphasis on the activities of the Levites and the prophets. Indeed, in Deuteronomy Moses is presented as the archetypal prophet, the only one with whom God spoke face-to-face (34:10).

According to Deuteronomy, the death of Moses was a turning point in the people's history. It was both the end of an era and the beginning of a new one. No longer were the Israelites slaves waiting to be free. They were ready to enter and claim the Promised Land. The preparations for Moses' death and his valedictory addresses dominate both the narrative structure and the content of Deuteronomy. In anticipation of his death, Moses wrote down all the laws entrusted to him by God and handed them to the Levites for safekeeping (31:9). In addition, in order to ensure the peaceful transfer of authority and power in Israel, Moses appointed Joshua his divinely chosen successor (31:14, 23; 34:9). Joshua was to enter the Promised Land, but Moses was to die on account of his lack of faith "at the waters of Meribath-Kadesh in the wilderness of Zin" (32:51).

Moses' exit from this world is related in loving detail. Although he himself would never set foot in the land, when the time came he ascended the summit of Mount Nebo, from which God allowed him to see the land from north to south and east to west (32:52; 34:1-4). Finally, Moses died at God's command with vigor undiminished at the ripe old age of 120 years.[259] God personally buried Moses in a valley in the land of Moab. Significantly, his place of burial was and is unknown, thus precluding the development of a cult of Moses asso-

---

258. On the Deuteronomistic reforms see Albertz, pp. 195-242, and Mordechai Cogan, "Into Exile: From the Assyrian Conquest of Israel to the Fall of Babylon," in *The Oxford History of the Biblical World*, ed. Michael D. Coogan (New York and Oxford: Oxford University Press, 1998), pp. 321-65, esp. 342-47.

259. Taking its cue from the life of Moses, Judaism views 120 years as the ideal life span. Indeed, the common wish is that one should live "until one hundred and twenty," which has been interpreted by some whimsically as "until one hundred like twenty."

ciated with his grave site (34:5-7). Moses may have been the archetypal prophet and Jew, but he was also just a human being who was doing God's bidding (34:10-12). After the Israelites had mourned his death for thirty days, Joshua assumed his mantle of authority and prepared to lead the Israelites into the Promised Land (34:8b-9; Josh. 1).

In spite of the relatively expansive detail concerning the death of Moses in the Hebrew Bible, in midrashic eyes there remained much room for the addition of material to complete the portrait of Moses. The midrashim about Moses' death combine two main themes: Moses' humanity and his special status. The former is made manifest by his all-too-human attempts to avoid dying, and the latter by the extraordinary treatment he received at the hands of God, of the angels, indeed of all creation.

When Moses found out that his death was approaching, he drew a circle around himself and refused to budge.[260] He implored God, begging him to let him reap some of the fruits of his toils, since he had known nothing but suffering in leading the people out of Egypt and through the desert. If God had sworn not to let him enter the Promised Land, then why could he not dwell with the tribe of Reuben and the half-tribe of Manasseh in Transjordan while Joshua ruled in Israel? Failing that, why would God not let him be buried in the Holy Land? After all, was not Moses the greatest human being who ever lived? In answer to this, God enumerated his sins other than his lack of faith at Meribah, which included among others the murder of the Egyptian taskmaster. Since God proved unresponsive to his entreaties, Moses implored the earth, the heavens, the sea, and the mountains to intercede on his behalf, once again to no avail. In order to prolong his life, he was willing to become the disciple of his student Joshua. When God granted him that request, the degradation he was subject to made him long for death.

Once Moses accepted the inevitability of his death, he worked to ensure a smooth transition for Joshua and the Israelites. This included his blessing the tribes of Israel and asking them for forgiveness. God took him on the mountain and showed him the Holy Land from afar and let him see the future. Nonetheless, when Sammael, the Angel of Death, approached with glee to take his life, Moses administered him such a beating that Sammael's life had to be saved by divine intervention.[261] Finally God and the angels Michael, Gabriel, and Zagzagel took Moses and laid him out on his bier. After Moses folded his arms in

260. This discussion is based mainly on *Deuteronomy Rabbah* 11:5, 10, and *Midrash Tanhuma*, Parashat Va'ethannan, as well as on the midrashim gathered in Ginzberg, 2:417-81.

261. For a literary analysis of this midrash, its development and variations, see Rella Kushelevsky, *Moses and the Angel of Death*, translated from the Hebrew by Ruth Bar-Ilan, Studies on Themes and Motifs in Literature 4 (New York: Peter Lang, 1995).

anticipation of the end, God coaxed his soul out of his body and, kissing him, took his life. Thus died Moses, most beloved of God.

The Legacy of Moses

How to interpret the Mosaic commandments and traditions within the context of Judaism has led both to a creative and to an intragroup tension within Judaism. To a great extent the discussion has been occasioned by external historical circumstances. Judaism is a religious tradition that has been forged in the furnace of an oftentimes tragic history. Historical crises have occasioned radical changes in the manner in which the religion is expressed and in the forms that expression takes. Among the crises that have had the greatest and most radical impact on the development of Judaism have been the destruction of the First Temple and its concomitant exile, the destruction of the Second Temple, and the European Enlightenment.[262]

The crisis attendant upon the destruction of the First Temple (586 B.C.E.) led to a reformulation of henotheistic Israelite religion into the universal monotheism that has become associated with Judaism. While the general tendency of Christian scholarship has been to emphasize the radical nature of the breaks with the past, Jewish scholarship has been somewhat more sympathetic to pointing out how the roots of the changes were present in preexilic Israel.

The destruction of the Second Temple (70 C.E.) and the failure of the Bar Kokhba revolt against Rome (132-35 C.E.) led to a redefinition of Judaism as a synagogue- and home-centered religion rather than a temple-centered one. The power of the ancient priesthood was broken, and authority was now invested in learned men, known as rabbis, who spent their time debating fine points of law and in effect completely reinventing and reinterpreting the biblical traditions for changed historical, economic, political, and social circumstances. In order to bolster their authority, they developed the fiction that God had actually revealed two Torahs to Moses at Mount Sinai. The first was the written Torah that had served as the source of Jewish tradition and authority since the time of Moses in their opinion, since around the time of Ezra in the fifth century in the opinion of most modern scholars. The second Torah was the oral Torah, by which the rabbis understood their own interpretative tradition. While the great compilation of the oral Torah, the Talmud, records extensive rabbinic debates and disagreements

---

262. This is not to claim that these were the only crises that had a radical impact on Judaism. Other such crises include the exile from Spain in 1492, the failure of Shabbatean messianism in the seventeenth century, and the Holocaust in the mid–twentieth century. This list can, of course, be expanded.

about the interpretation of the Torah, both written and oral, the rabbis' ultimate source of authority was invariably an appeal to the authority of Moses.

Although the fiction of the oral Torah would enable the claim to be made that Jewish law was eternal and everlasting, the rabbis themselves seem to have had a more differentiated understanding of the process of religious change and accommodation. In the famous story of the oven of Akhnai, the rabbis made clear that the ultimate authority for interpreting the traditions does not lie with God but with the people into whose hands he has entrusted his teachings.[263] In this familiar midrash, a number of rabbis were discussing a fine point of Jewish law. All assembled held to one view, with the exception of Rabbi Eliezer, who refused to be swayed by the overwhelming majority opinion. So he called on a carob tree to prove that his interpretation of the halakah, the religious law, was correct. The tree was uprooted and repositioned a hundred cubits away. But the other rabbis would not accept the evidence of a tree. So he called on a channel of water to prove that his interpretation was correct. Even though the water flowed backward, the other rabbis would not accept its evidence. Nor would they accept the evidence brought by the walls of the house that threatened to cave in. Finally, in desperation Eliezer called on heaven to support his interpretation. A heavenly voice sounded from heaven and asked how the other rabbis could disagree with Eliezer, whose interpretations were invariably correct. But Rabbi Joshua challenged the heavenly voice by arguing that "[i]t is not in the heavens" (Deut. 30:12), understanding the reference to be to the Torah. In other words, God gave Israel the Torah, and now it is up to the sages to interpret it, not up to God. A postscript to this midrash records that Rabbi Nathan once ran across the prophet Elijah, who according to legend walks the earth in anticipation of the coming of the Messiah. Nathan asked Elijah what God's reaction to this confrontation was. Elijah's answer was that God was overjoyed that his children had outsmarted him. They had learned well and knew how to apply divine law on their own.

Following the injunction to "build a fence around the Torah,"[264] the rabbis of the talmudic age developed a series of additional laws and customs whose purpose was to protect the essential 613 commandments that they distilled from the Torah. These 613 commandments were the essence of Judaism according to them. And it was these sacred commandments that they attempted to protect with their fences.

An illustration of their methodology may be found in the manner in which the rabbis interpreted the biblical injunction not to boil a kid in its mother's milk. This is the only commandment that appears three times in the Torah (Exod. 23:19; 34:26; Deut. 14:21); hence it must have expressed an essential religious or

263. *BT Bava Metzia* 59b.
264. *BT Avot* 1:1.

cultic concept in ancient Israel. Whatever the original meaning of the injunction,[265] the rabbis attempted to protect it by reading it literally. Better that one of the ancillary rabbinic injunctions should be transgressed than one of the Torah's. Thus, in order to avoid boiling a kid in its mother's milk, they effected a number of separations that would ensure that the essential injunction of the Torah not be transgressed, the end result of which was the development of some of the central principles of the elaborate rules of keeping kosher (Heb. *kashrût*) that have served to distinguish Jews from their environment over the course of the centuries. First they effected a separation in substance by forbidding the eating of milk and meat dishes together. Next they effected a separation in space by establishing separate dishes for milk and meat foods. And finally they ordained a separation in time by legislating a waiting period between eating meat dishes and milk dishes. Although the specific details of, for instance, the waiting period between meat and milk vary with the specific community and branch of Judaism, it is the principle that is important in this case.

The Enlightenment and its concomitant rise of scientific and rational thought presented a theological challenge not only to Christianity but also to Judaism. In addition, it led to the gradual emancipation of Jews in western European society. Judaism was torn between those who would hold fast to time-honored traditions and those who sought to modernize the faith. These diametrically opposed attempts to define a positive Judaism are to be contrasted with the great temptation that was held out to Jews wanting to be on the fast track to social acceptance, namely, conversion to Christianity.[266] The failure of this search for social acceptance as neo-Christians was exemplified by the rise of racial anti-Semitism in the late nineteenth century.

One of the major challenges posed by the attempt to modernize Judaism was a reevaluation of the hegemony of rabbinic Judaism. There had been previous attempts to break away from rabbinic authority and its claims to divine inspiration on the basis of a supposed revelation to Moses of the oral law. Among these attempts, the Karaite movement of the eighth century C.E. and beyond was one of the strongest. Be that as it may, the intellectual ferment of nineteenth-century Germany was eventually to give rise to the three major movements in modern Judaism, with their conflicting approaches to the issue of Torah in the broadest sense of the word.[267]

265. See Robert Ratner and Bruce Zuckerman, "'A Kid in Milk': New Photographs of *KTU* 1.23, Line 14," *Hebrew Union College Annual* 57 (1986): 15-60.

266. As the poet Heinrich Heine (1797-1856) famously declared, "The certificate of baptism is the entry ticket to European culture." Cited from Ritchie Robertson, *Heine*, Jewish Thinkers (London: Peter Halban, 1988), p. 84.

267. A good survey of the history, development, and theology of modern Jewish movements until the early 1980s is provided in Marc Lee Raphael, *Profiles in American Ju-*

Besides rejecting the revelatory claims of the rabbis' oral law, the early re-formers called the legal basis of Judaism into question. What they stressed was Judaism's nature as an ethical monotheism. The laws and customs as distilled by the rabbis were a secondary expression of the prophetic and moral insights to be gleaned from the text. For these reformers, Moses the lawgiver became Moses the prophet. The ethical norms of Judaism, now associated with the fig-ure of Moses, took the place of the heretofore obligatory legal structures. In this manner the Reform movement was born on German soil, although it thrived transplanted to the fertile ground of the New World.

The embattled traditionalists fought back by insisting on the primacy of the dual Sinaitic revelations. The rallying cry of Samson Raphael Hirsch, the founder of neo-Orthodoxy, was "Torah *with* secular knowledge." This freed tra-ditional Jews from their intellectual ghettos by allowing them to remain faithful to their inherited tradition while pursuing secular knowledge. In the case of a conflict between the two, precedence would, however, have to be given to rab-binic tradition.

Those who tried to steer a middle course between the need for moderniza-ization and the desire to continue working within the system of rabbinic hala-kah founded the Conservative movement, which is conservative with respect to the Reform movement but liberal with respect to Orthodoxy. While viewing it-self as a halakic movement, Conservative Judaism has been able to show appre-ciably more flexibility than Orthodoxy in the reinterpretation of rabbinic law in the modern world. The small Reconstructionist movement, an offshoot of Conservative Judaism, while based on an understanding of Judaism as an evolving civilization, has provided a home for a modern mystical or spiritual approach to Jewish life. Martin Buber's charismatic and mystical presentation of Moses would probably be an image comfortable to many Reconstruc-tionists.[268]

Although the Reform movement has turned back to more traditional practice in recent years, its basic theology is still based on individual choice and the nonbinding nature of the law. Its perception of Moses as a prophet has led to a marked social engagement in Reform Judaism. Orthodox Judaism is an en-tity that defines itself as based in the rabbinic tradition, although within that tradition there is no unanimity as far as ultimate authority goes. It is frag-mented into many different subgroups, ranging from various Hasidic sects on its right wing to the centrist "modern Orthodox" on its left. Conservative Juda-

---

daism: The Reform, Conservative, Orthodox, and Reconstructionist Traditions in Historical Perspective (San Francisco: Harper & Row, 1984).

268. See Martin Buber, *Moses: The Revelation and the Covenant* (New York and Evanston: Harper & Row, 1958, 1946); and F. Herzog, pp. 256-57.

ism has continued to try to hew to the middle path, agreeing with Orthodoxy in insisting on the binding nature of the halakah but siding with the Reform movement when using that religious law to allow practices unthinkable to earlier generations, such as the full religious equality of women. The field of contention, however, remains the individual movements' attitudes toward Mosaic law and practice, the whole development of which is traced to the divine revelation of God to Moses at Mount Sinai, whether that is to be understood literally or metaphorically.[269]

269. I would like to thank the editors of this volume for their thoughtful comments and suggestions, and my former fellow student, Prof. Choon-Leong Seow, for suggesting that I undertake this project. In addition, I would like to express my gratitude to my first teacher in matters biblical, Prof. Charles D. Isbell, who kindly looked over my manuscript and offered valuable insights, as well as to my former students Nicholas Osen, who provided me with bibliographic references and engaged me in some stimulating discussions on the subject of Moses, and Susan Haber, who provided some last-minute bibliographic aid. All mistakes and shortcomings are of course my own responsibility. My research was supported by a generous grant from the Centre for Jewish Studies at York University. And last but not least, my colleague, Prof. Douglas Freake, generously gave of his time to enable me to complete this project.

Shakyamuni: Buddhism's Founder in Ten Acts

RICHARD S. COHEN

Introduction: The Historical Buddha in Contexts

Four Buddhas: Amitabha, Konakamana, Kalachakra, Shakyamuni

- In 402 c.e. Buddhism was coming into its own in China. Introduced five centuries earlier by Indian and Central Asian merchants eager for trade with the glorious Han dynasty, Buddhism had been treated with curiosity and contempt by Chinese nobles and Confucian scholars. By the fifth century, however, the Han was no more; it had splintered into sharply divided warrior states. Buddhism flourished in this dynamic new environment: monks worked miracles for kings; in return, kings established Buddhist institutes, centers for ritual, education, and art. On September 11, 402, a monk named Hui-yüan gathered 123 monks and lay followers for a solemn ceremony. The congregation kneeled before an image of Amitabha, a complete and perfect buddha who resides in Sukhavati, a paradise to the west. Hui-yüan taught that innumerable buddhas populate the universe, each inhabiting his own particular world, and among all these buddhas' worlds, Amitabha's Sukhavati is the most perfect. Lighting incense and sprinkling flowers, Hui-yüan's congregation vowed collectively to seek rebirth in Amitabha's Buddhist paradise.
- The fourteenth year of Emperor Ashoka's reign fell sometime around 254 b.c.e. Just six years earlier, Ashoka had conquered the eastern Indian territory of Kalinga (south of modern Calcutta) in a battle so bloody that it

121

turned his heart from war to religion. Hundreds of thousands died according to the traditional account. With this battle Ashoka established his preeminence over the Indian subcontinent. The extent of his empire was not matched again until the British raj, more than two millennia later. This powerful king now sought to pacify his peoples through religion, Dharma, rather than through arms. He legislated morality, established hospitals and veterinary clinics, and mediated between competing sects. By the end of his reign, Ashoka went so far as to forbid the killing of animals, from ants to rhinoceroses. But we are concerned with the fourteenth year of Ashoka's reign. For it was in this year that he doubled the size of a brick memorial dedicated to a buddha named Konakamana, who lived during an ancient golden age in which the human life span was thirty thousand years. Ashoka knew that thousands of centuries had passed since Konakamana Buddha taught the truth and established a community of monks. Ashoka also knew that Konakamana's truths had been long forgotten and his community had been long defunct. Ashoka does not tell us why he enlarged this memorial, the relic of a long, long dead buddha.

- Over the course of three days in July 1985, Tenzin Gyatso, His Holiness the Fourteenth Dalai Lama, broke with tradition. In Madison, Wisconsin, surrounded by a congregation coming from many countries, cultures, and ethnicities, the Dalai Lama taught an esoteric practice for the first time outside of Asia. He introduced his audience to a profound method for transforming themselves into living buddhas. Those members of the audience who would pursue these teachings with unwavering rigor could become a buddha named Kalachakra in this very life, in this very body. Well, almost this body. Actually, Kalachakra Buddha is blue black in color; he possesses four faces and twenty-four arms; he stands trampling on demons while he embraces and unites sexually with a consort. Though the Dalai Lama's teachings were unprecedented in Madison, the size of his American audience paled by comparison with the one hundred thousand people who attended a similar ceremony in Bodh Gaya, India, in 1971. Teachings and rituals associated with Kalachakra Buddha have long held great import for Tibetans. On the one hand, the religion of Kalachakra gives the serious practitioner a rapid means to realize Buddhism's highest ideal, complete and perfect buddhahood. On the other hand, Tibetan Buddhists believe that their presence at the Dalai Lama's ritual performance guarantees them rebirth in Shambala, a secret paradise on earth in which the religion of Kalachakra Buddha is the state religion.

- The Dalai Lama's Kalachakra initiation in Bodh Gaya attracted a multi-

Bodh Gaya, India
(photo by Richard S. Cohen)

tude. Nearly two and one-half millennia earlier, Bodh Gaya was the site of a singular achievement. For it was in Bodh Gaya, under an enormous Bodhi tree, that a young warrior realized the ultimate truth and became the buddha known as *Shakyamuni*. Buddhists believe that many buddhas have walked the earth over the ages. But when non-Buddhists refer to "the buddha," they usually mean this man who sat under a tree circa 453 B.C.E. Shakyamuni's religion had a long history in India, remaining a vital cultural presence for nearly two thousand years. However, by the thirteenth century C.E. Buddhism was in severe decline. Monuments, which the faithful had once erected in Bodh Gaya to celebrate Shakyamuni, were neglected and crumbling. In the sixteenth century the temple built around Shakyamuni's tree of awakening even came under the administration of Hindu priests. Fast forward to 1891, when Anagarika Dharmapala, the son of a wealthy furniture dealer in Sri Lanka, visited Bodh Gaya. Distressed by the sorry neglect of this most central pilgrimage site, he founded the Maha Bodhi Society with the aim of fostering its restoration. Dharmapala's motives were missionary as well as devotional. Trained in the church schools of Sri Lanka's colonial masters, he imagined that a renewed Bodh Gaya would serve as a center for the propagation of Shakyamuni's teachings. Indeed, these teachings were particularly timely, for, in Dharmapala's view, Shakyamuni Buddha was a man for the scientific era. He was a mortal, not a god; his doctrines were the products of rational analysis, not divine inspiration; his ethics were supported by reason, not legislated by divinity. Shakyamuni Buddha attained his transformative experience through individual effort, intelligence, and fortitude, and thus achieved something that every other human being could achieve as well.

What Is a Buddha?

Amitabha, Konakamana, Kalachakra, Shakyamuni. Each is a buddha, literally one who has awakened. The term "buddha" is an honorific title given to any individual who has thoroughly realized ultimate truth to the highest degree. Although Buddhists universally regard Shakyamuni Buddha as the historical founder of their religious system in the current age, there is no evidence that Buddhists ever deemed Shakyamuni to be unique as a buddha. The rock-cut edicts of Emperor Ashoka provide the earliest extant evidence for Buddhism in India, and as I detailed above, Ashoka patronized a cult dedicated to a buddha other than Shakyamuni. One might say that buddhahood is true only if it is replicable, just as a scientific discovery is accepted only after experimental verification.

Broadly speaking, the buddhas' perfection has two dimensions: wisdom and compassion. First, the title buddha itself defines buddhahood as a cognitive state. Buddhas possess insight and knowledge the rest of us lack. Thus the Sanskrit term *buddha,* concretely denoting "awakening from a slumber," is related to metaphorical expressions for mental acuity such as *buddhi,* intelligence, and *bodhi,* enlightenment. As awakened beings, Amitabha, Konakamana, Kalachakra, and Shakyamuni possess an omniscient consciousness that utterly surpasses the ken of common humanity; their knowledge is bounded by neither space nor time; potentially they can perceive every facet of every datum — moral, material, emotional, intellectual — always. In short, as buddhas, Amitabha, Konakamana, Kalachakra, and Shakyamuni are capable of knowing everything worth knowing about everybody, past, present, and future. But crucially, this is not knowledge for its own sake: it is practical and liberative. The attainment of transcendent awareness enables buddhas to slough off the hindrances of mundane attachment. They extirpate the root causes of suffering. Even when they are *in* the world, they are no longer *of* the world. Considered from the perspective of their wisdom, there is little to distinguish these four buddhas one from the other. Their shared buddhahood makes them embodiments of the timeless truth. Thus, if one were to open a philosophical treatise that examined Amitabha, Konakamana, Kalachakra, and Shakyamuni from the perspective of their "Body of Truth," one would find that body described in the singular: the Truth-Body of the buddhas.

The second dimension of the buddhas' perfection is compassion. Omniscience benefits a buddha himself, but it also makes him a supremely effective teacher. A buddha's compassion, the ground from which he interacts with others, is as consummate as his wisdom. When a person sets out on the impossibly arduous path to become a buddha, he does not say, "I want to become a buddha," but rather, "I want to become a buddha for the sake of living beings." Buddhist traditions often use the simile of a bird to express these twin perfections. A one-winged bird cannot fly, whereas the twin wings of wisdom and compassion enable a buddha to soar aloft. And so Buddhist traditions consistently emphasize the ongoing and active roles buddhas play in the lives of their adherents. Consider the following vignettes: Amitabha Buddha created Sukhavati, a paradise within which to follow the Buddhist path; Kalachakra Buddha empowered an esoteric and dangerous rite by means of which practitioners can traverse the entire spiritual path in a single lifetime; Shakyamuni Buddha walked the dusty paths of India for forty-five years, teaching by word and deed. Notice also that although every one of these buddhas is revered as a teacher of truths and a creator of means for spiritual realization, the longer vignettes presented at this chapter's beginning highlighted the activities of their devotees as well: Amitabha *and* Hui-yüan, Kalachakra *and* the Fourteenth Dalai Lama, Shakyamuni *and* Dharmapala.

Though equal in wisdom, these individual buddhas can be differentiated through how they are encountered by and are meaningful to human followers. If one opened a philosophical treatise that examined Amitabha, Konakamana, Kalachakra, and Shakyamuni from the perspective of the material body by means of which they assist others, one would find differences and distinctions among these buddhas described in minute detail.

Shakyamuni the Founder

For Buddhists, every buddha is *both* the embodiment of a reality beyond time *and* an active participant in time. From the perspective of Western scholarship, however, the belief that Shakyamuni was only one among numerous buddhas cannot be substantiated. Shakyamuni was a historical individual; Amitabha, Konakamana, Kalachakra, and every other buddha (there are many!) were not. Granted, established facts about Shakyamuni's life are few: we are not certain when he lived or when he died; we do not know precisely what he taught; we do not really know how people regarded him in his own day. Despite this level of ignorance, however, few, if any, scholars doubt Shakyamuni's historical authenticity.

Another way of saying that Shakyamuni is Buddhism's founder is to say that every Buddhist culture, tradition, school, and society delights in his sacred biography. The birth of Shakyamuni, his abandonment of home and kin to become a mendicant, his spiritual awakening under the Bodhi tree, and his death at age eighty are all common themes in Buddhist lore. By contrast, some Buddhists celebrate Amitabha's accomplishments while others look on his tale as a fantasy. Fewer accept Kalachakra. And though most Buddhists believe in Konakamana's past terrestrial existence, most also ignore him. One way of distinguishing Shakyamuni from these other buddhas is through typology: Amitabha is a "celestial buddha," Kalachakra a "primordial buddha," and Konakamana a "buddha of the past." Some Buddhists consider buddhas of these various types to be more powerful than Shakyamuni, or more accessible to devotees. Nevertheless, though Shakyamuni is not the most important buddha for every community, as Buddhism's founder in the current age he always does have a place.

Despite this universal interest in Shakyamuni's life, there is no Buddhist equivalent to the Christian Gospels, written within fifty to one hundred years of the crucifixion, or even Ibn Ishaq's *Life of the Messenger of God*, composed little more than a century after Muhammad. No single story of this founder was written within the first century or two after he attained complete and final nirvana. Rather, a unified sacred biography evolved slowly over centuries. Particular discourses Shakyamuni gave, or particular miraculous deeds he is reputed to have performed, or places he frequented on a regular basis provided occasions for the telling of stories about his life. A pilgrim to the town of Gaya, for example, might go to the spot at which Shakyamuni gave the "Fire Sermon" and, while there, recollect the circumstances surrounding that discourse. Another pilgrim, visiting Vulture Peak where he taught the "Perfection of Wisdom," might reflect on how Shakyamuni's life incorporated that perfection. Still another might visit Vaishali, where Shakyamuni was offered a bowl of honey by a monkey, or Shravasti, where he defeated rival teachers in a contest of magical power. Over the course of centuries, local stories associated with these many life-events came together and were synthetically unified into a cohesive sacred biography.

Actually, the distinction to be drawn between Buddhism and Christianity or Judaism is even more radical. For biographical data on their founder, all Christians rely primarily on the four Gospels, and Jews on the Pentateuch. Few scholars of Judaism and Christianity regard the Pentateuch and Gospels as objective chronicles of past events, but many agree on their singular importance for recovering that past. By contrast, there is no one biographical text that all Buddhists accept as valid. Full biographies *were* written, but *many* were written, and not all agree about the facts of Shakyamuni's life or how to interpret those facts. This multiplicity is due in part to the fact that Buddhism was itself evolving at the same time as the evolution of Shakyamuni's legend. During the centuries after Shakyamuni's death, Buddhist communities fell into arguments over issues such as his nature as a buddha, how he became one, and what happened to him after death. The arguments were intimately connected with matters of biography, for Shakyamuni's biography itself was the paradigmatic model through which Buddhist truths were known, understood, and taught. Buddhology and biography cannot be disentangled: communities that disagreed over what it meant for Shakyamuni to be a buddha naturally disagreed over how he lived his life as a buddha; vice versa, variant conceptions of his acts as buddha required variant conceptions of his buddhahood. By reading these many biographies, it is possible to come up with some bona fide facts about his life, but distressingly few. And one must be careful. There are traditional biographies of Shakyamuni that appear to be virtually free of any mythological overlay; these almost read as modern, objective records of a great man's life. Although such nonmythologized representations of Shakyamuni appeal to modern sensibilities, one must keep in mind that they are actually no less ideological than highly miraculous accounts. What appears to be concern for accurate historical reportage in these biographies is a function of their theological conception of buddha, a conception that highlights Shakyamuni's humanity rather than his superhumanity.

Shakyamuni Buddha was born circa 488 B.C.E. with the given name

Shakyamuni buddha
(National Museum, New Delhi; photo by Richard S. Cohen)

Siddhartha (or Sarvarthasiddha) Gotama.[1] Though Siddhartha is often referred to as a "prince," he was not the son of a king. Rather, the Shakya family into which he was born was a tribal clan that occupied a territory in the Himalayan foothills, near the current Indo-Nepalese border. In Kapilavastu, the clan's center, Siddhartha's father was an elder, perhaps even *primus inter pares*. The Shakyas are remembered as a proud and wealthy people. Young Siddhartha

1. Scholars are not certain of Shakyamuni Buddha's dates. The traditional sources support two chronologies. The long chronology — based on Sri Lankan sources — places Ashoka's coronation 218 years after Shakyamuni's nirvana; according to this chronology, the buddha lived circa 566-486 B.C.E. The short chronology — based on Sanskrit and Chinese sources — places Ashoka's coronation 100 years after Shakyamuni's nirvana; according to this chronology, the buddha lived circa 488-368 B.C.E. This chapter focuses on Buddhism in India, using Indian sources. Accordingly I use the short chronology. The arguments surrounding this contentious and unresolvable issue can be found in Heinz Bechert, ed., *The Dating of the Historical Buddha* (Göttingen: Vandenhoeck & Ruprecht, 1991-92).

was raised to a life of pleasure and ease, reveling in his vigor and youth. The traditional story tells that his life was so sheltered that even as a young adult he remained utterly unfamiliar with old age, disease, or death. But at age twenty-nine, Siddhartha finally encountered these woes of human existence. As the story goes, Siddhartha was on a jaunt to a pleasure grove when he saw an elderly man ravaged by time. Siddhartha had never seen an old man before, and was troubled to learn that all humans are subject to age. Dumbfounded by the implications of this encounter, Siddhartha became even more disturbed when, on the next day, he headed out to the pleasure grove only to see a diseased man for the first time, afflicted by dropsy, frail and weak. Yet the inevitabilities of age and disease were overshadowed by the lesson Siddhartha received on his next day's outing, when he beheld his first funeral procession, learning that all must die. This is not the end of the story, for on the fourth day Siddhartha saw an ascetic monk, who glowed with the peace of one completely at peace with time. Thus at the same moment that Siddhartha came to know the inevitability of suffering, he also came to know that suffering only *seems* inescapable. Inspired by his vision of the renunciant, the prince decided to seek peace for himself, freedom beyond all suffering and change.

Thus Siddhartha abandoned the royal pleasance. His youthful hedonism gave way to six years of zealous asceticism. Again, history here is inextricable from story: Siddhartha's austerities are said to have been so severe that, according to one account, he ate only one juniper berry and rice grain per day. He became so thin that he could wrap his hand around his spine. This regimen went on for six years, until he realized that extreme physical mortifications were no more likely to lead to permanent peace than the joyful abandon of his youth. He then sought a middle path.

A visitor to India can still visit the spot where Siddhartha's six years of self-torture began in hope and ended with repudiation. This same visitor can then walk several miles from that lonely place to Bodh Gaya, where, at the age of thirty-five, Prince Siddhartha became Buddha Shakyamuni. (*Shakyamuni* translates as "sage of the Shakya clan.") From a doctrinal point of view, Siddhartha's dissatisfaction with the world was predicated on a cosmology founded on the twin concepts of samsara and karma. "Samsara" is a term used to describe the cosmos inhabited by the unawakened. The literal translation, "wandering about," is a clinical depiction of this world. Living beings wander from birth to death to a new birth in a new body. The cosmos within which we wander consists of five states — divine, human, animal, ghostly, and infernal — and there is no certainty as to which state one will enter upon death. One can be certain only that pleasures are fleeting and pain will be followed by more pain. Siddhartha sought release. He found his way out, first by contemplating the unsatisfactoriness of samsara, and then by elucidating its cause: karma. Literally "action," karma is the force that drives beings to wander ceaselessly through samsara. Evil offenses force one toward a rebirth in the hells of cold and heat; good, meritorious deeds force one toward the shining heavens. But even the gods fall from celestial joys, and maybe directly down to a hell!

For six years Siddhartha sought to gain permanent release from the prison of his body by torturing and disciplining that body. He had no lasting peace to show for it. To find his way beyond samsara, he had to discover a path beyond bodily action. His "trick" was to see that karma, at its base, is a function of the mind. Thus, one of the most popular collections of Shakyamuni's sayings, the *Dharmapada*, begins: "All things originate in mind, are distinguished by mind, are created by mind."[2] Although the naive view holds that the movements of conscious volition are ineffective if not translated into physical activity, the awakened know that conscious volition itself is the heart of action. The will powers samsara. One is stuck in samsara because one desires; karmic bondage arises from an act of mind as well as from deeds one does, impelled by blind desire. Suffering is very real, but that suffering can be stopped. Siddhartha reasoned that if he could control his will, he could then bring an end to desire. Detached, he could still act in the world, but he would no longer create new karma. Upon his death there would be nothing to force him to wander about ever again. He would attain nirvana beyond the mundane cosmos. Under the tree in Bodh Gaya, Siddhartha discovered the truth that enabled him to will without attachment, to act without creating karma, to become a fully awakened buddha.

The next forty-five years found Shakyamuni wandering the north Indian countryside preaching by word and example. His first sutra (= doctrinal discourse) was spoken to a group of five renunciants who had attended him during his severe ascetic phase and then abandoned him when he sought a new way to liberation. In this discourse, entitled *The Turning of the Wheel of Law,* Shakyamuni taught four principles known to the liberated, the so-called Four Noble Truths: (1) the persistence of suffering, (2) suffering's root causes, (3) the fact that suffering can be brought to an end, and (4) the practical means for ending suffering once and for all. A medical metaphor is often used to characterize this set of truths. Shakyamuni is the master physician who has (1) recognized the etiology of a disease, known as "existence"; (2) identified the vectors of that disease; (3) demonstrated a cure for the disease; and (4) prescribed a regimen for treatment. Hearing the four truths, this group of disciples also attained liberation from samsara. These five became the first members of Shakyamuni's *sangha,* the Buddhist monastic order. Many were to follow. Shakyamuni's life as a buddha centered on this *sangha,* which he cultivated

---

2. *The Buddhist Hybrid Sanskrit Dharmapada,* ed. N. S. Shukla (Patna: K. P. Jayaswal Research Institute, 1979), p. 1.

through discourses on doctrine and correct action. He was equally conscientious about developing a cadre of lay disciples, individuals who did not leave their homes to seek final liberation but nevertheless affirmed Buddhist ideals and supported the monks and nuns. Finally at age eighty, Shakyamuni died, one of the most exceptional men in history.

Shakyamuni and Other Founders

At first glance Shakyamuni's biography places him well within the company of the other religious founders discussed in this book. Like Moses, he left his native home and was a stranger in a strange land when he encountered the absolute. Moses saw a burning bush and spoke with God among the Midianites; Siddhartha was far from Kapilavastu when he comprehended the roots of suffering. Like Jesus, Shakyamuni's realization of the highest humanity has led followers to view him as more than human. Four centuries after Jesus' death, the Council of Chalcedon declared him to be "actually God and actually man"; five centuries after Shakyamuni, *The Lotus Sutra* declared him to be "ever present and unperishing." According to this text, Shakyamuni's death was a sham, an act to spur recalcitrant disciples to action. Like Muhammad, Shakyamuni wrote nothing himself; his words were collected and remembered by devoted followers. But whereas the Qur'an is held to have been compiled in an unalterable form in Arabic about twenty years after the Prophet's death, the Buddhist canon remained in a state of flux for a millennium. And by contrast with Uthman's edict to burn every leaf and codex that differed from the official Qur'an, Shakyamuni is remembered as authorizing the translation of his words into local languages. Not only that, new sutras were also composed throughout this period, accepted by some as Shakyamuni Buddha's own words and rejected by others as forgeries. Like Confucius, Shakyamuni played the role of political adviser. But whereas Confucius wandered from state to state actively seeking a ministerial position through which to effect his social vision, Shakyamuni renounced his own royal power in favor of a homeless life.

Despite these parallels, a superficially comparative approach to Shakyamuni's life would destroy any hope of exploring Buddhism from a perspective sensitive to traditional Buddhist concerns about this religious founder. For there is one fundamental difference between Buddha and the other figures discussed in this book. Consider Jesus. After his baptism on the river's edge, Jesus heard a voice from heaven: "You are my favored son — I fully approve of you" (Mark 1:11).[3] Je-

---

3. Robert W. Funk et al., *The Five Gospels: The Search for the Authentic Words of Jesus* (San Francisco: HarperSanFrancisco, 1997), p. 39.

sus alone heard this voice. More important, only Jesus could ever have been addressed by this voice saying *these* words. Christianity is predicated on the singularity of Jesus, God's only Son. His life ending in crucifixion is a unique turning point for the cosmic order, never to be repeated. This tenet is articulated in the popular verse, John 3:16: "This is how God loved the world: God gave up an only son, so that everybody who believes in him will not be lost but have real life."[4]

One will never find Shakyamuni making such a claim for his own personal life and death. Indeed, numerous Buddhist scriptures reject such claims. One excellent example is the *Discourse on Serene Faith,* in which Shariputra, a disciple renowned for his insight, proclaims Shakyamuni's preeminent uniqueness: "It is clear to me, Lord, that there never has been, never will be and is not now an ascetic or Brahmin who is better or more enlightened than the Lord."[5] Shariputra is correct in one sense, for other buddhas are *just as* enlightened as Shakyamuni, neither more nor less. Still, far from soaking in the praise, Shakyamuni mockingly challenges Shariputra's shortsighted faith that discounts buddhas of past and future altogether.

And Shakyamuni does not differ from only Jesus in this regard. The personally unique status of Muhammad and Moses is crucial to the traditions they are claimed to have founded. As the Seal of the Prophets, Muhammad is a singular figure (Qur'an 33:40). Muslims accept Abraham, Moses, and Jesus as prophets, but hold that only Muhammad received Allah's revelation in its most perfect and complete formulation. After Muhammad there can be no need for another prophet; to question his status as the last prophet is to question Allah's own perfection. Similarly, Moses is unique, his exceptional role for Judaism being summed up in the Torah's final verses: "And there has not arisen a prophet in Israel like Moses, whom the Lord knew face to face" (Deut. 34:10).

One might have wondered why, at this chapter's beginning, I introduced Shakyamuni Buddha in the company of Amitabha, Konakamana, and Kalachakra. Why emphasize commonalities among these buddhas rather than the obvious stark difference? Indeed, the grand theme guiding *The Rivers of Paradise* is that Buddhism — alongside Judaism, Islam, Confucianism, and Christianity — is a great personality religion, one that originated in, and centers around, the person, life, and experience of a single individual, i.e., Shakyamuni Buddha. This sounds like a very simple, straightforward project to implement, especially given that other buddhas, Amitabha et al., are not founders on this model. But now we see that to consider what a buddha is *for Buddhists,* who Shakyamuni is as a founder *for Buddhists,* is neither so simple nor

---

4. Funk et al., p. 408.

5. Maurice Walshe, trans., *The Long Discourses of the Buddha: A Translation of the Dīgha Nikāya* (Boston: Wisdom Publications, 1995), p. 417.

straightforward. A nuanced account of Shakyamuni as founder must emphasize his relationship with other buddhas, because for Buddhists, Shakyamuni's
nonuniqueness as buddha is central to his status as founder. This is why I first
presented Shakyamuni in the company of Amitabha, Konakamana, and
Kalachakra. Shakyamuni *is* Buddhism's founder. Perhaps for a Western scholar
seeking either Buddhism's origins or an essential commonality between Buddhism and other world religions, Shakyamuni's historical singularity as a
founder may be the crucial fact. But if one truly seeks to foster global understanding through sensitivity to the differences among religions, then one must
acknowledge that Shakyamuni's function as founder has not given him a singular status for Buddhists, who ironically use his teachings as a means for seeking,
worshiping, emulating, and encountering *other* buddhas. Rather than attempting to conform Shakyamuni to a category that is not appropriate for him, it will
be much more interesting and valuable to see how Shakyamuni is *not* a religious founder on the model of Moses, Jesus, or Muhammad.

Further, this point is not just apropos to the buddha; it holds for Buddhism as well. Historically Buddhism gained prominence in India as a missionary religion dedicated to fostering the happiness of the many through the dissemination of particular rituals and doctrines. Centuries after Shakyamuni's
death, Buddhist monks and lay devotees began to influence the religious lives of
peoples we now call the Thai, Burmese, Sri Lankans, Japanese, Laotians, Viet-
namese, Mongolians, Chinese, Nepalese, Tibetans, Cambodians, Bhutanese
(though they went by other names at the time). As diverse societies came to
hear of the buddhas, to consider their teachings, to sample their rituals, Buddhist ideals, doctrines, and practices adapted to disparate social structures and
cultural patterns. Just as Shakyamuni Buddha cannot be disengaged from the
many buddhas, so what we call Buddhism, capital *B*, is in fact an array of many
buddhisms, inextricably embedded within distinct locales. There ever only have
been buddhisms, small *b*. Even in Shakyamuni's day, sociocultural factors
played an important role in the formulation of doctrine, practice, and community. Shakyamuni's own Buddhism was ever just one buddhism.

Why?

This introduction has sought to sketch an intellectual landscape within which
Shakyamuni Buddha can be understood as a religious founder. We have seen
that buddhas are perfected in terms of cognitive development and social activity, wisdom and compassion. From the point of view of wisdom, buddhas are
ideal types or generic figures who embody the universal Truth; the historical dimension of their lives is beside the point. Yet, although all buddhas are equal in

their wisdom, they differ through their compassionate deeds. Thus Shakyamuni is the founder, and his acts as founder circumscribe his accomplishments as a buddha. But from the Buddhist point of view, status as the terrestrial founder of a religious order is only one thing a buddha might do, and not the most illustrious or effective by a long shot. Shakyamuni's historical acts as religious founder define him, but that role has to be placed within a much broader context: the infinite compassionate activities of all buddhas. This is the principle that permits Amitabha, Konakamana, Kalachakra, and Shakyamuni all to be buddhas and yet to play such different and unique roles within Buddhist traditions.

At this point you must be wondering why I am so concerned to problematize and contextualize Shakyamuni's historical role as Buddhism's founder. What does it benefit us to highlight the tension between a modern "scientific" approach to Shakyamuni as buddha and a traditional Buddhist approach? My reason for taking so much time to highlight these distinctions has much to do with the broader program of *The Rivers of Paradise*. Centuries ago Buddhism entered Sri Lanka, China, Tibet, and so on. Now, at the beginning of the third millennium of the common era, the buddhas are becoming meaningful to a new community of interest, albeit not as the founders of a path to devotion, faith, or salvation. This new community is Western academia. Yet another new buddhism is forming within academia's confines, adapting to a society that demands that one publish or perish and a culture whose highest value is the careful manipulation of data. Given this context, although the discussions of rituals, stories, doctrines, texts, communities, and institutions that follow are meant to introduce readers to Buddhism, that is not all they actually do. These discussions do not merely represent or reiterate data. They are creative. They play a role in the dynamic processes of creating new meanings for a new buddha. Thus, in keeping with this volume's broader aims, I hope to enable the reader to enter into a dialogue with Buddhism, allowing the religion's diverse concerns, categories, texts, and institutions to guide the conversation. My aim is to make Buddhism meaningful to this new community of interest by revealing what some Buddhists themselves have found meaningful about Shakyamuni Buddha as the founder of their religion.

If we are not self-conscious about prior assumptions we may bring to a study of Buddhism's founder and how our assumptions may differ from those traditionally held, we have no defense if accused of intellectual imperialism or epistemic violence. Thus the remainder of this introduction will explore this tension in three steps. First, we need to consider the categories through which Western scholars commonly analyze religious founders. In this regard the sociological writings of Max Weber are of singular importance. The second step is practical. Does the Weberian typology provide an adequate basis for understanding Shakyamuni Buddha? What does Weberian typology hide or obscure? Third, how can we represent Shakyamuni Buddha in a way that fulfills scholarly needs for historical accuracy and yet remains sensitive to traditional Buddhist understandings? Once this step is reached, we will be able to explore the doctrines, practices, and social formations associated with Shakyamuni as founder.

The Weberian Angle

Within the study of religious authority, Max Weber holds a singular position. Born in Thuringia in 1864, this remarkable son of a wealthy industrialist can be considered the father of the sociological study of religion. Sociology, for Weber, was a scientific attempt to understand and interpret "social action," i.e., how people act in relation to other people as well as the meanings they attribute to their actions. Weber's sociological study of religion sought to interpret religion's effect on people's lives, in terms of both what people do and why they do it. Given this orientation, Weber focused on individual motivation rather than group dynamics. That is to say, his sociology sought empathetically to grasp how individuals consider their actions meaningful. He did not view people as mere functions within a social process, swept along by a tide outside their control.

This emphasis on individual motivation created a problem, however, for Weber was heir to two intellectual currents that coursed during the nineteenth century. The first was *Geisteswissenschaften*, the cultural sciences, which sought to understand the meaningfulness of subjective human action. The second was positivism. Chiefly associated with the physical sciences, positivism seeks knowledge from empirical facts, independent of human subjectivity. Positivist sociology held that all human behavior can be explained through generalized universal laws, which are "value-free." Consider, for example, a glass of water. You may subjectively judge the water in this glass to be "hot" or "cold." Such a value judgment is notoriously unstable: if you move your hand from 100-degree into 90-degree water, the second glass feels cool, but a movement from 80 degrees to 90 degrees warms the hand. Positivism sought to avoid such subjective value judgments. Rather than speak of "hot" and "cold," the positivist views temperature as the statistical average of molecular movement and explains the experience of changing heat as a subjective manifestation of the second law of thermodynamics, i.e., entropy within a system will increase to the maximum limit. The experience of "cooling" or "warming" is merely an epiphenomenon of heat transfer toward greater systemic entropy: values attributed to the system have no bearing whatsoever on the physical processes at work within the system.

One can readily see the reason for conflict between the approach to sociology as a cultural science, which explained action through reference to individual experience and meaning, and positivist sociology, which sought generalizable laws for human activity apart from any individual subject. Weber sought to reconcile these two, to draw generalizable laws from the study of human subjectivity. In order to accomplish this, he developed a theory of the "ideal type," the social equivalent of "temperature." A physicist will not attempt to describe the individual movement of every particular water molecule in the glass: temperature is a collective phenomenon best explained in terms of statistical analysis. It would be impossible to determine a "temperature" if there were no individual molecules in motion, but to read a "temperature," that physicist must generalize beyond the level of individual molecules. Similarly, an "ideal type" is an abstract model. An ideal type does not attempt to account for the particular social actions of any real, specific individual person. Rather an ideal type elucidates general classes of human activity, providing a norm by which a scholar can understand and analyze subjective behavioral realities. In this way Weber sought to construct valid causal hypotheses vis-à-vis human activity while circumventing the hermeneutic difficulties that arise within the study of subjective meaning.

The use of typology is not in itself problematic. In fact, I have already presented Shakyamuni Buddha as something of an ideal type. For Buddhists, the fine particularities of Shakyamuni's life are less important than his fulfillment of the generalized duties of a buddha. From a Buddhist perspective, Shakyamuni realizes the type *buddha*. Weber, too, treated Shakyamuni as participating in an ideal type, but for Weber Shakyamuni was a *prophet*. Here is the point at which conflict arises. As a Weberian prophet, Shakyamuni can be individually compared or contrasted with other prophets, such as Moses and Jesus. We gain a greater ability to generalize across cultures through the Weberian type. Perhaps we even gain the ability to specify general laws about the foundation and formation of religions. But the price we pay is the reduction of cultural specificity and native context. Is the gain worth the loss? The only way to answer this is to see what it would mean for Shakyamuni to be of the ideal-type prophet.

Shakyamuni as Prophet

Weber defines the prophet as "a purely individual bearer of charisma, who by virtue of his mission proclaims a religious doctrine or divine commandment."[6]

---

6. Max Weber, *The Sociology of Religion*, trans. E. Fischoff (Boston: Beacon Press, 1964 [1922]), p. 46.

This definition seems straightforward enough. We can paraphrase Weber: a prophet is somebody who, possessing great personal authority without having any evident preestablished basis for that authority beyond himself, takes it upon himself to bring truth to the world. According to traditional accounts, Shakyamuni realized the absolute only after he had tried and rejected several other spiritual paths available to him in fifth century B.C.E. India. Beneath the tree of awakening, this man developed a new meditative technique, directly perceived a "new" truth, changed his mode of being in the world, and gained a personal power that lay at the heart of his authority as teacher and leader of a monastic order. Shakyamuni possessed authority as a prophet, but it was an authority born of internal experience, not external institution. Similarly, the Christian Gospels record that Jesus' mission began after a voice from heaven called to him alone: "You are my favored son — I fully approve of you." No other person heard this divine pronouncement, but it was only after this experience that Jesus went out as a prophet among the people. Neither Jesus nor buddha had institutional, economic, or political underpinnings for their authority: their power came solely from themselves. In both cases personal power was also inextricably linked to a personal experience of the absolute. Indeed, this link between experience, religious meaning, and authority is central. For Weber, the "hallmark of prophecy" is that "personal revelation" is the basis of salvific authority.[7]

It certainly is possible to plug Shakyamuni into the Weberian ideal type of the prophet and to make comparisons based on that analysis. Insofar as Weberian analysis strives toward positivist truth, its analyses begin from "givens," data accepted by all parties as fact. Weber's givens, presupposed to have a transcultural, transhistorical reality, are *individuality* and *experience*. Thus, to treat Shakyamuni as a prophet, a scholar must single him out as "purely individual" and empathetically comprehend his "experience." Again, this can be done. But one wonders: What is the ideological basis for Weber's emphasis on individuality and experience? Can it be disentangled from the legacy of a sixteenth-century fervor for "justification by faith" that sought holiness outside the established ecclesiastical orders? How much does it rely on the theology of Friedrich Schleiermacher (1768-1834), who almost single-handedly invented the concept of "religious experience" in the late eighteenth century? In short, to what extent is Weber's ideal type a specifically Protestant ideal? What would be at stake if one were to conform the buddha to this type? It "feels" far more ideologically charged to categorize Jesus as a "buddha" than to categorize Shakyamuni as a "prophet." But is that feeling justified? Is the ideal-type "prophet" as value-free as Weber may have believed? Though

7. Weber, p. 54.

pertinent, I will put these questions aside in favor of one other, far more crucial question. Weber defines the "prophet" in terms of individuality and experience. Have Buddhists themselves traditionally posited individuality and experience as fundamental categories? Indeed, the potential for conflict can be phrased in even stronger terms. What if Buddhism actively problematizes, mistrusts, or even teaches the invalidity of notions such as individuality and experience?

In fact, Buddhists have not traditionally treated their buddhas as individuals and have always been suspicious of experience. We have already found that Shakyamuni differs from other figures Weber calls prophets in that he is not viewed by Buddhists as purely individual or absolutely unique. There is only one Seal of the Prophets; there are many buddhas. Weber is conscious that a conflict such as this could arise, and preemptively asserts that "no radical distinction will be drawn between a 'renewer of religion' who preaches an older revelation and a 'founder of religion' who claims to bring completely new deliverances. The two types merge into one another."[8] Here Weber would have us ignore one index by which Shakyamuni can be differentiated from Moses, Muhammad, and Jesus. Or more to the point, Weber would tell his readers to ignore the Buddhists' own conceptualization of buddhahood. Buddhists believe that Konakamana (remember, the buddha whose monument Ashoka enlarged) established Buddhism when humans' life span was thirty thousand years, that in the intervening myriad centuries this religion was lost, only to be "rediscovered" by Shakyamuni circa 453 B.C.E. Moreover, Konakamana was not the only buddha to precede Shakyamuni on earth as a founder; others came before Konakamana and still more will follow Shakyamuni. The buddhas are countless. But according to Weber, this doctrine should have no bearing on our comprehension of the buddha as a religious founder. Something might be gained by following this scholarly strategy, but something might also be lost.

Why does Weber seem to require us to so transgress actual Buddhist representations of the buddhas? Recall that Weber's sociological approach to religion attempts to reconcile a meaning-based understanding of religious action with a positivist search for universal truths. Thus Weber's ideal types are necessarily abstract and ahistorical, detached from the messy details that clutter up the lives of religious communities on the ground. He is less concerned with how Buddhists themselves have actually approached Shakyamuni than with aspects of buddhahood that are most generalizable *beyond* Buddhism. Thus Weber sets up a dichotomy. On the one hand is the "pure individual," solid, definite, singular. On the other hand are qualities or activities abstracted from that individual; these are the human truths. This equation is placed in jeopardy by

8. Weber, p. 46.

Buddhism's belief in multiple buddhas: if there is no individual, there can be no abstract truths of religious behavior.

Indeed, how might Shakyamuni be judged a pure individual? For Jesus et al. the criteria are clear: the traditions that look upon them as founders emphasize their uniqueness. But a scholar seeking Shakyamuni's individuality cannot disentangle even the prosaic details of his life and career on earth from his role as a religious type. Let us take, for example, the seeming "fact" that Shakyamuni was eighty when he died. We cannot assume that the general understandings of temporal passage, life span, and death within which a Buddhist receives this information are the same as that within which you read it now. In fact, Buddhists have traditionally viewed human history as going back millions of years. Terrestrial time is a process of moral and spiritual decline. As human values and goodness diminish over the course of centuries, so the life span of human beings shortens. Thus, many mythological millennia ago, at the time of Konakamana Buddha, humans lived thirty thousand years. Even long before Konakamana was Vipashyin Buddha, when humans lived eighty thousand years. Now, at the time of Shakyamuni Buddha, the life span is a mere one hundred years. So why did Shakyamuni not remain on earth for this full century? The scholastics tell us that buddhas need live out only three-quarters of their ideal span. Did Shakyamuni really live for eighty years? Is the scholastic doctrine a response to this *fact*? Or is the age of eighty itself attributed to Shakyamuni in accord with a Buddhist (or generally Indic) system of numerological values? We do not know; we cannot know. Shakyamuni's death after eighty years may be as much a matter of scholastic norms as it is of human mortality.

This example of Shakyamuni's life span can be multiplied. Buddhist literature is replete with instances in which Shakyamuni is about to do something, but before acting he stops and wonders, "Where did buddhas in the past perform this deed?" or "What did buddhas in the past do in this instance?" These clichés are telling indeed, for they starkly demonstrate that from a Buddhist point of view no aspect of Shakyamuni's life was purely individual; his actions, teachings, associations, accomplishments were all predetermined by the fact that he was a buddha. Traditional biographies often represent the details of his life as determined by his participation in an ideal type. Every buddha who comes to earth and is born in India shares a life. For instance, every one of their mothers dies seven days after giving birth; every one awakens under a tree in Bodh Gaya, albeit the type of tree differs from buddha to buddha; every one teaches the same first sermon in the same place. To signal this compulsion of terrestrial buddhas' lives to conform to a single, common, paradigmatic ideal, Sanskrit literature uses a particular discourse marker: *dharmatā*. When something is *dharmata*, it is natural, regular, in the order of things. Insofar as the events in buddhas' lives are *dharmata,* we might say that the very nature of the world requires buddhas to act just as they do. A buddha who does not live an archetypical buddha's life is no buddha at all. (Recall that there are different buddha subtypes. Buddhas such as Amitabha and Kalachakra are not terrestrial, and therefore not required to conform to this pattern.)

If Buddhists do not valorize terrestrial buddhas as pure individuals, they are even more skeptical when it comes to experience. Weber understands experience to be self-evident and inexpressibly personal. His attempts to "understand" others across time and space, as well as his attempts to discover positivist truths about social action, suggest that he took a realist's view: sense experience provides valid information about reality. By contrast, Buddhism equates the naive acceptance of sense experience with ignorance; at the root of desire is a perverse equation between personal experience of the world and reality. Naive positivism is ignorance. Shakyamuni became liberated when he discovered that karma leading to rebirth is created by the will acting upon faulty understanding of the world's nature. Things are *not* really as they appear; liberation can occur only after one has unlearned habitual modes of experience. In fact, these reservations about gross experience developed over the centuries into a thoroughgoing skepticism about all experience. In the most arcane articulation, a buddha's wisdom, what he "experienced" under the tree, what gave him the charisma to be a Weberian prophet, is said to be *the creative nonexperiencing of no experience.* Thus for the Buddhists of Tibet, for instance, "the relation between . . . enlightenment and experience is not at all clear," in the words of Janet Gyatso.[9]

I have already suggested that biography is driven by typology: Shakyamuni the historical founder can never be separated from Shakyamuni the transhistorical exemplum. And so, this skepticism vis-à-vis sense experience has also found its way into traditional discussions of Shakyamuni the founder. One particularly graphic example is found in a sutra aptly named *On the Buddha's Secrets.* As is the case with other texts I have cited, this text is attributed to Shakyamuni, but most certainly was composed centuries after his death. This sutra's unknown author has Shakyamuni reveal a profound secret about himself from the perspective of perfect wisdom. The text claims that Shakyamuni never directly taught anything to anybody. From the hour of his awakening until the moment of his death, Buddhism's founder never spoke, never uttered a single syllable. Rather, Shakyamuni spent these decades under his tree suffused in awakening's bliss. According to this presentation of the buddha's secrets, whatever sermons and discourses unawakened folk believed they heard from Shakyamuni's lips were actually creations of their own ignorant minds. The fact that these imaginings came

---

9. Janet Gyatso, "Healing Burns with Fire: The Facilitations of Experience in Tibetan Buddhism," *Journal of the American Academy of Religion* 67, no. 1 (March 1999): 113.

across as doctrinal and moral truths can be attributed to the fact that they reflect Shakyamuni's silent perfection. In short, once one understands the buddha's secret, one knows that he never actively participated in the world and never actively founded anything. The religion that counts Shakyamuni as its founder was, in actuality, created through the mistaken perceptions of unawakened but faithful individuals who merely imagined that the buddha was teaching them.[10] The buddha is ever only what others make of him.

Let me emphasize that the conceptualization of Shakyamuni in the *On the Buddha's Secrets* is not common to all Buddhists. In fact, there is virtually no doctrine of any sophistication on which all Buddhists agree. Buddhism has no central church, no single leader, no single canon of scriptures. This is one reason why we must be reluctant to apply the Weberian ideal type of the prophet to Shakyamuni. The buddha we can know is only what his followers have made of him, which has been radically multiple, not purely individual. Weber, too, would make something of Shakyamuni. Seeking universal truths about human action, Weber needs a pure individual. To find one, he must re-create the buddha as he might have been before tradition mythologized him: a charismatic teacher of truth. But this is certainly a new buddha, and one that is no less made up than the others. Remember, we know of Shakyamuni's life from synthetic redactions of localized lore separated by centuries from Shakyamuni himself. To imagine that one can strip away two and one-half millennia of Buddhist tradition to reveal the pure individual who stands at the head of every tradition is both historically improbable and theoretically naive. This scholarly tactic requires one to devalue the plurality of traditions and their often divergent, often contentious claims to authority. And again one wonders, what unstated ideological and theological tendencies would make such a project seem natural and appropriate? Why does Weber think he can inquire about the buddha without also necessarily asking, "buddha for whom?"

An Alternative Approach to the Buddha

How do we resolve this conflict between history and theology so that we can move forward to a discussion of buddha as founder? History, as I use the term, is the attempt to comprehend human phenomena within the specificity of their sociocultural, geographic, and temporal contexts; theology, by con-

---

10. This is an interpretive paraphrase of citations in *Madhyamakaśāstra of Nāgārjuna with the Commentary: Prasannapadā by Candrakīrti,* ed. P. L. Vaidya and S. Tripathi (Darbhanga, India: Mithila Institute of Post-Graduate Studies and Research in Sanskrit Learning, 1987), pp. 265-66.

trast, situates social phenomena within the context of an essential, unchanging absolute or paradigm. Buddhist conceptions of the buddha and the Weberian conception of the prophet are both "theological." The buddha and the prophet function as ideal types precisely because they are constructed in such a way as to hush the ambient noise that surrounds real human activity. From the theological perspective, both typologies highlight essential characteristics, enabling one to perceive deep, universal truths. From the historian's perspective, by contrast, they create mere caricatures of a human being. Good scholarship in the study of religion is properly historical. If universal truths are to be found, they will be reached at the end of the scholar's investigation, not at the beginning; theological essences cannot provide a starting point for historical studies of religion. A historian's interest in such abstractions, rather, is confined to the consideration of how they give meaning to particular peoples in specific localized contexts. Thus the historian contextualizes norms that theologians designate as context-free, and historicizes norms that theologians set beyond the confines of history.

Looking at both Weber and Buddhism, we find theology. But which one enables history? On the one hand, there is the Weberian "prophet": an individual whose experience of the ultimate gives him the personal power and authority, charisma, to reject tradition and set out a compelling new path to salvation. On the other hand, the Buddhist "buddha" stands beyond all individuality, for perfection is perfection. All buddhas are equally wise, all equally compassionate. Not only is individuality impossible, it is undesirable, for individuality represents deviation from the perfected norm.

On the face of it, Weber's typology appears the more historical. Weber points us in the direction of somebody who happened to be born, to have a transformative experience, to teach and establish an organization, and then to die. These are commonplace events, able to be comprehended (if not performed) by almost anybody. Traditional Buddhist representations, by contrast, place Shakyamuni beyond all the happenstances of history: he is superhuman perfection. Nevertheless, the Buddhist view of Shakyamuni as founder allows for the better historical representation of Buddhism as a religion. This is because Weber constructs his ideal type by abstracting Shakyamuni from the processes of history and segregating him from all traditional communities. The lepidopterist comes to mind: a collector of beauty who must pin his beloved butterflies through the heart in order to closely observe their morphologies. But the historian's ideal of comprehending human phenomena within localized contexts cannot be realized if we approach Shakyamuni isolated from specific communities of interest. The so-called "search for the historical buddha," which necessarily stands at the beginning of Weber's study, reveals more about the sources of our sources than about Shakyamuni himself. But there exists a vast body of data, covering more than two millennia and all the world, which reveals how actual Buddhist communities have looked upon Shakyamuni as their founder.

Shakyamuni as Founder: The Ten Deeds a Buddha Must Perform Before Entering Nirvana

At the beginning of this chapter I introduced Shakyamuni in the company of his peers, plunging the reader into the sea of concentrated meanings and multiple values within which the term "buddha" floats. We saw that the multiplicity of buddhas inspires typological analysis at one level, while it invalidates all particularist typologies at another. Still, the encounter with Weber made clear that although every typology may be violable, we must nevertheless choose one. Not to choose at all is itself a distinctly theological choice. What matters most are the criteria upon which we choose. And so, in the remainder of this chapter I intend to represent Shakyamuni as founder, to show how Buddhism originated in, and centers around, Shakyamuni's person, life, and experience. But I will take my notions of origination, of personhood, of life, and of experience from Buddhists themselves.

As a buddha, Shakyamuni is neither "celestial" like Amitabha nor "primordial" like Kalachakra. Rather, like (the mythological) Konakamana before him, Shakyamuni is a "terrestrial buddha," a "historical buddha." He is a founder, and this status carries an existential burden. For as we have seen, Buddhists believe the lives of all terrestrial buddhas conform to a single predetermined pattern. Indeed, the earliest extant sacred biography associated with Shakyamuni, *The Great Story (Mahāvadāna Sūtra)*, actually recounts the life of another buddha altogether, named Vipashyin, who awakened when the human life span was eighty thousand years. This text presents Vipashyin's life as a model for that of Shakyamuni (and five other buddhas), not Shakyamuni's life as a model for Vipashyin.

To consider Shakyamuni as Buddhism's founder is to take seriously the fact that every living Buddhist tradition delights in his legend. *The Great Story* presents a pattern for the buddhas' sacred biography, but it was left to later scholastic authors to systematize that pattern. Buddhist traditions can be distinguished by how they particularize the buddhas' life as a set of *dharmata* (cosmically necessary) events. There are several such lists. The Theravada tradition of modern Sri Lanka, for instance, specifies thirty deeds in common for all buddhas; Tibetans, by contrast, homologize all terrestrial buddhas through twelve deeds. The Mulasarvastivada tradition, a sect that had great prominence in classical India, stipulates ten activities that all buddhas must accomplish before they can be said to have done their work as buddhas on earth. These lists of shared activities give us the best possible point of entry into an examination of

Shakyamuni as founder, because they reveal in detail what particular historical Buddhist communities considered a buddha's essential accomplishments as a participant in human society. These lists disclose, without ambiguity, how Buddhists looked upon Shakyamuni as their religion's founder, and why he was valued as such. The question of whether Shakyamuni "actually" performed any of the acts itemized on these lists is not raised by this study.

Buddhism has no central church, no single leader, no single canon of scriptures. Accordingly, although lists are common, and the logic underlying them universal, every particular list of shared deeds is somewhat idiosyncratic. My basis for choosing one list over the others is pragmatic. Which list enables the most effective introduction to Buddhism for this volume, *The Rivers of Paradise?* The Mulasarvastivada sect's ten acts. These ten may have been systematized as few as three hundred years after Shakyamuni's death, or as many as one thousand years. One cannot say. Moreover, the Mulasarvastivada list is probably not the oldest, nor has it been the most influential; but since no other scheme is significantly older or more universal, these caveats hardly matter. These ten are to be preferred over all the others because they are the most explicit about presenting the buddha as a religious founder. This list of ten is recorded in several works of Mulasarvastivada literature. Here I paraphrase the Sanskrit *Divine Stories*, which recounts episodes from the life of Shakyamuni and his followers.

It is the rule *(dharmata)* that living, breathing buddhas have ten essential duties. A buddha will not attain nirvana until:

- standing on the shore of Lake Anavatapta, he and his disciples recount rewards and punishments resulting from actions they performed in previous lives;
- he trains everybody he is able to train;
- he lives out at least three-quarters of a full life span;
- he establishes his parents in the Dharma;
- he delineates a congregational boundary;
- he displays a great miracle in the town of Shravasti;
- he shows himself descending from the heavens in the town of Samkashya;
- he appoints two chief disciples;
- he inspires another member of his retinue to aspire for the unexcelled, complete and perfect awakening of a buddha; and
- he predicts that somebody within his retinue will become a buddha in the future.[11]

11. *The Divyāvadāna*, ed. E. B. Cowell and R. A. Neil (Delhi: Indological Book House, 1987 [1886]), p. 150.

Note the logic. Final and perfect nirvana is absolute freedom from samsara, the abhorred domain of suffering, old age, disease, death, and rebirth. A buddha seeks nirvana as his ultimate aim. In order to gain this freedom, he must necessarily develop liberative wisdom: insight into the true nature of himself and his desires. This insight enables the awakened buddha to extirpate the roots of ignorance that have kept him circling in samsara and allows him never again to become entangled in karma's bonds. Once somebody has this insight, there would seem no reason for him to ever eat, defecate, stand, walk, or talk again. Yet the *Divine Stories'* author tells us that a buddha who has gained perfect wisdom has not done all he has to do. Insight is not enough. A buddha *cannot* realize nirvana until he accomplishes his role as a religious founder in full. A buddha must *necessarily* participate in social activities; he must predict, inspire, train, delineate and appoint, show, recount, and display. The ten acts named here are the deeds whereby this particular Buddhist tradition knew Shakyamuni to be its charismatic founder. More generally, these ten deeds point to Shakyamuni as a teacher, administrator, and wonder-worker, as a member of a family and member of a "church." In setting Shakyamuni apart as superhuman, these ten enable us to see him as very human indeed. In the pages that follow, I will take each of these ten deeds as the basis for an exploration of some aspect of Buddhist history, community, practice, or doctrine. Each of these ten essential duties is a highly compressed expression of an issue that has motivated and inspired Buddhists over the ages. By unpacking these events within a broad framework, we can come to generalize about the unique concerns and processes dynamically expressed in Buddhist history.

Act 1: Living Beings and the World in Which They Live

> It is *dharmata* that a living, breathing buddha will not attain nirvana until, standing on the shore of Lake Anavatapta, he and his disciples recount rewards and punishments resulting from actions they performed in previous lives.

Several weeks after Shakyamuni awakened, he sought his first disciples. Using divine vision, he saw that his own former teachers had died but that the five ascetics who had accompanied him during his exquisite bouts of self-denial were living near the village of Sarnath, 150 miles to the west. Shakyamuni traveled the long road. Far from being glad to see their old friend, however, these five, when they spied Shakyamuni at a distance, decided to snub him. In his ascetic phase Siddhartha had been a hero to the five. But once he gave up ascesis, having recognized that it was not the path to liberation, the Shakya became a backslider in their eyes, a spiritual weakling who did not deserve even common courtesies. Nevertheless, as Shakyamuni approached, his personal charisma was inescapable. Forgetting their hasty compact, one of the five offered the buddha a seat, one offered him water, and a third inquired about his health. Soon Shakyamuni was returning their hospitality through the gift of his first teaching, *Turning the Wheel of Law (Dharmacakrapravartana Sūtra)*. We will come to the content of this sutra later. For now suffice it to say, these five "got it." They realized the truth by which one becomes free from the poisons that contaminate samsaric existence: hatred, desire, and ignorance. Recall that Buddhists consider the number of buddhas to be potentially infinite because the Dharma is universal, impersonal, and accessible to all, albeit with great difficulty. However, mere realization of liberative truth does not create a *complete and perfect buddha;* though liberated, these five were not buddhas. Rather, Buddhism calls them *arhats,* literally "worthies." Like a buddha, an arhat has entirely freed himself from samsara's afflictions. But status as an arhat falls short of buddhahood for two reasons. First, an arhat's insight is shallower than that of a buddha; his knowledge is less broad. Second, a mere arhat does not maximize his worth as a teacher or storehouse of spiritual merit. A buddha is completely wise and completely compassionate. An arhat, by contrast, need only be wise and compassionate enough to effect his escape from samsara. The conversion of these five and their attainment of arhatship mark the beginning of Shakyamuni's career as a teacher. Traditional biographies remember him as swiftly swelling the ranks of arhats — fifty here, one hundred there — until the congregation of arhats numbered more than one thousand.

Years later Shakyamuni recollected that it was incumbent upon him, as a buddha, to travel with a group of 500 arhats to the shores of Lake Anavatapta. He could not attain complete and final nirvana until this deed was done. It was no picnic! Lake Anavatapta (lit. "not well heated") is located high in the Himalaya's northernmost reaches, on the far side from India. Given that these worthies were beyond desire, they did not complain about the cold. And besides, though frigid, Anavatapta is an especially beautiful spot for an arhat summit: its waters, filled with golden jewel-encrusted lotuses the size of chariot wheels, are the source of India's great rivers, including the Ganges. But don't book *your* ticket too soon, for the only agency that can fly you to Anavatapta is magic. This congress of 500 arhats by the lake was exclusive indeed.

The meeting at Lake Anavatapta is not counted as essential to Shakyamuni's role as buddha because of the stark beauty it evokes: yellow-red robes in somber silhouette against a background of snowy peaks. Rather, this event is privileged because its paradoxes betoken vast spiritual power. Anavatapta's far shores are virtually unattainable, yet 500 men stood there and told stories. These 500 were Shakyamuni's contemporaries, yet they vividly recounted details from their past lives. As arhats, they had sought and attained liberation from the effects of worldly acts, yet their stories lionize the effects of worldly acts. In fact, as the Mulasarvastivadin list of ten deeds has it, the gathering of arhats on Anavatapta's shores was a celebration of karma's workings, an opportunity for these arhats to explicitly tie their current attainments to actions performed by bodies long dead. The meeting on Lake Anavatapta's shore illustrates that the seemingly most unattainable goals can be attained; the seemingly impossible has already been realized by others whose own progress started in the simplest of acts. Thus, within this story of Shakyamuni's life we hear other stories:

Shariputra, one of Shakyamuni's two chief disciples, tells that he was fortunate enough to come into contact with the buddha, to become an arhat, because in a previous life he paid obeisance to other holy men. The good karma produced through his acts of reverence and devotion to these past worthies gave him the merit necessary to be in the right place at the right time when a full and perfect buddha was born.

Uruvilvakashyapa, an early convert, tells of a previous life in which he came upon a stupa, a burial mound, containing the remains of an ancient buddha named Kashyapa. This memorial had fallen into disrepair, but Uruvilvakashyapa rebuilt it (possibly providing a model for Emperor Ashoka, who enlarged the stupa of Konakamana Buddha). As a result of this simple ritual act, Uruvilvakashyapa enjoyed a divine rebirth for many millennia. When he returned to the earth as a human being, he was born into a prominent and wealthy family. Uruvilvakashyapa credits to this devotional act to Kashyapa's stupa his ability to become a monk in Shakyamuni's community and a perfected arhat.

The worthy Shaivali tells how he constructed a stupa for Kashyapa Buddha; Revata relates a story in which he offered medicine to monks in Vipashyin Buddha's *sangha;* in a previous life, Vagisha looked upon a stupa for Vipashyin Buddha with reverence and burnt incense in worship. Every one of these arhats ties his ultimate liberation back to a simple act of piety. Perhaps they could not have gained liberation except through a careful knowledge of Shakyamuni's Dharma. What we learn here is that they would not have met Shakyamuni except as the fruit of a good deed done toward another buddha in the past. Neither Shaivali, Revata, Vagisha, nor Shariputra, nor Uruvilvakashyapa, nor any of the remaining 495 arhats will ever be born again, thanks, ultimately, to proper action.

When the other arhats ask Shakyamuni for his own stories, he takes the discussion in another direction altogether. Rather than recounting his own past triumphs, Shakyamuni's tales of past lives have him going to hell as the result of his moral failings. We learn that Shakyamuni once lured his brother into a forest and then killed him, greedily coveting the entire inheritance for himself. In another life Shakyamuni was a young brahmin who befouled a saintly man's food out of jealousy. Other lives have him lying, encouraging immorality, and committing more murder. Though it may be surprising to see Buddhist literature highlight Shakyamuni's failings, there would have been little didactic benefit from the buddha recounting his own past good deeds on Anavatapta's shore. There exists an entire genre of Buddhist literature dedicated to Shakyamuni's positive development as a holy man throughout his past lives: the *jataka* tales. But to show the power of karma, whereby the one who is now known to be morally perfect once merited hell — now that's a story! These tales of Shakyamuni's weakness are like early acts in a play that people watch again and again because they know and anticipate the happy ending.

Let us now move beyond the stories themselves and into the physical and spiritual world they illuminate. For the event at Anavatapta was deemed crucial to Shakyamuni's identity as a terrestrial buddha precisely because these stories illustrate the nature of the cosmos and the efficacy of religious action therein. First, these stories point toward the structure of samsara, the realm of action, retribution, and rebirth. Uruvilvakashyapa says he went to heaven for several millennia as a result of his rebuilding the memorial to Vipashyin Buddha; later he became a human being. Shakyamuni sent himself to hell through his evil deeds. Yet other tales of Shakyamuni's previous lives tell of his deeds as a rabbit, a tree spirit, a monkey, or a king. These stories assume a cosmos divided into domains that contain living beings of distinctly different types. Buddhists call this cosmos *samsara*. They envision it as a spinning wheel, a Wheel of Becoming. A god named Death, Mara, grasps this wheel tightly in his claws and fangs, engulfing samsara. At the wheel's hub one finds hatred, desire, and ignorance, the impulses that force beings around this pointless circle of death and redeath. Held in Mara's grip, propelled by psycho-moral failings, samsara has five principal divisions.

Within samsara, the most desirable domains are the heavens, which can be reached only through great merit. In these paradises gods inhabit glorious palaces; their senses are filled with unimaginable bliss; their every desire is swiftly realized. But unlike the Christian heaven, which is otherworldly and lasts forever, Buddhist heavens are on a continuum with samsara's other destinations. Gods die, to be reborn according to their merit. Moreover, gods usually do not win a second consecutive life in heaven. They are so engrossed in the enjoyment of selfish pleasures that millennia pass before they remember that their divine abode is a reward for good karma. They recall this only in their last week of life, for gods know when they will die as well as their future fate. The greatest suffering in all of samsara is said to be that of a god who knows he will be reborn in the hells, at the far end of the moral cosmos. There in the hells the dissolute and meritless meet untold tortures involving knives, or boiling, or intense cold. Again, Buddhist hells differ from the Christian hell in that they are purgatorial; they are temporary abodes in which to experience the effects of previous evil deeds. Unlike with the heavens, however, one can get stuck in the hells indefinitely; after all, this realm is a breeding ground for further acts of ill will, malevolence, and hatred. Nevertheless, I have also heard a Tibetan monk teach that the very first step Shakyamuni took toward buddhahood was in a hell, where a benevolent thought flickered briefly in his head.[12] Superior to the hells, a third samsaric destination is the realm of the "hungry ghosts," beings with impossibly thin necks and impossibly large bellies, whose overwhelming hungers are insatiable. And one step above the ghosts we find the animals, fated to suffer early death due to either human exploitation or the law of the jungle. Finally, the fifth possible destiny is our own. Birth as a human being is looked upon as favorable, perhaps the most favorable. Humanity allows for joy. But no human is so happy as to forget the inevitability of suffering, whose recognition is the beginning of the spiritual path. Only human beings are likely to ask: "Is this as good as it gets?" and then to seek an answer.

This is the state of affairs in which we find ourselves. This is the bad hand we have been dealt but nevertheless have to play for all it is worth. According to Buddhist literature, there is no basis for inquiring about a dealer in this cosmic poker game, a prime mover of this wheel, a God existing before or beyond time. The game is here; the rules are set. Scholars often describe karma's workings as an impersonal and ineluctable law, on the model of the second law of thermodynamics, or Murphy's Law. One cannot suspend this law any more than one can a law of physics. Even Mara, the lord of samsara, cannot escape the effects of his actions; he will die and be replaced by another Mara. The impersonality of karma has a curious corollary: Buddhists make no attempt to explain samsara's ultimate origin. There is no myth that tells the beginning of time. Samsara has *always* existed. Still, though samsara has no known beginning, it need not be endless. This is not a mere game of chance. One *can* win. Witness the 500 arhats gathered on the shore of Lake Anavatapta.

Let us take a closer look at one of their stories for indications of how to win at the game of life. Here is the tale told by an arhat named Vagisha:

> Ninety cosmic aeons have passed since I last experienced a bad rebirth.
> Rather, I have been born as god and human being due to my spiritual merit.

---

12. This story is found in the *Sutra of the Wise and the Foolish,* a collection of Buddhist tales popular throughout Central and East Asia. For the story see *Sutra of the Wise and the Foolish,* trans. Stanley Frye (Dharamsala, India: Library of Tibetan Works and Archives, 1981), p. 222.

Not that I was a particularly good man. My merit is due to a single simple encounter: I saw the *stupa* of Vipashyin Buddha and venerated it. I covered the *stupa* with perfumes, garlands, unguents, which I purchased for sixty cowrie shells, and because of which I will never fall into an evil state again. For a mere pittance, I have received great good fortune. I have become an *arhat*, cooled the passions, and attained nirvana. Truly, if I performed worship to Vipashyin's *stupa*, having perceived a perfect buddha therein, that caused great excellence. Therefore, someone who knows the many virtues of a perfect buddha should perform honor to *stupas*: this will bear great fruit.[13]

The arhat Vagisha begins his tale aeons in the past, when he encountered a stupa dedicated to the still more ancient Vipashyin Buddha. Stupas are monuments dedicated to a saint or a buddha. Typically they contain sacred relics, vestiges of their resident holy man, that are interred in a casket deep within their core. The author of Vagisha's story would have considered this stupa's relics to have still been very much alive, infused with Vipashyin Buddha's own moral virtue, absolute wisdom, and profound benevolence. Thus, to comprehend this text one must understand that, for its audience, the encounter with a buddha's stupa is tantamount to a direct bodily encounter with the buddha himself. Indeed, Vagisha tells us as much when he says he perceived a perfect buddha therein. It is almost surprising how abbreviated this tale is. Vagisha saw Vipashyin Buddha's stupa and performed some simple rituals. The next thing we know, Vagisha is a liberated arhat. Note that the author makes no mention of meditation, or mystical experience, or even personal realization of truths about the world. Rather he matter-of-factly declares that it was his reverence for the stupa that bore this great fruit. How is it that karma can make mere rituals of reverence so powerful that they seem to catapult Vagisha to the state of a liberated arhat, beyond Mara's grasp?

Karma is thought of as a "law," so let us look to a professional "lawbook," a treatise on Buddhist doctrine: the *Compendium of Metaphysics (Abhidharma-kośa)*, written in the early fifth century C.E. by a scholar-monk named Vasubandhu. This text became a standard part of the monastic curriculum in India and influenced Buddhism's intellectual development in China, Japan, and Tibet as well. The *Compendium's* analysis of karmic law starts from the commonplace connection all Buddhists make between action and the mind: action is volition, first, and secondarily the physical and verbal deeds produced by volition. This fundamental predication of action as a mental event has crucial ramifications. With the exception of somatic reactions (for which the motivating volition is insignificant), all karma has a moral aspect: it can be good, bad, or indetermi-

---

13. *Le Congrès du Lac Anavatapta (Views de Saints Bouddhiques)*, ed. Marcel Hofinger (Louvain-la-Neuve: Institut Orientaliste, 1982), pp. 62-63.

nate. Good actions produce merit, leading to a desirable recompense; bad actions lead variously to the hells, the realm of hungry ghosts, or the animal kingdom. Thus, when Vasubandhu speaks of generosity, for instance, he characterizes it as a good volition and the resulting bodily or vocal action, having a desirable recompense. Applying this principle to Vagisha, we would not look to the mere lighting of incense or to bodily prostration as the force behind his liberation. Rather, his narration emphasizes that his worship of Vipashyin's stupa was motivated by his perception of a perfect buddha therein. An attitude of reverence and devotion, even faith, underlay Vagisha's physical deeds. Recall, by contrast, the stories Shakyamuni told on Anavatapta's shore: his past mental attitudes of jealousy, hatred, and ill will sent him down to the hells.

All is still not clear. One moment Vagisha is worshiping Vipashyin's stupa, the next moment (albeit ninety cosmic aeons later) he is an arhat. This aspect of Vagisha's story does not quite fit a simple ledger-book understanding of karmic recompense. Living beings circle in samsara because of their accumulated karma. But here it seems that a ritual act, albeit one of devotion to a buddha, erased Vagisha's karma. What happened? Does not karma's "law" require Vagisha to receive his retributions, felicitous or miserable? Did this karmic act abrogate karmic law? To address these questions, let us peer deeper into the *Compendium of Metaphysics.* Generosity, for Vasubandhu, is the paradigmatic meritorious action. Through Vasubandhu's analysis of generosity, we can understand the deeper mechanisms at work in Vagisha's story.

Every act of gift giving has three elements: giver, recipient, and gift. We have just seen that the giver's motivations have a profound effect on an action's karmic outcome. But for Buddhists the recipient's identity is just as important a factor in determining the quality and quantity of the karmic benefit derived from an act of giving. An agricultural metaphor is commonly used in explanation. Generally, a lazy farmer who neglects his daily chores should not expect a bumper crop. But if such a farmer is clever enough to plant his seeds in rich loam and lucky enough to receive rains in a timely fashion, he may nevertheless receive a bumper crop, even if he spends most days drinking at the bar. In fact, although this farmer is himself good for nothing, he will reap a richer harvest than an industrious worker who plants seeds in bad soil, has no system for irrigation, and receives no rain. A clever, skillful giver "plants" his "seeds" in the best possible "field of merit." The better the field, the more wide-ranging and immediate the effects. To illustrate the "excellence of the field of merit" as a factor influencing karmic recompense, Vasubandhu tells of a monk who instantly became a woman because he insulted the community of monks, saying, "You are nothing but women!" For me, the most striking example of this principle comes from an account of modern Burma: There is a monk who abandoned his monastic residence, choosing instead to live in a cave. Because this monk renounced even the barest of quarters, local people began to look upon him as especially holy, and therefore a superior field of merit. Even though he had already relinquished one monastery, wealthy patrons built three more in his honor. All four stand empty, a testament to this monk's virtue.[14] Within Vagisha's story, Vipashyin Buddha is the field of merit. In fact, buddhas are the supreme fields of merit, according to Vasubandhu's *Compendium*. A volition directed toward that field becomes supercharged (to mix metaphors). The transformation undergone by the giver, far from being subtle, is overt and absolute. In fact, Vasubandhu suggests that proper action — mental, physical, and verbal — directed toward a buddha advances one through the stages of the spiritual path straightaway, catapulting one straight to the ultimate fruit. He writes: "The learned rely upon the blessed one and his Dharma, even with the marrow of their bones. For, by mere faith, those who completely trust in the buddha overcome heaps of evils. They overcome splendid divine and human births. They arrive at their final refuge in nirvana. This is why buddhas are considered the unsurpassed field of merit."[15]

Does Vasubandhu's claim that faith in the buddhas overcomes the effects of evil deeds abrogate the law of karma? Let's leave that answer to the buddhalogicians. This analysis of Vagisha's story has enabled us to understand why a particular community of Buddhists believed that it was necessary for Shakyamuni to gather with his arhats on the shores of Lake Anavatapta in order to tell stories about the relationship between their present attainments and deeds done in previous lives. Mythological trappings here — the meeting occurs in a place inaccessible to the average person; the gathered arhats display knowledge not held by the average person — are a rhetorical device for marking this event's seriousness. On the shore of Lake Anavatapta, people whom the buddha led to perfection tell some basic truths about playing the game of life: namely, the law of karma can be inexorable and unforgiving, but the faithful worship of a buddha gives one the power to escape Mara's grasp. One can imagine a merchant, living in fourth century C.E. India, considering himself fortunate indeed that Shakyamuni had come to earth one thousand years earlier, giving him the opportunity to pay homage to a buddha's stupa. Epigraphic sources record the names of many such Buddhists. From what we can tell, moreover, these religious folk were rather excited about the prospect of passing several cosmic aeons in the heavens until their attainment of arhatship under a future buddha.

14. Melford E. Spiro, *Buddhism and Society* (Berkeley: University of California Press, 1970), p. 414.

15. *Abhidharmakośa and Bhāṣya of Ācārya Vasubandhu with Sphuṭārthā Commentary of Ācārya Yaśomitra*, ed. Dwarikadas Sastri (Varanasi: Bauddha Bharati, 1987), verse 7.34, p. 1099.

Act 2: Suffering and Its Origin

It is *dharmata* that a living, breathing buddha will not attain nirvana until he trains everybody he is able to train.

Shakyamuni's final day is remembered as a scene of remarkable calm. Surrounded by well-wishers, monks, lay devotees, even gods, Shakyamuni placidly uttered his last words, lay down, and died. That final utterance — "Whatever is constituted through karma necessarily passes away" — held nothing new. This message was the doctrinal heart of the *Dharma-vinaya* (doctrine and discipline) that Shakyamuni promoted while wandering the roads of northern India for forty-five years.

In fact, months earlier Shakyamuni had already declared his mission nearly complete. During the rainy season of his eightieth year he became so ill, his pains so sharp, that Ananda, the buddha's personal attendant and closest friend, feared he would die. But despite great suffering, Shakyamuni willed his life to continue. At that time the community of monks *(bhikṣu-sangha)* was scattered throughout northern India. The buddha deemed it "improper" to achieve complete, final nirvana without the *sangha* at his side. When told of this plan, Ananda misinterpreted his master's resolve. Ananda thought Shakyamuni was holding on to life because he had not yet given the complete course of his teachings. When Ananda told the buddha of his concern — not only that he feared to lose his beloved master but also that he was anxious for Shakyamuni to give the *sangha* a final exhortation and final instructions — Shakyamuni blew up at him. "Do you really think, Ananda, that I am a closefisted teacher who conceals teachings? Do you believe there are still truths I did not yet teach to others?"[16]

Shakyamuni had kept nothing back. And on the last day of his life this was confirmed. Reclining on his deathbed, which had been laid between two *sal* trees at the outskirts of Kushinagara village, Shakyamuni exhorted his community: "Ask, O monks, do not hold back! If someone has doubts or confusion about the buddha, the Dharma, or the sangha, or about suffering, its cause, its cessation, or the path: ask and I will answer!"[17] Silence followed, broken finally by Ananda stating the obvious: not a single member of the buddha's community doubted or was confused. Shakyamuni applauded Ananda's words. He told Ananda that what his friend suspected through faith, he himself knew through the unsurpassed insight of a buddha: every member of his community had

16. *Das Mahāparinirvāṇasūtra*, ed. E. Waldschmidt (Berlin: Akademie-Verlag, 1950-51), p. 196.

17. *Das Mahāparinirvāṇasūtra*, pp. 390-92.

been trained as thoroughly as possible. Shakyamuni accomplished one of the ten tasks that a living, breathing buddha *must* accomplish, and was thus free to attain complete, final nirvana.

Although this task was the final necessary confirmation of Shakyamuni's success as a religious founder, it directs us toward the early days of his career. Mulasarvastivadin Buddhists in India believed that Shakyamuni would not have entered nirvana until everybody who could be trained was trained. But to understand this tenet we might look back to Shakyamuni's first discourse, in which he turned the wheel of Dharma for five companions in Sarnath's deer park. The *Turning the Wheel of Law Sutra* begins with Shakyamuni glossing lessons learned from his own life. From birth until the renunciation of family and home at the age of twenty-nine Siddhartha enjoyed a life of luxurious pampering. Like a god, he experienced no obvious pain and gave no thought to his future, in this life or the next. Once he realized the inevitability of old age, disease, and death, however, Siddhartha left home, after which he passed six years torturing his body in a search for immortality. The fact that neither hedonism nor asceticism gave him lasting wisdom, happiness, or freedom becomes the starting point for Shakyamuni's teaching: "There are two extremes that should not be followed, discussed, or indulged by one who has gone forth from the home. What are these two? On the one hand, there is attachment to the indulgence of sense pleasures within the passions; this is low, common, vulgar, and the way of ordinary people. On the other hand, there is attachment to self-mortification; this is painful, ignoble, and yields no profit."[18] Having set the scene thus, Shakyamuni then tells his audience that once he abandoned these two extremes he discovered a "middle path" toward insight, wisdom, awakening, and ultimately nirvana. His realization of this middle path came from recognizing a set of fundamental truths, the so-called Four Noble Truths: suffering, the origin of suffering, the cessation of suffering, the path leading to the cessation of suffering. In short, the four truths Shakyamuni taught in his first sermon are Buddhism's *theodicy*, for they rationalize the possibility of liberation in the face of samsaric evils.[19] These four truths are among the few doctrines that all Buddhist communities share, albeit interpretations thereof vary greatly from place to place. The remainder of this section will focus on the first two of these four

18. *The Gilgit Manuscript of the Saṅghabhedavastu*, ed. Raniero Gnoli (Rome: Instituto Italiano per il Medio ed Estremo Oriente, 1978), 1:134.

19. The term "theodicy" — literally "the justice of God" — was coined by Gottfried Leibniz (1646-1716) to describe the philosophical reconciliation between belief in a perfectly benevolent, omnipotent God and the undeniable fact of evil. Contemporary scholars of religion have broadened the scope of Leibniz's "theodicy" such that the term can be used for philosophical/scholastic inquiries into the ultimate origins of evil in general, without any necessary reference to a God.

truths: suffering and its origin. The following sections will treat the third and fourth truths, in turn.

Buddhist theodicy, the religious explanation for how the world got to be the sorry place it is, begins with the fact of suffering. The First Noble Truth is *duḥkha*, a term that connotes suffering, unsatisfactoriness, dis-ease, unacceptability, imperfection. Ultimately, for Buddhism, *duhkha* is not a fact about the world, but rather a fact about living beings' (mis)apprehensions thereof. Beings cause their own suffering. But to know how that is so, we must understand the nature of nature itself. The theodicy of *duhkha* begins with a metaphysical analysis of samsaric existence. Let us look at how *duhkha* is explained in the *Turning the Wheel of Law Sutra*: "What is the Noble Truth of *duhkha*? Birth is *duhkha*. Old age is *duhkha*. Disease is *duhkha*. Death is *duhkha*. Separation from the pleasant is *duhkha*. Contact with the unpleasant is *duhkha*. Not getting what you want, though you strive after it: that too is *duhkha*. In brief, the five aggregates, which are the basis for clinging to existence, are *duhkha*."[20] Here Shakyamuni presents several explanations for why samsara is unsatisfactory. The first two are clear enough. Physical pains associated with biological existence are inescapable, even for Shakyamuni himself. Additionally, mental anguish awaits anybody who expects the world to conform precisely to his will. While writing about this Buddhist truth, my body suffers minor itches and aches; I struggle to find the correct word; sometimes I work for an hour and then erase everything. These quotidian annoyances are the background noise of samsaric existence; the death of one's child, war, and chronic illness are the first truth's crescendo. Let me emphasize that most Buddhists do not take the truth of *duhkha* to mean that everything is miserable always, that nobody is ever happy, or that ecstasies are impossible. Quite to the contrary, *duhkha* is made all the more poignant by the fact that happiness *is* possible. Satisfaction, unfortunately, always gives way to dissatisfaction. Cosmologically this is expressed by the belief that it is much easier to fall from the heavens than to rise from the hells.

Buddhism succeeded as a missionary religion in part because its theodicy starts from premises that are readily confirmed through empirical observation: change involves suffering. If Buddhism's analysis of samsara never transcended this level of naive experience, however, it would have had no more profound impact than a bumper sticker reading "Shit happens." But after characterizing *duhkha* according to physical and mental factors, Shakyamuni's sutra presents a third characterization: the five aggregates, which are the basis for clinging to existence, are unsatisfactory. This statement brings us to the core of Buddhism's analysis of samsara. Needless to add, this point requires further elaboration.

20. *The Gilgit Manuscript of the Saṅghabhedavastu*, 1:137.

Let me begin this analysis with a question. When I complain that "my back aches" or "I'm hungry," who is being talked about? Who, or what, is the "I" to which such statements refer? Is the "I" my back or stomach? Is it my hair, neck, skin, or eyes? My forty-six chromosomes? Is the "I" something physical at all? Perhaps the "I" is contained in my upbringing, name, education, religious affiliation, ethnicity, sexual preference? Is it emotional or mental in nature? Perhaps my perceptions, imaginings, thoughts, loves, hates, fears, longings? Perhaps the "I" is self-awareness itself: I think, therefore "I" ache? Page after page could be scribbled with possibilities. But the project is doomed. What makes me "me" cannot be reduced to a single physical phenomenon, or social phenomenon, or mental phenomenon. Not *one* of these is correct. When I say "my back aches" or "I'm hungry," the "I" to which these statements refer cannot be reduced to a single mundane referent.

If the basis of my individuality is not mundane, perhaps "I" can be identified through an *ultimate* referent. Perhaps the "I" to which these statements refer is a soul, like that described by Augustine in a 415 C.E. letter to Jerome, where he writes that the soul is immortal and incorporeal and that its fall into sin is due not to God but to its own free choice. After all, when articulating these complaints, I do have the sense that the "I" to which they refer is the same entity that, as a boy in 1968, believed he invented the word "magnetism." Was not that selfsame person in my mother's womb in 1962? Somehow "I" have not changed, even though everything about me — body, mind, knowledge, emotions — has. That thing which Augustine names the soul is called the *ātman* in Sanskrit. Hindu literature speaks of this atman as unchanging, immortal, and real. For Hinduism this atman is the essential Self/soul inherent in every person. Indeed, before Siddhartha discovered the Buddhist middle path, he believed this of the atman as well. This Shakya prince tortured his body attempting to subdue the atman, believing that such Self-control would free the atman from the prison of nescience, liberating it into the immortal, changeless bliss that is its proper being.

But according to the buddha's biography, Siddhartha renounced raw asceticism en route to his recognition of Buddhist truths. His rejection of asceticism was not just a matter of changing his religious practice. It had a metaphysical component as well. One cannot achieve liberation through controlling the atman because there is no atman. The belief in the existence of an atman is the core mistake resulting in the *duhkha* of samsara. Above I asked who, or what, is the "I" referred to in the complaints "my back aches" and "I'm hungry." Shakyamuni sought that answer for six painful years. Finally he discovered the answer by rejecting the question. Beings suffer because they ask this question, because they pursue its answer, because they expect a solution. The belief that there is an "I" that suffers is the fundamental mistake underlying samsaric suffering. This doctrine is known in Sanskrit as *anātman*, no-Self: there is no real, existent, independent, unchanging, ontologically stable "I."

The question then becomes, whence do beings get the notion that they have a stable Self? This brings us back to the *Turning the Wheel of Law Sutra*. The first two types of *duhkha* Shakyamuni describes are physical and mental. The third is existential: "the five aggregates, which form the basis for clinging to existence, are unsatisfactory." These five aggregates are the basis for clinging to existence because they are the basis for the mistaken belief in an atman. *Anatman*, no-Self, is *the* characteristic Buddhist doctrine, explained by analyzing the "I" into five parts or aggregates *(skandha)*: (1) matter, (2) sensations, (3) perceptions, (4) karmic constituents, (5) consciousness. To understand how these five *skandhas* become the basis for a mistaken notion of Self, let us first consider each in turn. The aggregate of *matter* is straightforward: it includes bodies as well as the material world in which those bodies live. The aggregate *sensation* refers to the feelings bodies experience through contact with the material world. The third aggregate, *perception*, is the cognitive faculty whereby one identifies sensations and categorizes them: this taste on my tongue belongs to a "bagel," that visual impression is a banana tree. *Karmic constituents*, the fourth *skandha*, are comprised of volitions produced in reaction to perceptions. Recall that karma, at base, is a matter of will. When I have the *sensation* of a tickling on my *material* skin and *perceive* that it is a mosquito, the repugnance I feel impels me to kill the mosquito: this volition is a *karmic constituent*. Actually, there is more than one karmic constituent involved in this act, for this volition to kill includes other mental factors, such as anger, ignorance, a false sense of self, and conceit. Finally *consciousness*, the fifth aggregate, is the most difficult of the *skandhas* to characterize because, unlike the others, it does not really *do* anything. Consciousness is a bare awareness, abstract mental action, without which there could not be sensation, perception, or volition. In short, according to Shakyamuni, the "I" to which the statement "I'm hungry" refers is not an individual identity but a series of five constituents, one physical, four mental. For comparative purposes, note how far this diverges from Cartesian modernism. For Buddhism mind and body may be distinguished but not divided.

Living beings make a cognitive error when they imagine the existence of a Self. The Self is a by-product of the *skandhas'* psychophysical processes. I think "I'm hungry" when a consciousness of my stomach's void yields a sensation. This leads to the perception "hunger." This impels me to get up and make soup. However, when my stomach grumbles, I do not analyze this process into aggregate moments. For me there is just one simple equation: "I" + hunger = feed! The perceived sensation becomes a basis for the conception of a personal identity, as well as volitions directed toward the gratification of that identity. In reality, however, this "I" is merely an epiphenomenon of the aggregates. The Self is a second-order perception, born of a mind that synthesizes experiences across time into a narrative whole. That is to say, at one moment "I" am hungry, at another moment "I" am itchy. The Self comes into existence when a mental consciousness senses a connection between these two "I's" and conceives a common identity uniting them. The mistake comes when that conventional, nominal, and synthetic Self comes to be conceived as really real, or as preexisting the psychophysical process that created it. The atman is a mind-ache far more pernicious than any backache. Perception gives way to karmic conditioning: karma is what keeps beings stuck in samsara. Just as hunger impels me to make soup or a backache impels me to shift my position, the perceived sensation of a real Self impels me to protect and preserve that Self at virtually any cost. In short, the imagined existence of a Self conditions me to circle in samsara. To refer back to the buddha's first sutra: "The five aggregates, which are the basis for clinging to existence, are *duhkha*."

Let us get our bearings. Shakyamuni, on his deathbed, invited the assembled monks to allay any doubts and confusions concerning the Four Noble Truths: suffering, its cause, its cessation, and the path. None of the monks in Kushinagara asked a question. We are seeking to learn what those monks had learned and to know what they knew. We have discovered that the first truth, *duhkha*, implies a metaphysical analysis of samsaric existence. Samsara is unsatisfactory and imperfect and involves suffering. One of the fundamental markers of this imperfection is the unceasing changeableness of things. Recall that "samsara" literally means wandering around: impermanence *(anitya)* is a constituent factor of samsara. Thus Buddhist scriptures directly equate these two: whatever is impermanent is *duhkha*, unsatisfactory. The next stage in the Buddhist explication of samsara is to explain why it is so unstable. If there was such a thing as a permanent, immutable Self, then things would not change and pleasure would never give way to pain. But within samsara there is no Self, or permanence, or stable ultimate. Archimedes, the Greek physicist, said, "Give me a lever long enough and a place to stand and I will move the earth." One might imagine Shakyamuni saying the same thing: "Give me a stable place in samsara and I will find permanent satisfaction therein." For Buddhism, that utopia is nowhere to be found.

Whereas the First Noble Truth analyzes the nature of the world in which we live — samsara is unsatisfactory, impermanent, and insubstantial — the Second Noble Truth turns its attention away from our environment to living beings themselves. In striving to understand how suffering arises, it asks: What is wrong with beings such that they remain stuck in samsara? This Noble Truth blames the victims, for the victims *are* responsible for their own suffering. The *Turning the Wheel of Law Sutra* reads: "What is the Noble Truth of the arising of *duhkha?* The thirst for continuing existence that accompanies pleasure and passion, delighting in this and that."[21] "Thirst" *(tṛṣṇā)* here is a synonym for will or volition, the importance of which we already know. The most pernicious volition is the thirst for continuing existence. But just as analysis of the First Noble Truth revealed that perceived suffering was only the most obvious manifestation of a more thoroughgoing problem with samsara — namely, that what we consider a unitary Self can be analyzed into five aggregate parts — so thirst is only the most obvious explanation for the arising of *duhkha.* At the analytic heart of the Second Noble Truth one finds an insidious and entrenched root: ignorance *(avidya).* Because of ignorance, people make mistakes when they perceive sensations. And because volitions are based on perceptions, a wrong perception can result in a dangerous volition. These mistakes can be both empirical and metaphysical. Thus Buddhists speak of "four misapprehensions" caused by fundamental ignorance, resulting in the unquenchable thirst for continuing existence: the mistaken perception of the impermanent as permanent, the mistaken perception of the Self-less as possessing a Self, the mistaken perception of the repugnant as delightful, and the mistaken perception of the unsatisfactory as satisfactory.

An image drawn from contemporary culture may help clarify the linkages between impermanence and *anatman* and thirst and ignorance. When one watches a movie, one is really viewing celluloid moving in front of a projection lamp at twenty-four frames per second. Yet, although this process can be given a simple material explanation, one's experience of the movie is not an experience of well-lit frames, but of living characters who arouse myriad feelings, sensations, and emotions, which often linger long after the movie is over. A movie is meaningful only to the extent that its celluloid is viewed by an audience that mentally processes the visual sensations and perceptions into a story, and forgets that it is "just a movie." Nevertheless, although a good film may teach or inspire or weigh on one's mind, one would be judged misguided, even delusional, if one developed so obsessive an emotional attachment to movie characters that one believed it possible to meet Rhett Butler himself or Holly Golightly herself. It *is* just a movie. The celluloid film can be cut into thousands of individual frames; those frames can then be separated and scattered across all the earth. If someone picks up a single random frame of celluloid, where is Rhett's swagger or Holly's pizzazz? Out of context, could a single frame of colored film inspire love or fear? In the final analysis the film is rubbish to be disposed of in an ecologically sound manner and forgotten. What we call the Self can similarly be cut into "frames," the five *skandhas;* each of these parts, in turn, changes from moment to moment to moment. The Self comes about when a mental conscious-

---

21. *The Gilgit Manuscript of the Saṅghabhedavastu,* 1:137.

ness, reflecting on this process, mistakenly imagines a continuity between "frames" and then reifies that imagined continuity into a reality. One might revere this continuing personal existence as the hero of one's life-movie, but it is no more real than Rhett Butler or Holly Golightly. Passionate attachment to the impermanent, unsatisfying, Self-less stuff of samsara is misguided, even delusional. Because of attachment, pain leads only to more pain.

If ignorance is the source of *duhkha,* what then is the source of ignorance? A monotheistic religion might answer this question by attributing this lack of thorough insight to God or to Satan. After all, Yahweh could have made Adam omniscient. But he did not. In fact, he made the Tree of Knowledge off-limits. Genesis suggests that we were much better off when we were ignorant of our ignorance, and we have Eden's snake to thank for the *duhkha* implicated in self-awareness. But for Buddhism time has no beginning; samsara, no Creator. The roots of ignorance, rather, are fixed within ignorance itself. The name for this doctrine is *codependent origination (pratītyasamutpāda).* Nothing about samsara can be attributed to a cause outside samsara. Everything within samsara comes about through the adventitious recycling and realignment of elements always already present within samsara. This was the doctrine to which Shakyamuni referred when he uttered these final words: "Whatever is constituted through karma necessarily passes away." Nothing in samsara is self-originated or wholly self-contained. Were such a thing to exist, it would be unproduced and not be subject to change. Everything in samsara exists through the concatenation of causes and conditions, physical and mental. As causes and conditions change, so entities are created and destroyed. The psychophysical bases that sustained Shakyamuni's terrestrial existence came to an end eighty years after his birth. To expect that it would be otherwise is to demonstrate one's ignorance. Why mourn?

Codependent origination is the Janus face of no-Self. On the one hand there is no Self, because self-identities are composite, conditional, relational, made up of parts. On the other hand, because everything in samsara is composite, everything in samsara is devoid of independent self-existence. Ignorance of this circle of equivalences is the ultimate source of misery. Not surprisingly Buddhist scholastics developed a complex schema through which to explain samsaric causality, which presents codependent origination as a chain of twelve links joined in a beginningless circle. The power in this illustrative analysis lies in the fact that it coordinates the First and Second Noble Truths, setting the processes of *duhkha,* samsaric existence, and ignorance into a lucid pattern. Indeed, Shakyamuni's biography grants this doctrine a privileged position. For Siddhartha became Shakyamuni, man became buddha, by understanding the interconnections among these twelve links. According to this doctrine (the links are in italics):

1. because of *ignorance,* for which no origin is postulated, beings create *karmic volitions;*
2. because beings create *karmic volitions* through their thoughts, words, and physical actions, they maintain a *consciousness* that continues between births;
3. because *consciousness* continues between births, it can enter a womb and enliven the *mental and physical attributes* of a developing embryo;
4. a living being must have *mental and physical attributes* in order to have *sense organs;*
5. without the *sense organs* there could be no *contact* with mental or physical stimuli;
6. the *contact* between sense organs and sense stimuli enables the experience of *sensations;*
7. *sensations* of pleasure and pain are the necessary precondition for *thirst,* the desire to increase pleasure and stop pain;
8. when one *thirsts* to enjoy positive experiences and escape negative ones, one *grasps* after continuing samsaric existence;
9. the result of *grasping* for samsaric existence is *becoming,* the continuance of psychophysical processes from life to life;
10. the processes of *becoming* naturally result in *rebirth* after death;
11. whenever one takes *rebirth,* one is guaranteed to experience:
12. *old age, death, sorrow, lamentation, suffering, distress, and dismay.*

Not only does this doctrine incorporate the interrelationships among the five aggregates (the psychophysical basis for samsaric misery), but it shows how those aggregates are inextricably linked to impermanence, to suffering, and to the causes of *duhkha,* thirst and ignorance. Well, not quite inextricable. Under the Bodhi tree Shakyamuni saw the twelve limbs of codependent origination. But he also saw that he could break this chain. If he could do away with ignorance, he could do away with the karma that fueled samsaric existence. If he could have sensations but not thirst, then the grasping that leads, ultimately, to rebirth and redeath could be eradicated.

When Shakyamuni ascertained that nobody at his deathbed was in need of further training, he perceived that the gathered monks had thoroughly comprehended that whatever is in samsara exists within a web of mutable relations. To understand what happens when those relations are brought to an end, we must move on to the next deed required of a living, breathing buddha.

Act 3: Nirvana and Its Aftermath

> It is *dharmata* that a living, breathing buddha will not attain nirvana until he lives out at least three-quarters of a full life span.

One must feel sorry for Ananda: he can be blamed for the buddha's timely death. In the final year of Shakyamuni's life, not long after he criticized Ananda for thinking him a closefisted teacher, the buddha hinted to Ananda that he need not pass away. Shakyamuni and Ananda were sitting in a grove on the outskirts of Vaishali — two old friends who had shared many adventures during their long lives. Shakyamuni remarked aloud upon India's vibrant beauty and the sweetness of human life. And then, in an offhand manner, the buddha observed that someone who possesses superhuman powers can stay alive for thousands of years, through the entire course of a cosmic age. While developing perfect wisdom and compassion, Shakyamuni had also perfected his control over matter and mind to such a degree that he could perform seemingly miraculous feats. In the past he had flown. He had shot fire out of his shoulders and water out of his feet. He had even created duplicates of himself so numerous that the universe appeared to be filled with buddhas from top to bottom. Now, having completed more than three-quarters of the full 100-year life span for a human being of his day, Shakyamuni seemed ambivalent about his accomplishments. He had fulfilled his duties as a buddha and could attain complete, final nirvana whenever he wanted. But for a second, even a third time, Shakyamuni remarked on the sweetness of human life and his own ability to preserve that life indefinitely. Not taking the hint, Ananda listened without remark.

Shakyamuni's observations were not lost on Mara, however. This divine lord of samsara and champion of passion had long considered Shakyamuni his nemesis: whenever an arhat gained nirvana, Mara lost another subject from his domain. Though Mara could not cause Shakyamuni to fall from buddhahood, he could hasten Shakyamuni's own nirvana. So after Ananda left the buddha's side, Mara approached, showed proper reverence, and said: "Pass away, Lord! This is the time for the buddha's nirvana." Mara reminded Shakyamuni that when he had first awakened, they made a pact. The buddha would attain final nirvana after he accomplished every goal he set for himself as a religious founder, after he was secure in the knowledge that his disciples remembered his words, comprehended his teachings, and obeyed his disciplines. That is, after his religion was widespread and popular. Shakyamuni had accomplished all this. And thus, whereas Shakyamuni seems to have wanted Ananda to ask him to remain alive indefinitely, the buddha instead heeded Mara's request that he pass beyond samsara, and promised to enter final nirvana three months hence. Later Shakyamuni told Ananda of the encounter with Mara. One can almost see the lightbulb turn on in Ananda's head as he wails and whines, "Please stay alive! Please stay alive!" Too late.[22]

This richly textured anecdote works on several levels, confounding and contextualizing the First and Second Noble Truths. We should have expected to see the buddha as passionless, unattached, and perfectly placid. But Shakyamuni here is melancholy with nostalgia. He accomplished his every aim as a religious founder; he left home to bring an end to birth and death; he preached, organized, exhorted, and disciplined. Now on the verge of his ultimate liberation, he looks back to human life as sweet, samsara as vibrant with beauty. It goes without saying that this representation of Shakyamuni's ambivalence about his final nirvana tells us far more about his followers' feelings than his own. This same paradox underlies the ambivalent requirement that every terrestrial buddha perform ten worldly acts before his nirvana. Until a buddha passes away, his personal aims are not fulfilled, but as soon as he achieves nirvana he is no longer present. The sweetest of humans, the most vibrantly beautiful of men, is gone. One might compare Shakyamuni here with Jesus as presented in the Gospel according to Mark. At the midpoint of this Gospel, Jesus bravely prophesies his passion: he will suffer, be put to death, and rise (from the dead) (8:31). Yet in Gethsemane Jesus pleads for God to relieve him of the chalice of death (14:36), and with his last breath Jesus despairs because of God's abandonment (15:34). Christian theology would make little sense without Jesus' death and resurrection. Nevertheless, this death is ever treated as a tragedy of unequaled magnitude. Without his death, Jesus is not the Christian Christ; without nirvana, Shakyamuni is no buddha, just a great man, a wise teacher, a compassionate friend. In both cases, followers' ambivalence vis-à-vis the founder's necessary absence is transferred onto the psychology of the founders themselves. That Ananda bewails Shakyamuni's nirvana, "Please stay alive," is rhetorically flat. That Shakyamuni himself claims that "human life is sweet" and all but asks Ananda to request him to enjoy it indefinitely, poignantly highlights frailties common to humanity even as it demonstrates that such frailties need not detract from spiritual majesty.

The requirement that a buddha live out three-quarters of his life span is a shorthand for Buddhist ambivalence about the inevitability and finality of Shakyamuni's nirvana: go, he must, but not too soon. This pool of attachment to Shakyamuni beyond death was a wellspring for religious creativity within Buddhism. Later in this section I will introduce several strategies Buddhists used to make the absent buddha present. One such strategy, mentioned above in the discussion of Vagisha, is the offering of devotion to a memorial stupa which has been enlivened with a buddha's relics. The imaginative force of

22. These events are described in *Das Mahāparinirvāṇasūtra*, pp. 204-20.

Shakyamuni's presence thus constituted only becomes evident in light of notions of his absence as defined by the doctrinal concept of nirvana.

To comprehend what is at stake in the nirvana of a buddha, let us return to the *Turning the Wheel of Law Sutra* for the Third Noble Truth: "What is the Noble Truth of the cessation of *duhkha?* The total eradication of that very thirst for continuing existence which accompanies pleasure and passion, delighting in this and that. It is salvation, abandonment, exhaustion, passionlessness, cessation, pacification, disappearance."[23] Note that the Third Noble Truth is cessation *(nirodha)*, not nirvana. This seems a minor distinction, but it points to an important matter of terminology. The term "nirvana," as used in colloquial English, usually refers to what Buddhists call "nirvana that is final and complete in all its parts" *(mahāparinirvāṇa)*, because nothing comes after it. This *mahāparinirvana*, attained at death, can be still more formally designated as "nirvana without any residue," because it is achieved only when all residual karma from the buddha's previous lives is used up; its attainment is simultaneous with the dissolution of the five aggregates. I shall discuss this nirvana at greater length below. Nirvana without residue is preceded by "nirvana *with* residue," also known as nirvana-in-this-world: the direct fruit of realizing and perfecting the Third Noble Truth.

Let us turn to the night of Shakyamuni's awakening, to see how he achieved the cessation of *duhkha.* Siddhartha awakened over the course of a night, conventionally split into three "watches." During the first watch he focused his superhuman eye on his own past lives. Above we saw several arhats describe the thread, tying actions performed in one life with results in another. During this watch Siddhartha surveyed the fabric of his own karmic existence as woven out of hundreds of thousands of lives. In the second watch of the night he turned his gaze from himself to others. He saw that karma controlled the destinies of all living beings, from gods to humans to the denizens of hell. Finally, in the third watch, he intuited the inner logic of karma and samsara, and systematized Buddhism's characteristic doctrines: the Four Noble Truths, *anatman*, codependent origination. At last he shouted, "My birth is finished. I have lived the holy life. What had to be done is done. I will not be born into another existence." Now Shakyamuni Buddha, he was "awakened," for when the veils of ignorance fell from his eyes he saw samsara for what it is — unsatisfactory, impermanent, and insubstantial — and he no longer clung to the stuff of samsara. He had attained nirvana, but a this-worldly nirvana. Although he would never again create karmic volitions through ignorant grasping, he still had karmic residues left from previous lives. Now he could become a virtuoso of karma. He could lucidly express his will in order to accomplish his aims, and

23. *The Gilgit Manuscript of the Saṅghabhedavastu*, 1:137.

he could do so without becoming stuck. A simile is often used to explain how a buddha acts in the world after his awakening. The buddha is likened to a magician who creates the illusion of an unimaginably beautiful woman. You or I might think this woman is real, and become besotted with lust. But only the most foolish magician would fall into this trap by forgetting that she is an illusion, his own creation. Though Shakyamuni remained *in* the world for forty-five years after his awakening, his attainment of this-worldly nirvana meant that he was no longer *of* the world. He could eat, teach, even work magic, without imputing a false substantiality upon himself, his deeds, or his audience.

Forty-five years later we find Shakyamuni offering to use his superhuman abilities to prolong his life beyond the span determined by the effluvia of old karma. Without Ananda's cooperation, however, the buddha had no excuse to exercise this power. Thus he passed his last three months visiting old haunts as he slowly journeyed to Kushinagara and his complete, final nirvana. "Nirvana" translates literally as "blowing out," as when a wind snuffs out a weak flame. Whereas nirvana-in-this-world is attained when all desires are quenched, complete and final nirvana is coincident with the elimination of all suffering and all further samsaric existence. This differs from death. For the common human being, death does not radically rupture the psychophysical process associated with the five aggregates. At death a body made of "gross matter" gives way to one made of "subtle matter," continuing the karmic process. This is why, to reiterate a point from above, the First Noble Truth equates the five aggregates with *duhkha:* they are the objective bases for the thirst for continuing existence. But with Shakyamuni's final breath, he no longer had *karmic constituents.* The fuel that powered his body, his sensations, his perceptions, and his consciousness, was used up.

Imagine a lit candle whose wick has burned out and whose wax is now gone. The flame goes out. Would one say that the flame extinguished itself? Or that the lack of wick or wax *put* it out? The active voice is just not appropriate here. Something happened, but one cannot point to a cause or agent for the event. Rather, the flame went out because the conditions for its continuing existence simply ceased to be. The cessation of *duhkha* occasions nirvana but does not cause nirvana. In fact, complete and final nirvana has no cause, because whatever has a cause is subject to conditioning, and by definition nirvana is the unconditioned. Indeed, according to Buddhist ways of thinking about life and death, the attainment of complete and final nirvana should not even be called "death." Death is one moment in the five aggregates' ongoing process, an important moment of transition from life to life. Complete and final nirvana, by contrast, comes about through cessation of all karmic causes and conditions. *Mahaparinirvana* occurs when the causes of *duhkha,* and therefore *duhkha* itself, are no more.

When a candle's flame goes out, bereft of wax and wick, where does the flame actually "go"? Metaphors of place are common in representations of nirvana. Thus English translations have the buddha "approach nirvana," "enter nirvana," or "attain nirvana." Similarly, Buddhist writings use the image of "the city of nirvana" with a certain frequency. Such metaphors inspire comparisons between nirvana and the heavens or paradise. But this is conceptually incorrect. For Buddhists, heavens and paradises are part of samsara. Final nirvana, by contrast, is not a place a buddha goes after death, nor is it a state he attains, a fruit of his practice, or a reward for his virtue. Were nirvana a place or state or reward, it would then be brought into existence in dependence upon specific causes; it would be conditioned, subject to vagaries of time and circumstance. However, none of these things are true of nirvana. Nirvana is more profitably compared to empty space: infinite, omnipresent, unchanging, without variation, unconditioned, calm, and real. Neither space nor nirvana has a beginning or end. Neither has positive attributes or characteristics. Indeed, nirvana is so difficult to characterize because it is essentially abstract. Paradoxically, attempts to concretize nirvana through the predication of attributes only obfuscate nirvana's inconceivable truth. Just as empty space can be defined only through differentiation from materiality, so nirvana's reality can be expressed only by differentiating it from samsara. Samsara is characterized by suffering, impermanence, and insubstantiality, but there is no suffering in nirvana, it is not impermanent, nor is it insubstantial. Samsara is conditioned by causality. Nirvana is unconditioned and uncaused. Samsara is fueled by thirst, born of ignorance. Nirvana is attained through liberation, born of wisdom. Samsaric processes are characterized by the bricolage of becoming. Nirvana is what remains when everything is subtracted.

In one famous encounter, a monk named Malunkyaputra threatened to give up his robes if the buddha did not address several ultimate questions that had theretofore been left unanswered. Among these, Malunkyaputra asked, "Does the buddha exist after attaining nirvana? Or not exist? Or both exist and not exist? Or neither exist nor not exist?" Malunkyaputra's threat was to no avail. Shakyamuni still refused to answer. He rejected these questions as irrelevant because their answers would not deepen Malunkyaputra's understanding of *duhkha* or karma. Even if Shakyamuni's answers are unavailable, the questions themselves bear further reflection. Hold the question in your mind — Does the buddha exist after attaining nirvana? — and ask yourself whether you can conceive of existence without it being spatial in some way. Were the buddha to exist after nirvana, it would have to be *somewhere*. Similarly, nonexistence can only be imagined as a lack of presence. Without spatial and temporal dimensionality, "existence" and its lack are inconceivable. Although scholastic philosophers might deplore inaccuracies involved in conceptualizing nirvana through spatial predicates, the majority of Buddhists through the ages have not been scholastic philosophers. Buddhists have long wondered, "Where is the buddha now that he attained nirvana?" And they have usually answered that question with "He is accessible right here, right now." Indeed, although Buddhists all accept Shakyamuni's complete and final nirvana as a fact, few have ever let that stand in the way of their religiosity. Ananda did not ask Shakyamuni to prolong his life, but Buddhists have taken it upon themselves to re-present the buddha ever since his nirvana. They have done so in spatial terms because they have wanted to interact with the buddha, to have access to him, to be in his presence. The history of Buddhism can be written as a history of these re-presentations: creative abrogations of final nirvana's finality.

Indeed, traditional tellings of Shakyamuni's biography do not end with his realization of *mahaparinirvana* in Kushinagara. Events surrounding the disposition of his body are integral to his life's story. Those gathered at Shakyamuni's side at his final nirvana witnessed a material body becoming progressively empty of personal vitality. The buddha was gone, but his material body remained to be cremated, the customary form of disposal for a revered holy man. Almost immediately after Shakyamuni's cremation, however, a dispute arose over who would possess the remaining relics of tooth and bone not consumed by the fire. The people of Kushinagara claimed these relics for themselves, since Shakyamuni had chosen their territory for his final nirvana. But the people of seven other territories swiftly learned of Shakyamuni's passing, and all demanded the relics. At first, the people of Kushinagara refused. Finally, to stave off a war over the relics, all eight peoples reached an entente. Shakyamuni's remains were distributed equally. Each of the eight measures of tooth and bone was then housed in a memorial stupa. Though the buddha was in nirvana, he was also present at each of these eight memorials.

Why would people have been willing to go to war over charred bone fragments from a dead holy man? One can certainly adduce socioeconomic factors, such as prestige, or income from a popular pilgrimage site. But in line with this chapter's focus on native explanation, we might instead revisit the conception of the buddha as a "field of merit," the doctrine that the qualities of a gift's recipient influence the karmic fruits of giving. On the shore of Lake Anavatapta, Vagisha claimed that he gained the ability to become an arhat merely by making a cheap gift of scented water and garlands to a stupa housing Vipashyin Buddha's remains. Similarly, a donative inscription found at Ajanta, a fifth century c.e. Indian monastery, declares that wise people engage in acts of intense devotion to the buddhas because the offering of even a single flower guarantees them heavenly rebirths and final liberation. According to this inscription's author, the wise know that, among all fields of merit, buddhas are the most fertile. Conflict over Shakyamuni's relics arose because people conceived them as being charged with spiritual power that could be accessed and harnessed through the appropriate exercise of ritual technology. One of the most striking examples of a king's employment of a relic comes from first century B.C.E. Sri Lanka, where King Dutthagamini is remembered as having installed a relic of Shakyamuni in his spear before marching out to battle with the Tamils. Dutthagamini won.

When one considers the posthumous conflict over Shakyamuni's remains in light of the Noble Truths, there seems to be a notable confusion. The doctrine of no-Self holds that what we commonly consider a "person" is really the psychophysical integration of five distinct components. If Shakyamuni, when alive, is only tentatively a "person," then after death his bones, separated from all vital energies, should certainly be seen for the mere physical objects they are. At best, relics might be mementos of the man Shakyamuni was, but certainly not equivalents for the buddha himself. On this chain of reasoning, it would seem inconsistent for Buddhists to revere relics as a field of merit. Be that as it may, however, the simple fact is that Shakyamuni's relics were conceived as being infused with Shakyamuni's life, as endowed with his vitality, as enclosures for his person, and as houses for his presence. Thus Vasubandhu's *Compendium of Metaphysics* claims that the karmic retribution for destroying a stupa containing buddha relics equals that for harming a flesh-and-blood buddha: immediately upon death, the perpetrator is doomed to rebirth in the lowest hell. Similarly, the reward for building a reliquary stupa is the same as that for providing a monastery to shelter the buddha's flesh and blood: a glorious rebirth in the high heavens. In the long run, little was lost by Ananda's failure to ask Shakyamuni to remain alive indefinitely: Buddhists simply never let him go.

One of the most complete explorations of a buddha's continuing life-after-nirvana is found in a sutra entitled *On Commissioning Buddha Image*.[24] As the title suggests, this scripture does not discuss bodily relics per se. Rather it treats images, and explains that one who commissions a buddha image will receive "heaps of merit, piles of merit, immeasurable, extraordinary, heaps of merit seemingly without end." In line with the tales told on Lake Anavatapta's shore, this sutra also promises donors that they will "attain buddhahood, and quickly approach peaceful *parinirvana*." How is this possible? The sutra asks this same rhetorical question, and then answers it. "What is the cause for the limitless power that arises as the fruit of fashioning a buddha image? I say, O monks, although the blessed lord buddha has entered into *mahaparinirvana*, when one sees an image of the buddha it is as if he has entered not into

---

24. Adelheid Mette, "Zwei kleine Fragmente aus Gilgit — 1: Tathāgatabimbakārāpaṇa-sūtra (Gilgit-Ms. No. 18), 2: Devatāsūtra und Alpadevatāsūtra (aus Gilgit-Ms. No. 13)," *Studien zur Indologie und Iranistik* 7 (1981): 133-51.

mahaparinirvana." Simply put, he who has eyes will see the buddha where he sees an image. In an important sense, the very word "image" here is misleading. One might commonly think of an "image" as lifeless matter made into a simulacrum of a human being by human agency. But in this case an "image" is one more living material form taken by a buddha. This idea is very clearly expressed in an inscription from Buddhist Central Asia: "Hail to the buddhas having the bodies of buddha-images!"[25]

Let us conclude this section. The requirement that a buddha live out three-quarters of a common human life span introduces a fascinating and crucial dimension of Buddhism. In his capacity as a religious teacher, Shakyamuni is most closely associated with doctrines contained in the first two Noble Truths: to escape samsara's sufferings one must gain insight into no-Self, for that wisdom alone enables one to end the craving that fuels karmic existence. The Third Noble Truth holds that such cessation is possible. *Mahaparinirvana,* the complete dissolution of all associations with samsara, is the "logical" consequence of this third truth. But we have seen that simultaneous with this systematic, scholastic doctrine, Buddhists also believed Shakyamuni's presence continues after his nirvana. His power inheres in physical objects which can be associated with him. Bodily remains left from the cremation pyre are the most obvious relics, but other traces of his terrestrial existence came to be treated as living equivalents as well. A partial list would include golden statues, reliefs pressed in wet clay, the tree he sat under on the eve of awakening, his robes and bowl, manuscripts containing his sutras, palm leaves scratched with the formula of codependent origination. These things were not Shakyamuni's equivalents merely because as icons or as symbols they referred to him. Rather, like bodily relics, these objects' power was believed to inhere directly in their materiality. Their stuff was the stuff of buddhahood. *On Commissioning Buddha Images* explains: "Somebody who makes a *stupa* or image of the blessed one enjoys sovereignty over heaven and earth perpetually, for a span equal to the number of atoms in the *stupa* or image. In fact, the blessed one showed relics belonging to previous buddhas and [his own] bodily remains because each and every single minute atom produces a marvelous heap of merit."[26] This is a very different understanding of what a buddha is, and why he gains nirvana, from that posed by the strictly scholastic interpretation based on the Noble Truths. According to this sutra, the buddha lives and dies precisely because he wants to serve as a source for relics. Paradoxically, the belief that the buddha has completely passed away and the belief that he may be perpetually present are both conse-

---

25. H. W. Bailey, "Hvatanica IV," *Bulletin of the London School of Oriental and African Studies* 10 (1940-42): 895.
26. Mette, p. 138.

quences of the doctrine of *mahaparinirvana*. Shakyamuni's absence allowed for his presence to expand materially without limits, but that material expansion was possible only because he had gone entirely beyond samsara.

Act 4: Morality, Meditation, and Discernment

> It is *dharmata* that a living, breathing buddha will not attain nirvana until he establishes his parents in the Truth.

Leading up to his final life on earth, Shakyamuni realized a fancy that captures every child's imagination at least once: he chose his own parents. The buddha was a god, king over Tushita Heaven, before he took birth as Siddhartha Gotama. As the time approached for the great being's final life, he surveyed the earth for the best couple belonging to the best family living in the best place, just as other incipient buddhas did prior to their final births. He espied Shuddhodana, the leader of the royal Shakya clan, and his wife, Mahamaya, who was beautiful, moral, and had once expressed the desire to be the mother of a buddha. Shakyamuni-to-be would make her wish come true. Ten lunar months after conception, Mahamaya was standing in a garden grove, holding a tree, when young Siddhartha passed painlessly through her side. The gods Indra and Brahma caught him, while warm and cool waters fell from the heavens washing and refreshing mother and child. To end the scene, the newborn boy took seven steps in each of the four cardinal directions, declaring this to be his final birth.

Thrilled, young Siddhartha's parents soon learned that the birth of so remarkable a child carries a dear cost. His given name, Siddhartha, literally means that he was the fulfillment of his parents' every wish. But Mahamaya died seven days after giving birth, as is the fate of every terrestrial buddha's mother. She was reborn in a heaven, to be sure. But the god-of-gods was now a baby on earth. Shuddhodana found himself in a tenuous position as well. In India it is customary for a child to bow before and touch the feet of his elders as a sign of obeisance. But in Siddhartha's presence, Shuddhodana was the lesser. On the day of his birth, Siddhartha was brought to a shrine dedicated to the Shakyas' guardian deity. Though the Shakyas customarily prostrated themselves to the deity, on this day the god bent down to a baby. In a later miraculous incident, Shuddhodana found himself so taken with awe that he, the father, fell at the feet of his own son. What inspired Shuddhodana to act so? Although the sun had nearly set, the shadow of a tree under which Siddhartha sat remained steady as if it were still noon.

Shuddhodana was merely caught up in the moment when he saw the unmoving shadow. For, despite this brief excitement over Siddhartha's spiritual merit, Shuddhodana wanted his son to become a world-conquering king. He was mortified when Siddhartha abandoned family and renounced worldly power in search of liberation. Six years after his awakening, Shakyamuni returned home to Kapilavastu, swiftly winning many converts among his former friends and kin. Yet Shuddhodana remained aloof. He had seen a statue come to life; he had seen the miraculous shadow. Shuddhodana reflected that his son had been honored by gods in the past, yet here in Kapilavastu his retinue was entirely human. Full of pride, Shuddhodana paid no heed to his son's teachings.

Once the buddha recognized the source of his father's pride, however, he staged a grand scene. Late one night Shakyamuni entered a windowless chamber having four doors and invited a great assembly of gods to hear a discourse on the Dharma. Seated on a high throne, Shakyamuni was surrounded by thousands of shining, resplendent, perfect, and glorious gods. Celestial sentries were placed at the four doors to guard against intrusions by mere humans. The trap was set. When Shuddhodana came near the building, he saw an unearthly glow escaping from beneath its doors. He heard the sweet timbre of the buddha's voice. But he could not enter. Trying all four doors, Shuddhodana was turned away, rebuffed again and again. The sentries' own glory whetted Shuddhodana's appetite for the wonders within. Finally Shakyamuni discerned that Shuddhodana's head would explode were he kept apart from the divine assembly any longer. The buddha revealed himself. Eyes and heart satisfied, Shuddhodana's mind was ripe to hear the Four Noble Truths. Then and there, Shuddhodana destroyed the belief in a Self with the thunderbolt of knowledge. He celebrated, proclaiming that his own son had done something for him that nobody else had ever done: not his father, mother, or king, not the gods, ancestors, renunciants, priests, or any other kinsman. Shakyamuni had done something for himself as well, since a buddha cannot attain nirvana until he converts his father to the Truth.[27]

Few stories in the Buddhist canon match this one for its revelation of the buddha's modus operandi as a teacher, which combines deft wit with limitless power. Buddhas are practical jokers on a cosmic scale — place the emphasis on *practical.* There is nothing mean-spirited or self-aggrandizing in the "con" Shakyamuni works on his father. He has one intention only: to set his father onto the path toward wisdom, awakening, and ultimate liberation. This path is the final one of the four truths. And though it comes at the end of the list, in a practical sense it belongs at the beginning, for dissatisfaction with life naively lived leads one to start out on the road to the city of nirvana. More formally, the Fourth Noble Truth is described as a path having eight parts. Thus the *Turning the Wheel of Law Sutra* declares:

27. *The Gilgit Manuscript of the Saṅghabhedavastu,* 1:195-99.

What is the Noble Truth of the path leading to the cessation of *duhkha?* It is the Noble Eight-Limbed Path, i.e., 1) correct view, 2) correct intention, 3) correct speech, 4) correct action, 5) correct livelihood, 6) correct effort, 7) correct mindfulness, 8) correct concentration. . . . Cultivate the Noble Eight-Limbed Path in order to comprehend *duhkha!* . . . Cultivate the Noble Eight-Limbed Path in order to destroy craving! . . . Cultivate the Noble Eight-Limbed Path in order to realize the cessation of *duhkha!*[28]

In an important sense, the entirety of what we call "Buddhism" can be comprehended as the imaginative elaboration of this "path" metaphor. Although the *Turning the Wheel of Law Sutra* describes the Buddhist path as having eight parts, scholastic thinkers traditionally rearrange the parts and organize them under three general headings. Buddhist practice is a matter of *morality* (correct speech, action, livelihood), *mental discipline* (correct effort, mindfulness, concentration), and *wisdom* (correct view, intention). Let us consider each of these three in turn.

Morality is the foundation of the religious life. Unless one lives morally, one cannot have the serenity or mental stability necessary for pursuing deeper truths. This is one reason that a buddha must fix his parents on the path to liberation before attaining nirvana himself. Compassion does not allow a buddha to "enjoy" nirvana while his own parents continue to inflict suffering on themselves; as a perfect buddha, Shakyamuni was also a perfect son. More specifically, morality is defined as the intentional and willful restraint of one's body, speech, and mind from the commission of actions that would cause harm to oneself or to others. Functionally, one is expected to avoid ten unwholesome activities: murder, theft, sexual misconduct, false speech, slanderous speech, harsh speech, frivolous speech, covetousness, ill will, and false views. This list of ten unwholesome activities should *not* be compared with the Hebrew Bible's Ten Commandments. One is culpable for violating biblical commandments insofar as one accepts them as God's law. But the ten activities listed above are not interdicted by order of the buddha. Their violation is not sinful, but stupid. When one kills or calumniates another, that activity injures the other, to be sure. But because karma is fundamentally a matter of volition, such a deed is perhaps even more deleterious to its perpetrator.

Although avoidance of harm, *ahimsa,* is the foundation of the Buddhist moral life, it is also possible to increase the karmic benefits of morality by taking on vows or commitments to abide by specific moral restraints. It is good not to kill others. But within a karmic calculus it is far better to vow that one will avoid killing others, and then to abide by this vow. The act of vowing intensifies and stabilizes the volition. There is a recognition that not all beings are ca-

28. *The Gilgit Manuscript of the Saṅghabhedavastu,* 1:137-38.

pable of making the same commitments. This is another point of disjunction with the biblical commandments. All Hebrews are required to observe God's orders, but Buddhism places no one under an obligation to accept any vow of moral restraint. Indeed, a butcher who vows not to kill will do himself more harm than good. A butcher truly concerned about his karma will find another line of work before he makes this vow.

Because the moral restraints are voluntary, their acceptance has served as an index through which to distinguish communities of interest within Buddhism. A dedicated layman or laywoman, for instance, is known by his or her adherence to a set of five restraints, the so-called *pañcaśīla* (an abridgment of the ten unwholesome actions listed above): not to kill, not to take what is not given, not to commit sexual misconduct, not to lie, and the avoidance of intoxicants. Dedicated lay folk may also visit a monastery twice a month to study or make merit, at which time they will take an additional three restraints upon themselves, such as not to eat after the noon hour. Note the situational nature of morality. The articulation of a vow — "For today only, I will not eat after 12:00 P.M." — creates a universe in which karmic effects accrue to activities that normally have no moral value. Whereas it usually makes no difference whether or not a layman eats after 12:00, on the day he makes this vow the act of eating after 12:00 is karmically harmful, even immoral. The definition of certain specific actions as moral or immoral can be situational, personal, and fluid.

Indeed, not to belabor the point, even suicide and killing another are appropriate when not acting so would result in even greater harm. In a previous life Shakyamuni-to-be was the captain of a ship carrying five hundred merchants and their wares to a distant port. Unbeknownst to the traders, one of their number was a thief, who intended to murder them in their sleep and take their fortune for himself. A sea-god warned the captain of the evil that was about to transpire on his ship. After some deliberation, Shakyamuni-to-be realized that radical action was necessary:

> He thought, "There is no means to prevent this man from slaying the merchants and going to the great hells but to kill him." And he thought, "If I were to report this to the merchants, they would kill and slay him with angry thoughts and all go to the great hells themselves." And he thought, "If I were to kill this person, I would likewise burn in the great hells for 100,000 eons because of it. Yet I can bear to experience the pain of the great hells, that this person not slay these five hundred merchants and not develop so much evil karma. I will kill this person myself."

As a result of this quick action, the would-be robber was reborn in paradise and the buddha-to-be, far from going to hell himself, was freed from 100,000 aeons of samsaric suffering.[29] This story celebrates the killing of the evil man because, had the captain not acted thus, five hundred merchants would have been murdered. Here is the interesting twist: Shakyamuni-to-be did not kill the pirate in order to save the traders' lives; rather his compassion was directed toward the would-be assailant. Shakyamuni-to-be was motivated by a desire to prevent the thief from committing grievous evil. Through an act of moral murder, Shakyamuni-to-be saved the thief from himself.

Beyond the laity Buddhism has novices — monks-in-training or students being educated at monastic schools — who are subject to ten rules. Beyond these groups are the fully ordained monks and nuns. As we have already seen, the Buddhist religious life is not simply a matter of restraint. Buddhist lore overwhelmingly celebrates the positive virtue of generosity, especially when directed toward fertile fields of merit such as the buddha or his community of monks. Indeed, whereas the buddha is deemed the supreme source of merit because he is perfectly wise and compassionate, even ordinary monks are treated with great respect, precisely because of the great number of moral restraints they undertake. Numbers of rules differ from sect to sect within Buddhism, but the monks of contemporary Sri Lanka and Thailand, for instance, are subject to 227 rules. These monastic regulations range from broad-scale restraints, such as celibacy, to micro-level controls over personal behavior: monks may not slurp and belch when they eat, nor may they smile so broadly as to show their teeth. Nuns are under an even larger burden, constrained by 311 rules of conduct. The social world being such as it is, this superabundance of restraint does not make nuns a greater source of spiritual merit than monks.

After Shakyamuni had gained his first converts and was certain that, as arhats, they thoroughly comprehended the Dharma, he sent them out to spread his teachings "for the good of the many, for the happiness of the many, out of compassion for the world." The buddha's inclusion of correct speech, correct action, and correct livelihood as "limbs" of the Path demonstrates that social harmony is fundamental to Buddhist definitions of worldly good and worldly happiness. However, Buddhism is not early Confucianism: social harmony is not an end in itself. Though one must be existentially right with the world, liberation requires renunciation. True separation from the world is impossible, however, as long as one imagines substance where there is no substance or permanence where there is no permanence. To cease grasping, one must be able to see the world as it really is, and that, in turn, requires intensive training. He who has eyes, let him see. But one does not simply "have" the eyes. Correct sight is a matter of cultivation, which is the focus of Buddhist teachings on mental discipline.

---

29. *The Skill in Means (Upāyakauśalya) Sūtra*, trans. Mark Tatz (Delhi: Motilal Banarsidass, 1994), p. 74.

What we commonly call "meditation" in English is *bhāvanā* in Sanskrit, "cultivation" or "mental culture." *Bhavana* has two aspects: mental quiescence and liberative insight. The former can be thought of as a skill or craft, and is not specific to Buddhism. In fact, Shakyamuni's biographies record that he learned the techniques of mental quiescence from other teachers. Insight, by contrast, is uniquely Buddhist, for it is the fruit of a controlled mind that focuses on Buddhist truths. To gain insight, one begins with a mind that is tranquil and imperturbable, on the one hand, but supple and alert, on the other. Thoroughgoing insight into reality requires a mind that can focus on a mental image or idea with complete clarity and without wavering. The teachings of quietude promote this intense ability to concentrate, commonly spoken of as "one-pointed consciousness." The elements of the Noble Eightfold Path associated with mental discipline — correct effort, correct mindfulness, and correct concentration — are grouped together because these three are necessary factors for the stabilization of the mind.

In order to describe the processes of concentration associated with undistracted quiescence, Buddhists rely on a cosmological model. The contemporary imagination conceptualizes the universe as a series of exponentially increasing magnitudes of space, expanding from home to city to country to planet to solar system to galaxy to galactic cluster to supercluster. The ability to apprehend or study these domains requires increasingly powerful and sensitive instruments. Similarly, meditative concentration brings the mind into ever deeper inner worlds within inner worlds. The processes of concentration begin by fixing attention upon a material object such as a circle of color or the sensation of one's own breath in the nostril. This object merely serves as a convenient basis for stabilizing the mind. Success is first achieved when one is able to quiet the random distractions that carry the untamed mind this way and that. Although concentration techniques begin with material objects, the gross material world falls away when one-pointed awareness is attained. The mind, stable in itself, moves beyond the senses to a state of mental activity that focuses on the awareness of the awareness of a material object. This is called the first stage of trance *(dhyāna)*. This trance is an enstatic state: one has penetrated the inner reaches of the material world. Beyond this trance are three more, each attained through ever deepening concentration. By penetrating the awareness of materiality, one attains a second level of trance, characterized by effervescent joy; the third level moves one beyond joy into stable bliss, and the fourth trance brings one to a place of absolutely stable equanimity. But this is not the end of the inner cosmos. Beyond these four trances are four levels of existence utterly detached from all materiality: infinite space, infinite consciousness, absolute nothingness, and neither-perception-nor-nonperception. This final trance, neither-perception-nor-nonperception, brings one to the edge of samsara, the very limit of existence. This is the deepest, most profound, and most mentally detached of states. But lack of perception is not the equivalent of inerrant perception. The former is a temporary escape from *duhkha,* the latter is *duhkha's* solution.

Before moving to the third aspect of the Buddhist path — insight, characterized by correct view and correct intention — we may consider one important corollary of advanced mental discipline; namely, that the cultivation of concentration endows a meditator with superhuman abilities and psychic powers. The Sanskrit term for such abilities is *abhijñā,* which translates literally as "higher knowledge." To maintain the quasi-technological comparison, one may imagine that facility with deep mental concentration enables the development of *abhijna* in the same way that possession of a scanning electron microscope enables the skillful biochemical manipulation of genetic materials. Both technologies allow one to see worldly stuff at the level of its component parts and give one the ability to manipulate that stuff deliberately, to recombine its elements, and thus, seemingly, to make magic. As the science fiction writer Arthur C. Clarke once observed, "Any sufficiently advanced technology is indistinguishable from magic."

Just as recombinant DNA techniques can be used to cure diseases or create new viruses, the thaumaturgic skills that accompany deep awareness are sources of ambivalence for Buddhist authors. The ability to remember one's past lives, for instance, was not unique to Shakyamuni or Buddhist arhats. Similarly, the ability to walk on water, swim through dry land, or fly up and touch the moon is available to anybody with the know-how. Insight has no role in it. The Fourth Noble Truth proposes that unwavering one-pointed concentration is a prerequisite for progress across the full length of the Buddhist path. But the magical abilities one gains along the way can be used for ill or, at the least, can become traps if treated as ends in themselves. The third stage on the path, wisdom, ensures that one does not become sidetracked thus. Correct view — whereby one does not mistakenly imagine a Self where there is no Self, or stability where things are unstable — leading to correct volition — which grasps after neither being nor becoming — is the end of the path. This path begins with morality, willing the right things, and ends with wisdom, willing in the right way.

We have already spent some time on the rudiments of Buddhist wisdom. So, rather than recontextualizing those points within this discussion of the path, let us conclude this section by returning to the buddha as the perfecter of the Noble Eightfold Path. Above I noted that Buddhist literature demonstrates a certain ambivalence about thaumaturgic powers. In fact, only four actions require a monk's immediate expulsion from the order: killing, lying, stealing, and claiming possession of superhuman abilities. Be that as it may, we have also seen that such psychic powers are central to Shakyamuni's success as a buddha. Shakyamuni's awakening relied directly on his recollection of past lives; these lives provided the raw data through which he deduced links between karma, *anatman,* and codependent origination as he worked out the Four Noble Truths. These powers hold equal importance, however, for defining Shakyamuni's roles as teacher and religious founder. Perfectly wise and perfectly compassionate, a buddha not only knows what it takes to introduce somebody to the Dharma, he also possesses the ability to do what has to be done to accomplish that conversion. There is a Sanskrit term for a buddha's combination of ready wit and superhuman power: *upāya-kauśalya* (skill-in-means). When Shakyamuni invited the gods to Kapilavastu so as to overcome his father's pride, he was practicing skill-in-means. The buddha-to-be's decision to kill the evil merchant in order to prevent him from killing five hundred others is another instance of skill-in-means. So too, the story of Shakyamuni's skill-in-means in the conversion of his mother places his superhuman abilities to the fore. Mahamaya died seven days after Siddhartha's birth, and was immediately reborn, a goddess in heaven. Years later Shakyamuni used his abilities to move between worlds in order to go to that heaven, where he spent three months setting his mother on the path of Dharma. Had Shakyamuni lacked insight into the Four Noble Truths, his ability to transport himself to heaven would have been a mere amusement, since he would have had nothing worthwhile to offer his mother. But insight, too, was not enough. Had Shakyamuni lacked superhuman abilities, his mother would have been truly lost when she died; her status as Shakyamuni's mother would have been greatly to her detriment rather than her benefit. Shakyamuni, too, would have been lost, since he would have then failed to accomplish the full complement of deeds required of a living buddha.

Act 5: Founding an Institution

> It is *dharmata* that a living, breathing buddha will not attain nirvana until he delineates a congregational boundary.

This expectation differs from the others so far encountered. The gathering of arhats on the shore of Lake Anavatapta and the conversions of Shakyamuni's parents, for example, were onetime events. Although they pointed us toward Buddhism's inner structures, these acts were also remarkable for the pageantry of their unique occurrences. The requirement explored in this section lacks such a bold display; the associated stories are rather drab and down-to-earth. In a sense this is appropriate. This requirement of living, breathing buddhas points less to the buddhas' own personal glory than to their structural role as founders of a religious institution that flourishes even in their absence. Buddhism's monastic community is purported to be the longest continuously existing human institution, a remarkable feat in light of the fact that Buddhism has no overarching structures for regulating group belief or individual morality. All issues of discipline, practice, and doctrine are dealt with on the local level by groups of men acting as a corporate body. The inclusion on the list of ten necessary deeds that a buddha must establish a distinct monastic community by delineating a spatial boundary demonstrates a fundamental fact about Buddhist social history: this religion's longevity can be attributed, in large part, to its dynamic rules for the establishment and regulation of communities of monks. In fact, Buddhist traditions are themselves fully aware of the fundamental importance of their rules for community formation and administration. The early biography of the buddhas, *The Great Story*, tells that ninety-one cosmic aeons ago Vipashyin Buddha taught his monks the Dharma and then sent them in the four directions to spread it. Vipashyin gave these monks only one order: every six years they must reunite as a group in order to recite the monastic rules. Note, although the members of Vipashyin's *sangha* traveled the world as teachers, when they rejoined together as a community they focused on straightening the orthopraxy of their daily lives, not the orthodoxy of their teachings. Perhaps people are more forgetful now than in Vipashyin's day: Shakyamuni's monks recite an abridgment of their rules on a biweekly basis.

What is a congregational boundary (*sīmā*), and why is it so crucial that a buddha designate one? The answer to the first question is straightforward; the second, more important question brings us directly to the heart of how Buddhists define the *sangha* and situate it within social structures. The answer to both begins with a story. One of Shakyamuni's most important disciples was a wealthy banker named Anathapindada. As the story goes, Anathapindada first met Shakyamuni at the house of a friend who had invited the buddha and monks for a meal. Anathapindada saw his friend preparing a great feast, but no wedding was imminent, nor had the king announced a visit. Anathapindada asked his friend about the preparations, and so learned that a buddha and *sangha* were coming for a meal. Anathapindada had never heard this word, *sangha*, before in such a context, but for some reason it thrilled him. Covered with goose bumps, he asked his friend what he meant by this word. The answer given is a cliché, found not only in this story but throughout Buddhist literature:

There are sons of good family belonging to warrior families who cut off their beards and hair, put on red robes, and with proper faith follow in renunciation the blessed one, who himself went forth from the home to the homeless life. Similarly, there are sons of good family belonging to priestly families, to merchant families, and to artisan families, who cut off their beards and hair, put on red robes, and with proper faith follow in renunciation the blessed one, who himself went forth from the home to the homeless life. This is called the *sangha*.[30]

Shakyamuni had been awakened for only three years when Anathapindada's friend is purported to have described the *sangha* thus. Indeed, the first monastic residences had only just been established. Before Shakyamuni's monks had monasteries, they lived where and as they pleased, in the woods, under rock overhangs, in graveyards, or in huts temporarily erected. These were men who abandoned everything they possessed, every association with kin and social life, out of faith in Shakyamuni as a buddha. They were rootless wanderers united by their dedication to liberative truth and in need of unlearning the spiritual naïveté of worldly life.

Although in Anathapindada's day Buddhist monks may have been predominantly wanderers, when the Mulasarvastivada's list of ten necessary deeds was composed much had changed. By that time, what had been described to Anathapindada as the *sangha* was more properly termed "the *sangha* of the four directions." This new term retains the archaic notion of monks as wayfarers without a home. But notice here that a monk's lack of fixed abode becomes a noteworthy marker of his identity within the broader assemblage of Buddhist renunciants. When Mulasarvastivada theologians stipulated that a buddha must demarcate a monastic boundary before he can attain nirvana, the majority of monks were not wanderers at all but rather were affiliated with specific monasteries set in specific places. These monks, usually called "residents," delimited their institutional identity in spatial terms, through the location of the monasteries in which they resided. Thus there was a *sangha* of the town of Shravasti, a *sangha* of Vaishali, a *sangha* of the Western Mountain. Even more properly, every monastery (or cluster of residences) was considered to possess its own *sangha*. And each of these separate *sanghas* was distinguished from the others by its location as defined through specific geographical boundaries. These boundaries, called *sima*, could delimit a large space — up to about nine square miles — using natural demarcations. Thus a monastic rule book records Shakyamuni's explanation of the *sima*: "The blessed one said: 'Resident monks and visiting monks should set fixed markers for a large boundary in all four directions. To the East, the marker can be a wall, tree, rock, rampart, or moun-

---

30. *The Gilgit Manuscript of the Śayanāsanavastu and the Adhikaraṇavastu, Being the Fifteenth and Sixteenth Sections of the Vinaya of the Mūlasarvāstivādin*, ed. Raniero Gnoli (Rome: Instituto Italiano per il Medio ed Estremo Oriente, 1978), p. 15.

tain-slope; to the South, West, and North, the marker can be a wall, tree, rock, rampart, or mountain-slope. . . . Following that, a single monk should make a motion and an action of the *sangha* may be performed.'"[31] Alternately a *sima* could be small and adopt things such as a road, a designated rock, or pillars erected and set in the ground to mark its boundaries.

The *sima* is the basic unit of social life for Buddhist renunciants. Without a *sima* there is no community of monks, only a haphazard collection of individuals who may (or may not) share doctrinal, practical, and moral ideals. Actually Buddhists use the term *sangha* in several ways: (1) this term identifies the general assemblage of Buddhist monks, in line with the clichéd description given to Anathapindada above; (2) this term specifies those Buddhists who have attained a clear understanding of *duhkha* and its causes; (3) this term is a catchall for all Buddhists, both lay and monastic; finally (4) a *sangha* is a unit of renunciant social life, defined as the set of individual monks located within the circumscribed limits of a *sima* at the time in which there is an occasion for monks to act as a corporate group. It goes without saying that human institutions persist only insofar as there are rules for their organization and mechanisms for enforcing those rules. For Buddhist monks to establish, change, enforce, or affirm their rules of behavior, and therefore act as members of a social institution, they must first delimit a *sima*. As the text stipulates in the paragraph above, after *sima* boundaries are set, one monk should make a motion and an action of the corporate *sangha* may be performed.

Thus, for instance, Buddhist monks are required to gather fortnightly to recite the *pratimoksha*, the disciplinary rules of monastic life. This ceremony is permitted to take place only when the entire local *sangha* is present. Whoever is present within the *sima* when the ceremony begins must be present at the ceremony; whoever is outside the *sima* is not deemed to be a member of that *sangha* for that time. Similarly, if a disciplinary action has to be taken against a specific monk — for instance, suppose there is a monk who brags about psychic powers he does not really possess and therefore merits expulsion from the monastic community — the entire body of monks residing within the *sima* must be present. Not only must every monk be present, but all monks must assent unanimously to an order of expulsion. Individual dissent is not allowed, for the *sangha* is constituted as a single corporate body and must act as such. A *sangha* functions in undivided unanimity or does not function at all. A seventh-century pilgrim from China describes the strict adherence to this discipline in a monastery he visited on India's eastern coast: "When any business happened, it

---

31. *Mūlasarvāstivādavinayavastu*, ed. S. Bagchi (Darbhanga, India: Mithila Institute of Post-Graduate Studies and Research in Sanskrit Learning, 1970), 2:115.

was settled by the assembly; and if any priest decided anything by himself alone
. . . without regarding the will of the assembly he was expelled."[32]

Socially speaking, a *sangha* is a group of individual monks gathered in
one place at one time working in unison to accomplish an action that has bearing on themselves as members of a community. This has proven a remarkably
dynamic and adaptive social structure. The fact that every monk within a community must assent — if only through silent acceptance — to the doings of the
corporate body unifies the community, strengthening it. Indeed, the will of the
community is absolute over its members. But membership itself is fluid: one
can vote with one's feet and leave a *sangha* with which one disagrees. Buddhist
lawbooks say as much, advising monks that at the time of the biweekly recitation of monastic rules they should be in a place in which the residents are pure
and share their views, not one in which the residents are quarrelsome or argu-
mentative. From a bird's-eye view, the longevity of the Buddhist *sangha* lies in
the fact that one monk's "troublemaker" is another monk's "friend," and there
is no final arbiter or supreme authority to say which perception is correct.
Members of different *sanghas* could disagree over religious practice or, less importantly, doctrine; they could calumniate each other, or even attempt to excommunicate each other. But ultimately, because there is no internal mechanism by which one monastery's monks could be definitely affirmed as proper
and the other's as heretical, as long as the renunciants living in opposing monasteries retained material support, both could exist and call themselves "Buddhist." Highly successful, Buddhism's formula for community formation reads:
allow heterogeneity between *sanghas* but require homogeneity within each
sangha.

Though this formula is neither authoritarian nor universalist, it is also
not anarchic. The potential for endless schism and differentiation within the
broader Buddhist community is limited by the fact that the Buddhist *sangha* is
a *social* institution woven into a web of parallel institutions — economic, political, familial, medical, cultural, environmental — that have no necessary stake
in the *sangha*'s perpetuation. Societies in which monks are part of the larger social fabric have distinct expectations about what it means to be a professional
Buddhist. Insofar as an individual monk, or community of monks, transgresses
those expectations, that monk or *sangha* stands to lose material support. And
such support is necessary, for the majority of monasteries have not been economically self-sufficient. Instead, they have relied on local donors and local rulers for steady donations. And though, historically, some monasteries have be-

---

32. I-Tsing, *A Record of the Buddhist Religion as Practiced in India and the Malay Ar-
chipelago (AD 671-695)*, trans. J. Takakusu (Delhi: Munshiram Manoharlal, 1982 [1896]),
pp. 62-63.

come quite wealthy — owning fields and slaves, gold and silver — even these institutions retain their charters and bounty only through the assent of the reigning king. Even the wealthiest of monks is still a *bhikshu,* a term that translates as "beggar," one who lives on alms. Thus monastic rule books represent Shakyamuni as fervent in his pursuit of a monastic "good neighbor" policy. The sole rationale for many restrictions on conduct is that certain behaviors violate the circumspect decorum lay folk expect of renunciants. A monk must not speak while eating, for instance. This is ordered not because table manners possess an intrinsic moral worth, but rather because when monks spoke while eating, people complained to the buddha, saying that such behavior is acceptable for the rude, crude masses but not for monks. For the same reason, a monk may not rub his genitals against a tree, sleep on a high bed, or splash while bathing. Indeed, even practices that seem to cut right to the heart of the lay/monk distinction — yogic meditation and the biweekly recitation of the *pratimoksha,* for instance — may have been made normative for monks in response to lay demands. According to sacred biography, Shakyamuni requires his monks to perform these acts only after lay followers complain that members of other religious groups engage in these practices but his do not. In short, there is a complex dynamic play of expectations, obligations, and actions that enables Buddhist monks to disagree among themselves over rules of behavior, doctrine, and religious practice, but that functionally limits those disagreements by acknowledging that a *sangha* cannot survive without the laity's respect. Buddhism is what society at large allows Buddhism to be. Indeed, monks seem to have been concerned to lower lay expectation over the limits of acceptable conduct. The Khotanese *Book of Zambasta,* for instance, states explicitly that householders will be corrupted and lose faith in the buddha if they become aware of precisely what is required of monks. A monk who reveals the rules to the laity is thought to commit a grave sin.[33]

When scholars desire to describe the state of the *sangha* as an institution within the broadloom of social institutions, they often use the term "domestication." Domestication connotes the successes of agriculture and animal husbandry: the taming or refinement of wild biological entities, enabling a better, safer, richer life. This same connotation carries over into the term as used for the *bhikshu-sangha.* Here are men who entered something of a "state of nature," following the buddha from the home to the homeless life. These same men nevertheless re-formed a community of their own and affirmed the importance of binding that community to lay society by conforming their behaviors to its ideals. Why? Following the metaphor of "domestication," we would expect that by

---

33. *The Book of Zambasta: A Khotanese Poem on Buddhism,* ed. and trans. R. E. Emmerick (London and New York: Oxford University Press, 1968), p. 341.

acting so, Buddhist monks furthered their own aims as well as those of their supporters. The former, because Buddhism does not generally promote severe asceticism. Monks who lack material necessities — food, robes, a begging bowl, medicine, etc. — cannot pursue higher religious attainments. The latter, because, as we have already seen, the rationale for supporting the *sangha* was expressed in terms of merit making. From the lay point of view, the *sangha* is a depository for gifts, a "field of merit," the "fertility" of which is directly related to the moral purity of its members. For a *sangha* to be pure, its members must gather to recite their rules and to punish those who have fallen. This gathering, in turn, requires a *sima*. Thus, in a sense, the *sima* is not merely the boundary of a monastic enclosure, nor the basic unit of social life for Buddhist renunciants. Rather it is a line that marks the very possibility of Buddhist society, civilization, and culture. As a ritual act, the establishment of a *sima* is the condition of possibility for the *sangha*'s domestication.

One scholar, Ivan Strenski, has discussed these points very neatly. Strenski writes: domestication occurs "whenever the *sangha* participates with the laity in institutions" through the mechanism of gift exchange; "Buddhist society was formed in the process of ritual giving."[34] Indeed, the symbiotic give-and-take of exchange between laity and monks can be seen in many stories found in Sanskrit Buddhist literature. One tells of a small monastery, home to a monk who assiduously sweeps, cleans, and polishes its buildings and maintains a lush garden of trees and flowers, attracting the sweet songs of birds. Once a traveling salesman spent the night at this monastery. He was so impressed by the site's tranquil beauty that he made a munificent gift to the *sangha*.[35] In this case a desire for merit was *not* the motivating factor in the gift, but rather the donor's wish to express his pleasure at a thing of beauty created and maintained by this monk. Another story, however, is quite explicit in its calculus. In this case lay Buddhists in a certain area are flush with faith, and build a number of small monasteries. There are not enough monks to fill all the dwellings, so thieves use the empty buildings as hideouts. The householders complain to Shakyamuni that, although they build monasteries for the *sangha,* they are not gaining the expected merit. (Remember, quantity of merit depends as much on the moral quality of a donation's recipient as on the mental volition of its giver.) To remedy the situation, Shakyamuni orders the monks to move from monastery to monastery during the course of the day, so that each structure is used by a Buddhist monk at least once daily.[36] In still

---

34. Ivan Strenski, "On Generalized Exchange and the Domestication of the *Sangha*," in *Religion in Relation: Method, Application, and Moral Location* (Columbia: University of South Carolina Press, 1993), pp. 134, 141.

35. *Mūlasarvāstivādavinayavastu*, 1:225-26.

36. *The Gilgit Manuscript of the Śayanāsanavastu*, p. 35.

another story, a lay Buddhist builds a monastery, hoping for merit, but no monks use it. When he asks why his gift goes unused, he is told that building a monastery is insufficient. In this area there are more monasteries than monks to fill them. To attract monks he must also satisfy their other material needs with robes and other goods.[37] In still another story, the lay devotee Anathapindada is laying out the ground plan of a Buddhist monastery. He is told that as he chalks in the foundation on earth, a foundation is simultaneously being laid in heaven for the celestial palace in which he will enjoy his next life. Inspired, Anathapindada enlarges the building.[38]

These stories might give the impression that Buddhist acts of giving were motivated only by a crassly commercial calculation of interest on the part of the laity and monks alike. To counter such an impression, one could cite acts of truly disinterested gift exchange: for instance, the Burmese monk who has received numerous dwellings precisely because he refuses to occupy any of them. But rather than a superficial citation of examples and counterexamples, there is a more nuanced point to be taken from these various tales. As a domesticated institution, the *bhikshu-sangha* exists to satisfy mundane needs and transmundane aspirations equally. Certainly monasteries provide a stable place within which students can study the Four Noble Truths and cultivate the arduous discipline of mind and body necessary for their full realization. As such, monasteries have long served as schools, preservers of Buddhist lore and literature, logic, music, magic, and art. But at the same time, monasteries are established and supported by the laity out of their own quotidian concerns for health and wealth, bouncing babies and bountiful harvests. One poignant example takes place in the Indian city of Mathura. As the story goes, a *yaksha* (a superhuman being who lives in the earth or a tree) named Gardabha was eating the children of Mathura to satisfy his blood lust. (Think of this as a way of imagining a disease that preys upon infants.) The people of Mathura turned to Shakyamuni for assistance, telling him that they held no personal animosity against Gardabha, but they wanted the *yaksha* to leave their children in peace. Shakyamuni adjudicates their grievance: if these devotees will construct a monastery for the local community of monks and dedicate it in Gardabha's honor, the *yaksha* will cause their children no more harm.[39] In contemporary terms, we would say that building a monastery in Gardabha's honor is a form of ritual medicine. In fact, this story concludes by claiming that twenty-five hundred *yakshas* were tamed in Mathura through the building of twenty-five hundred monasteries. A range of activities might have transpired in Mathura's monas-

37. *The Gilgit Manuscript of the Śayanāsanavastu,* p. 37.
38. *The Gilgit Manuscript of the Śayanāsanavastu,* p. 24.
39. *Mūlasarvāstivādavinayavastu,* 1:18.

teries: education, meditation, recitation of scripture, creation and worshiping of images, the composition of popular didactic stories; on occasion, monasteries even served secular functions as banks, pawnshops, mints, and armories. But at the same time, the very existence of these monasteries stood as a guarantor of welfare for the entire local society, as a palliative against disease, as security for the king, as a promise of a felicitous rebirth, as a gathering place for festivals, as a repository of wisdom. In short, the scholar who wrote that "in its essence and inner core, Buddhism was and is a movement of monastic ascetics" is mistaken.[40] As a *religion*, Buddhism is a social institution that mediates the relationship between human and superhuman realities. The lay folk who constructed Gardabha's monastery are just as "Buddhist" as the renunciants who inhabited that monastery; the concern of Mathura's laity to protect their children is a legitimately "Buddhist" concern. Domestication of the *sangha*, initiated by the buddha's first demarcation of a *sima*, promises an institutionalized social solidarity inclusive of, at least, monks, nuns, lay folk, and deities.

Acts 6 and 7: The Great Miracle and the Descent: Buddhism's "Rite of Passage"

> It is *dharmata* that a living, breathing buddha will not attain nirvana until he demonstrates a great miracle near the town of Shravasti.

> It is *dharmata* that a living, breathing buddha will not attain nirvana until he shows himself descending from heaven with the gods near the town of Samkashya.

The buddha is supposed to be perfect in wisdom, perfect in understanding, perfect in knowledge. And the buddha is supposed to be able to utilize these perfections in his personal interactions, making him the perfect teacher. One might imagine that so great a man could never have failed to make his mark on the minds of others. However, Shakyamuni's sacred biography records a curious incident, soon after his awakening, that suggests otherwise. According to this story, Shakyamuni spent the first seven weeks of his buddhahood in a state of blissful awareness, not yet ready to share his Dharma with the world. When these seven weeks came to an end, he then surveyed the world for somebody to teach. He perceived that the five renunciants who had attended him during his

---

40. Edward Conze, *Buddhism: Its Essence and Development* (New York: Harper Torchbooks, 1975), p. 70.

years as an ascetic were dwelling about 130 miles to the west, in a deer park near the town of Varanasi. The buddha set out to turn the Wheel of Dharma for the first time. But no sooner did Shakyamuni start on the road than he met a potential convert, a wanderer named Upagu who, like Shakyamuni himself, had left his home and family in search of ultimate liberation. It would seem that Upagu should easily have been won over to the buddha's way. But as the story goes, Upagu quickly left the buddha, possibly thinking him something of a madman. In the popular telling, Upagu himself initiated their conversation by remarking on the clarity of the buddha's visage and by asking about the buddha's teacher. In return, Shakyamuni declared (I paraphrase), "I have no teacher, for there is none other in the world like me. I, and I alone in all the world, have realized complete awakening. I am unequaled, the teacher of gods and men, the conqueror of death, the victor." Not knowing what to make of such a statement, Upagu responded with a shrug, "perhaps," and walked away, making certain to take a different path.

This incident has struck many as odd. Why would Buddhists preserve such a tale, in which Shakyamuni fails during his first encounter with a potential convert? Upagu was the ideal interlocutor. He had left his home and was seeking freedom. Shakyamuni, for his part, possessed the very Dharma that Upagu desired, and would have shared it had Upagu asked. What happened? The answer can be summed up in a Sanskrit term, the one word used to describe this wandering mendicant: Upagu is called an *Ajivika*. The Ajivikas were rivals of the Buddhists, whose contending claims for metaphysical knowledge are often the butt of jokes in Buddhist literature. Given the distance of twenty-five centuries, one might not see much difference between the Ajivikas and Buddhists. Both groups centered their teachings on the workings of karma (albeit with rather divergent interpretations); both groups championed the renunciation of worldly life; both groups claimed that their leaders possessed superhuman powers, immense spiritual merit, and insight without equal; both groups rejected the mainstream texts and rituals of India's brahmin priests. Both groups, in short, were closely related in their teachings, their truths, their methods, their goals, and their positions vis-à-vis the broader social sphere. Their competing claims to authority and legitimacy resulted in sectarian sniping from both camps. In other words, from the Buddhist point of view, Shakyamuni's inability to capture Upagu's mind did not indicate the buddha's shortcomings, but rather this Ajivika's own spiritual myopia.

This encounter with Upagu shows us a Buddhism concerned to belittle the intelligence of its competitors. Upagu was blind to the truth even when he saw it clearly with his own eyes. More generally the tale of this strange encounter points our gaze toward the broader historical context within which Buddhism originated and developed. The previous section discussed the premium the Buddhist *sangha* placed on conforming to worldly expectations, and the internal mechanisms it developed to enforce this conformity: the ritual demarcation of a *sima* is the condition of possibility for the *sangha*'s domestication, its institutionalized interaction with the laity. But Buddhist renunciants were certainly not the only renunciants to wander the byways of fifth, fourth, or third century B.C.E. India.

Our sources do not allow us to penetrate with any level of detail into the social history of India at the time of Shakyamuni or the following centuries. However, certain caricatures are possible. The period during which the buddha's teachings were first articulated, preserved, reformed, and redacted was a time of critical transformation within the Gangetic plain. More than one millennium earlier, waves of migrants, the Indo-Aryans, started to cross through the mountain passes of Afghanistan in approach to the Indian plains. We know little about these people, and what little we do know comes from their sacred books, the Vedas, collections of hymns and lore to be used in the performance of sacred ritual. The Indo-Aryans raised horses and cows; they were successful warriors, possessing swift two-wheeled chariots; they believed their Vedic literature was divinely inspired, and therefore had to be preserved with the utmost accuracy; they had a generalized understanding that society was composed of four classes of people, ranked hierarchically: (1) the brahmin priests; (2) the rulers and warriors; (3) the common people, especially farmers; and (4) at the bottom of the hierarchy, the servants and artisans. By the year 1000 B.C.E. the Indo-Aryans began to settle in the Gangetic valley, to wander less and farm more. A striking illustration of this transition is found in the development of the Sanskrit language. In the earlier period the word *grama* was used to indicate a nomadic group, including warriors and baggage trains. As the Indo-Aryans settled, *grama* became the word for "town." As farming techniques improved, greater surpluses became available, enabling towns to become cities. By the fifth century B.C.E. the plains of northern and central India had been divided into myriad tribal kingdoms and sixteen major kingdoms. These kingdoms were linked by both the necessities of trade and the animosities of war. But war and trade, farming and banking, the luxuries of the urban elite contrasted with the despair of the urban poor raised concerns that traditional Indo-Aryan priests, Vedas, and rituals could not address. Certain individuals, dissatisfied with the religious/ideological status quo, left their homes and families. They wandered out of the cities to become *shramanas,* literally "strivers," seeking liberation from relentless samsara. One can speak of a "*shramanic* movement" of the late fifth century. This movement was comprised of men who exerted themselves in the practice of austerities toward the realization of truth, and who often defined themselves in opposition to the established religious order of the brahmins, Vedas, and sacrifices. Thus an Indian grammarian presents the construction *shramana*-and-*brahmana,* ascetic-and-priest, as an example of ceaseless animosity, on a par with cat-and-mouse or snake-and-mongoose.

Shakyamuni and Upagu were both *shramanas.* The prominent memory of an encounter between the freshly awakened buddha and the obtuse Ajivika demonstrates that animosity did not divide only *shramanas* from brahmins, but *shramanas* from each other as well. They were competitors for religious legitimacy and for social legitimacy. They contended with each other for members, each group seeking to inspire young men to adopt a *shramanic* path, as well as to attract converts from other established *shramanic* groups. They also contended with each other for material support, each group striving to represent itself as the most fecund "field of merit."

No story from the buddha's life demonstrates the stakes of this competition more than that surrounding the sixth act required of a living, breathing buddha, his demonstration of a great miracle. In fact, this "great miracle" (which Shakyamuni performed in the north Indian town of Shravasti sixteen years after his attainment of buddhahood) is the first part in a long narrative cycle that concludes with the seventh act required of a living, breathing buddha, i.e., his descent from heaven accompanied by the gods near the town of Samkashya. For Buddhists these two events mark crucial moments in the buddha's life and project as a religious founder. This story cycle represents Buddhism's own myth of its formation as a religion, as a thoroughly domesticated source for social and spiritual legitimacy. These tales do not offer a myth of origins, of birth, but a myth of adulthood, of Buddhism coming into its own as a full-fledged socioreligious order. I use "myth" here in the sense given it by the French critic Roland Barthes, who wrote that "myth has the task of giving an historical intention a natural justification, and making contingency appear eternal."[41] In other words, these stories are "mythological" in the sense that they seek to exhibit the buddha, his Dharma, and his *sangha* as the ideal person, the ideal teaching, the ideal community, naturally and eternally superior to all others in history. In Shravasti and Samkashya, Shakyamuni revealed his great power, his supreme power, his supernatural power: power that could transcend and transfigure the *dharmata,* the natural order to which buddha himself is supposed to be subject. The patterned action by which this power was first revealed and then modulated provides a native Buddhist model for the founding and institutionalization of a Buddhist community and cosmos.

The stories associated with the great miracle at Shravasti and the descent at Samkashya revolve around a set of themes one often finds linked in Buddhist literature: giving, worship, and spiritual power. These concerns are expressed in

41. Roland Barthes, *Mythologies,* trans. A. Lavers (New York: Hill & Wang, 1972), p. 142.

the first paragraph of the particular account I will follow, located in the Indian collection of *Divine Stories*.[42] The tale begins in the city of Rajagriha. Shakyamuni dwells in a park on the outskirts of town while a group of six Ajivika teachers live nearby. The contrast between the religious figures could not be more stark. Shakyamuni is presented as receiving a steady stream of visitors, human and divine, who eagerly elevate him in veneration and load him down with material goods. The Ajivikas, by contrast, had been the toast of the town before Shakyamuni arrived, but now they were completely ignored. The Ajivikas received nothing from anybody, and so began to hatch a nefarious plan. While scheming among themselves, one said: "We possess superhuman powers. The shramana Gotama also represents himself as possessing superhuman powers. Let us challenge him to a magic contest! If he performs one miracle, we'll perform two; if he performs sixteen, we'll perform thirty-two."

It goes without saying that this Buddhist text would not admit that these Ajivikas really did possess such powers. Indeed, each is shown as knowing in his heart that he lacks magical ability. Nevertheless, through a device of deus ex machina the god Mara decides he will use these foolish Ajivikas for his own purposes. Mara had long wanted to embarrass Shakyamuni, to make him a less sought-after teacher and to undermine his acceptance as a field of merit. So Mara takes on the form of an Ajivika and performs a superhuman feat (no problem for a god), convincing all the other Ajivikas that they do, finally, have Shakyamuni right where they want him; for the Ajivikas believe that Shakyamuni, like themselves, is a fraud. Anticipating victory, the Ajivika teachers propose to the local king, Bimbisara, that he host a contest of magical abilities between themselves and Shakyamuni. Bimbisara refuses to countenance the contest, and, to make a long story short, the Ajivikas decide to lie in wait for the buddha in the city of Shravasti, whose ruler, King Prasenajit, is willing to host such a contest.

The scene now shifts to Shravasti. As part of the buildup to the big event, the *Divine Stories* relates a series of tales demonstrating the true breadth of Shakyamuni's majesty. In one tale a *shramana* named Subhadra tells the Ajivikas to forget their folly. He has seen gods wash the dirty robe of a student of Shariputra, one of Shakyamuni's own students, yet those same gods did not even offer Subhadra a glass of water. "We are not even the equal of the student of Shakyamuni's student," Subhadra concludes. A second story tells of an act, performed by Shakyamuni's good friend Ananda, whereby a prince whose hands and feet had been cut off was made whole again. But after these and many other marvels, and after still further twists and turns to the plot, Shakyamuni finally performed his great miracle:

---

42. *The Divyāvadāna*, pp. 143-66.

Shakyamuni miracle
(Lahore Museum, Pakistan; photo by Richard S. Cohen)

At the buddha's command, two snake-deities conjured a lotus flower, whose thousand petals were as large as wagon wheels, entirely golden, and studded with jewels. They placed it before the buddha, who sat on the lotus's center. Sitting in the lotus-position, his body erect, and his awareness full-front, the buddha then conjured a lotus above the first lotus. There, too, sat a second buddha, legs crossed. The same thing happened in front of the buddha, behind him, and to his sides. In this way, the buddha conjured a mass of buddhas reaching as high as the highest heaven. These buddhas formed an assembly. Some of the conjured buddhas walked, some stood, some sat, some reclined. Additionally, some burst into flame, and some performed the miracles of fire, light, rain, and lightning. Some asked questions; others replied. Thus, empowered by the buddha, the entire world, from the gods in the highest heaven even to young children, beheld this panoply of buddhas without any obstruction.

Lacking all superhuman power, the Ajivikas could not match this display.

The place to begin our consideration of this event at Shravasti is the setting for the day's events: a challenge by the buddha's opponents who are distressed that his popularity was growing at their expense. More specifically, and rather explicitly, this is a fight over resources. Gods and men shower the *sangha* with gifts while they ignore the Ajivikas' needs. This contrast is intensified and put into higher relief by the time of year in which this competition is set. The great miracle at Shravasti took place in the inferno of the Indian summer. But this season is not only notable for its increased incidence of heatstroke. This season also marks a crucial moment in the Buddhist liturgical calendar. The full moon of the Indian month Asalha (June/July) is the beginning of the annual monsoon rains' retreat. This retreat is a three-month period during which Buddhist monks (as well as other *shramanic* groups) are required to stay put where they are, in a single locale, to interact with a single community of local patrons. Generally a monk is not supposed to leave the area enclosed by the *sima* even for a day during these three months. Moreover, in some contemporary Buddhist countries, it is not unusual for laymen to take ordination as monks temporarily during this period. Lay devotees visit their local monasteries with greater frequency during the rains as well. In brief, the rains' retreat provides the paradigmatic occasion for the development of specific, lasting contacts between the *sangha* and lay society. Whereas the great miracle took place at the beginning of the rains' retreat, the buddha's descent from heaven at Samkashya marks the rainy season's finale, bringing this annual cycle to a close. The sixth and seventh actions required of a buddha, in his capacity as religious founder, bracket the single most important period in the Buddhist liturgical year.

In the previous discussion of the *sima,* we saw that Buddhist cultures, societies, and civilizations emerge out of the union between the *sangha* and laity in the ritual of gift exchange. Buddhist societies form in the process of ritual giving. In fact, such ritual giving creates two species of relationship, both of which are necessary for domestication. First, there are the direct interpersonal relationships, a corollary of the exchange partners' shared presence. To put this point more plainly, for Buddhist societies to form, monks and lay donors must necessarily be personally accessible to one another. However, such direct, interpersonal relationships are limited in scope, involving only the individuals on either side of the exchange. For full socialization these restricted transactions must coalesce into a generalized network of exchange that redounds to the broader social good. In the words of Ivan Strenski: "We have a circle of giving, beginning with the lay donor, passing to the *sangha,* then from the *sangha* to other recipients, and ultimately . . . either in this or the next life to the initial giver." The *sangha* and its lay supporters are "linked in a theoretically open system of indebtedness, the momentum of which tends to build up systems of social solidarity."[43] To return to Shakyamuni's bodily display at Shravasti, the question is: How did this performance contribute to the localization and domestication of the Buddhist *sangha,* the institutionalization of specific patterns of exchange relationships across the many sectors of a Buddhist society?

The answer: Domestication begins with the valorization of presence. And the buddha's success in Shravasti demonstrated, quite simply, that Shakyamuni and his disciples were good people to have around. The stakes of this contest were clear and unambiguous. Which *shramana* teacher could claim supremacy on earth? Which would be able to gain the highest social standing for his order at this crucial time when local communities were formed and established? Shakyamuni's great miracle confirmed that the buddha (and by extension his followers) had the highest "potential energy" and greatest spiritual efficacy of all *shramana* groups. In fact, the scope of Shakyamuni's accomplishment is signaled by the exact phrase used to describe his miracle: "While in a superhuman state, the buddha displayed a miracle of power." Nothing in the human world is beyond the power of a being who can perform this act, and so anybody who does not take refuge in that being is a fool. The *Divine Stories* forcefully underscores this latter point. After the buddha concluded his display, a god named Panchika became enraged at the Ajivikas because they had harassed the buddha and *sangha* for so long. Using his own superhuman powers, Panchika created a great storm, with wind, rain, and lightning. Whoever ran to Shakyamuni and asked for refuge (both literally and figuratively) remained completely dry; whoever sought refuge under trees, behind walls, or in groves was beaten down by

43. Strenski, pp. 146, 143.

Panchika's tempest. Finally, the Ajivikas' leader panicked in the realization that he had lost his followers to Shakyamuni. He drowned himself, after being mocked by a eunuch. Thus the *Divine Stories* ends this tale by explicitly representing the buddha's display of power as a basis for increasing the ranks of Buddhists.

The title buddha is often conceptualized in terms of cognitive abilities, wisdom, teaching. But the Shravasti miracle had little to do with the buddha's superior wisdom or the quality of the doctrines and practices he taught. It was a matter of sheer power, and by extension the benefits resulting from superior power. In fact, although this so-called great miracle is the supreme use of the buddha's magical powers, Buddhist scholastics identify two other "miracles" performed by a buddha: telepathy and teaching. The word I am translating here as "miracle" is *prātihārya*. Given this broadened context, in which magical power is listed with telepathy and teaching, it may be better to set aside the conventional English gloss for *pratiharya*, "miracle," and instead adopt the more literal translation, namely, "means of conversion." Shakyamuni's performance in Shravasti was the greatest use of thaumaturgic power as a means for converting human beings. This latter translation tallies with the etymology of *pratiharya,* which in its most basic sense signifies something that immediately and forcibly carries something else away; in this case, that latter something, the something carried away, was the minds of Shakyamuni's audience.

I imagine it must be captivating to witness a multiplication of buddhas on lotus blossoms, whereby the universe is filled with a solid mass of buddhas from top to bottom and side to side. But Buddhist literature remembers Shakyamuni as performing many stunning marvels throughout his life. And moreover, although the Ajivikas were phonies, Buddhism allows that buddhas are *not* the only human beings possessed of superhuman powers. So why do Buddhists deem this display in particular as the epitome of Shakyamuni's performance as an "evangelist"? The literature I am using reserves the designation "great miracle" or "great means of conversion" solely for this multiplication of buddhas. To understand why this particular display provides an unparalleled basis of support for the Buddhist *sangha,* one must note how Shakyamuni presented himself bodily to his audience. According to the story, every one of the Shravasti buddhas acted, spoke, and taught as if it was the "real," "original" buddha. Each of the conjured buddhas adopted a personal posture (e.g., walking, standing, sitting, and reclining); each performed lesser miracles by bursting into flame or shooting fire and water out of its body; and each taught by asking and answering questions. Each, for the duration of its existence, was animate and present, performing actions independent of those of the "original" Shakyamuni. The *Divine Stories* is careful to explain that this power is special to a buddha. Shakyamuni's superhuman powers exceeded those of every other magical adept in that his "creations" are able to act independently of himself — he can converse with them or they can converse with one another — whereas the creations of lesser magicians must always directly mimic the actions of their creator. The simulacra of a lesser adept speak only when he speaks; they stand only when he stands. In fact, a second telling of this tale adds an additional layer of complexity to the event. According to this second text, the so-called "created" buddhas could, themselves, create additional buddhas.[44] In other words, each and every buddha present could potentially perform his own great miracle. If one takes doctrine seriously, the implications are startling: Buddhists could have believed (some did believe!) that Shakyamuni, the "historical" buddha, was actually the magical creation of a still more primordial buddha figure. In light of this latter doctrine, any talk of a *real* or *original* buddha becomes moot. For all these reasons, Shravasti's great miracle is *the* performance that is special and unique to a buddha.

Not only does the buddha display the unsurpassed range of his abilities through this performance, but at a doctrinal level, too, the great miracle reveals a buddha's supremacy even over the laws of nature. As I have tried to suggest, each buddha in the mass of buddhas did not merely resemble Shakyamuni: each was a bodily equivalent for Shakyamuni in every existentially significant way. However, the existential equality of these multiple buddhas contravenes a fundamental Buddhist doctrine, namely, that two buddhas cannot exist in the same world at the same time. Thus, if each Shravasti buddha was imagined by his audience to be a full and perfect buddha, and was revered as such, Shakyamuni's performance would be truly a miracle in the Humean sense. The Scottish philosopher David Hume (1711-76) defined the miracle as "a violation of the laws of nature."[45] And the performance at Shravasti thus conceived would violate a principal canon of Buddhist "natural law." In Shravasti Shakyamuni demonstrated that two buddhas *could* simultaneously exist in some way, and not merely as two buddhas one on top of the other: the universe appeared to be filled in its entirety with the mass of buddhas Shakyamuni conjured. In this light Shakyamuni's great miracle blurred the line between his status as a mundane, bodily being and as supermundane being, beyond all natural laws.

For Shravasti's masses this was a unique, unheard-of, miraculous performance wherein the cosmos was revealed in its entirety, and shown to be filled with living buddhas. Moreover, this bodily display had an explicit social impact.

---

44. *Le Traité de la Grande Vertu de Sagesse de Nāgārjuna (Mahāprajñāpāramitāśāstra)*, trans. Étienne Lamotte (Louvain: Institut Orientaliste, 1944-80), 1:469.

45. David Hume, *An Enquiry concerning Human Understanding*, ed. L. A. Selby Bigge (Oxford: Clarendon, 1902), p. 114.

The contest between the buddha and rival Ajivikas took place directly before the rains' retreat. Shakyamuni's successful great miracle immediately and forcibly carried away the minds of his audience. Whatever social risk the buddha's *sangha* had been under by the challenge of the six Ajivikas was utterly removed. The buddha revealed the highest social worth of his buddhahood.

In Shravasti, during the rains' retreat, monks and lay folk developed an accommodation with one another, forming a local Buddhist community. Such local communities are often designated using a collective noun, the "four assemblies," i.e., monks, nuns, laymen, and laywomen. The buddha's descent from heaven accompanied by gods occurred three months later, at the formal end of the rains' retreat period. By contrast with Shravasti's emphasis on conversion and community formation, the details told of Shakyamuni's actions at Samkashya reveal that the social context had changed. The display of a miracle at Shravasti gained converts for Shakyamuni and enabled his monks to claim spiritual priority over competing *shramanas*. In Shravasti Shakyamuni's cosmic revelation confirmed that he and his *sangha* were desirable neighbors indeed, worthy of high privilege within a network of exchange. In Samkashya, by contrast, Shakyamuni's descent clarified the proper organization for exchange relationships and established the hierarchy of individuals and groups within the Buddhist *sangha*. In Samkashya Shakyamuni displayed a cosmological tableau in which buddha, gods, and humans were all set in their proper places as he descended on a jeweled staircase flanked by such supreme divinities as Indra and Brahma.

The story continues. The people of Shravasti rejoiced at the Ajivikas' humiliation, and redoubled their donations to the buddha and his disciples. But Shakyamuni became concerned that it would seem as if he had performed his miracle solely for the sake of wealth and honor. In order to prevent such gossip, he left the earth and flew to heaven. He spent the three months of the rains' retreat in Trayastrimsha Heaven, the divine realm into which his mother had been reborn after her young death. The buddha passed the rainy season teaching the Dharma to his mother and her fellow gods. (During this three-month period he completed one of his ten acts, since his father had been converted already, ten years earlier.)

Thus, while the so-called four assemblies came together on earth, in heaven a second Buddhist community was being formed. In fact, Shakyamuni did not remain only among the gods of Trayastrimsha Heaven. Buddhists conceive of "heaven" in the plural; the divine realms have many levels, many divisions. Before Shakyamuni returned to earth, he journeyed to all the diverse realms of divinity, meeting many groups of gods, teaching and converting them all.

The descent at Samkashya was the occasion upon which these two *sanghas* — human and divine — came together as one. According to the traditional telling, the human community was dismayed by Shakyamuni's extended absence. The monks, the nuns, the laymen, and the laywomen had not seen him for three long months; they were distressed; they desired his presence; they thirsted to see him again. So the members of these four assemblies approached a monk named Maudgalyayana, one of Shakyamuni's chief disciples, renowned for his magical abilities. The four assemblies implored Maudgalyayana to use his magical abilities to fly to heaven and beg the buddha to return. After all, these humans argued, whenever a god desires to worship the buddha in the buddha's own presence, that god can easily descend to earth, but most humans cannot ascend to heaven at will. Maudgalyayana acceded to this request and flew to heaven. The buddha agreed to return. The text then focuses with close precision on the details of Shakyamuni's descent:

> Indra, the Lord over Trayastrimsha Heaven, asked the buddha how he would go to Earth.
>
> The buddha replied, "I will descend."
>
> "Will you descend using magical powers or your own feet?"
>
> "With my feet."
>
> Indra then instructed Vishvakarman, the divine craftsman: "Vishvakarman, fashion three staircases: one of gold, one of cat's-eye, and one of crystal." Vishvakarman fashioned three staircases according to Indra's instructions.
>
> Then the buddha went to the cat's-eye staircase. To the right, Brahma, Chief Among All Gods, descended from the golden staircase accompanied by the gods of the Form Realm, carrying one hundred thousand jeweled flywhisks. To the buddha's left, Indra, Lord of Trayastrimsha Heaven, descended from the crystal staircase accompanied by the gods of the Desire Realm, carrying parasols of one hundred spokes.
>
> Then the buddha considered, "If I descend on foot my rivals will claim, 'The *shramana* Gotama went to heaven through magic. But because he saw the goddesses' beautiful bodies, his magical powers have weakened. Now he descends on foot.' If I descend through magic, then the preparations of this host of divine beings will bear no fruit. Perhaps I should descend partially by foot and partially by using magical powers."
>
> The buddha descended in stages by foot, in stages through his magical powers.[46]

46. *The Tibetan Tripitaka, Peking Edition*, ed. Daisetz T. Suzuki (Kyoto: Tibetan Tripitaka Research Institute, 1955-61), 44:157-4-3 to 157-5-2.

Here one sees that even the most banal detail of Shakyamuni's activity as a founder — his means of locomotion to earth — is a matter of social and religious negotiation. The many constituencies that participate in the performative enactment of Shakyamuni's buddhahood have a stake in these details. The gods prepare a majestic, albeit mundane, means for the buddha's descent: if he does not go on foot, their actions lose their efficacy and he would fail his divine *sangha*. The Ajivika rivals still seek some way to disgrace the buddha. In order to maintain the coherence of his human *sangha*, he must again demonstrate his superhuman power.

Indeed, Shakyamuni's bodily performance at Samkashya reveals his humanity and superhumanity as equally fundamental to his role as buddha. Shakyamuni is both human and superhuman; his society includes humans and gods alike. Buddhist literature traditionally calls the event at Samkashya "descending with the gods" rather than "the descent of buddha," precisely because Shakyamuni is himself only a single player in a much grander drama. One of the greatest works of Sanskrit literature, Ashvaghosha's *Life of the Buddha,* captures this moment with characteristic grace. As Shakyamuni descends, "the gods . . . follow him with their eyes, as if they are falling to earth, and the various kings on earth, raising their faces to the sky, receive him."[47] Beholding buddha, gods and men meet face-to-face on the staircase from heaven.

The narration in the text I am following is less idealized than that of Ashvaghosha. This text reflects the more practical difficulties this cosmic encounter would occasion for gods and humans alike if Shakyamuni were not present to mediate:

> Smelling the filth 50 miles below, the gods could not bear the stench, so the buddha created the perfume of sandalwood, which the humans smelled as well. Then the buddha considered, "Suppose men see the daughters of gods, or women see the sons of gods: they will vomit hot blood and die. Certainly, this would happen. I should therefore present a miraculous vision in which men see only the sons of gods and women see only the daughters of gods." The buddha then fashioned a miraculous vision such that men only saw the sons of gods and women saw only the daughters of gods.[48]

Here even the humans' vision of the gods and the gods' perception of the humans are part of Shakyamuni's own performance. Shakyamuni controls every

47. *The Buddhacarita or Acts of the Buddha,* trans. E. H. Johnston (Delhi: Motilal Banarsidass, 1984 [1936]), 3:56.
48. *The Tibetan Tripitaka,* 44:157-5-3 to 157-5-6.

aspect of the bodily display in the interest of developing a stable social structure, inclusive of humans and gods.

This story is richer yet. Not only does the buddha bring humans and gods together, but this event also serves as an occasion for fixing hierarchies within the Buddhist community. This latter theme is treated in almost every textual version of the descent story. The most explicit statement of it is found in the *Book of Zambasta,* from Khotan in Central Asia: "The monks, the nuns, all the laymen, all the laywomen then made an agreement with one another: 'When the buddha descends here, whoever can worship him first will be chief of all among us.'"[49] That is to say, whoever greeted buddha first was to be considered his foremost disciple, and the assembly of which that disciple was a part — monk, nun, layman, laywoman — was to be considered foremost among the four assemblies. The actions and reactions of the buddha's human disciples to what they saw in Samkashya hold fundamental importance for this event's institutional meaning.

The text treats this theme by describing the actions of two of Shakyamuni's disciples at this time. First we learn that while the buddha was descending, a monk named Subhuti sat beside a tree to meditate. Looking up, Subhuti witnessed Shakyamuni's great bliss as he descended. Having seen Shakyamuni's bliss, Subhuti decided that such bliss outstripped any joy one might attain through a favorable rebirth as a human, or even as a god. Inspired, he intensified his meditation, attending to the following verse: "All conditioned things are impermanent, unstable, unreliable, and characterized by changeability. Have done with all conditioned things! Their legacy is sadness! Their legacy is undesirable! Hold fast to liberation!" At this moment Subhuti realized the truth of no-Self, *anatman*. In gratitude he quickly knelt and offered reverence to the buddha.

The second disciple to be discussed is a nun named Utpalavarna. Her name translates as "smells like a lotus." In brief, Utpalavarna conceived a desire to be the first of Shakyamuni's human disciples to pay him honor at the base of the divine staircase. To realize this goal, she uses her own magic. She transforms herself into a glorious king surrounded by sons and ministers. Fooled, the common people made way for Utpalavarna, allowing her to stand at the bottom of the staircase. Unfortunately for her, another of Shakyamuni's followers recognized her by her smell. Utpalavarna accomplished her goal of being the first at the staircase's foot, but she paid a stiff price for this honor. According to the text, Shakyamuni castigated her for using her spiritual powers in his presence and sent her away.

Utpalavarna's use of her own magical abilities thwarted Shakyamuni's at-

49. *The Book of Zambasta,* p. 357.

tempt to control all physical, bodily representations in this encounter between the humans and gods. Her use of her body could have had dire consequences for the society Shakyamuni was creating through his performance. One can imagine the problems that would have arisen had Utpalavarna's preeminence received canonical sanction. During Shakyamuni's sojourn in heaven, the monks, nuns, laymen, and laywomen coalesced into a local community; the four assemblies became a corporate body. But a society headed by nuns would have been inconceivable. Had Utpalavarna been considered successful, the community of Buddhist renunciants would have become as socially repugnant as the Ajivikas that Shakyamuni defeated in Shravasti. The *Divine Stories* emphasizes that Shakyamuni's rivals were unworthy to receive offerings, not only because they lacked superhuman powers, but more importantly because they were fundamentally antisocial. Remember, before the Ajivikas' leader killed himself, he was insulted by a eunuch, a social outcast. The details and entailments of the buddha's bodily display in Samkashya promised a *sangha* whose institution would not only *not* violate fundamental social canons, but would actively legitimate and conserve those canons.

The reentry of Shakyamuni into the lives of his disciples was a definitive moment at which a social cosmos that had lost its linchpin was formed anew. The physical location of individuals and groups in this tableau at Samkashya defined their proper positions within the Buddhist social hierarchy. Indeed, as members of the Buddhist community were jockeying for position at the foot of the triple staircase, so the events on the stairs were a graphic performance of the cosmological hierarchy. The symbolism is unambiguous and in need of little clarification. For three months in the heavens, Buddha sat on a throne while the many gods sat on the ground at his feet. And as the terrestrial relationships established during the rains' retreat culminated, so the buddha's relationship with divine beings came to its fullest expression in this act of descent. Both human and superhuman, the buddha displayed himself to all the world at the center of his community, one that included gods and men and women. The event at Shravasti established the buddha's spiritual authority; his descent at Samkashya transformed that personal power into active social authority, ordering the generalized network of exchange relationships that constitutes a Buddhist society.

Act 8: Schismatic Disciples and the Ironies of Early Buddhist History

It is *dharmata* that a living, breathing buddha will not attain nirvana until he appoints two chief disciples.

If the great miracle that Shakyamuni performed in Shravasti reveals anything about this religious founder, it is that when he chose to be everywhere at once, he could be. However, notwithstanding the grand dramas of Shravasti and Samkashya, Buddhist literature typically represents Shakyamuni as withdrawn from the day-to-day toils of administering a group of occasionally fractious renunciants. The Pali author Buddhaghosa describes the buddha's daily routine as centered around his dwelling, known as the *gandhakuti,* or "perfumed chamber." In the morning Shakyamuni would leave his *gandhakuti* for a round of begging and a communal breakfast. Then, as he reentered his chamber, he would exhort the monks to practice. He would retire inside the *gandhakuti* for most of the day. Late afternoon and evening brought lay and monastic visitors to his doorstep. Heavenly visitors came later in the night. There is no doubt that Shakyamuni was his *sangha's* leader. The buddha's word was final in any dispute over proper conduct, proper doctrine, or proper practice. But when it came to the mundane responsibilities of educating monks and administering a monastic organization, Shakyamuni often relied on the two men he appointed as his chief disciples: Shariputra and Maudgalyayana.

We have encountered both Shariputra and Maudgalyayana earlier in this chapter. Among the individual achievements we have seen are these: Shariputra stood on the shore of Lake Anavatapta, and associated his good fortune in meeting Shakyamuni with his worship of holy men in lives past; Maudgalyayana requested the heaven-dwelling Shakyamuni to return to earth. But as a pair of disciples, these two are recollected as the two members of the *sangha* who were most capable of leading the *sangha* in the buddha's stead. Shariputra was known by a military nickname, General of the Dharma, in part because he was second only to Shakyamuni in the attainment of wisdom. Maudgalyayana gained renown as Master of Superhuman Powers, because only Shakyamuni was more powerful. Shariputra's superior wisdom enabled him to lead disciples to the edge of insight, to show them the empty vanity of desire and the futility of samsara. Maudgalyayana's control over the workings of mind (for Buddhism, superhuman powers are fundamentally psychic in nature) enabled him to take disciples the rest of the way toward awakening, to extirpate all remaining moral impediments and mental defilements. According to one of the more interesting sets of traditional metaphors, Shariputra is likened to a "mother" who brings a disciple into the world of Dharma, while Maudgalyayana is likened to a "wet nurse" who nourishes the disciple through his formative development.

There are many stories to tell about Shariputra and Maudgalyayana and their central role in the life of the Buddhist *sangha.* But one tale above all explains why these two chief disciples were so crucial to the buddha's success as a religious founder. This incident takes place late in Shakyamuni's life, though it has its roots early in his youth. As a child, Siddhartha, the buddha-to-be, was jealously scorned by his cousin Devadatta. Everything Devadatta did well, Siddhartha did better; everything Devadatta wanted, Siddhartha already had. In middle age Devadatta schemed to become leader of the Shakya clan. When his plan was thwarted, he was forced to become a Buddhist monk. Devadatta's hatred of his cousin became a disruptive force within the *sangha*. There are stories of Devadatta trying to kill Shakyamuni by loosing a mad elephant upon the buddha, by putting poison beneath his fingernails and trying to scratch the buddha, by catapulting a boulder at the buddha. But the most disastrous event in Devadatta's saga occurred when he made an effort to depose the buddha and have himself named the *sangha*'s head. In fact, Devadatta did manage to attract a cadre of monks away from Shakyamuni, thus threatening an irrevocable split in the *sangha*. This is where Shariputra and Maudgalyayana enter the story. For the buddha did not go himself to retrieve the errant monks. He sent the two chief disciples in his stead. Shariputra, through his skillful teaching, reminded Devadatta's followers of the profundity of Shakyamuni's Dharma. Maudgalyayana reawakened their faith in Shakyamuni through his performance of amazing, miraculous feats. Together, Shariputra and Maudgalyayana thwarted Devadatta's coup, brought his schism to an end, and returned orthodoxy and orthopraxy to Shakyamuni's united *sangha*.

It was so important that a buddha appoint two chief disciples before he entered nirvana precisely because he was bound to enter nirvana. The presence of two figures, whose excellence had been sanctioned by the buddha, guaranteed that transcendent wisdom, practical knowledge, and the power to utilize that knowledge toward ultimate ends would continue in the buddha's absence. Shariputra's and Maudgalyayana's success against Devadatta was a dress rehearsal for the tasks they would face after Shakyamuni's nirvana, when the *sangha* would have to continue without the daily exhortations and charismatic teachings of its founder.

But, as fate would have it, Shariputra and Maudgalyayana both died several years before Shakyamuni. Shariputra is said to have attained nirvana peacefully at the break of dawn. Maudgalyayana met his end one fortnight later, beaten to death by the followers of a rival religious teacher; it is said that as Maudgalyayana's bones were ground to dust, his mind remained tranquil and focused. Thus, once again we see the ironic encounter between the theological imagination and historical happenstance. The tradition makes it *dharmata* for a buddha to appoint two chief disciples, calling attention to the fact that even a buddha cannot run the *sangha* alone. Yet those two disciples predeceased the buddha, leaving the *sangha* without a universally acknowledged chain of leadership after Shakyamuni's final nirvana.

Indeed, the problem goes even further. For although Buddhist traditions valorize consensus and unanimity within the *sangha,* they are also highly ambivalent about institutionalizing an authority with the power to enforce such consensus. Shariputra and Maudgalyayana died before Shakyamuni. Without these two chief disciples to succeed him, Shakyamuni stated that the rules of monastic conduct should be considered the master in his place, after his final nirvana. This rule is given in the *Mahaparinirvana Sutra,* the story of the buddha's last days. But immediately after Shakyamuni proclaims the abiding importance of the rules of conduct, he then issues an order permitting monks to suspend petty rules and minor precepts as they see fit. Talk about ambivalence! The sutra does not explain what is meant by "petty rules and minor precepts." Thus the *sangha* is left: (1) without a central leader; (2) with a notion that certain teachings/practices must be maintained; (3) with permission to change certain teachings/practices; and (4) without specific guidelines as to how to distinguish an essential teaching/practice from one that is petty or minor.

The difficulties of telling the *sangha's* early history after Shakyamuni's death are no different from the difficulties of telling the buddha's life. In both cases we possess stories and legends that were compiled and edited *after* the *sangha* had split along sectarian lines. Indeed, the institutional history of Buddhism after Shakyamuni's nirvana is punctuated by a series of increasingly divisive splits over wisdom, practice, conduct, and religious goals. The continuing history of the Buddhist *sangha* can be read as the fascinating account of a tugof-war between, on the one hand, individuals or groups seeking to conserve what they considered the core of Shakyamuni's religion and, on the other hand, the forces of social, cultural, political, and economic change, the simple fact of time.

This anxiety to conserve finds its way into Buddhist legend in stories of a so-called First Council. Most Buddhist traditions hold that Shakyamuni's remaining great disciples held a convocation in the town of Rajagriha during the very first rains' retreat after his nirvana. The purpose of this First Council was to fix a corpus of teachings, monastic rules, and formal doctrines that could provide the core for a unified *sangha.* As the story goes, this council was comprised of 500 monks, all arhats (recollect that an arhat is an individual who has freed himself from hatred, desire, and ignorance, and will attain nirvana upon death). It was presided over by Mahakashyapa, an early convert and the most accomplished monk still alive. As president of the council, Mahakashyapa invited Ananda to mount the pulpit and recite the sutras. The conceit is that Ananda, the buddha's personal attendant, possessed a perfect memory and had been present at Shakyamuni's every Dharma discourse. Ananda was thus able to remember every word the buddha had spoken on the Truth; he was able to note the city, village, or grove in which the Dharma was articulated; he was able to recollect the buddha's interlocutors, their questions and reactions. This is why Buddhist sutras typically begin with the statement "Thus have I heard"; the "I" is supposed to guarantee the first-person witness of Ananda himself to the sutra's veracity. Once Ananda had finished repeating all the buddha's sutras, and his words were approved by the gathered arhats, it was held that the canon of sutras (in Sanskrit, the *sūtra-piṭaka*, "basket of sutras") was established. Following Ananda's performance, Upali, the foremost scholar of monastic rules, was called upon to restate every rule of conduct, to describe where and why the buddha established each rule, and to enumerate particular penalties for violating rules. In this way Upali articulated a canon of conduct (in Sanskrit, *vinaya-piṭaka*, "basket of *vinaya*"), which was accepted by all 500 arhats as the single basis for communal life. The monks decided to forgo the buddha's permission to cancel petty rules and minor precepts as they saw fit. Then, finally, Mahakashyapa himself articulated the canon of lists *(mātṛkā-piṭaka* or *abhidharma-piṭaka),* scholastic summaries of the doctrine.

The historicity of this First Council is not taken for granted by contemporary scholarship. Nevertheless, one can certainly see the council's rhetorical value. It could be claimed that within a year of buddha's complete and final nirvana, every one of his teachings and rules was recited, affirmed by 500 perfect men, and set in its appropriate canonical "basket," sutra, *vinaya*, or *matrika/ abhidharma*. And yet the same institutional memory that lauds this "orthodox" meeting also tells us of a "dissident" monk who rejected the council's authority. Thus one reads of a Buddhist monk named Purana, himself the leader of 500 disciples, who was in the south when the meeting was called and did not participate. When the members of the First Council ordered Purana to "submit" to the teachings and precepts they had established, Purana demurred: "I am sure that this council has done a good job. But I will follow the teachings and precepts as *I* received them from the buddha, and as I remember them."[50] The council's 500 had no response, for they held no direct authority over Purana. In short, the historicity of the First Council is open to question. But even if we could be sure that a council of 500 arhats really did convene in the year after Shakyamuni's death, we would still not know how many figures like Purana there might also have been: important leaders of subgroups within the *sangha* who followed a Dharma and *vinaya* that owed nothing to the grand convocation.

Again, even if we were to accept the historicity of the First Council, we still would not have any certainty as to the precise texts that were included therein. The great French Buddhologist Étienne Lamotte put this point best:

---

50. This is a paraphrase of the story as told in the Pali vinaya. See *The Book of the Discipline*, vol. 5: *Cullavagga*, trans. I. B. Horner (Oxford: Pali Text Society, 1988), pp. 401-2.

"The sources disagree over the extent of the canonical texts recited in Rājagṛha, and each school claims that it was its own canon which was compiled by the elders of the [first] council. . . . It would be absurd to claim that all those canons were fixed at the very beginnings of Buddhism, in a period when the schools had not yet been formed. Furthermore, those canons were not fixed until quite late [e.g., fifth century C.E.], if at all."[51] Indeed, it could not have been otherwise. For unlike Islam, which claims that the Qur'an must be in Arabic to be considered the word of Allah, Buddhism seems to have always permitted the translation of Shakyamuni's words into local dialects. The story chartering this practice goes as follows: Once upon a time, two monks from priestly families suggested that the buddha stop using the vernacular of common folk and teach only in the high-culture cadences of Vedic Sanskrit. Shakyamuni rejected this suggestion. He severely reprimanded the monks, explaining that, although priests would still understand his teachings, most listeners would not. This story ends with the buddha permitting each of his monks to learn and recite the buddha's words in his own regional language. To the extent that an original canon might ever have existed, it did not survive the incremental spread of Buddhism from dialectal region to dialectal region. Eventually several canons were fixed in several languages. The differences among these canons are as numerous as the commonalities.

The difficulties the Buddhists faced in the maintenance of a unified *sangha,* and the difficulties contemporary scholars face in reconstructing this early period of Buddhist history, come to a head in the set of stories telling of a Second Council. Following the First Council there was a Second Council, dated to 116 years after the buddha's nirvana. Whereas the First Council is presented as establishing a basis for the *sangha's* orthodoxy and orthopraxy, stories surrounding this Second Council concern the attempt to reunify a fractured *sangha.* This council was initiated by a wandering monk named Yashas. One day Yashas arrived in the town of Vaishali, where he saw the local monks engaging in practices that he considered violations of the *vinaya.* For instance, the Vaishalian monks solicited donations of gold and silver from the laity; they farmed the land; they drank young palm wine. Yashas ordered Vaishali's monks to stop. They refused. In response, Yashas initiated a legal proceeding to discipline the members of Vaishali's *sangha,* or failing that, to excommunicate them.

This is a fascinating event for what it reveals about the sectarian representations of religious history. Many, varied accounts of this Second Council have come down to us, but they can be put in two camps. There are those accounts which present Yashas as a guardian of orthoprax tradition. As represented by

51. Étienne Lamotte, *History of Indian Buddhism,* trans. Sara Webb-Boin (Louvain: Peeters Press, 1988), pp. 129-30.

these texts, Yashas discovered lax, corrupt monks who had fallen away from the *vinaya* established in the First Council. Yashas was righteous in his attempt to reform the order. But a second set of texts pertaining to this story gives the perspective of the Vaishali monks themselves. According to this second view, Yashas exceeded his authority. In prosecuting the monks of Vaishali, he sought to expand the ancient *vinaya* beyond the text as established in Mahakashyapa's First Council. Here is an account of the Second Council from the *Questions of Shariputra Sutra,* a text that gives the Vaishalians' side of the story.

> At that moment, there was an old monk who was avid for glory and prone to disputing. He copied and arranged our Vinaya, developing and increasing what Mahākāśyapa had codified and which is called "The Vinaya of the Great Assembly" *(Mahāsāṃghavinaya).* He collected from outside some materials which had been neglected [until then], with the aim of deceiving beginners. He thus formed a separate party which quarreled with [the Great Assembly]. There were some monks who asked the king to pass judgement. The king brought the two schools together and set about taking a vote with black and white slips of wood, proclaiming that those who approved of the old Vinaya could take the black slips, and those who favored for the new Vinaya, the white slips. Then those who took the black slips were more than ten thousand, while those who took the white slips were a mere hundred or so. The king considered that [the doctrines of the two schools] both [represented] the word of the Buddha and that since their preferences were not the same, [the monks of both groups] should not live together. Since those who studied the old [Vinaya] were in the majority, they were called the *Mahāsāṃghikas* ("members of the majority") for that reason; those who studied the new [Vinaya] formed the minority, but they were all *Sthaviras* ("elders"): hence they were called *Sthaviras.*[52]

Here is a brief account of the same events as told by the group that called itself the *Sthavira-vada,* the School of the Elders, who look upon Yashas as a champion:

> In order to subdue the wicked monks, many Sthaviras came to Vaiśālī. . . . After having annihilated the wicked monks [in debate], and after having crushed the sinful doctrine, the Sthaviras selected 700 arhats, choosing the best ones, in order to purify their own doctrine, and held a council. . . . The wicked monks [of Vaishali], who had been excommunicated by the Sthaviras, gained another party; and many people, holding the wrong doctrine, ten

52. Cited in Lamotte, *History of Indian Buddhism,* p. 172.

thousand, assembled and (also) held a council. Therefore this Dharma council is called the "Great Assembly."[53]

Both accounts agree that a dispute over monastic conduct ended in an irrevocable split within the *sangha* between one group that called itself the Sthaviravada — this can be translated as "the Way of the Elders," or more loosely, "the Orthodox Way" — and a second group that called itself the Mahasamghika — "the Great Assembly," or simply, "the Majority." Both accounts agree that the avowed Mahasamghikas far outnumbered the avowed Sthaviras.

Which account is correct? Until recently the second telling, that of the Sthavira school, was accepted as more accurate. The fact that this group's rules are more rigorous than those of the Mahasamghikas, combined with the Sthavira school's primary self-definition as the preserver of orthodoxy, held powerful sway over the scholarly imagination and gave its texts priority in the reconstruction of Buddhist history. Recent additional research, however, has tilted opinion away from the Sthavira account, toward that of the Mahasamghikas, the group sympathetic to Vaishali's *sangha*. In the words of Jan Nattier and Charles Prebish: "The sole cause of the initial schism in Buddhism history pertained to matters of Vinaya, but rather than representing a reaction of orthodox Buddhists to Mahāsāmghika laxity, . . . [this schism] represents a reaction on the part of the future Mahāsāmghika to unwarranted expansion of the root Vinaya text on the part of the future Sthaviras (who, in so doing, ultimately provoked the schism they were so diligently seeking to avert)."[54]

In the name of tradition, the new Sthaviras initiated a period of radical change in the history of Buddhism. Yashas's suit against the monks of Vaishali resulted in the *sangha*'s division into two *nikayas* (lit. "groupings," usually translated "schools" or "sects"): the Sthavira-vada *nikaya* and the Mahasamghika *nikaya*. But even had Yashas not instigated this break, there had long been centrifugal forces acting on the *sangha*. Above I noted the example of the monk Purana, the leader of a proto-sect who was unwilling to acknowledge the First Council or the canon it is purported to have established. Certainly Purana would not have been the only monk to have asserted his right to teach disciples on his own authoritative knowledge of Shakyamuni's truths. Beyond the issue of multiple claims to authority, differences of language, of location, and of monastic rules, as well as burgeoning differences over doctrine and religious practice, all contributed to the further division of the *sangha* into numerous

---

53. *The Dīpavaṃsa*, trans. Hermann Oldenberg (New Delhi: Asian Education Services, 1982 [1879]), p. 140.

54. Janice J. Nattier and Charles S. Prebish, "Mahāsāmghika Origins: The Beginnings of Buddhist Sectarianism," *History of Religions* 16 (1977): 238-39.

nikayas. Though the absolute number of *nikayas* is not known, it is popularly held that within three centuries of Shakyamuni's nirvana the *sangha* had split into at least eighteen separate *nikayas.* Some of these were distinguished by little more than geography. For instance, there was an "Eastern Mountain *nikaya*" and a "Western Mountain *nikaya*"; these two professed similar doctrines and practices but had their monastic centers built on neighboring mountains. Other *nikayas* were distinguished by unique doctrines. The name of the Sarvastivada *nikaya,* for instance, translates as "the School which Professes that Everything Exists"; this means that according to Sarvastivada doctrine, the past, the present, and the future all exist simultaneously. Members of the Pudgala-vada *nikaya* held that there was a real, ineffable Soul that persists from life to life; because this doctrine seems to contradict the fundamental teaching of *anatman,* members of the Pudgala-vada are often castigated as heretics.

It is the rule: a buddha cannot attain nirvana until he appoints two chief disciples. Shakyamuni named Shariputra and Maudgalyayana to these posts early in his career. The complexities entailed by this act foreground the ironies of Buddhism's early history. Shariputra was a chief disciple because he approximated Shakyamuni in wisdom; Maudgalyayana gained his position through his psychic abilities. The naming of these two as chief disciples highlighted Shakyamuni's own complete perfection at the same time that it demonstrated that others could, at least, approach his ideal. But Shariputra and Maudgalyayana were not merely symbolic epitomes; they held functional roles, running the *sangha's* day-to-day operations on Shakyamuni's behalf. Shakyamuni could not attain nirvana until he named them. But the fact that they attained nirvana before he did undermined all expectations that they would follow him as the *sangha's* recognized leaders. In lieu of such human authorities, it would seem that the Dharma and *vinaya* were named as Shakyamuni's successors. But which Dharma and *vinaya*? Which canon? Early Buddhism was a religion in which wanderers settled and settlers wandered. The Dharma and the *vinaya* were brought to every corner of the Indian subcontinent. As these teachings spread, linguistic differences, as well as localized cultural differences, brought about the development of distinct buddhisms, each of which made its own claims to orthodoxy and orthopraxy. Indeed, scholarship on the Second Council suggests that the invention of stricter new rules for the monastic life may have been as revolutionary a force in Buddhist history as the lax ignorance of old rules. And the story of the Second Council demonstrates that no authority could fix a canon for all Buddhists. In the *Questions of Shariputra Sutra's* telling of these events, the disputing sides go to the king to adjudicate their dispute. But how does the king respond? He throws up his hands in dismay. As far as he can tell, both groups are Buddhists. He orders that, since these fractious monks cannot live together in harmony, they should just live apart.

Act 9: The Bodhisattva's Vow

It is *dharmata* that a living, breathing buddha will not attain nirvana until he inspires another member of his retinue to aspire for
the unexcelled, complete, and perfect awakening of a buddha.

The literature of the Mulasarvastivada *nikaya* — the *nikaya* responsible for the
doctrine that a buddha must perform ten acts before he can win nirvana —
does not specify a uniquely "first time" a follower of Shakyamuni aspired for
the unexcelled, complete, and perfect awakening of a buddha. This theme is repeated throughout the literature. One noteworthy instance reads as follows:

Once upon a time, there was a poor washerwoman who offered a small
lamp to the buddha. As she presented this gift, the washerwoman also spoke a
vow:

By the merit I obtain as a result of this offering, may I become a buddha just
like this blessed lord Shakyamuni in every way. Just as Shakyamuni came into
the world as a teacher of students when human beings lived for one hundred
years, so too may I become teacher of students when human beings live for
one hundred years. Just as the excellent pair Shariputra and Maudgalyayana
are his chief disciples, so may I have chief disciples, Shariputra and Maudgalyayana. As Ananda is his attendant, so may I have an attendant, Ananda. As
Shuddhodana and Mahamaya are his father and mother, so may my parents
be Shuddhodana and Mahamaya. As Kapilavastu was the city of his youth, so
may I have a Kapilavastu. As Rahulabhadra is his son, thus too may I have a
son, Rahulabhadra. And, as his relics will be distributed after his final nirvana, so too may I obtain final nirvana and have my relics distributed.

Very soon thereafter Shakyamuni predicted that all would come to pass
just as the washerwoman requested, from the fact that she would become a fully
awakened buddha named Shakyamuni when the human life span is one hundred years, to the fact that her relics would be distributed after her final nirvana.

There is quite a lot to wonder about here. But before delving into the significance of this story, let us also note its epilogue. The local king, Prasenajit
Kosala, heard that Shakyamuni prophesied that a mere washerwoman would
become a buddha. He was astonished at how her trifling gift could bring so
great a reward. Prasenajit complained: "I have performed long and costly rituals in your honor. I have fed your sangha for months on end. But never have
you said that I will become an unexcelled, complete, and perfect buddha!
Please, lord, announce that I too will become a perfect buddha!"

Shakyamuni responded:

Complete and perfect awakening is profound, great king. It is profound. Its traces are difficult to see and difficult to perceive. It is incomprehensible. Nor can one comprehend its scope. It is fine and subtle and can only be recognized when one has the discretion of a sage. It isn't easy to attain. You cannot attain it by a single act of giving. Ten gifts will not win you awakening, nor one hundred gifts, nor even one hundred thousand gifts. Rather, great king, when you give, you must give with the express intention of attaining unexcelled, complete and perfect awakening. You must make donations with this aim. You must visit holy men with this aim. You must revere and serve religious teachers with this very aim: to attain unexcelled, complete and perfect awakening.[55]

This story is quite a bit like several others presented throughout this chapter. The idea that merit from a mere act of giving could enable one to attain a supreme spiritual goal was the substance of the story Vagisha told on the shore of Lake Anavatapta. The fact that Buddhist doctrine equates action with intention — it places greater emphasis on the aim toward which an act is performed than on the details of the physical deed — has also been discussed at some length, especially in relation to the Second Noble Truth, the cause of *duhkha*. We have met the cast of characters named by the washerwoman as well, and we have seen their roles in the grand drama of Shakyamuni's life as buddha.

What is unique and striking within this present story is the content of the washerwoman's mental deed. Her vow brings a specific theory of karmic action together with a specific conception of the most exalted aspiration toward which karmic action can be applied. She wants to be a religious founder on the exact model of Shakyamuni. Certainly her vow in this regard is somewhat unimaginative; the author could have used different names, at least. (I will return to this point at the beginning of the next section.) But this story serves as a useful introduction to the ninth act required of Shakyamuni as a founder precisely because it is so mechanistic, its characterizations so stark. A poor low-caste woman possesses insight that a powerful male king lacks. The readers of this story are shown that somebody who has the wisdom to voice an exalted wish can make Shakyamuni's life her own, down to names of her future family and companions. Complete and perfect awakening is profound; its traces are subtle and difficult to recognize. But somebody who even glimpses the nature of real-

---

55. This is a paraphrase of the events recounted in the *Mūlasarvāstivādavinaya-vastu*, 1:57-58.

ity can set out to attain the unexcelled, complete, and perfect awakening of a buddha, teach the Dharma, and found a *sangha* in *exactly* the same way as Shakyamuni. To use more specific terminology, such a person can set out on the *bodhisattva* path.

In fact, the set of doctrinal and institutional assumptions comprehended within this story have been central to the present chapter's representation of Shakyamuni as founder. The chapter began with the claim that, for Buddhists, Shakyamuni's value as a religious founder cannot be disentangled from the expectation that he is only one of countless buddhas. The chapter has been structured by a more refined version of this same doctrine, namely, that all the buddhas born on this earth necessarily live lives of great similitude. The washerwoman's vow is unusual only in that it tries to substitute "exactitude" for "great similitude" in creating a parallel life. Nevertheless, before any terrestrial buddha can perform his ten requisite deeds, earning him the right to attain final nirvana, before he can awaken, and even before he can reincarnate a final time, he must take a first step toward buddhahood by making a vow and entering the bodhisattva path. The washerwoman's dedication of merit was one form of what would be called a "bodhisattva vow." The bodhisattva figure has been one of the Buddhists' most important objects of conjecture, conceptualization, and contemplation. The path of the bodhisattva has been measured for length and metered for time, its every step explained in detail. Accomplishments of the bodhisattvas are the subjects of songs and prayers, and have even affected the very notion of what it means to be a buddha. Indeed, disparate doctrines and practices surrounding the bodhisattva figure have led to important institutional divisions within the *sangha*. In order to accommodate the important range of developments that arise out of the Buddhists' prolonged interest in the bodhisattva, I will split my discussion into two halves. Here, under consideration of the ninth act — i.e., at least one of Shakyamuni's followers must become a bodhisattva — I will treat formative conceptualizations of this figure as a model of the religious practitioner. In the context of the tenth necessary act, I will treat the broad doctrinal and institutional ramifications of an increasing importance placed on the taking of the bodhisattva vow as a model for religious practice.

Examination of the bodhisattva might begin with some of our earliest tangible evidence for Buddhist doctrines and practices, an inscription composed during the reign of Emperor Ashoka in the mid–third century B.C.E. According to this record, Ashoka doubled the size of a brick memorial stupa dedicated to Konakamana, a buddha who was believed to have taught the Dharma and established a *sangha* millions of years in the past. This inscription shows us that within two centuries of Shakyamuni's death a cult had arisen for buddhas other than Shakyamuni, and that this cult was so prominent it was supported by the greatest ruler of the day. Although we know little else about the third century B.C.E. cult of Konakamana, we can be relatively certain that such worship would not have arisen had there not been a more general speculative interest in the figure of the buddha as a religious type, a speculation that was closely connected with the imagination of buddha as a focus of devotion. Buddhahood, as the epitome of spiritual perfection, had to be a generalized state that could be attained by religious virtuosi who ardently perfected themselves throughout the course of myriad lifetimes. Such aspirants were called "bodhisattvas": literally people "attached to awakening," or idiomatically buddhas-in-training. Indeed, just as numerous speculative systems developed to explain the nature of buddhahood, so the bodhisattva as a religious type also came under scrutiny. What did one have to do to become a bodhisattva? What were the stages in the bodhisattva's progress? How long did it take?

Early speculation on the bodhisattva was especially fostered by the *jataka* tales, a genre of literature that was not directly included in the three canonical baskets (sutra, *vinaya,* and *matrika*) but has nevertheless held foundational importance for Buddhism. *Jataka* is a generic term for the stories of Shakyamuni's births while he was a bodhisattva. As we saw on the shore of Lake Anavatapta, Shakyamuni is remembered as sometimes speaking of births in which he committed great evils against his friends and teachers. But far more commonly, *jatakas* represent Shakyamuni's forward momentum as a bodhisattva. Once the buddha was an elephant who saved a party of lost travelers from starvation by throwing himself off a cliff so they could survive on his massive corpse; once the buddha was a young quail who saved an entire forest from destruction by convincing a wildfire to turn back and leave the animals in peace; once the buddha was a monkey who taught a human king the principles of legal justice. Sometimes the bodhisattva was a hare, sometimes a beggar, and sometimes a child prodigy. In every one of these triumphant *jatakas,* the bodhisattva shows himself to be the greatest of beings; he also possesses the wisdom to use his greatness for others' benefit as well as his own. Many *jatakas* fit into the category of "fable"; many are common Indian folktales, overlaid with the Buddhist conceit that the tale's hero is the bodhisattva, Shakyamuni-to-be. Indeed, the fundamental importance of the *jatakas* is revealed not only by the sheer number of such tales and their broad diffusion throughout the Buddhist world, but also by the fact that stone illustrations of these birth stories are found in the very earliest stratum of Buddhist archaeological remains. Probably from the time of Shakyamuni himself, *jataka* stories have provided monks and lay folk alike with an imaginative basis for conceiving what it means to train for buddhahood.

Whereas most *jataka* tales simply represent the bodhisattva as generous, patient, moral, or valorous in some way, several are concerned with bodhisattvahood itself and comment directly on Shakyamuni-to-be's progress along the path to buddhahood. One such *jataka* tells of an encounter between the bodhisattva when he was a young brahmin named Megha and a buddha named Dipankara. Just as the washerwoman at the beginning of this section made an offering to Shakyamuni and stated her desire to become a buddha, so in this *jataka* tale the bodhisattva Megha makes an offering of flowers and vows to become a buddha in the future. The version of this story preserved in the Mulasarvastivada canon is rather abbreviated. Here is a translation of the vow taken from the literature of the Mahasamghika *nikaya*, a text entitled *The Great Subject (Mahāvastu):*

Ah! May I too in some future time become a *tathāgata*, an *arhat*, a perfect buddha, gifted with knowledge and conduct, a *sugata*, an unsurpassed knower of the world, a driver of tameable men, a teacher of gods and men, as this exalted Dīpaṅkara now is. So may I become endowed with the thirty-two marks of a great man, with his minor characteristics, and with his radiant body. May I become endowed with the eighteen special attributes of a buddha, strong with a buddha's ten powers, and confident with the four grounds of self-confidence as this exalted Dīpaṅkara now is. So may I set rolling the incomparable wheel of Dharma as does now the exalted Dīpaṅkara. So may I preserve a body of disciples in harmony. So may gods and men deem me worthy to be heard and believed. Having thus crossed, may I lead others across; emancipated, may I emancipate others; comforted, may I comfort others, as this exalted Dīpaṅkara now does. May I become this for the happiness and welfare of mankind, out of compassion for the world, for the sake of the great multitude, for the happiness and welfare of gods and men.[56]

Just as Shakyamuni predicted that everything the washerwoman requested would come to pass, here too Dipankara declares that young Megha is a valid bodhisattva who, in some future time, will become a buddha named Shakyamuni.

The importance of this telling lies in its detailed, mature theory of buddhahood, and hence of bodhisattvahood. For Megha to achieve his end, he must train in such a way as to transform his body, his mind, and his range of abilities; he must develop special powers and attributes. Yet throughout this period of training Megha must not imagine that he is working for his own benefit alone. As a bodhisattva, Megha sets out on the road to final nirvana, his own highest good, as a way of expressing his concern for others' welfare and happiness. Thus, in its most generalized formulation, this bodhisattva vow is articu-

56. *The Mahāvastu*, trans. J. J. Jones (London: Pali Text Society, 1987), 1:194.

lated as follows: "May I become a buddha for the sake of other living beings." The bodhisattva's spiritual progress, and the buddha's spiritual perfection, cannot be realized without his or her altruistic participation in the world. Inspired in part by the spiritual heroism of the *jataka* tales, Buddhists came to imagine the bodhisattva path as the progressive accomplishment of a fixed set of perfections. The precise numbers and names of the requisite perfections differ from *nikaya* to *nikaya*. For instance, the Sthavira-vada *nikaya* stipulates that the bodhisattva perfect himself in ten ways, each one of which reveals the fiber of his moral character (e.g., generosity, morality, renunciation, resolution). The Sarvastivada *nikaya*, by contrast, came up with a list of six perfections: generosity, morality, patience, energy, meditation, and wisdom.

Let us look somewhat more closely at how these six perfections are integrated into the actual practice of the bodhisattva. The Sarvastivada holds that Shakyamuni took his first step on the bodhisattva path in the virtually infinite past, over 300,000,000,000,000,000,000,000,000,000,000,000,000,000,000, 000,000,000,000 years ago. (This number is known to Buddhist literature as "three incalculable aeons.") At that time, born a merchant, he encountered a buddha named Shakyamuni and uttered a vow: "May I become a buddha just like you in every way." In fact, the vow associated with this ancient merchant was almost word for word the same as the vow put in the mouth of the poor washerwoman. According to the literature, the merchant requested that his future name be Shakyamuni, that he become a buddha when humans live for a brief span, and so on. The karmic ramifications of the merchant's vow were enormous. For, from the moment he spoke these words, the merchant's every act of virtue and wisdom was not merely a random act of kindness but moved him farther along the grand concourse of spiritual progress toward buddhahood.

When this ancient merchant first encountered the ancient Shakyamuni, he became aware of a superior goal for which to strive, buddhahood. But he was not yet familiar with a means for attaining that result. Over the ensuing time span, known as an "incalculable aeon" (equal to 10^{59} years), this now-bodhisattva met and worshiped 75,000 more buddhas, being guided by each one on the practices of morality, meditation, and wisdom. By the end of this first incalculable aeon of his training as a bodhisattva, he was well on his way to buddhahood, and yet was not certain that he would actually realize his goal. The first aeon of training was followed by a second period of 10^{59} years, during which the bodhisattva encountered tens of thousands of additional buddhas. The last buddha Shakyamuni-to-be met during this second incalculably long period was Dipankara. In fact, the encounter with Dipankara is a milestone in this bodhisattva's progress, because Dipankara was the first buddha to prophesy that the bodhisattva would *definitely* be successful in his quest. This prediction marks the division between the second and third segments of the bodhisattva path. The bodhisattva begins a third incalculable aeon of training with the knowledge that he *will* become a buddha. Technically, such a bodhisattva is called *avaivartika,* meaning that he cannot desist from his practice or regress from his aim. This prediction marks a turning point in the bodhisattva's social self-representation as well. Though Shakyamuni-to-be was a bodhisattva in deed before his meeting with Dipankara, it was felt that one deserves to be called bodhisattva publicly only after one attains the *avaivartika* stage.

After the third period of 10^{59} years has been completed, the bodhisattva has very nearly accomplished his aim. But to become a full and perfect buddha he must then set out actively to accomplish each of the six perfections. He does this over the course of a mere one hundred aeons. *Generosity:* he sacrifices his body again and again for the sake of others; *morality:* he forsakes his life rather than violate a moral code; *patience:* he bears all punishments and ridicule with equanimity, no matter how undeserved; *energy:* he shows inexhaustible energy, as when he stood on one leg for seven days and nights, without closing his eyes, while singing praises of a buddha named Pushya; *meditation:* he learns and explores all possible states of trance; *wisdom:* he sees the truths of no-Self and codependent origination.

Throughout the course of his training in the six perfections, the bodhisattva was born in many different regions of samsara. (In fact, adherents to the Mahasamghika *nikaya* even held that he took birth in the hells, albeit of his own free will, in order to assist beings' escape from their horrendous sufferings.) The tale told of his penultimate life as a human being is one of the most popular in all of Buddhist lore. This life found the bodhisattva born as a prince named Vishvantara, who was unstinting in generosity. Vishvantara was beloved by all his subjects: nobody in his kingdom lacked anything, for whenever a supplicant came to him with a request, he fulfilled it. Once a legate from a rival kingdom requested Vishvantara's white elephant, a magical animal believed by all to be the source of the kingdom's prosperity. He presented the elephant without a second thought. Though the people of the kingdom were ready to praise his largesse when it benefited them, they were horrified when he gave away the elephant. Fearing that his generosity was getting out of control, the people had him banished to the forest, along with his wife and two children. While in the forest (to make a long story short), an evil brahmin requested his two children, making no secret that he intended to work them as servants. Vishvantara was simultaneously overjoyed and saddened by the request, with which he complied. Then the god Indra, intrigued by the fact that Vishvantara would give away his own children so freely, took on a human form and requested Vishvantara's wife. Perfect in generosity, he again complied. The story

Maitreya
(photo by Richard S. Cohen)

ends on a happy note for all, however: Vishvantara's children and wife were returned to him, and he was accepted back among his subjects.

Following the bodhisattva's penultimate human life as Vishvantara, he was reborn as a god, the divine king of Tushita Heaven. As the time approached for the great being's final life, he surveyed the earth for the best couple belonging to the best family living in the best place, just as other incipient buddhas did prior to their final births. He espied Shuddhodana, the leader of the noble Shakya clan, and his wife, Mahamaya, who was beautiful, moral, and had once vowed to become the mother of a buddha. Shakyamuni-to-be would make her wish come true. The bodhisattva then handed his crown to another bodhisattva, named Maitreya, who will himself come to earth as a buddha millions of years hence. Just as countless buddhas preceded Shakyamuni, so will countless buddhas follow him, Maitreya being the very next in line. And just as past buddhas, such as Konakamana, received reverence and honor, so there is a long tradition of worship directed toward the bodhisattva Maitreya.

The Buddhist conceptualization of the bodhisattva is certainly one of the grand moments in the history of human imagination. The predicates of true perfection, the duration of the bodhisattva's training and profundity of his practice, combine to present buddhahood as an accomplishment that, though attainable by all in theory, is the province of only a select few in reality. In fact, one should be clear that the term "bodhisattva," as discussed in the literature of the *nikayas,* refers quite specifically to Shakyamuni (or less often, Maitreya) during the period of his training before he was a buddha. When members of these *nikayas* speculated about bodhisattvahood, the theories they developed were almost exclusively retrospective — i.e., explaining how Shakyamuni perfected himself — rather than prospective — i.e., instructing living Buddhists how to travel on the bodhisattva path. Although the list of the buddha's necessary deeds stipulates that he must inspire a follower to aspire for the complete and perfect awakening of a buddha, *nowhere* in the literature of the *nikayas* does one find a prescriptive expectation that Buddhists should, or must, conceive such a desire. However, beginning in the second or first century B.C.E., it seems that a small cadre of Buddhists, owing allegiance to a number of *nikayas* and living in various locales around the Indian subcontinent, did begin to look upon the bodhisattva vow as something they themselves might utter; the bodhisattva path became a course of action they themselves chose to follow. Let us now move on to a discussion of the tenth and final act required of a buddha, in which we will investigate the important doctrinal and institutional ramifications of this radical development.

Act 10: From the Bodhisattva Vehicle to the Great Vehicle

It is *dharmata* that a living, breathing buddha will not attain nirvana until he predicts that somebody within his retinue will become a buddha in the future.

At the beginning of the previous section we saw King Prasenajit Kosala complain bitterly that his largesse to Shakyamuni and the *sangha* reaped little reward when compared with the great prophecy the washerwoman received in return for a single, small flame. We also saw Shakyamuni's response: a buddha will predict the future buddhahood of a donor only if that donor makes his offerings as a bodhisattva, with the express intention of attaining unexcelled, complete, and perfect awakening. Indeed, reading this story in light of the theories of the bodhisattva path just presented, we can surmise that the old poor woman was rather advanced on her journey. The fact that she received a prophecy portends that she had come to the end of her second incalculable aeon of bodhisattva practice — at least. She had met with hundreds of thousands of buddhas over millions of years. Despite her current low social status, she was a spiritual giant. How could a mere king compete?

Apropos our present inquiry, however, this story is less interesting for the competition between the old woman and the king than for the precise formulation of the washerwoman's bodhisattva vow. When one considers her words in light of Shakyamuni's *jatakas,* one finds that this vow is not unique. A Buddhist hearing the washerwoman's tale would know that her vow was modeled on that spoken by Shakyamuni himself when, as an ancient merchant, he met a buddha for the first time and began traveling the path to buddhahood. A Buddhist hearing this tale would take away the message that entry onto the bodhisattva path was not simply a matter of making gifts or practicing morality and meditation: one could become a bodhisattva only when one was willing to emulate Shakyamuni in full. For this old washerwoman, a character in a story, the ancient merchant's statement to the ancient Shakyamuni — "May I become a buddha just like you in every way" — was not only a *model of* religious practice but served as a *model for* that practice as well. The events of Shakyamuni's former lives were not just tales to remember and retell in laudatory verse, they were privileged models for how to act as a bodhisattva.

The washerwoman of this story is an advanced bodhisattva, despite her humble appearance. But although she is modeled on Shakyamuni-the-bodhisattva, the Buddhists who wrote her story — members of the Mulasarvastivada *nikaya* — would not have expected many in their group to follow her example. For the earliest *sangha,* the bodhisattva ideal was strictly retrospective in nature. For the first two centuries of Buddhism's development, a monk who sought religious perfection would not have imagined that he should emulate Shakyamuni in full. Rather, he would have pursued liberation as an arhat. He would have striven to eliminate all moral defilements (i.e., craving, hatred, and ignorance). He would have expected that as an arhat he would be free of all desires, create no additional karma, and attain nirvana once his current store of karma was emptied; he would "go out," like a flame whose fuel was completely used up. Indeed, from the little glimpses we have had of the bodhisattva path, we can see just how different the arhat ideal is from the bodhisattva. The arhat seeks nirvana, which he must necessarily accomplish alone; the bodhisattva seeks *bodhi*, awakening, for the sake of living beings. The arhat's path and goal both entail the elimination of karmic attachments to samsara through the accumulation of insight; the bodhisattva actively cultivates such attachments, for his pursuit of wisdom is not privileged over his pursuit of compassion. The arhat strives for the quickest possible liberation; the bodhisattva's liberation is deferred to the almost infinite future. The differences can be so great that a later text, *The Questions of Upali Sutra*, states: "A pure precept observed by disciples [striving for arhatship] may be a great breach of discipline for bodhisattvas, while a pure precept observed by bodhisattvas may be a great breach of discipline for disciples [striving for arhatship]."[57]

Yet, at some time around the second or first century B.C.E., developing theories about Shakyamuni's former lives as a bodhisattva began to inspire living Buddhists to pursue the inconceivably long training required for a buddha's complete perfection. This was a revolutionary development in the history of Buddhism that can only be explained in relation to a complex range of doctrinal and social factors.

An investigation of the doctrinal factors that account for the increasing importance of the bodhisattva as an active religious ideal must begin with the Second Council, and the first lasting split within the *sangha*. Earlier we saw that the division between the Sthavira *nikaya* and the Mahasamghika *nikaya* centered on a dispute over monastic rules. It seems that the so-called Elders had attempted to create a stricter definition of monastic practice by formulating rules not found in other versions of the shared *vinaya*. Separated institutionally, members of the various *nikayas* also developed contrasting doctrines about the arhat, the buddha, and the bodhisattva. When representing the arhat as a religious figure, I have so far followed the model of the Sthavira-vada and Sarvastivada *nikayas*: schools that teach that a disciple who realizes the Four Noble Truths in full is the buddha's equal vis-à-vis fundamental liberating knowledge. These two schools certainly acknowledge the buddha's superiority to the arhat in terms of the scope of his powers and virtues, but not in terms of his ultimate goal. Thus for these two schools, the attainment of arhatship is sufficient for complete liberation. Members of the Mahasamghika *nikaya*, by contrast, came to regard the arhat as imperfect. Mahadeva, an early teacher of the Mahasamghika *nikaya*, is said to have presented the arhat as fallible in four ways: (1) an arhat can have nocturnal emissions; (2) an arhat might still be ig-

---

57. *A Treasury of Mahāyāna Sūtras: Selections from the Mahāratnakūṭa Sūtra*, ed. Garma C. C. Chang (University Park: Pennsylvania State University Press, 1983), p. 268.

norant with respect to worldly matters; (3) an arhat may have doubts; and (4) an arhat relies on others for teachings, rather than realizing the truth through his own efforts. Whereas none of these four theses represents the arhat as a false saint — i.e., that arhats do not really attain nirvana — these four theses do point to a potential for fallibility on the part of the arhat. They lower the status of the arhat, creating doubt as to whether his liberation is assured.

For the members of the Mahasamghika *nikaya*, these uncertainties over the arhat's perfection were interwoven with a *docetic* doctrine of buddhahood. All Buddhists hold that buddhas possess superhuman powers and abilities beyond imagining. But the Mahasamghikas took this belief to the next level by proposing that the Shakyamuni who wandered the byways of India for forty-five years was not a real, flesh-and-blood being at all. The members of this school taught that the human being people imagined to be Shakyamuni was in truth a magical creation sent to earth by the real Shakyamuni, who was permanently engaged in meditation while dwelling in transcendent nirvana. The birth of young Siddhartha was just a deception created by the real buddha; the prince's renunciation was a deception; the bodhisattva's awakening was a sham, for he was already a buddha when he pretended to awaken; he ate food offered to him, although he did not need material nourishment; he showed himself as wracked by aging, though he is ageless; even the buddha's attainment of final nirvana was an illusion: not being born, he did not have to die. For the Mahasamghika *nikaya*, the buddha, Shakyamuni, was an omniscient, transcendental being who strategically adapted himself to worldly conventions in order to make himself available as a teacher.

Even if the Mahasamghika *nikaya* had not problematized arhatship as an ultimate religious aim, this apotheosis of the buddha raises additional questions about that goal. The Sthavira-vada and Sarvastivada *nikayas* taught that the arhat's nirvana was equal to the nirvana of the buddha: both were definitively free of samsara. By contrast, this Mahasamghika representation of buddhahood renders the nirvana of the buddha as a state qualitatively superior to the nirvana of the arhat. Relying on these doctrinal differences, some Buddhists became convinced that even if the arhat were assured of liberation, that liberation would so pale by comparison with the state of buddhahood as to be undesirable. Inspired by this doctrine of transcendental buddhahood, not interested in the limited accomplishments of the arhat, these Buddhists began to take their own first steps toward becoming bodhisattvas on the path to supreme perfection. Borrowing a metaphor from the realm of transportation, they characterized themselves as riding the vehicle of bodhisattvas *(bodhisattva-yāna)*; those who did not strive for buddhahood were characterized as riding on an alternate vehicle, that of the disciples *(śrāvaka-yāna)*.

The doctrinal developments that inspired interest in the bodhisattva as a model *for* religious action were complemented by several social factors, perhaps chief among which was the increased prominence the *bodhisattva-yana* gave to the laity. According to Étienne Lamotte, the bodhisattva ideal directly expressed the religious aspirations of Buddhism's laity. Lamotte's version of this theory is strong. As he puts it, Buddhist lay folk became increasingly unwilling to allow monks and nuns to arrogate spiritual privileges to themselves; the laity demanded equal religious rights. (Doctrinal literature from the *nikayas* generally holds, for instance, that a layman cannot attain arhatship; a layman with advanced spiritual aspirations must join the monastic *sangha*.) In Lamotte's analysis, the bodhisattva path gave characteristically lay practices (e.g., generosity) the same overall importance as characteristically monastic practices (e.g., meditation), thereby eliminating the religious hierarchy, which privileged the life of the renunciant over that of the layman.[58] The bodhisattva could be married, hold a job, raise a family, and be no less accomplished a bodhisattva. There are several problems with Lamotte's thesis in its very strong form. It is incorrect to propose that the burgeoning importance of bodhisattvahood had an "anti-clerical" bias or was essentially caused by lay religious aspirations. Indeed, the distinctions between the laity and the monks were not as clear-cut as Lamotte supposes. For instance, epigraphic evidence reveals that religious generosity was not the sole province of the laity; Buddhist monks and nuns also actively participated in the practice of giving. Yet, even if lay religious aspirations cannot be privileged as the single reason for the *bodhisattva-yana*'s success, this vehicle did certainly offer the laity greater religious prestige than that offered by the vehicle of disciples.

The development of interest in the bodhisattva as a model *for* religious action is a complex phenomenon. The layman's desire to be regarded as a religious actor in his own right — not merely as a member of the monks' "support staff" — is one factor. But an equally important development directs us to the opposite pole of social values. A second social factor that lent early impetus toward bodhisattvahood can be found within Buddhist monastic communities, among groups of renunciants who considered themselves reformers of monastic practice. These bodhisattvas saw their fellow monks as having fallen away from the original ideals of the renunciant's life. The monastic bodhisattvas accused their brethren of being hypocrites, materialists, hedonists, and sloppy accountants; they said they were lazy, unstudied in the rules of conduct, and ignorant of the joys of the true ascetic's simple life. These renunciant bodhisattvas seem to have favored the practice of living in forests, an ascetic practice that is optional for all Buddhist monks. For these bodhisattva monks, the monastic

---

58. Étienne Lamotte, "Sur la formation du Mahāyāna," in *Asiatica: Festschrift F. Weller*, ed. Johannes Schubert (Leipzig: Otto Harrassowitz, 1954), pp. 377-96.

vows and the bodhisattva's vows are not in conflict. To the contrary, articulation of the intention to become a buddha for the sake of all living beings is a marker of just how seriously one takes one's life as a monk.

Since our time line here is somewhat muddy, let me attempt to clear the water. *Jataka* stories recounting Shakyamuni's former births as a bodhisattva were probably told by the buddha himself. These stories could not have served as more than mere fables without the existence of some theoretical apparatus for explaining bodhisattvahood as a religious state, and some incipient notion of the course by which a bodhisattva becomes a buddha. In the centuries following Shakyamuni's nirvana, a variety of historical factors allowed for the competitive coexistence of numerous buddhisms. (If the near success of Devadatta's schism is any indication, even during the buddha's life Shakyamuni's buddhism was only one of several.) Within 150 years of Shakyamuni's nirvana, these various groups institutionalized their divisions in line with the *vinaya's* rules for forming separate *sanghas.* Numerous formal *nikayas* began to take shape; these *nikayas* were divided in part by practice, but also by doctrine. Maybe 250 years after Shakyamuni's nirvana, a few renunciants associated with these *nikayas,* as well as some members of the *nikayas'* local lay communities, began to turn their eyes toward a new religious goal, to speak a new vow: "May I become a buddha for the sake of living beings." They even began to conceive of themselves as riding a new vehicle. This *bodhisattva-yana* had a diffuse origin; it cannot be tied to a single doctrinal development, a single sociological group, a single *nikaya,* a single location, or a single founder. Its members were not federated through an institutional form: these bodhisattvas did *not* form a new *nikaya* unto themselves. Rather, while conserving the characteristically divided institutions of traditional Buddhist social life, these bodhisattvas became united by a common vision, for which *nikaya* membership was beside the point. They held, as one, that bodhisattvahood, and ultimately buddhahood, was the most legitimate aspiration for a follower of Shakyamuni.

The fact that the *bodhisattva-yana* developed diffusely, simultaneously in many centers, makes it difficult to speak of an "origin" per se or even of a single *bodhisattva-yana.* However, there is one aspect of religious life that these scattered bodhisattvas did share in common: a desire to learn more about how they should live, practice, and think as bodhisattvas. The old canons had little to say about the bodhisattva figure, and what information those canons did provide was overly general and retrospective. What were the bodhisattvas to do?

To understand the answer, let us recall the First Council. The rhetorical force of this quasi-historical meeting is to be found in the Buddhist's expectation that institutions that share a single orthodoxy and orthopraxy are more stable than institutions in which everybody can think and do as they please. Yet, even if such a council did take place, we know that the unity it attempted to undergird did not last long, for the earliest historical data available to us reveal the presence of competing claims to authority. Recall Lamotte's words previously quoted: "Each [*nikaya*] claims that it was its own canon which was compiled by the elders of the [first] council. [But] it would be absurd to claim that all those canons were fixed at the very beginnings of Buddhism, in a period when the [*nikayas*] had not yet been formed." To put the point bluntly, in the centuries after Shakyamuni's nirvana, members of the many *nikayas* composed new sutras and freely edited sutras already in their possession, but they presented their work as "original." The bodhisattvas were no exception to this practice. By the first century B.C.E., a new corpus of Buddhist literature was being written, a new genre that focused directly on the path of the bodhisattva, the practices of the bodhisattva, and the attainments of the bodhisattva.

The very earliest stratum of works specifically related to a *bodhisattva-yana* is lost. However, we possess texts from perhaps the second stratum, circa first century C.E. At this time the bodhisattva movement was still diffuse and numerically insignificant. But it had given itself a distinctive name: the Mahayana (the Great Vehicle). Its literary works were called Mahayana sutras, the term "sutra" implying a claim to canonical validity. The Mahayana began as a minor reform movement within the constraints of *nikaya* Buddhism. It soon developed into a new, unique, and separate form of Buddhism. One cannot overemphasize how important the rise of the Mahayana is within the history of Buddhism throughout the world. Regrettably, this chapter's treatment of the Mahayana will be too brief.

The wide range of subjects one finds in the body of early Mahayana sutras is suggestive of the diverse origins out of which the Mahayana arose. These sutras show that Mahayanists were concerned to re-form Buddhism on a number of fronts: doctrinal, sociological, soteriological, cultic, mythological. Andrew Rawlinson has given probably the best characterization of this phenomenon. He states that the Mahayana had a "multi-origin." The Mahayana began with the secret, oral transmission of the texts that came to be called Mahayana sutras. A Buddhist who wished to join a group that transmitted these teachings did not have to foreswear other formal institutional affiliations; anybody who was genuinely moved by a particular Mahayana sutra, and therefore believed it to be the valid teaching of the buddha, was welcome to join.[59] This model can accommodate the fact that certain Mahayana sutras severely criticize Buddhists who have not taken the bodhisattva vow, while other sutras contain no such polemic. This model can allow for the clearly monastic milieu

59. Andrew Rawlinson, "The Problem of the Origin of the Mahāyāna," in *Traditions in Contact and Change*, ed. Peter Slater and Donald Wiebe (Waterloo, Ont.: Wilfrid Laurier University Press, 1983), p. 169.

of some Mahayana sutras, while not being troubled by the fact that other sutras champion lay bodhisattvas. This model can allow us to accept that early Mahayanists might have engaged in a variety of competing devotional practices (e.g., worship of memorial stupas, worship of Mahayana sutras, worship of the sutras' public reciters). This model can enable us to embrace a vision of the early Mahayana as heterogeneous, with bodhisattvas even disputing other bodhisattvas in an open-ended process of decentralized change.

It is important to note that the Mahayana should not be considered a *nikaya*. The individucal *nikayas* are parallel institutions within Buddhism, in that each *nikaya* possesses a unique canon and each claims its canon was originally set by the First Council. The Mahayana does not possess a canon as such, nor does it claim that its sutras were spoken by (or even known by) the arhats at the First Council. Rather the Mahayana claimed that any Buddhist whose religious life remained wholly encompassed by teachings and practices found in the *nikaya*'s canons — and especially, any Buddhist who did not take the bodhisattva vow — was practicing a lesser form of Buddhism. The Mahayanists sometimes denigrated forms of Buddhism that did not center on the bodhisattva path by stigmatizing them as belonging to a Lesser Vehicle, the Hinayana. But even so, the Mahayana did not reject the *nikayas'* canons *in toto*. An example: Tibetan Buddhists are avid champions of Mahayana ideals, and yet their monks follow the *vinaya* of the Mulasarvastivada *nikaya*.

In fact, several early Mahayana sutras have their roots in the canons of specific *nikayas*. For instance, the Eastern Mountain *nikaya* had a text called "The Perfection of Wisdom," and there is an entire subgenre of Mahayana literature called the "Perfection of Wisdom sutras." However, as the Mahayana developed its distinctive practices, doctrines, and mythologies, Mahayanists severed explicit links between their sutra literature and that of the *nikayas*. The Mahayanists claimed their sutras *came* directly from the mouth of buddha, as Mahayana sutras. Thus the Mahayanists did not consider their form of Buddhism to be "later" or "invented." But this put them in a difficult hermeneutical position, for the Mahayanists also acknowledged (as they had to) that their sutras were unknown to the majority of Buddhists and had no place in the canonical recitations of early Buddhism. To solve this dilemma, Mahayana sutras reveal a range of doctrinal strategies for explaining how Shakyamuni could have spoken the Mahayana sutras and yet nobody but Mahayanists ever heard them. Some sutras were revealed only to advanced bodhisattvas while Shakyamuni was dwelling in heaven (remember that all Buddhists believe Shakyamuni spent time in heaven teaching Dharma). Some sutras claim to have been taught in a general assembly. It is explained that members of those assemblies who had not taken bodhisattva vows ignored these teachings, and so did not recall the discourse. Some sutras were supposedly hidden under the oceans, in the lairs of snake deities, until they were recovered. Some sutras acknowledged that they were composed by latter-day Dharma reciters. This did not invalidate those sutras, however, because Mahayana doctrine holds that Shakyamuni's birth and death were both fictive acts; the buddha remains accessible to those who can hear him. Though composed long after Shakyamuni's illusory death, these sutras were nevertheless the words of buddha.

Mahayana Buddhism's intellectual and social histories are far too rich to fit within the brief space allotted for them by this chapter. However, before concluding, I would like to offer a brief glimpse at how Mahayana sutras offered a conception of Shakyamuni-as-founder that differed radically from what I have unpacked through consideration of the ten necessary acts. Recall the formula that begins the list of ten acts: "It is the rule *(dharmata)* that living, breathing buddhas have ten essential duties. A buddha will not attain nirvana until . . ." Nirvana, here, is the buddha's goal. He must participate in samsara as a founder to attain this goal, but once a buddha has realized nirvana, he is utterly abstracted from samsara. This formula's use of the term *dharmata* indicates that every individual buddha's career is subordinated to a natural and necessary order. A "buddha" whose life does not conform to this order is not truly a buddha, and will not truly gain nirvana.

For the Mahayana, a buddha trains over an immeasurably long career because buddhahood is immeasurable in scope. Every buddha's grandeur is unbounded in its infinitude. It is impossible that any buddha could actually be subject to an abstract, external principle of order like *dharmata*. To the contrary, the buddhas invent the very notion that there is a natural and proper way for a buddha to live his life. Thus the Mahayana reenvisions Shakyamuni's earthly career. His every action, from birth to death, is said to have been a scripted fiction intended to inspire the unenlightened to pursue the religious path. Shakyamuni's life followed certain patterns, not because it had to, but because the buddha created the expectation that a buddha would live a certain paradigmatic life. In fact, Shakyamuni gained awakening in the unimaginable past. The Mahayana's *Lotus Sutra* puts this point very plainly: "If this universe was reduced to atoms, and if each atom was a cosmic age, the time since my achievement of buddhahood would exceed even this. . . . My life span is an innumerable number of incalculable aeons, ever enduring, never perishing."[60] Although Shakyamuni takes the explicit form of a buddha only sometimes, he is perpetually engaged in striving to demonstrate the Dharma. This same sutra explains that Shakyamuni strategically refrains

---

60. *Scripture of the Lotus Blossom of the Fine Dharma (The Lotus Sūtra)*, trans. Leon Hurvitz (New York: Columbia University Press, 1976), pp. 238-39.

from taking an overt form as buddha too often or for too long: if people were aware that he is both immortal and omnipresent, they would lose the impetus to practice themselves. Knowing that an infinitely wise, infinitely powerful, and infinitely compassionate buddha was always available to satisfy their wants, beings would allow themselves to become spiritual infants. On this view, Shakyamuni's actions as a terrestrial religious founder are only a very small part of his everlasting involvement in the work of training beings toward perfection.

Given the infinitude of buddhahood, the Mahayana found it necessary to explain how there could be more than one buddha. The answer is brilliant, simple, and consonant with the Mahayana's rhetoric of apotheosis. We have seen that the Buddhist imagination is highly spatial. Living beings inhabit a cosmo-moral universe in which karma determines the environment within which an individual lives and acts; the Wheel of Becoming (discussed above, in relation to the first act) offers a generalized map of the universe at the same time that it demonstrates the benefits of good karma and the horrors of bad. This cosmological imagination became an important factor in the Mahayanist conception of buddhahood. The bodhisattva's training, in its evolved Mahayana formulation, is not to be looked upon simply as an incredibly long period during which a bodhisattva develops wisdom and compassion. Rather, this path became conceptualized in terms of world creation. Over the course of countless aeons, the bodhisattva creates a "buddha-field," a particular universe within which he will be the sole buddha and over which he will wield absolute control. Thus the Mahayana's cosmology envisions a multiverse filled with an ever expanding number of buddha-fields. Every time a bodhisattva becomes a buddha, a new buddha-field pops into existence. In an important sense the Mahayana's buddha is not merely immortal and omnipresent within his buddha-field, he is also the creator "god" of his very own universe.

Some buddhas (e.g., Amitabha, presented at this chapter's beginning) create buddha-fields in which only the spiritual elite are born. Every being in Amitabha's buddha-field, named Sukhavati (the Land of Bliss), is close to complete perfection. According to the *Longer Land of Bliss Sutra*, when Amitabha Buddha was still just a bodhisattva, he set out to create the most perfect buddha-field that any buddha had ever created. He "assembled . . . a perfect buddha-field that was by far much superior to, nobler, more exalted, and more immeasurable than all the perfect arrays of wondrous qualities and ornaments from the buddha-fields of eighty-one hundred thousand million trillion buddhas."[61] Among the perfections of Amitabha's Land of Bliss: "All the living

---

61. Luis O. Gómez, *The Land of Bliss: The Paradise of the Buddha of Measureless Light* (Honolulu: University of Hawaii Press, 1996), p. 68.

beings who are reborn in [his] buddha-field [are] only one more birth away from unsurpassable, perfect, full awakening,"[62] unless they consciously postpone their full awakening out of compassion for others.

The buddha-field is the cosmological materialization of its creator's perfection. Amitabha wanted his buddha-field to directly reflect his own perfection to the highest degree. Does this mean that Amitabha is a more perfect buddha than Shakyamuni? Just look around you: Shakyamuni's buddha-field, our world, seems so very imperfect. How do Buddhists explain this imperfection? What is their theodicy? Buddha-fields are categorized as either pure, impure, or mixed. While Amitabha's Land of Bliss is the epitome of a pure buddha-field, Shakyamuni's world (called the Saha-loka) is a prime example of an impure buddha-field. Paradoxically, the Saha-loka's seeming imperfection was taken to illustrate Shakyamuni's personal greatness rather than his failings. It is easy to run a universe (like that of Amitabha) in which all the beings are dedicated to Dharma. But Shakyamuni created a buddha-field dedicated to the training of imperfect beings, many of whom have no interest in Dharma. Don't we have greater regard for the teacher who inspires a room of D students to earn A's than for the teacher of an honors class whose students eagerly meet their teacher's already high expectations? The seeming imperfections of our world are signs of the exceeding perfection of Shakyamuni's compassion. This is explained by the *White Lotus of Compassion Sutra*: "Bodhisattvas bring forth a pure buddha-field through the power of their vows; bodhisattvas bring forth an impure buddha-field through the power of their vows. A bodhisattva, a great being, brings forth an imperfect buddha-field because he possesses great compassion."[63] And still other Mahayana sutras describe Shakyamuni as being praised by other buddhas precisely because he dedicated his buddhahood to training the spiritually deficient. In the *Shorter Land of Bliss Sutra*, Shakyamuni says,

> Just as I at present here extol the inconceivable wondrous qualities of other buddhas, blessed ones, so in the same manner, all those other buddhas, blessed ones, extol these inconceivable wondrous qualities of mine, saying: "A most difficult task has been accomplished by the blessed one, Śākyamuni, the sage of the Śākyas, the monarch of the Śākyas. After he awakened to unsurpassable, perfect, and full awakening in this Saha world, he taught a Dharma that the whole world was reluctant to accept, at a time when the cosmic age was in a period of decay, when living beings were in a period of decay,

62. Gómez, pp. 71-72.

63. *Karuṇāpuṇḍarīka: The White Lotus of Compassion*, ed. Isshi Yamada (New Delhi: Heritage Publishers, 1989), 2:51-52.

when views and opinions corrupted human beings, when the length of human life had declined, when the afflictions vitiated human beings."[64]

This description of Shakyamuni brings us full circle back to the washerwoman-bodhisattva. Like the ancient merchant Shakyamuni once was, the washerwoman too vowed to become a buddha at a time in which human beings live for a mere one hundred years. This is simply shorthand for characterizing that world, and ours, as one of decay, corruption, and affliction. Taken together, the ninth and tenth acts required of a living buddha — that he inspire one member of his congregation to take a bodhisattva vow, and that he predict the future buddhahood of one member of his congregation — point to the high value all Buddhists placed on the bodhisattva as a religious figure. For all Buddhists the bodhisattva is the spiritual hero par excellence. We have also seen, however, that whereas the Buddhism of the *nikayas* regarded bodhisattvahood as one of numerous possible modalities within which to be a Buddhist, the Mahayana developed a distinct set of doctrines, myths, and practices based on the expectation that bodhisattvahood was the only truly legitimate course for a Buddhist to follow. It is not proper, however, to speak of Mahayana Buddhism as a radical transformation of Buddhism *away* from its "original" roots. I hope that, throughout this chapter, I have demonstrated the intellectual fallacies involved in any attempt to reconstruct the history of Buddhism along such essentialist lines. One can neither posit an essentially pure Buddhism to be found at this religion's origin nor examine its historical development in light of a teleological model. The Mahayana was neither a "necessary" development nor a faulty "corruption." Certainly the rise of the Mahayana represents a radical reform within Buddhism, but one that the scholar can see as having strong roots in a multiplicity of the parallel traditions that hearken to Shakyamuni as their founder.

Glossary of Sanskrit Terms, Names, and Titles

abhidharma	the higher teaching; systematic recapitulation of doctrine included as one of the three baskets of the Dharma
abhijñā	superhuman powers attained through meditative techniques
ahiṃsā	nonharm; the central principle of Buddhist ethics is to harm neither oneself nor others

64. Gómez, p. 21.

Ājīvika	a type of *shramana* that would have competed with the Buddhists for disciples, alms, and renown
Amitābha	a buddha best known for his vow to create a perfect buddha-field, named Sukhavati, the Land of Bliss; Amitabha is especially popular in East Asia
Ānanda	the buddha's personal attendant and closest friend
Anāthapiṇḍada	the most renowned of Shakyamuni's lay followers
anātman	no-Self; the doctrine that there is no aspect of a person that is permanent or unchanging
Anavatapta	a mythological lake located in the Himalaya Mountains
anitya	impermanence
arhat	a Buddhist saint; one who has escaped from desire
Aśoka	a king who ruled much of the Indian subcontinent circa 268-233 B.C.E. Ashoka was a great patron of Buddhism, and used his royal power to help spread the Dharma
Aśvaghoṣa	second century C.E. author of the *Acts of the Buddha,* an epic retelling of Shakyamuni's early life
ātman	self or soul
avaivartika	the stage in a bodhisattva's training in which it will be impossible for him to ever again regress from progress toward buddhahood; an *avaivartika* bodhisattva is *certain* that he will become a buddha
avidyā	ignorance
bhāvanā	mental cultivation or meditation
bhikṣu	a Buddhist monk
bhikṣu-saṅgha	the community of Buddhist monks
Bodh Gaya	the place in which Shakyamuni Buddha achieved enlightenment
bodhi	enlightenment
bodhisattva	a being who is attached to *bodhi;* a buddha in training
bodhisattva-yāna	the vehicle of the bodhisattvas; a form of Buddhism that focuses on development of the special practices and insights of bodhisattvas, with buddhahood as the ultimate goal
Brahmā	a class of powerful gods
brahmin	a Hindu priest
buddha-field	a universe created by a buddha during his training as a bodhisattva; a buddha is responsible for the spiritual progress of all the beings within his buddha-field

Devadatta	Shakyamuni's cousin and occasional nemesis
Dharma	fundamental reality; the basic orderliness of the cosmos; the religion taught by a buddha
Dharmacakrapravartana Sūtra	The *Sutra Which Turns the Wheel of Law,* Shakyamuni's first sutra
dharmatā	the way things really are; the natural order
dhyāna	a meditative concentration
Dīpaṅkara	the former buddha who first prophesied that the bodhisattva Megha would become a buddha named Shakyamuni
Divyāvadāna	*Divine Stories;* a collection of stories associated with Shakyamuni's life, compiled by Buddhists belonging to the Mulasarvastivada *nikaya*
duḥkha	unsatisfactoriness and the associated suffering; the First Noble Truth
Eight-Limbed Path	the Fourth Noble Truth: correct view, correct intention, correct speech, correct action, correct livelihood, correct effort, correct mindfulness, correct concentration
First Council	a legendary meeting held soon after Shakyamuni's final nirvana in which his words were recalled, repeated, and arranged into three baskets: the sutras, *vinaya,* and *abhidharma*
four assemblies	monks, nuns, laymen, and laywomen
gandhakuṭī	the "perfumed chamber" in which Shakyamuni dwelled
Gotama	the patronym of Shakyamuni Buddha's clan
Hīnayāna	the "Lesser Vehicle," a pejorative epithet used by members of the Mahayana for those Buddhists who do not identify their religious values with the bodhisattva ideal
incalculable aeon	10^{59} years
jātaka	tales told of past lives, especially those of the buddha
Kālachakra	a buddha worshiped within Tibetan Buddhism
Kapilavastu	Shakyamuni Buddha's birthplace
karma	action
Kāśyapa	a buddha who is believed to have lived and taught on earth millions of years in the past
Konākamana	a buddha who is believed to have lived and taught on earth millions of years in the past
Kuśinagara	the site of Shakyamuni's attainment of complete and final nirvana

Mahākāśyapa	one of Shakyamuni's important disciples; the leader of the First Council and speaker of the *abhidharma-pitaka*
Mahāmāyā	Shakyamuni's mother
mahāparinirvāṇa	nirvana that is complete in all its parts and finally attained at "death"; also known as "nirvana without any residue"
Mahāsāṃghika	"the Great Assembly," the majority faction at the Second Council
Mahāvastu	*The Great Subject,* a text dedicated to Shakyamuni's sacred biography
Mahāyāna	the Great Vehicle
Maitreya	the next buddha to be born on earth
Māra	the personification of death; the lord over the realm of desire
Maudgalyāyana	one of Shakyamuni's two chief disciples, known for his magical abilities
Mūlasarvāstivāda	the *nikaya* responsible for the doctrine that a buddha must perform ten actions before he can attain final nirvana; we know of this *nikaya*'s stories through two Sanskrit works: the Mulasarvastivada *vinaya* and the *Divyavadana*
nikāya	a sect of early Buddhism
nirodha	cessation; the Third Noble Truth
pañcaśīla	the five moral precepts typically followed by the Buddhist laity: not to kill, not to steal, not to lie, not to perform sexual misconduct, not to use intoxicants
prātihārya	miracle, especially used for miracles performed in order to attract people to the Buddhist religion
prātimokṣa	an abbreviation of the Buddhist monastic rule, recited fortnightly
pratītyasamutpāda	codependent origination
Rāhula	Shakyamuni Buddha's son
Sahā-loka	the name of Shakyamuni's buddha-field
Śākyamuni	"the sage of the Shakyas," the buddha of the current age
Sāṃkāśya	the town near which Shakyamuni is reputed to have descended from heaven, accompanied by a retinue of gods
saṃsāra	the realm of rebirth
saṅgha	the community of Buddhist monks and nuns

Śāriputra	one of Shakyamuni's two chief disciples; nicknamed the General of the Dharma, he was known for his wisdom
Sarnath	the village near which Shakyamuni gave the teaching in which he turned the Wheel of Law for the first time
Sarvāstivāda	one of the *nikayas;* its hallmark teaching is that the past, present, and future all exist simultaneously
Second Council	a council that was held approximately one hundred years after Shakyamuni's death; the reasons for this council are unclear, but this gathering led to a split within the *sangha* between the Mahasamghika and Sthavira-vada *nikayas*
Siddhārtha	Shakyamuni's given name, sometimes rendered Sarvarthasiddha
sīmā	the boundary line that demarcates a monastic "parish"
six perfections	the principal values associated with a bodhisattva's training: generosity, morality, patience, energy, concentration, wisdom
skandha	aggregate; Buddhist doctrine analyzes the "I" into five *skandhas:* matter, sensations, perceptions, karmic constituents, consciousness, each of which is thought to be in a constant state of flux
śramaṇa	a "striver"; somebody who leaves his home and family in pursuit of liberative truth
śrāvakayāna	the vehicle of the disciples; a form of Buddhism that focuses on direct teachings from Shakyamuni, with arhatship as its highest goal
Śrāvasti	the town near which Shakyamuni defeated six rivals in a magic contest
Sthavira-vāda	the School of the Elders; also known as Theravada
stūpa	a memorial to a holy man, often containing a bodily relic
Śuddhodana	Shakyamuni Buddha's father
Sugata	the "Well-Gone One," an epithet of buddha
Sukhāvatī	the "Land of Bliss"; the perfect buddha-field created by Amitabha during his training as a bodhisattva
sūtra	a sermon or speech given by a buddha
sūtra-piṭaka	the basket of sutras within a Buddhist canon
tathāgata	the "Thus-Come One," an epithet of buddha

Trāyastriṃśa	heaven of the thirty-three gods; Indra is the king over this heaven, in which Shakyamuni's mother Mahamaya was born after her early death
tṛṣṇa	thirst, especially the thirst for continuing existence
Tuṣita	the heaven ruled over by Maitreya, the bodhisattva who is destined to be the next terrestrial buddha
Upagu	an Ajivika; a renunciant Shakyamuni met soon after he attained buddhahood, who demonstrated no interest in Shakyamuni's Dharma
Upāli	a disciple of Shakyamuni, particularly renowned for his practice of the *vinaya;* he is reputed to have recited the basket of *vinaya* at the First Council
upāya-kauśalya	skill-in-means; the technique a buddha uses to bring others to a realization of Dharma
Vasubandhu	fifth century C.E. author of the *Compendium of Metaphysics*
vinaya	the rules of monastic life
vinaya-piṭaka	the collection of *vinaya* texts within a Buddhist canon
Vipaśyin	a buddha who is believed to have lived and taught on earth millions of years in the past
Viśvaṃtara	Shakyamuni's name during his penultimate life as a human being; as Vishvantara, the bodhisattva was renowned for his generosity

Confucius

MARK CSIKSZENTMIHALYI

For many people in the modern West, the image of ancient China conjured up by the name Confucius is the very definition of an eternal but static traditional society. There the rhythms of life were constant, lacking both conflict and innovation, regulated by the Edenic wisdom of the sage. People were a cross between the peasants of Pearl S. Buck's *Good Earth* and the monks of James Hilton's *Lost Horizon*. Their lives were simple, pastoral, and solidified in aspic.

While in many ways a charming tableau, this "Blue Willow pattern" China is little more than chinoiserie. Originally produced at the start of the sixteenth century to suit the tastes of philosophers and missionaries searching for a universal natural theology, it needed little modification to meet the needs of foreign governments and trading companies eager to justify their influence in China in the nineteenth century. These groups did not see Confucius as a character in the tableau, but rather credited him with its design. Epiphanius Wilson (1845-1916) explained the influence of the designer in this way: "the flat mediocrity of his character and his teachings has been stamped forever upon a people who, while they are kind, gentle, forbearing, and full of family piety, are palpably lacking . . . in any religious feeling, generally so-called."[1] Outsiders held Confucius responsible not only for the lack of religious feeling that justified attempts to convert the Chinese, but also for the benevolent docility that invited

---

1. From the introduction to Wilson's 1900 translation entitled *The Wisdom of Confucius* (reprint, New York: Crown, 1982), p. 5.

The author would like to thank Winston Davis, Philip J. Ivanhoe, Michael McClymond, David Noel Freedman, and Cameron Richardson for their comments on an earlier draft of this chapter.

the intervention of solicitous foreign powers. Wilson does not mention how Confucius could "stamp" these characteristics on so many people for so long, yet this image of an entire race having been transformed by the "mediocre" founding figure of Confucius has persisted into the present. From caricatures of "heathen Chinese" to the avuncular platitudes mouthed by Swedish actor Warner Oland as the detective Charlie Chan in a series of 1930s movies, what some Westerners saw as essential Chinese characteristics were continually transposed into effects of the mysteriously universal influence of Confucius.[2] Although this image of Confucius and the pattern he created did not come out of thin air, it was to a large extent constructed to match the expectations of those who consumed it.

That modern Western representations of Confucius are in part based on past stereotypes is not especially controversial. Much more complex is the question of what to do about it, because as difficult as dismantling this image is, it is even more difficult to agree on a replacement. One possibility is to assume that an indigenous portrait of Confucius will be more accurate, and this chapter begins by examining a modern Chinese account of the life of Confucius. Yet the creation of images of ancient China in the West since the sixteenth century has simply been a continuation of an even more venerable industry of constructing such images in China, one that has continued into the present. Rival constructions of Confucius have arisen in preimperial, imperial, and modern China, and, as we will see below, the Chinese viewed Confucius in drastically different ways at different times. An entry on Confucius in a major dictionary published in the People's Republic of China in 1965, for example, notes that the Confucian idea of benevolence was "in reality geared toward safeguarding the order of the aristocratic class" and that China's "feudal governors" made Confucius into an idol.[3] Again Confucius gets credit as the designer of the pattern of ancient China, but the compilers of this dictionary portray him as a feudal ideologue in the service of the slave-owning class. After twenty-five hundred years, it appears that no culture or group enjoys an unambiguous claim to knowing who the sage really was.

The question, "Who was Confucius?" has been and will continue to be an important one both inside and outside East Asia. Today, as Confucianism is regaining status in mainland China and is seen as a potential challenge to democracy by some Americans, older images of Confucius — as a philosopher and

2. After Oland's death in 1938, he was replaced by the American actor Sidney Toler. The "sayings" mouthed by these actors, such as "Grain of sand in eye may hide mountain" (from the 1935 *Charlie Chan in Paris*), spawned the still common idea that Chinese wisdom comes in the form of trite and ungrammatical maxims.

3. *Sea of Words (Cihai)* dictionary (1965), p. 2127.

teacher, a ritual specialist, a religious prophet, and an uncrowned king — are selectively invoked to legitimate or attack new versions of the tradition. The fact that many of these images disagree with each other or recast Confucius in the mold of exemplary figures from other traditions should not come as a surprise, because similar processes have been going on for millennia. As the noted historian Gu Jiegang once commented: "Each era has its own Confucius, and moreover, each era has various disparate types of Confucius."[4] In the same way, the development of Confucianism will continue to be influenced by portrayals of Confucius in the next millennium.

Because of this link between the history of the man and the future character of the tradition, the quest for a "historical Confucius" has been a constant throughout most of Chinese history. This chapter will concern itself as much with that quest as with Confucius himself because, at the end of the day, the two may never really be separated. It will consist of two main parts, an exploration of the formation of the narrative of Confucius's life, followed by a look at the way that narrative both informed and was changed by Confucian traditions.

Tracing the origins of the stories regarding Confucius is no simple task. After introducing a modern version of his biography, we will compare its content to its earliest precursor, which dates to the end of the second century B.C.E. Yet even studying the earliest biography would not be sufficient introduction to the early development of the story of Confucius, because such biographies have never been the only source for information about his life. Because Confucius has traditionally been seen as the compiler of a set of canonical texts, these texts provide a source for information about Confucius that was considered in some ways more telling than summaries of the events of his life. Therefore biographical accounts have always been read in counterpoint with the texts attributed to him, either as author or editor, especially the *Analects* (in Chinese, *Lunyu*) and the *Spring and Autumn (Chunqiu)*. Historically, these canonical sources were mined for details about the teachings and life of Confucius, and as a result the biography of Confucius existed in a dialectical tension with the texts of the canon: the understanding of Confucius's life was strongly informed by these canonical texts, while biographical details changed the way the texts of the canon were interpreted. Therefore the chapter continues by examining the picture of Confucius implicit in the *Analects* and the *Spring and Autumn* traditions. We will see how these texts, for reasons connected with the circumstances of their composition, paint two very different pictures of the sage: a ritualist and teacher, and a prophet and "uncrowned king."

---

4. Laurence A. Schneider, trans., "A Translation of Ku Chieh-kang's Essay 'The Confucius of the Spring and Autumn Era and the Confucius of the Han Era,'" *Phi Theta Papers* (1965): 105-47, p. 110.

After the arrival of Buddhism in the first century c.e., the Chinese began to reimagine Confucius as a religious founder in light of the example of the Buddha. Once those who identified themselves as members of the traditions begun by Confucius began to self-consciously differentiate themselves from members of other traditions that they perceived to be of the same type, the quest for a historical Confucius was undertaken alongside a similar inquiry into the origins of their Confucian traditions. In short, the character of the tradition began to influence the understanding of the man. We will look closely at two important readings of Confucius, the post-Buddhist Confucianism of Zhu Xi (1130-1200) and the reading of Confucius in light of the example of Christ by Kang Youwei (1858-1927). In important ways the encounter with foreign religions forced the Chinese to reconceptualize their relationship with Confucius and view him as the intentional creator of a quasi-religious movement.

Once Confucianism began to be conceptualized as similar to other religious traditions, defining the relationship between the various forms of Confucianism and their supposed founder became increasingly important. For this reason the chapter will conclude with an examination of Confucius in a comparative context by exploring the reception of Confucius by twentieth-century sociologists like Max Weber (1864-1920), and will ask the question: How should the sage be compared to founders of other religious traditions? If Confucius were simply the creator of a timeless traditional pattern for Chinese society, then this question would be relatively simple to answer. Given the diversity of historical images and appropriations of Confucius, however, any answer to that question must take this wide range of representations into account.

A Modern Account of the Life of Confucius

> better gift can no man make to a nation
> than the sense of Kung fu Tseu
> who was called Chung Ni
> nor in historiography nor in making anthologies
> Ezra Pound, *Canto* LXXVI (1948)[5]

We begin the search for a less stereotyped Confucius with a representative account of his life from a standard Chinese reference source, the popular *Word Source (Ciyuan)* dictionary. Besides the useful details it provides, there are two important aspects of this entry that are worth noting at the outset. First, it nowhere expresses doubt about the reliability of any of the data it provides. This is

---

5. Ezra Pound, *The Cantos* (New York: New Directions, 1973), p. 454.

revealing, since it will become clear later that many points in the account are either of doubtful authenticity or the subject of long-standing historical debates. The entry also provides a good introduction to many traditional sources for information about Confucius, since it draws on most of them at different points to supply different types of detail. Second, the entry mostly cleaves to one side of what we will see is a major interpretive divide between depictions of Confucius as an apolitical instructor in self-cultivation through ritual and a prophetic figure with political concerns. The *Word Source*'s portrayal of Confucius is of a teacher and an official, but one who was limited in the latter capacity by both his high principles and the shortsightedness of the rulers of his day. The following modern account consists of segments of the basic account of the life of Confucius from the *Word Source*, followed by explanatory paragraphs that trace the information to its origins in Chinese historical sources.

Confucius lived from 551 to 479 B.C.E.[6]

This dates Confucius to the later days of the Zhou (trad. 1027-221 B.C.E.), the classical period of Chinese history. Through the efforts of King Wu and his younger brother Dan, known as the Duke of Zhou, the Zhou clan was able to break the hold of the Shang (trad. 1523-1027 B.C.E.) and establish themselves as the rulers of a set of principalities. While many call the Shang and Zhou China's first historical dynasties, they were much less economically centralized or culturally homogeneous than later dynasties beginning with the Qin (221-202 B.C.E.). This was especially the case for the Zhou after the incursions of western border nations forced the movement of the capital east from Hao to Luoyang, and Zhou control over their principalities significantly decreased. It is against the politically decentralized background of what has become known as the Eastern Zhou period (771-221 B.C.E.) that a set of newly independent states competed for authority.

One of these states was Lu, originally the area where King Wu had enfeoffed the Duke of Zhou. The Duke of Zhou spent little time there because of his role as regent following the death of his brother, but the Duke of Zhou's son Boqin, known as the Duke of Lu, ruled the state for forty-six years. Most of what we know about the later history of the state of Lu comes from a terse chronicle traditionally believed to have been compiled by Confucius. The *Spring and Autumn* (*Chunqiu*, a synecdoche for its year-by-year structure) begins with the reign of Duke Yin in 722 B.C.E. and proceeds chronologically, ending with the four dukes whose reigns overlapped with the life of Confucius:

---

6. The dictionary *Word Source* (*Ciyuan*) has a long publishing history, but this translation is based on the Taibei Yuanliu edition of 1988, p. 421.

Xiang (r. 572-542 B.C.E.), Zhao (r. 541-510 B.C.E.), Ding (r. 509-495 B.C.E.), and Ai (r. 494-468 B.C.E.). Recording intrigues, wars, treaties, and speeches, this chronicle paints a picture of a period of turmoil, during which the rulers of the different states were in a constant competition for political and strategic advantage. During the life of Confucius, the dukes of Lu shared power with, and were occasionally eclipsed by, their own chancellors drawn from the collateral Ji line. In his lifetime Confucius repeatedly clashed with members of the Ji clan, and his disapproval of their usurpation of the rightful power of the dukes of Lu is an important theme in writings attributed to him.

The traditional dates for the life of Confucius appear first in historical materials that became attached to the *Spring and Autumn* chronicle at least several centuries after his death. The *Spring and Autumn* exists in three versions, each attached to one of three commentaries: the Zuo, Gongyang, and Guliang. While the material in the commentaries is of indefinite age, all three were in circulation during the first century B.C.E. The dates for the birth and death of Confucius are recorded in these commentaries. The Gongyang and Guliang commentaries record his birth, accompanied by auspicious eclipses, in 551 B.C.E. The Zuo commentary records the death of Confucius in 479 B.C.E.[7] These records are the basis for the dates given in the dictionary entry.

> *His name was Kong Qiu, and his courtesy name was Zhong Ni. Originally from the county of Zou, his family was old nobility from the state of Song, descended from the ruling clan of the Shang Dynasty.*

Jesuit missionaries coined the word "Confucius" as a Latin version of "Kong fuzi," a combination of the surname Kong and the honorific suffix *fuzi*. The surname Kong was inherited from his father, and the name Qiu, or "Hill," comes from the fact that his forehead had an indentation, according to one early tradition. His "courtesy" name, a more personal second name, combines "Zhong," a prefix for second-born children, and "Ni," the name of a hill where his parents were reputed to have made offerings before his birth.

---

7. The Zuo commentary extends to 468 B.C.E., while the Gongyang and the Guliang commentaries both extend to 480 B.C.E. That the Zuo version covers events that postdate the traditional death of Confucius was explained by the early commentator Du Yu (222-84 C.E.) as the result of the master's disciples' completion of his work on the basis of the archives of Lu. See his commentary following the entry on the death of Confucius, in his *Corrected Meaning of the Zuo Commentary to the Spring and Autumn (Chunqiu Zuozhuan zhengyi)*, in Ruan Yuan, *Commentary and Subcommentary to the Thirteen Classics (Shisanjing zhushu)* (Beijing: Zhonghua, 1979), p. 2177. A good English introduction to this text is Burton Watson, trans., *The Tso Chuan: Selections from China's Oldest Narrative History* (New York: Columbia University Press, 1989).

Early sources relate that the sage came from a good family that had fallen on hard times. This idea that Confucius came from faded nobility dovetails with the common trope that at the time of his birth, the nouveaux riches and military strongmen of the Eastern Zhou were elbowing out the hereditary aristocracy. In a rare autobiographical comment in the *Analects,* the central early collection of anecdotes about the sage, Confucius explains his wide abilities in terms of his family's poverty: "When I was young, I was poor, and so I am able in many minor matters."[8]

Further adding to his hardship was the fact that his father, "Third-born" Lianghe, died while Confucius was a young child. Although Lianghe and his family lived in the village of Zou (modern Qufu in Shandong Province) in the state of Lu, his grandfather Fangshu had come from the state of Song to the southwest. Some sources connect the Kong family's exile in Lu with the defeat of Song by the state of Zheng and Chu recorded in the *Spring and Autumn* entry for 607 B.C.E. Others connect the Kong family with the elder brother of Duke Li of Song (r. 858-831 B.C.E.), a claim made in a speech recorded in the Zuo commentary to the *Spring and Autumn.* This latter tradition holds that an eighth century B.C.E. ancestor of Confucius served as a minister in Song, and his contemporaries celebrated this ancestor for his abject self-deprecation.[9] Regardless of the exact identity of his Song ancestors, the exile of Confucius's great-grandfather is a theme continually recapitulated in his own later life.

These details about Confucius's name and family do not derive from the *Spring and Autumn* or its commentaries, but from the writing of Sima Qian (ca. 145–ca. 86 B.C.E.), the compiler of the prototype for historical writing in East Asia, the *Historical Record (Shiji).* Sima Qian weighed many different sources against each other, tried to reconcile their implicit chronologies, and assembled those he thought reliable. The influence of his *Historical Record* is such that this section of the modern entry accepts its conclusions almost verbatim.

---

8. References to the *Analects* utilize the numbering system of D. C. Lau, *Confucius: "The Analects"* (Harmondsworth: Penguin Books, 1979), and, where there are textual complications, reference will be made to Cheng Shude, *Collected Explanations of the "Analects" (Lunyü jishi),* 4 vols. (Beijing: Zhonghua, 1990). This passage is from *Analects* 9.6, and the Chinese text may be found in Cheng, vol. 2, p. 583. Confucius goes on to point out that reaching moral perfection does not require such a background. To find the context for this and other quotations from the *Analects,* Lau's is a good English translation (for *Analects* 9.6, see p. 97).

9. An inscription on a bronze tripod attributed to this ancestor recorded his attitude at the time of each of three successive official appointments: "At the first I bowed my head, at the second I bowed at the waist, and at the third I prostrated myself." See the *Corrected Meaning of the Zuo Commentary to the Spring and Autumn,* in Ruan, p. 2051.

> *In the state of Lu, Confucius held various minor offices like Assistant in the Rites (charged with directing ceremonies), Foodstuffs Scribe (managing provisions), and Scribe in the Field (managing animals).*

This section of the *Word Source* dictionary entry illustrates the tradition that Confucius was not appreciated by the rulers of his day. This information also comes from the *Historical Record* and makes the point that even as historically important a personage as Confucius was able to occupy only minor offices in his own state. These offices might best be characterized as technical or clerical, calling on talents that Confucius himself noted a person did not require to reach moral perfection. Specific information about Confucius's official service appears in two different early texts. The idea that he served as Assistant in the Rites *(Xiangli)* comes from an entry in the Zuo commentary to the *Spring and Autumn* for 535 B.C.E. According to this story, a minister of Lu named Master Meng Xi was on his deathbed and could not act as Assistant in the Rites, and so sent his successor to study the rites with the young Confucius.[10] That Confucius served in the other two offices is a tradition that comes from the *Mencius (Mengzi)*, a text in many ways like the *Analects* but centered on a figure generally regarded as the most important early developer of Confucius's thought, Mencius (trad. 372-289 B.C.E.). As Foodstuffs Scribe *(Weili)* and Scribe in the Field *(Chengtian)*, Confucius was involved with "managing the scribes that kept the books at the granary" and was "overseer of those who bring the six kinds of domestic animal to pasture," according to an early commentator to the *Mencius*.[11] As we will see, another early tradition recounts Confucius reaching the highest ministerial position, that of chancellor *(Xiang)* of Lu, but that tradition is omitted in the *Word Source* dictionary entry. The identification of the offices in which Confucius served continues to be a source of controversy not only because of differences among the earliest accounts, but also because some have interpreted his lack of official advancement as proof of the inability of Lu's benighted rulers to recognize merit. For these people, accepting Confucius's service in higher office would have raised the question: If some of his merits were recognized, why did he not go on to wield even more authority?

10. *Corrected Meaning of the Zuo Commentary to the Spring and Autumn*, in Ruan, p. 2051, repeated in Sima Qian, *Historical Record (Shiji)* (Beijing: Zhonghua, 1959), 47.1907-8.

11. The six domestic animals are horses, cattle, sheep, pigs, dogs, and chickens. The commentator on the *Mencius* who explained these terms was Zhao Qi (d. 201 C.E.). See Yang Bojun, *Explanation and Commentary of the "Mencius" (Mengzi shizhu)* (Beijing: Zhonghua, 1984), p. 244. A good English translation of the *Mencius* is D. C. Lau, *Mencius* (Harmondsworth: Penguin Books, 1970) (see his p. 155 for Lau's translation of this passage).

That Confucius held such minor offices and executed his duties without rancor serves to illustrate an essential aspect of his views on government service. This is the point that Mencius derived from the sage's work as a humble overseer. He writes that when serving as Foodstuffs Scribe, Confucius said: "It is just a matter of keeping the supply numbers correct." As Scribe in the Field, Confucius said: "It is just a matter of the cattle and sheep growing up strong and healthy." Mencius uses the example of Confucius to argue that all officials must strive to fulfill their job descriptions, but limit themselves to those descriptions. He concludes that it is shameful "for a person to be established at court and not put the Way into effect."[12] The implicit argument is that Confucius understood what holding petty offices required, and also what it meant to put the Way into practice. Since Confucius could apply his understanding in the former case, how much more would he have excelled in a position of greater authority.

> Under Duke Ding of Lu, he served as Steward of Zhongdu and as Director against Brigands, but because he was dissatisfied with the policies carried out by Ji Huanzi, he left and made a circuit of the feudal states of Wei, Song, Chen, Cai, and Chu. None of their rulers made use of him, and he returned to die in the state of Lu.

The motif that Confucius made a circuit of the various states but was not utilized by their rulers is central to the story of his life. On one hand, it shows that Confucius was willing to put good government into effect in any state whose ruler was willing to accept his counsel. Confucius's loyalty was neither to his family's home state of Song nor to his birthplace in Lu, but rather to the principles behind the program he tried to set up. On the other hand, it also emphasizes the degree to which he was constrained and frustrated by the high standards that prompted him to leave any state whose ruler refused to adopt them. Confucius even had to leave the state of a sympathetic ruler when the chancellor Ji Huanzi acted improperly. The pathos of this image of frustrated idealism has appealed to officials throughout Chinese history.

To the list of occupations held by Confucius are added Director against Brigands *(Sikou)* of Lu and steward *(Zai)* of the district of Zhongdu. These rather different offices are the subject of a disagreement in the early sources. The Zuo commentary to the *Spring and Autumn* records that Confucius was in

---

12. The term "Way" *(dao)* as used by Confucius and Mencius is a normative concept that refers to the best process for living or governing. The same term is adopted by some Taoists as shorthand for the unitary phenomenon behind all processes. For this passage in *Mencius,* see Yang, p. 243.

the former office when Duke Ding of Lu began his reign in 509 B.C.E., but the *Historical Record* records that he was appointed to the latter office by Duke Ding and only later assumed the former office. The most likely explanation of these and other disagreements about chronology is that many anecdotes, of varying authenticity, about Confucius in each of these offices came into circulation over the several centuries before the authors of the Zuo commentary and *Historical Record* began to collect and reconcile them into coherent chronologies. In other words, the facts about Confucius's life are a mixture of truth and fiction, but standards according to which the two might be differentiated had already disappeared by the time these works were assembled in the Han dynasty (206 B.C.E.–220 C.E.).

The same is true for the circuitous trips he took through the states of Wei, Song, Chen, Cai, and Chu. This information may have come from stories in a genre popular in the Eastern Zhou period: the parable of political intrigue that illustrated psychological or political principles.[13] Some tales in this genre have been incorporated into the Zuo commentary to the *Spring and Autumn,* with terse didactic comments appended. These comments are sometimes attributed to Confucius, resulting in his association with the actors and places of the tales themselves. Scholars disagree about whether these intrigues were historical or merely didactic, and it is likely that they were of varying historicity. Even with the reliable ones, however, the insertion of a judgment attributed to Confucius might sometimes have occurred well after the fact. Therefore it is possible that the task of constructing a feasible route for Confucius's travels might involve a confusion of myths for historical data.

> *During his later life [Confucius] gathered disciples and schooled them in the general style of a private academy. Traditionally he had 3000 disciples, with 72 personally learning the Six Attainments from him.*[14] *Ancient scholars have argued that he revised the* Poetry *and* History, *arranged the* Ritual *and* Music, *praised the* Zhou Changes *[i.e.,* I Ching*], and compiled the* Spring and Autumn. *Although these claims are not completely reliable, he was conversant with the ancient classics and capable of having carried out any of those types of editing work. Because of the movement formed by his disciples, which after his death was transformed into the Confucian [i.e., "Ru"] academic school, he has had a great impact on later generations.*

13. For a study of an early collection of such tales, see J. I. Crump, Jr., *Chan-kuo ts'e* (Oxford: Clarendon, 1970).

14. The "Six Attainments" mentioned here refer to rites, music, archery, charioteering, writing, and mathematics.

In this last section of the entry lies the first hint of the establishment of something that survived Confucius's death. The entry separates the institutional and the textual legacies of the sage. The report of the number of first- and second-generation disciples covers the former, a tradition we see as early as the *Historical Record*. The tradition, encapsulated in the reference to the "academic school" established by the disciples, holds that these disciples went on to collect the master's words and assemble them into works such as the *Analects*, which were transmitted through a formal master-disciple lineage. The textual legacy of Confucius also includes the "Six Classics" connected with him in the various ways outlined above. The entry accurately reflects the fact that tradition connects Confucius to the classics *Poetry* (*Shi* or *Shijing*), *History* (*Shu*, *Shujing*, or *Shangshu*), *Record of Ritual* (*Liji*), *Record of Music* (*Yueji*), *Changes* (*Zhouyi*, *Yi*, or *Yijing*), and *Spring and Autumn*. Five of these works (the *Record of Music* had been lost) became the basis for the official examinations during the Han dynasty. This precedent retroactively made Confucius, in effect, the medium between the semidivine sages of antiquity and the scholar-officials of the present.

Several reasons exist for the intertwining of the institutional and textual legacies of Confucius. Most of what is known about the community of disciples derives from descriptions in the canonical texts, and the texts themselves do not address a theoretical reader, but rulers and members of this community of disciples. Almost every section of the *Analects*, the work today most closely associated with Confucian doctrine, describes Confucius interacting with others, either the rulers he encountered on his travels or the disciples of his later career as teacher. Writings from both phases of his life share the important formal similarity that they portray the master's teaching in particular situations. Throughout the *Analects* the words *zi yue*, "the Master said," continually reiterate the claim that the authoritative figure Kongzi, "Master Kong," offered words of guidance as instruction to disciples or advice to princes.

The context of the words of Confucius has certainly colored their reception in both China and the West. Traditionally, Confucius's teachings have served as a foundation for the Chinese educational and civil examination systems, institutions often identified with the term "Confucianism." This association resulted in the canonization of Confucius throughout much of Chinese dynastic history, and also in his status as scapegoat during the Cultural Revolution of 1966-76, particularly during its "Criticize Lin [Biao] and Criticize Confucius" campaign. In the West Immanuel Kant dismissed Confucius's ethics as "nothing outside a moral doctrine designed for princes," while Max Weber saw him as an "academic teaching philosopher." The contention that Confucius invented an "academic school" known as Confucianism (as the term *Ru* — a "scholar" or "classicist" — is usually translated) is consistent with the idea that Confucius was primarily a teacher, even if it denies the legitimacy of a host of other institutions that claim him as their founder. Yet this identification is often made simply because Confucius has come to be identified as the founder of the scholarly and official tradition that bears his name.

This is one reason it is a mistake to use "Confucius" and "Confucianism" interchangeably, as is sometimes done today. As with any religious founder, later traditions that ground their authority in the name of a celebrated founder do not always accurately reflect the founder's intentions. Yet there are even problems with making comparisons with other "founded" traditions, for the founder and the religion here are both problematic. Confucius is a shadowy historical figure, and for most phases of Chinese history he has been the personification of the shifting set of canonical texts associated with him. Confucianism, if it existed before Chinese contact with the celebrated isms outside China, was integrated into familial and governmental structures in a way that differentiated it from many traditions labeled "religions" in the West. For these reasons the precise relationship between Confucius and Confucianism is a shifting target, dependent on both what canon is associated with Confucius and how strictly Confucianism is defined.

In common with most contemporary reference sources, the *Word Source* dictionary simplifies this complex relationship and portrays Confucius as the intentional founder of the Confucian academic school. The details it includes are selected from a variety of sources, yet the entry excludes other details from the very same sources. Indeed, given that Confucius lived two and a half millennia ago, there is almost no indication that any of the details of his life are known with anything less than certainty. To delve more carefully into the question of who Confucius was, and what made him and his teachings so valuable and vital to the life of China, it is necessary to return to the original sources. The next sections of this chapter separate out the images of Confucius presented in three of these sources: the *Historical Record,* the *Analects,* and the commentaries to the *Spring and Autumn.*

Historical Record: The Earliest Account of the Life of Confucius

> Confucius had hardly passed off the stage of life before his merits began to be acknowledged. . . . His disciples proclaimed their estimation of him as superior to all the sages whom China had ever seen. Before long this view of him took possession of the empire; and since the Han dynasty, he has been the man whom sovereign and people have delighted to honour.
>
> James Legge, Protestant missionary, 1895[15]

15. James Legge, trans., *The Chinese Classics* (Oxford: Clarendon, 1895), 2:38.

All historians trying to reconstruct Confucius's biography have faced the problem of a long gap in the historical record. There is a paucity of information concerning him that may be definitively dated to the two and a half centuries between his death (traditionally estimated to have been around 479 B.C.E.) and the emergence of detailed biographical accounts in the Han dynasty (206 B.C.E.–220 C.E.), when he became widely celebrated as a culture hero. During this gap, narratives about the sage were passed down from master to disciple as part of an esoteric transmission centered in Confucius's temple in the small state of Lu. Yet, when these narratives emerge in written records that have survived to the present day, their content is somewhat inconsistent and appears to have been refashioned or at least selected in a manner pertinent to the concerns of the newly established Han dynasty. Before returning to the account of Confucius's life that is widely accepted today, it is worth taking a closer look at how the fluid set of narratives and details that surrounded the man might have developed.

Confucius was not the only "sage" to emerge from the Eastern Zhou. In fact, many motifs in Confucius stories appear in similar narratives about figures that predate him. For example, when Confucius was eight years old, Prince Jicha of the state of Wu made a circuit of several states, including Lu, to announce the accession of a new ruler. The Zuo commentary to the *Spring and Autumn* records that Jicha had prescient words of advice for each ruler of these states. But most of the narrative concerns his reaction to various pieces of classical music and dance performed for him in the state of Lu. Prince Jicha, on hearing each, identified the state of origin and offered prophetic words about that state. When his Lu hosts performed the "Greater Elegance" odes, a section of the *Poetry* from the early Zhou period, the prince said: "Tremendous indeed! So harmonious! The melody exhibits plainness of form. Such was the virtue of King Wen!"[16] This ability to perceive and recognize the mind behind the composition of classical music is also found in an anecdote about Confucius included in the *Historical Record*. In that story Confucius was practicing a tune on the zither, and his music teacher prompted him to go on to another piece. Confucius continually refused, as he first mastered the melody, then the technique, then the intention of the music. Finally his teacher prompted him again:

> After a while he said:
> "Now you have mastered its intent, you can move on to another piece."
> Confucius said:
> "But I have not yet grasped how he was as a man."

16. From the entry for year twenty-nine of the reign of Duke Xiang, see *Corrected Meaning of the Zuo Commentary to the Spring and Autumn*, in Ruan, p. 2007.

Later . . . [Confucius] said:

"I have grasped how he was as a man, dark complected and tall, eyes like he was looking for distant animals, as if he were governing the states on all sides. Only King Wen could have composed this!"

His music teacher Master Xiang rose from his mat and bowed twice. He said:

"I must tell you that these are the songs of King Wen."[17]

The similarity between these two accounts suggests the possibility that some anecdotes about Confucius were actually refashioned from tropes associated with other early sages. Even if this was not so, it demonstrates that significant aspects of the behavior associated with Confucius were characteristic of a class of prescient advisers in his time.

The pre-Confucian figure that Confucius most resembled was the Duke of Zhou. As seen above, the Duke of Zhou was also associated with the state of Lu and the preservation of the ancient rites and music. Several of his characteristics are similar to those of Confucius, from his period of exile from Zhou because others slandered him after his brother's death to his ability to foretell future events based on his knowledge of the past. He was reputed to have been so dedicated to governing and training gentlemen that when showering, he had to leave three times to attend to his charges, grasping his wet hair in his hand, before he could finish and tie it up. A third century B.C.E. text called the *Spring and Autumn of Master Lü (Lüshi chunqiu)* identifies the Duke of Zhou's strategy for governing the state of Lu as: "Treat relatives with familial affection, and promote kindness."[18] Many aspects of the picture of the Duke of Zhou are similar to those of Confucius, with the obvious exception that the broad political power that the former enjoyed was only aspired to by the latter.

Whether or not Prince Jicha of Wu and the Duke of Zhou were models for details in Confucius's life, it is clear that he shared important traits with many great ministers and sages of early China. The multiple versions of the master that existed as early as this first biography, and the differing messages to be read between the lines of texts he is thought to have written, are both evidence that his biography is to some extent a composite one. This variety has provided a rich palette for those who have sought to paint images of the sage, and is an indispensable part of the explanation of the historical diversity of such images. The composite nature of the earliest descriptions of Confucius does not, however, mean that there is no way to know who Confucius really

17. *Historical Record*, 47.1925.

18. In section 11.5; see Xu Weiyu, *Collected Explanations of the Spring and Autumn of Master Lü (Lüshi chungiu jishi)* (Taibei: Zhongguoshudian, 1985), 11.15a. p. 455. A version of this statement is found in *Analects* 18.10.

was. It does give rise to a more complex question: If narratives about Confucius emerged from a fluid set of stories of exemplary sages, is there any way to gauge the period from which a particular detail emerged?

Occasionally it is possible to make an educated guess at the age of a particular detail in his biography because some elements appear to address issues particular to earlier periods. For example, the historical Master Kong was likely born in the middle of the sixth century B.C.E., a time when the cultural unity imposed by the Zhou clan had mostly receded into memory. Such is the importance of Confucius in Chinese culture that the subperiod in which he lived is named after a text many thought he wrote. This era, the Spring and Autumn era (from 722 through 481 B.C.E.), saw the decline of the Zhou clan's authority and the ascendance of increasingly independent principalities. It is likely that some aspects of the sage's writings that stress his interest in reviving the Zhou order reflect the political situation of this Spring and Autumn era.

Many sources attest to Confucius's desire to revive the institutions of the Zhou, a period that he saw as a "Golden Age."[19] In particular, he identified with the Duke of Zhou, whom he saw as the epitome of the gifted sage (*Analects* 8.11), and who appeared to him in his dreams (7.5). Confucius's dedication to a particular set of norms and behavior associated with the rule of the Zhou caused him to be sought out by Spring and Autumn era rulers and students. As a result, the traditionalist undertone to much of his writing may best be understood in terms of the political and religious situation of the late Spring and Autumn era.

Yet Zhou revivalism is only one aspect of these writings, and in all likelihood only some works attributed to Confucius are actually Spring and Autumn era texts. Many passages probably date to the subsequent period of disunity, known as the Warring States (480-222 B.C.E.). Writings from this period treat court ritual and statecraft, important concerns in the eyes of the regional court officials who might patronize itinerant scholars who had mastered these subjects. This is the context of exchanges between Confucius and his disciples concerning matters of court etiquette, such as the following from the *Record of Ritual:*

Zengzi said:

"If a person has begun a funeral for a deceased parent and has already started onto the road, but is there informed of the death of the ruler, what should the person do?"

The Master said:

19. For Confucius's relationship with the Zhou, see Philip J. Ivanhoe, *Confucian Moral Self Cultivation* (New York: Peter Lang, 1993), pp. 9-10.

"The person should continue until the tomb is sealed, change his clothes, and then go on."[20]

Such exchanges outline the high standards of behavior to which a person needed to conform to be considered a "gentleman" *(junzi),* standards that demonstrated a moral fitness for exercising authority. The many dialogues that include information on the character and methods of self-cultivation of the gentleman address concerns dominant in the texts written in the Warring States period.

What remains of both Spring and Autumn and Warring States strata constitute a set of dialogues that draw on the authority of Confucius in matters of tradition and ritual, but are less concerned with the details of his life per se. Although part of the picture of Confucius's life derives from Spring and Autumn and Warring States texts, much of it was fixed centuries after his death in the early imperial period that began in 221 B.C.E.

The enormous changes that China underwent because of the centralization and unification brought about by the emperors of the Qin (221-206 B.C.E.) and Han dynasties fundamentally shifted the social and economic organization of Chinese society. They also affected the ways different social groups cited and appropriated the authority of Confucius. Qin was the state to emerge out of the "Warring States" with aspirations to empire and a powerful centralized army that could eventually defeat its rivals. The scale of the founding emperor's military might is reflected in the enormity of the recently excavated terra-cotta army that guarded his tomb. Despite the authoritarian nature of the Qin dynasty, the emperor did consult experts from the old state of Lu on traditional sacrifices, and is spoken of in surviving Qin stele inscriptions using the Confucian term "sage." Yet Han writers such as Jia Yi (200-168 B.C.E.), looking back on the Qin, criticized it for its blindness to the fundamental values espoused by Confucius. After the fall of the Qin, a debate between those who adopted the Qin model and advocated harsh and impartially applied penal law as a means to social order, and those who pursued this goal by supporting the development of individual moral character, raged inside and outside the Han court at Chang'an (modern Xi'an). The latter faction looked to the sage-kings of antiquity as ideal examples of administration based on moral example rather than punishments, and looked to Confucius as their foundational theoretician.

In this context the events of Confucius's life took on greater importance, and as a result the Han saw the creation of what is now the oldest ex-

---

20. "Zengzi Asks" ("Zengzi wen"), chap. 7 of the *Record of Ritual.* Compare the translation by James Legge (p. 335) of *The Chinese Classics,* vol. 28 of Max Müller's Sacred Books of the East series.

tant biography of the sage. While some aspects of this biography are found in sources that date to Confucius's time, largely they derive from a store of anecdotes in general circulation before they became fixed around 100 B.C.E. in Sima Qian's *Historical Record*. A man who deeply admired Confucius, Sima Qian worked with a myriad of official and unofficial sources, piecing together many accounts that included the names, family and birthplace information, dates, number of disciples, and most of the major events that could be found in the archives to which he had access. While the sources he used are mostly lost, the details that Sima selected from them still exist, continuously transmitted over the generations and incorporated into modern sources such as the *Word Source* dictionary entry above. Many anecdotes collated in Sima Qian's *Historical Record* also appear in collections like the *Analects* and the *Mencius,* but he gave no hint that these collections existed in anything like their current form.[21] Because of the wide influence of his *Historical Record,* many centuries of scholars have regarded Sima Qian's account of Confucius's life as authoritative, and it became what D. C. Lau called the "standard source" for Confucius's life.[22] Most modern biographies rely heavily on that account for important facts about the life of the sage.

Yet, because Sima Qian wrote this biography several centuries after Master Kong's death, the intervening generations may have lost, altered, or concocted many of the details of his life. His *Historical Record* biography of Confucius appears to draw on disparate, and occasionally contradictory, sources of information to provide a comprehensive version of Confucius's life. Sima begins his account with the birth narrative, a standard feature found in his biographical treatments:

> Master Kong was born in the state of Lu, in the village Changping located in the county of Zou. His ancestor from the state of Song was called Kong Fangshu. Fangshu begat First-born Xia. First-born Xia begat Third-born Lianghe. Late in his life [Lianghe] married a woman from the Yan clan, and begat Master Kong. After asking for blessings at the Ni hill she had Kongzi (i.e. Master Kong). It was in the twenty-second year of Duke Xiang of Lu (i.e. 551 B.C.E.) that Kongzi was born. Because there was an indentation on the

---

21. Indeed, as Zhu Weizheng has convincingly shown, there is little evidence that the *Analects* existed in anything resembling its current form prior to the first century B.C.E. ("'Lunyu' jieji cuoshuo" [Jottings on the collation of the *Analects*], *Kongzi yanjiu* 1 [1986]: 44). This throws open to question the dominant attitude that material about Confucius in the *Analects* predates or is more authoritative than the accounts selected and transcribed by Sima Qian.

22. Lau, *Confucius: "The Analects,"* p. 161.

top of his head he was called by the personal name "Hill." He was given the courtesy name Second-born Ni, and had the surname of the Kong clan.[23]

Besides the interesting supernatural role of the Ni hill, a role commemorated in both the personal and courtesy names given to Confucius, what makes this short passage noteworthy is the way it mentions Confucius's birth three separate times, the first time relating his parentage, the second time the particular circumstances of his birth, and the third time the year of his birth. Since the three birth references do not use the same name for Confucius, it is likely that Sima Qian followed his usual procedure of collating accounts from several different sources. This collage technique may be seen in the biography as a whole, which arranges Confucius's dialogues with princes and disciples in what Sima Qian saw to be a rough chronological order, covering his journey from Lu to Zhou, his return to Lu, and his subsequent circuit through the states of Qi, Wei, Song, Zheng, Chen, Cai, and She in search of a patron who would employ him.

Sima Qian's principle of collation appears to have been, in part, based on certain didactic messages he sought to communicate to his readers. In recounting Confucius's travels, he is concerned with displaying the moral and therefore political soundness of the sage's methods. According to Sima's account, in the rare cases where a local feudal lord gave Confucius some authority, he demonstrated his ability quickly. In 495 B.C.E., after three months as Lu's Grand Director against Brigands, having carried out a strategic execution, social order was restored: "merchants of lamb and pork did not inflate their prices, and men and women walked on opposite sides of the street."[24] Later in the master's career the king of Chu was considering enfeoffing Confucius, but the king's minister dissuaded him on the grounds that a person of such virtue and possessed of such able disciples would soon be able to expand his influence and usurp the state of Chu.[25] For Sima Qian, not only did Confucius exercise political influence, but others who perceived his abilities to be a potential threat to their own authority denied him further influence. One of the most interesting examples of Confucius's method of administration in the biography is the episode regarding Duke Ding's diplomatic mission to the state of Qi. When the ministers there twice arranged ritually inappropriate performances for the heads of state,

---

23. This biography is in the "Kongzi shijia" chapter of the *Historical Record,* beginning on p. 1905 of the Zhonghua edition. Sima Qian for the most part had treatments of individuals in his "liezhuan" chapters, yet he places Confucius among the treatments of "shijia," the hereditary noble lineages. The Tang commentator Zhang Shoujie explains that this is due to the fact that scholars in particular and those who use the Six Attainments in general revere Confucius and call him the epitome of the sage.

24. *Historical Record,* 47.1917.

25. *Historical Record,* 47.1932.

尼丘禱嗣

"Asking for blessings at Ni Hill," a scene from before Confucius's birth
(from Gu Yuan's [fl. 1826-1848] Qing dynasty *Shengji tu*, 1826; Beijing: Xianzhuang)

251

Confucius twice rushed forward to object. The second time, the assorted entertainers were summarily executed on Confucius's suggestion. The result was that
the Qi hosts, realizing that they were using the "barbarian way" rather than the
"gentleman's way," ceded back the land they had previously captured from the
state of Lu. These stories all stress the effectiveness of the administration of
government based on the demonstration of moral rectitude advocated by Confucius. At the same time, they also illustrate well Sima Qian's own belief in the
adversity a person of moral superiority must face in gaining power.[26]

It is worth noting that these stories are not entirely consistent. Sima
Qian's Confucius is quite willing to execute people for infractions that many of
modern sensibilities might forgive, a practice that does not appear to be consistent with his rejection of the harsh application of penal law in the *Analects* and
other texts. Another apparent conflict involves Confucius's military expertise,
since at one point he disclaims knowledge of this field but at another his disciple Ran Qiu claims to have learned successful military strategies from him.[27]
These contradictions are artifacts of Sima's collation method of writing history,
and reveal that the earliest biography already appears to incorporate different
elements of an already thriving set of legends.

While the intervening millennia have witnessed many chronologies and
attempts to assess individual biographical data, discussions of Confucius's life
for the most part depend on the materials Sima Qian transcribed at the end of
the second century B.C.E. Scholars today still accept some of these details, but
routinely discount other aspects of Sima Qian's account of Confucius's life. As
early as the eighteenth century, scholars downplayed the strain of Sima Qian's
biographical treatment that depicts Confucius as a prodigy who is distinct from
others in his physical appearance and sensory acuity. These characteristics were
widely accepted by Sima's contemporaries (as explored below in the section on
portrayals of Confucius as prophet), but were not destined to survive. According to Sima Qian, Confucius was born with a deformity on his head, grew to
such a height that others always called him "the tall man" and marveled at him,
and had bodily features that caused him to resemble a composite sketch of the
sages of the past.[28] Another narrative holds that as a small child he displayed an

---

26. *Historical Record*, 47.1915. Sima Qian himself was castrated by Emperor Wu for
coming to the defense of a Chinese general who had surrendered to the enemy. A detailed
study of Sima Qian's life and his emulation of Confucius may be found in Stephen
Durrant, *The Cloudy Mirror: Tension and Conflict in the Writings of Sima Qian* (Albany:
State University of New York Press, 1995). For a more detailed examination of this specific
incident, see Marcel Granet, *Danses et légendes de la Chine ancienne*, vol. 1 (Paris: F. Alcan,
1926), pp. 171-213.

27. Compare *Historical Record*, 47.1926 and 1934.

28. *Historical Record*, 47.1905, 1909, and 1921.

The fruits of Confucius's virtuous administration, from the
Ming dynasty blockprint *Kongzi Shengtuji*. Note the merchant
refraining from cheating his customer in the foreground and
the appropriate segregation of male and female travellers further back.
(Tianjin Yangliuqing Publisher, 1997)

unusual interest in and knowledge of the rites, a trait that influenced at least
one member of the Lu nobility to seek his guidance in ritual forms.[29] Perhaps
because of this knowledge, he displayed a Sherlock Holmes–like ability to identify forms of arrows and the composers of music.[30] In one instance he could in-
tuit that a recently discovered entombed animal was a sheep, and in another
could guess correctly the source of a fire.[31] These features were consistent with
the developing image of Confucius as exceptional, and as an almost messianic
"uncrowned king," an image examined at greater length later in the chapter.

The dismissal of these supernormal features in Sima Qian's portrait of
Confucius is based on several factors, including an emphasis by Qing dynasty
(1644-1911) philologists on Confucius's textual and ritual expertise, the exposure of the Chinese to the European notion of superstition, and a need to differentiate Confucianism from other religions and popular beliefs. In the twentieth century Westerners also tended to downplay such features, although this
grew out of a slightly different set of concerns. These considerations may have

29. *Historical Record*, 47.1906, 1909.
30. *Historical Record*, 47.1922, 1925.
31. *Historical Record*, 47.1912, 1927.

"Confucius playing at presenting a sacrificial vessel"
(Gu Yuan, *Shengji tu,* 1826; Beijing: Xianzhuang)

led to the ascendancy of the *Analects* as the twentieth century's standard source for Confucius's life. In this respect the statement from the *Word Source* dictionary typifies the twentieth-century attitude: "His words and deeds can for the most part be seen in the book compiled by his first- and second-generation disciples, the *Analects*."[32] While the majority of the accepted details of Confucius's life still derive from the *Historical Record,* modern scholars generally reject details inconsistent with the portrayal of the *Analects.* Because of the importance of this text, the message it ascribes to Confucius is worth examining in detail.

The Confucius of the *Analects* will be examined with two different ends in mind. The first will be to outline his theory of ethical self-cultivation. Late imperial and modern scholars have taken the *Analects* as their primary source material and used it to recast Confucius at least partially in their own image. This has resulted in Confucianism being pictured, according to Herbert Fingarette, "either as an empirical, humanist, this-worldly teaching or as a parallel to Platonist-rationalist doctrines."[33] The second goal is to look behind this image at the context of his teachings and derive from the *Analects* a picture of early Confucian social organization.

Analects: Confucius as a Teacher of Ethics

> "Simply by being filial to those to whom one should and being friendly to one's elder and younger brothers, one is putting governance into practice."
>
> Confucius in the *Analects,* quoting the classic *History* [34]

In the *Analects* a nameless interlocutor asks Confucius about his lack of participation in government. Confucius responds, in the paraphrase of the prominent modern scholar of Confucianism, Tu Wei-ming, that "taking care of family affairs is itself active participation in politics."[35] In other words, by acting virtuously and serving as an exemplar for others, one can transform society even without taking part in government. While many early sources are concerned with Confucius's possible influence in government, many modern scholars portray a Confucius who did not exercise direct political influence but advocated the transformation of society through the modification of individual be-

32. *Word Source,* p. 421.

33. Herbert Fingarette, *Confucius — The Secular as Sacred* (New York: Harper and Row, 1972), p. 1.

34. *Analects* 2.21; Cheng, vol. 1, pp. 121-25.

35. Tu Wei-ming, *Centrality and Commonality: An Essay on Confucian Religiousness* (Albany: State University of New York Press, 1989), p. 115.

havior. This section examines the ideal of the gentleman that lies at the core of the ethical theory of the *Analects*.

This focus on the ideal of the gentleman is the unifying element in the *Analects*. The *Analects* was collected from a body of diverse sayings and anecdotes written on bamboo slips and circulated in the late Spring and Autumn and Warring States periods. The earliest reference to the text is from the Han dynasty, around the time Sima Qian wrote his biography of the master. According to the bibliographic survey included in Ban Gu's (32-92 C.E.) *History of the Han (Hanshu)*, by the first century C.E. three versions of the *Analects* were in existence, an *Ancient (gu)* version in twenty-one chapters, a *State of Qi* version in twenty-two chapters, and a *State of Lu* version in twenty chapters. Elsewhere the *History of the Han* tells of an imperial tutor who assembled his own composite around 45 B.C.E., after finding that the versions in circulation contained different numbers of chapters.[36] The current *Analects* has twenty chapters, and the consensus is that Zheng Xuan (127-200 C.E.) collated it from these three versions some six centuries after Confucius's death.

Despite its status as a composite text, the *Analects* is coherent in several important ways, including that much of the text is in the form of a dialogue. Its concise quotations or exchanges between the master and his disciples and feudal lords are occasionally peppered with historical anecdotes without dialogue. The arrangement of the text is not strictly topical, and thus it reads more like an anthology of maxims and conversations than the composition of a single writer. Indeed, the reverential but occasionally humorous portrayal of Confucius in the *Analects* is most likely the work of several generations of disciples, compiled from notes, memories, and creative attributions.

Out of the many stories and sayings concerning Confucius in circulation in the late Warring States period and the Qin and Han dynasties, only certain kinds of texts were selected to be included in the *Analects* anthology. The selection criterion was the usefulness of a particular text in the contexts of educating the crown prince and training other aristocrats who lived their lives in strict accordance with the rites that governed the court. It was in such contexts that the *Analects* first gained popularity and began to enjoy canonical status. One of the earliest commentaries on the *Analects* was written around 73 B.C.E. by the Grand Tutor to the Heir-Apparent, the Marquis Sheng of Xia. Over the next century, officials who served in the same office of Grand Tutor to the Heir-Apparent and officials possessed of a detailed knowledge of the rites produced many new arrangements of the text and a number of commentaries.[37] Indeed,

---

36. Ban Gu, *History of the Han (Hanshu)* (Beijing: Zhonghua, 1962), 81.3352.

37. See Mark Csikszentmihalyi, "Confucius and the *Analects* in the Han," in *Essays on Confucius and the "Analects,"* ed. Bryan W. Van Norden (Oxford, forthcoming).

many passages in the *Analects* may be read as a guide to proper ritual behavior for princes and officials charged with maintaining court etiquette.

One reason for the interest in Confucius during the first century B.C.E. may have been a resurgence of Zhou revivalism during the period. The accession of Emperor Xuan in 74 B.C.E. marked the beginning of a period that, according to historian Michael Loewe, saw the Han imperial court cease modeling itself on the example of the Qin dynasty and begin looking back to the Zhou.[38] Thus the renewal of interest in Confucius in the Han was based on his stature as an expert on the Zhou and on the nature of Zhou ritual forms. The tutors in ritual forms who compiled the *Analects* likely selected those aspects of the lore of Confucius that best fit their idea of what the heir apparent and officers charged with ritual duties needed to know to mirror their idealized counterparts during the Zhou period.

The content of the *Analects* that circulates today reflects these selection criteria. The Confucius of the *Analects* is an expert on ritual and the leader of a group of disciples whose instruction is his foremost concern. He trains these disciples and occasionally advises the nobility to become "gentlemen," people who engage in ritual self-cultivation and are not governed by desires for wealth, sex, or official position. So, for the official, the Confucius of the *Analects* has these words of advice: "In serving your lord, treat his affairs reverently, and consider your meals later."[39] The *Analects* does not present this as a rule to be followed blindly, but as an example of the advice Confucius gave in a particular situation. It does not provide rules to follow as much as scenes from an exemplary life that illustrate the changes in priorities that Confucius sought to convince prospective officials they needed to make. The *Analects* details this process of self-cultivation and the resulting attributes that would allow a ruler to set an example for his people and engender a well-governed and prosperous state. The picture of Confucius in the *Analects* links individual self-cultivation and service in government, implying that moral perfection includes the ability to govern well.

These dual goals are reflected in the dual audiences with which the *Analects* portrays Confucius as being concerned. In the *Analects* Confucius balances the goal of modifying individual behavior against that of exercising concrete political influence. He counsels his community of disciples on how to attain the first goal, encouraging them to cultivate their virtue. An example is his explanation of the importance of the attitude behind proper familial behavior in book two of the *Analects*:

---

38. Michael Loewe, "The Former Han Dynasty," in *The Cambridge History of China,* vol. 1, *The Ch'in and Han Empires, 221 B.C.–A.D. 220,* ed. Denis Twitchett and Michael Loewe (Cambridge: Cambridge University Press, 1986), p. 198.

39. *Analects* 15.38; see Cheng, vol. 4, pp. 1125-26.

[The disciple] Ziyou asked about filial piety.

The Master said,

"To be considered filially pious today requires nothing more than being able to provide nourishment [for one's parents]. Yet providing nourishment is something that one might even do for dogs and horses. Without reverence, what is the difference between the two?"[40]

Instructing his disciple Ziyou, Confucius stresses that an individual must have the proper moral motivation for acting.

By contrast, when addressing the rulers of his age, Confucius gave moral advice directed to the end of promoting order and authority in the state. He thought good government depended on the proper behavior of rulers toward their subjects:

Duke Ai asked:

"What should I do in order to have my people follow me?"

The Master answered:

"If you promote the upright and place them ahead of the corrupt, then your people will follow you. . . ."[41]

The contrast between the ruler's interest in compelling the people to follow him and Confucius's redirection of the conversation to focus on the quality of the ruler's actions illustrates the pedagogical strategy implicit in the dialogue form. The reader, with Duke Ai, begins the dialogue thinking it will treat the issue of how a ruler is to hold on to political power. Contrary to expectation, Confucius argues that such concerns are at best secondary to the imperative to consistently act to reward trustworthiness, and persuades the reader (and perhaps Duke Ai) that the political must become personal.

The two audiences of Confucius in the *Analects,* then, are ultimately given the same guidance, even though the original ends for which they sought advice were different. The idea that the conduct of the ruler is central to the well-being of the state was not original with Confucius, but was incipient in the pre-Confucian notion of virtue *(de).* This notion that moral behavior leads to political power by creating a sense of obligation or gratitude in others is what binds together the advice offered to the two audiences in the *Analects.* Confucius drew on this ancient concept of virtue, what David S. Nivison has called "moral force,"[42] connecting it

---

40. *Analects* 2.7; see Cheng, vol. 1, pp. 85-88.

41. *Analects* 2.19; Cheng, vol. 1, pp. 117-19.

42. David Nivison, *The Ways of Confucianism: Investigations in Chinese Philosophy,* ed. Bryan Van Norden (Chicago: Open Court, 1996), p. 26.

to the ideal of the gentleman. The moral perfection of the gentleman was the goal of both adviser and ruler. What was original in the writings now attributed to Confucius was the approach to moral perfection that they outlined.

The process of self-cultivation in the *Analects* focuses on a set of personal virtues that include benevolence (*ren*, a sensitivity to others), righteousness (*yi*, an obligation to act fairly), wisdom (*zhi*, an ability to assess circumstances), and trustworthiness (*xin*, being true to one's word). Self-cultivation also consists of locating oneself correctly with respect to one's family through filial piety (*xiao*, caring for relatives as befits one's role) and with respect to one's community through ritual propriety (*li*, regulating speech and demeanor as befits one's status). Thus the Confucian gentleman engages in the *personal* task of eliminating selfishness, and is also committed to the *collective* transformation of family and society.

The first concern of the Confucius of the *Analects* is individual moral development through the cultivation of virtues. To describe this process, he shifts the connotations of the term "gentleman" from that of nobility as determined by social class to nobility as the product of moral education.[43] The *Analects* uses the term "gentleman" to describe the individual engaged in self-cultivation, and it appears much more often than the related term for one who had reached moral perfection, the "sage" *(sheng)*. Confucius's focus on the *process* of self-cultivation on the individual level does not mean that he was not concerned with broader issues. Instead it suggests that the textual selection process that produced the *Analects* favored those sayings concerned with the cultivation of virtues and only indirectly, at most, with political emancipation or personal salvation. While Confucius promoted an attitude of engagement in society, it could not be at the expense of acting contrary to one's virtue.

Of the ideal personal characteristics of the gentleman, the most essential is probably benevolence, acting with awareness of the desires of others. Several passages illustrate the gravity Confucius accorded this characteristic, for the *Analects* argues that it is all-encompassing, informing every action the gentleman takes (4.5; 6.7), and states that a gentleman would rather die than compromise it (15.9). Sometimes the *Analects* defines benevolence simply as "caring for others" (12.22; 13.19). This caring, as in the quotation from book two earlier in this section, must be more than simply providing materially as one does for dogs and horses. It must also include a realization of the fundamental similarity between the actor and his or her object, and so must be predicated on the more complex principle of reflexivity. The master says the method of benevo-

---

43. See Hsü Cho-yun, *Ancient China in Transition: An Analysis of Social Mobility, 722-222 B.C.* (Stanford: Stanford University Press, 1965), pp. 158-74, for a discussion of the shift in the meaning of the term "gentleman."

lence is "the ability to take what is near as an analogy" (6.30), and describes benevolence in a formulation similar to that of the Golden Rule: "Do not impose upon others what you yourself do not desire" (12.2).[44] So, to be benevolent one cares for others in the way one would want to be cared for oneself, with a realization that their personhood is of the same kind as one's own.

The resemblance of this formula for reflexivity to influential ethical formulations in other traditions has led many to abstract the idea of benevolence from the social context in which the *Analects* grounds it. This is misleading, because the *Analects* ties its few concrete examples of benevolence very closely to conventional behavior. A person demonstrates benevolence by treating people on the street as important guests and common people as if they were attendants at a sacrifice (12.2), by being reticent in speaking (12.3), and by being respectful where one dwells, reverent where one works, and loyal where one mixes with others (13.19). By contrast, it involves the rejection of using clever speech and projecting a pleasing countenance (1.3; 17.17), dwelling in extremes of poverty or wealth (4.2), and being in a state of anxiety (9.29; 14.28). In other words, benevolence does not entail creating novel behavior or original social relationships; it simply means relating to others in what is an uncommon but nevertheless already established way.[45] This is the sense in which it consists of "overcoming oneself and returning to ritual propriety" (12.1). The close connection between benevolence and ritual propriety links the former to a set of social conventions and distinguishes it from simply acting spontaneously. This is why the master describes benevolence as a medium between "learning widely and earnestly taking aim, inquiring incisively and reflecting on what is at hand" (19.6). Benevolence, then, is the disposition to seek out and learn the best kind of behavior to use with particular persons, and to rely on a recognition of their fundamental likeness to oneself.

The second personal virtue of the *Analects* is righteousness. Some schol-

---

44. David Hall and Roger Ames argue that Confucius is altering understanding of the "self": "One acts by extending the perimeter and the parameters of one's own person to embrace the defining condition, perceived attitudes, and the background of the other person in order to effectively become 'two' perspectives grounded in one judgment" (*Thinking through Confucius* [Albany: State University of New York Press, 1987], p. 117). For a comparison of the Confucian and Western formulations of the Golden Rule, see Philip J. Ivanhoe, "Reweaving the 'One Thread' of the *Analects*," *Philosophy East and West* 40, no. 1 (January 1990): 17-33.

45. Benjamin Schwartz has emphasized the relationship between benevolence and ritual performance: "Only through the established channels of [ritual propriety] can one's inner self-mastery make itself manifest to society and lead within to the higher moral excellence of [benevolence]" (*The World of Thought in Ancient China* [Cambridge: Harvard University Press, 1985], p. 77).

ars have argued that righteousness is not a virtue per se but rather a characteristic of "right acts." This is indeed one sense of the term, but the Confucian picture of a righteous individual entails a character that is unbiased and unselfish and thus disposed to the performance of "right acts."[46] Therefore righteousness is an ideal characteristic of a legal authority, although it is pertinent to other decision-making contexts. Righteousness requires one to ignore personal advantage or relationships when making decisions, to forgo profit (14.12), and to act dutifully even when one sees the possibility of personal gain by acting otherwise (16.10; 19.1). The master goes so far as to shun wealth and rank attained by going against righteousness (7.16). Besides creating an attitude that does not allow one to take advantage of one's office for personal gain, righteousness also impels one to make personal sacrifices to serve in office. To avoid public service is to be "without righteousness" (18.7). In many ways righteousness is an attitude of fairness. The *Analects* says righteousness often informs acts directed to the common people (5.16; 6.22), and that it leads to an attitude of acceptance on their part (13.4). Some later texts written in the tradition of Confucius see righteousness in conflict with other virtues that might cause a ruler, out of benevolence or filial consideration, to act with partiality, but the *Analects* for the most part does not recognize such conflicts between virtues.

The virtue of wisdom is the characteristic that allows the gentleman to correctly appraise a situation or a person. In the *Analects* wisdom allows a gentleman to see the advantage in benevolent behavior (4.2), as suggested by the master's rhetorical question: "How can a person be considered wise who does not dwell in benevolence?" (4.1).[47] The cultivation of wisdom, then, requires the development of a type of moral discernment. It allows the gentleman to distinguish between alternate ways to expend his energies (6.22), discern crooked and straight behavior in others (12.22), and discriminate between those who may be reformed and those who may not (15.8). Wisdom brings resoluteness and freedom from doubt (9.29; 14.28), or at least clarity as to when one has enough information to know a thing with certainty. Wisdom is also defined as saying "that you know something when you know it, and saying you do not know something when you do not know it" (2.17). In this sense wisdom is the

---

46. An example of the position that righteousness is a characteristic of acts is found in D. C. Lau's introduction to his translation of the *Analects* (p. 27). Contrast this with the rebuttal of Lau's position by Hall and Ames, who argue that righteousness "cannot solely be a matter of applying some externally derived norm" (Hall and Ames, p. 95; see also pp. 102-5).

47. Often in the *Analects* benevolence and wisdom are paired (e.g., 4.2; 5.19; 6.22; 6.23; 15.33). The relationship is not always clear, but at one point good rulership is said to consist of several steps, the first two of which are "reaching to" an action with wisdom and then "being able to maintain it" with benevolence (15.33).

characteristic that allows the gentleman to be confident of the appropriateness of a particular action.

Finally, the characteristic of trustworthiness qualifies a gentleman to advise a ruler and a ruler to rule his subjects. It applies to interactions between individuals, since one must be trustworthy with one's friends (1.4; 5.26), but it also is of paramount importance in dealing with people of different standing. Trustworthiness is crucial to rulership (1.5; 12.7), and it is the quality that keeps subordinates from grudging their effort (19.10; 20.1). The gentleman's trustworthiness leads others to give him responsibility (17.6), and leads the ruler to be willing to hear words of advice that would otherwise prove unwelcome (19.10). Trustworthiness refers not only to the truth of words, but to the congruence of deeds with words, since one's action may or may not match one's initial declaration (5.10). Thus trustworthiness may not be practiced in isolation, but must be embodied in interactions between friends and between superior and inferior.

Because the *Analects* was culled from a wider collection of sayings following Confucius's death, its ethics is not as systematic as the outline of the virtues presented above. Other expressions might be considered personal virtues (e.g., reverence or courage), and it is possible that even the limited number of virtues discussed above are not open to synthesis into a consistent "ethics." Further, it is unclear whether the *Analects* endorses the development of such characteristics in all people in a society, or if they are suitable only for people of a certain social class or role. These caveats are particularly relevant with respect to those portions of the *Analects* that differentiate the virtues of the superior from the comparable qualities in the common people. A ruler who is mature will have subjects who are reverent, a ruler who exercises filial kindness will have loyal subjects (2.20), a ruler who loves righteousness will meet with acceptance in his people, and a ruler who loves trustworthiness will meet with sincerity in his people (13.4). In other words, the characteristics of the gentleman build on general human qualities but also surpass these qualities, because they are specific to the optimal type of behavior for a person occupying a particular social role. As such, one might think of these virtues, like the excellences of Aristotle, as a distillation of certain culturally defined patterns of behavior.

While individual moral development is at the center of the *Analects*, its prescriptions cannot take effect in a vacuum. That is because the genuine cultivation of the personal virtues requires the internalization of two key cultural patterns: filial piety and ritual propriety. The tension between reforming the individual virtues and advancing these social norms accounts for the different readings of Confucius across history. Today many read the Confucius of the *Analects* as advocating the former, the cultivation of a set of personal virtues, as a means of indirectly achieving the latter, the transformation of society. Thus

Confucius is portrayed as a proponent of self-cultivation who also championed the linked collective values of filial piety and ritual propriety.

One of the existing social norms that the Confucius of the *Analects* emphasized was the imperative to behave appropriately with respect to one's parents. Once, when Master Meng Yi asked Confucius about being filial, the sage answered that one should "never go against [the rites]." Then one of his disciples prompted this explanation of his answer:

> Fan Chi asked:
> "What do you mean by that?"
> The Master said:
> "During their lives, serve them according to what is ritually proper. When they are dead, bury them according to what is ritually proper, and sacrifice to them according to what is ritually proper."[48]

Because ritual obligations to parents continue after they are dead, the proper behavior toward parents is more than a subset of general ritual obligations. The basis for this attitude was the belief in the postmortem existence of the parents, since filial piety is what the legendary sage-king Yu showed in his sacrifices to the demons *(gui)* and spirits *(shen)* of his ancestors (8.21). Yet this explanation for filial piety is only one of several present in the *Analects*. At one point the *Analects* explains the origin of the three-year mourning period a child observes after the death of a parent as the period of the same length through which the parents had given their child support (17.21). D. C. Lau explains the implication of this as follows: "This may be taken to mean that the observance of the three-year mourning period is, in some sense, a repayment of the love received from one's parents in the first years of one's life. If this is so, it is not difficult to see why the obligations we owe to other people should also be in proportion to the closeness of our relationship to them."[49] Filial piety is the archetype of the ritual relationship one has with other members of society. The natural allegiance one has to one's parents is the model for the consideration one shows to others, the degree of which depends on one's degree of affiliation to them.

The term "ritual propriety" summarizes a wider set of model behaviors and ideal relationships with members of one's community. Confucius's portentous words reflect the importance of ritual propriety: "If something goes against ritual propriety, do not look at it, listen to it, speak of it, or act on it."[50]

---

48. *Analects* 2.5; see Cheng, vol. 1, pp. 81-83.
49. Lau, *Confucius: "The Analects,"* p. 19.
50. This is a paraphrase of *Analects* 12.1; Cheng, vol. 3, pp. 817-24.

Ritual propriety was not simply a willingness to submit to a set of symbolic conventions, it also played a central role in the cultivation of individual virtues.

The code of behavior passed down from the golden age of the Zhou dynasty, called the rites (*li*, the same term also translated here as "ritual propriety"), was essential to Confucian self-cultivation. The *Analects* depicts Confucius both teaching and conducting the rites in the manner that he believed they had been conducted in antiquity. Detailed restrictions such as "the gentleman avoids using reddish black trim" (10.6) were in no way seen as trivial. This level of minutia, which Ezra Pound saw as "verses re length of the night-gown and the predilection for ginger,"[51] must have played an important part in the daily life of the master himself. The *Analects* has Confucius arranging funerals (9.16; 10.22), playing the stone chimes (14.39), serving in the ducal court as a "counselor" (10.2; 14.21), and serving at the lord's home as "usher" (10.3). He is well versed in matters of sacrificial vessels (15.1), formal dress (10.6), ritual music (15.11; 17.19), and in all manners of ritually correct mien and deportment. While he may occasionally alter a detail of the rites out of frugality (9.3), mostly he insists on adherence to the letter of the rites (3.18; 17.18). In short, he is the very model of a ritual expert.

For Confucius, however, the rites did much more than provide a script to facilitate smooth social interaction. By restricting appetites and desires, the rites allow their practitioners cognitive space to reflect on their actions and cultivate the personal virtues. The definition given by Confucius to his disciple Yan Hui, already alluded to in the discussion of the personal virtues above, provides an example of the link between the rites and the regulation of desires: "Overcoming the self and returning to the rites constitutes benevolence."[52] This is the conjunction of the social and the personal, the way in which ritual propriety also affects the moral character of the individual.

Acquiring the virtue of ritual propriety is in this sense a prerequisite for the practice of ethical self-cultivation. While Confucius appreciated the fact that ritual forms had symbolic aspects, participation in the rites was a symbolic act that also concretely moved a person toward the ideal of the gentleman. This is ritual in the sense understood by sociological theorists such as Mauss and Bourdieu: ritual as personally transformative.[53] Ritual practice on the individ-

---

51. Ezra Pound, *Confucius* (New York: New Directions, 1951), p. 191.

52. *Analects* 12.1; Cheng, vol. 3, pp. 817-24.

53. Talal Asad summarizes this position: "As in the case of medieval monastic programs, discourse and gesture are viewed as part of the social process of learning to develop aptitudes, not as orderly symbols that stand in an objective world in contrast to contingent feelings" (*Genealogies of Religion* [Baltimore: Johns Hopkins University Press, 1993], p. 77). It is not surprising that this way of looking at ritual is particularly suitable to China, since Mauss was influenced by Marcel Granet's analysis of Chinese ritual in developing his notion of "bodily techniques" and *habitus*.

ual level therefore has important consequences for the society as a whole, according to Philip J. Ivanhoe: "The rites were not intended merely to elicit particular kinds of behavior, the goal was to instill certain attitudes and dispositions in the practitioner. Confucius believed that only the reflective practice of the rites could produce the particular set of attitudes and dispositions needed for a harmonious, meaningful and flourishing society."[54] Indeed, while Confucius attends to a number of virtues, the *Analects* is just as concerned with the rites as the unique way of nourishing those virtues and transmitting them from one generation to the next. Thus the rites are not only a key to understanding ethics in the *Analects*, they are also essential to understanding the social context in which Confucius taught ethics.

Confucian Social Organization in the *Analects*

> In all arrangements with the stands, the chief attention was given to the bones. Some bones were considered nobler, and some meaner. . . . The nobler guests received the nobler bones, and the lower, the less noble; the nobler did not receive very much, and the lower were not left without any: — impartiality was thus shown.
>
> James Legge, trans., *Classic of Ritual*, 1895[55]

Beyond the ethical system that is often abstracted from the *Analects* lies a world in which Master Kong and his later disciples sought to use their knowledge of this system to earn a living. Contemporary attempts to appropriate and update the virtues of the Confucian gentleman often sunder them from their social context. Yet it is arguable that these virtues would be unintelligible if stripped of ritual considerations such as those of "nobler" and "less noble" bones. In the *Analects* we can find concrete illustrations of the close relationship between Confucian ritual and the ethics outlined in the previous section. Continuing to rely on the evidence of the *Analects*, this section examines the relationship between Confucius and his disciples, and the social and economic structure of their community.

The relationship between Confucius and his disciples was founded on his transmission of the knowledge of the rites, a knowledge that was valuable to late Spring and Autumn and Warring States period rulers who were anxious for polit-

---

54. Ivanhoe, *Confucian Moral Self Cultivation*, pp. 15-16. Ivanhoe outlines two functions of the rites: restraining excess behavior to instill humility and keeping virtuous tendencies from becoming overbearing.

55. *The Texts of Confucianism*, trans. James Legge, part IV, Sacred Books of the East, vol. 28 (London: Oxford University Press, 1985), p. 248.

ical legitimacy. According to Sima Qian, Confucius showed an early interest in ritual forms, playing at performing the rites as a small child. When he was still a teenager, one of his first students in the rites was a chancellor of Lu. After Confucius studied in Zhou, he gathered more disciples, and it is at this point in its account of the sage's life that the *Historical Record* makes the first reference to Confucius and his students as a group. An adviser to the ruler of Qi berates the "scholars" *(Ru)* around Confucius in these terms: "Now, Master Kong makes demeanor and dress so intricate, accumulating rituals for ascending and descending and formalized rules for when to hasten and walk with open arms. It would be impossible to understand his teachings over several generations — a single lifetime is insufficient to master his rites!"[56] Such criticism of the Confucian obsession with ritual forms can also be found in other Warring States texts, and Sima Qian implies that it was the reason the ruler of Qi cooled to Confucius's expertise. The *Historical Record* indicates that, after he fell out of favor, Confucius devoted himself to the study of the classics of *Poetry* and *Documents,* as well as *Ritual* and *Music,* as his "disciples grew more numerous, arriving from more distant places, all to receive their training from him."[57] For the Han writers making these claims, the reason Confucius attracted so many students must have seemed obvious, because during the Han the study of the classics had become the main road to a government salary. While it is doubtful that the link between scholarship and employment was as direct in earlier periods, these accounts suggest that one goal of Confucius's program appears to have been a fitness for certain types of employment. Later accounts have Confucius directly teaching 23, 70, 72, or 77 disciples, with thousands more coming to study from him indirectly. Sima Qian makes it clear that his ritual expertise acted as the magnet that attracted students to him.

For Confucius, gaining ritual knowledge was a necessary step in cultivating the characteristics of the gentleman. The dialogue form of the *Analects* shows that the teaching method he used was individual and informal. In his provocative treatment of early Confucianism, Robert Eno has described Confucius and his later disciples as forming "study groups" where "students concentrated on the tasks of self-ritualization, and delighting in the rewards of participation in a brotherhood preoccupied with perfecting highminded and aesthetic skills. The syllabus they studied was varied, and included martial arts and textual study, along with formulaic and aesthetic ritual study. But, in fact, all elements of the syllabus were directed toward the end of ritualizing every aspect of speech and conduct."[58] Eno's description illustrates the concerns of the

---

56. *Historical Record,* 47.1911.
57. *Historical Record,* 47.1914.
58. Robert Eno, *The Confucian Creation of Heaven: Philosophy and the Defense of Ritual Mastery* (Albany: State University of New York Press, 1990), p. 63.

compilers of the *Analects* very well, although the social phenomena he describes are somewhat speculative. It also captures the degree to which ritual training combined the acquisition of a vocational skill that qualified disciples for employment with a program of personal development and self-transformation.

By claiming mastery over knowledge of Zhou ritual forms, Confucius gained not only students but also the patronage of rulers. Because the compilers of the *Analects* accepted the insistence on a ritual medium of exchange as an element of what made Confucius an exemplary instructor, that text preserves many examples of the economic transactions that were the basis for the system of patronage itself. The currency that Confucius recognized was not gold or copper coin, but instead one that derived its value from its use in the context of ritual sacrifice. The Confucius of the *Analects* accepted meat from the nobility that he served and from those who sought counsel from him. A person who was perceptive enough to understand the value of this currency was a person Confucius felt he could instruct: "I have never failed to instruct a person who freely presented me with a bundle of dried meat."[59] This is also the type of gift he received from his lord, which he took great trouble to accept in the ritually correct way: "When his lord presented him with food [Confucius] always straightened his mat and first tasted [the food]. When his lord presented him with raw meat, he always cooked it and used it as an offering. When his lord presented him with a live animal, he always reared it."[60] Such gifts were important not only because their role in ritual sacrifice gave them value, but also because Confucius's acceptance of them meant that he eschewed more conventional standards of value.

The use of sacrificial meats as a medium of exchange was also a rejection of the valuation of salary, luxury items, and sex. While Confucius would accept some gifts that were not meat, he preferred meat because it was the ritually correct form of exchange for his services. This was the case even if the monetary value of the gift was high: "Even if it was a carriage and horses, if it was not sacrificial meat he did not make a ritual bow."[61] As this passage implies, some of these references to meat included sacrificial offerings left out for the required period. In this context Confucius also received meat, but he "did not keep his sacrificial meat for more than three days."[62] The final category of gift mentioned in the text is the nonmeat gift that was so incorrect it should not even be accepted: "The

---

59. *Analects* 7.7; Cheng, vol. 2, pp. 445-48. Several lines of commentary hold that this ceremonial gift is specific to persons of a certain age.

60. *Analects* 10.18 (selection); Cheng, vol. 2, pp. 715-19.

61. *Analects* 10.23; Cheng, vol. 2, pp. 722-23.

62. *Analects* 10.9; Cheng, vol. 2, pp. 698-99.

people in the state of Qi made a gift of female entertainers. [The minister] Ji Huanzi accepted them and for three days did not come to court. Confucius left."[63] Here Confucius is in the service of a ruler whose appetite for the ritual propriety is subsidiary to other appetites. The master's departure clearly implies that there are some gifts that should not be accepted. Interestingly, in the version of this story in Sima Qian's biography of Confucius, the master considers staying if the duke would at least offer sacrificial meat to his minister, but then ends up leaving when Ji Huanzi not only spends three days with the dancers but neglects to offer any sacrificial meat. According to this Han dynasty account, when informed of the master's departure, Ji Huanzi sighed and said: "The Master has found fault with me on account of slave girls!"[64]

While the meat economy outlined above probably operated parallel to an economy in which the lord paid Confucius in grain or currency, there is no question that becoming a disciple of Confucius meant trading one economy for the other. This is one of the clearest lessons that Confucius sought to teach, and it appears across the different strata of the *Analects*. An official salary is secondary to the virtue of benevolence (4.5) and to reverently attending to official affairs (15.38). The Confucian gentleman must not be "ashamed of ugly clothes and nasty food,"[65] and so "in matters of food does not seek satiety, and in matters of residence does not seek security."[66] The teacher must instruct the disciple to reject the standard values of wealth and position, and instead to derive value from ritual context. This is the lesson learned by the disciple Zigong, who wanted to dispense with the sacrifice of a live sheep to announce the new moon. Confucius chastises him: "You care for the sheep, I care for the rites."[67] For the disciple, ritual value must always take precedence.

Indeed, in one sense Confucius is not a "teacher" by occupation because there was no fixed payment for his lessons. As seen above, the interaction between Confucius and those who would learn from him instead occurs on the level of ritual gift exchange. The *Analects* provides several fascinating glimpses into the special social and economic relationship between Confucius and his disciples. In many ways this relationship appears to have been modeled on that between a father and his sons. This is made explicit when his disciple Yan Yuan (also called Yan Hui) dies and the other disciples give him a lavish burial that Confucius saw as ritually incorrect. Confucius laments: "Hui regarded me as a father, but I have

63. *Analects* 18.4; Cheng, vol. 4, pp. 1258-61.

64. *Historical Record*, 47.1918.

65. *Analects* 4.9 (selection); Cheng, vol. 1, pp. 246-47.

66. *Analects* 1.14 (selection); Cheng, vol. 1, pp. 52-54. The security probably refers to a sense of attachment to a fixed home, something that is not proper to a man of Confucius's class (14.2).

67. *Analects* 3.17; Cheng, vol. 1, pp. 191-97.

**Confucius leaving Lu in protest after the ruler
accepts a gift of 80 female entertainers**

(from the Ming dynasty blockprint *Kongzi Shengtuji;* Tianjin Yangliuqing, 1997)

been unable to regard him as a son."[68] There is no stronger bond in the *Analects* than that between a father and a son, and it appears that Confucius acted *in loco parentis* for his disciples once they left home to join him.

Two stories about Confucius assuming responsibility for his disciples imply that there was also a stronger economic link between the master and his disciples than the tribute mentioned earlier. In one a disciple asks Confucius for grain to support the mother of another disciple sent as an emissary to a neighboring state. Confucius counsels giving less grain than requested by the mother, observing that her son left with fancy horses and clothes and that "the gentleman supplements those in distress but does not maintain the wealthy."[69] Another request for aid comes from the father of Yan Yuan, who asks Confucius for his carriage in order to pay for or use as a second, outer coffin for his re-

---

68. *Analects* 11.11; Cheng, vol. 3, pp. 759-60. A similar statement is found in the second chapter of the Han dynasty *Record of Ritual (Liji)*, where, following the death of Confucius, the disciple Zigong notes that Confucius mourned for his disciples Yan Yuan and Zhong You as if they were his sons, except that he did not wear the father's mourning clothes. Zigong suggests that his disciples mourn Confucius as a father but observe the same exception to the rites.

69. *Analects* 6.4; Cheng, vol. 2, pp. 371-75.

cently deceased son.[70] Confucius turns down this request, observing that for ritual reasons he himself had not even been able to use his carriage as an outer coffin at his own son's funeral: "I was not able to walk and thereby use [my carriage] as an outer coffin [for my son], because walking would not have befitted my former status as Counselor."[71] In both cases, then, Confucius denies the request for assistance, not because of a potential monetary loss but rather on the basis of either a personal moral judgment or ritual requirements. These two passages also show the biological parents of disciples requesting assistance from Confucius in a way that suggests he accepted economic responsibility for his disciples, or perhaps even acted as custodian of the wealth of the group.[72]

These stories, coupled with Confucius's statements about the gentleman's rejection of materialistic desires, suggest that the earliest Confucians sought to set themselves apart from ordinary society by suspending accepted economic criteria of value and replacing them with criteria derived from a ritual system of exchange. Once internalized, this alternate value structure functioned to guarantee that disciples who became officials did not use their position to cause economic hardship for others. Disciples were often asked to serve as stewards (*zai*) of the estates of wealthy landowners (6.5; 6.9; 6.14), but they were expected by Confucius to continue to follow the alternate system of value, even if it meant not following their employer's wishes. The case of the disciple Ran You (a.k.a. Ran Qiu) illustrates this point well. Ran You was in the service of the Ji clan, a group often criticized in the *Analects*. At one point, when the Ji are planning to attack a dependency of the state of Lu, Confucius harshly criticizes Ran You. Ran You's former teacher says that because Ran failed to restrain his benighted employers and did not help them cultivate their civil virtue, Ran is the Ji clan's real enemy (16.1). On another occasion Ran You helps the clan collect taxes and add to their already exceptional wealth. In the *Analects* Confucius excoriates him:

70. A convincing alternative reading of this entire passage was given early this century by Huan Maoyong. Huan made eight objections to the usual reading that Yan's father planned to sell the carriage and buy an outer coffin, attributed to Kong An'guo and made orthodox by Zhu Xi. Instead, Huan argued that Yan Yuan's father was requesting the use of the carriage not at the burial but as a traditional bier-cum-outer-coffin at the funeral that takes place before the burial. See Cheng, vol. 3, p. 752.

71. *Analects* 11.8; Cheng, vol. 3, pp. 752-57. The interpretation of this passage by E. Bruce Brooks and A. Taeko Brooks (*The Original "Analects": Sayings of Confucius and His Successors* [New York: Columbia University Press, 1998], p. 71) is that it is concerned with the succession of Confucius.

72. Upon being presented with a thousand measures of grain, "the master accepted it without a word of decline and then divided the grain between those of his disciples who were destitute," according to the Han or WeiJin period text *Kongcongzi*; see Yoav Ariel, *K'ung-Ts'ung-tzu: The K'ung Family Masters' Anthology* (Princeton: Princeton University Press, 1989), p. 87.

The Ji clan was wealthier than the Duke of Zhou, but [Ran] Qiu still helped them amass greater wealth by collecting taxes. The Master said:

"[Ran You] is not my follower! It is now suitable for the younger disciples to shriek at him and play the drums to chastise him."[73]

This unusually blunt criticism makes clear the importance of the disciples' continued withdrawal from the regular economy. For working to increase his employer's wealth, Ran You is cast out from the community.

From an anthropological perspective, the alternate system of exchange promoted by Confucius is consistent with the existence of alternate types of ceremonial exchange found in other societies. The distinction between the aristocratic *kula* exchange and the monetary *gimwali* described by the anthropologist Bronislaw Malinowski in his *Argonauts of the Western Pacific* might be compared to the regular and ritual exchange systems outlined above. When faced with a gift of a carriage and horses, in accordance with what some commentators call the economy of the "circulation of wealth" *(tongcai)*, Confucius does not respond to it as a matter of ritual. Yet, when a carriage allows him to move in the manner prescribed by ritual for his office, he will not part with it even to enhance the funeral of his son or favorite disciple. Marcel Mauss notes with respect to the ritual exchange system of ancient India: "The gift is thus something that must be given, that must be received and that is, at the same time, dangerous to accept. The gift itself constitutes an irrevocable link especially when it is a gift of food."[74] The meat economy is just such an alternate system. From a Maussian perspective, the notion of credit derives from the ritual exchange system rather than the "circulation of wealth" economy, and indeed this is consistent with Confucius's assistance with funerals and emphasis on the support network created by filial piety. Confucius, like Mauss himself, sought to reestablish a ritual order in which "the rich should come once more . . . [t]o consider themselves treasurers, as it were, of their fellow-citizens."[75] On a social

---

73. *Analects* 11.17. Confucius's rationale for what some commentators call Ran's expulsion from the group is expressed in the Zuo commentary to the *Spring and Autumn* record of the eleventh year of Duke Ai. That text expresses the likelihood that once a person has abandoned the rites, then even once the tax is collected he will not be satisfied. See Cheng, vol. 3, pp. 774-77.

74. Marcel Mauss, *The Gift: Forms and Functions of Exchange in Archaic Societies* (Glencoe, Ill.: Free Press, 1954), p. 50. While the exchange theory of Mauss, later developed by Lévi-Strauss, usually postulates a return gift for each gift given, the idea of a gift presented and a service rendered seems consistent in this case where services are ostensibly given voluntarily. Mauss himself considers the possibility of a service creating the obligation to give a gift in his discussion of the Roman *nexum*.

75. Mauss, p. 66.

level the function of the meat economy may be to invert the social hierarchy, as Weiner's more recent studies of *kula* exchange have suggested.[76]

From a slightly different perspective, an anthropologist might regard the promotion of the meat economy as a political strategy to make a group cohesive and distinguish it from outsiders. Such a strategy is not unique to Confucian society, and indeed Max Weber saw it as characteristic of a certain type of religious founder. In *The Sociology of Religion* Weber notes that the typical prophet propagates ideas for his own sake and "not for fees,"[77] and elsewhere notes that this is one of the main elements of charismatic authority: "In its 'pure' form, charisma is never a source of private gain for its holders in the sense of economic exploitation by the making of a deal. Nor is it a source of income in the form of pecuniary compensation, and just as little does it involve an orderly taxation for the material requirements of its mission. If the mission is one of peace, individual patrons provide the necessary means for charismatic structures; or those to whom the charisma is addressed provide honorific gifts, donations, or other voluntary contributions."[78] The Confucius of the *Analects* was interested in establishing exactly this kind of alternative set of social economic relationships that is characteristic of charismatic authority, something Weber called "the very force that disregards economy."[79] The portrayal of Confucius in the *Analects* was not simply of a teacher by occupation, but of a teacher engaged in building a social and economic arrangement independent of conventional society. For the moment it is enough to note that this appears to run against the grain of Weber's picture of Confucius as an "academic teaching philosopher." In the social organization of the Confucian group described in the *Analects,* the master wields something akin to what Weber called charismatic authority, a point we will revisit in the final section of this chapter.

At the same time, in light of the Confucius stories that did not make it into the *Analects,* it is also safe to say that charismatic authority was not the characteristic of Confucius that most interested the ritual experts who put that anthology together. Their descriptions of the social and economic relations between the master and his disciples preserve suggestions that the authority of the sage was not simply a function of the brilliance of his ethical thought. But the

---

76. Annette Weiner contends that the *kula* can "transcend kinship in order to achieve political autonomy without the backing and ranking of a particular kin group or ancestors" (*Inalienable Possessions: The Paradox of Keeping-While-Giving* [Berkeley: University of California Press, 1992], p. 132).

77. Max Weber, *The Sociology of Religion,* trans. E. Fischoff (Boston: Beacon Press, 1963), p. 48.

78. *From Max Weber: Essays in Sociology,* trans. H. H. Gerth and C. Wright Mills (New York: Oxford University Press, 1946), p. 247.

79. *From Max Weber,* p. 248.

prophetic, charismatic, and even messianic aspects of Confucius are brought out more fully in texts that circulated alongside the *Analects*. In those texts one finds images of Confucius that have been championed by other groups in Chinese history, and which contradict many characteristics of the ritualist and teacher familiar from the *Analects* and widely accepted today.

Spring and Autumn: The Image of Confucius as Prophet

Confucius said: "I wrote the *Classic of Filial Piety* because uncrowned kings have recourse to neither the reward of noble rank nor to capital punishment by the executioner's axe. Therefore I have laid out the Way of the enlightened king." . . . Zengzi left his mat and sat down [nearer to Confucius]. Confucius said: "Be seated. Let me explain to you. Obedient grandchildren are a means to avoid catastrophes. Offerings to the former kings are a means to rely on their power."

> A fragment of the *Classic of Filial Piety: Drawguard for
> Targeting the Mandate (Xiaojing gouming jue),*
> a Confucian apocryphal book preserved
> in a Tang dynasty collection[80]

In contrast to the academic teacher for whom participation in government consisted of proper family behavior, the Confucius of the *Classic of Filial Piety: Drawguard for Targeting the Mandate* explains proper family behavior as a tool to control the natural and political order. The set of texts known as the "apocryphal books" *(weishu)* portray Confucius as having had exceptional or supernatural powers and explicit political ambitions. These ambitions led him to establish an esoteric transmission of his most important teachings. While the apocryphal books generally postdate the Han dynasty biography of Confucius written by Sima Qian and the collation of the different versions of the *Analects* by the later Han writer Zheng Xuan, they expand on themes that were already popular in the Han. Such alternate images of Master Kong have gained and lost favor at different times in Chinese history, but are worth examining to paint a fuller picture of the range of early representations of the master.

The explicitly political Confucius of the apocryphal books is just one of several alternate constructions of Confucius that have been important at differ-

---

80. Under the heading "Study" in the *Taiping yulan,* quoted in Huang Shi, *Weft Texts of the "Spring and Autumn," "Analects," and "Classic of Filial Piety" (Chunqiu wei, Lunyu wei, Xiaojing wei)* (Shanghai: Guji, 1993), 3.32-33. A drawguard *(jue)* was a stone or ivory tool worn on the archer's right thumb when drawing a bowstring.

ent times or for particular social groups throughout Chinese history. While they vary in several important ways from the Confucius of the *Analects*, there is as yet no objective basis upon which to conclude that they are necessarily less authentic than that book's teacher of ritual-based ethics. This section will center on the Confucius of the *Spring and Autumn* and its related traditions, and will also treat the Confucius who studied the *Changes* (*Yi*, a.k.a. *I Ching*).

While many images of Confucius based on the *Analects* portray his objectives as primarily academic in nature, the tradition of Confucius as the "uncrowned king" focused on his ability to rule and his attempts to transform the Chinese polity. Writers in predynastic China used the phrase "pure" or "unrecognized" *(su)* king, more commonly translated "uncrowned" king, to denote a person with kingly virtue who did not gain a position of rulership.[81] By the Han, writers used the term to refer to Confucius. The Han critic Wang Chong (27–ca. 97 C.E.) employs the term to identify Confucius: "Confucius did not rule as king, but his work as uncrowned king may be seen in the *Spring and Autumn*."[82] In other words, while he did not himself govern China, through his writings Confucius could prepare it for the government of a future sage-king.

While most authorities hold that Confucius did not rise to high office,[83] whether he sought to do so or to gain political authority by other means is unclear. Despite the perception that he spoke only to his students and to the princes of his period, even the *Analects* contains stories of his addressing others. The Japanese scholar Asano Yûichi has noted that Confucius's willingness to consider serving regional strongmen (17.5; 17.7) and speak with a border official (3.24) and a madman (18.5) shows that he was interested in effecting change on a broader level. Consider these portentous words in the *Analects* spoken by said border official to the disciples following his meeting with the sage: "The world has been without the Way for a long while, but Heaven is going to use [Confucius] as the wooden clapper of a bell."[84] While commentators disagree about whether the border official is speaking of Confucius's dissemination of his message or his

81. Cf. chap. 13 of the Taoist classic *Zhuangzi*.

82. Chap. 80 of Wang Chong's *Lunheng*.

83. While there are reports that Confucius did serve in high office, for the most part early sources depict him as having been employed as an official in charge of ritual functions. While many scholars criticize the claim in the *Historical Record* that Confucius once rose to the equivalent of prime minister of the state of Lu, its claim that he served as Grand Director against Brigands (*Da sikou*) is, by contrast, accepted since it is substantiated in the *Analects*. Nevertheless, there is little to indicate what interest or expertise, beyond a general focus on character formation, the sage may have had in such a post. Instead the pervasive attitude in the *Analects* and other early sources is frustration that Confucius's talents are not appreciated by the rulers of his time combined with a tacit appreciation of the reticence to serve rulers who did not meet the sage's high standards.

84. *Analects* 3.24; Cheng, vol. 1, pp. 219-22.

eventual occupation of high office, there is little question the official is making a prediction that Confucius will transform the populace in line with the desires of heaven. This is certainly Yang Xiong's (53 B.C.E.–18 C.E.) reading of the passage in his *Model Sayings (Fayan)*, a text patterned on the *Analects:* "Was not Heaven's Way embodied in Confucius? Confucius is the one who transmitted it. Is it not embodied in us Confucians? If his words continue to be transmitted, then would not this cause us Confucians to become metal bells with wooden tongues?"[85] Yang Xiong recycles the border official's imagery, asserting that in getting the attention of the people of the world, Confucius is simply the tool of heaven. In this sense Confucius and his disciples are nothing more than the wooden clapper of a bell, their message dictated by a higher authority. There are several places in the *Analects* where Confucius appears to claim special dispensation based on his relationship with heaven (7.23; 9.5; 11.23). This is perhaps the basis of his confidence that if given the opportunity, he would be able to re-create the golden age of the Zhou: "If there was someone who would make use of me, could I not make a Zhou in the East?" (17.5). These aspects of the *Analects* seem to support a different conclusion regarding the relationship between personal self-cultivation and social transformation outlined earlier. In these passages social transformation is not a secondary effect of the widespread acceptance of Confucius's ethical program, but instead is the explicit goal of Confucius, a goal he sought to achieve through political means. This image of Confucius, the master as "uncrowned king," gained favor in the Han period.

These explicit statements worked in tandem with records of omens that implicitly identified Confucius as an ideal ruler. The story that from birth he was marked as different from other mortals proved his exceptional nature in the eyes of those who saw him as destined to rule China. In the apocryphal books the circumstances in which he was born and the physical signs on his body at birth both demonstrated his destiny as the "uncrowned king." While some of these characteristics (e.g., his detached earlobes, like the Buddha) are probably late additions,[86] early versions of these stories are present in the *Historical Record*. The apocryphal books have elaborate narratives about Confucius's mother being told of the location of her son's birth in a dream, but the *Historical Record* simply has her making offerings at the Ni hill before giving

---

85. Cheng, vol. 1, p. 221.

86. Huang, 1.35. Julia K. Murray has noted the connection between some of the legends about the marks on the body of Confucius and legends about Buddha. In the case of the forty-nine bodily signs of Confucius noted in the thirteenth century, Murray writes: "Inspired by the thirty-two marks that distinguished the Buddha Sakyamuni's body from that of ordinary mortals, the attribution of a larger number to Confucius also implied that he was superior to the Buddha" ("Illustrations of the Life of Confucius: Their Evolution, Functions, and Significance in Late Ming China," *Artibus Asiae* 56, no. 1/2 [1997]: 81).

birth.[87] The apocryphal books describe Confucius's physical peculiarities in detail, which is consistent with the prominence of physiognomy among traditional Chinese omenological practices. The apocryphal book *Analects: Picking Out the Simulacrum of the Fu Star (Lunyu tifuxiang)* tells us that Confucius was the uncrowned king, and that his disciples Yan Yuan and Zigong filled the traditional offices of Minister over the Masses and Minister of Works, respectively. As evidence, the text recounts their various physical peculiarities, including Zigong's long tongue (three *cun* — a little less than three inches), which he used to preach across the four seas — not unlike the wooden clapper of a bell.[88] Another such text, preserved in a tenth century C.E. compendium, records that Confucius was born with characters inscribed on his chest to the effect that he would govern and transform his generation.[89] Many writers saw these physical signs as omens that he was indeed destined to rule, just as Sima Qian did in his discussions of Confucius's abnormal height and deformity in the *Historical Record*'s early account of his life. These were heaven-sent proofs of Confucius's political authority, and in the minds of Han writers substantiated the sage's identification as the "uncrowned king."

The events surrounding the revival of the dynasty by the emperor Guangwu (r. 25-57 C.E.), predicted and facilitated by the prophecies of Confucius, serve as a good illustration of the political authority attributed to Confucius during the Han dynasty. As the Japanese scholar Itano Chôhachi has shown, in the crucial dispute following the short-lived Xin dynasty (9-23 C.E.) that culminated in the restoration of the Han, both sides sought to legitimate their authority by citing prophecies appearing in both exoteric sources like the *Spring and Autumn* and esoteric texts such as *Kong Qiu's Secret Classic*.[90] Thus the Han was witness to two types of prophetic text: canonical texts associated with Confucius were read as source manuals for the interpretation of omens, and the apocryphal books were read as the products of an esoteric transmission that paralleled the canonical texts. These novel readings of old texts and new auxiliary "classics" often made use of what some scholars have called the "correlative cosmology" of the Han period. This cosmology allowed Han systematizers to reduce the observable world to sets of natural categories, the

---

87. Huang, 1.23. According to the dream, Confucius was to be born in Kongsan, the traditional birthplace of the sage Yi Yin.

88. Huang, 2.2-3. The title of this text is somewhat ambiguous, but I take *fu* to refer to one of the stars of the Big Dipper. The reference to offices comes from the *Taiping yulan*, dating from the tenth century, and the one to Zigong's tongue from a commentary to the *Wenxuan*, datable to the seventh century C.E.

89. Huang, 1.24.

90. Itano Chôhachi, "The T'u-ch'an Prophetic Books and the Establishment of Confucianism," *Memoirs of the Research Department of the Toyo Bunko* 34 (1976): 50-56.

elements of like categories influencing each other according to patterns that human beings could only indirectly observe. They applied these correlations, expressed in categories like *yin* and *yang* or the five phases *(wuxing)*, to both the natural world and to the realm of human affairs; to the past and, sometimes, to the prediction of the future. Through this correlative system and the universe of connections it provided, these systematizers were able to find messages of all types that had been encoded in seemingly ordinary phenomena.

The idea that Confucius's doctrines were secret, or in some sense encoded, comes through clearly in the apocryphal books. The sage used subtle or secret words *(weiyan)* so that those not conversant in the Way would be unable to understand them. This language might be spoken or it might be wordless, but the ability to communicate in it was akin to a special sensitivity or perceptual acuity. A seventh-century collection contains a fragment of an apocryphal book to the *Analects* that explains how a disciple of Confucius composed the *Analects:* "Zi Xia made public the selected secret words of Confucius to make the case he was the 'uncrowned king.'"[91] In this view all the teachings of Confucius were once esoteric, but a disciple made a part of them public. The claim is that the *Analects* was only a part of Confucius's secret transmission, and the fact that the apocryphal books arose centuries later than did the *Analects* does not mean that they are less genuine. Those who saw Confucius in this light interpreted the fact that his "subtle words" had been kept secret to mean that they were *more* valuable than the doctrines found in the *Analects.*

The idea of an esoteric transmission from Confucius, however, can be found much earlier than the apocrypha. A text that dates to 239 B.C.E., the *Spring and Autumn of Master Lü,* portrays Confucius as able to communicate without speech with another worthy named Master Wen Boxue. Confucius explains the nature of their communication: "If one is that sort of man, one's eyes meet and the Way is established in a way that cannot be conveyed by appearance or sound."[92] The idea of secret language is also associated with Confucius in the encyclopedic text *Master Huainan (Huainanzi),* which was presented to the throne in 139 B.C.E.:

> The Duke of Bai said:
> "If one threw water into water, how could anyone find it?"
> Confucius said:
> "If it was a mix of the [water] of the Zi and Sheng rivers, then Yi Ya would know by tasting it."

91. Huang, 2.6.
92. Xu Weiyu, 18.10a. This example of the wordless communication of Confucius is preceded by a similar example having to do with the Duke of Zhou.

The Duke of Bai said:

"In that case, is it true that a person can never make use of secret language?"

Confucius said:

"How could one say that a person cannot? Who understands what it is to which words refer? The person who understands what it is to which words refer does not use words to have words with another person."[93]

Confucius is not only saying that it is possible to communicate without using language, but also that the person who is not as sensitive as a sage will not notice such communication.

By the Han dynasty, many of those writers and officials who identified with Confucius saw the Confucian apocryphal books and commentaries to the *Spring and Autumn* as texts that contained secrets hidden from the uninitiated in the same way that the master's manner of wordless speaking concealed his true message from those who were not sages. Han scholars like Dong Zhongshu (179-104 B.C.E.) read the *Spring and Autumn* as containing Confucius's secret transmission, and this tradition, associated with the "New Text" (*jinwen*) school of Confucianism, extended the notion to the other major works associated with the sage. Around 150 B.C.E. the commentary to the *Spring and Autumn* attributed to Master Gongyang explained why those who fared well in the chronicle were deserving and why those who fared ill were blameworthy. This exercise involved quite a bit of "reading between the lines," and interpretations often hinged on Confucius's choice of a particular word, assuming that the master crafted the text as a code.

Many apocryphal books incorporated the correlative cosmology of the Han and were essentially omenological dictionaries, guides to deciphering astronomical or divinatory patterns. These patterns were, in the same manner as the *Spring and Autumn*, natural codes broken by Confucius, and the texts the keys that subsequent scholars could use in deciphering the hidden truths of the natural world. According to one apocryphal book, "Confucius understood astronomy and divined good and bad fortune. If the person to whom he was talking was not one of his own men, then even though he spoke to them, he did so opaquely."[94] This image of Confucius as responsible for the propagation of secret knowledge was already present at the time the text of the *Analects* was being fixed. The bibliographic survey of the history of the Han, which still separates the three versions of the *Analects*, also lists a text called the *Charts and Codes of Confucius and His Disciples (Kongzi turen tufa)*. Early sources explain the phrase *tufa* in conjunction with the ministers of doomed states who can

93. Chap. 12 of the *Huainanzi*.
94. Huang, 1.173.

"read the writing on the wall."[95] This and texts like *Kong Qiu's Secret Classic*, mentioned earlier, show that texts claiming esoteric transmissions from Confucius existed from a very early time.

The picture of a Confucius who encoded his political message in the *Spring and Autumn* and whose authority derived from physical markings that identified him as a born ruler is just one of several early versions of Confucius that competed during the formative period of Confucius legends. A related image surrounds the master's interest in the divination classic *Changes*. Because of the following passage in Sima Qian's biography of the sage, many later generations of scholars have identified Confucius as the author of the commentaries to the classic:

> Only in his old age did Confucius take pleasure in the *Changes*. He ordered the [commentaries on the] *Decision, Appended Judgments, Images, Discussion of the Trigrams*, and *Words of the Text*. He read the *Changes* so much that the cords that held the slips of text together broke three times. He said:
> "At this rate, if I had several more years, I would become proficient at the *Changes!*"[96]

Recent archaeological discoveries show that when Sima Qian was writing, the association between Confucius and the *Changes* was already well established. Consider the following passage from the *Appended Commentary (Xici)*, a text now known to have existed in 168 B.C.E., where Confucius uses a trope from early Taoist texts to explain the value of the *Changes*:

> The Master said:
> "Writing cannot completely capture words, and words themselves cannot completely capture intentions."
> "Therefore, is it possible to understand the meaning of the intentions of the sages?"
> The Master said:
> "The sages established the images to completely embody their intentions, and explained the trigrams to completely capture true and false circumstances. . . ."[97]

95. Chap. 16 of the *Lüshi chunqiu*.

96. *Historical Record*, 47.1937. The translation of the names of the commentaries follows the popular Wilhelm/Baynes edition of the *Changes* (see succeeding note).

97. Cf. Richard Wilhelm, *The I Ching or Book of Changes*, trans. C. Baynes (Princeton: Princeton University Press, 1977), p. 322. This section of the "Appended" commentary was also found at Mawangdui in 1973 and so dates to the second century B.C.E. at the latest.

Confucius explains to his unidentified interlocutor that the images used to express the patterns of milfoil stalks used in this type of divination (patterns derived from "trigrams," triplets of solid or broken lines) constitute a mode of transmission that is superior to the written word. That Confucius, late in life, came to an appreciation of the *Changes* because it was a repository for the symbolic messages of the ancient sages, is yet another picture of the sage. This picture, which shares certain assumptions with the "uncrowned king" narratives, is very different from the one that developed into the ritual expert and teacher of the *Analects*.

The explanation given by Confucius in his discussion of the value of the *Changes* is similar in many ways to the reasoning that Han Confucians used in connection with his writing of the *Spring and Autumn*. Confucius treasured the *Changes* because it contained a secret transmission of the intentions of King Wen of Zhou. Similarly, Han scholars read the *Spring and Autumn* as containing a secret transmission from Confucius. In this way the Han image of Confucius the divination expert reinforced that of the uncrowned king.[98]

The images of Confucius associated with both the *Spring and Autumn* and the *Changes* have in common the fact that they suit the promotion of the value of a particular text. The Confucius of the *Spring and Autumn* tradition happened to make that text the key to understanding the political method of the "uncrowned king," while that of the *Changes* tradition suggested that the symbols of divination were actually a legacy of the ancient sage-kings. In this sense these images were of a kind with the ritual master of the *Analects*, who sought to school kings and disciples in the ritual self-cultivation that would allow them to prosper. In each case the valuable expertise of Confucius was a reflection of the contents of the text.

From the third through the first century B.C.E., a picture of Confucius as an ambitious reformer, impelled, protected, and given distinguishing features by heaven, enjoyed popularity. His divine markings and concern with a secret transmission reflected concerns of a period when the reading of omens was increasingly central to Chinese political life. This picture is very different from that of Confucius as a teacher of ritual, and was used to political ends by a different group of people than the imperial tutors who culled the latter from a larger set of sayings to assemble the *Analects*. Both these groups, then, appropriated Confucius to valorize their own work and the texts they used.

There existed a variety of images of Confucius during the early imperial period. When viewed against some of the other images of Confucius that were pres-

98. The role of the "Taoist" notion of the inadequacy of words and Han Confucianism is treated at greater length in Mark Csikszentmihalyi, "Chia I's 'Techniques of the Tao' and the Han Confucian Appropriation of Technical Discourse," *Asia Major* 10, no. 1-2 (1997): 49-67.

ent as well, the modern image of Confucius certainly seems both more human and less politically ambitious. If the principle of selection of the *Analects* had been different, perhaps scholars would view Confucius in a different way today (or, more likely, would use another text as the standard source). At the same time, these early alternate constructions of Confucius should not be considered more or less authoritative than the now standard image of Confucius as ritualist and teacher. The claim that Han courtiers or Qing dynasty literati reformulated the life of Confucius to valorize their own pursuits might just as well be applied to diviners or omenologists who placed Confucius at the head of their genealogy.

Now that we have examined the images of Confucius in three of these major sources for information on his life, the *Historical Record,* the *Analects,* and the commentaries to the *Spring and Autumn,* it is worth briefly returning to the *Word Source* dictionary entry that drew from each of them. What is so interesting about the entry, and the many modern presentations of the life of Confucius that it resembles, is the way it draws details out of widely divergent sources and assembles them into a coherent narrative. After examining the diverse early narratives about Confucius, it should be apparent that the modern version of Confucius is actually assembled from parts of three very different Confuciuses, constructed by different communities to different ends. Instead of asking which image is right, it might be more instructive to ask: What are the historical processes that led to one particular image from this broad spectrum being singled out? The next two sections will examine two influential stages in the process of sifting out what has become the dominant synthesis of these early images.

Zhu Xi and Post-Buddhist Readings of Confucius

> We can state that this history of learning was initiated by Confucius, and that the most accomplished organizer and synthesizer of this history was Zhu Xi. This is what I mean by treasuring similarity and disparaging dissimilarity. It is analogous to the total absence of any proponent of new religious doctrines after Jesus in the Christian tradition.
>
> Qian Mu (1895-1990), "Historical Perspective on Chu Hsi's Learning"[99]

Chinese scholars of the late imperial period, and many modern scholars like Qian Mu, have seen themselves as continuing a tradition that Confucius had begun. Late imperial writers cast Confucius as primarily, and sometimes ex-

---

99. In Chan Wing-tsit, ed., *Chu Hsi and Neo-Confucianism* (Honolulu: University of Hawaii Press, 1986), pp. 39-40.

clusively, concerned with the transmission and understanding of ritual texts. This picture was generally consistent with the perspective of the *Analects*, which Zhu Xi elevated to canonical status in the Song dynasty (960-1279 C.E.), along with the *Mencius* and two chapters of the *Record of Ritual*. Zhu Xi's influence on the development of Confucianism has been so profound that his readings of many passages of the *Analects* are still the basis for most modern translations. A reader of Lin Yutang's (1895-1976) description of Confucianism as the "religion of the *li* [i.e., ritual]"[100] may well catch a glimpse of Zhu's emphasis on Confucian ritualism. Yet the *Analects* is but one possible source for details of the life of the master, and ritual, although a central facet, does not exhaust the information about him even in the *Analects*. After examining many images of Confucius in the preimperial and early imperial periods, it remains to be seen why this aspect was singled out as authoritative in the late imperial period.

The emphasis on ritualism was the result of several factors, but one of the most important was the central role of ritual in the conceptual systems of the classical textual scholars of late imperial China. The Song dynasty scholarship of Zhu Xi (a.k.a. Chu Hsi) had an enormous impact on the study of the classics into the early modern period of Chinese history. Zhu Xi was the son of a local official and early in his life was exposed to Chan Buddhism, the tradition that became known as Zen when it reached Japan. Around the age of twenty, however, he read the Confucian scholarship of the Cheng brothers (Hao, 1032-85, and Yi, 1033-1107), which led him formally to reject Buddhism and turn his attention to pre-Buddhist classical scholarship. In his 1177 commentary to the *Analects*, Zhu focused on the cultivation of benevolence, the measure of which was the social conduct that resulted from it. Because of this emphasis on benevolence, some scholars have seen Zhu's Confucius as more socially engaged than the enlightened exemplars of his Buddhist contemporaries. At the same time, Zhu's version of the Confucian gentleman attained benevolence through the knowledge of the heavenly "principle" *(li)* that had been understood by past sages, and so Zhu's program of self-cultivation was, at its heart, based on ritual and the study of the classics. In reading *Analects* 12.1, when Confucius says that benevolence consists of "overcoming oneself and returning to ritual propriety," Zhu defined "oneself" as "the body's selfish desires" and "ritual propriety" as "the patterns of the Heavenly principle."[101] The study of ritual is then the way to reach the transcendent heavenly principle, the knowledge of which allows one to act morally.

---

100. Lin Yutang, *The Wisdom of Confucius* (New York: Random House, 1938), pp. 13-17.

101. Zhu Xi, *Collected Commentaries on the Paragraphs and Sentences of the Four Books (Sishu zhangju jizhu)* (Beijing: Zhonghua, 1983), p. 131.

When Zhu Xi's interpretation of the *Analects* became the basis of the imperial examination system, this somewhat scholastic approach to the text became the method used in most late imperial readings. From the Song through the Qing, scholars paid increasing attention to those ancient texts whose primary concern was the ritual code, such as the *Record of Ritual*. As Chow Kai-wing has recently argued, the discourse on rites went on to become the dominant intellectual trend in China during the Qing dynasty.[102] There are many reasons for the dominance of ritualism as an intellectual focus during the Qing, not the least of which was the fact that many topics that dealt more directly with politics were directly or indirectly censored by the occupying Manchu mandarins. At the same time, the recourse to the rites of the past was an implicitly nativist move that dovetailed with the philosophical interests in ritual characteristic of Song writers like Zhu Xi and the Cheng brothers. Chow notes that "The triumph of the alien regime not only helped keep the Confucian purist movement alive but also gave it new impetus. The convergence of anti-Manchu sentiment with the resurgent [Cheng-Zhu] school added fuel to the quest for authentic Confucian rituals."[103] The political situation for scholars in the Qing restricted them to discussing the past, but their need to address the present gave them an impetus to discover what was authentically Chinese in that past. In this sense Qing Confucian revivalism found a model in the Zhou revivalism of Confucius. The net result was that the Qing literatus viewed Confucius as the paradigm for the Chinese scholar, and the life of the sage was increasingly read in a way that mirrored the lives of those doing the reading.

Another reason that Qing literati located Confucius at the beginning of a scholastic lineage may have been due to the influence of Buddhism. While Buddhism had yet to arrive from India in Sima Qian's time, it had become a major social force by the time of the Tang (618-907 C.E.) and Song dynasties. While Buddhism adapted to Chinese society, Chinese writers disagreed about how to classify it vis-à-vis indigenous Chinese traditions like Confucianism and Taoism. In the sixth century C.E., for example, debates were held that pitted Buddhist monks against Taoists. Some records of these debates compare Confucianism to Buddhism and Taoism, and others simply subsume Taoism under the name Confucianism when it is compared to Buddhism.[104] In other words, it

102. Chow Kai-wing, *The Rise of Confucian Ritualism in Late Imperial China: Ethics, Classics, and Lineage Discourse* (Stanford: Stanford University Press, 1994).

103. Chow, p. 98.

104. Examples of these different typologies are the *Laughing at the Tao Discussions (Xiao Dao lun)* and the *Two Teachings Discussions (Er jiao lun),* respectively. See Livia Kohn, *Laughing at the Tao: Debates among Buddhists and Taoists in Medieval China* (Princeton: Princeton University Press, 1995), pp. 24-34.

was the introduction of a foreign "teaching" *(jiao)* that led the Chinese to label Confucianism an indigenous "teaching," and in so doing caused it to be reconceptualized along the lines of Buddhism.

Buddhism influenced the portrayal of Confucius in the visual arts and altered the form in which later traditions encountered him. Julia Murray has pointed out that the early development of the genre of narrative illustrations of Confucius's life (such as the ones reproduced in this chapter) was closely associated with Buddhism. The illustrations themselves were formally modeled on illustrations of the life of the Buddha Sakyamuni.[105] During the Tang and Song dynasties, artists increasingly depicted Confucius in a style homologous to that used to portray the Buddha.

Intellectual historians today generally appreciate the influence of Buddhism on the thought of the Song dynasty "Study of the Way" *(Daoxue)* school of Confucianism associated with Zhu Xi, but it is less commonplace for them to acknowledge its influence on the way late imperial scholars conceptualized Confucius and the traditions associated with him. The increasing importance of transmission of the "Way" from Confucius to later scholars derived in part from the Mahayana Buddhist conception of Shakyamuni's expedient use of the sutras to transmit the Dharma. Late imperial scholars engaged in the interpretation of the Confucian classics took this transmission as an implicit model for a tradition that viewed Confucius as its "founder." In the words of the Qing scholar Pi Xirui (1850-1908), the author of *History of the Study of the Classics (Jingxue lishi)*, "The first age of the study of the classics began with Confucius's editing of the Six Classics."[106] Consequently, when scholars like Pi constructed genealogies from which they claimed authority, Confucius was always placed at the beginning. Thomas A. Wilson traces similar practices to the Buddhist emphasis on the transmission of the Dharma, and writes that this tendency began with the "Study of the Way" school associated with Zhu Xi: "[Genealogy] characterized the manner in which first the ['Study of the Way'] adherents and later their opponents ordered the raw data of the Confucian past and constructed a doctrinally unified and ideologically compelling lineage of sages and worthies that simultaneously served to define and legitimate their school's interpretation of the Confucian tradition."[107] In

---

105. See Julia K. Murray, "Buddhism and Early Narrative Illustration in China," *Archives of Asian Art* 48 (1995): 17-31.

106. Pi Xirui, *History of the Study of the Classics (Jingxue lishi)* (Taibei: Yiwen, 1987), p. 1. Here the "six classics" refer to the Five Classics plus the lost classic of *Music*. Pi notes that some of these texts did predate Confucius, but that it was only after he edited them that they became classics.

107. Thomas A. Wilson, *Genealogy of the Way: The Construction and Uses of the Confucian Tradition in Late Imperial China* (Stanford: Stanford University Press, 1995), p. 77.

late imperial China, issues of national identity, academic and political authority were bound up in the identification of Confucius as a ritualist and a teacher.[108] The emphasis on ritual in late imperial China, a result of political factors as well as the influence of Buddhism, led to a redefinition of Confucius as the founder of a line of ritual experts. The result was that the *Analects*, which had been selected on the principle of its utility as a textbook on ritual, enjoyed ever greater popularity.

What is particularly significant about this development is that the late imperial conception of Confucius as the founder of an intellectual lineage is an instance of Confucius being portrayed as an innovator. Confucius himself always looked back to the former sages for inspiration, identifying himself as part of a transmission from ancient times. In the *Analects* he even identifies himself as a "transmitter, not a creator" (7.1). Yet it is in the context of the scholarly tradition that later scholars saw him as a founder. John Berthrong has noted that "The title of First Teacher has always been the proudest and most uncontested title for Confucius."[109] When Europeans first came to China, they took this image of Confucius as First Teacher and generalized it to the idea that Confucius was the designer of the more general pattern of Chinese society.

For Europeans and American missionaries, a primary question was whether Confucianism, as it had been conceptualized following the arrival of Buddhism in China, was a religion in the sense that Christianity was. Could Confucius the First Teacher be compared with (and therefore seen to be in competition with) Christ the Savior? As we shall see, whether out of admiration for Confucian ethical precepts or a belief in Christ's exceptionalism, many missionaries were ambivalent about equating the role of the two founders in their respective traditions. Narratives of the life of Christ influenced some Chinese scholars, like the Qing dynasty reformer Kang Youwei, to reinterpret the biography and teachings of Confucius.

Kang Youwei and Christian Influence on Readings of Confucius

It is true further that Father Martini, another Jesuit, in his *Sinica historia* ascribes a great antiquity to Confucius, which has led many

108. Miyazaki Ichisada, *New Research on the "Analects"* (*Rongo no shin kenkyû*) (Tokyo: Iwanami, 1974), p. 33, draws similar conclusions about the Song dynasty emphasis on transmission of the Way, and also points to the influence of Buddhism as a cause of the increased emphasis on ritual and the *Classic of Ritual*, which corresponded with the important Buddhist genre of *vinaya*.

109. John Berthrong, *All under Heaven: Transforming Paradigms in Confucian-Christian Dialogue* (Albany: State University of New York Press, 1994), p. 72.

into atheism. . . . Nevertheless Nicolas Trigault, better informed than Ruggieri or Martini, writes in his *De christiana expeditione apud Sinas* that printing was in use in China not more than two centuries earlier than in Europe, and that Confucius flourished not more than five hundred years before Christ.

The New Science of Giambattista Vico[110]

Writing in 1725, Vico vigorously disputed the idea that Confucius lived before the flood, a notion that he said had led some to abandon their Christian faith and conclude that the flood spread only over the "lands of the Hebrews." Vico's idea that Europeans might see Confucianism as a challenge to or disproof of Christianity was not uncommon in the first stages of Europe's exposure to Confucianism, but it soon gave way to an interpretation of the two traditions as harmonious. The encounter between the Jesuits and the Chinese is only one moment that shaped the way Europeans and Chinese began to conceive of Confucius as a "philosophical" rather than a "religious" thinker.

It was the late imperial picture of Confucius as ritualist that came to Europe at the end of the sixteenth century, where some Enlightenment thinkers seized on it. The initial images of China came through the lens of Christian missionaries, and foreign observers distinguished the "scholastic" founder of Confucianism from the "religious" founder of Buddhism. Missionaries like Matteo Ricci (1552-1610) came to see Buddhism and Taoism as heresies that had polluted Confucianism. Lionel Jensen has argued that this elevation of Confucianism over the other traditions encountered in China was part of an attempt to prove the existence of an original monotheism in China that traced itself to the pure faith of Confucius.[111] Some Jesuits held that Confucius intuited correct ethical principles but used different words like *shangdi* (highest ancestor) or *tianzhu* (ruler of the heavens) for God because he was unaware of Jesus for chronological reasons. At least one reviewer of the first translation of the *Analects* into a European language, the *Confucius Sinarum Philosophus* of 1687, saw it as in no way contradicting what Europeans called "natural law": "God has spread in the souls of the infidels the same lights which lead us to virtue, which, insofar as the exterior of action is concerned, are not at all different from Christian values."[112] While the Jesuits took Buddhism and Taoism to be reli-

---

110. *The New Science of Giambattista Vico,* trans. T. G. Bergin and M. H. Fisch (Baltimore: Johns Hopkins University Press, 1976), p. 33.

111. Lionel M. Jensen, *Manufacturing Confucianism: Chinese Traditions and Universal Civilization* (Durham, N.C.: Duke University Press, 1997), p. 111.

112. Pierre-Sylvain Régis in the *Journal des sçavans* of January 5, 1688, cited in D. E. Mungello, *Curious Land: Jesuit Accommodation and the Origins of Sinology* (Honolulu: University of Hawaii Press, 1989), p. 290. Mungello's comments (pp. 276-77) on the biog-

gious and therefore heterodox, they received Confucius as a philosopher who prefigured Christianity as well as anyone could have without access to Christ's teachings.

The writings of the nineteenth-century missionary James Legge, the most influential missionary translator of Confucius, reveal a variation on this attitude. Legge saw Confucianism as lacking the necessary condition for religiosity as he understood it, allegiance to a divine being. Yet he acknowledged that it did have other aspects of a religion. He complained that the early Confucians substituted a "mere principle of order or fitness of things" for the concept of God, and that as a result "It has left the people in the mass to become an easy prey to the idolatrous fooleries of Buddhism. Yea, the *unreligiousness* of the [Confucian] teachers has helped to deprave still more the religion of the nation, such as it is, and has made of its services a miserable pageant of irreverent forms."[113] Legge had no choice but to begrudgingly classify the ceremonies of the Confucians as religious, but their emphasis on ritual at the expense of belief in a divine being resulted in his strange classification of Confucianism as an unreligious religion. By contrast, the Buddhist worship of "idols" classifies it as a religion, albeit an ultimately mistaken one. The earlier ideal of Confucius as the discoverer of a natural theology vanished in late imperial Confucianism. In 1905 the Sinologist Herbert Giles said of the Chinese that "all idea of the early God of their forefathers has long since ceased to vivify their religious instincts."[114] At the end of the twentieth century, many scholars continued to see Confucius as a secular philosopher, accepting the portraits of Confucian scholasticism and Confucianist irreligion painted by these missionaries.

The reception of the teachings of Confucius by Christians did not just affect those who read their reports in the West. In the context of the colonial expansion of the West into China in the nineteenth century, some intellectuals in both China and Japan sought to revitalize indigenous traditions to serve a role equivalent to the one Christianity had played in the technological and military development of the West. With his 1897 work *Confucius as a Reformer (Kongzi gaizhi kao)*, the influential scholar Kang Youwei sought to remove the costume of an ineffectual pedant that traditional Qing dynasty scholars had used to disguise the sage, and reveal his true identity as a reformer. To do so, he turned back to the texts associated with the "New Text" movement, especially the commentaries to the *Spring and Autumn* and the apocryphal books. He used the alternate construction of Confucius in those texts to reject the orthodox Zhu Xi

---

raphy of Confucius included in the *Confucius Sinarum Philosophus* are particularly telling in this regard.

113. Legge, 2:73, emphasis in original.

114. Giles, *Religions of Ancient China* (Chicago: Open Court, 1905), p. 60.

reading of Confucius that emerged from the Song dynasty, and to promote an image of Confucius centered on the sage's advocacy of social justice. Kang shows that the attempts of European missionaries to interpret Confucius changed the way the Chinese themselves viewed him.

Kang Youwei was born in 1858 into an intellectual family in Nanhai, a city in Guangdong Province, and was classically trained at a time when the level of Western technological and military development was both threatening and alluring. Kang encountered books about Western thought and society at an early age, some of them through the agency of Christian missionaries. This exposure influenced the type of political and cultural reforms that he promoted. Kang had to be careful about how he presented his case for reform, however, because of the deeply conservative governmental structure of the Qing dynasty. His classical training allowed him to focus on the progressive aspects of Chinese tradition, and ultimately he was able to argue that the reforms he proposed had the authority of no less traditional a figure than Confucius.

Kang Youwei's 1902 commentary on the *Analects* describes Confucius as a prophet who foresaw the changes that China was undergoing at the start of the twentieth century. He read the Gongyang commentary to the *Spring and Autumn* as a Chinese proof text for the idea that society passes through three stages. The specific passage in the commentary that Kang used was actually an explanation of the differences between portions of the *Spring and Autumn* chronicle. Because the entire text had purportedly been written by Confucius, the commentary explained the differences as reflecting, respectively, what Confucius had seen, what he had heard, and what he had transmitted to him.[115] In Kang's version of these "three ages" (*sanshi*), the categories become the "chaotic" (*juluan*), the "promoting peace" (*shengping*), and the "great peace" (*taiping*) ages. These ages are very similar to the three eras of Buddhism, in which the period following the death of the Buddha was divided into the ages of the true law, the copied law, and the degeneration of the law. There also were overtones of Christian premillennial dispensationalism that divided history into a series of divinely ordained stages or "dispensations," often based on a literal interpretation of the Bible.

Regardless of the influences for his idea of the three ages of history, Kang characteristically justified the theory by finding precedent for it in the teachings

---

115. The Gongyang ages are: (1) the "seen" (*jian*) age: what had been directly observed by Confucius during the reigns of three of the dukes of the state of Lu from 541 to 479 B.C.E.; (2) the "heard" (*wen*) age: what he had heard from eyewitnesses during the reigns of the three dukes from 608 to 542 B.C.E.; and (3) the "transmitted" (*zhuanwen*) age: what had been passed down from the period of the dukes from 722 to 609 B.C.E. See the very end of the *Subcommentary to the Gongyang Commentary to the Spring and Autumn* (*Chunqiu Zuozhuan zhengyi*) in Ruan, p. 2200.

of Confucius. Kang wrote that his three ages resembled the stages that Confucius taught his disciples to use to understand the future by following a close study of the record of the past. Kang saw this understanding displayed in an exchange between Confucius and his disciple Zi Zhang from chapter 2 of the *Analects:*

> Zi Zhang asked: "Can ten generations from the present be known?"
>
> Confucius said: "The Yin dynasty based itself on the rites of the Xia dynasty. What [the Yin] added and subtracted can be known. The Zhou dynasty based itself on the rites of the Yin dynasty. What [the Zhou] added and subtracted can be known. In this way, whatever entity continues the Zhou, no matter whether it is a hundred generations from the present, can be known."[116]

Confucius's response can be read as an admonition not to predict the future except through the study of the patterns of the past. Kang's interpretation acknowledged this reading, but also went further and claimed for Confucius the title of originator of this method. The method of predicting the future through the past bore similarities to the newly influential theory of evolution, and Kang borrowed the intellectual authority of that theory to claim that Confucius had been able thereby to predict the changes that naturally develop in a society over time. He stressed what he called the "deductions" that Confucius could make, and argued that they allowed him to penetrate the future:

> When Confucius wrote the *Spring and Autumn* he illuminated the three ages. In the "chaotic" period he concentrated on the affairs of state and paid little attention to foreign affairs. In the "promoting peace" period he concentrated on foreign affairs and paid scant attention to the barbarian nations. In the "great peace" period, he treated all entities, no matter their distance or size, the same way. In other words, he did it according to evolutionary principles. Confucius was born in a "chaotic" age, but today people have navigated the globe, have transformed Europe and America, and so perhaps we are moving into a period of "promoting peace." In time, all points on the globe, regardless of distance or size, will be as one. National boundaries will become obsolete, there will no longer be divisions among peoples, local customs will become regularized, and then there will be the unity of "great peace." Confucius already predicted all of this.[117]

116. *Analects* 2.22. See Cheng, vol. 1, pp. 127-32.
117. Kang Youwei, *Lunyu zhu* (Commentary to the *Analects*) (Beijing: Zhonghua, 1984), p. 28.

Thus, to Kang's mind the *Spring and Autumn Annals* contained the kernel of Confucius's method, one that allowed the master to predict the future. These predictions could even be applied to changes at the beginning of the twentieth century. Kang wrote that it is only in certain texts like the Confucian apocrypha that Confucius secreted the methods and description of the age of "great peace." Kang makes this explicit in another section of the commentary: "The 'uncrowned king' received the omens of the Mandate [of Heaven]. The Great Sage was not born for nothing. He necessarily would have a method of governance to pass down, and at his birth there would necessarily be a [Heavenly] response to it. Later, the unicorn arrived, a book called the *Extending the opening chart (Yankong tu)* flew like a bird, and then Confucius wrote the *Spring and Autumn.* He did this to give his method of the 'three ages' to the people of the future."[118] Kang's use of the rich omenological imagery of the Gongyang commentary to the *Spring and Autumn* allows him to portray Confucius as a prophet whose knowledge of the past allowed him to predict the future and prepare a method useful even to the rulers of Kang's day. This revival of the *Spring and Autumn's* alternate construction of Confucius illustrates the way generations of scholars and officials have used the rich palette of images of Confucius to different ends, even in relatively recent times.

Kang's attempts at reform had a deep impact on Chinese history. His direct influence on Emperor Guangxu (r. 1875-1908) led to a series of explicit measures intended to transform China into a constitutional monarchy. For several months beginning in the summer of 1898, Kang succeeded in imposing reforms in education and political administration along the lines of the same European models that had already greatly influenced the emperor Meiji in Japan. In September of that year, however, the powerful Empress Dowager (i.e., the widow of the previous emperor) Cixi staged a coup d'état and Kang, still only forty years old, fled to Japan while Cixi reversed most of the reforms. After the Chinese defeat at the hands of Japanese, European, and American troops following the Boxer Rebellion of 1900, the voices of Kang and his student Liang Qichao (1873-1929) were among those that revived a constitutional movement in the period from 1905 through 1911. The embattled Manchu rulers, however, adopted only token changes, causing most reformers to move behind the more radical republicanism espoused by Sun Zhongshan (i.e., Sun Yat-sen, 1866-1925). Following the death of Emperor Guangxu in 1908 and Sun's success in

---

118. Kang, p. 129. The Gongyang commentary to the *Spring and Autumn* interprets the capture of a unicorn in 481 B.C.E. to be a sign that Confucius would not rule in his lifetime. Later that year the commentary records that heaven presented the master with the *Extending the Opening Chart* (perhaps the pun extends to the use of Confucius's surname — extending Confucius) to allow him to read the future.

deposing the Qing dynasty in 1911, history largely bypassed Kang's brand of constitutional monarchy.

Kang's revival of the image of Confucius as a reformer and quasi-messianic figure affected readings of the sage in the twentieth century. One example of its influence was on an essay written by the prominent intellectual historian Hu Shi (1891-1962) that portrayed Confucius as a prophetic figure who played a role similar to that of Jesus in China. Lionel Jensen describes the homology drawn by Hu between Confucius and Jesus in this way: "Hu Shi, through a very sophisticated analysis that compared the ancient messianic beliefs of the Shang and the Jews with the humanitarian teachings of Kongzi and Jesus, used indigenous texts to identify what was common in the historical paths of China and the West, and thus to bind their futures in a common universal civilization."[119] In the late Qing and modern periods, then, Christ served as a prototype for several influential Chinese images of Confucius as a salvific figure.

The appropriation of Confucius in such diverse ways points out the different types of people who claimed him as an ancestor, and how the reasons for doing so changed over time. Confucianists have read Confucius in so many different ways, in part because of the changes in the groups we associate with Confucian traditions.

After surveying the range of images of Confucius across Chinese history, from the ritualist of the *Analects* to the prophet of the *Spring and Autumn*, it remains to be seen just how these multiple varieties of Confucianism relate to the material conditions of Chinese society. The final two sections of this chapter approach this issue directly by addressing the problem of defining Confucianism in terms of the ideal image of the Chinese scholar-official and locating Confucius in a comparative context.

Defining "Confucianism" across Chinese History

After the playing of more ancient music, the President returned to the palace in his automobile.

Conclusion of a newspaper report of the autumnal
sacrifice to Confucius, September 22, 1917[120]

119. Jensen, p. 221. Hu's view was also accepted by the sociologist C. K. Yang (*Religion in Chinese Society: A Study of Contemporary Social Functions of Religions and Some of Their Historical Factors* [Berkeley: University of California Press, 1961], 233).

120. Cited in Paul Carus, "Ceremony Celebrated under the Chinese Republic in Honor of Confucius," *Open Court* 32, no. 3 (March 1918): 172.

On a hot day in September 1989, several friends and I attended the annual celebration of Confucius's birthday at the temple to Confucius in Taibei, the capital
of Taiwan. Jammed behind several rows of onlookers, hemmed in along the
side of the courtyard, we watched the ceremonial dancers and musicians clad in
traditional costumes slowly perform. At one point attendants wheeled in one of
several sacrificial animals and set it only a foot or so behind me, an enormous
glazed boar that appeared to be watching the ritual with about as much comprehension as did our motley coterie of foreign observers. The ceremony ended
and the onlookers dispersed into the surrounding maze of busy urban streets
lined with shops and restaurants. The otherworldliness and precision of the observance simply evaporated, and life in noisy, hectic, modern Taibei resumed
again. I left the celebration completely confused — unable to connect what I
had witnessed with the humanistic moral philosophy I had learned to associate
with Confucius during college.

The English term "Confucianism" conflates several distinct terms in Chinese, glossing over the fact that members of diverse traditions see themselves as
part of Confucius's lineage. "Confucianism" minimally connotes a tradition that
acknowledges allegiance to one or more aspects of Confucius's legacy. In this
broad sense Confucianism includes the commentators on the classics associated
with Confucius (e.g., *jingxue* or *daoxue*), the members of a bureaucracy that used
these same classics as texts for their entrance examinations (*guanyuan*), the
scholars engaged in moral-political discourse who revered Confucius and the ancient sage-kings (*rujia*), traditional ceremony and sacrifice to Confucius as just
described (*rujiao*), and even the contemporary movement to promote "social values" such as filial piety to redress dislocations caused by rapid industrialization.
While sometimes these categories overlap, for the most part they represent distinct social entities that over time have sought to represent Confucius in terms
consistent with their interests.

Even beyond the identification of these individual social groups, Confucius's name is inextricably tied to the institutional structure of Chinese government into the early twentieth century. Whether justified or not, in the West
"Confucianism" still conjures the image of a meritocratic bureaucracy made up
of scholar-officials whose motivation derives from a sense of responsibility inculcated by the value system that Confucius invented. The pejorative use of the
term may suggest that these scholar-officials lack a sense of responsibility and
exercise their authority without formal oversight. In this sense "Confucianism"
is not an intellectual lineage or tradition that traces itself back to Confucius,
but the political system that relied on those lineages or traditions to transmit a
set of cultural values.

With all these diverse connotations to the term "Confucianism," it is no
wonder that arguments flourish about how to categorize it. Rather than focus

on each of the "Confucianisms" alluded to above, this section will describe some common touchstones used by most of those traditions that viewed Confucius as a founder. This section will concentrate on two interrelated dimensions of the relationship between Confucius and Chinese society: the official promotion of the study of texts associated with Confucius and the state's connection to temples and sacrifices to Confucius. In its broadest sense Confucianism is used to connote the entirety of the Chinese bureaucracy, but that identification mistakes the state's use of the legacy of Confucius for all other uses. State sponsorship of Confucianism was primarily associated with the educational system and with ritual observance, and it was these aspects of the legacy of Confucius that formed the basis for the link between the sage and scholar-officials throughout Chinese history.

The earliest site of religious observance relating to Confucius was his own house, outside the capital city of the state of Lu. The first accounts of this observance come from transmitted records and an eyewitness account that are summarized in Sima Qian's *Historical Record*. Writing around 100 B.C.E., Sima describes the scene at Confucius's burial site near the Si River in the state of Lu:

> Over a hundred of his disciples and others from the state of Lu passed back and forth from the grave and built dwellings there. Because of this, it was called "Kongtown." The practice of presenting sacrifices at Confucius's grave at set times each year was passed from generation to generation in the state of Lu. Scholars also discussed the rites, held banquets and staged archery contests at Confucius's grave. Confucius's gravesite was one *qing* (i.e., 11.4 acres) in area. In later generations, the hall where he stayed and the wing where the disciples dwelled became the temple. Confucius's clothing, hat, zither, carriage, and documents were stored there, and have remained there continuously over the two hundred and some years to the current Han Dynasty. When Emperor Gao passed through Lu, he performed the *tailao* sacrifice (i.e., killing a cow, sheep, and pig) there. When feudal lords and high officials arrive, they always first present themselves there and only then take up their official duties.[121]

This description is probably more accurate regarding the situation in the late second century B.C.E., when Sima Qian was gathering his materials, than in the immediate aftermath of the master's death some three hundred years earlier. In Sima Qian's own era, some accounts verify some aspects of it,[122] and

---

121. *Historical Record*, 47.1945-46.
122. For example, the sacrifice by Emperor Gao is dated to 195 B.C.E. by Ban Gu. See *Hanshu* 1.76.

his own visit to the site confirmed other aspects of the description of Kongtown. Sima writes: "When I went to the state of Lu I observed the carriage, clothing, and ritual vessels [of Confucius] in the Hall of the Temple. Students came to periodically practice the rites at his house. I felt sincerely reverent, and reluctantly hesitated before leaving."[123] Over time the temple complex grew, and by the time the Qing dynasty classicist Sun Jiagan (1682-1752) visited it, it had become considerably more ornate. In his *Record of Southern Travels (Nanyouji)*, Sun describes the scene upon entrance to the Temple: "There were molded statues of the sage and his disciples, and three statues of Confucius carved from stone. A carriage, clothing, and ritual vessels were stored on the floor of the sage's family home."[124] It is impossible to tell if these are the same relics observed by Sima Qian so many years earlier, but the similarity is striking.

The Han authorities established the precedent of gaining legitimacy by paying homage to Confucius, and state sponsorship of ceremonies at the temple of Confucius has been an expression of state orthodoxy since their time.[125] In Lu, traditions surrounding Confucius appear to have been carried on by members of the sage's family like Kong Ba, a thirteenth-generation descendant who was ennobled in 48 B.C.E. after asking the emperor to follow the precedent set by Emperor Gao and sacrifice to Confucius.[126] After Emperor Gao visited the temple, however, no emperor personally visited the site until Emperor Ming combined the sacrifice to Confucius with sacrifices to the sage's seventy-two disciples there in 59 C.E. Observances at the master's birthplace were first augmented by official sacrifices at the capital in 241 C.E. The emperors of the Tang dynasty (618-907 C.E.) established an official network of Confucian temples in all prefectural and county schools.[127] The connection between the state-sponsored educational system and Confucius existed on two levels. First, the state based the curriculum of the official examinations on texts associated with Confucius, although the specific texts changed over time as a function of the changes in the canon. Second, those at regional schools and at the Imperial University sacrificed to Confucius as the founder of the scholarly traditions.

The political tides that swept East Asia in the twentieth century have

---

123. *Historical Record,* 47.1947.

124. Takigawa Kametarô, *Examining the Evidence of the Assembled Commentaries to the "Historical Record" (Shiki kaichû kôshô)* (Tokyo: Tôhô Bunka Gakuin, 1932-34), 47.89.

125. See Thomas A. Wilson, "The Ritual Formation of Confucian Orthodoxy and the Descendants of the Sage," *Journal of Asian Studies* 55, no. 3 (August 1996): 564.

126. Léon Vandermeersch, "Aspects rituels de la popularisation du Confucianisme sous les Han," in *Thought and Law in Qin and Han China,* ed. Wilt Idema and Erik Zürcher (Leiden: Brill, 1990), p. 100.

127. Wilson, *Genealogy of the Way,* p. 33.

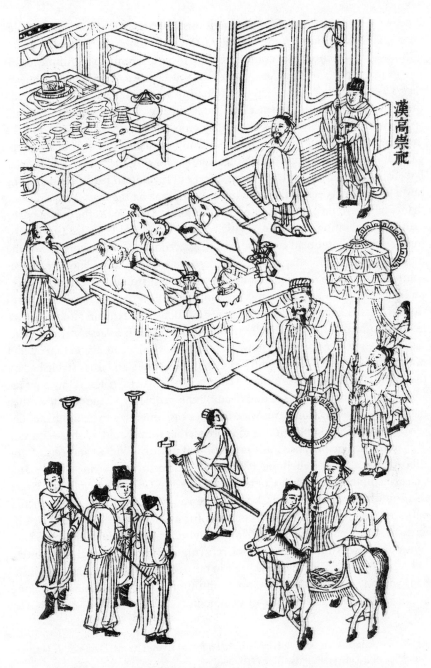

漢高崇祀

The sacrifice of Emperor Gao of Han at the temple of Confucius;
note the cow, sheep, and pig laid out for the *tailao* sacrifice.

(from Gu Yuan's *Shengji tu*, 1826; Beijing: Xianzhuang)

greatly affected the fortunes of the traditions identified with Confucius. As detailed in the description of the "Teacher's Day" celebration in Taiwan at the beginning of this section, observances and sacrifices to Confucius continue to this day in many parts of East Asia, including South Korea. The island of Taiwan serves as a bastion of Confucian traditionalism where grade-schoolers still read the "Four Books" made canonical by Zhu Xi during the Song dynasty. In mainland China Confucianism has alternately enjoyed support and disfavor in the modern period. Kang Youwei promoted Confucianism as an official state religion, and arguably it approached this status following the success of the May Fourth Movement in 1911. However, the 1949 revolution led by Mao Zedong saw a precipitous decline in the status of Confucius on the mainland, a decline that accelerated during the Cultural Revolution of 1966-76. At the height of the Cultural Revolution came the "Criticize Lin [Biao] and Criticize Confucius" campaign that combined criticism of a disgraced party leader with that of the most famous historical apologist for the slave-owning class. Those in power compelled figures such as the famous intellectual historian Feng Youlan to repudiate his previous scholarship on Confucius. Feng's early work compares Confucius to Socrates, and he wrote that Confucius "was the first to popularize learning and culture" in China.[128] In the 1974 collection *Selected Articles Criticizing Lin Piao and Confucius,* however, one finds Feng's confession that he had not previously understood Lenin's idea that the social standards established by the ruling class existed to exploit the common people. He writes: "Only after realizing this did I come to see that 'leading the people by virtue' and the other means advocated by Confucius were in every case intended to benumb and deceive the working people more and more so that they would neither want nor dare to resist. The purpose was to uproot and destroy all ideas and acts of 'insubordination and rebellion.'"[129] Feng's self-criticism echoes the state-sanctioned attitude toward Confucius during the Cultural Revolution. Since that time, however, mainland China has seen a revival in interest in Confucius, perhaps partially as a symbol to counter official corruption. Despite their differences, politicians in mainland China, Taiwan, and the Chinese diaspora have continued to see Confucius as a powerful symbol of the traditional social order. In every case the state will define itself in terms of Confucianism, either consonant with or in opposition to it, thus continuing the long tradition of linking political authority to the figure of Confucius.

128. Feng Youlan, *A History of Chinese Philosophy,* vol. 1, trans. Derk Bodde (Princeton: Princeton University Press, 1954), p. 54.

129. Feng, "A Criticism of Confucius and Self-Criticism of My Own Past Veneration for Confucius," in Feng Youlan et al., *Selected Articles Criticizing Lin Piao and Confucius* (Peking: Foreign Languages Press, 1974), pp. 88-106.

This link raises the central problem for anyone trying to understand the role of Confucius in Confucianism. If the state appropriated Confucius because of the authority lent by his name, is Confucianism properly defined as the teachings of Master Kong or as the state ideology that has appropriated his name?

The answer hinges on which Confucianism the question is being asked about. The ritual tradition that resulted in the composition of the *Analects*, the scholarly tradition of Qing literati, the social reformation of the *Spring and Autumn* tradition all had different elements at their core. It was in late imperial and modern times that political, religious, and scholarly traditions were consolidated under a single rubric and that the authority of Confucius, whose biography had been to a large extent fleshed out from a set of canonical writings, began to surpass that of the writings themselves. Since that development the construction of a new Confucius has been a necessity for any attempt to adapt or appropriate Confucianism. As a result, his life, the works that those in subsequent eras have thought he wrote or edited, and even the words of his disciples and their students all serve to provide a set of data from which future eras will create new understandings of Confucius and Confucianism. The memory of Confucius, whether real or imagined, is now the central element in Confucianism, and for this reason we must include it in both considerations of the role of Confucianism in Chinese society and in arguments about its future role in the world.

While the central elements of traditions known today as Confucian may not have been "founded" for their first centuries of existence, in their latter stages many of them were redefined in terms of their establishment by Confucius. Confucianism — as the collective label for a set of diverse traditions — has developed so that it now has this in common with the other major founded religions. With this observation of commonality comes the inevitable invitation to compare the role of Confucius to that of founders in other traditions, a task that should seem perilous at the outset due to the historical plurality of Confuciuses reviewed above. Nevertheless, there are certain parameters within which all these images fit, and this affords the possibility of comparison.

Comparing Confucius

The worthiness of others is like a small hill that may be surmounted. Confucius is like the sun or the moon in that he cannot be surmounted. . . . One cannot reach the level of my Master in just the same way that one cannot put a stairway to the sky and climb up to it.

The disciple Zigong in the *Analects*[130]

130. *Analects* 19.23 and 19.25; see Cheng, vol. 4, pp. 1340-44.

The terms used by Confucius's disciple Zigong may evoke comparisons between Confucius and other founders, and between Confucianism and other religious traditions. In light of the distinctions examined in the previous section, such comparisons must be approached gingerly. Does it make sense to portray Confucius as the "founder" of Confucianism, or would it be more accurate to locate the institutional beginnings of Confucianism well after the period during which his personal influence could affect it? Clearly, this line of analysis begs the question of what constitutes a founder, and may even raise the issue of whether such a definition is worth making. From some perspectives ideological and genealogical considerations are secondary elements of superstructure and might only serve to obscure the fundamental economic or power relations of Chinese society. Nevertheless, over particular segments of their existence, traditions have a static element, whether it is a nostalgic portrait of a bygone era, texts or rituals of a golden age, the "old ways" carried away from a vanished homeland, or the paradigmatic life of a founder.

In the twentieth century comparisons between Confucius and other religious founders were especially important to sociologists who sought to integrate traditional China into more global social models and typologies. Any exploration of this issue must begin with Max Weber, whose attentiveness to the particularities of different traditions was so great that few scholars since have even ventured to revisit his examinations of the subject. This section begins by looking at Weber's idea that charisma was not something Confucius had but was intrinsic to the Chinese bureaucracy, an idea that has influenced subsequent sociological writing on Confucianism. This idea was behind his categorization of Confucius as an academic and not a prophet, a notion that he derived from source materials that described late imperial China. Because of these limitations, Weber overlooked the genuinely religious dimensions of the fifth century B.C.E. master-disciple group headed by Confucius, specifically its recourse to the immanent order of *tian* (heaven) and the reflection of that order in the system of ritual self-cultivation.

Before Max Weber died in 1920, he wrote extensively on the subject of comparative sociology, paying special attention to the case of China. He became well versed in the writings of "missionaries, travelers and Western diplomatic officials" who observed China,[131] according to which he painted his picture of Chinese society largely defined by its Taoist and Confucian heritage. Weber's *Confucianism and Taoism* (retitled by its translator, Hans H. Gerth, as *The Religion of China*) is in part a description of these Chinese religions, but it is also an implicit comparison between Confucianism and Puri-

---

131. According to C. K. Yang's introduction to Max Weber, *The Religion of China*, trans. H. H. Gerth (Glencoe, Ill.: Free Press, 1951), p. xix.

tanism intended to prove his theory that cultural and religious factors determine economic systems. Specifically Weber argued that Confucianism did not foster conditions necessary for the development of capitalism, for "Confucian rationalism meant rational adjustment to the world; Puritan rationalism meant rational mastery of the world."[132] This thesis, developed in his *Protestant Ethic and the Spirit of Capitalism,* has been enormously influential. In the case of China it has attracted criticism because Confucianism-influenced societies have been among the most rapidly expanding capitalist economies of recent decades.[133] Others have disagreed with Weber's characterization of Confucianism but have adapted his overall thesis by arguing that Confucianism led to the development of a successful type of capitalism characterized by familism, loyalty, and group thinking.[134] Whatever the relationship between religion and economic structure, Weber's characterization of Confucius was suited to his broader argument that non-Protestant religions encouraged passive adjustment to the world.

A major part of Weber's argument with respect to China was that Confucius was not a prophet but simply an "academic teaching philosopher." The distinctive feature of prophecy was that it allowed an individual to aspire to improve his or her lot. Weber wrote: "A true prophecy creates and systematically orients conduct toward one internal measure of value. In the face of this the 'world' is viewed as material to be fashioned ethically according to the norm. Confucianism in contrast meant adjustment to the outside, to the conditions of the 'world.'"[135] Weber went further than denying Confucianism a prophetic character, and at times even denied it religious characteristics altogether. C. K. Yang wrote that "Weber treated Confucianism more as an ethical doctrine than as a theistic religion."[136] This characterization continues a trend seen in some earlier missionaries' accounts of Confucianism, and is worth considering critically.

The notion that Confucius was not a prophet was important to Weber's overall argument, but certain difficulties of translation inevitably arise in applying Weber's typology of religious leadership to China. For example, he defines the important category of prophet in terms of proclamation of salvation

---

132. Weber, *The Religion of China,* p. 248.

133. See the discussion of this thesis by Winston Davis, "The Weber Thesis and the Economic Development of Japan," in Davis, *Japanese Religion and Society: Paradigms of Structure and Change* (Albany: State University of New York Press, 1992), pp. 113-51.

134. See, for example, John Wong, "Promoting Confucianism for Socioeconomic Development: The Singapore Experience," in *Confucian Traditions in East Asian Modernity,* ed. Tu Wei-ming (Cambridge: Harvard University Press, 1996).

135. Weber, *The Religion of China,* p. 235.

136. Yang's introduction to Weber, *The Religion of China,* p. xix.

and charismatic authentication through magic or ecstasy,[137] terms applied to Confucius's China with difficulty. As missionaries like Legge noted, salvation, understood in any but the most this-worldly sense, is not something Confucius cared to address. Weber, in fact, numbered Plato and Confucius among the founders of "schools of philosophy," a category he explicitly contrasted with that of the prophet: "[Both Confucius and Plato] were simply academic teaching philosophers, who differed chiefly in that Confucius was centrally concerned and Plato only occasionally concerned to influence princes in the direction of particular social reforms."[138] Weber argues that such academic teaching philosophers lacked the "vital emotional preaching" distinctive of prophecy, and by implication makes the claim that Confucius was not a charismatic leader. Indeed, Weber's picture of China places such emphasis on bureaucracy that he locates charismatic leadership in offices rather than in individuals, e.g., the office of the emperor.[139] It is in this context that Weber makes one of his most prescient observations about Chinese religion, that it is, in C. K. Yang's formulation, "diffuse" rather than "institutional," and does not have a hierarchy independent of other social institutions like clan or state.[140] To the extent that it is possible to understand the term "prophet" in the context of a diffuse religion without a distinct apostolic succession, Weber thought the goals of Confucius were too academic to deem him a prophet.

Revisiting Weber's typology today, we see a number of limitations inherent in his characterization of Confucius. The distinction between the "religious prophet" and the "philosophical ethicist," for example, is not as well defined as it may first appear. As shown above, one reason many in the West have seen Confucius as simply a "moral philosopher" is that those elements of interest to modern Western readers looking for a naturalistic moral philosophy have been isolated from the broader framework — a framework that might indeed fit many definitions of religion. Legge's description of Confucianism as "unreligious" applies only if one assumes a nineteenth-century definition of religion that centers on the belief in "spiritual beings," and the moral and devotional aspects of these beings.[141] Despite the work of scholars such as Asano

137. Weber, *The Sociology of Religion,* pp. 46-59.

138. Weber, *The Sociology of Religion,* p. 53.

139. *From Max Weber,* p. 247; Weber, *The Religion of China,* p. 128.

140. To invoke a biological simile, diffused religion is something like a virus, adopting the cellular structure of the host organism as its own. By contrast institutional religion is more like a separate organ or organism. See Weber, *The Religion of China,* p. 143; and Yang, pp. 278-340.

141. This example comes from E. B. Tylor. He saw the most primitive societies as those that saw spiritual beings everywhere, and the most developed religions as those that recognized only one spiritual being. The purpose of the study of religions was to bring be-

Yûichi, Rodney Taylor, Tu Wei-ming, and Herbert Fingarette, many other scholars still measure the scope of Confucianism by this definition.

Other images of Confucius, such as those described above that derive from the *Spring and Autumn* traditions about Confucius, bear stronger resemblances to the religious types Weber discusses. Why did Weber ignore these aspects in favor of the image of Confucius as the ritualist and teacher? One explanation is that Weber's source material exposed him to the literatus Confucius of late imperial China, and he assumed that this account was true of all times. Given Weber's conception of Chinese society as fundamentally static, the identification of the Confucius of the late nineteenth century with the Confucius of the fifth century B.C.E. made perfect sense.

Bryan S. Turner has argued that "Weber's Orientalism" constrained his reception of Chinese history. In common with many interpreters of China from the Enlightenment through at least Ezra Pound, Weber accepted the notion of an underlying social continuity throughout Chinese history, a thesis implicit in China's official histories.[142] Turner notes the implications of this assumption: "One particular feature of Weber's apparently static model of Asia is that Weber typically quotes historical evidence from widely scattered epochs to demonstrate some feature of a social structure. The implication of not treating historical chronology seriously is that the social structure of Asia is frozen."[143] Once a person assumes this static model, he or she may use evidence from any period or movement to prove a thesis. With the widespread dislocations of the Six Dy-

---

lievers in animistic and polytheistic religions into the bright light of the monotheistic day. Unfortunately, many people still define religion as Tylor's "belief in spiritual beings," even though the idea of evolution of belief has shrunk into the background. In the twentieth century, figures like Freud and Marx posited reductionist theories of religion predicated on such narrow conceptions of religion. However, others such as Emile Durkheim and Mary Douglas began to stress the more experiential aspects of religion, aspects that existed to some extent independently of doctrinal elements such as the belief in God or gods. Theorists like Victor Turner and Stanley Jeyaraja Tambiah have begun to recognize the importance of performative actions in religion, science, and magic. No longer can Tylor's narrow definition be seen as adequate — religions with deities developed them to enforce a preexisting moral code. And no longer can Confucianism's alleged lack of "deities" disqualify it as a religion despite the presence of other elements of a religious tradition.

142. This weakness may characterize any approach that focuses on the primacy of culture. Discussions of the role of Confucianism in the contemporary geopolitical context have also been characterized by this ahistorical approach. Recent examples of this problem are Richard Bernstein and Ross H. Munro, *The Coming Conflict with China* (New York: Knopf, 1997), and Samuel Huntington, *The Clash of Civilisations and the Remaking of World Order* (New York: Simon & Schuster, 1996).

143. Bryan S. Turner, *For Weber: Essays on the Sociology of Fate* (Boston: Routledge & Kegan Paul, 1981), pp. 277-78.

nasties period (220-589 C.E.), the economic transformation of the Song dynasty, and the changes in Chinese identity in the wake of contact with other nations in the Qing dynasty, Chinese history actually exhibits great variation. The Orientalist assumption denies this variety, and so becomes a means by which data may be collected to support a variety of mutually incompatible hypotheses. If Weber had examined other images of Confucius, especially the earliest stratum, he might have recognized features of founders other than Plato.

This notion of an unchanging Confucianism also affected social theorists who came after Weber. The eminent anthropologist Anthony F. C. Wallace, for example, saw Confucianism less as a distinct religion than as the glue that held together other Chinese religions. Wallace, who divided the world into four distinct "religious culture areas" characterized by shamanic, communal, Olympian, and monotheistic religions, saw Chinese religion as monotheistically organized around the figure of Confucius:

> Chinese monotheism, apart from the devotees of Islam, Buddha, Tao, and other particular monotheistic faiths, is an eclectic mixture of communal (particularly ancestral), Olympian, and monotheistic cults, held together by the teachings and symbolic figure of Confucius, who functions as a kind of humane focus of divine wisdom. Confucian sanctioning of all cults and of the state seems — at least to this Western observer — to serve the same unifying function for religious diversity as does a monotheistic theology, and hence "Chinese religion" is here classified as monotheistic.[144]

Wallace's claim is not that Confucius is a Chinese "Godhead" but rather that the universal recognition of his authority unifies a diverse set of religions, and thus Confucius serves as the *functional equivalent* of a monotheistic theology. What is interesting about this view is that it does not really ask the question whether Confucianism itself is theistic. As in Weber's view, it is the bureaucratic nature of Confucianism that is central, and it is Confucius who gets the credit for having designed the pattern for the bureaucracy.

Roland Robertson adopts and expands this view of a Confucius at the center of a kind of Chinese monotheism in his influential *Sociological Interpretation of Religion* (1970). Robertson contrasts monotheistic religions with more pluralistic Olympian religions, saying that in the former, the deities of the latter are "transcended by belief in a single supreme entity or being, who either controls other supernatural beings or expresses himself in terms of them." Drawing largely on representations of Chinese religion supplied by Weber and Wallace, Robertson argues that the "unifying function of Confucianism" qualifies it for

144. Wallace, *Culture and Personality* (New York: Random House, 1964), p. 101.

inclusion among the monotheistic religions.[145] How this fits the definition of monotheism that Robertson provides is not clear, but it is likely that for him the "entity" of Confucianism "controlled" the other "entities" of the diverse religions of China. In other words, the implication is that the same definitions applied to the relationships between deities in the West are applicable to the relationships between religions in China.

Robertson's account of a "Chinese monotheism" depends on seeing claims about the unifying function of Confucius through Weberian eyes. Although Robertson draws liberally on Wallace, there are a couple of subtle variations that result in significant differences in the claims the two authors make. First, where Wallace spoke of the unifying function of the "figure of Confucius," Robertson follows Weber more closely in changing this to the function of "Confucianism." Second, Wallace's felicitous characterization of Confucius as the "humane focus of divine wisdom" is supplemented by the more Weberian statement that "the function of Confucianism and the religious orientations it subsumed was to sanction the existing harmony of the social order."[146] Yet the most significant evidence of Weber's thinking about China is the assumption that the image of Confucius is interchangeable with the role of Confucianism throughout Chinese history.

These examples illustrate the profound way in which Weber's idea that Confucianism has always located charismatic leadership in bureaucracy has affected the way twentieth-century sociology has understood Confucianism. The range of images of Confucius throughout Chinese history, however, belies the idea that Confucius was ever reducible to an icon of the bureaucracy. Indeed, there are several important senses in which some images of Confucius exhibited Weberian charismatic authority. Philip J. Ivanhoe has compared the Confucian notion of exemplary virtue, a quality attributed to him by many of his later followers, to Weberian "moral charisma."[147] Another example, explored earlier, is the disengagement of Confucius and his followers from the money economy. Weber's prophet similarly eschews a regular salary, since "charismatic domination is the very opposite of bureaucratic domination," and "rejects as undignified any pecuniary gain that is methodical and rational."[148] Since Weber saw Confucian China as fundamentally a bureaucratic entity, and Confucius as an academic teacher, it is unsurprising that he was not aware of the social organization of the master-disciple group and did not apply the category of

145. Roland Robertson, *The Sociological Interpretation of Religion* (New York: Schocken Books, 1970), p. 83.

146. Robertson, p. 87.

147. Ivanhoe, *Confucian Moral Self Cultivation*, pp. 1-7.

148. *From Max Weber*, p. 247.

prophet to Confucius. Yet this blinded him to the differences between the late Zhou Confucius and the late Qing literati who remade him in their image. Even the Confucius of the *Analects* (let alone the "uncrowned king") could not be described as a Qing dynasty bureaucrat. Confucius disparaged the quest for an official position for the sake of status and emphasized that because in his circle a thing's value derives from its ritual context, his disciples should delight in gifts of sacrificial meat.

Many central claims of the traditions collectively known as Confucianism, such as Confucius's conscious distancing from and traditionalist critique of the status quo, might even be read as critical of bureaucratic authority. It is also possible to see other images of Confucius, especially those from traditions that held that the *Spring and Autumn* and apocryphal books contained his blueprint for rulership, as even closer to Weber's ideal of the prophet. Since Weber accepted the self-identification that late imperial scholar-officials made with Confucius, he looked at "Confucians" and saw a Confucius whose authority derived from official position. Because his sources exposed him primarily to that particular image of Confucius, possible religious aspects of Confucius's leadership were not available to him.

Since many of the institutional aspects and affiliations of Confucianism postdate Confucius, Weber's attention to institutions obscured not only the economic dimension of early Confucian social organization but also the degree to which the master's authority traditionally derived from "supernatural, superhuman, or at least specifically exceptional qualities"[149] — in Weberian terms, charisma. Having established that Confucius and Confucianism are two distinct entities, we should not be surprised that the political institutions of Confucianism in late imperial China do a poor job of describing its founder in the preimperial era. Beyond the supernatural aspects of Confucius in Han dynasty sources and the exceptional characteristics emphasized in Sima Qian's *Historical Record* outlined above, there exists a stratum in the *Analects* that attributes a magical efficacy to the gentleman and the virtuous ruler.

For Confucius the magical dimension of the sage's ability derived from his special connection with heaven, and as such, his original program was to transform society according to a natural model. One passage in the *Analects* likens the transformative powers that the gentleman has over the common people to the wind blowing the grass (12.19), and another likens them to the command of the Pole Star over other stars in the night sky (2.1). These are similar to the supernatural metaphors invoked by the disciple Zigong else-

149. From Weber's definition of charisma as found in *Theory of Social and Economic Organization* (New York: Oxford Univeristy Press, 1947), p. 329.

where, comparing Confucius to the moon, sun, and sky (19.24; 19.25). Taken figuratively, these powers refer to the suasive effect the gentleman may have on others, like his ability to civilize barbarians (9.14), but the effect of the exemplar as portrayed in the *Analects* is usually more direct and spontaneous (2.21; 12.22; 13.4; 14.42). Asano Yûichi, in his recent evaluation of Weber's picture of Confucius, has argued that these features are exactly what Weber meant by the term "charisma": "Confucius' reception of special knowledge of ritual studies and exceptional virtue from Heaven is witnessed by the portents present on his physical body, and is something that he received from Heaven above and transmits to those below — this constitutes his charisma."[150] Asano's point is that early sources portray Confucius as a "charismatic" founder, though most contemporary readers do not read them that way. Elsewhere Asano's view of Confucius as heading a resistance movement is perhaps extreme, but he illustrates well how the same sources used by scholars in constructing less politically threatening images of Confucius through the ages might be used to portray Confucius in a radically different light. Asano illustrates how even the Confucius of the *Analects* possesses features that fit Weber's definition of charisma rather well.

Beyond the presence or absence of charisma, Weber's characterization of Confucius as "academic" implies that his ethical system did not have a religious dimension. The role of heaven *(tian)* in his program of ethical self-cultivation, however, makes it somewhat similar to the ethics of some of Weber's "prophetic" founders. While modern thinkers often see ritual as an aspect of culture rather than nature, for Confucius it had quite a bit to do with heaven. Confucius thought that people act ritually according to their roles. The determining factor in social roles is the set of hierarchies: superior and inferior, father and son, husband and wife. Keith Knapp puts it this way: "The rites produced order within a ritual by explicitly displaying the hierarchical status and duties of each participant. For example, the mourning rites display the hierarchy inherent within the family by having sons perform the most severe austerities, those of three years' mourning, for their parents, as do wives for their husbands. However, a husband only mourns his wife and son for a year."[151] The rites are an affirmation of a hierarchical system, and participation in them is tantamount to accepting one's role in that system. For the Confucian, heaven determines these hierarchies.

150. Asano Yûichi, *The Myth of Confucius (Kôshi shinwa)* (Tokyo: Iwanami, 1997), p. 28.
151. Keith Knapp, "New Approaches to Teaching Early Confucianism," *Teaching Theology and Religion* 2, no. 1 (1999): 48.

The *Analects* does not confine the role of heaven to establishing the set of hierarchies that the rites exemplify, but depicts it as part of the larger backdrop to the ethical teachings of Confucius. Some see Confucius as preoccupied with ritual because in the *Analects* he adopts a position that human agency can affect only certain aspects of the future. For example, Confucius believes that no one controls his own life span, telling his disciple Sima Niu that "life and death are a matter of fate, wealth and honor depend on Heaven" (12.5). Confucius then stresses to Sima that while these aspects of life are out of our control, the favor of one's peers is a matter of human agency and may be gained through ritual propriety. Yet ritual propriety does not guarantee a good outcome to one's life. In the *Analects* Confucius claims a type of special consideration from heaven. When in prison in Kuang, Confucius says: "Now that King Wen is no more, does not culture *(wen)* reside in me? If Heaven is going to destroy this culture, people will not be able to get any of it after I am dead. If Heaven is not yet to destroy this culture, then what can the men of Kuang do to me?"[152] That heaven might intend the cultural patterns to be destroyed shows that the *Analects* embeds the ethics of Confucius in a larger cosmology in which the outcome of human action is never completely decided by humans themselves. Rodney Taylor has argued that heaven is central "not only to Confucius but to the entire Confucian tradition in the life and practice of the individual, community, and state."[153] While Weber and other writers have portrayed Confucius's ritually based ethics as essentially a secular system, in the context of Confucius's acceptance of this cosmology and the natural social hierarchies it dictates, this categorization is difficult to justify.

We have seen that who Confucius was depends in large part on to whom one listens. As traditions have developed over time, different texts associated with Confucius have come to the forefront and in turn affected the image of the master. In the formative period of the development of traditions about the master's life, from his death in the fifth century B.C.E. through the Han dynasty, several different groups were already attempting to appropriate the authority of the figure of Confucius. Some saw texts associated with him, like the *Spring and Autumn* and the *Changes,* as expressive of a secret transmission, one that might (in the case of the former) legitimate a future ruler or (for the latter) express the intentions of the sage-kings of the Zhou dynasty. Others attempted to crystallize the traditions of ritual self-cultivation associated with Confucius into a text

152. *Analects* 9.5; see Cheng, vol. 2, pp. 576-79.
153. Rodney Taylor, "The Religious Character of the Confucian Tradition," *Philosophy East and West* 48, no. 1 (January 1998): 89.

called the *Analects,* and use it to train high officials. When Confucius was appropriated as a lineage founder by the textually oriented scholar-officials of late imperial China, and then deemed "unreligious" by European missionaries, the myriad of images of Confucius were whittled down to the one that became Weber's "academic teaching philosopher." Had Weber access to the other early versions, he might have recognized in them an alternate system of ceremonial exchange and a charismatic authority more like what he saw in other religious founders.

In the end Weber's insights into the differences between Chinese religions and other religious traditions are important, as are the similarities drawn above between some images of Confucius and other religious founders. Yet neither should obscure the fundamental problem of comparison that arises from treating "Confucianism" as a religion. Because the term represents such a complex of sociologically diverse phenomena, any single conclusion regarding the place of Confucius within the tradition is bound to apply at best to only one of its aspects. Moreover, this survey of the historical development of stories about Confucius highlights the degree to which the lack of definitive evidence about Confucius's life has made it a tabula rasa upon which different groups could sketch and erase different images of the master. Those inside and outside of China have recognized Confucius as the founder of numerous traditions — a "First Teacher" whose descendants still annotate the classics that he promoted, a philosopher whose ethical precepts educators teach at academies across the globe, a ritual expert at whose temples state authorities have carried out the *tailao* sacrifice — and yet no one can say definitively that he founded any of these traditions. Because of the variety of Confucianisms, and their diffuse character, we may best say that Confucianism had a variety of founders that can all be referred to by the name Confucius.

This conclusion is important in light of attempts to define Confucianism in a narrow way and then invoke or deride it as means to secure political authority. Reducing it to a bureaucratic structure, a justification of paternalistic governance, or a caricature of aristocratic apologetics misrepresents it as a single strand that must be rejected or accepted in its entirety. If Confucianism is instead accepted as a multivocal tradition, the many resources it contains for addressing modern problems might be better employed. The incorruptible steward of the *Analects,* for example, would have much to say to officials negotiating the transition from command to market economies. The disciple who saw Confucius as the sun and moon might provide a pithy rejoinder to the missionary who assumes that he or she was "palpably lacking" in any religious feeling. The ethicist who embeds a notion of virtue within a web of familial and social relationships might have advice about what to preserve amidst the changes in family structure that have accompanied rapid industrialization. And the scholar-officials of late imperial China who saw Confucius as the founder of their line are examples of engaged scholarship that might repay attention from academics who see themselves as marginalized. In this way the many different strands of Confucian traditions that have informed Chinese life for two and a half millennia may continue to exert vital and diverse influences in the future.

Jesus

MICHAEL J. McCLYMOND

Introduction

On the vast subject of Jesus, one might think that nothing new could ever or would ever be said. Yet recently a great deal has changed. Only two or three decades ago, most scholars approached the biblical texts with the assumption that very little can actually be known regarding Jesus. Rudolf Bultmann, representing the earlier viewpoint, made the famous assertion: "I do indeed think that we can now know almost nothing concerning the life and personality of Jesus, since the early Christian sources show no interest in either, are moreover fragmentary and often legendary; and other sources about Jesus do not exist."[1] As a spokesperson for the more recent school of thought, E. P. Sanders has declared: "The dominant view today seems to be that we can know pretty well what Jesus was out to accomplish, that we can know a lot about what he said, and that those two things make sense within the world of first-century Judaism."[2] The Jewish scholar Paul Winter makes a similar claim: "The last decade [of the 1970s] has seen an amazing transformation. Now, the Jesus of history seems more accessible than ever. Like archaeologists swarming over a prime location, the historians and theologians have turned with gusto to the original documents, parallel historical records and the geographical sites, and at every turn have found a clearer and clearer picture emerging of Jesus of Nazareth."[3]

---

1. Rudolf Bultmann, *Jesus and the Word* (New York: Scribner, 1934), p. 14.
2. E. P. Sanders, *Jesus and Judaism* (Philadelphia: Fortress, 1985), p. 2.
3. Paul Winter, *The Search for the Real Jesus* (London, 1982); cited in James H. Charlesworth, "Jesus Research Expands with Chaotic Creativity," in Charlesworth and

Sanders and Winter are not alone. A host of English-language scholars have blazed a new trail back to the first century, including such authors as Dale Allison, Marcus Borg, James H. Charlesworth, John Dominic Crossan, Craig Evans, John P. Meier, Ben F. Meyer, E. P. Sanders, Morton Smith, Geza Vermes, Ben Witherington, and N. Thomas Wright.[4] In varying ways all of these writers have attempted what Bultmann and his followers thought impossible: a reconstruction of Jesus' life history, teachings, actions, and early following based on a judicious reading of the ancient sources. Many today are convinced that we can know as much about Jesus as we can about any figure of the ancient world. While we do not have the fullness of biographical detail and the variety of independent firsthand accounts that are available for recent public figures, such as Winston Churchill or Mother Teresa of Calcutta, we nonetheless have a great deal more data on Jesus than we do for such ancient figures as Alexander the Great.[5]

An outsider to the academic guild is bound to wonder: Why the big change from severe skepticism to cautious confidence? Is this simply an indication that religion professors are in their own way as faddish as Parisian clothiers, who prefer a new look every once in a while? Without denying the reality of academic fads, much of the current thinking regarding Jesus is founded on new sources of information and newer methods of interpreting the old sources. The last half-century has witnessed the deciphering and eventual publication of the Dead Sea Scrolls — a revolutionary event in the study of ancient Jewish culture. Archaeology in the ancient Near East has also become more closely intertwined with the study of ancient texts, often confirming or disconfirming the conjectures of textual scholars and pointing out promising new directions for

---

Walter P. Weaver, *Images of Jesus Today* (Philadelphia: Trinity Press International, 1994), p. 11.

4. In addition to the authors already mentioned, a more complete list of important recent authors would have to include: Raymond E. Brown, Bruce Chilton, F. G. Downing, James Dunn, Harvey Falk, Paula Fredriksen, Robert Funk, A. E. Harvey, Richard Hayes, Richard Horsley, Luke Timothy Johnson, Pheme Perkins, John Riches, Ellis Rivkin, Gerd Thiessen, and David Wenham.

5. E. P. Sanders, *The Historical Figure of Jesus* (London: Allen Lane/Penguin Press, 1993), pp. xiii-xiv, 1-6, 56. Marcus Borg writes: "We can be relatively sure of the *kinds* of things he said, and of the main themes and thrust of his teaching. We can also be relatively sure of the kinds of things that he did: healings, association with outcasts, the deliberate calling of twelve disciples, a mission directed to Israel, a final purposeful journey to Jerusalem. Moreover, as we shall see, we can be relatively certain of the kind of person he was: a charismatic who was a healer, sage, prophet, and revitalization movement founder. By incorporating all of this, and not preoccupying ourselves with the question of whether Jesus said *exactly* the particular words attributed to him, we can sketch a fairly full and historically defensible portrait of Jesus" (*Jesus: A New Vision; Spirit, Culture, and the Life of Discipleship* [San Francisco: Harper San Francisco, 1987], p. 15).

inquiry.[6] Today's student of the Hebrew Bible, New Testament, or early Judaism can learn much from studies of the material culture of the ancients. The social sciences, too, have played a large part in encouraging new forms of interpretation. A cadre of capable scholars has applied social-scientific methods to the investigation of biblical texts, using such categories as social class, gender, kinship, patron-client relations, ethnocentrism, purity rules, urban-rural distinctions, and marginalization to open up new perspectives on old texts.[7] The comparative study of millenarian movements throughout the world has shed light on Judaic and New Testament apocalypticism.[8]

Last but by no means least among the factors, recent investigations into first-century Judaism have unveiled a very rich and varied picture of religious life that defies the stereotypes regarding "the scribes and Pharisees" that prevailed in most of nineteenth- and early twentieth-century scholarship on Jesus. A number of major works have argued that Jesus had more in common with the Jewish religious leaders than previously imagined.[9] Christian scholars have more than ever relied on work done by Jewish colleagues, while numerous Jew-

---

6. A discussion of recent archaeological findings and their significance for the intepretation of the New Testament is given in James Charlesworth, *Jesus within Judaism: New Light from Exciting Archaeological Discoveries,* Anchor Bible Reference Library (New York: Doubleday, 1988).

7. One of the pioneering works in applying a social-scientific approach to the Hebrew Bible was Norman K. Gottwald, *The Tribes of Yahweh: A Sociology of the Religion of Liberated Israel, 1250-1050 B.C.E.* (Maryknoll, N.Y.: Orbis, 1979). A path-making work in New Testament studies was Abraham J. Malherbe, *Social Aspects of Early Christianity* (Baton Rouge: Louisiana State University Press, 1977). Gerd Theissen has written numerous works on the sociology of the New Testament, including *The Sociology of Early Palestinian Christianity* (Philadelphia: Fortress, 1978), and the summary volume (with Annette Merz) *The Historical Jesus: A Comprehensive Guide* (Minneapolis: Fortress, 1998). Theissen's work has been critiqued in Richard A. Horsley, *Sociology and the Jesus Movement* (New York: Crossroad, 1989). The writings of Bruce Malina also deserve mention, especially *The New Testament World: Insights from Cultural Anthropology* (Atlanta: John Knox, 1981) and *The Social World of Jesus and the Gospels* (London and New York: Routledge, 1996).

8. Among the recent comparative studies of millennialism are the following: the essays contained in Sylvia L. Thrupp, ed., *Millennial Dreams in Action: Studies in Revolutionary Religious Movements* (New York: Schocken Books, 1970); the articles in *The Encyclopedia of Apocalypticism,* ed. John J. Collins, Bernard McGinn, and Stephen J. Stein, 3 vols. (New York: Continuum, 1998); Hillel Schwartz, "Millenarianism: An Overview," in *The Encyclopedia of Religion,* ed. Mircea Eliade (New York: Macmillan, 1987), 9:521-32; Michael Barkun, *Disaster and the Millennium* (New Haven: Yale University Press, 1974); and Bryan R. Wilson, *Magic and the Millennium: A Sociological Study of Religious Movements of Protest among Tribal and Third-World Peoples* (New York: Harper & Row, 1973).

9. See Sanders, *Jesus and Judaism,* and Hyam Maccoby, *Judaism in the First Century* (London: Sheldon Press, 1989).

ish writers have sought to reclaim Jesus as a major teacher within the Judaic tradition. According to one account, more was written about Jesus in Hebrew from about 1950 to 1975 than during the preceding eighteen hundred years![10] A spate of recent books have all emphasized the *Jewishness* of Jesus.[11] This stress on the Judaic context is crucial to the major reconstructions of Jesus' life and activity by E. P. Sanders, John P. Meier, and N. Thomas Wright, though, as we will see in what follows, it is less salient in the works on Jesus by such figures as Burton L. Mack and John Dominic Crossan.

Everyone who studies Jesus is stepping into a stream that has been flowing for generations.[12] It may be helpful therefore to survey, at least in its broad outlines, the path that has already been traced in studies of the historical Jesus during the last two hundred years or so. Prior to the late 1700s it is very difficult to find any attempts at a biography or a life of Christ. The apocrypha of early Christianity sought to fill in the missing years of Jesus' life, and the medieval period witnessed miracle plays and Gospel paraphrases based on episodes in the biblical texts. A life of Christ in the modern sense only arrives near the middle of the nineteenth century.[13] Yet when we consider the last 150 years, there is a great deal to be learned from earlier investigations. To a remarkable degree the issues, motifs, agendas, and dilemmas of earlier researchers continue to find expression in the more recent works.[14]

---

10. Pinchas Lapide, *Israelis, Jews, and Jesus* (Garden City, N.Y.: Doubleday, 1979), pp. 31-32, cited in Donald A. Hagner, *The Jewish Reclamation of Jesus: An Analysis and Critique of Modern Jewish Study of Jesus* (Grand Rapids: Zondervan, Academie Books, 1984), p. 25.

11. See especially: Geza Vermes, *Jesus the Jew: An Historian's Reading of the Gospels* (New York: Macmillan, 1973), along with other books by Vermes; Pinchas Lapide and Ulrich Luz, *Jesus in Two Perspectives: A Jewish-Christian Dialogue* (Minneapolis: Augsburg, 1985); and Harvey Falk, *Jesus the Pharisee: A New Look at the Jewishness of Jesus* (New York and Mahwah, N.J.: Paulist, 1985).

12. On the study of Jesus throughout the history of Christianity, see Harvey K. McArthur, *The Quest through the Centuries: The Search for the Historical Jesus* (Philadelphia: Fortress, 1966), and Warren S. Kissinger, "Historical Overview," in Kissinger, *The Lives of Jesus: A History and Bibliography* (New York and London: Garland, 1985), pp. 3-111.

13. Henry J. Cadbury, *The Peril of Modernizing Jesus* (New York: Macmillan, 1937), p. 17.

14. Throughout this introductory section of the chapter I am indebted to N. Thomas Wright's insightful article, "Jesus, Quest for the Historical," in *Anchor Bible Dictionary,* ed. David Noel Freedman et al., 6 vols. (New York: Doubleday, 1992), 3:796-802. Another broad overview, focusing on current issues, may be found in William R. Telford, "Major Trends and Interpretive Issues in the Study of Jesus," in *Studying the Historical Jesus: Evaluations of the State of Current Research,* ed. Bruce Chilton and Craig A. Evans (Leiden: Brill, 1994), pp. 33-74.

The book that did more than any other to sum up nineteenth-century scholarship on the life of Jesus, and to set the tone for twentieth-century research, was Albert Schweitzer's *Quest of the Historical Jesus,* first published in German in 1906 and subsequently translated into English in 1910. Indeed, Schweitzer's work was so influential that it may have spawned some common misunderstandings regarding historical-Jesus research. It is not accurate to suggest, as Schweitzer did, that Hermann Samuel Reimarus (1694-1768) began the quest for the historical Jesus, since he in fact drew extensively on the work of earlier writers and particularly the English Deists.[15] Moreover, as N. T. Wright points out, the general impression of a single overarching quest for the historical Jesus does not do justice to the diversity of methods and aims among the individual researchers of the nineteenth and twentieth centuries. While some were motivated by a desire to lay a firm historical foundation for the church's faith, others were in search of a more-or-less objective account of the first-century Jesus, and still others had the aim of discrediting Christianity. From the mid-1800s up to the present, there have been innumerable books on Jesus that, in the words of Crossan, were theology disguised as history or autobiography in the form of biography.[16] Perhaps the only thing these authors had in common was that each produced a text discussing Jesus!

The phase of development from Reimarus to Schweitzer, sometimes designated the "first quest" for the historical Jesus, began during an Enlightenment and post-Enlightenment era in which Christian orthodoxy was under assault from rationalism. In differing ways the authors who wrote on the life of Jesus sought to respond to the charge that Christianity was a superstition grounded on an untenable belief in miracles and divine intervention in the world. H. S. Reimarus in essence argued that Jesus was a Jewish revolutionary whose disciples, after his failure and death, conceived the notion that he was divine. They stole his body and then promulgated a new idea regarding his life and significance, according to which the world would end with the arrival of a divine being upon the clouds of heaven. Thus Christianity originated in a kind of double mistake in which Jesus first failed as a revolutionary and then his followers mistakenly expected the immediate end of the world. Reimarus's hypotheses con-

---

15. The story of Reimarus's impact on the learned world is as complex as it is interesting. Following Reimarus's death in 1768, the German man of letters Gotthold Ephraim Lessing published as the "Wolfenbüttel Fragments" in 1774-78 several anonymous extracts from a vast manuscript left behind by Reimarus under the title *Apologie oder Schutzschrift für die vernünftigen Verehrer Gottes.* A part of the *Apologie* has been translated into English with a helpful introduction in Charles H. Talbert, ed., *Reimarus: Fragments,* trans. Ralph S. Fraser (Philadelphia: Fortress, 1970).

16. John Dominic Crossan, *The Historical Jesus: The Life of a Mediterranean Jewish Peasant* (San Francisco: Harper San Francisco, 1991), p. xxviii.

tinue to hold significance for many later writers who see the delayed return of the Messiah as a key factor in the early development of Christianity, and for those few who have carried forward the interpretation of Jesus as a revolutionary.[17]

Like Reimarus, David Friedrich Strauss (1808-74) was preoccupied with the issues posed by the apparently supernatural or miraculous aspects of the New Testament narratives. Yet for him a critical rereading of the biblical texts still allowed one to find truth within them. One had to realize that the Gospels are myth rather than history, and must be read in accordance with their literary genre. Supernatural events did not and do not occur — here Strauss is at one with the later scholar Bultmann — and the mythical events contained in the New Testament are simply nonhistorical projections of the early faith of the Christian community. While Strauss took steps to win the favor of the academic authorities, the publication of his *Life of Jesus* (1835) alienated the conservatives in Germany and brought a swift end to his university career. He entered politics, continued to publish, and continued to influence academic life through the challenging questions posed in his earlier writings.[18]

While Strauss was finding myth in the Gospel texts, many other writers were in effect using the Gospels to create myth, that is, to fashion a mythicized Jesus that conformed closely to the cultural expectations of well-educated, late nineteenth-century western Europeans. Jesus was not in opposition to the culture of his day, or our own. Instead he was the flower of humanity, revealing the essential genius that lies in the heart of each man and woman. The kingdom of God was not an external realm of laws and regulations but a matter of pure hearts and proper intentions. Almost nothing was said to indicate that Jesus was opposed to the social world of his day or predicted its judgment by God and its ultimate demise. For some, especially in North America, the kingdom of God was a program of human betterment that could and would progress through time if only Jesus' followers devoted their energies to the cause. The Je-

17. For an interpretation of Jesus in light of first-century Jewish Zealotism, see S. G. F. Brandon, *Jesus and the Zealots: A Study of the Political Factor in Primitive Christianity* (New York: Scribner, 1967), esp. pp. 350-58. Brandon's view is discussed and critiqued in Oscar Cullmann, *Jesus and the Revolutionaries,* trans. Gareth Putnam (New York: Harper & Row, 1970); and J. P. M. Sweet, "The Zealots and Jesus," and Ernst Bammel, "The Revolution Theory from Reimarus to Brandon," in *Jesus and the Politics of His Day,* ed. Ernst Bammel and C. F. D. Moule (Cambridge: Cambridge University Press, 1984), pp. 1-9, 11-68 respectively.

18. On Strauss see James C. Livingston, *Modern Christian Thought: From the Enlightenment to Vatican II* (New York: Macmillan; London: Collier Macmillan, 1971), pp. 173-80, and Albert Schweitzer, *The Quest of the Historical Jesus: A Critical Study of Its Progress from Reimarus to Wrede* (New York: Macmillan, 1968), pp. 68-120.

sus of the late nineteenth century was less a savior than a teacher, and his most important instructions were embodied in the "Sermon on the Mount" (Matt. 5–7) and other passages of ethical exhortation.[19] Yet, unlike the Jesus of the eighteenth-century Enlightenment, the Jesus of nineteenth-century romanticism both exhibited and inculcated a life of sentiment and feeling. In his *Life of Jesus* (1863), the Frenchman Ernest Renan referred to Jesus as a "sublime person" who "every day still presides over the destiny of the world," so that "his worship will constantly renew its youth, the tale of his life will cause endless tears, his sufferings will soften the best hearts." Given the popularity of books like Renan's — which sold 60,000 copies during its first six months — one may conclude that a sentimentalized portrayal of Jesus appealed to large segments of the populace, and especially during an era when the traditional Christ of church and dogma seemed less compelling.[20]

While the popular biographies of Jesus were sprouting up like mushrooms after a warm summer storm, technical studies of the Gospel texts were also proliferating and becoming increasingly refined during the late nineteenth century. H. J. Holtzmann proposed the theory that Mark's Gospel was chronologically prior to Matthew and Luke and served as a source for the two later Gospels — a view still held by the great majority of New Testament scholars. Thus he laid the groundwork for many later studies of the sources of the Gospels. The ministry of Jesus fell into a series of clear-cut and comprehensible stages, with the decisive turning point in the episode at Caesarea Philippi (Mark 8:27–9:1). Holtzmann's influence has continued to be felt through his portrayal of the ministry of Jesus and his belief that source criticism is a primary tool for reconstructing the course of events that lay behind the birth of Christianity.[21]

A slender book by Johannes Weiss (1863-1914), published in German in 1892 and later translated into English,[22] provoked a major rethinking of the meaning of "the kingdom of God" in the teaching of Jesus. Together with

19. See Daniel L. Pals, *The Victorian "Lives" of Jesus* (San Antonio: Trinity University Press, 1982).

20. Ernest Renan, *Life of Jesus,* pp. 392-93, cited in Jaroslav Pelikan, *Jesus through the Centuries: His Place in the History of Culture* (New York: Harper & Row, 1985), p. 199.

21. Heinrich Julius Holtzmann was not the first to propose a two-source theory of Mark and Q, and yet he was a leading figure in what David L. Dungan has called a "period of consolidation" in the mid–nineteenth century. See Dungan, *A History of the Synoptic Problem: The Canon, the Text, the Composition, and the Interpretations of the Gospels,* Anchor Bible Reference Library, ed. David Noel Freedman (New York: Doubleday, 1999), esp. pp. 326-29.

22. Johannes Weiss, *Die Predigt Jesu vom Reiche Gottes* (Göttingen: Vandenhoeck & Ruprecht, 1892), and later editions, translated as *Jesus' Proclamation of the Kingdom of God* (Chico, Calif.: Scholars Press, 1985).

Schweitzer's book on the quest, Weiss's work led to a rediscovery of Jesus' teaching on the last things, the apocalyptic and eschatological elements that had been largely ignored in most nineteenth-century scholarship. (Intellectual history has its ironies: Weiss was the son-in-law of Albrecht Ritschl, perhaps the foremost liberal Protestant thinker in Germany at the time, and Weiss's work propelled scholarship regarding the kingdom of God in a new and unanticipated direction.) Jesus, according to Weiss, announced the imminent ending of the world. Yet the great cataclysm did not materialize as predicted. Although various efforts have been made to address Weiss's arguments, the basic issues he posed have remained dominant throughout twentieth-century scholarship, as seen especially in the recent works by E. P. Sanders and Dale Allison.

Schweitzer's *Quest*,[23] which summed up so much of previous scholarship and anticipates so many twentieth-century trends, is probably still the single most influential book on the subject. Its lively style set it apart from the colorless prose of most academic works, and its forceful argumentation chiseled out a new image of Jesus. Schweitzer argued that Jesus chose to keep his own messiahship a secret, disclosing it only to the disciples at the transfiguration and then commanding them to tell no one of the experience. Judas then broke the silence by revealing the secret to the chief priests. At the beginning of his ministry, Jesus had expected the Son of Man to appear in short order, and when this hope was not realized, he went to his death in order to bring upon himself the "messianic woes" that had to be endured before the Jewish people could be delivered. "The Jesus of Nazareth who . . . preached the ethic of the Kingdom of God, who founded the Kingdom of Heaven upon earth," argues Schweitzer, "never had any existence." Yet this negative assertion is coupled with the positive affirmation that "Jesus means something to our world because a mighty spiritual force streams forth from Him and flows through our time also." The eschatological sayings regarding the kingdom of God, despite or perhaps even because of their oddity for modern people, "raise the man who dares to meet their challenge . . . above his world and his time, making him inwardly free."[24]

One era of research ended and another began with Schweitzer, who posed so forthrightly the question, in N. T. Wright's words, of "how such a strange and remote Jesus could be relevant in a different culture and time."[25] In many ways this issue continues to dominate scholarship on Jesus up to the present time. What Schweitzer did was to sharpen an awareness of the cultural distance between ancient and modern times. When we scrutinize the paintings of bibli-

23. Albert Schweitzer, *The Quest of the Historical Jesus: A Critical Study of Its Progress from Reimarus to Wrede*, trans. W. Montgomery (New York: Macmillan, 1961 [1910]).

24. Schweitzer, *Quest*, pp. 398-99, 402.

25. Wright, "Jesus," p. 798.

cal scenes done by medieval and early modern artists, we can usually spot any number of anachronisms: Adam is reclining in a garden scene that is obviously Flemish, Mary Magdalene wears a Florentine headdress, and Rembrandt's Jerusalem has the look of a seventeenth-century town. Yet when one reads prose descriptions of Jesus' inner thoughts and feelings, attitudes toward others, self-consciousness, and ultimate purposes, it is not quite as easy to detect what is unhistorical.

Where the Gospel texts remain silent — as, for instance, regarding Jesus' boyhood and youth, and his thoughts and inner life — it is easy for us to fill in the lacunae with material from our own time and culture. During the missing years Jesus was doing what *we* would have done, and during his ministry he was thinking the thoughts that would have occurred to *us*. Even the most renowned of historians have modernized Jesus, or at least have been accused of doing so. One of the classic texts of German Protestantism, Adolf von Harnack's *What Is Christianity?* (1900), evoked a telling critique from a Roman Catholic critic: "The Christ that Harnack sees, looking back through nineteen centuries of Catholic darkness, is only the reflection of the Liberal Protestant face, seen at the bottom of a deep well."[26]

Today, as in times past, most writers approach Jesus with at least a tacit assumption of his relevance to the present time. To quote Cadbury again: "We are anxious (often quite unconsciously and without any formal Christian acceptance of him) to secure his authority for our own point of view. We flatter ourselves by praising his universality, his modernness, his insight, since we mean by these things merely our own judgment in the areas where we are quoting him."[27] Few indeed are the authors who say that Jesus' significance is confined to the first century, that he has no message for later generations or for the present age. Yet often there seems to be a trade-off between historical authenticity and contemporary relevance: the more firmly Jesus is embedded in the first century, the less clearly his words and deeds apply to the present time, while the more clearly his words and deeds apply to the present time, the less firmly he is embedded in the first century. One could argue that scholars should strive for complete objectivity in their research, but today there is a general recognition in the academy that all forms of human inquiry are shaped by the preconceptions and interests of the researchers themselves. The inquirer is a part of the inquiry, and not separate from it. Given the diversity of the approaches and answers given to many of the basic questions regarding Jesus, one might conclude that this particular field of inquiry shows the subjectivity and personal disposition of the researcher as much as any area of study. Schweitzer's

---

26. George Tyrrell, *Christianity at the Cross Roads* (London: Longmans, 1909), p. 44.
27. Cadbury, p. 43.

abiding significance is that he made it much harder for scholars to lapse into unconscious anachronism in their interpretations. Those who read Jesus as a man of the twentieth century had to do so in defiance of Schweitzer's image of Jesus as a first-century Palestinian Jewish apocalypticist.

During roughly the first half of the twentieth century, the dominant trends in scholarship were not favorable toward an investigation of the historical Jesus. Some have referred to this as the era of "no quest." Perhaps in part this was due to a failure of nerve subsequent to Schweitzer: How *could* a Jewish apocalyptic prophet speak to the people of the early twentieth century? In part the neglect of the topic was also due to theological movements, emanating in the German-language countries, which made the life of Jesus largely irrelevant for Christian faith. In the so-called dialectical theology of Karl Barth, Emil Brunner, and Friedrich Gogarten during the 1920s and 1930s, the earthly Jesus met his end on the cross, and at the cross God also rejected and passed judgment against human religiousness and piety. Jesus' earthly life is thus irrelevant, and preoccupation with it can in fact become an impediment to Christian faith and theological reflection. Moreover, the prevailing philosophy of existentialism highlighted the call to human decision, not the rational basis on which decisions were to be made. Faith was more a "leap" than a historical judgment. A verse from the letters of Paul was often cited to make the point: "Even though we once knew Christ from a human point of view, we know him no longer in that way" (2 Cor. 5:16).[28]

Rudolf Bultmann (1884-1976), one of the dominating figures in twentieth-century New Testament studies, had a dampening effect on historical Jesus research. His detailed literary analyses of the synoptic Gospels attempted to show that the sayings and stories attributed to Jesus actually took their origin in the circumstances of the early Christian movement. Contending parties in the church sought to buttress their positions by coining stories in which Jesus supported their point of view. Furthermore, Bultmann argued in a celebrated essay that the New Testament texts presuppose a prescientific outlook that is unacceptable to contemporary persons. "It is impossible," Bultmann quipped, "to use electric light and the wireless . . . and at the same time believe in the New Testament world of spirits and miracles."[29] In consequence he called for a "demythologization" of the New Testament that would strip away its miraculous elements and preserve its enduring meaning — which happened to coincide with the ideas of the existentialist philosopher Martin Heidegger (1889-1976).

---

28. Unless otherwise noted, this and all subsequent biblical quotations are from the New Revised Standard Version.

29. Rudolf Bultmann, "The New Testament and Mythology," in Bultmann et al., *Kerygma and Myth: A Theological Debate* (New York: Harper & Row, 1961), pp. 1-44, citing 5.

Both the form criticism of the Gospel texts and the program of demythologiza-tion represented an effort *not* to find Jesus. One of the personal factors driving Bultmann was an idiosyncratic interpretation of Lutheran theology: to find Je-sus by historical inquiry would be a human "work," and we must be saved "by faith" and not "by works." In Bultmann's 1934 book *Jesus and the Word,* not much remains of the first-century Jesus except an ongoing challenge for today's generation to live in existential authenticity. Little is said regarding his actions; only his sayings remain, and even these, when filtered through the sieve of Bultmann's critical method, yield only a modicum of material that certainly goes back to Jesus. To reconstruct the life and personality of Jesus himself is neither desirable nor possible. Since Bultmann relied heavily on the Greek and Hellenistic backdrop to explain the rise of early Christianity, Jesus' Jewish con-text was only of tangential interest in his research.[30]

Following a common pattern in German academic life, Bultmann's school of thought gave rise to a self-conscious movement of post-Bultmannians who parted company with their eminent teacher on a number of fundamentals. A lecture delivered by Ernst Käsemann in 1953 is generally re-garded as the opening of a "new quest" for the historical Jesus. While Käsemann agreed with Bultmann that no one could write a "life of Jesus," he maintained nonetheless that Christianity should not be severed from its historic roots. The earthly Jesus remains essential to the faith of the Christian church. Without the historical Jesus, faith in a heavenly Christ can easily become otherworldly, ethe-real, and "docetic." In certain respects, however, the post-Bultmannians contin-ued much of Bultmann's tradition. The apple fell near the tree. Günther Bornkamm's *Jesus of Nazareth* (German 1956; English 1960) kept the miracu-lous out of the picture and portrayed a Jesus who did not use messianic titles for himself. Bornkamm's Jesus spoke of an eschatological fulfillment in the present time rather than in the future. All in all, it was the message of Jesus rather than the events of his life that remained the primary focus. Nonetheless, Bornkamm parted company with Bultmann on the call of the twelve apostles. According to the former, this was an actual occurrence during the lifetime of Je-sus and not a retrojection from the fact of twelve leaders during the time of the primitive church.

Beginning in the mid-1980s, the "Jesus Seminar," under the direction of the American scholars Robert Funk and John Dominic Crossan, has continued in the general direction established in the post-Bultmannian "new quest" for the historical Jesus. A principal concern has been to establish insofar as possible

30. Bultmann made it his principle never to visit any of the sites of the Holy Land — "a bad old German tradition with dangerous results," in the words of Martin Hengel (in Richard Ostling, "Who Was Jesus?" *Time,* August 15, 1988, pp. 37-42, quoting 38).

the actual words spoken by Jesus. Several dozen scholars have been active participants in the seminar.[31] At their regular meetings the individual Gospel sayings are discussed, debated, and then voted on according to a scale of probability ranging from a high likelihood of genuineness to a near certitude of spuriousness. Members of the Jesus Seminar use one of four different colored beads to indicate their judgment regarding each saying, according to the following formula: red — Jesus said this or something very much like it; pink — he probably said something like this; gray — he did not say this but the idea is close to being his own; black — he did not say this and it represents a later and differing perspective. One member suggested a more down-to-earth interpretation of the colors: red — "that's Jesus!"; pink — "sure sounds like Jesus"; gray — "well, maybe"; and black — "there's been some mistake."[32] The summary conclusion reached by the Jesus Seminar is that only about 18 percent of the sayings attributed to Jesus in the Gospels were actually spoken by him. If this assertion is disturbing to Christian believers, then Funk and the others stress that theological preconceptions should not stand in the way of an open inquiry into the ancient texts. The seminar's stated rule is: "Beware of finding a Jesus entirely congenial to you."[33]

The findings of the Jesus Seminar have frequently been promulgated through print, radio, and television interviews, and its founder has acknowledged that his work is motivated by a desire to overcome "the tyranny of . . . Schweitzer's eschatological Jesus."[34] As Robert Funk noted in his opening statement to the seminar in 1985: "We are having increasing difficulty these days in accepting the biblical account of the creation and of the apocalyptic conclusion in anything like a literal sense. . . . What we need is a new fiction. . . . In sum, a new narrative of Jesus, a new Gospel, if you will, that places Jesus differently in the grand scheme, the epic story."[35] To be relevant today, then, Jesus has to be interpreted as non-eschatological. At least some of the seminar's participants have a social agenda underlying their scholarship, namely, to rescue Jesus from conservative Christianity

---

31. A roster of the "fellows" of the Jesus Seminar is given in Robert W. Funk, Roy W. Hoover, and the Jesus Seminar, *The Five Gospels: The Search for the Authentic Words of Jesus* (New York: Macmillan, 1993), pp. 533-37.

32. Funk et al., *The Five Gospels*, pp. 36-37. This volume contains the results of the seminar's deliberations on all the sayings attributed to Jesus in the synoptic Gospels and the noncanonical *Gospel of Thomas*.

33. Funk et al., *The Five Gospels*, p. 5.

34. Funk et al., *The Five Gospels*, p. 4.

35. Robert Funk, in *Foundations and Facets Forum* 1, no. 1 (1985): 11-12, cited in Luke Timothy Johnson, *The Real Jesus: Misguided Quest for the Historical Jesus and the Truth of the Traditional Gospels* (San Francisco: Harper San Francisco, 1996), p. 8. Johnson's book is a rebuttal of the methods and conclusions of the Jesus Seminar.

and especially from fundamentalists and evangelicals. They oppose a literal reading of the Gospels and belief in a literal return of Jesus. In general the seminar participants portray Jesus as a first-century iconoclast and antitraditionalist. He was, in Funk's words, "no goody two-shoes" but "a sort of flower child with an idealistic view of life that is virtually impossible to achieve."[36] The movie director Paul Verhoeven, whose credits include *RoboCop, Basic Instinct,* and *Showgirls,* has been in conversation with some members of the seminar about producing a film that would embody and publicize their point of view regarding Jesus.[37]

Connected with the Jesus Seminar and its portrayal of Jesus as a cultural iconoclast is an emphasis on the Hellenistic background of the Gospels and especially Cynic philosophy. This viewpoint represents a reversal of the generally accepted idea, at least since Schweitzer, that the more we put Jesus into his historical context, the more Jewish he will turn out to be. John Dominic Crossan and F. Gerald Downing have both argued that the wandering ministry of Jesus can best be understood according to the model of the Cynic philosopher-sage.[38] The ancient Cynic was an individual who theoretically questioned and practically denied the cultural values and civilized presuppositions of his society. He appeared everywhere ragged and dirty, carrying wallet, staff, and cloak, and always insuring that his right shoulder remained bare. He never wore shoes and allowed his hair and beard to be long and unkempt. The dress code dramatized his rejection of the material values of society. In one little bag (something like a rucksack) the Cynic carried everything necessary for his vagabond life, and so the bag itself served as an important symbol of self-sufficiency. The basic assumption, as Crossan notes, is that "the one who has nothing and wants nothing is totally free."[39] The most famous story regarding the Cynics comes from a much earlier period, when the victorious general Alexander the Great encountered the Cynic philosopher Diogenes and asked him if there was anything that he might do for him. "Stand a bit away from the sun" was the answer he got, because Alexander was standing in his light.[40]

One of the most radical new interpretations of Jesus and the Gospels comes from Burton L. Mack, who argues that the Jewish strands in the Gospels

36. Robert Funk, in *Atlanta Journal-Constitution,* September 30, 1989, cited in Johnson, pp. 12-13.

37. Johnson, pp. 15-16.

38. See Crossan, *The Historical Jesus,* and, more concisely, *Jesus: A Revolutionary Biography* (San Francisco: Harper Collins, 1994); F. G. Downing, *Jesus and the Threat of Freedom* (London: SCM, 1987) and *Cynics and Christian Origins* (Edinburgh: T. & T. Clark, 1992).

39. Crossan, *The Historical Jesus,* pp. 115, 117-18, 120.

40. Recounted in Cicero, *Tusculan Disputations,* Loeb Classical Library (London: William Heinemann; New York: Putnam, 1927), 5.92.

are later accretions and that the earliest traditions show Jesus as closely akin to the wandering Cynic preachers. Jesus, according to Mack, was in no sense an apocalyptic or eschatological prophet. Instead he was a popular sage, a wordsmith who uttered pithy aphorisms that shocked his hearers and forced them to reflect on themselves and their social and personal situations. His death by crucifixion was not significantly related to his life and teachings.[41] Moreover, the eschatological imagery in the New Testament texts actually originated subsequent to Jesus. In effect Mack has reversed the customary order of development. Now the Hellenistic or sapiential traditions come earlier, while the Jewish and apocalyptic elements come later. The Gospel of Mark served to create a "myth" of a cosmic Savior that in no sense corresponded to the earthly life of Jesus.[42]

Among the benefits of the recent studies of Jesus and Cynicism by Crossan and Downing is that they have led to a closer consideration of the non-Jewish background to the Gospels. In the light of their argument, it is not so easy to isolate Palestinian Judaism from the wider cultural influences and resonances of Greco-Roman antiquity. At the same time, Downing's argument is weakened by the lack of evidence for a Cynic presence in Galilee in Jesus' day and by the fact that his argument for parallels between Jesus' teaching and that of the Cynics relies on texts that come from different geographical regions and chronological periods. Crossan, moreover, in his argument for Jesus as a Palestinian Jewish Cynic, has to admit that there are discrepancies between the New Testament injunctions for the apostolic preachers and the basic ground rules that applied to the Cynic preachers. Both sets of texts agree that one is to wear no sandals and waste no time in greetings and gossip along the way. Yet the Gospel texts forbid the use of staff and wallet, while the Cynics required it, and indeed, constantly harp on the importance of cloak, staff, and bag or wallet.[43] Another problem is that the Cynics were extremely individualistic and probably were never gathered together into any sort of social grouping — a decisive point of difference from the early movement around Jesus.[44] Finally there is

---

41. Marcus Borg writes: "There is a friendly joke circulating among Jesus scholars: Burton Mack's Jesus was killed in a car accident on a freeway in Los Angeles. The point: for Mack, there is no significant connection between what Jesus was like and the fact that he was executed. His death was, in an important sense, accidental" (*Jesus in Contemporary Scholarship* [Valley Forge, Pa.: Trinity Press International, 1994], p. 38 n. 28).

42. Burton L. Mack, *A Myth of Innocence: Mark and Christian Origins* (Philadelphia: Fortress, 1988) and *Who Wrote the New Testament? The Making of the Christian Myth* (San Francisco: Harper San Francisco, 1995).

43. Crossan, *The Historical Jesus*, pp. 117-18; cf. Horsley, *Sociology*, p. 117.

44. Charlesworth, "Jesus Research Expands," p. 16. Compare the statement of Sean Freyne that the early Jesus movement did not "espouse the kind of social and personal

also a religious element in the Gospel instructions that is lacking in the Cynic texts. Jesus' disciples were not self-sufficient but rather dependent on God to provide for their necessities. Material provision was to come through generous individuals who would provide food and lodging during the preaching expeditions, and this was a reflection of God's active care for those engaged in the task of proclaiming the kingdom of God.[45]

The Jesus Seminar and the Cynic interpretation of Jesus stand in a certain tension with a broader phenomenon of the 1980s and 1990s that has been dubbed "the third quest" for the historical Jesus (in distinction from the "old quest" prior to Schweitzer and the "new quest" of the post-Bultmannians). N. Thomas Wright correctly stresses that this third quest is more diffuse than cohesive: "The current wave of books about Jesus offers a bewildering range of competing hypotheses. There is no unifying theological agenda; no final agreement about method; certainly no common set of results. But there are certain features which justify a unifying label."[46] Probably the most distinctive feature of the third quest is its reliance on our greatly expanded knowledge of Second Temple Judaism as background for understanding Jesus. This stress on the Jewish context brings the third-quest authors in accord with Reimarus and Schweitzer, and sets them against most nineteenth-century scholars, Bultmann, the post-Bultmannians, and the Cynic-Hellenistic interpretation of Jesus propounded by Crossan and some others in the Jesus Seminar. To oversimplify somewhat, the ideological fault line in Jesus studies today runs between two tectonic plates, the one representing Jesus as a Jewish apocalypticist and the other as a Hellenistic Cynic. Much of the fire and friction in recent scholarship comes from the pressure exerted by these two viewpoints against one another.

The third-quest authors, such as E. P. Sanders, Ben F. Meyer, A. E. Harvey, and Marcus Borg (who also is a participant in the Jesus Seminar), are seriously engaged in rereading first-century sources such as Josephus and situating Jesus in relation to the social, political, economic, and religious forces of his day. Sanders seeks answers to a set of basic questions, such as: What was Jesus' intention in his life and ministry? What was his relationship to his contemporaries? Why did he die, and why did Christianity begin? The methods used by these authors are based less on theological considerations than on the ordinary canons of historical inquiry: hypothesis and verification, the testing of sources, the use

---

withdrawal that was associated with various kinds of Cynicism. . . . Rather it proposed an alternative way of life that adopted and adapted the kinship and familial values which were being eroded in the larger culture" ("The Geography, Politics, and Economics of Galilee and the Quest for the Historical Jesus," in *Studying the Historical Jesus,* pp. 75-121, quoting 120).

45. See Matt. 10:5-15, 24-33; 19:27-30.

46. Wright, "Jesus," p. 800.

of material culture to supplement textual data, and so forth. Ben F. Meyer has written a work on Jesus' aims that highlights the restoration of Israel as the theme that underlies the proclamation of the kingdom of God. He argues that there was a distinction between Jesus' public and private messages, and that he intended for his public actions (such as table fellowship with sinners) to allow the question of his role or identity to emerge. Jesus envisaged a new community that would come into being, involving a renewal of the covenant and the promise of the forgiveness of sins. Contrary to Bultmann and the Bultmannian school, Meyer affirms that the early Christian community in its interpretation of Jesus was simply deciphering the powerful clues and indications concerning his identity that he himself bequeathed to it.[47]

A. E. Harvey's Bampton Lectures at Oxford University, published in 1982, proceed from the assumption that Jesus must be understood in terms of the "historical constraints" that operated within the particular culture of his place and time. Beginning with the crucifixion, he argues that the Gospel accounts concerning it are consistent with what is independently known regarding Roman and Jewish practice in the first century. Regarding the religious law or Torah, Harvey notes that while Jesus started from the common assumption of the legitimacy and authority of the Jewish legal requirements, he "put his teaching in the form of instructions appropriate to exceptional circumstances."[48] This consideration leads Harvey to a further examination of Jesus' sense of time and eschatology and the significance of his miracles. He concludes that Jesus was known as Messiah, though without any divine overtones, during his own lifetime. Since the constraint of monotheism meant that no Jew would or could have thought of himself as God, we must think of Jesus as possessing a uniqueness in his actions rather than in his being per se.

Marcus Borg, in his numerous books and articles on Jesus,[49] may be regarded as a third-quest author who also embodies some of the emphases of the Jesus Seminar. In particular he stresses that Jesus was non-eschatological and that his message set him at odds with the "politics of holiness" that characterized the religious leaders of his day. Jesus emerges as a cultural critic and icono-

---

47. Ben F. Meyer, *The Aims of Jesus* (London: SCM, 1979). For a condensation of Meyer's position, see his article "Jesus," in *Anchor Bible Dictionary*, 3:773-96.

48. A. E. Harvey, *Jesus and the Constraints of History* (Philadelphia: Westminster, 1982), p. 65.

49. Among his works on Jesus are the following: *Conflict, Holiness, and Politics in the Teachings of Jesus* (New York: Mellen, 1984); *Jesus* (see n. 5 above); *Jesus in Contemporary Scholarship;* (with N. T. Wright) *The Meaning of Jesus: Two Visions* (San Francisco: Harper San Francisco, 1998); and the essay "An Orthodoxy Reconsidered: The 'End-of-the-World' Jesus," in *The Glory of Christ in the New Testament,* ed. N. T. Wright and L. D. Hurst (Oxford: Clarendon, 1987), pp. 207-17.

Warner Sallman, *Head of Christ*
(Jessie C. Wilson Galleries, Anderson University)

clast, and not an apocalyptic prophet. On the other hand, Borg is more attentive than is Crossan to the Jewish background. Jesus did not intend to create a new religion, but rather wished to effect a "revitalization" of the Jewish tradition in which he was reared. His actions and teaching took place in the Jewish context of Torah and Temple: "His challenge . . . was not a complete overthrowing or disregard of tradition. . . . He was a Jew who treasured his tradition. He quoted Scripture, explicitly affirmed the Ten Commandments, and so far as we know observed the Jewish law all his life."[50] At the same time, Jesus challenged the "conventional wisdom" that established clear-cut and insuperable boundaries between good people and bad, men and women, and Jews and Gentiles. Jesus spoke of a compassionate God and required his disciples to follow a "way of transformation" that involved a dying to their old way of thinking and being, the implanting of a new heart, and a practice of centering in God's Spirit. More than other recent authors on Jesus, Borg stresses Jesus' spirituality and his call for others to imitate his spirituality.

E. P. Sanders, in several major works, has placed special emphasis on Jesus' relation to first-century Judaism.[51] He views Jesus with a historian's eye, and not through the lens of piety or theology. At the same time, Sanders is confident that the Gospels contain a good deal of reliable historical information. Sanders, along with other third questers, is generally unhappy with an approach to Jesus that stresses only his words and engages in an overly subtle analysis of the possible transmissional history of the reported sayings. Not all of our questions are answerable at this point. "Our sources contain information about Jesus," says Sanders, "but we cannot get at it by dogmatically deciding that some sentences are completely accurate and some are fiction. The truth will usually lie somewhere in between."[52]

Sanders's general method is to start from the actions rather than the words of Jesus, and to construct an overall picture of Jesus by beginning first with the events in Jesus' life that may be regarded as indubitable: that he was baptized by John the Baptist, that he was a Galilean who preached and healed, that he was crucified by the Roman authorities, and so on. Sanders lays special emphasis on Jesus' action in the Temple, which was less a "cleansing" of the Temple than a symbolic destruction of it. This one episode is an indication that Jesus' message fell within the general bounds of the first-century "Jewish restoration eschatology," according to which God would act in history to reestablish

50. Borg, *Jesus*, p. 114.

51. Sanders's most important books include the following: *The Historical Figure of Jesus; Jesus and Judaism; Jewish Law from Jesus to the Mishnah* (London: SCM, 1990); and *Judaism: Practice and Belief, 63 B.C.E.–66 C.E.* (London: SCM; Philadelphia: Trinity Press International, 1992).

52. Sanders, *Historical Figure*, p. 56.

his kingdom and erect a new Temple in Jerusalem. The action in the Temple was probably the specific event that triggered Jesus' arrest and crucifixion under the Romans. Certain questions are left unresolved by Sanders, such as the hotly debated issue of whether Jesus referred to himself as "the Son of Man." The reported disputes between Jesus and the Pharisees are for the most part a reflection of later church-synagogue controversies, according to Sanders. Yet there are some reliable sayings of Jesus that indicate that he departed from at least some of the central Jewish teachings, such as the imperative of attending to the burial of one's parents.[53]

A massive and as yet uncompleted study of the historical Jesus, *A Marginal Jew,* is currently being written by John Meier, with two volumes already written and at least one more forthcoming. Meier's work is probably the most meticulous and exhaustive of any of the third-quest authors. The endnotes to his chapters provide an encyclopedic survey of previous authors and opinions on each topic he treats. The "historical Jesus," as Meier explains, is always a "scientific construct" or "theoretical abstraction" that prescinds from what the Christian faith or later church teaching says about Jesus. It neither affirms nor denies the theological claims. To explain his project, Meier whimsically imagines a discussion among a Catholic, Protestant, Jew, and agnostic who are locked in the bowels of the Harvard Divinity School and must remain there on a spartan diet until they have hammered out a consensus document on who Jesus was and what he intended. *A Marginal Jew* is Meier's effort to anticipate the conclusions reached by such an "unpapal conclave."[54]

Meier regards Jesus as "marginal" in several senses. He was merely a "blip" on the radar screen of ancient history. He willingly forsook an honorable place in society and adopted an unusual way of life. He broke with the beliefs of his day in such teachings as voluntary celibacy and the impermissibility of divorce. He came from the periphery of society and had no upper-class claim to legitimate himself in the eyes of the aristocracy of his day. Finally, by the end of his life "he had managed to make himself appear obnoxious, dangerous, or suspicious to everyone from pious Pharisees through political high priests to an ever vigilant Pilate," and so was pushed altogether out of society by his gruesome and embarrassing death.[55] Generally Meier's portrayal of Jesus, or what we have of it thus far, is in accord with other recent authors who stress Jesus' Jewish background. Meier is skeptical regarding the noncanonical *Gospel of Thomas,*

53. "Let the dead bury their own dead" (Luke 9:60), discussed in Sanders, *Jesus and Judaism,* pp. 252-55.

54. John P. Meier, *A Marginal Jew: Rethinking the Historical Jesus,* 2 vols. to date, Anchor Bible Reference Library, ed. David Noel Freedman (New York: Doubleday, 1991-), 1:1.

55. Meier, *A Marginal Jew,* 1:7-9.

holding that it does not add any significant new historical information to the picture of Jesus contained in the canonical Gospels.[56] Differing from E. P. Sanders, Meier maintains that the kingdom of God in the teaching of Jesus is not wholly futuristic but contains a present aspect as well. Thus the kingdom is both a present and a future reality, both experienced and anticipated.[57] In his monumental treatment of Jesus and the miraculous in the second volume of *A Marginal Jew*, Meier argues that Jesus was known in the first instance as a doer of "startling deeds" rather than simply a teacher or visionary.[58]

The discussion thus far has treated only the scholarly works on Jesus. During the last several decades Jesus has continued to be a figure of immense importance for popular culture. John H. Hayes has written on the various images of Jesus during the twentieth century. These include Bruce Barton's bestseller *The Man Nobody Knows* (1925), portraying Jesus as a successful leader and organizer and "the friendliest man who has ever lived . . . the type of man whom you would have chosen as a companion on a fishing trip."[59] Hugh Schonfield's *Passover Plot* (1965) viewed Jesus as a man sincerely convinced that he was the Messiah, who followed the "nightmarish conception" and "frightening logic of a sick mind" by planning his own arrest and crucifixion. Albert Cleage's *Black Messiah* (1968) presents the man from Galilee as "the non-white leader of a non-white people struggling for national liberation against the rule of a white nation, Rome."[60] Levi H. Dowling's *Aquarian Gospel of Jesus the Christ* (1911) and Elizabeth Clare Prophet's *Lost Years of Jesus* (1984) represent Jesus as a spiritual master propounding a mystical and esoteric religion. Writers such as D. H. Lawrence in *The Man Who Died* (1928) and Nikos Kazantzakis in *The Last Temptation of Christ* (1961) created imaginative renderings of Jesus' life in which he struggles to deny his sexual desire or else finds fulfillment through gratifying it.

The British comedy troupe Monty Python produced *The Life of Brian* (1979), a movie about a certain first-century Jewish carpenter who bears a strong resemblance to someone better known. As Brian runs to escape his all-too-eager followers and their impertinent questions, his shoe inadvertently falls off, and there ensues a dialogue among the disciples. *First Man:* "He has given us a sign!" *Second Man:* "He has given us a shoe!" *First Man:* "The shoe is the

56. Meier, *A Marginal Jew*, 1:123-41.

57. Meier, *A Marginal Jew*, 2:237-506.

58. Meier, *A Marginal Jew*, 2:509-1038. The quoted phrase is from Josephus, *Antiquities* 18.3.3.

59. According to the Gospels (e.g., Luke 5:1-11), Jesus *did* go on fishing trips, and yet they were laborious rather than recreational!

60. John H. Hayes, *Son of God to Superstar: Twentieth-Century Interpretations of Jesus* (Nashville: Abingdon, 1976), pp. 82, 187-88, 184, 170.

sign — let us follow his example." *Second Man:* "What?!" *First Man:* "Let us like him hold up one shoe and let the other be upon our foot. For this is his sign that all who follow him shall do likewise." *Third Man:* "No, no, no, the shoe is a sign that we must gather shoes together in abundance." *Woman:* "Cast off the shoe! Follow the gourd [touched by Brian]!" This tongue-in-cheek episode can be read as a Bultmannian gloss on Christian origins — the church's interpreta- tion of Jesus derived from its own independent interests and preoccupations.

Along with the scholarly books and the popular books and films, there is a good deal of pseudoscholarship on Jesus that finds its way into print. Con- sider for instance Barbara Thiering's *Jesus the Man* (1975), which makes the fol- lowing remarkable claims: that Jesus was betrothed to Mary Magdalene at 10 P.M. on Tuesday June 6 in the year 30; that the Last Supper took place on March 19, 33, between 6 and 10 P.M.; that Jesus swooned on the cross (after receiving poison to relieve his pain) and was revived by friends; that Mary Magdalene subsequently had a daughter by Jesus; that this daughter was named Tamar; that Jesus had another child by Mary Magdalene, named Jesus Justus, born in March 41; that Jesus thereafter separated from Mary Magdalene and was last heard of in Rome in 64; and that his manner of death is unknown.[61] No less fanciful in character is Faber-Kaiser's *Jesus Died in Kashmir* (1977), which is based in part on local legends in northern India. The author asserts that Jesus did not die on the cross but recovered from his crucifixion wounds, traveled eastward (accompanied by his mother and the apostle Thomas) in search of the ten lost tribes of Israel, settled down in Kashmir, begat children, and died of natural causes at a ripe old age. The living descendants of Jesus in Kashmir pos- sess a genealogical table that traces their ancestry from Jesus.[62] Such books as *Jesus the Man* and *Jesus Died in Kashmir* do perhaps serve a purpose, in that they force a consideration of the foundational issues regarding the reliability of sources and the appropriate methods of historical inquiry.

Sources and Methods of Study

In this section there are two questions to consider: What textual sources should be used in developing a picture of the life and teachings of Jesus? And, after a decision is made on the sources to be used, what methods for studying these textual sources are most likely to result in reliable conclusions regarding Jesus?

61. Barbara Thiering, *Jesus the Man* (New York: Doubleday, 1975), pp. 88, 103-4, 115-16, 133, 146-48, 221-22, 229, 237, 254, 262-63, discussed by Telford, p. 46.
62. A. Faber-Kaiser, *Jesus Died in Kashmir: Jesus, Moses, and the Ten Lost Tribes of Is- rael* (London: Gordon Cremonesi, 1977).

One of the most characteristic developments in biblical studies during the last generation has been the growing interest in and appeal to noncanonical materials in constructing a picture of Jesus' life. Helmut Koester has claimed that the noncanonical writings are "just as important" as the New Testament texts for the study of early Christianity and "contain many traditions which can be traced back to the time of the very origins of Christianity."[63] At the outset it is important carefully to distinguish the different kinds of writings that lie outside of the biblical canon and to weigh the historical value of each individually. They differ greatly in character and in their relationship to the contents of the New Testament Gospels. *First,* there are references to Jesus in non-Christian sources, such as Greco-Roman authors (Suetonius, Pliny the Younger, Tacitus, etc.), the Jewish Talmud, and the rabbinical writings. Josephus's famous paragraph on Jesus, in his *Antiquities of the Jews,* is an especially important, though debated, text. *Second,* there are the agrapha, a term that refers to sayings attributed to Jesus that are not contained in any of the canonical Gospels. These sayings come from a wide variety of sources — from noncanonical gospels (such as the *Gospel of Thomas,* the *Gospel of the Nazoreans*), from early Christian authors (such as the author of *1 Clement,* Justin, Clement of Alexandria, Origen, Tatian, Eusebius, and many others), and from ancient Greek texts (such as the Oxyrhynchus Papyri). *Third,* there are the noncanonical gospels taken as a whole, which include not only sayings of Jesus but also narratives about him and reflections or exhortations on his life and significance. We will briefly consider each of these possible noncanonical sources in turn. It is impossible in this brief chapter to enumerate all the relevant noncanonical materials, let alone to summarize the extraordinarily complex debates about these texts and their significance for understanding the historical Jesus. The footnotes provide references for further study.[64]

The Talmud, though put into written form centuries after the life of Jesus, contains some ancient traditions and therefore could shed some light on Jesus. A number of statements may be found regarding a certain Jesus (or Yeshua), and yet the references are brief or oblique and there is often doubt as to whether they pertain to Jesus of Nazareth. An apparent reference to Mary, the mother of Jesus, who "played the harlot with carpenters,"[65] is clearly an anti-

---

63. Helmut Koester, *Introduction to the New Testament,* 2 vols. (Philadelphia: Fortress; Berlin and New York: Walter de Gruyter, 1982), 2:13.

64. Here I am indebted to the fine summary of recent scholarship in Chilton and Evans, *Studying the Historical Jesus,* and in particular the following chapters: Craig A. Evans, "Jesus in Non-Christian Sources," pp. 443-78; Evans, "Appendix: The Recently Published Dead Sea Scrolls and the Historical Jesus," pp. 547-65; and James H. Charlesworth and Craig A. Evans, "Jesus in the Agrapha and Apocryphal Gospels," pp. 479-533.

65. *b. Sanh.* 106a. This and the other Talmudic and Judaic references in this chapter are taken from the following texts: *The Babylonian Talmud,* ed. I. Epstein, trans. Maurice

Christian polemic that presupposes the Gospels of Matthew and Luke, and not an ancient and independent source of information. The same should probably be said with regard to the traditions about Jesus in Egypt,[66] Jesus' five disciples,[67] Jesus' practice of magic or sorcery,[68] and the various allusions to Jesus as a teacher or pupil figure.[69] One of the most important passages speaks of Jesus' death and the reason for it: "On the eve of the Passover Yeshu [the Nazarean] was hanged. For forty days before the execution took place, a herald went forth and cried, 'He is going forth to be stoned because he has practised sorcery and enticed Israel to apostasy. Any one who can say anything in his favour, let him come forward and plead on his behalf.' But since nothing was brought forward in his favour he was hanged on the eve of the Passover!"[70] In general it can be said that the rabbinical writings add no significant biographical detail to the picture of Jesus derived from other sources that are more detailed and reliable.[71]

Among the classical Greek and Roman writers who allude to Jesus is Suetonius, who, in *The Lives of the Caesars* (ca. 120 C.E.), refers to the expulsion of the Jews from Rome in 49 C.E. during the reign of Claudius: "[Claudius] expelled the Jews from Rome who, instigated by Chrestus, continually caused unrest."[72] The wording here may reflect an error arising from the confusion of "Chrestus" — a common slave name — with the title "Christus," a word that would not have been familiar to many of the Romans. In any case the passage

Simon et al., 39 vols. (n.p.: Rebecca Benet Publications, 1959); *The Talmud of the Land of Israel: A Preliminary Translation and Explanation,* trans. Tzvee Zahary et al., 35 vols. (Chicago and London: University of Chicago Press, 1982-93); *The Mishnah,* trans. with notes by Herbert Danby (London: Oxford University Press, 1933); *The Tosefta,* ed. Jacob Neusner et al., 6 vols. (Hoboken, N.J.: Ktav Publishing House, 1977-86); Jacob Neusner, *The Fathers According to Rabbi Nathan: An Analytical Translation and Explanation* (Atlanta: Scholars Press, 1986). Following the usual scholarly conventions, the initial letter "b" stands for *The Babylonian Talmud,* "y" stands for *The Jerusalem Talmud* or *The Talmud of the Lord of Israel,* "m" stands for *The Mishnah,* "t" stands for *The Tosefta,* and "Abot de-Rabbi Nathan" stands for *The Fathers According to Rabbi Nathan.*

66. *b. Sanh.* 107b; *b. Sota* 47a.

67. *b. Sanh.* 43b.

68. *b. Sanh.* 107b; *b. Sota* 47a; *t. Shabb.* 11:15.

69. *b. Ber.* 17b; *b. Sanh.* 107b.

70. *b. Sanh.* 43a.

71. The same can be said regarding the picture of Jesus presented in the Qur'an and other Islamic sources. Non-Muslim scholars are generally in agreement that the Islamic teachings on Jesus are literarily dependent on the New Testament and/or other early Christian writings. Hence they cannot serve as independent sources of information regarding Jesus.

72. Suetonius, *Divus Claudius* 25.4; cited in Evans, "Jesus in Non-Christian Sources," p. 457.

indicates that by the early second century some knowledge of "Chrestus" had spread among the Romans. One of the more interesting passages in the Roman writers comes from Pliny the Younger, who was governor of Bithynia and in the year 110 wrote to the emperor Trajan requesting advice on how to deal with the Christians. He purports to tell the Caesar what the Christians had told him: "They [the Christians] declared that the sum of their guilt or error had amounted only to this, that on an appointed day they had been accustomed to meet before daybreak, and to recite a hymn antiphonally to Christ, as to a god." Pliny goes on to say that the Christians made it their practice "to bind themselves by an oath, not for the commission of any crime but to abstain from theft, robbery, adultery and breach of faith . . . [and] to depart and meet again to take food."[73] None of this is information that could not be gleaned from the pages of the New Testament. Yet the passage suggests that an exalted image of Jesus (singing "as to a god") was widespread among Christians at this early stage.

One of the hostile witnesses to early Christianity in the second century was the philosopher Celsus, whose treatise *The True Doctrine* survives only in the spirited rebuttal *Against Celsus,* written by Origen in the mid–third century. There are numerous references in Celsus to Jesus as a sorcerer who deceived the people with his magic.[74] These statements echo the earlier assertion of Justin Martyr regarding the Jewish rejection of Jesus: "But though they saw such works, they asserted it was a magical art. For they dared to call Him a magician, and a deceiver of the people."[75] This particular accusation is already found in the Gospel texts (e.g., Matt. 12:22-32) where Jesus is charged with casting out demons by the power of Satan. The statements by Celsus along with the parallel Jewish statements on "sorcery" corroborate the impression given by the New Testament that Jesus was widely known by Christians and non-Christians alike as the performer of supernatural deeds. The key difference of opinion was over the *source* of Jesus' spiritual powers, whether from God or from the devil and the forces of darkness.[76]

---

73. Pliny the Younger, *Epistles,* bk. 10, letter 96, in Henry Bettenson, ed., *Documents of the Christian Church,* 2nd ed. (London: Oxford University Press, 1963), pp. 3-4.

74. See Origen, *Contra Celsum* 1.6, 38, 46, 68, 71; 2.9, 14, 16; 3.1; 5.51; 6.42; cited in Evans, "Jesus in Non-Christian Sources," p. 460.

75. Justin Martyr, *Dialogue with Trypho* 69, in Alexander Roberts and James Donaldson, eds., *The Ante-Nicene Fathers,* 10 vols. (Grand Rapids: Eerdmans, 1985 [1885]), 1:233.

76. There are other notable references to Jesus in classical authors, as for instance in Lucian of Samosata (ca. 115–ca. 200), who writes of those who "revered him [Jesus] as a god, used him as a lawgiver, and set him down as a protector" (*Passing of Peregrinus* 11.13). Lucian refers disdainfully to early Christian egalitarianism ("their first lawgiver persuaded

The most important early non-Christian reference to Jesus is found in a key paragraph in Josephus's *Antiquities,* probably written during the 90s C.E. The text as it has come down to us contains certain statements that almost certainly could not have been penned by Josephus himself, including an apparent confession of faith in Jesus as "the Messiah." While some scholars believe the entire paragraph is a Christian interpolation, inserted into the text to make Josephus more palatable for ecclesiastical consumption, a more plausible theory is that much of the paragraph derives from Josephus while certain statements were sandwiched in at a later time. The celebrated passage, sometimes known as the *Testimonium Flavianum,* is given below, with the likely Christian interpolations rendered in italics:

> About this time there lived Jesus, a wise man, *if indeed one ought to call him a man.* For he was one who wrought surprising feats and was a teacher of such people as accept the truth gladly. He won over many Jews and many of the Greeks. *He was the Messiah.* When Pilate, upon hearing him accused by men of the highest standing amongst us, had condemned him to be crucified, those who had in the first place come to love him did not give up their affection for him. *On the third day he appeared to them restored to life, for the prophets of God had prophesied these and countless other marvellous things about him.* And the tribe of the Christians, so called after him, has still to this day not disappeared.[77]

As John Meier has argued, the three highlighted passages above are the only assertions that suggest a Christian point of view regarding Jesus. Their deletion, moreover, creates a compact and fluent set of statements that is fairly neutral in its tone. Thus the most economical and least complicated theory would seem to be that Josephus wrote a paragraph that lacked these three segments.[78]

---

them that they are all brothers of one another") and to martyrdom ("the poor wretches despise death and most even willingly give themselves up"). Another sneering comment comes from Cornelius Tacitus (ca. 56–ca. 118), who in *Annals* 15.44 speaks of the Christians as "those hated for their vice" and followers of a "pernicious superstition" (citations from Evans, "Jesus in Non-Christian Sources," pp. 461-65). Tacitus confirms that Jesus died under the authority of Pontius Pilate, and that he was the founder of a religious movement called after his name. On this whole subject of outsiders' perceptions of Jesus and the early Christians, see the fascinating book by Robert Louis Wilken, *The Christians as the Romans Saw Them* (New Haven: Yale University Press, 1984).

77. Josephus, *Antiquities* 18.63; cited from *Josephus,* English translation by H. St. J. Thackeray, Ralph Marcus, Allen Wikgren, and L. H. Feldman, Loeb Classical Library, 9 vols. (Cambridge: Harvard University Press, 1926-83).

78. Meier discusses the *Testimonium,* with customary thoroughness, in *A Marginal Jew,* 1:56-88.

One notes that Josephus's text does not exaggerate the role played by the Jewish leaders in Jesus' arrest, trial, and crucifixion. If the entire passage were a later Christian invention, one might have expected the Jewish leaders to be portrayed as outright villains. Also the text lacks the animus toward Jesus that is conspicuous in the later rabbinical texts that we have already considered. Thus the *Testimonium* reads as we might expect if it had been written (apart from its later interpolations) by a first-century Jew prior to the emergence of Jewish-Christian animosities. Craig Evans argues that a later and quite incidental reference in *Antiquities* to Jesus, mentioned in connection with "James the brother of Jesus who was called the Christ,"[79] seems to demand some prior explanation of Jesus by Josephus, and that the *Testimonium* can be taken as the implied reference. Thus the later passage lends support to the authenticity of the former. Josephus has significance for current scholarship in that some have recently called into question the Gospels' presentation of Jesus' death as the outcome of his public teaching. Burton Mack has argued that the causes leading to Jesus' death are obscure, and that the bond created by the Gospel of Mark between Jesus' teachings or miracles and his death is fictional in character.[80] David Seeley claims that "Mark concocted the Jewish conspiracy against Jesus for his own, redactional reasons."[81] Yet the implication of the *Testimonium* is that Jesus' actions and teachings were linked with his arrest and accusation, and that the "first men" of the Jews played a role of some kind in his death.[82]

79. Josephus, *Antiquities* 20.200; Evans, "Jesus in Non-Christian Sources," pp. 468-73.

80. Mack, *A Myth of Innocence,* p. 282.

81. David Seeley, "Was Jesus like a Philosopher? The Evidence of Martyrological and Wisdom Motifs in Q, Pre-Pauline Traditions, and Mark," in *Society of Biblical Literature 1989 Seminar Papers,* ed. David J. Lull (Atlanta: Scholars Press, 1989), pp. 540-49, citing 548. Both cited in Evans, "Jesus in Non-Christian Sources," pp. 471-72.

82. Before leaving the topic of non-Christian sources, I should mention some recent discussions concerning the Dead Sea Scrolls (summarized in Evans, "Dead Sea Scrolls," pp. 547-65, esp. 553-54, 563-65). A stir was caused by the recent publication of the remaining scrolls from Cave 4 at Qumran. The original texts are given in Robert H. Eisenman and J. M. Robinson, *A Facsimile Edition of the Dead Sea Scrolls,* 2 vols. (Washington: Biblical Archaeology Society, 1991), and a selection of them with translations is found in Robert H. Eisenman and M. O. Wise, *The Dead Sea Scrolls Uncovered: The First Complete Translation and Interpretation of Fifty Key Documents Withheld for Over Thirty-five Years* (Shaftesbury: Element, 1992). The text catalogued as 4Q285 quickly became controversial when Eisenman claimed that it speaks of a slain Messiah (Eisenman and Robinson, pp. 224, 321, 409, 739, 1352; and Eisenman and Wise, pp. 27-29). He translated the key passage as "they will put to death the Leader of the Community, the Branch of David." Yet the context suggests that it is not the Messiah who is overcome, but rather the enemies who are overcome by the Messiah. Thus the translation should read: "The Prince of the Community, the Branch of David, will put him to death." Another text worth mentioning is 4Q491,

Regarding the agrapha, or noncanonical sayings attributed to Jesus, there is probably less reliable historical information to be gleaned than in the case of the various non-Christian sources on the life of Jesus. Joachim Jeremias considered hundreds of different sayings attributed to Jesus in a wide variety of ancient texts, and isolated only eighteen that were worthy of serious consideration as possibly authentic.[83] A more recent survey of the agrapha is even less optimistic.[84] To give the reader a feel for the agrapha, a few examples will be cited along with the respective sources. "Blessed is the man who has suffered; he has found the Life" *(Gospel of Thomas)*. "Woe to the Pharisees, for they are like a dog sleeping in the oxen's manger, which neither eats nor allows the oxen to eat" *(Gospel of Thomas)*. "He himself will give you your clothing" (Oxyrhynchus Papyri). "If you are in my bosom and do not the will of my Father in heaven, I will cast you out of my bosom" (Codex 1424 at Matt. 7:5). "As you prove yourselves kind, so you will experience kindness" *(1 Clement)*. "Save yourself and your life" (Theodotus, as reported in Clement of Alexandria). "There will be schisms and heresies" (Justin Martyr). "I choose for myself the best, the best are they whom my Father in heaven gives me" *(Gospel of the Nazoreans)*. "The one who has not forgiven seventy times seven times is not worthy of me" *(Liber Graduum)*. "They who are with me have not understood me" *(Acts of Peter)*. "Let your Holy Spirit come upon us and cleanse us" (Codex 700 to Luke 11:2). "It is more blessed to give than to receive" (Acts 20:35).[85]

The final agraphon above — considered such because it is not from the canonical Gospels, though it is in the New Testament — is the most likely of the group to be authentic.[86] Yet in many cases the agrapha are simply embellishments or variations of sayings that are already attested in the synoptic Gospels or elsewhere in the New Testament. Furthermore, even if the eighteen or so agrapha that Jeremias considered were added to the "database" on Jesus, this

---

discussed by Morton Smith in "Two Ascended into Heaven — Jesus and the Author of 4Q491," in *Jesus and the Dead Sea Scrolls*, ed. James H. Charlesworth (New York: Doubleday, 1992), pp. 290-301. The text seems to describe a human being who ascends into heaven and there takes a seat among celestial beings. This text could have some relevance for the Gospel verse "'you will see the Son of Man seated at the right hand of the Power,' and 'coming with the clouds of heaven'" (Mark 14:62), since it provides evidence that notions of heavenly exaltation were entertained in certain branches of Judaism in Jesus' day.

83. Joachim Jeremias, *The Unknown Sayings of Jesus* (London: SPCK, 1957). See also the older classic in German, A. Resch, *Agrapha: Aussercanonische Schriftfragmente*, Texte und Untersuchungen 15 (Leipzig: Hinrichs, 1906).

84. O. Hofius, "Unknown Sayings of Jesus," in *The Gospel and the Gospels*, ed. Peter Stuhlmacher (Grand Rapids: Eerdmans, 1991), pp. 336-60.

85. Cited from Charlesworth and Evans, pp. 484-86.

86. Charlesworth and Evans, p. 487 n. 22.

would not appreciably alter the general picture that we have of Jesus' life and teachings.[87] Hofius concludes that there is little evidence that substantial material on a level of quality approximating that of the synoptic Gospels survived outside of the New Testament canon. Quoting Jeremias with approval, Hofius declares that the "four canonical Gospels embrace with great completeness almost all the early Church knew of the sayings and deeds of Jesus in the second half of the first century."[88] Nonetheless, the agrapha have pertinence for our understanding of early Christianity. If a saying proves to be inauthentic, then one can imaginatively reconstruct the historical setting and social group that might have been responsible for creating such a saying and attributing it to Jesus. The agrapha, like the apocryphal gospels generally, enrich our understanding of the variants of Christianity (or Christianities) that flourished during the early centuries.

Many of the noncanonical or apocryphal gospels have been well known among scholars for decades or centuries, and yet it is only within the last generation that many have argued that they should be taken seriously as sources for the life of Jesus. Bultmann considered the apocryphal texts to be nothing more than "legendary adaptations and expansions"[89] of the material already contained within the canonical Gospels. Certain features of the apocryphal gospels seem plainly to be legendary. In the *Gospel of Philip*, for instance, Jesus goes into the dye works of Levi, takes seventy-two different colors, throws them into the vat, and they all come out white. Stranger still, Joseph the carpenter grows a tree from which he makes the cross on which Jesus is later hanged.[90] The *Gospel of Peter* also features a talking cross and angels whose heads reach into heaven.[91] Yet today, many apocryphal texts are taken more seriously as historical sources. Particularly important for current study is the *Gospel of Thomas*, written in the Coptic language and included in the Nag Hammadi library unearthed in Egypt in the late 1940s.[92] (This *Gospel of Thomas* is not to be confused with the so-

---

87. Meier, *A Marginal Jew*, 1:114.

88. Hofius, p. 357, citing Joachim Jeremias, "Die Zuverlässigkeit der Evangelien-Überlieferung," *Junge Kirche* 6 (1938): 580, quoted in Charlesworth and Evans, p. 490.

89. Rudolf Bultmann, *History of the Synoptic Tradition*, trans. John Marsh (New York: Harper & Row, 1963), p. 374.

90. Meier, *A Marginal Jew*, 1:123-24, referring to the *Gospel of Philip* 63:25-30, and 73:8-15.

91. John Dominic Crossan has proposed a complex theory according to which the second-century *Gospel of Peter* is a revision of a much earlier "Cross Gospel," which was in fact so early that it served as the sole basis for the passion narrative in the Gospel of Mark. Meier (*A Marginal Jew*, 1:116-18) and Charlesworth and Evans (pp. 503-14) demonstrate the weaknesses in Crossan's theory.

92. For a collection of these texts in English translation, see James M. Robinson, ed., *The Nag Hammadi Library in English*, 3rd ed. (San Francisco: Harper & Row, 1988).

called *Infancy Gospel of Thomas,* a quite different text that was known prior to the discovery of the Nag Hammadi writings.) A cadre of contemporary scholars, led by professors and graduates of Harvard University and Claremont Graduate School, has published a flurry of books and articles asserting that the *Gospel of Thomas* is nothing less than a "fifth Gospel," which embodies traditions as early and as reliable as those contained within the synoptic Gospels.

A key claim made by *Thomas*'s champions is that it is independent of the canonical texts, and that the sayings it records may be set over against those of the synoptics as a test of the genuineness and authenticity of the latter.[93] Obviously if *Thomas* is just a reworking of themes contained in the synoptics, was written several decades later, and was inspired and influenced by the canonical texts, then this severely limits its role in shedding any new light on Jesus. If, however, *Thomas* is as early or almost as early as the synoptics, and is literarily independent of them (i.e., composed without knowledge of the written synoptic Gospels), then it might tell us a good deal regarding Jesus and his teaching not already known from canonical texts. One of the distinctive features of *Thomas,* as compared with all four New Testament Gospels, is the almost complete absence of any narrative framework or recounting of Jesus' actions. *Thomas* is basically a compilation of 114 sayings attributed to Jesus.[94]

A number of features of the *Gospel of Thomas* weigh against regarding it as independent of the synoptic Gospels. It appears to quote or allude to some sixteen different New Testament books — all four canonical Gospels, Acts, many of the epistles, and Revelation — and could be simply a collage of canonical and noncanonical materials, often interpreted allegorically, assembled to advance second- and third-century gnostic ideas. To circumvent the problem of *Thomas*'s allusions to the canonical texts, Crossan and some other scholars have attempted to extract an early version of *Thomas* from the

---

93. A defense of these claims may be found in Stephen J. Patterson, *The Gospel of Thomas and Jesus* (Sonoma, Calif.: Polebridge Press, 1993), and Richard Valantasis, *The Gospel of Thomas,* New Testament Readings (London and New York: Routledge, 1997). Some of the recent authors overstate their case, however, in claiming that a "consensus is emerging in American scholarship that the *Gospel of Thomas* is a text independent of the Synoptics and that it was compiled in the mid to late first century" (Stevan L. Davies, "The Christology and Protology of *The Gospel of Thomas,*" *Journal of Biblical Literature* 111 [1992]: 663, quoted in Charlesworth and Evans, p. 497 n. 41). Marcus Borg makes a similar claim regarding a "consensus" in *Jesus in Contemporary Scholarship,* p. 165.

94. John Meier argues that Matthew, Mark, Luke, and John fall into a distinct literary genre of "gospel" that necessarily includes reference to Jesus' deeds, death, and resurrection, as well as his teaching. On this basis Thomas does not qualify as a "gospel" (*A Marginal Jew,* 1:143-45 n. 15). Helmut Koester by contrast seems to define a "gospel" as including all writings that pertain to Jesus of Nazareth (*Ancient Christian Gospels: Their History and Development* [London: SCM; Philadelphia: Trinity Press, 1990], pp. 44-47).

Coptic and Greek texts now extant. Yet the problems besetting an early dating of the *Gospel of Thomas* run deep. *Thomas* not only contains *sayings* that are distinctive to Matthew, Luke, and John, but even *redactional* elements as well. That is, the sayings in *Thomas* are arranged in ways that suggest the unmistakable influence of the canonical Gospels. The Gospel of Matthew, for instance, links together the three themes of almsgiving, prayer, and fasting (Matt. 6:1-18), and *Thomas* echoes this. And since *Thomas* views almsgiving, prayer, and fasting in a negative light, this probably links *Thomas* with a later gnostic antipathy toward Jewish piety and once again shows it to be secondary to Matthew. These and other considerations have led a number of scholars to view the *Gospel of Thomas* as later than the synoptic Gospels and as derivative from them.[95]

After reviewing the complex arguments regarding the various possible sources for the life of Jesus, John Meier makes the following remarks:

> For all practical purposes, then, our early, independent sources for the historical Jesus boil down to the Four Gospels, a few scattered data elsewhere in the NT, and Josephus. Contrary to some scholars, I do not think that the rabbinic material, the *agrapha*, the apocryphal gospels, and the Nag Hammadi codices (in particular the *Gospel of Thomas*) offer us reliable new information or authentic sayings that are independent of the NT. What we see in these later documents is rather the reaction to or reworking of NT writings by Jewish rabbis engaged in polemics, imaginative Christians reflecting popular piety and legend, and gnostic Christians developing a mystic speculative system. . . . We are left alone — some would say forlorn — with the Four Gospels, plus scattered tidbits. It is only natural for scholars — to say nothing of popularizers — to want more, to want other access roads to the historical Jesus. This understandable but not always critical desire is, I think, what has recently led to the high evaluation, in some quarters, of the apocryphal gospels and the Nag Hammadi codices as sources for the quest. It is a case of the wish being father to the thought.[96]

If the canonical Gospels are the only substantive sources that we presently possess for an investigation of Jesus, then it is important to consider carefully the nature of the canonical texts and the possible methods of inquiry to be used in

---

95. E. P. Sanders says: "I share the general scholarly view that very, very little in the apocryphal gospels could conceivably go back to the time of Jesus. They are legendary and mythological. Of all the apocryphal material, only some of the sayings in the Gospel of Thomas are worth consideration" (*Historical Figure,* p. 64).

96. Meier, *A Marginal Jew,* 1:140.

studying them. To this topic we will turn briefly before launching into a consideration of Jesus' life, sayings, actions, and influence.

The question of the authenticity or inauthenticity of the synoptic Gospels is one of the neuralgic points of modern scholarship. The issues have long been debated, no consensus has yet emerged, and nothing that I write here could or would be satisfactory to all interested parties. You cannot please all the scholars all the time, and sometimes it seems that you cannot please even some of them some of the time! Traditional or orthodox Christians of varying types may be inclined to dismiss the whole question of authenticity in the canonical Gospels, affirming that these texts are the word of God in written form and are therefore incapable of containing any errors or distortions regarding Jesus. Here we encounter a difference between the characteristic attitude of the believer — accepting, trusting, and doubtful of self — and that of the historian — cautious, questioning, and doubtful of the sources. The tension between these two ways of approaching the biblical texts is one of the fundamental issues in modern Christianity and in other religions (e.g., Judaism and Islam) that purport to be based on a written revelation of God's will.[97] The issue is like a subterranean stream flowing beneath the vast scholarship on the Bible and Christianity, now emerging, later submerging, but never absent and never far from ground level.

Yet one need not be a skeptic to perceive some of the fundamental issues of historical reliability that crop up in the synoptic Gospels. All one has to do is read *closely*. As Crossan has correctly observed, if one approaches the Gospels "vertically," that is, reading straight through one before moving on to the next, the dominant impression one gains is that of coherence and harmony. Yet if one approaches them "horizontally," pausing to consider each saying or episode in the life of Jesus and comparing it with the accounts given in the other Gospels, one sees a great deal of divergence between the passages.[98] The small differences in each passage add up, and patterns become visible in each Gospel. This has given rise to a whole field of research known as redaction criticism, which examines the ways in which the material concerning Jesus is transmitted and shaped in each respective Gospel. Thus, to give one of many possible examples, the Gospel of Matthew replaces Jesus' references to the "kingdom of God" with the phrase the "kingdom of heaven," and this is probably a reflection of the Jewish veneration for the name of God and desire to avoid putting it into print.

Little has been said thus far regarding the Gospel of John. The observant reader may have noted already in this chapter that I have sometimes used the

---

97. An excellent analysis of the issues is found in Van A. Harvey, *The Historian and the Believer: The Morality of Historical Knowledge and Christian Belief* (New York: Macmillan, 1966).

98. Crossan, *Jesus*, p. x.

expression "synoptic Gospels" where one might have expected "canonical Gospels." Concerning the Fourth Gospel, there are few scholars today of any theological background who would be prepared to assert that it is on a par with Matthew, Mark, and Luke in its value as a historical source for the life of Jesus. The Christ of John speaks in a radically different way than the Jesus of the synoptics — not in parables, not in pithy phrases that show the coloring of first-century Palestine, and only rarely in talk about "the kingdom of God." Instead the Christ of John engages in extended soliloquies that revolve around himself and his unique identity. Only in John do we find the remarkable assertions: "I am the bread of life" (6:35), "I am the light of the world" (8:12), "I am the true vine" (15:1), and so on. The nearest we come to this in the synoptic Gospels is probably in the "Son of Man" sayings, whose authenticity is highly contested. Yet John goes much further than the other canonical Gospels in bringing Jesus himself and his identity into the foreground. The proclaimer becomes the proclaimed. That is, Jesus in the Gospel of John is as much the content of the message as the herald who announces the message. That said, a number of scholars have demonstrated that the author of the Gospel of John exhibits a knowledge of Palestinian geography and Jewish custom that is unequaled in the other canonical Gospels.[99] This militates against reading John as a very late first-century or even early second-century text that reflects not the circumstances of Jesus' time but a Gentile culture and a Hellenizing tendency.[100] Still, the historical reminiscences contained in John are not enough to offset the other factors already mentioned, and for this reason the picture of Jesus presented in this chapter will be based almost exclusively on the synoptic Gospels rather than the Gospel of John.

This brings us at length to some questions that are critical for everything else that follows in this chapter on Jesus: Exactly what *kinds* of texts are the synoptic Gospels of the New Testament? What are their distinctive literary *features*? What, if anything, can we learn from the present form of the texts about the compositional *process* that led to the Gospels in their present form? And finally, how should the answers to the above questions influence our judgment regard-

---

99. On historical tradition in John, see the following: C. H. Dodd, *The Fourth Gospel* (Cambridge: Cambridge University Press, 1960), pp. 444-53, and Dodd, *Historical Tradition in the Fourth Gospel* (Cambridge: Cambridge University Press, 1963); Raymond Brown, *The Gospel according to John,* 2 vols., Anchor Bible, ed. David Noel Freedman (Garden City, N.Y.: Doubleday, 1966-70), esp. 1:xli-li; and A. J. B. Higgins, *The Historicity of the Fourth Gospel* (London: Lutterworth, 1960).

100. For an interpretation of John in light of the Gnostic, Hermetic, Mandaean, or Manichaean background, see the classic studies by Wilhelm Bousset, *Kyrios Christos,* trans. John E. Steely (New York and Nashville: Abingdon, 1970 [German 1913]), pp. 211-44; and Rudolf Bultmann, *The Gospel of John* (Oxford: Basil Blackwell, 1971 [German 1941]).

ing the general historical *reliability* of the picture of Jesus presented in the synoptic Gospels? Seas of ink have been spilled over mountains of paper in answering each of these questions. Only the briefest and most cursory account is possible here. As in the earlier discussion of the non-Christian sources on Jesus and the noncanonical Gospels, the reader is referred to the notes that contain references for further study.[101]

There are a number of foundational principles to keep in mind regarding the synoptic Gospels and their portrayal of Jesus. First, the earliest Christians probably did not write out a full narrative of Jesus' life, but rather preserved individual units (called pericopes or pericopae, lit. "cut around") about his life and deeds. These units were later moved and arranged by editors and authors. This means that we cannot be completely certain regarding the immediate context of Jesus' sayings and actions. Second, much of the material included in the Gospels has been significantly revised and shaped by the concerns of the early Christians who gathered together the traditions concerning Jesus. Third, the Gospels were written anonymously. That is, their inscriptions of authorship were not a part of the earliest versions of the text, but were added later. Fourth, as we have mentioned already, the Gospel of John is quite different from the other three Gospels, and it is primarily in the latter that we must seek information about Jesus. Fifth, the Gospels lack many of the characteristics of biography, and we should especially distinguish them from modern biographies.

To understand the Gospels it may be helpful to envision the immediate aftermath of the crucifixion. After Jesus' death his followers fled or hid, but their hopes were renewed when they had a vision of him alive again. Convinced that the kingdom Jesus predicted would soon arrive in full force, they waited in Jerusalem and sought to convince others that Jesus was the promised Messiah. Given their situation, it is unlikely that they sat down together at this early stage, collectively ransacked their memories, and in this sort of deliberate fashion composed a biography of Jesus. Since they expected that he would soon be among them, the question of how best to preserve the knowledge of his life for future generations was probably not in their minds. Yet, even at this earliest stage, while trying to communicate their own convictions regarding Jesus to others, they must have often told stories of Jesus' actions and words. It is likely that these stories were not initially written down, but circulated for some time in oral form. Thus the sayings and doings of Jesus were preserved, though perhaps in a somewhat different context than that of Jesus' own life, namely, in the context of the teaching and practice of the earliest Christian communities. As

---

101. Most general introductions to the New Testament discuss the authorship, composition, and dating of the Gospels. An unusually lucid summary is given in Sanders, *Historical Figure*, pp. 57-66, to which I am indebted here.

time passed, and as Jesus' expected return did not occur, the traditions about Jesus were then put into written form.

The process that produced the New Testament Gospels is not fully known to us. It is a question of drawing inferences from the finished product, like an architect inspecting a completed house from the front lawn and making conjectures regarding its foundation and frame. Based on the study of the synoptic Gospels, it is plausible to think that the material regarding Jesus was organized into discrete segments or pericopes. One of the key questions that confronts the contemporary scholar of the Gospels is the issue of the editing or redaction of these pericopes. In other words: How did the authors of the Gospels make decisions to include or exclude, to abridge or amplify, the units of tradition that were passed down to them? How did they decide on the order of presentation? It is clear that they did shift these units around. This is obvious when we see that the same saying or act of Jesus is presented in different contexts in different Gospels. The authors of the Gospels probably did not know the immediate context and circumstances of the individual stories and sayings of Jesus. This was not a part of the tradition that was passed down to them. Thus they organized the pericopes according to principles of their own devising.

It is possible that there were proto-gospels that preceded the present synoptic Gospels of Matthew, Mark, and Luke.[102] Most scholars believe that Mark was the first of the New Testament Gospels to be written. Scholars refer to this as the theory of "Markan priority." (A few believe that Matthew was written earlier than Mark, and this is known as "Matthean priority" or the Griesbach hypothesis.) A likely basis for many of the sayings attributed to Jesus in the Gospels was a source called "Q" (from *Quelle*, the German word for source). Thus Mark (if it did come first) and Q (if it really existed) were two major sources for the Gospel of Matthew and the Gospel of Luke. Some material is unique to Matthew and some to Luke, however, and so scholars have hypothesized the existence of "M" (a Matthean source) and "L" (a Lukan source) to account for this fact. The final texts of the Gospels as we have them today were probably composed between the years 70 and 90, though some scholars put Mark earlier, in the early to mid 60s, prior to the crisis of the Jewish War (64-70 C.E.).[103]

102. There is a much-debated statement by the second-century author Papias, quoted in Eusebius's *Ecclesiastical History* (3.39.16), regarding an Aramaic or Hebrew version of the Gospel of Matthew that preceded the Greek. See F. C. Grant, "Matthew, Gospel of," in *Interpreter's Dictionary of the Bible*, ed. George Arthur Buttrick, 4 vols. (New York and Nashville: Abingdon, 1962), 3:303-4, and William R. Schoedel, "Papias," in *Anchor Bible Dictionary*, 5:140-42.

103. Robert H. Gundry, in his monumental study *Mark: A Commentary on His Apology for the Cross* (Grand Rapids: Eerdmans, 1993), sifts the available evidence and

Concerning the sayings of Jesus included in the Gospels, we should note that the earliest Christians believed that Jesus had ascended into heaven and they could communicate with him in prayer. They spoke to him, and sometimes he spoke back through visions or voices. Some of their prayers evoked verbal answers that could then be attributed to "the Lord." Thus in 2 Corinthians 12:7-9, Paul prays that God will remove an unnamed ailment, a "thorn in the flesh," and Paul recounts that the Lord responded: "My grace is sufficient for you, for power is made perfect in weakness." This is in effect a direct quotation of the heavenly Lord.[104] While there is considerable debate over the amount and quality of historical information in the Gospel of John, some scholars have regarded the discourses of Jesus there as consisting in sayings of the "heavenly Lord," transmitted through recognized prophets. If that is the case, then the Fourth Gospel would be based on the assumption of a continuity between the sayings of the earthly Jesus and the Spirit-inspired utterances that came from the heavenly, exalted Jesus through the early Christian prophets.[105]

The authors of the Gospels are not known with certainty. The Gospels presently have headings — "according to Matthew," etc. Yet the canonical Gospels may well have remained untitled until the second half of the second century. The Gospels were quoted frequently in the surviving Christian literature of the second century, but they are quoted anonymously rather than by a writer's name. Rather suddenly this changes about the year 180. By this time there were any number of gospels, and not merely the four that were ultimately accepted by Christians as canonical. So it became necessary at this point to specify which gospels were to be accepted, and the naming of the canonical Gospels was a way to deal with the issue. All this suggests that the four New Testament Gospels were not commonly known in the believing community under the names Matthew, Mark, Luke, and John until late in the second century. It seems unlikely that Christian authors knew the names of the authors of the

---

concludes that the Gospel of Mark was probably composed prior to the outbreak of the Jewish War in 66 C.E., and possibly as early as 60-62 C.E. (pp. 1026-45, esp. p. 1042). John A. T. Robinson, in *Redating the New Testament* (Philadelphia: Westminster Press, 1976), argued that some of the Gospels were written as early as the 50s, based on his judgment that the fall of Jerusalem in 70 C.E. is never alluded to in the New Testament, and that therefore the entire canon of the New Testament was completed by 70 C.E.

104. Sanders, *Historical Figure*, p. 62.

105. Supporting the theory that the sayings of the early Christian prophets were attributed to Jesus is M. Eugene Boring, in "How May We Identify Oracles of Christian Prophets in the Synoptic Tradition? Mark 3:28-29 as a Test Case," *Journal of Biblical Literature* 91 (1972): 501-21. A rebuttal may be found in D. Hill, "On the Evidence for the Creative Role of Christian Prophets," *New Testament Studies* 20 (1974), while David E. Aune, in *Prophecy in Early Christianity and the Ancient Mediterranean World* (Grand Rapids: Eerdmans, 1983), pp. 233-45, regards Boring's theory as unsubstantiated.

Gospels for a century or so but did not mention them in any of the surviving literature. It is more plausible to suppose that the names were those settled on by "Christian detectives" who did their work carefully and shrewdly, but whose assignments of names to the Gospel authors were educated guesses rather than well-established traditions.[106] In any case it is clear that the authors of the Gospels wanted to diminish interest in the question of *who* wrote them and focus all attention on *what* was written. We should also keep in mind that in ancient times, the claim of an anonymous work was often higher than that of a named work. An anonymous book, like an unsigned article in the *Encyclopaedia Britannica,* could have a claim to complete knowledge and reliability.[107]

One of the most fundamental questions that can be posed regarding the Gospels is the following: Did Jesus really utter the sayings attributed to him? Are these Jesus' own words (translated from Aramaic into Greek)? Or are the sayings to be understood as early Christian modifications and adaptations of things that Jesus said at various times and places? Or should some of the sayings attributed to Jesus be regarded as plain and simple creations of the early church? As one can infer from the questions themselves, there is a spectrum of possible opinions on this topic. To address the issue, scholars have proposed various "criteria of authenticity" to determine which Gospel sayings are most likely to go back to Jesus himself.[108] Prior to the rise of modern critical studies

106. Sanders, *Historical Figure,* p. 65. Contrary to the majority view, as expressed by Sanders, Martin Hengel argues that the four canonical Gospels were circulated with titles attached beginning in the first decades after their composition ("The Titles of the Gospels and the Gospel of Mark," in *Studies in the Gospel of Mark* [Philadelphia: Fortress, 1985], pp. 64-84, esp. 81-84).

107. An intriguing discussion of the phenomenon of anonymous authorship may be found in Michel Foucault's essay "What Is an Author?" in *The Foucault Reader,* ed. Paul Rabinow (New York: Pantheon Books, 1984), pp. 101-20. Foucault provides a new angle on the modern preoccupation with determining the authors of unsigned texts.

108. See the discussion in Crossan, *The Historical Jesus,* pp. xxvii-xxxiv, 427-66; Meier, *A Marginal Jew,* 1:168-84; Dale C. Allison, *Jesus of Nazareth: Millenarian Prophet* (Minneapolis: Fortress, 1998), pp. 1-77; and Craig A. Evans, "Authenticity Criteria in Life of Jesus Research," *Christian Scholars' Review* 19 (1986): 6-31. Other important recent discussions of authenticity criteria are found in Norman Perrin, *Rediscovering the Teaching of Jesus* (New York and Evanston: Harper & Row, 1967), pp. 39-47; D. G. A. Calvert, "An Examination of the Criteria for Distinguishing the Authentic Words of Jesus," *New Testament Studies* 18 (1972): 209-19; Morna D. Hooker, "On Using the Wrong Tool," *Theology* 75 (1972): 570-81; Richard N. Longenecker, "Literary Criteria in Life of Jesus Research: An Evaluation and Proposal," in *Current Issues in Biblical and Patristic Interpretation,* ed. Gerald F. Hawthorne (Grand Rapids: Eerdmans, 1975), pp. 217-29; and Robert H. Stein, "The 'Criteria' for Authenticity," in *Gospel Perspectives: Studies of History and Tradition in the Four Gospels,* vol. 1, ed. R. T. France and David Wenham (Sheffield: JSOT, 1980), pp. 225-63.

of the Bible, the only criterion for authenticity was the presence of a particular saying in the canonical Gospels. What was in the Gospels was assumed to be genuine; what was not in the New Testament was thereby suspect. Once this assumption was shaken during the 1700s and early 1800s, other tests had to be used. In the earlier phase of the quest for the historical Jesus there were few if any carefully formulated criteria for determining the presence of authentic tradition within the Gospels. Miracle stories were often assumed to be unhistorical or legendary in character, and at times this seems to have been the only functioning criterion. (One thinks of the "Jefferson Bible" that contained the teachings of Jesus minus the miraculous elements in the Gospel narratives.)

It is important for the sake of clarity to distinguish between authenticity in the historical sense and relevance in an interpretive or theological sense. The criteria of authenticity are a part of the attempt to determine what material in the attributed sayings actually derives from Jesus and what aspects of the narratives accurately describe the actual events of Jesus' life. The relevance or authority of the material judged as authentic is another question, not directly addressed by the criteria of authenticity.[109] Among the proposed criteria that have received widespread attention are those of multiple attestation, dissimilarity, embarrassment, Semitic or Palestinian background, and coherence. Each of these will be briefly described and critiqued in turn.

The criterion of multiple attestation arose in connection with source criticism, and essentially it asserts that the claim of any saying is strengthened when it is attested in more than one source (Mark and the hypothetic sources — see above — Q, M, and L). One of the possible difficulties with this criterion is that it relies on the "two-source theory" (i.e., Mark and Q as sources for Matthew and Luke), and this particular theory is not universally accepted. Also the criterion of multiple attestation can prove only that a multiply attested tradition is early and widespread, and not that it is necessarily authentic.

One of the criteria most widely touted in the mid–twentieth century was the so-called "criterion of dissimilarity." Norman Perrin went so far as to refer to it as "the fundamental criterion for authenticity upon which all reconstructions of the life of Jesus must be built."[110] The basic description of the criterion is given in the words of Rudolf Bultmann: "We can only count on possessing a genuine similitude of Jesus where, on the one hand, expression is given to the contrast between Jewish morality and piety and the distinctive eschatological temper which characterized the preaching of Jesus; and where on the other hand we find no specifically Christian features."[111] Note that this criterion rests

109. Evans, "Authenticity Criteria," pp. 7-8.
110. Perrin, *Rediscovering*, p. 39.
111. Bultmann, *Synoptic Tradition*, p. 205. Perrin's description of the criterion is

on a double dissimilarity: Jesus' teaching is assumed to be unlike that of both first-century Judaism and nascent Christianity.

Bultmann's statement rests on a number of debatable assumptions. It presupposes that "Jewish morality and piety" in the first century were noneschatological in character, in contradistinction to the "eschatological temper" of Jesus' message. Yet in light of the newer studies of first-century Judaism during the last several decades, it seems no longer possible to uphold a dichotomy between "piety" and "eschatology." Only a misleading stereotype regarding Judaism — as a religion of literalistic and picayune adherence to law, lacking a deeper sense of divine presence and activity — could sustain such a dichotomy between Jesus and Judaism. Bultmann also assumes that the voice of the authentic Jesus stands against that of the earliest Christians. Yet this is unwarranted as a general methodological principle. Only if on independent grounds we already have evidence that the earliest Christians diverged from Jesus' teaching can we assume that the sayings of Jesus, to be judged authentic, must differ from the characteristic thoughts and symbols used by Jesus' first followers. In other words, a rift between Jesus and his followers cannot be built in as a methodological principle before one has done the necessary investigation of the sources. It may be a conclusion, but it cannot serve as a presupposition.

There are still other reasons to doubt the utility of the criterion of dissimilarity. It isolates Jesus from his immediate environment, and tends to portray Jesus as a non-Jew and as a leader without followers.[112] Just as crucially, the criterion runs into the objection that we simply do not know enough to apply it effectively. Our present knowledge of first-century Judaism is quite imperfect, and in many cases our only attestation for important Judaic ideas and practices lies in texts that date from the 200s, 300s, 400s, or even later. So in these cases our general picture of Judaism in the first century has to be created by extrapolating backward from the later texts. Often we are uncertain as to when certain practices began (e.g., the water baptism of proselytes — Gentile converts to Judaism). Likewise we run into the same problem in trying to distinguish Jesus from his first followers. There does not seem to be enough evidence to allow us to reconstruct the founder and his first followers in independence of one another.[113]

The criterion of embarrassment focuses on sayings or actions that would have embarrassed or created difficulty for the earliest Christians. The point of

---

quite similar to Bultmann's: "The earliest form of a saying we can reach may be regarded as authentic if it can be shown to be dissimilar to characteristic emphases both of ancient Judaism and of the early church" (*Rediscovering*, p. 39).

112. Charlesworth, *Jesus within Judaism*, p. 167.

113. Hooker, pp. 570-81.

the criterion is that the primitive church would hardly have gone out of its way to create material that brought embarrassment or else weakened its position. On the contrary, one might expect that embarrassing material that came from Jesus would be suppressed or at least softened in the later stages of the Gospel tradition. Perhaps the classic instance is the baptism of Jesus by John the Baptist, an act that would seem to make Jesus a disciple of John and perhaps even imply that Jesus needed a baptism for the "remission of sins" — an idea clearly in contradiction to the early Christian teaching on the sinlessness of Jesus. It is virtually unthinkable that anyone in the first or second generation of the Christian church would have invented a story of Jesus' baptism by John. The criterion of embarrassment can function as a strong positive test for certain conspicuously embarrassing episodes and sayings. For this reason it may provide a few foundation stones on which to build: Jesus was certainly baptized by John. Yet the absence of embarrassment connected with a text does not prove that text to be inauthentic.

The criterion of Semitic or Palestinian background rests on the idea that any saying is likely to be genuine if it clearly shows traces of the Aramaic language (e.g., the word *Abba*, "Father," for God), characteristic Semitic thought forms (e.g., antithetical parallelism), or elements of the first-century Palestinian culture (e.g., references to customs connected with farming, taxation, etc.). Yet this criterion too may be criticized. Since the earliest Christian community was itself Semitic and Palestinian, the presence of these features does not guarantee that the tradition in question goes back to Jesus. Furthermore, this criterion cannot be used in the other direction, to argue that sayings that lack Semitic or Palestinian elements should be treated as inauthentic. The absence of Semitic features might simply be an indication that the original teaching of Jesus has been fully translated into Hellenistic language or culture forms, which is not enough to allow one to claim that it is inauthentic.

Subordinate to the other criteria of authenticity is the criterion of consistency (or coherence). Norman Perrin sums it up in this way: "Material which is consistent with or coheres with material established as authentic by other means may also be accepted."[114] This criterion assumes the others, since it begins from the presumption that some body of tradition has already been determined to be authentic. One of the possible problems here is circularity, since the scholar starts from what is assumed to be characteristic of Jesus and then uses this to filter the data for reconstructing the historical Jesus. It is easy to use the criterion of consistency to dismiss material that might serve as evidence against one's pet theories. This would be a case of theory controlling data, not

114. Norman Perrin, *What Is Redaction Criticism?* (Philadelphia: Fortress, 1969), p. 71.

data controlling theory. Another problem with the criterion of consistency is that it seems to assume that Jesus himself was perfectly self-consistent in his public statements. Great teachers are commonly known for adapting themselves to their changing audiences, and so authentic material that derives from Jesus himself could easily carry the appearance of inconsistency and contradiction. Meier comments that "Jesus would hardly be unique among the great thinkers or leaders of world history if his sayings and actions did not always seem totally consistent to us."[115]

When all is said and done, an application of the authenticity criteria does not provide a watertight argument for or against the authenticity of the individual sayings attributed to Jesus. Some decades ago Ernst Käsemann acknowledged that "we possess absolutely no kind of formal criteria by which we can identify the authentic Jesus material."[116] E. P. Sanders is on the right track, in my view, when he says that "our sources contain information about Jesus, but we cannot get at it by dogmatically deciding that some sentences are completely accurate and some are fiction."[117] Sanders further notes that "there are no hard and fast laws of the development of the Synoptic tradition. On all counts the tradition developed in opposite directions. It became both longer and shorter, both more and less detailed, and both more and less Semitic."[118] This means that no one can construct a trajectory of the early literary development that is complete and detailed and nuanced enough to allow definitive judgments regarding what in the Gospels does or does not go back to Jesus. At best the criteria of authenticity can help to ascertain the varying degrees of historical plausibility or implausibility that attach to particular sayings or events in the Gospels.

For the reasons just indicated, the elaborate scheme that John Dominic Crossan uses for authenticating Gospel traditions involves a number of doubtful procedures.[119] A great deal of weight rests on his stratigraphy of Jesus traditions, which are sorted into four time periods: 30-60, 60-80, 80-120, 120-50 c.e.

---

115. Meier, *A Marginal Jew,* 1:176. Similarly Gerd Theissen writes: "We have to develop a historical sense for the degree of coherence and incoherence which we may expect in a given epoch and in the writings of an individual author or in his orally transmitted words" ("Historical Scepticism and the Criteria of Jesus Research," *Scottish Journal of Theology* 49 [1996]: 156 n. 10).

116. Ernst Käsemann, "The Problem of the Historical Jesus," in *Essays on New Testamant Themes,* Studies in Biblical Theology (London: SCM, 1964), pp. 15-47, citing 35.

117. Sanders, *Historical Figure,* p. 56.

118. E. P. Sanders, *The Tendencies of the Synoptic Tradition* (Cambridge: Cambridge University Press, 1969), p. 272. Sanders draws from this the conclusion, underlined in the original: "For this reason, dogmatic statements that a certain characteristic proves a certain passage to be earlier than another are never justified" (p. 272).

119. See Crossan, *The Historical Jesus,* pp. xxvii-xxxiv, 427-66.

Many scholars will not even definitely declare to which century the *Gospel of Thomas* belongs, let alone what portion of the first or second century. "One wonders," writes Dale Allison, "how he dares to be so confident about such uncertain things."[120] A degree of arbitrariness attaches to his dating system. Why, after all, should a text written in 81 be classified with one written in 119, rather than with one written in 79? Another very basic problem with Crossan's approach is that it seems to tie each tradition's authenticity to the date at which it found its way into writing. Yet there is no necessary connection between the date at which an oral tradition is first written down and the antiquity or authenticity of the tradition that is preserved in that written version. Some very old traditions related to Jesus may have circulated in oral form for many decades prior to being written down, while other traditions may have been coined many years after Jesus and then immediately put into writing. Crossan has said that his "methodology does not claim a spurious objectivity,"[121] yet his discussion of authenticity does not lay enough emphasis on the uncertainty of the many judgments that have to be made and the element of subjectivity that enters into all such discussions.

The completed New Testament Gospels can be compared to jigsaw puzzles. While one can use various methods to piece it together — e.g., starting with the pieces of a single color, building inward from the edge pieces of the puzzle, etc. — once the puzzle has come together, no one can tell what method was used to do it. Allison observes: "We cannot separate chemical compounds with a knife. Nor can we tell at the end of a river what came from the fountainhead and what from later tributaries." The complex tradition histories that scholars have proposed for particular sayings of Jesus cannot be falsified, and this should lead us to wonder to what extent the tradition histories are largely educated guesses or imaginative exercises.[122] The truth seems to be that *everyone* makes some kind of conjecture regarding the nature of Jesus and his teaching prior to examining the individual sayings. This is a point that Crossan himself has made: "Nobody initiates historical Jesus research without any ideas about Jesus. It is therefore a little ingenuous [*sic*] to start from certain texts and act as if one discovered the historical Jesus at the other end of one's analysis. There is and should be always an initial hypothesis that one tests against the data."[123] The upshot is that a general picture of Jesus is not assembled piecemeal from the tidbits of authenticated tradition. Instead there is a larger para-

---

120. Allison, p. 16. See Allison's entire critique of Crossan's method on pp. 10-33.

121. Crossan, *The Historical Jesus*, p. xxxiv.

122. Allison, pp. 29-33.

123. Crossan, "Materials and Methods in Historical Jesus Research," *Forum* 4 (1988): 10, quoted in Allison, p. 36.

digm or gestalt that comes prior to the examination of the various traditions. The mark of a good paradigm is its explanatory power. Over time it proves itself more capable than other possible paradigms of accounting for the existing data and assimilating any new data that come along.

To enunciate my own paradigm of interpretation in this chapter, I would agree in general terms with E. P. Sanders that "enough evidence points toward Jewish eschatology as the general framework of Jesus' ministry that we may examine the particulars in the light of that framework."[124] At the same time, in what follows I hope to show that Jesus was not merely "eschatological" but also "sapiential." These two aspects of the life and teaching of Jesus, so often set against one another in recent interpretations, should rather be related and coordinated. Jesus was an "eschatological sage." That is, his wisdom teaching must be interpreted against the backdrop of eschatology, and vice versa. Furthermore, I would agree broadly with James Charlesworth that there is substantial continuity between Jesus and his first followers: "The dreams, ideas, symbols, and terms of his earliest followers were inherited directly from Jesus."[125] Certainly the traditions embodied in the Gospels have been decisively shaped by the interests and concerns of the first- and second-generation Christians. They chose what to transmit and how to transmit it. Yet there is a difference between authoring or inventing sayings or stories and editing or otherwise modifying existing traditions. E. P. Sanders agrees with Charlesworth at this point: "The gospel writers did not wildly invent material. They developed it, shaped it, and directed it in the ways they wished."[126] Since some of the major features of the Gospel narratives are definitely grounded in the events of Jesus' lifetime,[127] this indicates that the many unnamed persons responsible for editing and transmitting the early traditions regarding Jesus were concerned with historical authenticity. They were not creators of the traditions, but custodians.

124. Sanders, *Jesus and Judaism*, p. 10.
125. Charlesworth, *Jesus within Judaism*, pp. 167, 3.
126. Sanders, *Historical Figure*, p. 193.
127. Here the "criterion of embarrassment" can be put to work. Among the passages that would be quite embarrassing to early Christian leaders (e.g., Peter, the Twelve, Mary, the brothers of Jesus) are the following: the disciples' failure to understand Jesus, and their sharp rebuke by Jesus (Mark 8:14-21); Jesus telling Peter that he was acting on Satan's behalf (Mark 8:31-33); Jesus' apparently dismissive statements about his immediate family members (Matt. 12:46-50); James and John's request to sit on thrones at either side of Jesus (Mark 10:35-45); Judas's inclusion as one of the Twelve (Mark 3:13-19); Peter's denials of Jesus (Mark 14:66-72); the rejection of Jesus by his own family members (Mark 3:21; John 7:1-9); the disciples' timid behavior after Jesus' death (John 20:19); and the refusal of the apostles to believe the first reports of Jesus' resurrection (Mark 16:14, longer ending; Luke 24:9-11; John 20:26-29). In each of these cases it is highly implausible to think that the episode was invented during the period of the early church.

Summary Biography

As a basis for what follows, we may begin with a brief chronological survey of Jesus' life. A few events of his life may be regarded as all but indisputable, and together they form a solid foundation for understanding him and his influence.[128] Jesus was born around 4 B.C.E., before the time of the death of Herod the Great. He spent his childhood and early adult years in Nazareth, a Galilean village. He was baptized by John the Baptist. He called disciples. He taught in the towns, villages, and countryside of Galilee, and apparently not in the cities. He preached "the kingdom of God." About the year 30 C.E. he went to Jerusalem for Passover. He created a disturbance in the Temple area. He had a final meal with his disciples. He was arrested and interrogated by Jewish authorities, specifically the high priest. He was executed on the orders of the Roman prefect, Pontius Pilate. There are a number of equally secure facts regarding the aftermath of Jesus' life. His disciples at first fled. They saw him again (in some sense) following his death. As a consequence, they believed that he would return to found the kingdom. They formed a community to await his return and sought to win others to faith in him as God's Messiah.

It is possible to elaborate further on the above points. The summary here will serve as a bridge into the fuller discussion of the various aspects of Jesus' life in the subsequent sections of this chapter.[129] Opinions differ regarding the tradition of Jesus' birth in Bethlehem; some scholars see this as grounded in actual events, while others view this as a later theological embellishment.[130] His family was Jewish, as is clear from the names of his parents (Joseph and Mary) and his brothers (Jacob, Joses, Judas, and Simon). Jesus' father was a building artisan or a carpenter (Matt. 13:55), as Jesus may himself have been prior to his

128. Sanders, *Historical Figure*, pp. 10-11.

129. The following is based on Sanders, *Historical Figure*, pp. 11-14, and Koester, *Introduction*, 2:73-86.

130. Crossan sees the infancy narratives in the Gospels as "overtures, condensed intertwinings of the dominant themes in the respective gospels to which they serve as introduction and summary" (*Jesus*, p. 5). He compares the twin births of Jesus and John the Baptist in Luke, showing the structural similarities (pp. 6-10): (1) the angelic announcements to Zechariah and Mary (1:5-25, 26-38); (2) the publicized birth of each child (1:57-58; 2:7-14); (3) the circumcision and naming (1:59-63; 2:21); (4) the public presentation and prophecy of destiny for each child (1:65-79; 2:25-38); and (5) the description of the child's growth (1:80; 2:40-52). Crossan also points out the parallels between the infancy story of Moses in Exodus and that of Jesus (p. 15). Concerning the virginal conception of Jesus, Crossan calls this "a confessional statement about Jesus' status and not a biological statement about Mary's body" (p. 23); cf. Raymond Brown, *The Birth of the Messiah: A Commentary on the Infancy Narratives in Matthew and Luke* (Garden City, N.Y.: Doubleday, 1977), pp. 32-37, and Meier, *A Marginal Jew*, 1:208-30.

public career. Jesus' mother tongue was Galilean Aramaic, or perhaps a Hebrew dialect that had survived in Galilee. Like many of his contemporaries, Jesus presumably could speak Greek, yet the sayings that are preserved in Greek and attributed to him derive from an Aramaic original. Thus Aramaic must have been the language he used in his public discourses. No reliable information has been transmitted regarding Jesus' education, yet it is quite possible that he was able to read and write.[131] There is one Gospel passage (Luke 4:16-20) that speaks of him reading aloud in the synagogue.

A possibility exists that virtually all of Jesus' active ministry, with the exception of the last few weeks, was carried out in Herod Antipas's Galilee. How often Jesus traveled to Jerusalem remains unclear, since the synoptic Gospels seem to know of only one journey to Jerusalem and the Gospel of John speaks of multiple journeys. It seems that Jesus was not an urbanite. The cities of Galilee — Sepphoris, Tiberias, and Scythopolis (Heb. Beth-Shean) — do not figure in the Gospel accounts of Jesus' activities. Doubtless Jesus knew of Sepphoris, which was only a few miles from Nazareth, but he may have regarded his own mission as being directed to the Jews of the villages and small towns in Galilee. Nazareth itself was a small village, tucked away in the hill country, not adjacent to the Sea of Galilee. Yet Jesus taught principally in the towns and villages on the sea, and fishermen were among his first followers. Rural images frequently appear in the teaching attributed to him.

When Jesus was a young man, perhaps in his late twenties, John the Baptist began to preach a message of repentance in light of the coming judgment. Jesus heard John and felt called to accept baptism at his hands. All four Gospels point to Jesus' baptism as a decisive and life-changing event. Jesus "saw the heavens torn apart and the Spirit descending like a dove on him," and he also heard a voice saying "You are my Son, the Beloved" (Mark 1:9-11). Herod Antipas had John arrested because he had criticized his marriage to Herodias (so say the Gospels) and/or because he feared that John's preaching might lead to insurrection (so Josephus). At about this time Jesus began his public ministry. Whereas John had worked outside of the settled areas, Jesus went from town to town and usually preached in the synagogues on the Sabbath days. He called a small number of people to be his disciples, including a group that became known as "the Twelve." Unlike John, Jesus not only preached but also healed the sick. The crowds that may have gathered to see miraculous healings also stayed to hear Jesus teach in parables and explain the "kingdom of God."

131. Koester expresses the point more strongly: "He was certainly able to read and write" (*Introduction*, p. 74). Yet it is not clear how one can draw this conclusion, in the absence of any clear traditions regarding Jesus' education. Meier argues that Jesus probably possessed very good reading skills (*A Marginal Jew*, 1:268-78).

Jesus was known among his contemporaries for his activity as an exorcist. This does not imply that Jesus' special authority derived specifically from extraordinary psychological abilities or supernatural powers. On the contrary, the sayings connected with the exorcisms indicate that Jesus viewed them as the visible sign of a victory over Satan and the beginning of the rule of God. "But if it is by the Spirit of God that I cast out demons, then the kingdom of God has come to you" (Matt. 12:28). This suggests that Jesus viewed himself as the decisive and effective mediator of the beginning of God's rule.

The announcement of God's kingdom or rule was indeed one of the most important aspects of Jesus' career, one that he took over from his kinsman and predecessor John the Baptizer. Yet Jesus' emphasis seems to have been different from John's. Unlike John, Jesus did not stress a future coming of God for judgment but rather a call to participate here and now in the kingdom of God. The difference between Jesus and John is shown in that John's disciples fasted while Jesus' did not (at least during his life; Mark 2:18-20). The parables of Jesus are central to Jesus' proclamation of God's rule, in that each parable expresses a particular aspect of God's rule. Not mere illustrations of timeless truths, the parables are statements through which the rule of God becomes a living word addressed to Jesus' hearers. To the followers of Jesus it has been given to understand the parables and to act upon them (Matt. 13:10-17).

In Jesus' parables it becomes clear that the coming of God's rule is God's own act and that human action does not influence its miraculous arrival in any way (Mark 4:26-29). Moreover, God's action contradicts the human criteria of moral standards (Luke 16:1-9) and religious values (Luke 18:9-14), and lies beyond the category of just rewards (Matt. 20:1-16). Love is not limited by human expectations, but rather exceeds all that might be expected (Luke 15:11-32). Characteristically the parables of Jesus involve an element of surprise. The stories begin often enough within the framework of customary ideas but conclude with a twist in the plotline and an assertion of unconventional wisdom. What kind of farmer would do nothing during the entire growing season, allowing the weeds to sprout up with the crops (Matt. 13:30)? Or when did a rich man ever invite hooligans and street people to his lavish party when the distinguished guests declined the invitations (Matt. 22:10)? Or what father would be so undignified as to run down the street joyfully to embrace a wastrel child that had just squandered his entire patrimony (Luke 15:20)? Jesus' parables underscore the mystery and incalculability associated with the coming of God's rule.

The command to love one's neighbor, which already held a central place within Judaism (Lev. 19:18), was affirmed and emphasized by Jesus as well (Mark 12:31). Yet Jesus rejected a practice of loving others that rested on reciprocity with one's peers or on membership within a particular social group, i.e., loving others because they love you or loving the people of one's own familial, social, or ethnic group. Jesus explicitly commanded love for one's enemies (Matt. 5:44). Power and force are not the way that God's kingdom will be established (Matt. 26:52-54). Moreover, the person who wants to follow Jesus must be prepared to suffer, and even to lose his or her life (Mark 8:34-35). Discipleship means to give up one's security (Luke 9:62), one's possessions (Luke 14:33), and one's identification with family and kin (Luke 14:26).

Jesus' itinerant ministry probably lasted from one to three years, and was concluded by Jesus' visit to Jerusalem during Passover (Matt. 21–27; Mark 11–15; Luke 19–23). Jesus rode into the city on an ass, and some people hailed him at that time as the "son of David." When he went into the Temple precincts, he attacked the money changers and those who sold doves to be used in Temple sacrifice. The high priest and his advisers determined that Jesus was dangerous and had to die. After Jesus shared a final meal with his followers (which the synoptic Gospels present as a Passover meal), he went apart to pray, and was then betrayed by one of his followers to the high priest's guards. He was tried in some fashion, and was then turned over to the Roman prefect with the recommendation that he be executed. After a hearing to consider the case, the prefect ordered the execution, and Jesus was put to death by crucifixion as an insurgent, along with two others.

He died after a relatively brief period of suffering on the cross. A few of his followers placed him in a tomb. According to reports that circulated among his early followers, some of the disciples returned to the tomb about two days following his burial to find an empty tomb. Then his followers saw him again in some fashion, and became convinced that Jesus was alive again, that God had acted in his death to bring salvation, and that Jesus would return again in glory and power. The early community used titles to describe Jesus, such as "Anointed" ("Messiah" in Hebrew or "Christ" in Greek), "Lord," and "Son of God." As the decades passed, the followers of Jesus became more and more distinct from Judaism at large, and finally emerged as a largely Gentile Christian church. Yet at the time the Gospels were written, this parting of the ways between Jewish and Gentile Christians, on the one hand, and all other Jews, on the other hand, was still occurring.

A number of uncertainties plague the chronology of Jesus' life, and they are the sorts of problems that plague almost all studies of ancient history.[132] Unable to appeal to any universally accepted calendar, and often unable to gain access to archives that provided a fixed chronological reference, ancient authors provided dates that were often uncertain. Matthew seems to place Jesus' birth late in Herod's reign (6-4 B.C.E.), while Luke seems to conflict with this by placing the birth during the census under Quirinius, who was not legate of Syria

132. Sanders, *Historical Figure*, pp. 52-55, 282-90.

while Herod was alive. Yet the general time and place parameters of Jesus' birth are fairly clear. The Gospels mention Augustus Caesar (31 B.C.E.–14 C.E.) at the time of Jesus' birth and Tiberius (14-37 C.E.) later in his life. When Jesus was executed, Pontius Pilate was prefect of Judea (26-36 C.E.) and Caiaphas was high priest (18-36 C.E.). Thus the conclusion is that Jesus was killed between 26 and 36 — based on three "big names" in Palestine of Tiberius, Pilate, and Caiaphas.

Taking into account this broad information, and Luke's dating (Luke 3:1) of the beginning of John's ministry in the fifteenth year of Tiberius, together with additional information from the chronology of Paul's life, most scholars are content to say that Jesus was executed sometime between 29 and 33. The exact date of Jesus' birth is not known, since there is no information in the Gospels regarding the day and the month. The Gospels would seem to be in conflict over the exact day of Jesus' death. The synoptic Gospels agree in their presentation that Jesus died on 15 Nisan, while the Gospel of John seems to place it one day earlier, on 14 Nisan.

It is difficult to find categories by which to describe Jesus' ministry and self-presentation. To construct the various contexts of Jesus' specific activities, often we must rely on inferences from the sayings attributed to him. Moreover, what we learn regarding Jesus only partially fits the known categories for understanding a religious office or mission at that time. Messianic or christological titles, such as "Messiah"/"Christ," "Son of David," "Son of God," "Son of Man," and "Lord," were applied to Jesus by the earliest Christians, but scholars debate whether Jesus applied any such title or titles to himself. The title "priest" or "high priest" is applied to Jesus relatively late, and only in very limited circles of early Christianity (such as the Epistle to the Hebrews). Philosophical influences were present in Palestine beginning with the Hellenistic period, and yet Jesus was not in any sense a wandering philosopher or a school philosopher. Not until the time of the Christian apologists in the early second century was there an effort to combine Jesus' teachings with philosophical insights. Furthermore, Jesus does not fit the general profile of the apocalyptic seer or visionary. He did not present the specific timetable of future events that is characteristic of ancient apocalyptic authors, nor is there any tradition of Jesus taking a celestial journey. There is no evidence that he ever used the written medium of communication — something very important within apocalypticism.

In many respects Jesus' words and actions reflected the earlier Israelite traditions of the prophets and wisdom teachers. Like the prophets of old, Jesus made clear and unequivocal declarations concerning God's will, rather than elaborate and casuistic judgments regarding right and wrong in specific circumstances. Like the earlier wisdom teachers, he preferred simple sayings, proverbs, metaphors, and parables to the speculative and spiritualizing literature that became more common in Judaism during the Hellenistic period. Yet despite Jesus' recourse to prophetic and wisdom traditions that were centuries removed from his day, there is no artificiality or archaizing tendency in his teachings. Rather, his words and actions come across as a renewal of much earlier Israelite traditions.

At the same time, many of the typical signs of a prophet or wisdom teacher are absent from the reports about Jesus. There is no tradition recording Jesus' call to prophethood in the customary sense, nor are there reports of visions of God, voices from heaven, or other kinds of stories about his receiving a prophetic commission. (The story of Jesus' baptism bears only a partial analogy to the earlier stories of prophetic calling.) Jesus does not introduce his sayings with the common prophetic formula "Thus says the Lord." Regarding Jesus' dress or external behavior, there are no traditions (as there are with John the Baptizer) that connect him with the classical prophets. In Jesus' wisdom teaching there is no appeal to the antiquity of sayings given by earlier sages and teachers, or to their reliable transmission across generations. Consequently it is clear that Jesus' preaching is quite different from rabbinical instruction. As Helmut Koester notes: "The visible documentation of Jesus' authority thus remains an enigma. Whoever wants to understand Jesus' authority is referred absolutely to his words and to that which they say and announce."[133]

Contexts — Geographical, Political, Cultural, and Religious

Like all human lives, the life of Jesus occurred in the context of a specific time, place, culture, and society, and it cannot be grasped apart from the particulars of that context. What follows is a brief portrait of this context, highlighting the features of first-century Palestinian Jewish society that would appear to be most pertinent for interpreting the life of Jesus.

In terms of its natural features, the land of Israel/Palestine may be divided into four natural regions.[134] These are the Mediterranean coastal plain, the hilly territory of northern and central Israel, the Great Rift Valley, and the Negev Desert. The coastal plain is a narrow strip about 115 miles in length which widens to a breadth of about 20 miles in the south. In the northern part of the country, the mountains of Galilee are the highest portion of the land, rising to the peak of Har Meron (or, in Arabic, Jebel Jarmaq), which is 3,963 feet in elevation. Toward the east these mountains grade off into an escarpment that overlooks the rift valley. The mountains of Galilee are separated from the hills

---

133. Koester, *Introduction*, 2:78.
134. Eliahu Elath, "Israel," in *The New Encyclopaedia Britannica*, 30 vols. (Chicago: Encyclopaedia Britannica, 1983), 9:1059-60 (Macropaedia).

of Samaria and Judea to the south by the Plain of Esdraelon (ʿEmeq Yizreʿel), which, running from the northwest to the southeast, connects the coastal plains with the rift valley. The hills of Samaria and Judea culminate in the spur of Mount Carmel (1,791 feet), which reaches almost to the coast of Haifa.

The Great Rift Valley forms part of a massive fissure in the earth's crust that runs from beyond the northern border of Israel down the length of the country to the Gulf of Aqaba in the south, and then down the Red Sea and East Africa. The Jordan River runs southward through this rift, from the region of Dan, on Israel's northern border, where the river is 500 feet above sea level, into the Sea of Galilee (also known as Lake Tiberias or Yam Kinneret; 696 feet below sea level), and then into the Dead Sea, which is 1,302 feet below sea level and represents the lowest point on the earth's surface. Thus the Jordan River, which is the principal drainage system in the region, flows into both the freshwater Sea of Galilee and the intensely saline Dead Sea. The Negev Desert, in the southern part of Israel, forms an arrow-shaped wedge of land that comes to a point at the port of Elat on the Gulf of Aqaba.

The land of Israel, situated between the subtropical and arid zone prevailing in Egypt to the south, and the subtropical and wet zone in Lebanon to the north, experiences great climatic contrasts. Rainfall is light in the south, amounting to only an inch per year in the territory south of the Dead Sea, but more plentiful in the north — up to forty-four inches per year fall in the region of Upper Galilee. The most readily cultivated regions have a rainfall of a dozen or more inches per year. The annual rainfall occurs over a period of some forty to sixty days, spread over a season of about seven months between October and April. Dry and hot weather prevails during the summer months, though in the coastal regions the sea breezes exert a moderating influence. In the summer the sun ascends high in the sky (over eighty degrees above the horizon), and radiation reaches the ground in 98 percent of all the potential hours of sunshine. The temperature depends on the elevation and the distance from the sea. The mean annual temperature in the coastal areas is from 68 to 70 degrees Fahrenheit, while at Elat in the far south the temperatures are around 59 degrees in January and may rise to 120 degrees in August. The relative humidity is highest near the coast and higher at night in summer than in winter. The Jordan Valley is hotter and drier than the coast, and the hilly regions experience occasional snows in winter. In attempting to picture the life of Jesus, one should bear in mind the varied landscape of Israel. Within a few short verses the Gospel of Mark begins with Jesus' sojourn in the "wilderness" (1:12) — a barren region that in parts is an uninhabitable moonscape of white rock and blazing sun — and then shifts scenes rapidly to the lush region surrounding the Sea of Galilee where Jesus announces the kingdom of God and calls his first followers (1:14-20).

Along with its variation in climate, the land of Israel has a wide variation in its plant and animal life. The original evergreen forests disappeared long ago because of the many centuries of cultivation and the depredations of goats.[135] The hills are mostly covered with wild shrub vegetation. Only desert scrub grows in the Negev and on the sand dunes of the coastal plains. Yet north of Beersheba, most of the land may be cultivated or used for hill grazing. Animal life is similarly varied. The mammals that are indigenous to the region include wild cats, wild boars, gazelles, ibex, jackals, hyenas, hares, coneys, badgers, and tiger weasels. The reptiles include the agama and gecko lizards, the viper, and the carpet viper. The birds include the partridge, tropical cuckoo, bustard, sand grouse, and desert lark. There are many different kinds of fish and insects. Invasions of desert locusts sometimes occur. This background information gives some local coloring to the statement of Mark's Gospel that Jesus "was in the wilderness . . . [and] was with the wild beasts" (1:13).

Three non-Jewish writers of ancient times — Strabo, Pliny the Elder, and Tacitus — all touch on ancient Palestine in their writings.[136] Strabo (ca. 64 B.C.E.–20 C.E.) speaks of various regions in Judea, and claims that the land is inhabited by a mixture of Egyptian, Arabian, and Phoenician tribes. He mentions a lake known to produce excellent fish, but he seems to have confused the Sea of Galilee with the Dead Sea (or Lake Meron) when he goes on to say that the same lake also produces aromatic rush, reeds, and balsam. From this it is clear that Strabo had no firsthand acquaintance of Palestine, and the same is true of Pliny (23-79 C.E.) and Tacitus (ca. 55 C.E.–ca. 117 C.E.). By contrast, the New Testament Gospels are familiar with the threefold division of Jewish territory — Galilee, Perea, and Judea. John and Luke are aware of Samaria as intervening between Galilee and Judea (John 4:1-4; Luke 9:51-52).[137] In addition, Idumea is known to Mark as being adjacent to Jewish territory (Mark 3:8). These divisions were established firmly in the early Roman period and were maintained under Herod, though they date back to the Hasmonean wars of conquest. Differences occur, however, in the ways the synoptic Gospels and the Gospel of John present Jerusalem. The synoptic Gospels concentrate their attention on Galilee, except for Jesus' brief and final visit to Jerusalem, while John treats Jerusalem and Judea as the center of Jesus' ministry, with Galilee as a place of retreat for Jesus and his disciples.

Among the other important place references in the New Testament Gos-

135. Robert H. Gundry notes that there is another explanation for the disappearance of the forests: with the introduction of the railroads, Palestinian forests were cut down for firewood to burn in locomotives (letter to the author, September 8, 1999).

136. For my description of the economic, political, and cultural context of first-century Palestine, I am dependent on Freyne, "Geography," pp. 75-121.

137. At the same time, it seems from the phrasing of Luke 17:11 that Luke has located Samaria alongside of Galilee, and not between Galilee and Judea.

pels are the following: Nazareth is mentioned in all of them as the place of Jesus' upbringing, even though Matthew and Luke place the birth of Jesus in Bethlehem. Capernaum stands out as the real center of Jesus' ministry in the synoptic Gospels, as emphasized by the special woe pronounced against it for rejecting Jesus (Matt. 11:23) and the fact that Matthew refers to it as Jesus' own city (9:1). The Gospel of John, by contrast, seems to have a special predilection for Cana (John 2:1-2; 4:46), even though John also mentions Capernaum (2:12). As often noted, the Fourth Gospel, despite its high theological tones, shows a much better acquaintance with the geography of Palestine and the topography of Jerusalem than do the synoptics. There are references to Aenon near Salim (3:23) and Sychar, a city of Samaria (4:5). The Gospel of John shows knowledge of such places as the pool of Bethesda with its five porticoes, Solomon's portico in the Temple district, and the exact location of Golgotha. On this basis some have concluded that the author of the Fourth Gospel may have been a native of Jerusalem.

Despite the numerous place references, the New Testament Gospels provide relatively little in the way of a specific description of land and water, and this sets them apart from the writings of Josephus. The rabbinical writings show a keen sense of the boundaries of the land, since many aspects of Jewish law (e.g., tithing) applied only within the borders of Israel. The interests of the Gospel authors lie elsewhere. Still, one of the more puzzling things is the absence of reference to Sepphoris and Tiberias, the former refurbished and the latter founded during the lifetime of Jesus. Both were major commercial and administrative centers in Lower Galilee. This point plays some role in how one interprets Jesus' teaching, for if Jesus had visited Sepphoris and Tiberias, then it becomes more likely that he would have gained some firsthand acquaintance with Greek culture and philosophy. Those who interpret Jesus as a kind of Jewish Cynic have sometimes conjectured that he gained his exposure to Greek thought while on business in Sepphoris — a city unnamed in the Gospels.

In the Gospels, and especially in Mark, Jesus seems to move with relative ease between different regions of Palestine, seemingly indifferent to the tensions between these areas. According to Josephus, Jewish and Gentile relations deteriorated in the period after Jesus' life and hostilities broke out in the Greek cities of Palestine in the years immediately prior to the general Jewish revolt.[138] Sean Freyne has raised the question of how we are to think about interregional movements in the late 20s, the period of Jesus' ministry, teachings, and travels. Palestine, like other parts of the Mediterranean world, enjoyed relative peace during the reign of Tiberius. In Galilee Herod Antipas had political quarrels only with the Nabateans. The Phoenician cities, the territory of Herod Philip,

---

138. Josephus, *Jewish War* 2.556-65.

and the Decapolis would all have been accessible to Jewish traders and craftsmen, and the Herodian cities of Lower Galilee would have been more friendly to Gentiles than they were some decades later.

The archaeological data lend support to this general picture, for an analysis of pottery during the period shows a thriving export industry of Kefar Hanania wares to the surrounding cities, including those in the Golan as well as Ptolemais and Caesarea Philippi. Significantly, no wares emanating from Galilee have been found in sites south of the Nazareth ridge. The discovery of Tyrian coinage in the sites of Upper Galilee also points to commercial movement between the regions. In sum, the political realities and the material remains make free movement between Jews and Gentiles in the north quite plausible for the period of Jesus' life. These movements are more plausible for the period of Jesus than for the time of the proposed dating of the Gospel of Mark. Thus the Gospel of Mark would seem to reflect the circumstances that were likely to have prevailed during Jesus' own lifetime, rather than those that existed during the 60s and later decades.

The Gospel of Matthew portrays Jesus' ministry as largely confined to the Jewish population. Jesus declares that he did not intend to go "among the Gentiles" but rather "to the lost sheep of the house of Israel" (Matt. 10:5-6; 15:24). The Gospel of Mark seems to present Jesus as going to the territories and villages of the largely Gentile regions, but not into the cities themselves. Moreover, Mark also indicates that Jesus, despite his healing powers, was not welcome to the people of Gerasa, who on hearing of his successful exorcism of the "legion" of demons asked him to depart from their territory (Mark 5:17). Thus even Mark's narrative does not completely efface the cultural divide of Jew and Gentile. In light of the above, the silence regarding Sepphoris and Tiberias becomes all the more puzzling. If the reason for the omission is Jesus' lack of success after preaching and healing in these areas, then one might have expected a series of woes against these cities like those spoken against Chorazin, Bethsaida, and Capernaum. If Jesus' stated mission was to go to the dispersed Jews, and if he was generally willing to go into Gentile regions, then it is not clear why the two great Herodian cities of Sepphoris and Tiberias were not included in the mission.

Concerning the political life of Galilee during Jesus' day, the key question is how power was distributed, to wit: Who exercised political power in Galilee on behalf of Antipas, and toward whom was this power exercised? That is, what were the demands on and benefits accruing to different segments of society, and what sanctions could be employed to enforce the will of the ruling class? According to Josephus, our main authority for the period, Herod Antipas was allowed 200 talents in personal income from his territories.[139] Presumably this

---

139. Josephus, *Antiquities* 17.318-20; *Jewish War* 2.94-100.

was collected as a land tax or poll tax, as was the general custom throughout the Roman world. Paid in kind, this would have amounted to 440,000 bushels of wheat each year. In addition to this, tribute had to be paid to Rome, though we do not know the exact amount. Beyond these fixed taxes, it is likely that Herod Antipas could impose special levies for building projects or other public works. He could moreover force peasants to live in his new city — a form of compulsory labor that was prevalent throughout the empire and against which there was little redress. In addition to this, there were also customs, tolls, and sales taxes exacted on goods transported from one district to another. The burdens borne by the people and their daily hardships are seen in the calls of the Jerusalem populace to Archelaus to remove them, and in the complaints of the Jewish delegation to Rome about Herod's misrule.[140]

Herod the Great had raised an extra 100 talents in Galilee during his early years as governor of the region, and was rewarded by Rome.[141] On another occasion he sent part of his army to be billeted in Galilee for the winter, which was one of the most dreaded forms of imposition on the country people during antiquity.[142] Although there is no direct evidence for either of these practices during the reign of Herod Antipas, the threat of such exactions loomed over the peasants of the region. In light of this, it is surprising that taxation is not specifically mentioned by Josephus as an issue in Galilee as well as Judea. In Jerusalem the peasants sought to destroy the debt records. Josephus speaks of the serious complaints made in Rome against the Herodian tax system and the bribery and corruption connected with it.[143] No such incidents are recorded for Antipas's reign, and this makes it likely that he had learned a thing or two from the mistakes his father had made.

Another episode that reveals much of the economic and taxation situation is the threatened agricultural strike at Tiberias over Emperor Caligula's statue being placed in the Jerusalem Temple.[144] The account indicates that crops had not been sown during the period of political turmoil, and the *Antiquities* specifically notes that the Jewish leaders feared an outbreak of banditry because the peasants could not pay the tribute. This shows that the farming during that period was basically of a subsistence character and did not provide for surpluses from year to year. It is interesting to note that the payment of the tribute was not in dispute between the leaders and the peasants, but only the latter's inability to pay and the consequent threat of social upheaval.

140. Josephus, *Antiquities* 17.200-205; 17.304-14.
141. Josephus, *Antiquities* 14.271-76.
142. Josephus, *Antiquities* 14.406-12.
143. Josephus, *Antiquities* 17.304-14.
144. Josephus, *Antiquities* 18.261-309; *Jewish War* 2.184-203.

Under foreign rule the Jews of Palestine were saddled with a double burden — Roman taxes and the Jewish tithe. While among Christians the tithe has
often been regarded as a voluntary contribution, among the Jews it was a matter of divine law and so was regarded as compulsory. The combined level of
Jewish and Roman taxes may have reached as high as about 35 percent, which
would have been a crushing burden within a subsistence economy.[145] Since the
collection of revenue was left to tax farmers who often extorted and pocketed
more than the stipulated amount, the actual level of tax levied from the people
could have gone even higher. The impact on the Jewish people was severe, because they were in no position to change either of the two systems of taxation.
One was dictated by Rome, and the other by divine law. The difference between
them was that the Roman taxes were enforced by police power, while the Jewish
taxes were not. If one simply could not get by while paying both taxes, then one
seemingly had to disobey God's law. Thus it may not have been the appeal of
Gentile or Hellenistic ways of life but the stark realities of economic life that
drove many Jews away from strict observance of the Jewish law. The double tax
burden helped to swell the ranks of nonobservant Jews.[146]

The benefits that operated within the patronage system of the rulers and
the ruled were very unevenly distributed. This gives some local coloring to the
saying of Jesus reported in Matthew: "'What do you think, Simon? From whom
do kings of the earth take toll or tribute? From their children or from others?'
When Peter said, 'From others,' Jesus said to him, 'Then the children are free'"
(Matt. 17:25-26). During the reign of Herod Antipas, and that of his father,
Herod the Great, a considerable amount of land was in the form of royal estates, which would have been free from taxes owed by the owners. The money
or produce paid by the tenants as rent accrued to the owners of the land as a
part of their own income. Jesus' cryptic comment regarding the execution of
John the Baptist, "Elijah has come, and they did to him whatever they pleased"
(Mark 9:13), is, in the words of Sean Freyne, "a typical 'view from the bottom'
of how such power was seen to operate."[147] Josephus noted the popular belief
that the defeat of Herod Antipas by the Nabateans was divine retribution
against him for having John killed.

Richard Horsley, on the basis of the earlier work of Eric Hobsbawm, has
argued that the phenomenon of "social banditry" was endemic to the whole
Palestinian region under Roman rule, and that it reached epidemic levels just

---

145. Frederick C. Grant, *The Economic Background of the Gospels* (New York: Russell
& Russell, 1973 [1926]), pp. 87-110, esp. 105. Some recent scholars think Grant's figure of
35 percent is too high.

146. Borg, *Jesus,* p. 85.

147. Freyne, "Geography," p. 90.

before the revolt of 66 C.E.[148] This "social banditry" can be described as prepolitical in that it represents a spontaneous outburst of resentment against the ruling class with which the peasants can identify without being directly involved. It becomes revolutionary only when it takes place on such a massive scale that large numbers of the peasantry become involved and are supported by an apocalyptic or millennial worldview that suggests an alternative social order — as in the case of the 66 revolt.[149] Sean Freyne has called into question the advisability of treating all the episodes in question under the heading of "social banditry." Freyne notes that the threatened agricultural strike would seem to indicate that banditry was the direct and inevitable outcome of scarcity in production, together with an inability to meet the demands of tribute. In Horsley's presentation, by contrast, the banditry was symptomatic of more permanent social changes that were occurring, and this in turn would have immediate repercussions on one's interpretation of Jesus' ministry among the peasantry.[150]

The first century C.E. in Palestine witnessed the rise of a monetary economy rather than one based primarily on subsistence and barter. This new market worked to the advantage of the few rather than the many. The maintenance of status became a primary concern of those who controlled the land and its resources. Their aim was to obtain from their property a life of luxury, which they regarded as their right. There was simply no incentive or motivation for them to improve the lot of the peasants or lower classes. Thus the market economy, far from improving the situation, was exploitative and created a rift between the ruling elite and the vast majority of the population. This consideration puts into context the critique of Herod's court style that one finds in the preaching of both John the Baptist and Jesus: "Look, those who wear soft robes are in royal palaces" (Matt. 11:8). As the peasantry came under increased pressure to maintain the opulence of the rulers, hostility increased toward economic centers such as Sepphoris and Tiberias. Even though these cities provided markets for agricultural produce and manufactured goods, they could not disguise their exploitative character.

Jesus' immediate environment was more culturally diverse and cosmo-

---

148. Richard A. Horsley, *Jesus and the Spiral of Violence: Popular Jewish Resistance in Roman Palestine* (San Francisco: Harper & Row, 1987), and Horsley and John S. Hanson, *Bandits, Prophets, and Messiahs: Popular Movements in the Time of Jesus* (Minneapolis: Winston Press, 1985).

149. Horsley, *Jesus*, pp. 37-43.

150. Freyne, "Geography," p. 95; see also Freyne, "Bandits in Galilee: A Contribution to the Study of Social Conditions in First-Century Palestine," in *The Social World of Formative Christianity and Judaism*, Essays in Tribute to Howard Clark Kee, ed. Jacob Neusner et al. (Philadelphia: Fortress, 1988), pp. 50-68.

politan than has generally been recognized.[151] It is at least probable, and perhaps even likely, that Jesus had enough linguistic competence in Greek to converse in that language during his itinerant ministry. That Jesus' primary language was Aramaic has been argued from, among other things, the presence of some twenty-six Aramaic words in the New Testament Gospels. Some scholars argue that Hebrew was used as a vernacular by a sizable group in the population during this period. Mishnaic Hebrew is a probable language of first-century Palestine, and hence a possible language of Jesus. According to Luke 4:16-20, Jesus knew enough Hebrew to locate a passage from Isaiah in a Hebrew scroll and then read it aloud. While virtually no contemporary scholars have argued that Jesus spoke *only* Greek, a number of writers have concluded that Greek was widely used by the Jews in first-century Palestine. Perhaps a majority of them spoke Greek. Many Jews even chose Greek for memorializing their dead in their burial inscriptions. That even rabbis and their families phrased their epitaphs in Greek strongly indicates that Greek was the language of their daily life.

It is clear that Greek was the lingua franca of the Roman Empire as a whole. Stanley Porter writes: "Galilee was completely surrounded by hellenistic culture, with Acco-Ptolemais, Tyre and Sidon in the west and north-west, Panias–Caesarea Philippi, Hippos and Gadara in the north-east, east and south-east, and Scythopolis and Gaba in the south. Besides being connected by a number of waterways, there was a road system that utilized a series of valleys to interconnect the Galilean region. . . . As a result, Galilee was a center for import and export as well as general trade, resulting in a genuinely cosmopolitan flavor."[152] Jesus was from Nazareth, and spent a good part of his career in Lower Galilee around the cities of Nazareth, Nain, Cana, and Capernaum. Although Nazareth was only a small village of some 1,600 to 2,000 in population and relied heavily on agriculture as its economic base, it is not accurate to think that Jesus grew up in cultural and geographical isolation. Nazareth was situated alongside of, and overlooking, one of the busiest trade routes in ancient Palestine, the Via Maris, which stretched all the way from Damascus to the Mediterranean. Capernaum, a town of 12,000 to 15,000, was yet more culturally diverse than Nazareth. Matthew (perhaps also known as Levi), the tax collector in Capernaum, would probably have had to use Greek to conduct his duties with the local taxpayers and the officials of Herod Antipas. The fishermen disciples would also probably have needed to speak Greek in order to carry on their business of selling fish.

151. Stanley E. Porter, "Jesus and the Use of Greek in Galilee," in *Studying the Historical Jesus*, pp. 123-54.
152. Porter, p. 135.

The religious background of the Jewish people in first-century Palestine is an unusually rich and variegated topic which, if anything, has become even more complex and colorful in the academic literature of the last generation. Only a bare outline of a few of the major religious trends can be offered here.[153] Recent scholarship has recognized the enormous diversity within Judaism during the period from the Roman conquest of Palestine (63 B.C.E.) to the destruction of the Jewish Temple at the conclusion of the war against Rome (70 C.E.). For this period it is probably best to speak and think of "Judaism" in the plural. That is, there were competing "Judaisms" that shared certain common preoccupations — with Temple, with Torah, with ceremonial law and purity, and so forth — but held to diverse and even diametrically opposed opinions on all these topics. Some decades ago George Foot Moore published a classic study of Judaism in the first centuries of this era which presented rabbinical teaching as "normative Judaism."[154] While this may accurately describe the period from about the seventh to the nineteenth centuries, it does not do justice to the complexities of the first century. Jacob Neusner, in his innumerable books, has portrayed a "first age of diversity" in Judaism that is unrivaled for its breadth of outlook and variety of practice until the developments of the last two centuries.[155] To take a specific example of Judaic diversity, even a basic rite such as circumcision was understood quite differently in the Hebrew Bible, the writings of Paul, 1 Maccabees, Josephus, and Philo.[156] Similarly the concept of "Messiah," often thought to

---

153. A brief summary of scholarship on first-century Judaism may be found in the articles of the *Anchor Bible Dictionary,* including the following: J. Andrew Overman and William Scott Green, "Judaism (Greco-Roman Period)," 3:1027-54; Anthony Saldarini, "Pharisees," 5:289-303; Saldarini, "Sanhedrin," 5:975-80; Saldarini, "Scribes," 5:1012-16; Gary G. Porton, "Sadducees," 5:892-95. A lengthier treatment is given in Anthony J. Saldarini, *Pharisees, Scribes, and Sadducees in Palestinian Society: A Sociological Approach* (Wilmington, Del.: Michael Glazier, 1988), and Martin Hengel, *Judaism and Hellenism,* 2 vols. (Philadelphia: Fortress, 1974). A truly monumental study of the period is found in Emil Schürer, *The History of the Jewish People in the Age of Jesus Christ (175 B.C.E.–A.D. 135),* rev. and ed. Geza Vermes and Fergus Millar, 3 vols. (Edinburgh: T. & T. Clark, 1973-87). This new edition of an old classic removes some of the pro-Protestant and anti-Judaic bias found in Schürer's nineteenth-century text, and incorporates new material from more recent scholarship.

154. George Foot Moore, *Judaism in the First Centuries of the Christian Era: The Age of the Tannaim,* 3 vols. (Cambridge: Harvard University Press, 1927-30).

155. Jacob Neusner has written literally hundreds of works on Judaism. A convenient entry point into his writings is the short text, *The Way of Torah: An Introduction to Judaism,* 5th ed. (Belmont, Calif.: Wadsworth, 1993).

156. Jonathan Z. Smith, *Imagining Religion: From Babylon to Jonestown* (Chicago and London: University of Chicago Press, 1982), pp. 9-14.

be essential to all forms of Judaism, is in fact used in only some of the texts of this period, and then used inconsistently.[157]

The question then arises: What, if anything, tied together the various "Judaisms" that flourished during the first century of the present era? Certain broad and overarching concerns connected the differing groups: the Temple, the Torah or scripture, the role of nonscriptural or extrascriptural tradition, and apocalypticism. Not all groups shared these concerns to an equal degree. Each concern, if taken singly and separately, had the capacity to absorb or nullify all the others. Thus an apocalyptic Judaism could, and sometimes did, negate the importance of the Temple and of priestly ritual, while a Judaism based on Levitical tradition and ritual purity would often rely on noncanonical texts as a basis for its claims and practices. For some versions of Judaism the Temple in Jerusalem was a concrete physical reality with spiritual meaning. Others had spiritualized the entire conception of the Temple, so that in the end it had become a metaphor or an idealization. To give an overview, I will first treat the general Judaic concerns of Temple and Torah, and then move on to the specific groups such as the Pharisees, Sadducees, and Essenes or Qumran community.

The general importance of the Temple to first-century Judaism becomes apparent in the persistence of the Jewish people in rebuilding and maintaining the Temple and in the central place given to it in the literature of the day. It was the most prominent institution in Judea that was under Jewish control. As such, it had unmistakable symbolic meaning: "As the center of the cult of Yahweh, and the seat of native Jewish, as opposed to Roman, rule, it represented both the forgiveness of sins and the hope for national sovereignty."[158] The desecrations of the Temple by Antiochus Epiphanes (165 B.C.E.) and the Roman general Pompey (63 B.C.E.) are recorded respectively in the canonical book of Daniel and the noncanonical *Psalms of Solomon*. Offenses against the Temple contributed to the Jewish revolts against foreign domination in the Maccabean period (165 B.C.E.), the first revolt against Rome (66 C.E.), and the Bar Kokhba rebellion (133 C.E.). The Temple plays a central role even in the Mishnah, the first collection of rabbinical writings, put into writing about 130 years (ca. 200 C.E.) after the destruction of the Temple and the cessation of the sacrifices there. The opening paragraph of the Mishnah asks when the evening prayer (i.e., Shema) may be recited, and formulates an answer in terms of the activities of the priests in the Temple. This might be compared to Americans today debating the hour at which Abraham Lincoln delivered the Gettysburg Address! It indicates how

157. Jacob Neusner, William Scott Green, and Ernest S. Frerichs, eds., *Judaisms and Their Messiahs at the Turn of the Christian Era* (New York: Cambridge University Press, 1987).

158. Overman and Green, p. 1039.

central the Temple and its rituals had become to the religious life of the Jewish people during the preceding centuries.

The fierce controversies surrounding the Temple only serve to underscore its importance. People fight over what they care about, and concerning the Jerusalem Temple there were both profound concern and passionate argument. The Qumran community, which produced the Dead Sea Scrolls and will be described below, may have come into existence in the second century B.C.E. in response to a change in the priestly succession that rendered the existing Temple leadership illegitimate in the eyes of these sectarians. In their organization and ritual practice they sought to constitute themselves as a *true* priesthood that awaited the unveiling of a purified and restored Temple. Yet the Qumran community was not the only group critical of the Temple leadership. The mid–first century B.C.E. *Psalms of Solomon* attacks the priests as "sinners" and "lawless" persons who have stolen from the Temple's sanctuary and have no regard for the distinction between clean and unclean. Two other texts from the so-called Pseudepigrapha, the *Testament of Levi* and *The Lives of the Prophets,* make similar claims.[159]

The early movement surrounding Jesus seems also to have been critical of the Temple. In Mark's Gospel Jesus responded negatively to a statement praising the grandeur of the Temple: "Do you see these great buildings? Not one stone will be left here upon another; all will be thrown down" (Mark 13:2). When Jesus died, the Gospels report that the veil of the Temple was torn in two (Mark 15:38) — an event that might signify a devaluing of the Temple. Likewise the speech attributed to Stephen in the Acts of the Apostles includes a sharp critique of Temple-centered piety (7:48-53; cf. 6:13-14). The writings of Paul refer to the Temple, yet only as an image representing the spiritual community in Christ. The earthly structure fades from view. Likewise the Epistle to the Hebrews in the New Testament, in a fashion reminiscent of Philo (ca. 30 B.C.E.–45 C.E.), teaches that the earthly Temple is "a mere copy of the true one" which is in "heaven itself" (Heb. 9:24; cf. 8:2, 5). To sum up points made already, the various forms of first-century Judaism were alike in valuing the Temple, and yet they criticized the existing priesthood and sacrificial service in a variety of ways. Some called for a replacement of the current priests with more qualified persons; others awaited a divine intervention to overthrow the Temple leadership and establish a new Temple with new priests; and still others viewed the earthly edifice as secondary to a spiritual Temple not made with hands.[160]

---

159. See *Pss. Sol.* 1:8; 2:3-13; 4:1, 8, 12; 8:11ff.; *T. Levi* 10:3; 16:2-4; 14:4-6; *Liv. Pro.* 3:15ff.; these texts are included in James H. Charlesworth, ed., *The Old Testament Pseudepigrapha,* 2 vols. (Garden City, N.Y.: Doubleday, 1983-85). References from Overman and Green, p. 1040.

160. Despite the instruction in the book of Deuteronomy that all sacrifices were to

A telling phenomenon of Greco-Roman Judaism was the appearance of documents that retold the stories and history of the Bible. Sometimes this re-iteration of biblical stories took the form of copying a genre contained within the canonical writings (e.g., psalms, apocalypses, histories), while at other times the stories were a cross between biblical styles and the conventions of the ancient romance. J. Andrew Overman and William Scott Green note that these new writings, supplementing the Hebrew Bible, underscore "the need on the part of Jews both at home and in the diaspora to clarify who they were, whose they were, and what the future held for them."[161] By seizing hold of the past, they sought to orient themselves in the present. The interpretation of the past was a way for the Jewish people to redefine and redirect themselves in an age of uncertainty.

With regard to sacred scripture or Torah, no single text was used by all Jews during this period. Greek-speaking Jews rarely resorted to the Hebrew original, but instead used the Greek translation known as the Septuagint (or LXX). Some even thought this translation (or a part of it) had been directly inspired by God and possessed as much authority as the Hebrew original, an idea that became apparent as early as the *Letter of Aristeas* (ca. 150-100 B.C.E.). (English-speaking Christians have sometimes had a comparable veneration for the Authorized Version or King James Version of 1611.)[162] Rabbinical Judaism had its Targums — renderings of the Hebrew Bible into the Aramaic language — but always regarded these as interpretations of sacred scripture and not as original or authoritative texts. With regard to the Septuagint itself, this translation was not completed all at once (notwithstanding the legends regarding its origin), and so there were many different manuscripts. The Greek version of Isaiah, for instance, may be 100 to 150 years later than that of the Pentateuch.

Of all the Jewish groups of the first century C.E., the Pharisees (probably from Heb. *perushim,* "separated ones") are perhaps the best known because of

---

be offered at "the place that the LORD your God will choose" (Deut. 12:5, and parallels) — assumed to be Jerusalem — some groups built temples in other localities. Mount Gerizim, outside of Shechem, was an ancient site of worship that may have antedated the establishment of the Temple in Jerusalem. The Samaritans claimed that this mountain, rather than Mount Zion in Jerusalem, was the divinely appointed spot for worship, and they produced a version of the Hebrew Bible that supported their claim. In Egypt a priest named Onias (either III or IV) built a temple at Leontopolis sometime in the second century B.C.E., and it remained in operation until it was closed by the Romans in 74 C.E. (Overman and Green, p. 1040).

161. Overman and Green, p. 1051.

162. A seminary professor is said to have preached to a rural congregation from one of the newer Bible translations, and evoked this response from a disapproving parishioner: "If the King James Version was good enough for the apostle Paul, then it's good enough for me!"

the role they play as Jesus' chief opponents in many of the Gospel stories. While Josephus and early rabbinical literature also provide information on the Pharisees, all of the existing sources on them have to be used with caution and none presents a very complete picture. The aim of the Gospel writers was to present Jesus and not a detailed and accurate picture of the Pharisees and other Jewish groups. Josephus wrote with a view to commending the Pharisees to his Roman patrons and Gentile reading audience. The rabbinical writings appeared many generations after the pre–70 C.E. Pharisees, the crisis of the war against Rome, the destruction of the Temple, and other profound changes in Jewish life. The rabbis' presentation of the first-century Pharisees is often colored by a desire to promote their own later agendas. In fact, we have writings from only two persons who actually claim to be Pharisees: Saul of Tarsus or Paul the apostle, and Josephus.[163]

Josephus lists the Pharisees as one of three different sects or philosophical groups (Gk. *hairesis*) that existed among the Jews, with the others being the Sadducees and the Essenes.[164] Josephus describes these differing groups in terms of their respective beliefs on such matters as fate or free will, the immortality of the soul, and rewards and punishments after the present life. The Pharisees, he says, affirm both fate and free will, believe that the soul is imperishable, that the dead will be raised again, and that the wicked are punished eternally. They eschew a life of luxury, show respect for elders, and follow the guidance of reason. It is clear that Josephus's description attempts to commend the Pharisees to Gentile readers who would likely have looked with favor on a group said to be mildly ascetic and reasonable in its outlook. Throughout Josephus's narrative, the Pharisees appear as a kind of political interest group, currying favor with rulers. They belong to a retainer class that has no political power of its own but cultivates good relations with the ruling group. In time they gained and then lost the support of John Hyrcanus (ruler from 134 to 104 B.C.E.), and then again won over Queen Alexandra (76-67 B.C.E.). Unfortunately, it is not really possible from Josephus's narrative to reconstruct any clear picture of the Pharisees' agenda or what specific program they might have sought to implement.[165]

In the Gospel texts the Pharisees and Jesus contend over issues of purity, Sabbath observance, fasting, and tithing. A dispute over eating with unwashed hands becomes the occasion for Jesus to set forth a contrast between the Pharisees' "traditions of the elders" and the "commandments of God" (Mark 7:1-23; Matt. 15:1-20). In general the notion of Jesus disputing with the Pharisees over

---

163. Josephus, *Life* 9-12; Phil. 3:4-6.
164. Josephus, *Jewish War* 2.119-66; *Antiquities* 18.11-25.
165. Overman and Green, pp. 1041-42.

matters of ritual and purity is consistent with the later evidence of the Mishnah and Tosephta, where the Pharisees and the Sadducees have seven different disputes with one another that are largely concerned with purity. The Pharisees' agenda for the renewal of Judaism almost certainly centered on such matters as strict tithing, the observance of ritual purity by nonpriests, careful attention to the Sabbath and other holidays, and rules regarding the practice of sharing meals with others. Later rabbinic writings, such as *Tractate Demai* in *The Mishnah* (ca. 200 C.E.), make reference to a custom of "association" (Heb. *habura*) and to people known as "associates" *(haberim).*[166] While these references do not imply the existence of a unified group of *haberim,* they do attest to a practice among some Jews of sharing meals only with those who practiced strict tithing and insured that the food met the other standards for ritual purity. It is therefore possible and even likely that the Pharisees of the first century C.E., in striving for purity, limited their food consumption to meals that they had prepared themselves or that were offered to them by a handful of like-minded individuals.

Concerning the Sadducees, we are in an even weaker position than with the Pharisees in terms of historical documentation. The term itself may be derived from the name Zadok, the high priest at the time of David (2 Sam. 8:17; 15:24). Yet no surviving sources are written from the Sadducees' point of view, no Jewish movement from a later period claims descent from the Sadducees, and the sources that do mention the Sadducees tend to couple them with the Pharisees and rarely mention them separately. When Josephus wrote his major works, the Pharisees may have been gaining in influence, and his comments on the Sadducees may be biased against them. In the rabbinic literature the Sadducees are treated almost as outsiders.[167] The various sources all agree that they denied the resurrection of the dead.[168] Josephus adds that they do not believe in fate, accept no observance apart from the laws of the Torah, and reject the traditions of the Pharisees. In the New Testament the Sadducees are associated with the high priests and rulers of the Jews (Acts 23:6-8). These scant references do not justify the fuller picture of the Sadducees that is sometimes offered, namely, as a group of biblical literalists who had no oral traditions of their own in addition to the written Torah. This may or may not be accurate. Moreover, while the Sadducees played a role in the ruling elite, they should not simply be identified with it.[169]

Prior to the discovery of the Dead Sea Scrolls in the caves at Qumran in the 1940s, the Essenes were known largely through the references in Josephus,

166. *m. Dem.* 2:2-3.
167. Saldarini, *Pharisees,* p. 301.
168. Josephus, *Antiquities* 18.16; Mark 12:18; *Abot de-Rabbi Nathan* A.5.
169. Overman and Green, p. 1042.

along with some additional information in Philo and Pliny the Elder. Although there is still debate on the issue, the Dead Sea Scrolls are today almost universally accepted as documents from an Essene community that shared a kind of monastic life in the isolation of the desert.[170] Thus the Dead Sea Scrolls give a much more detailed picture of a first-century sect than was possible before the discovery and decipherment of the scrolls. The texts span a period running from the middle of the second century B.C.E. to the destruction of the community by the Romans (ca. 68 C.E.). Some of the distinctive practices of the Qumran community included a sharing of material possessions, a disparaging attitude toward marriage, and a habit of adopting children into the community. Some members were celibate — a rarity within Judaism. For such infractions as speaking against the group or violating its purity rules the community inflicted severe penalties (e.g., imprisonment for several years, permanent expulsion, mulcting or diminishing food and water rations). The sensational claims that New Testament figures such as John the Baptist, James the brother of Jesus, or Jesus himself are referred to in the Dead Sea Scrolls have not won support within the international scholarly community.

The documents show that the Qumran community was alienated from the Temple leadership in Jerusalem. The group may have withdrawn into the desert because its members rejected the Hasmoneans' claim to the high priesthood. There is extensive discussion of a certain "Wicked Priest" (whose identity is in dispute). Among the texts in the Dead Sea collection, the Damascus Document and Thanksgiving Hymns condemn the false priests who fail to observe the distinction between clean and unclean as "teachers of lies and seers of falsehood" who lead the people "to exchange the Law engraved on [the] heart . . . for the smooth things (which they speak)."[171] The War Scroll describes a final battle between the sons of light and the sons of darkness, and indicates that the community believed that the holy war would be followed by a new and reconstituted Temple in its true and pure form. Those at Qumran followed Levitical regulations that normally applied only to the Temple priests. They held a rank or order (Heb. *serek*) among themselves according to levels of purity or holiness approximating those of the Jerusalem Temple. Thus Qumran in its internal organization understood itself as the *true* Temple and ordered its life to accord with its tradition of how the Temple ought to be managed. The present corrupt leadership of the Temple would be overthrown and the true priests — the

---

170. A thorough discussion of the basic issues and debates regarding the Dead Sea Scrolls, written in the light of the most recently published texts, is found in Geza Vermes' introduction to *The Complete Dead Sea Scrolls in English* (New York and London: Allen Lane/Penguin Press, 1997), pp. 1-90.

171. Vermes, *Complete Dead Sea Scrolls*, Damascus Document 5.2 (p. 131), Thanksgiving Hymn 12 (p. 263).

Qumran community itself — would take its place. Yet there is not much evidence that the Qumran community ever had much influence on the rest of Jewish society.[172]

In addition to the three schools of thought described by Josephus, there were other first-century Jewish groups that might be described as popular movements: the so-called Fourth Philosophy, the Zealots, the *Sicarii* (or "dagger men"), various prophetic and messianic groups, as well as social bandits. All of these groups played some role in the rebellion against Rome, which is their common trait in Josephus's description of them. Many of these movements justified their actions in religious terms, as expressions of loyalty or obedience to the God of Israel. The Fourth Philosophy was basically a tax-resistance movement, as typified by a Galilean named Judas who urged his countrymen to resist paying the tax assessment and upbraided those who would go on "tolerating mortal masters, after having God for their Lord."[173] Judas, together with Zaddok the Pharisee, filled the nation with unrest and thus paved the way, in Josephus's view, for the catastrophe of the war against Rome. Josephus also describes groups of bandits or brigands, especially prevalent in Upper Galilee.[174] The social unrest also produced a series of popular or charismatic leaders, some referred to as "king" and others as "prophet" or "messiah." In the Galilean city of Sepphoris, Judas, son of Ezekias, a well-known brigand, led a raid and revolt at the death of Herod (ca. 4 B.C.E.). A servant of Herod named Simon was proclaimed king and led a popular uprising, plundering royal residences throughout the land until he was captured and beheaded.[175]

Other popular leaders described by Josephus were prophetic rather than opportunistic in character. They reiterated the message of the earlier prophets that Israel had strayed from obedience to God, had fallen under divine judgment, and needed to repent in order to be free from foreign domination. A certain Theudas persuaded a multitude to follow him to the Jordan River, where he said he could miraculously divide the river.[176] His movement ended speedily with his capture and execution. Another figure, known simply as "the Egyptian," managed to draw some 30,000 followers, whom he incited to storm the city of Jerusalem. Many were killed and captured, although the Egyptian escaped.[177] John the Baptist is also mentioned by Josephus as a figure who stood in the prophetic tradition of Isaiah or Elijah. The Zealots, as a distinct political

172. Overman and Green, pp. 1039, 1043.
173. Josephus, *Jewish War* 2.118, cited in Overman and Green, p. 1044.
174. Josephus, *Life* 77; *Jewish War* 4.84-120.
175. Josephus, *Antiquities* 17.271-85.
176. Josephus, *Antiquities* 20.97-98.
177. Josephus, *Jewish War* 2.261-63.

movement, probably did not coalesce until the 60s when war with Rome was imminent.[178]

Standing above the political interest groups and the movements of popular insurgence was the Sanhedrin, or chief council of the Jews in Jerusalem. The term itself comes from the Greek *synedrion* (lit. "a sitting down with"), a common term for a meeting or assembly. There is considerable debate over the nature and function of the Sanhedrin, which has been variously understood as a political council of the high priests, a legislative body in Jewish Palestine, a judicial supreme court, a grand jury for important legal cases, the council of the Pharisaic school, and a final court of appeals in deciding questions of Jewish law. There is even debate over whether there was one or more than one distinct group known under the title of Sanhedrin. There were likely many different assemblies and councils attached to the various Jewish groups, but only one supreme council in Jerusalem, composed of the most powerful and influential leaders at a given time. In the New Testament the term *synedrion* refers sometimes to local courts or councils that keep order and administer punishments (Matt. 5:22; 10:17; Mark 13:9). More often it refers to a supreme council in Jerusalem that acts as a judicial court, a political link to the Roman governor, and the guardian of public order. The high priest is said to preside over it, and its members include the chief priests, elders, scribes, and other leading citizens (Mark 15:1).

In Mark and Matthew the Sanhedrin condemns Jesus to death (Mark 14:64; Matt. 26:66), but then must approach the Roman governor to have him executed. In Luke no formal condemnation of Jesus is made until after the governor has been approached (Luke 22:71). The Gospel of John attributes a political motivation to the Sanhedrin, led by Caiaphas, which feared that Jesus might precipitate social unrest and provoke the Romans to destroy the nation (John 11:47-53). In the Acts of the Apostles the function of the Sanhedrin is of a piece with the picture presented in the Gospels. It upholds public order, guards the sanctity of the Temple, and metes out punishment to offenders (Acts 4–6; 23). It represents the nation to the Roman authorities (Acts 22:30), is composed of Sadducees and Pharisees, and is led by the high priest (Acts 5:21, 34).

---

178. Overman and Green, pp. 1044-45. These authors note (p. 1045) that there is only slender evidence for a distinctive "charismatic Judaism" in the persons of Honi the Circle-Maker (*m. Ta'an.* 3.8; *b. Ta'an.* 23a), Hananiah ben Dosa (*m. Ber.* 5.5; *t. Ber.* 3.20; *m. Sota* 9.15), and possibly Jesus of Nazareth. The rabbinic traditions attribute to the former two figures an unusual efficacy in prayer (for rain, or for healing) but not a special form of Judaism. Their actions do not set them apart from other Jewish figures of the era. Thus, contrary to Geza Vermes in *Jesus the Jew,* pp. 58-82, the accounts regarding Honi and Hananiah do not attest to a distinctive "charismatic Judaism" that can serve as a category within which to understand Jesus. See n. 271.

Under its direction are Temple officials, guards, and a prison, and so it resembles a typical Hellenistic-Roman regional or city council.[179]

Debates over the character of the Sanhedrin, its procedures, and its authority vis-à-vis the Roman governor have been driven by a desire to explain Jesus' arrest, trial, condemnation, and execution. Yet the Sanhedrin should be understood in terms of the general responsibilities assigned to ancient councils in cities and territories. A nation under Roman domination had to keep order among the populace, and this would have been a fairly routine matter in ancient Palestine. Governmental authority at that time did not follow the neat divisions of executive, legislative, and judicial powers that are familiar to those living in modern nation-states. Certainly there was no demarcation between the religious and the political spheres, as Anthony Saldarini notes: "The theory of two sanhedrins, one political and one religious, during this period is improbable in the extreme because political and religious life were one."[180] The Pharisees, Sadducees, and other groups may have had their own private assemblies, yet this does not mean there was more than one Sanhedrin. Ellis Rivkin may be correct in his argument that the Sanhedrin was an ad hoc group dependent on the will of the current ruler. He suggests further that it was not really a standing council, but one convoked from time to time under the firm hand of the Jewish high priest and his immediate associates.[181] Sean Freyne concludes that the Gospel narratives appear to give the Sanhedrin as a court greater importance and a more permanent role than in fact it possessed. This strengthens an impression that the death of Jesus was the formal responsibility of the Jewish establishment.[182]

The preceding discussion has shown the remarkable vitality and diversity of first-century Judaism. This diversity has considerable significance for interpreting the life of Jesus, because it suggests that he lived in an era when the basic concepts of Judaism were hotly contested and few practices or teachings were a matter of general agreement. Consequently one should not think of Jesus and his first followers as a tiny minority set over and against a unified Judaism or the Jewish people as a whole. This impression, though reinforced by the customary interpretations of certain New Testament texts, is erroneous in that it presumes a degree of religious consensus that did not exist among the Jewish people during this era. Even more basically, it fails to account for the Jewishness of Jesus' first followers. J. Andrew Overman and William Scott Green speak of

---

179. Saldarini, "Sanhedrin," pp. 975-77.

180. Saldarini, "Sanhedrin," p. 979.

181. Ellis Rivkin, *What Crucified Jesus? Messianism, Pharisaism, and the Development of Christianity* (New York: UAHC Press, 1997), pp. 50, 62-63, 72-73.

182. Freyne, "Geography," p. 100.

the earliest Christians as constituting a "Jesus-centered Judaism," and they observe: "It is anachronistic, though still commonplace, to identify the Jesus movement of 1st century Palestine as 'Christianity.' In its historical and religious context and in its varied forms, the Jesus movement was a type of *Judaism* and was viewed as such by non-Jews." The same authors note that there were significant internal differences within the Jesus movement: "Jesus-centered Judaism was not monolithic. The internal differences within this Judaism parallel those that distinguished other Judaisms from one another. Some variants of this Judaism stressed scripture, tradition, and aspects of Levitical piety, while others were dominated by apocalypticism."[183]

Having now portrayed, with broad brush strokes, the complex, variegated, contentious, passionate, and ultimately revolutionary context of first-century Palestine, we are now in a position to examine the specifics of Jesus' life, beginning with the appearance of Jesus' kinsman and predecessor, John the Baptist.

John the Baptist

The story of Jesus' adult life begins with that of John the Baptist.[184] John is named no fewer than eighty times in the canonical Gospels and nine times in Acts. Though each of the Gospels portrays John somewhat differently, they all proceed from the assumption that the beginning of Jesus' ministry and the beginning of the gospel message lie in John and his preaching. John the Baptist is thus a part of Jesus' identity. "Some key elements of John's preaching and praxis," writes Meier, "flowed into Jesus' ministry like so much baptismal water."[185] A scrutiny of the Gospels shows, however, that John's role is more ambiguous than at first appears. He did not oppose Jesus as did Herod Antipas and Pilate, and yet he is said to have posed to Jesus the skeptical question: "Are you the one who is to come, or are we to wait for another?" (Matt. 11:3; cf. Luke 7:19). The Gospel of John suggests that there was some measure of competition

183. Overman and Green, p. 1045. A detailed study of Jesus-centered Judaism is contained in Jean Daniélou, *The Theology of Jewish Christianity,* trans. John A. Baker (London: Darton, Longman & Todd; Chicago: Henry Regnery, 1964).

184. On John the Baptist see Meier, *A Marginal Jew,* 2:19-99, and Robert L. Webb, "John the Baptist and His Relationship to Jesus," in *Studying the Historical Jesus,* pp. 179-229.

185. Meier, *A Marginal Jew,* 2:7. Hendrikus Boers even argues that Jesus viewed John and not himself as the pivotal figure in the coming of God's kingdom. Thus Jesus points to John rather than the reverse. See Boers, *Who Was Jesus? The Historical Jesus and the Synoptic Gospels* (San Francisco: Harper & Row, 1989), pp. xii, 35, passim.

between the followers of John and those of Jesus, and that for a period these two figures were developing their ministries and followings alongside of one another (John 3:22–4:2). In light of the criterion of embarrassment, discussed above, it seems quite certain that there were actual events that stand behind these passages showing John the Baptist and his movement as independent of Jesus and his followers. At the same time, it is very certain that Jesus was baptized by John, and this indicates that at least for some period of time the two had a close affinity. Between John and Jesus there was an intricate and intriguing relationship that can be interpreted in a number of different ways.[186]

John, in general terms, was a leader of a sectarian baptizing movement centered in the wilderness of Judea — a place with eschatological as well as ascetic associations. In continuity with earlier prophetic and apocalyptic figures, John announced the imminent end of the world and the time of divine judgment. John also spoke of a "Coming One" who would carry out the judgment. He summoned people to repentance because the remaining time was short, and the end was drawing near.[187] The accounts of his preaching given in the Gospels carry a tone of urgency: "Even now the ax is lying at the root of the trees; every tree therefore that does not bear good fruit is cut down and thrown into the fire" (Matt. 3:10). While John's baptism bears some analogy to the water lustrations and ritual cleansings at Qumran in the desert, there is a decisive difference. This water ritual does not seem to have been administered more than once, and so it does not fit into the pattern of the Levitical laws that specified that ritual washing was to occur whenever a person became ceremonially unclean. Instead John's baptism seems to mark a once-for-all transition into a new religious state or identity.[188]

The Gospels agree in connecting John's baptism with repentance and forgiveness, calling it a "baptism of repentance for the forgiveness of sins" (Mark 1:4). The exact relationship between the water ritual and forgiveness is not, however, spelled out. Robert Webb suggests that the water ritual symbolized a per-

186. The image of John the Baptist played a role in the development of Christianity and specifically the monastic tradition, as discussed by Edmondo F. Lupieri, "John the Baptist: The First Monk," in Jordan Aumann et al., *Monasticism: A Historical Overview,* Word and Spirit 6 (Still River, Mass.: St. Bede's Publications, 1984), pp. 11-23.

187. Josephus, like the Gospels, portrays John as a preacher of divine judgment and repentance. See *Antiquities* 18.116-19.

188. Luke 1:80 says John "was in the wilderness until the day he appeared publicly to Israel," and some have connected this with Josephus's statement about the celibate Essenes who adopted and raised other people's children (*Jewish War* 282). Yet Webb, p. 207, observes: "Concrete evidence of John's membership in the Qumran community is lacking. And even if John had been a member at one time, aspects of his teaching are sufficiently different from that found in the Qumran scrolls, that one would be forced to conclude that John had broken away from them."

son's repentance and God's forgiveness, and that the forgiveness itself would be conferred at the final judgment rather than at baptism itself.[189] Baptism was thus an expression of hope. Josephus seems to support this interpretation when he states that John's baptism was not "to gain pardon for whatever sins they committed, but as a consecration of the body implying that the soul was already thoroughly cleansed by right behavior."[190] On the other hand, since John required baptism of his followers, the act of baptism (or even John himself) may have been viewed in some sense as a means of forgiveness and spiritual cleansing. This would have put John into competition with the Temple priests and their sacrifices, and may help to account for the controversy surrounding John.

The origins of John's mission are not spelled out in any detail in either the New Testament Gospels or Josephus. Yet Luke records a tradition that John was the only son of a Jerusalem priest who functioned in the Temple (Luke 1:5-80), and this would suggest that John's decision to preach in the wilderness represented a decisive break with family and tradition. Meier notes that John would have had "a solemn duty to follow his father in his function and to make sure that the priestly line was continued by marriage and children." Instead John seems to have "scandalously rejected his obligation" and "struck out into the desert to embrace the role of an Israelite prophet of judgment."[191] More than this cannot be asserted with confidence, although it is tempting to take a stab at writing a kind of first-century screenplay about the events that may have led John to take up his solitary calling. Another unanswered question regards the custom of baptizing itself. As already noted, the cleansing rites associated with the Jerusalem Temple and with Qumran afford only a partial analogy to John's baptism, while the Jewish custom of proselyte baptism (i.e., for Gentiles who wished to become Jews) is not clearly attested in this early period in the sources that might be expected to mention it. The likely conclusion is that John's baptism derived from his own eschatological vision and message, and represented something new arising from the hallowed custom of water rituals. The distinctive practice stuck in the minds of John's hearers and resulted in the designation by which he became forever known — the Baptist.[192]

The identity of John's "Coming One" has been disputed. John could have been thinking of a heavenly or apocalyptic "Son of Man," a human Messiah of some kind, or simply God himself coming in judgment at the end of the age.

189. Webb, p. 184.

190. Josephus, *Antiquities* 18.116-19.

191. Meier, *A Marginal Jew,* 2:24-25.

192. Meier, *A Marginal Jew,* 2:52-53. Regarding Jewish proselytes, there are abundant references to circumcision in Philo, Josephus, the New Testament, and the text on conversion to Judaism, *Joseph and Asenath*. Consequently the lack of reference to proselyte baptism seems to be a significant silence.

John in several passages says the "Coming One" was "more powerful" than he, and that he himself was "unworthy" — statements that are superfluous if John's implicit point of comparison is God himself. Also John speaks of untying "the thong of his sandals," and this too suggests that the "Coming One" was a human figure (Matt. 3:11-12; Mark 1:7-8; Luke 3:15-17; John 1:25-27). If the "Coming One" cannot be God, then whom did John have in mind? Perhaps John himself did not know. As Meier notes, the references to the "Coming One" in the Gospels are really too vague to have been coined by early Christians. They do not have the specificity one might expect if they were invented ad hoc to connect John with Jesus. The hazy statements about a "Coming One" are, after all, a rather odd way to herald a person if the identity of that person is definitely established.[193] The question posed by John to Jesus, "Are you the Coming One?" (cf. Matt. 11:3), is another argument in favor of the theory that John himself was uncertain regarding his predicted successor.

John may not have intended to form a distinct sect or gather a group of followers around himself, and yet his message and the baptism he offered initiated people into a new group that sought to prepare itself for the end of the world, or eschaton. It is possible that although John offered his message to all Jews, the baptism he offered was in effect an initiation into "true Israel," a people prepared for the "Coming One" and for the impending judgment by God. After their baptism, most of John's followers were likely to have returned to their ordinary lives and occupations (cf. Luke 3:10-14), but a few became John's disciples and remained with him in the desert. The Fourth Gospel indicates that some of Jesus' closest disciples, including the apostles Simon and Andrew, were followers of John before they became followers of Jesus (John 1:35-42), and there is little reason to think that this kind of tradition would have been invented after the fact.

Yet the Gospels stress not only the connection between John and Jesus, but the differences as well.[194] John was ascetic and self-denying, while Jesus was not (Matt. 3:4; 9:14-17; 11:18-19; Mark 1:6; 2:18; Luke 5:33-35; 7:33-34). John is portrayed in camel's hair garments and a leather belt, eating locusts and wild honey (Matt. 3:4), while Jesus is known for partaking in food and drink and is even accused of being "a glutton and a drunkard" (Matt. 11:18-19). John's disciples fasted, but Jesus' followers did not (at least during his lifetime; Matt. 9:14; Mark 2:18; Luke 5:33). Associated with John's fasting was prayer, and John had taught his disciples to pray while Jesus had not (Luke 11:1). John's activities were concentrated in the wilderness, while Jesus focused on towns and villages (Matt. 4:23; Mark 1:38-39; Luke 4:43-44). John did no miracles (John 10:41),

193. Meier, *A Marginal Jew*, 2:32-35.
194. Webb, pp. 226-27.

while Jesus' entire ministry was characterized by miracle working (Matt. 8:16; Mark 1:32-34; Luke 4:40-41). Thus the differences between John and Jesus are just as striking as the continuities.

To summarize, what then is the significance of John the Baptist for understanding the life of Jesus? Jesus began his public ministry within John's movement, and at first may have shared in John's general attitude and outlook. Yet Jesus moved beyond that initial ministry with John and came to differ from John. The outward differences in John's and Jesus' respective forms of life — ascetic denial versus moderate enjoyment, and social withdrawal versus social engagement — are relevant in assessing the two figures. The two forms of life represented two different notions of public ministry and two different conceptions of the kingdom of God. Jesus' withdrawal from John may have been associated with his work of healing and exorcism — activities that are never attributed to John.[195] Still more basically, Jesus' departure from John is seen in his teaching on the coming of God's kingdom: "But if it is by the finger of God that I cast out the demons, then the kingdom of God has come to you" (Luke 11:20). These words bear witness to the *presence* of the kingdom in connection with Jesus and his activity. Jesus' table celebrations with the despised and marginalized were also an indication of the kingdom's presence. What for John had been a hope and expectation that loomed in the future, for Jesus became a present reality to be enacted and acknowledged here and now. It was not just that John's future had become Jesus' present, for the *character* of the kingdom had shifted as well.[196]

John was also significant for Jesus because the Gospel accounts consistently portray Jesus' baptism as a major transition. "As far as our meager sources allow us to know," writes John Meier, "before his baptism by John, Jesus was a respectable, unexceptional, and unnoticed woodworker in Nazareth." Family and friends alike were offended by Jesus once he undertook his ministry, and not without reason. In all probability there was little if anything in his previous life that foreshadowed his later mission to Israel. Consequently "his baptism by John is so important because it is the only external, historically verifiable marker of this pivotal 'turning around' in Jesus' life — his 'conversion' in the root sense of the word."[197] The accounts of the baptism and temptation in

---

195. Paul W. Hollenbach has argued that Jesus was a kind of lapsed or apostate follower of John, and that Jesus' ministry changed when he realized that he had the power to exorcise and to heal (Webb, p. 224). See Hollenbach, "Social Aspects of John the Baptizer's Preaching Mission in the Context of Palestinian Judaism," in *Aufstieg und Niedergang der römischen Welt*, ed. W. Haase and E. Temporini (Berlin: Walter de Gruyter, 1979-), 2.19.1 (1979), pp. 850-75, and "John the Baptist," in *Anchor Bible Dictionary*, 3:887-99.

196. Webb, p. 224.

197. Meier, *A Marginal Jew*, 2:108-9.

the synoptic Gospels (Matt. 3:13–4:11; Mark 1:9-13; Luke 3:21-22; 4:1-13) indicate that Jesus had a powerful new experience of the divine realm. While these narratives are shot through with miraculous elements that transcend the ordinary realm of experience, they attest to Jesus' experience of a call by God and to his wrestling with the significance of this call. Such an experience may be highly individual and idiosyncratic, and yet if the traditions of Israelite prophecy have any application to Jesus, it is reasonable to presume that Jesus would have provided his disciples with some account of his private call by God.[198]

Once he had been baptized by John, Jesus began to announce that "the kingdom of God has come near" (Mark 1:15).

"The Kingdom of God"

Jesus proclaimed "the kingdom of God." Of this there is no doubt. Scholars who represent the entire spectrum of opinions on the historical Jesus concur that, in the words of Joachim Jeremias, "the central theme of the public proclamation of Jesus was the kingly reign of God."[199] This is one of the rare areas of genuine consensus in contemporary biblical studies. One might go further than this and assert that Jesus' proclamation of the kingdom of God was not only central to his teaching but serves as the point of integration for understanding the differing aspects of his life and ministry. Thus Perrin claims: "Jesus appeared as one who proclaimed the Kingdom; all else in his message and ministry serves a function in relation to that proclamation and derives its meaning from it."[200] The theme of God's kingdom or reign leads directly into all the enduring issues concerning Jesus — his understanding of God, the significance of his miracles, the parables and other sayings, his call to repentance and gathering together of followers, his fellowship with "sinners," the opposition he faced, the death he endured, the claim that he rose from the dead, and his own self-understanding. Because of its centrality and cruciality, the kingdom of God in the teaching of Jesus has evoked a rich literature of discussion and debate.[201]

198. Webb, pp. 225-26. The apostle Paul seems to have laid great stress on his private vision of Jesus as a basis for his authority as an apostle (Gal. 1:1, 11-17).

199. Joachim Jeremias, *New Testament Theology: The Proclamation of Jesus* (New York: Scribner, 1971), p. 96. Compare the statements of Rudolf Bultmann, that "the dominant concept of Jesus' message is the *Reign of God*" (*Theology of the New Testament*, 2 vols. [New York: Scribner's, 1951], 1:4), and of John Meier that "the kingdom of God is a central part of Jesus' proclamation" (*A Marginal Jew*, 2:289).

200. Perrin, *Rediscovering*, p. 54.

201. For a summary of the different views, see Wendell Willis, ed., *The Kingdom of God in Twentieth-Century Interpretation* (Peabody, Mass.: Hendrickson, 1987).

Elimo Philipp Njau, *The Baptism*
(London: Society for the Propagation of the Gospel)

Every presentation of the life and ministry of Jesus may be judged by the way in which the kingdom of God is understood. Some of the recent debates over the kingdom were noted above in the introduction to this chapter, yet more background is necessary before delving into the issues posed by the biblical texts.

While discussions of the kingdom of God make frequent use of the terms "eschatology" and "apocalyptic," these terms are not used in any consistent fashion, and therefore in some of the debates over the kingdom of God the participants may have been speaking past one another. As G. B. Caird has pointed out, some authors have resorted to "tactical definitions" of their terms and "in this way they built the conclusion of their argument into the meaning of the word 'eschatology.'"202 Albert Schweitzer would seem to be an example of this trend when he writes that "the term eschatology ought only to be applied when reference is made to the end of the world as expected in the near future."203 This way of defining words tends to obscure the evidence in the Gospels concerning the kingdom of God as a present reality and as unconnected with the end of the world. Confusion arises also in Marcus Borg's call for a "non-eschatological Jesus" where an "eschatological prophet" is understood as one "who proclaimed the end of the world *in his own time*."204 But what if Jesus had proclaimed a kingdom of God that was not tied to the immediate end of the world? Would such a kingdom then not be "eschatological"? Crossan too fosters misunderstanding when he broadens the term "eschatology" to refer to "world-negation" in all its variety — "mystical, utopian, ascetic, libertarian, or anarchistic" — and concludes that "Jesus was not an apocalyptic prophet like John the Baptist, but he was an eschatological or world-negating figure."205 Surely the term "eschatology" has to be understood more narrowly than "world-negation," or else everyone in religious history from first-century Jewish Zealots to medieval Catholic nuns and modern Hindu *saddhus* will turn out be "eschatological"!

The term "eschatology" was introduced in the early nineteenth century to refer to that part of theology that deals with Christian beliefs concerning death, the afterlife, judgment, and the resurrection of the dead.206 Today this term is almost always used more broadly "to refer to the whole constellation of beliefs

---

202. G. B. Caird, *The Language and Imagery of the Bible* (Grand Rapids and Cambridge, U.K.: Eerdmans, 1997 [1980]), p. 250. For a careful elaboration on the uses of the word "eschatology," see the whole section on "The Language of Eschatology" (pp. 243-71).

203. Albert Schweitzer, *Paul and His Interpreters* (London: A. and C. Black, 1912), p. 228; Caird, p. 250.

204. Borg, *Jesus*, p. 11, emphasis in original. The disavowal of "eschatology" is seen in Borg's essay "A Temperate Case for a Non-Eschatological Jesus," in *Jesus in Contemporary Scholarship*, pp. 47-68. At the same time, Borg qualifies his rejection of the term when he writes: "Though I deny imminent eschatology, I do not exclude eschatology altogether from Jesus' message. In addition to speaking of the kingdom of God as a present power, Jesus apparently used kingdom language to refer to the eschatological banquet with Abraham, Isaac, and Jacob . . . and seems to have affirmed a life beyond death . . . [and] a last judgment" (*Jesus in Contemporary Scholarship*, pp. 41-42 n. 79).

205. Crossan, *Jesus*, pp. 52-53.

206. Caird, p. 243, notes that the word was first used in Germany, and then carried over into English. The first recorded use in the *Oxford English Dictionary* was in 1845, by the American author G. Bush. Gerhard Sauter, in "The Concept and Task of Eschatology — Theological and Philosophical Reflections," *Scottish Journal of Theology* 41 (1988): 499-515, traces the term back to Abraham Calov, who used the rubric *eschatologia* for the final section of his *Systema locorum Theologicorum* (1677).

and conceptions about the end of history and the transformation of the world which particularly characterized early Judaism, and early Christianity, and Islam, i.e., *cosmic* eschatology."[207] Central to eschatology are the twin notions of the salvation of the righteous and the punishment of the wicked. Eschatology is a way of understanding the complete realization of salvation as a future event or series of future events that are nevertheless linked with the present moment. There is a relation between the present and the future, and also a tension between them. The present time could serve as the point of departure for the unfolding of the eschatological drama, or alternatively the time of fulfillment may be further deferred. The future may be anticipated in the present through a partial and incomplete fulfillment.

A fundamental issue in eschatology is the relation between material and spiritual realities. As we will see in what follows, the language of eschatology can be understood in a more literal fashion as referring to tangible, this-worldly objects and persons, or else in a more symbolic way as pertaining to intangible realities or ineffable experiences. Early Christianity, as compared with Judaism, tended to spiritualize the conceptions of the land, the holy city, and the Temple. The earthly blessing, multiplied descendants, and possession of land that God promised in his covenant with Abraham and his descendants (Gen. 12:1-3) became for early Christians a cipher for a spiritual homeland not to be identified with ancient Palestine (Heb. 11:8-16). Hope centered on the new heavens and new earth that God would create at the end of the age. On the other hand, some strands of early Christianity were strongly influenced by Judaism's emphasis on the renewal (not replacement) of this present earth and the exaltation of Jerusalem among the nations.[208] This was particularly true of the "Jesus-centered Judaism" or "Jewish Christianity" of the late first and early second centuries C.E.[209]

In much of the recent literature, authors have distinguished eschatology from apocalypticism.[210] The issue of definition is germane to the debates regard-

207. David Aune, "Eschatology (Early Christian)," in *Anchor Bible Dictionary*, 2:594-609, quoting 594.

208. Aune, "Eschatology (Early Christian)," pp. 594-95. See Rev. 14:1-5; 20:1-10; 21:1–22:5.

209. See Jean Daniélou, *The Theology of Jewish Christianity*, trans. and ed. John A. Baker (London: Darton, Longman & Todd; Chicago: Henry Regnery, 1964), 377-404.

210. Some writers distinguish "apocalyptic" as a literary genre (e.g., the book of Daniel, the *Book of Enoch*, the book of Revelation) from "apocalypticism" as a thought world or worldview (including belief in the predetermination of history, the conflict of good and evil, etc.). See the helpful treatment in Charlesworth, *Jesus within Judaism*, pp. 34-38. In this brief discussion I am not distinguishing the texts from the worldview or social context that engendered them. For a thorough treatment of the issues, see Collins, McGinn, and Stein, eds., *The Encyclopedia of Apocalypticism*.

ing Jesus' kingdom of God and whether it was eschatological, apocalyptic, both eschatological and apocalyptic, or neither of the two. Those who distinguish eschatology from apocalypticism typically view the former in a positive light and the latter negatively. The prophets anchored their hope for the future in the certainty that God had acted in past historical events, was still acting, and would continue to act. Where the people of Israel faced catastrophe, this was because God was acting in judgment and called upon the people to repent. Even in the darkest moments, hope was still possible because God could and would come to deliver his people from their suffering and travail. In the writings that reflect an apocalyptic understanding of history, written between about 200 B.C.E. and 70 C.E., the understanding of history and God's action in it changes markedly. Rather than considering each historical event and epoch separately and seeking to understand the work of God in that occasion, the apocalyptic authors conceived of history as a total series of events that, from the perspective of the final consummation, is already unified and sequential and complete, stretching from the creation of the universe to the final conflict and consummation.

In apocalypticism the important thing about history is that it is running its foreordained course to a predetermined climax in accordance with the divine plan. Earthly existence is overshadowed by supernatural forces of good and evil — angels and demons — that battle in the heavenly realms (cf. Rev. 12:7-12). This makes human beings spectators of rather than participants in the drama of history and its consummation. The interest of apocalypticism is directed almost entirely toward the conclusion of all things, and apocalyptic seers are preoccupied with the calculation of the time of the end and the delineation of the signs of its coming.[211] Apocalyptic writings are rife with visions of God, angels, demons, journeys into celestial regions, heavenly books that disclose the secrets of the future, and the recording of these esoteric visions in written form. Given these characteristics of apocalypticism, it is appropriate to follow the distinction observed by most Hebrew Bible scholars between "prophetic eschatology" and "apocalyptic eschatology." Where concepts differ, so should terminology. At the same time, one finds overlap between prophetic and apocalyptic eschatology, and so a watertight division is not really desirable or possible.[212]

---

211. Norman Perrin, *The Kingdom of God in the Teaching of Jesus* (Philadelphia: Westminster, 1963), pp. 176-77.

212. Aune, "Eschatology (Early Christian)," pp. 595-96. Once again there is a possibility of confusion over terms, since I began this discussion by asking about the relationship between "eschatology" and "apocalypticism," and now have resorted to a different usage, according to which "eschatology" is a larger term that embraces both "prophetic eschatology" and "apocalyptic eschatology." From this point on I will follow this latter convention.

James Charlesworth, with many others, sees apocalypticism as resulting from a collapse in the world of meaning. The apocalyptic texts are a lament over the failure of ordinary historical processes to resolve human problems. They are a eulogy over an exhausted, worn-out earth and the present age of suffering, and they culminate in a vision of a new age in which "the wolf shall live with the lamb" (Isa. 11:6) and peace will prevail throughout the world. One side of apocalypticism is irenic and conciliatory — the nations will finally be at peace with one another — while the other side is warlike and vengeful — the enemies of God's people (either all Gentiles, or some of them) will suffer ultimate defeat and receive punishment for their sins. Reactions to apocalypticism have varied, but a common modern response is to see it as escapist. It tells us that though the present world is filled with ineradicable evil, there is a realm beyond where God triumphs, the wicked suffer, and the righteous flourish. Furthermore, this other domain will soon overtake and replace the present world of evil. Once again, the lines are somewhat blurry inasmuch as the classical Hebrew prophets all announced that ultimate salvation was God's work and not a human accomplishment. Apocalypticism is in effect an intensification of the sense of human powerlessness in the face of evil.

Having thus distinguished prophetic eschatology from apocalyptic eschatology, one may assert that Jesus was not an apocalypticist in the usual sense. The apocalyptic authors were constantly exhorted to write down what they had seen in their visions (Rev. 1:11; 10:4), while we have no evidence that Jesus ever wrote anything. The apocalypticists were often scribes, preoccupied with the minutiae of encyclopedic and technical details (e.g., the exact appearance of the angels, calendrical calculations, etc.), while Jesus was a wandering teacher whose message emphasized such generalities as the approaching kingdom and the need for repentance. While the apocalypticists tended to be vengeful, calling on God to destroy the forces of evil and especially the Jews' enemies, Jesus sought to cultivate an attitude of compassion and outgoing love. "Love your enemies" (Matt. 5:44) was one of his most distinctive teachings (although he spoke of a God who came in judgment as well as in grace). The apocalypticists denigrated the earth, insisting that God would bring a purified or even a wholly new world. Jesus, by contrast, celebrated God's creation in many of his sayings, such as that about the lilies of the field that bloom so gloriously and yet so briefly (Matt. 6:28-30). While the apocalypticists tended to situate God further and further away from the living world of humanity, Jesus stressed the nearness of the compassionate Father, who should be addressed in an almost childlike way as *Abba*. Finally, Jesus spoke of the kingdom of God not as a separate reality that was approaching nearer, but as somehow already present in and through his own miracles and preaching.[213]

213. Charlesworth, *Jesus within Judaism*, pp. 34-39.

Though not apocalyptic, Jesus' teaching on the kingdom of God shows many characteristics of prophetic eschatology. This means that it is in continuity with the salient features of the earlier Hebrew prophets, canonical scriptures, and postbiblical Jewish texts. This will become clear if we examine just a few of the many relevant passages from the Hebrew Bible. According to the later part of the book of Isaiah (or Deutero-Isaiah), God will restore "Jacob" or the "tribes of Israel" through a figure known as the "Servant" (Isa. 49:5-6). "The outcasts of Israel" will be gathered together, along with the foreigners who keep the Sabbath and the covenant. These righteous Gentiles will make sacrifices on the altar, "for my house shall be called a house of prayer for all peoples" (56:1-8). Nations (Heb. *goyim*) will come to Israel's light, and her sons and daughters will come before God with "the wealth of the nations." The Temple will be glorified, foreigners will rebuild the walls of Jerusalem, and God announces that "I will glorify my glorious house." The Gentiles who do not submit will be destroyed (60:3-14). God will gather "all nations and tongues," and he will send out messengers to declare his glory "among the nations." The Jews who are dispersed among the nations will be brought as "an offering to the Lord," and some will become priests and Levites to God. A new heaven and a new earth is promised (66:18-24). In the latter days the mountain of the house of the Lord will be established as the highest mountain, where many nations will come to learn the law, the word of the Lord. Israel will defeat opposing nations and shall devote their gain to "the Lord of the whole earth" (Mic. 4). The Temple will be rebuilt (Isa. 44:28; Ezek. 40–43), the Gentiles will be subservient to Israel (Isa. 54:3; 60:16; 61:6), and dispersed Israel will be restored, sometimes, it is said, under the leadership of "David" (Ezek. 34; 37; 47:13–48:29).[214]

The Jewish postbiblical literature reiterates many of the eschatological themes contained in the Hebrew Bible. While God has chastised Israel by giving the nation into the hands of her enemies, what lies ahead is the punishment or subjugation of the nations. Israel will be regathered "from east and west" (Bar. 4:37; 5:5). The book of Ben Sira calls on God to crush and destroy Israel's enemies, to "gather all the tribes of Jacob," and to "give them their inheritance, as at the beginning" (Sir. 36:11). Elijah is ready to act, "to restore the tribes of Jacob" (Sir. 48:10). In 2 Maccabees Jonathan prays to God to "gather our scattered people," to "set free those who are slaves among the Gentiles," to "look upon those who are rejected and despised," and to "afflict those who oppress and are insolent" (2 Macc. 1:27ff.). The text expresses a "hope in God that he will soon gather us from everywhere under heaven into his holy place" (2 Macc. 2:18). The *Psalms of Solomon* speak of the gathering of Israel from east, west, and north, as well as "from the isles afar off." This shows that God takes pity on Is-

---

214. References from Sanders, *Jesus and Judaism*, p. 79.

rael (*Pss. Sol.* 11). God will gather "a holy people" and "divide them according to their tribes upon the land" (17:28-31; cf. 8:34). A benediction is pronounced upon those who see what God does for his people: "Blessed be they that shall be in those days, in that they shall see the good fortune of Israel which God shall bring to pass in the gathering of the tribes" (17:50). The *Testament of Moses* speaks of the twelve tribes (*T. Mos.* 3:4; 4:9), as well as the punishment of the Gentiles and happiness of Israel (10:7).

In the text of the War Scroll from Qumran, the twelve tribes will be represented in the Temple service (1QM 2.2ff.), all the tribes will supply troops for battle (2.7ff.), and the army will be marshaled by tribes (3.13; 5.1). The conquering Israelites are known as "the poor" (11.13; 13.13f.). In the Temple Scroll twelve loaves are offered by the heads of the tribes (11QTemple 18.14-16). A thousand come from each tribe, making a total of twelve thousand (57.5f.). An expectation of the reassembly of the twelve tribes continues even after the destruction of the Temple in 70 C.E., as shown in the book of Revelation (Rev. 21:12) and in rabbinical writings (*t. Sanh.* 13:10; R. Eliezer).[215]

If one broadly compares the Hebrew Bible with the postbiblical literature, one finds some differences in emphasis. While a prediction of and a hope for the salvation of Gentiles do not altogether disappear in the postbiblical writings, they have a stronger and sterner stress than the biblical literature on the punishment to be inflicted on Gentiles. The same duality continues into the rabbinical period, where there is debate on whether Gentiles can be saved and, if so, which ones have a "portion in the world to come."[216] There is also a variation in the way the Jewish restoration is conceived. The canonical authors tend to focus their attention on the "remnant" that is saved, and this suggests that many of the Jews are not included in the restoration. The later texts tend to speak of a restoration of Israel as such, and not on its reduction to a "remnant." At the same time, the texts at Qumran have hard-line passages where the final war is against both the Gentiles and the "wicked of the covenant" (1QM 1.2). The general thrust of the Commentary on Habakkuk seems to be that the "breakers of the covenant" will be destroyed (1QpHab 2.6). Yet even in the Dead Sea Scrolls the hard line is sometimes softened, as for example in the passage which seems to teach that the suffering of the wicked Israelites, if they begin to obey the commandments, will atone for their misdeeds (1QpHab 5.3-6).[217]

---

215. References from Sanders, *Jesus and Judaism*, pp. 96-97.

216. While there is a saying attributed to R. Eliezer the Great that Gentiles are excluded from the life to come, it is opposed in the same passage by the saying of R. Joshua that the righteous Gentiles will indeed have a share in the life to come (*t. Sanh.* 13.2).

217. Sanders, *Jesus and Judaism*, pp. 97-98.

Judaism during the Second Temple period, across a range of differing parties, held to the expectation of a coming restoration by God. It would involve such features as a regathering of the twelve tribes, a return from exile, a renewal of the covenant, a rebuilding of the Temple, and possibly a repentance on the part of Gentiles as well. This Jewish background is germane to the interpretation of the Gospels, where Jesus preached "the kingdom of God," gathered together a group of followers that became known as the Twelve, and near the end of his life took decisive and controversial action at the site of the Temple. All these aspects of Jesus' life take on fuller meaning vis-à-vis the Jewish background. His disagreements with his contemporaries should be understood in light of his agreements. In light of the background sketched out above, a first and overriding question regarding Jesus' eschatology is: What exactly did Jesus mean by "the kingdom of God"?

The exact phrase "the kingdom of God" is extremely rare prior to Jesus. This is rather surprising, given that the general concept of God as king over creation, God as reigning, and God as extending his rule even over his rebellious creatures is a quite familiar idea in the Hebrew Bible and other ancient Jewish writings. Yet the precise phrase used in the synoptic Gospels to capture this general concept, "the kingdom of God," almost never occurs elsewhere. It does not occur even once in the Hebrew Bible, and there are only a few instances in Jewish Apocrypha and Pseudepigrapha, the Dead Sea Scrolls, Philo, Josephus, and the Targums. In the book of Psalms one finds instead many affirmations that "Yahweh reigns," as shown especially in the so-called enthronement psalms (e.g., Pss. 93, 96, 99). Even in the New Testament exclusive of the synoptic Gospels, there are relatively few occurrences of the phrase "kingdom of God." In the letters whose authorship by Paul is undisputed, there are only seven instances, and even here the phrase seems often to be a summary of traditional material that antedated Paul. One concludes then that the prevalence of the phrase "kingdom of God" in the synoptic Gospels does not derive either from pre-Christian Judaism or from first-century Christianity.[218] Thus the phrase "kingdom of God" easily satisfies the (rather too stringent) criterion of dissimilarity as well as the criterion of multiple attestation. It occurs all through the Gospels — in individual sayings, as well as parables and narrative passages. Unquestionably, then, the "kingdom of God" was central to Jesus' teaching.

One of the distinctive features of Jesus' kingdom of God is its range of meaning. It does not seem to have a single, univocal, easily identifiable definition. In a general sense the phrase is "meant to conjure up the dynamic notion of God powerfully ruling over his creation, over his people, and over the history of both . . . the kingdom of God means God ruling as king. Hence his action

---

218. Meier, *A Marginal Jew,* 2:9-10, 238-39, 244, 274 n. 18, 277.

upon and his dynamic relationship to those ruled, rather than any delimited territory, is what is primary."[219] Meier here is expounding a commonly accepted viewpoint among recent scholars that "kingdom" is not to be conceived in a static, substantive, or reified fashion, as a thing-in-itself or as a specific locality. Instead it is dynamic and fluid, like God's entire relationship to the world in general and his people in particular. Hence the phrase "God's reign" might capture the original meaning better than the time-hallowed English words "kingdom of God."

Many of the parables in the Gospels explain differing aspects of the kingdom of God. Moreover, the sheer variety and detail shown in these parables suggest that Jesus' perspective on the kingdom of God was not widely shared by others, and so had to be carefully explained.[220] Among these are the following parables: the sower and the soils (Matt. 13:3-23), the wheat and the tares (Matt. 13:24-50), the unforgiving servant (Matt. 18:23-35), the workers in the field (Matt. 20:1-16), the slighted wedding invitation (Matt. 22:1-14), the wise and foolish maidens (Matt. 25:1-13), the seed growing secretly (Mark 4:26-29), the mustard seed (Mark 4:30-34), and the yeast and the dough (Luke 13:20-21).

Some of the parables lay emphasis on the present time, and so seem to teach the *presence* of the kingdom. The "strong man" (i.e., Satan) has already been bound (Mark 3:27). The disciples of Jesus are like a man who has found a "treasure hidden in a field" and promptly purchases that land (Matt. 13:44), or like a merchant who sells all his possessions to purchase "one pearl of great value" (Matt. 13:45-46). Jesus requires the disciples of the kingdom to practice forgiveness here and now toward one another (Matt. 18:23-35). The marriage feast is prepared and ready, but most of the invited guests "would not come" (Matt. 22:3). The kingdom of God is like scattered "seed" that secretly grows while the one who sowed it sleeps (Mark 4:26-27), or like yeast that is causing a lump of dough to rise (Luke 13:21). In addition to the parables, some of the individual sayings of Jesus that are best authenticated and most distinctive make reference to the presence of God's kingdom. "But if it is by the Spirit of God that I cast out demons, then the kingdom of God has come to you" (Matt. 12:28). "Go and tell John what you hear and see: the blind receive their sight, the lame walk, the lepers are cleansed, the deaf hear, the dead are raised, and the poor have good news brought to them" (Matt. 11:4-5). "Blessed are your eyes, for they see, and your ears, for they hear. Truly I tell you, many prophets and

219. Meier, *A Marginal Jew*, 2:240.

220. The parables of Jesus will be discussed below, but two classic studies relate Jesus' parables to differing conceptions of the kingdom of God as present or as future, respectively: C. H. Dodd, *The Parables of the Kingdom* (New York: Scribner, 1961), and Joachim Jeremias, *The Parables of Jesus*, trans. S. H. Hooke, 3rd rev. ed. (London: SCM, 1972).

righteous people longed to see what you see, but did not see it, and to hear what you hear, but did not hear it" (Matt. 13:16-17). "Today this scripture has been fulfilled in your hearing" (Luke 4:21). "The kingdom of God is not coming with things that can be observed; nor will they say, 'Look, here it is!' or 'There it is!' For, in fact, the kingdom of God is among you" (Luke 17:20-21).

It is also evident that other Gospel texts stress the *future* arrival of the kingdom of God. The so-called Lord's Prayer is a key piece of evidence that the kingdom was in some sense yet to come: "Your kingdom come. Your will be done, on earth as it is in heaven" (Matt. 6:10).[221] Likewise, the Beatitudes stress the blessings that are yet to come to Jesus' followers. Those who mourn "will be comforted," the meek "will inherit the earth," those who hunger for righteousness "will be filled," the merciful "will receive mercy," and the pure in heart "will see God" (Matt. 5:4-8). Jesus speaks of the kingdom of heaven as a banquet in which "many will come from east and west and will eat with Abraham and Isaac and Jacob," while others "will be thrown into the outer darkness, where there will be weeping and gnashing of teeth" (Matt. 8:11-12). Another saying regarding the coming of the kingdom implies that it is yet to come: "Truly I tell you, there are some standing here who will not taste death until they see that the kingdom of God has come with power" (Mark 9:1). One of the more intriguing sayings relates to drinking wine in the kingdom of God: "Truly I tell you, I will never again drink of the fruit of the vine until that day when I drink it new in the kingdom of God" (Mark 14:25). The pièce de résistance of Schweitzer's argument in *The Quest of the Historical Jesus* was a verse in Matthew that seemed to predict the end of the world before the apostles had even finished their initial preaching tour: "Truly I tell you, you will not have gone through all the towns of Israel before the Son of Man comes" (Matt. 10:23).[222]

Numerous sayings and parables attributed to Jesus convey a situation of immediate crisis or impending judgment. "Those eighteen who were killed when the tower of Siloam fell on them — do you think that they were worse offenders than all the others living in Jerusalem? No, I tell you; but unless you repent, you will all perish just as they did" (Luke 13:4-5). "Do not weep for me, but weep for yourselves and for your children. For the days are surely coming when they will say, 'Blessed are the barren, and the wombs that never bore, and the breasts that never nursed'" (Luke 23:28-29). The sayings that refer to "en-

---

221. The concluding petition, "lead us not into temptation" (Matt. 6:13 RSV), might also have eschatological significance if the word "temptation" (Gk. *peirasmos*) refers to the final time of testing for the world.

222. See the discussion of this saying that John Meier judges to be authentic: "There is no hint of Jesus' death as atoning sacrifice, to say nothing of an explicit affirmation of his resurrection, exaltation, or parousia. In all this there is something disconcerting to Christian expectations" (*A Marginal Jew*, 2:308).

Michelangelo, detail from *The Last Judgment,* showing
Christ, the Madonna, and John the Baptist
(Sistine Chapel, Vatican; Alinari/Art Resource, N.Y.)

tering" the kingdom of heaven must also be understood in terms of futurity: the kingdom is not yet (Matt. 5:20; 7:21; Mark 9:43-48; 10:15; 10:23). Last but not least in possible importance are the "Son of Man" sayings that refer to the future coming (or parousia) of this figure (Matt. 19:28; 24:27, 37; Mark 8:38; 13:26; 14:62; Luke 12:8-9; 17:24, 26).[223] Scholars have called into question the authenticity of some of the sayings and parables cited above. The "Son of Man" sayings in particular are fiercely contested.[224] Yet the remarkable volume and variety of the teachings concerning the kingdom of God give it a central place in interpreting Jesus.

The scholarship of the past century has generated divergent interpretations of Jesus' teaching on the kingdom of God. The so-called "consistent eschatology"

223. References from Aune, "Eschatology (Early Christian)," p. 601.

224. Marcus Borg reports that 80 percent of the voting members of the Jesus Seminar have judged the coming "Son of Man" sayings to be inauthentic (Borg, *Jesus in Contemporary Scholarship,* p. 40 n. 53). The "Son of Man" theme will be taken up again toward the conclusion of the chapter.

of Johannes Weiss and Albert Schweitzer stressed the imminence of the kingdom of God. It "made an end of the modern [i.e., nineteenth-century] view that Jesus founded the Kingdom. It did away with all activity, as exercised upon the Kingdom of God, and made the part of Jesus purely a waiting one."[225] E. P. Sanders agrees with Schweitzer, at least to the extent that the kingdom of God for Jesus primarily referred to a future event.[226] Yet, as if in counterpoise to Weiss and Schweitzer, the "realized eschatology" of C. H. Dodd stressed a completely different aspect of the kingdom of God in the Gospels.[227] Though recognizing that Jesus sometimes referred to the kingdom as future, Dodd argued that Jesus' emphasis on the presence of the kingdom was the truly distinctive feature of his teaching. The "kingdom of God" was not apocalyptic, but rather "the manifest and effective assertion of the divine sovereignty against all the evil of the world." In Jesus' teaching, "history had become the vehicle of the eternal."[228] For Dodd the problem posed by the early Jesus movement was not the delay of the parousia, as for Weiss and Schweitzer, but rather how the imminent return of Christ ever became an integral feature of early Christianity. For Dodd the Fourth Gospel and the Epistle to the Hebrews retained the original emphasis on realized eschatology as taught by Jesus.[229] Problems overshadowed both Schweitzer's and Dodd's proposals, to wit: If Jesus had erred so monumentally by predicting the end of the world in his own day, then why should the early Christians or anyone else have taken him seriously? Alternatively, what sense is there in speaking of an eschaton (i.e., an end of the world) that is already present or realized? Is not "realized eschatology" a contradiction in terms?

A number of scholars, dissatisfied with the antithetical alternatives provided by Schweitzer on the one hand and Dodd on the other, proposed a model of "proleptic" or "inaugurated eschatology." Included in this school of thought are Joachim Jeremias, Oscar Cullmann, W. G. Kümmel, and G. E. Ladd. These authors acknowledge a certain tension or paradox in a kingdom that was "already but not yet." Not all sought to resolve the tension in the same way, but they were agreed that neither the present nor the future aspect of the kingdom was to be subsumed or dissolved into the other.[230] Generally they appealed to a

225. Schweitzer, *Quest,* p. 357.

226. Sanders, *Jesus and Judaism,* pp. 153-54. Sanders qualifies this somewhat by adding: "Just as we cannot say precisely what Jesus thought would happen in the future, so also we cannot say just what he thought was taking place in the present" (p. 154).

227. A good deal of debate centered on a single Greek word, *eggizō* (Matt. 3:2; 4:17; 10:7; Mark 1:15; Luke 10:9, 11), which some translated as "the kingdom of God *draws near*" and others as "the kingdom of God *is upon* you."

228. Dodd, *Parables of the Kingdom,* pp. 34-35, 159.

229. Aune, "Eschatology (Early Christian)," p. 600.

230. G. B. Caird seems to hold that there is not a tension between these two aspects

preponderance of evidence in the Gospels which, in the words of David Aune, "strongly suggests that Jesus himself understood the kingdom as provisionally present in his own person and message but that complete arrival of the kingdom of God was the object of imminent expectation."[231]

The debate among the three viewpoints mentioned — "consistent (i.e., imminent) eschatology," "realized eschatology," and "proleptic" or "inaugurated eschatology" — occurred on the basis of a shared assumption that the kingdom of God has had or will have fulfillment at a particular point in time. Yet some recent authors suggest that Jesus' teaching on the kingdom should not at all be understood with reference to time. An influential presentation of this perspective was Norman Perrin's *Jesus and the Language of the Kingdom* (1976), which modified the author's earlier position. Here he questions whether it is "legitimate to think of Jesus' use of Kingdom of God in terms of 'present' and 'future' at all."[232] The kingdom of God was not a concept or idea but a symbol that pointed Jesus' hearers toward "the manifestation of the reality of which it speaks in the concrete actuality of their experience."[233] Perrin distinguished two kinds of symbols. The kingdom of God was not a "steno-symbol" that has a simple one-to-one relationship with its referent, but rather a "tensive symbol" that conveys a reality without exhausting it.[234]

In certain respects Perrin continued many of the emphases of Bultmann's existentialist interpretation of the New Testament. Eschatology translates into anthropology — statements not about the cosmos, or society, but about the individual and his or her experience. Marcus Borg too, at least in some of his statements, interprets the terminology of kingdom in terms of religious experience or what he calls "eschatological mysticism," according to which the new

---

of the kingdom of God, but rather a semantic confusion in the discussion regarding them: "The debate between those who hold that Jesus declared the kingdom of God to have arrived and those who hold that he declared it to be imminent is reducible to its simplest terms when we recognise that the parties to the debate have differently identified the referent. If Jesus was referring to the final vindication of God's purposes in the reign of justice and peace, where the righteous are to banquet with Abraham, Isaac and Jacob (Matt. 8:11; Luke 13:28-29), it is mere nonsense even to suggest that this was present on earth when Caiaphas was High Priest and Pilate Governor of Judaea. On the other hand, if Jesus was referring to the redemptive sovereignty of God let loose for the destruction of Satan and all his works (Matt. 12:28; Luke 11:20), it makes nonsense of the whole record of his ministry to argue that for him this lay still in the future. And we have only so to state the matter to see that on various occasions Jesus referred to both" (Caird, p. 12).

231. Aune, "Eschatology (Early Christian)," p. 601.

232. Norman Perrin, *Jesus and the Language of the Kingdom: Symbol and Metaphor in New Testament Interpretation* (Philadelphia: Fortress, 1976), p. 40.

233. Perrin, *Jesus,* p. 43.

234. Perrin, *Jesus,* pp. 29-32.

age is the other realm of religious experience and "the phrase Kingdom of God is thus a symbol for the presence and power of God as known in mystical experience." Somehow the kingdom exists in a fashion that transcends time.[235] Borg's conclusions regarding the kingdom of God, like those of Perrin, are grounded in an understanding of the symbolic or mythic function of eschatological language. "Language about 'the other world,'" writes Borg, "is necessarily metaphorical and analogical, simply because we must use language drawn from the visible world to try to speak of another world constituted by very different realities and energies."[236]

Crossan's approach to the kingdom of God, like that of Borg and the later Perrin, does not fit comfortably into any of the three categories of imminent, realized, or proleptic eschatology. At points Crossan moves away from the notion of temporal reference, as for instance in his mind-teasing words regarding the village of Emmaus, where the Gospel of Luke (24:13-35) situates one of Jesus' postresurrection appearances: "Emmaus never happened. Emmaus always happens."[237] Resurrection language for Crossan symbolizes something that cannot be tied down to the events of a certain morning in first-century Palestine. Like Dodd though, Crossan sees the kingdom of God as already embodied or fulfilled in some sense in Jesus' own time. The kingdom comes not in individual and mystical experience, as in Borg, but rather in the new *social* experience of Jesus' followers, a "kingdom of nuisances and nobodies." Perhaps the most distinctive thing about Jesus' ministry in Crossan's presentation is his practice of "open commensality" in which different social groups — rich and poor, male and female, observant Jew and nonobservant — shared their meals in common. This was truly revolutionary, a ritual enactment of an inclusive kingdom that challenged the existing social hierarchy. Crossan distinguishes the apocalyptic conception of the kingdom from his understanding of it as "sapiential" (from Lat. *sapientia,* "wisdom"). "One enters that kingdom," he writes, "by wisdom or goodness, by virtue, justice, or freedom."[238]

On any hotly contested topic, the participants are often more likely to be correct in their affirmations than in their denials. This would seem to be the

---

235. Borg, *Conflict,* pp. 253-54, 259, 261. Borg acknowledges his debt to Huston Smith's "primordial tradition," and uses this as a framework for understanding Jesus (*Jesus in Contemporary Scholarship,* pp. 127-39). Somewhat akin to Perrin and Borg, Bernard Brandon Scott asserts that "kingdom" has no conceptual content, and that Jesus "experienced Kingdom" — an experience that cannot be expressed in discursive speech (*Jesus, Symbol-Maker for the Kingdom* [Philadelphia: Fortress, 1983], pp. 10-12, 29, cited in Sanders, *Jesus and Judaism,* p. 125).

236. Borg, *Jesus,* p. 28.

237. Crossan, *Jesus,* p. 197.

238. Crossan, *Jesus,* p. 56.

case in the recent discussions of the kingdom of God. Each of the major authors offers something worth considering, some partial insight into the whole, or some new angle of vision on the complex topic of Jesus' preaching of the kingdom of God. After reviewing the biblical texts related to the topic, it should be clear that the inaugurated or proleptic eschatology model provides a firmer grasp on a wider range of texts than either the imminent or realized eschatology theories. The consistent or realized eschatology theories require one to ignore a great many relevant texts, or else hypothesize a massive and systematic editing of the Jesus traditions to create the double-sided appearance of the texts on the kingdom as present and as still to come. By far the simpler explanation is that Jesus himself spoke of the kingdom of God in both these ways, and this today is probably the viewpoint accepted by a majority of New Testament scholars. This conclusion does not, however, negate either Schweitzer's or Dodd's insights. It merely suggests the need to coordinate or synthesize them in some fashion.

Regarding the conception of the kingdom of God as somehow transcending time or temporal reference, one must acknowledge Borg's point that the language of the kingdom has a metaphorical or analogical character. While all language has its metaphorical aspect,[239] this seems to be especially true of language about transcendent or spiritual realities — God, heaven, angels, nirvana, and so on. Of the various statements regarding the kingdom of God in the Gospels, those that seem to present the kingdom as already present — e.g., "the kingdom of God is among you" (Luke 17:21) — are most easily interpreted in a symbolic or nontemporal fashion. Yet the statements regarding the coming kingdom are not so easily interpreted in this way. Perrin's nontemporal kingdom is closer to Dodd's realized kingdom than to Schweitzer's imminent kingdom. In response to Perrin, Meier comments: "It does not follow that the kingdom of God, simply because it is a multifaceted tensive symbol, does not or cannot, in individual instances, convey a reference to the time of the kingdom's arrival. A time frame, however vague or mythic, was part of the underlying story of the kingdom evoked by the tensive symbol."[240] God's reign, in the Jewish background of Jesus, was a richly textured story of a good and ordered universe, the rebellion of creatures against the Creator, God's choice of Israel to be

---

239. When I say to my friend "I follow you," the physical act of coming after something else stands for the intellectual act of understanding her statement. George Lakoff and Mark Johnson, in *Metaphors We Live By* (Chicago: University of Chicago Press, 1980), make the following claim: "Most people think they can get along perfectly well without metaphor. We have found, on the contrary, that metaphor is pervasive in everyday life. . . . Our ordinary conceptual system, in terms of which we both think and act, is fundamentally metaphorical in nature" (p. 3).

240. Meier, *A Marginal Jew*, 2:242.

his people, the Exodus from Egypt, the kingdom as established under David and Solomon, and so forth. It is reasonable then to think that Jesus' references to the kingdom of God evoked, in the first instance, not an individual's private experience, or a mystical state of consciousness, or some ineffable reality beyond the space-time universe, but this cosmic narrative in which the creation of the world, the call of Israel, the coming of Messiah, and the consummation all unfold in temporal succession.

Crossan is correct in insisting that Jesus' "open commensality" with the marginalized people of his society was a distinctive feature of his life and teaching — a point to which we will later return. Yet this does not in itself imply that Jesus saw God's reign as fully actualized in his own ministry, or as fully visible in general experience to those who have the eyes to see. An earlier generation of scholars used to refer to this way of viewing the kingdom as "immanentizing the eschaton," and it is one of the problems with Crossan's presentation of Jesus. He seems to have resolved the tension of the kingdom that is present and still to come by eliminating the kingdom's future aspect. Also, Crossan's assertion that one enters the kingdom "by wisdom or goodness" is misleading. The kingdom of God is understood in the Gospel texts as a divine gift rather than a human achievement. The human response, which starts as repentance rather than wisdom or goodness, is evoked by the announcement of the kingdom.

In a summary statement on the kingdom of God, Bruce Chilton draws together a number of key assertions that have been treated above:

> Jesus' preaching of the kingdom is in the first place an announcement of God's dynamic rule. Human response, which might generally be described under the category of repentance, is performed as response, not initiating cause. The fact that the kingdom is normally a challenge of the future removes the possibility of understanding it within immanental terms of reference alone. The kingdom is immanent in so far as God's rule impinges upon, and elicits a response from, those who live in the present. At the same time, the kingdom cannot be reduced to human expectations of the future, any more than it can be reduced to human activities in the present.[241]

The kingdom of God as announced by Jesus had a future aspect. It was not simply present, but was still to come. At the same time it was present insofar as it elicited a response from Jesus' contemporaries. This kingdom involved human activity, and yet as a response to the prior initiative of God. Much of this is concentrated and encapsulated in the simple prayer of Matthew 6:10: "Your king-

---

241. Bruce Chilton, "The Kingdom of God in Recent Discussion," in *Studying the Historical Jesus*, pp. 255-80, citing 265.

dom come! Your will be done, on earth as it is in heaven!" Jesus sought to announce and exhibit the kingdom of God in actions as well as words, as should become clear in the ensuing discussion of miracles.

Healings, Exorcisms, and Other Works of Wonder

A discussion of miracles draws one immediately into the contrasting attitudes of most ancient people, who believed that miracles can and do happen, and many modern scholars, who deny this. The whole modern historical-critical approach to the life of Jesus in the late 1700s and early 1800s began in large part as a reaction against or reinterpretation of the alleged miracles of Jesus. Reimarus understood the miracle accounts in the Gospels to be the result of perceptual errors: Jesus was not really walking on the water, but a fog on the water led the disciples to see it in this way. David Strauss took a yet more radical approach when he treated the Gospel narratives as essentially "mythic." Properly understood, these texts were not attesting to extraordinary events, but rather to extraordinary insights that had been clothed in the form of miraculous narratives. Among more recent authors one sometimes finds blanket assertions of the impossibility of miracles, or at least the impossibility for contemporary or better-educated persons to affirm them. In the 1940s Bultmann declared that "it is impossible to use electric light and the wireless . . . and at the same time believe in the New Testament world of spirits and miracles."[242] Similarly Gerd Theissen has recently written: "Today we can no longer regard miracle stories as evidence of divine intervention in the normal course of things."[243]

One wonders who is included in Theissen's "we." He and all contemporaries? He and his German university colleagues? A recent cross-cultural study indicated that about 75 percent of the world's population believes in the existence of demons and the reality of demonic possession.[244] These people do not all fall into any single, readily distinguishable category, but are rich and poor, non-Western and Western, Ph.D. recipients and illiterate. So what Bultmann said is impossible — to use electricity and believe in spirits or miracles — is evidently not impossible.[245] Several billion people prove otherwise. So if miracles

242. Bultmann, "New Testament and Mythology," p. 5.

243. Gerd Theissen, *The Miracle Stories of the Early Christian Tradition,* trans. Francis McDonagh, ed. John Riches (Philadelphia: Fortress, 1983), p. 34.

244. Crossan, *Jesus,* p. 85.

245. Though Bultmann denied that modern people can believe in miracles, he seems to have had no problem affirming this for the ancients. After admitting that the miracle stories in the Gospels have "embellishments," he added: "But there can be no doubt that Jesus did the kinds of deeds which were miracles to his mind and to the minds

cannot be ruled out of bounds at the very outset by some kind of scholarly fiat, then there remains an important question of historical method. How is a historian to approach his or her sources when these record astonishing events that find no parallel in ordinary experience, and that cannot be explained in terms of natural processes as generally understood? What is to be said regarding such phenomena as sudden healings, exorcisms of demons, predictions of future events, or mind reading?

Perhaps the best general principle is to have no fixed general principle. Individual cases must be treated individually. Ernst Troeltsch argued that historical inquiry is based on a "principle of analogy," according to which each event in history bears some resemblance to all other events in history.[246] While this principle is useful, if applied too strictly it can become a kind of straitjacket. After all, there are plenty of surprises in human experience. There is a story that the king of Siam, after meeting some travelers from faraway Holland, was at first inclined to trust these men. Yet when they told him that in their homeland it sometimes got so cold that the rivers became hard as stone, and one could even ride horses on top of them, he knew that the men were liars. It is better not to prejudge. A historian must assess the evidence that pertains to the case at hand and then deliver some general judgment as to what sort of event has transpired. The "mad monk" Rasputin is said to have prayed for the son of the Russian czar, and at the moment he prayed the bleeding of the hemophiliac child ceased. This was confirmed by the Russian court physician himself — a rather credible witness — and the phenomenon happened repeatedly.[247] In a case like this, the historian may avoid playing the theologian by discussing the religious claims of Rasputin, but he or she is entitled to assert that something extraordinary occurred — something that no doubt changed the thinking of the royal family, and so, the course of Russian history. With regard to the alleged miracles of Jesus, it is historically credible to make the same sort of claim: something extraordinary occurred. The multitudes that flocked around Jesus were drawn not only by his teaching, but also by what Josephus referred to as Jesus' "surprising feats."[248] The early attacks on Jesus as a "magician" or "sor-

---

of his contemporaries, that is, deeds which were attributed to a supernatural, divine cause; undoubtedly he healed the sick and cast out demons" (*Jesus and the Word*, p. 173).

246. Ernst Troeltsch, "Über historische und dogmatische Methode in der Theologie" (1898), in *Gesammelte Schriften* (Tübingen: J. C. B. Mohr, 1922), 2:729-53.

247. Alex De Jong, *The Life and Times of Grigorii Rasputin* (London: Collins, 1982), pp. 136-42.

248. Josephus, *Antiquities* 18.3.3. Among the notable recent discussions of Jesus' miracles are the following: Meier, *A Marginal Jew*, 2:509-1038; Barry L. Blackburn, "The Miracles of Jesus," in *Studying the Historical Jesus*, pp. 353-94; Harold E. Remus, "Miracles (NT)," in *Anchor Bible Dictionary*, 4:856-69; Sanders, *Historical Figure*, pp. 132-68;

cerer" corroborate the point that Jesus was known for his remarkable powers.[249]

To gain a clearer understanding of the miracle stories related to Jesus, it is helpful first to consider the ancient context. In Jesus' day, just as today, those who suffered from serious illnesses often hoped for some kind of sudden recovery. Sometimes they sought healing from medical professionals or physicians, and yet in ancient times their reputation was not very high. As he approached his end, Alexander the Great is said to have remarked: "I am dying with the help of too many physicians!"[250] The Gospel of Mark (5:26) describes a woman who had suffered for twelve years with a hemorrhage and "had endured much under many physicians, and had spent all that she had; and she was no better, but rather grew worse." Those who needed help often turned to healing specialists other than physicians. Specially gifted persons, thought to have supernatural powers, were available to help. If the ailing wished to stay out of the hands of the physicians, then they (or their family and friends) could ask God or the gods directly for healing.[251]

Miraculous healings were reported in the Greco-Roman era among Jews and Gentiles alike. Hanina ben Dosa lived about a generation after Jesus, and the best-known cure attributed to him parallels that of the centurion's servant by Jesus (Matt. 8:5-13). The son of the great Pharisee Gamaliel was sick, and so he sent two of his disciples from Jerusalem to Hanina in Galilee to ask him to come and heal the boy. Instead Hanina went upstairs and prayed, and told the visitors to return, for the boy was well. Upon their return they found that he had returned to health at the exact hour of Hanina's prayer.[252] Among the Greco-Romans, the god Asclepius was well known as a healer.[253] The city of

---

Reginald H. Fuller, *Interpreting the Miracles* (Philadelphia: Westminister, 1963); Morton Smith, *Jesus the Magician* (New York: Harper & Row, 1977); and David Wenham and Craig Blomberg, eds., *Gospel Perspectives*, vol. 6, *The Miracles of Jesus* (Sheffield: JSOT Press, 1986). A discussion of the philosophical issues involved in the debate over miracles is contained in Colin Brown, *Miracles and the Critical Mind* (Grand Rapids: Eerdmans, 1984).

249. Early Christian texts indicate that both Jewish and pagan opponents derided Jesus as a magician: Justin, *Dialogue* 69.5; *First Apology* 30; Origen, *Contra Celsum* 1.6, 28, 38, 68, 71; 2.9, 14, 16, 48-49; 3.27; 5.51, 57; 6.77; 7.77; Tertullian, *Apologeticus* 21.17; 23.7; Arnobius, *Adversus nationes* 1.43; Lactantius, *Divine Institutes* 4.15.1. Jewish sources refer to Jesus' "sorcery": *b. Sanh.* 43a; *b. 'Abod. Zar.* 27b; *y. Shabb.* 14.4, 14d; *t. Hul.* 2:22-23; *y. 'Abod. Zar.* 2.2, 40d-41a. References from Blackburn, p. 361 n. 40, and Remus, p. 861.

250. J. M. Cohen and M. J. Cohen, *The Penguin Dictionary of Quotations* (Harmondsworth, Middlesex, England: Penguin Books, 1960), p. 3.

251. Sanders, *Historical Figure*, p. 135.

252. *b. Berakot* 34b.

253. For a fuller discussion see Emma Jeannette Levy Edelstein, *Asclepius: A Collection and Interpretation of the Testimonies*, 2 vols. (Baltimore: Johns Hopkins University

Epidaurus might be described as the Lourdes of the ancient Hellenistic world. Six pillars there contained inscriptions that described a variety of miracles that were alleged to have occurred. Some are rather fantastic, such as one about a woman who after five years of pregnancy gave birth to a four-year-old child. Others are more down-to-earth, such as the story of a certain Demosthenes who was lame in the legs and came to the shrine on a stretcher. As he lay down to sleep, he had a vision of God instructing him to spend four months in the shrine so that he might be healed. He remained on, and toward the end of his stay was able to dispense with his two canes and walk without any aid.[254]

In the ancient Greco-Roman world, erratic behavior was commonly attributed to demonic possession. Demons, conceived as independent spiritual forces of evil, were thought to take up residence inside a human body and dominate that person's thoughts, feelings, utterances, and actions. The only remedy for this miserable condition was the expulsion of the demon, or exorcism. In an age in which the spiritually or mentally disturbed typically lived with their family members, it is not surprising that exorcists were among the healing specialists most frequently sought out. The Jews were especially well known as exorcists. Josephus records the story of an exorcism performed by a Jew named Eleazar in the presence of the Roman general (and later emperor) Vespasian, in which he used a ring with special roots within it and invoked the name and incantations of Solomon.[255] It is worth noting that the Gospels attribute the practice of exorcism to persons other than Jesus. In Mark certain unnamed exorcists are using Jesus' name to cast out demons, and the disciples at first are inclined to discourage this kind of copycat exorcising (Mark 9:38-40). Also in the Acts of the Apostles there is a story about a botched attempt at exorcism by some Jewish exorcists who addressed the spirits "by the Jesus whom Paul proclaims" (Acts 19:13-17). The recently translated Greek magical papyri, containing various spells and incantations, include one that indicates that Jesus' name was used by Hellenistic exorcists: "I conjure you by the god of the Hebrews, Jesus."[256]

A specific case of demonic possession and exorcism is described in a Greco-Roman narrative, Philostratus's *Life of Apollonius*, which recounts the career of one of the most famous wonder-workers of the ancient world. In one

Press, 1945); K. H. Rengstorff, *Die Anfänge der Auseinandersetzung zwischen Christusglaube und Asklepiosfrömmigkeit* (Münster, 1953), and "Asklepios the Healer," in Howard Clark Kee, *Miracle in the Early Christian World: A Study in Sociohistorical Method* (New Haven and London: Yale University Press, 1983), pp. 78-104.

254. Fuller, p. 22.

255. Josephus, *Antiquities* 8.46-49.

256. Hans Dieter Betz, ed., *The Greek Magical Papyri in Translation*, 2 vols. (Chicago: University of Chicago Press, 1986), 1:96 (lines 3019-20), cited in Blackburn, p. 361.

episode a youth breaks out into such loud and coarse laughter that it drowns out the voice of Apollonius, and this elicits the following explanation: "And in fact the youth was, without knowing it, possessed by a devil; for he would laugh at things that no one else laughed at, and then he would fall to weeping for no reason at all, and he would talk and sing to himself. Now most people thought that it was the boisterous humour of youth which led him into such excesses; but he was really the mouthpiece of a devil, though it only seemed a drunken frolic in which on that occasion he was indulging." The story goes on to describe how Apollonius addressed the demon in the youth as a master does a servant, ordered it to come out, and after that the youth returned to his senses, and even took up a life of philosophical sobriety, modeled after Apollonius himself![257] In rough analogy to this, the Gospel of Mark includes the following description of a demoniac: "They came to the other side of the sea, to the country of the Gerasenes. And when he had stepped out of the boat, immediately a man out of the tombs with an unclean spirit met him. He lived among the tombs; and no one could restrain him any more, even with a chain; for he had often been restrained with shackles and chains, but the chains he wrenched apart, and the shackles he broke in pieces; and no one had the strength to subdue him. Night and day among the tombs and on the mountains he was always howling and bruising himself with stones" (Mark 5:1-5). Like the young man in the tale of Apollonius, the possessed individual here is isolated, antisocial, disruptive, and seemingly unable to control his own behavior. Mark goes on to recount how Jesus directed the demons to leave the possessed man, and they entered into the swine. In the conclusion to the story, the man is "clothed and in his right mind" (5:15), and then goes out "to proclaim in the Decapolis how much Jesus had done for him" (5:20). The demons depart, and the disruptive person is calmed, brought out of isolation, and given a socially useful function.

The four New Testament Gospels narrate some thirty-three specific miracles performed by Jesus. This does not include parallels among the Gospels, summary statements of miracle-working activity, and the events connected with Jesus' conception and birth, baptism, transfiguration, resurrection, and ascension.[258] The summary statements regarding healing occur frequently, and these suggest that healing was quite prominent in Jesus' public ministry (see Matt. 4:23-24; 8:16-17; 14:14, 35-36; 15:30-31; 21:14; Mark 1:32-34, 39; 3:10-12; 6:5, 55-56; Luke 4:40-41; 6:18-19; 7:21; 9:11; John 2:23). The Gospels distinguish healings from exorcisms. Not all healings were conceived of as exorcisms, and not all mala-

---

257. Sanders, *Historical Figure*, pp. 137-38.

258. Blackburn, pp. 353-54. This also does not include the miraculous catches of fish (Luke 5:1-11; John 21:1-11; Matt. 17:24-27), which might be seen as due to supernatural knowledge.

dies were thought to be caused by evil spirits.[259] The synoptic Gospels record about a dozen healings of specific conditions: fever (Mark 1:29-31), leprosy (Mark 1:40-45; Luke 17:11-19), paralysis (Matt. 8:5-13; Mark 2:1-12), a withered hand (Mark 3:1-6), bent back (Luke 13:10-17), hemorrhage (Mark 5:24-34), deafness and dumbness (Mark 7:31-37), blindness (Mark 8:22-26; 10:46-52), dropsy or edema (Luke 14:1-6), a severed ear (Luke 22:50-51), and a sickness near death (Luke 7:1-10).[260]

There are many Gospel passages that speak of demons and of exorcism. Jesus is said to have cast out a demon from a man in a synagogue (Mark 1:23-28; Luke 4:31-37), from a man possessed by a whole legion of demons (Matt. 8:28-34; Mark 5:1-20; Luke 8:26-39), from the daughter of a Syro-Phoenician woman (Matt. 15:21-28; Mark 7:24-30), from an epileptic child (Matt. 17:18; Mark 9:25; Luke 9:42), from his own follower Mary Magdalene (Luke 8:2), and from many other persons (Matt. 4:24; 8:16; 9:32-34; Mark 1:32-34, 39; 3:11; Luke 4:41; 6:18; 13:32). He engaged in controversy with some of the Jewish leaders over the source of his exorcistic power, after he had been accused of casting out demons on behalf of Beelzebul or Satan (Mark 3:20-30; Matt. 12:22-37; Luke 11:14-23). The Gospels report exorcisms done by persons other than Jesus (Matt. 7:22; 10:1, 8; 12:27; Mark 3:15; 6:7, 13; 9:38; Luke 9:1, 49; 10:17; 11:19). Jesus refers to the accusation that John the Baptist was demon-possessed (Matt. 11:18; Luke 7:33), and another saying describes how unclean spirits in leaving the body of their host search for another place to dwell (Matt. 12:43; Luke 11:24). It is notable that demonic possession and exorcism are not themes in the Hebrew Bible,[261] and their presence in the New Testament did not derive from its influence. Moreover, John the Baptist is not said to have cast out demons. After Jesus' day, Theudas and "the Egyptian" promised miracles, but Josephus does not say that either of them exorcised. Honi and Hanina, the Jewish holy men of this period, were also not known as exorcists. A comparison of Jesus with these contemporaries makes it clear that his practice of exorcism was distinctive.[262]

In addition to the healings and exorcisms, the Gospels record miracles of revivification — the raising of Jairus's daughter (Mark 5:21-24, 35-43), the raising of the son of the widow (Luke 7:11-17), and the raising of Lazarus (John 11:1-44). Another category of action by Jesus is the so-called nature miracle, which includes the following: the calming of the sea storm (Mark

---

259. Theissen, *Miracle Stories*, pp. 85-86.

260. Borg, *Jesus*, pp. 61-62, 65, 73 n. 28.

261. The evil spirit that tormented King Saul is an exception to the rule (1 Sam. 16:14-23; 18:10-11; 19:9-10), but even here there is no exorcism, properly speaking.

262. Sanders, *Historical Figure*, pp. 149-50 (for biblical references), and 152-53.

4:35-41), the feeding of the five thousand (Mark 6:30-44), Jesus walking on the water (Mark 6:45-52), the feeding of the four thousand (Mark 8:1-10), the cursing of the fig tree (Mark 11:12-14, 20-21), the coin in the fish's mouth (Matt. 17:24-27), and the wine miracle at Cana (John 2:1-11). Recently John Meier has questioned whether "nature miracle" is really a helpful or appropriate category, given that these stories have no common elements that link them together.[263] Perhaps the term should be regarded as a kind of miscellany that includes all the extraordinary actions of Jesus that are not healings, exorcisms, or revivifications.

Often scholars have treated the nature miracles differently from the healings and exorcisms, typically because the latter can be explained as psychosomatic cures while the former cannot be explained in terms of any ordinary causes. Another notable difference is that the nature miracles, unlike the healings and exorcisms, are said to have occurred only in the presence of the disciples. They are for their eyes only. As private events, they are akin to the postresurrection appearances of Jesus. This also suggests that nature miracles were not known to have played any role in Jesus' public ministry. Often the nature miracles show close affinities to Hebrew Bible themes. Jesus' revivification and feeding miracles are paralleled in the lives of Elijah and Elisha (1 Kings 17:17-24; 2 Kings 4:8-44). The stilling of the storm depicts Jesus in a role reserved only for God in the Hebrew Bible (Job 38:8-11; Pss. 65:7; 89:9; 107:23-32; etc.).[264]

The Gospel texts presuppose that there was some kind of relationship between Jesus' miracles and the crowds. The crowds are never really explained — they are just presupposed to be there, surrounding Jesus. Though Jesus may have drawn crowds by his teaching, it seems more likely that his public appeal in the first instance was based on his reputation as a wonder-worker. The career of Jesus follows a clearly comprehensible progression, as follows: miracles-crowds-teaching-tumult-death.[265] The early part of Mark's Gospel especially stresses Jesus' miracles. About two-thirds of Mark, prior to the story of Jesus' final week in Jerusalem, concerns the miraculous.[266] While Mark regularly mentions that Jesus was teaching, he gives relatively little information on what Jesus might have taught. Matthew and Luke for their part offer large blocks of sayings and parables, and this may give the reader the impression that Jesus made his mark chiefly as a teacher. Yet the immediate impression made by the Gospel of Mark may be closer to the viewpoint of Jesus' first audience: he was known as a

263. Meier, *A Marginal Jew*, 2:874-77.
264. Blackburn, pp. 370-71, with n. 78.
265. Sanders, *Jesus and Judaism*, p. 164.
266. Borg, *Jesus*, p. 71.

worker of miracles.[267] John Meier notes that no miracles were attributed to John the Baptist, and adds: "To be blunt, without miracles, one wonders how much popularity this particular Jewish preacher and teacher [i.e., Jesus] would have enjoyed. Without miracles, many Palestinian Jews might have seen Jesus merely as a more 'upbeat' version of John the Baptist."[268]

One of the most characteristic features of Jesus' miracles is the way he connects them with his teaching on the kingdom of God. In controversy with the Jewish leaders, they accuse him of exorcising demons by the power of Satan, and he retorts: "But if it is by the finger of God that I cast out the demons, then the kingdom of God has come to you" (Luke 11:20; cf. Matt. 12:28). Bultmann regarded this utterance as claiming "the highest degree of authenticity which we can make for any saying of Jesus,"[269] because of the unusual way it combines the kingdom of God with the activity of exorcism. Gerd Theissen agrees with this: "Jesus is unique in religious history. He combines two conceptual worlds which had never been combined in this way before, the apocalyptic expectation of universal salvation in the future and the episodic realisation of salvation in the present through miracles."[270] This link between miracles and the kingdom of God is a point of distinction between Jesus and other ancient figures to whom wonderful deeds were attributed.[271]

The stories of Jesus' healing usually stress the faith of those seeking the

---

267. Burton Mack is one of the very few who hold that Jesus in his lifetime was not known as a wonder-worker. According to Mack, nothing in the Gospel miracle tradition has any basis in Jesus' life (*A Myth of Innocence*, esp. pp. 75-77, 91-93, 215-24).

268. Meier, *A Marginal Jew*, 2:4.

269. Bultmann, *Synoptic Tradition*, p. 162.

270. Theissen, *Miracle Stories*, p. 278. "Jesus sees his own miracles as events leading to something unprecedented. They anticipate a new world" (p. 280).

271. Geza Vermes, *Jesus the Jew*, pp. 58-82, interprets Jesus on analogy with other charismatic Jewish healers. Yet this misses the connection between Jesus' miracles and the kingdom of God. His interpretation suffers from other difficulties as well (Blackburn, pp. 376 n. 101, 379). (1) Only two figures are clearly Galilean — Jesus and Hanina — and this is hardly enough to create a whole category of Galilean miracle worker. (2) The source for Hanina's life (i.e., the Palestinian Talmud) dates to about three hundred years after his life. (3) Miracle working was probably only incidental to the lives of these Jewish sages. In fact, miracles were attributed to other Jewish sages as well, and so the boundaries of Vermes' religious type are blurry. Successful prayers for rain were attributed to Rabbi Aqiba as well. (4) Jesus never procured rain, which is the only miracle common to the other figures belonging to Vermes' type. (5) There is no evidence that any of them except Jesus conducted an itinerant ministry. (6) In the whole Gospel tradition, Jesus is only once portrayed as *praying* prior to the miracle, while for Honi and Hanina the situation is just the reverse. Meier notes that a person who prays for and awaits a miracle by God is not in the strict sense a "miracle-*worker*" (*A Marginal Jew*, 2:536). The Gospels present Jesus as working wonders by his own power. See note 178.

healing. The miracles were granted to those with "faith," which might refer to those who accepted Jesus' proclamation of the kingdom or, at the least, believed that he had received the power to bring healing. In Mark Jesus declared to the woman with the hemorrhage, "Daughter, your faith has made you well" (Mark 5:34). This statement is frequently repeated. Yet in the Gospel accounts it is not always a "faith healing" by virtue of the faith of the sick person. Sometimes it is the faith of those surrounding the sick person that is decisive. In the healing of the paralytic (Mark 2:1-12), Jesus healed when he "saw their faith" (v. 5), that is, the faith of those who brought the man to be healed. In a number of the healings we have a record of the Aramaic word used in the healing (e.g., *talitha cum*, Mark 5:41). Jesus rebuffed those who demanded a miraculous sign for him to legitimate himself (Mark 8:11-13), and he performed only a few miracles in Nazareth because of the villagers' unbelief (Mark 6:5). The Gospel statement regarding Jesus' inability to perform miracles at Nazareth — "he could do no deed of power there" — would have been jarring to early Christian sensibilities, and so the saying easily meets the criterion of embarrassment as discussed above. In conclusion then, neither the curious nor the hostile could expect miraculous aid from him. The further implication is that Jesus did not perform miracles as proofs of the truthfulness of his message or as a way of vindicating his own authority.

In response to Morton Smith's book *Jesus the Magician* (1978), there has been discussion regarding the terms "miracle" and "magic," whether the two are synonymous, and, if not, which might be better applied to Jesus' actions. Smith argued that Jesus belonged to the social type that encompassed such figures as Apollonius of Tyana and the nameless persons who used the formulas that appear in the Greek magical papyri. He bases this in part on certain details in the Gospels, such as curing by touch, sighing, the use of foreign language formulas, and exorcistic techniques (e.g., Jesus' asking for the name of the demon; Mark 5:9). Crossan has supported Smith's claim in suggesting that "magic" is simply a pejorative label applied to miracles that occur among groups considered marginal, disreputable, or somehow déclassé. "*We* have religion while *they* have magic," writes Crossan. "Magic is especially a term that upper-class religion uses to denigrate its lower-class counterpart."[272] The point is that the same phenomenon can be described appreciatively or disparagingly. (During wartime one hears of the "noble heroism of our troops" and the "savage fanaticism of the enemy," and yet the behavior may be almost identical.)

From an anthropological perspective, however, it is possible to classify

---

272. Crossan, *Jesus*, p. 104. Robert Grant writes: "In polemical writing, your magic is my miracle, and vice versa" (*Gnosticism and Early Christianity*, 2nd ed. [New York, 1966], p. 93, cited in Remus, p. 859).

different sorts of wonder-working along a kind of continuum with magic at one end and miracle at the other. Characteristically the magician is someone who possesses a more-or-less automatic power by virtue of secret formulas and rituals. In magic there is a resultant coercion of divine or spiritual powers by human beings, who in turn receive a tangible solution to some practical problem. Usually magic is marked by individualism or a kind of spiritual entrepreneurship, rather than an enduring community of faith. Religiously speaking, it has an ad hoc character. Miracle, by contrast, suggests faith in a personal deity to whom an individual submits his or her own will in prayer. It is also associated with a perduring religious community and a public manifestation of God's presence and power that is not dependent on any set ritual or formula. Along these lines, Howard Clark Kee has observed that preternatural phenomena take on a different significance depending on whether the context is Jewish monotheism or Greco-Roman polytheism. The framework of meaning is different in the two cases. When the focus lies on the communication of human beings with higher powers, the phenomenon is religious in character and the extraordinary event in question may be termed a miracle. When the focus lies on the functioning of forces that have been placed at the disposal of human beings, we find ourselves in the realm of magic.[273]

Magic and miracle, defined and distinguished in this way, represent ideal types that rarely occur in isolation from one another. Within the Greek magical papyri, which contain spells and incantations from the Hellenistic period, there are also prayers and humble supplications offered to the gods, and so these texts exhibit the characteristics of both magic and miracle as they have been defined here. Likewise, in the Gospels the actions attributed to Jesus sometimes have magical characteristics, as for instance when Jesus heals by spitting on the ground and forming clay to apply to the eyes of a blind man (John 9:6-7; cf. Mark 7:31-37). Saliva and other substances often play a role in facilitating the healings performed by magicians. Also when a woman is healed by simply touching the fringe of Jesus' garment, this is in accord with popular Hellenistic conceptions.[274] Yet in general the miracles attributed to Jesus are marked by their simplicity and lack of spoken verbal formulas or other elaborate ritual processes. They fit the overall pattern of miracle better than that of magic.[275] Furthermore, it is clear that Jesus understood his works of power to be directly

273. Kee, *Miracle*, pp. 62-64, 170, 211-18, and Howard Clark Kee, *Medicine, Miracle, and Magic*, in *New Testament Times*, Society for New Testament Studies Monograph Series, 55 (Cambridge and New York: Cambridge University Press, 1986), pp. 95-125.

274. Ernst Käsemann (*Essays*, p. 96) notes that the same notion of a healing garment later occurs with reference to Paul (Acts 19:12), and that even the shadow cast by Peter was thought to be able to heal the sick (Acts 5:15).

275. Meier, *A Marginal Jew*, 2:11-12.

related to the kingdom of God that he announced (Matt. 12:28), and the notion of magic has essentially nothing to do with the coming of God's reign. Perhaps Jesus could appropriately be called a wonder-worker, a term that acknowledges both his similarity to, and difference from, the magicians of the Hellenistic age.[276]

Many of the miracles attributed to Jesus are rich in symbolic significance. That is, quite apart from the historical value of the Gospel narratives, the events as described address fundamental issues faced by those living in the first century. The most detailed exorcistic account of all, in Mark 5, has a good deal of encoded information. It has both political and spiritual meanings. The name of the demon, or rather horde of demons, is "Legion" — a title that signifies Roman dominance. The demons are consigned to the swine, which were regarded as the most impure of all the impure animals. The swine are then cast into the sea — surely the dream of every Jewish resister of the Romans.[277] On another level the story speaks of deliverance from impurity or uncleanness. The details in the narrative all contribute to a sense of the man's defilement. His home is in the Gentile region. The spirits in him are "unclean." He lives "among the tombs," where contact with corpses would have made him ceremonially impure. Swine are feeding nearby. Even the comment that he was "gashing" or "bruising himself with stones" (v. 5) suggests a flow of blood on his skin that would have rendered him yet more impure. Everything in his environment bespeaks uncleanness. Yet Jesus exercises authority over this manifold impurity, the man is freed from demons, and his cleansing is consummated when he is told to "go home to your friends" (v. 19).[278]

In the eyes of his contemporaries, what would Jesus' miracles have signified? Modern people have generally misunderstood the ancient outlook on miracles. The defenders of Christianity have often adduced the miracles as proof that Jesus was more than merely human, and was none other than the incarnate Son of God. With the rise of Deism in the eighteenth century, some have viewed the miracles as obviously fictional and have concluded therefore that the Christian faith is based on a fraud. "Both of these extreme views,"

---

276. Did Jesus heal while he was in some kind of altered state of consciousness? There is a reference in Mark 3:20-21 to Jesus being "beside himself" (RSV). This could denote some kind of trance or visionary state, although the context in Mark does not make it altogether clear. Morton Smith takes this as a reference to Jesus' "abnormal behavior": "Magicians who want to make demons obey often scream their spells, gesticulate, and match the mad in fury" (*Jesus the Magician*, p. 32). Yet these verses in Mark are a rather slender basis for Smith's claim. For a critique of Smith's views, see Walter Wink, "Jesus as Magician," *Union Seminary Quarterly Review* 30 (1974): 3-14.

277. Crossan, *Jesus*, p. 90.

278. Borg, *Jesus*, p. 72 n. 12.

writes E. P. Sanders, "miss the ancient perspective, which saw miracles as strik-ing and significant, but not as indicating that the miracle-worker was anything other than fully human."[279] Blackburn notes that there is almost no evidence in the synoptic Gospels that Jesus ever performed his miracles to establish his sta-tus as God's spokesperson. While it is true that the Acts of the Apostles speaks of the miracles as showing that Jesus was "attested . . . by God" (Acts 2:22), this statement is in the context of the early Christian proclamation of Jesus and not in the context of Jesus' own life. To reiterate an earlier point, the really distinc-tive thing about Jesus' miracle working is its link with the coming reign of God. The saying in Luke 11:20 (Matt. 12:28) is unparalleled in either Jewish or early Christian literature: "But if it is by the finger of God that I cast out the demons, then the kingdom of God has come to you." Jesus viewed his own "startling deeds" (Josephus) as signs of the kingdom and its coming.

Teachings: Sayings and Parables

As a teacher Jesus was unconventional both in the style and the content of his message. At the same time, his teachings contain frequent references to and re-flections on the Hebrew scriptures, and this suggests that he did not fundamen-tally reject the legal and wisdom traditions that he inherited as a Jew, but rather built upon them in his own teaching. Some scholars have even questioned whether there is any specific element of Jesus' teaching that is completely un-paralleled among the Jewish sages of his day or the centuries immediately fol-lowing.[280] The task here is to unravel what was distinctive in Jesus as a teacher and set him apart from others and, on the other hand, what connected him to the traditions of his time and place. To anticipate the conclusion, if there is something unique about Jesus, it is probably the particular *combination* of ele-ments in his teachings and actions. Others, like the great Jewish sage Hillel, in-sisted on the need to love one's neighbor, and the first century had its exorcists, healers, and even some who announced that God would soon intervene to de-liver the people of Israel. Yet these elements are all combined in a characteristic

---

279. Sanders, *Historical Figure,* p. 132.

280. See the comparative study of Jesus with the great first-century Jewish sage Hillel: James H. Charlesworth and Loren L. Johns, eds., *Hillel and Jesus: Comparative Studies of Two Major Religious Leaders* (Minneapolis: Fortress, 1997). Perhaps the best-known point of comparison is between Jesus' "golden rule" ("Do to others as you would have them do to you," Matt. 7:12) and Hillel's reported response to a Gentile convert to Ju-daism who wanted a short summary of the Torah: "What is hateful to you, do not to your neighbor: that is the whole Torah, while the rest is the commentary thereof; go and learn it" (*b. Shabb.* 31a).

way in Jesus, and all enter into some relationship with his teaching on God's reign or kingdom.

In the first century a teacher would typically have been thought of as someone who offered instruction in a school. In Jesus' day there were some schools, especially in urban areas, where young people in their earlier years would spend their mornings learning the basics of reading and writing. After about age twelve, only the boys of wealthier families could continue their education, and it would have been customary for them to learn the classic texts and to seek to imitate famous orators of the past. Jesus, by contrast, did not establish a school with a philosophical doctrine or a special method of interpreting the Torah. His followers learned by observing what he said and did in different situations. Another distinctive of Jesus is that his message to the crowds and his message to his disciples do not seem to have differed. Sometimes, to be sure, the Gospels present Jesus giving further explanations of his sayings and actions to his most intimate followers (e.g., Matt. 13:1-53). Yet he was no esotericist, holding to a secret doctrine that was known only to a group of initiates.[281]

Jesus' call for others to follow him must be understood in its historical context. Most of those who accepted Jesus' preaching probably saw it as consistent with their accustomed way of life. At the same time, there was a group of disciples who made a break with their homes, families, villages, and a settled existence. In today's mobile society it is not all that shocking to hear of people who change their place of residence, exchange one job for another, or even leave behind family and friends in order to move to another part of the world. Yet, as Pheme Perkins notes: "In Jesus' time such forms of 'uprooting' were evidence that disasters like war and famine had destroyed the traditional society of villages and towns. In that society children followed the occupations of their parents unless displaced by natural disaster, war, or enslavement. People lived in the same community for generations. . . . The traditional villager would have been quite shocked to have Jesus and his followers break with the ancestral ways of life."[282] It comes as no surprise that the Gospels portray Jesus' relatives as concerned about him (Mark 3:21) and his enemies as accusing him of insanity (John 10:20). In that time and culture, any person who broke with his or her family and home territory would have experienced a loss of identity. Almost everything about a person was determined by the place of birth and the patterns of social relationship into which he or she was born. Yet Jesus defends himself

---

281. Pheme Perkins, *Jesus as Teacher* (Cambridge: Cambridge University Press, 1990), pp. 1-2.

282. Perkins, *Jesus as Teacher,* pp. 27-28. See also the discussion of Jesus' itinerancy as a teacher in Martin Hengel, *The Charismatic Leader and His Followers,* trans. J. C. G. Greig (Edinburgh: T. & T. Clark, 1981), pp. 35-37.

Rembrandt, *Christ Teaching (La Petite Tombe)*
(Kunstgeschictlichen Institut der Phillips-Universität; Foto marburg/Art Resource, N.Y.)

by insisting that his own preaching and healing are a sign that God's reign is destroying the power of Satan. He also insists that one's birth family and blood relationships are not ultimate. Eclipsing these in importance is one's relationship to God, and to other people through that relationship to God.[283] Jesus expressed this point rather stingingly when he announced: "'Who is my mother, and who are my brothers?' And pointing to his disciples, he said, 'Here are my mother and my brothers! For whoever does the will of my Father in heaven is my brother and sister and mother'" (Matt. 12:48-50).

Jesus' distinctiveness as a teacher can be grasped if we think of the context of first-century Palestine and the conventional wisdom that prevailed within this society.[284] At the heart of this ancient culture, as with almost any premodern culture, was a commitment to sacred traditions, or ways of thinking, acting, and feeling that were widely accepted within the society and seen as

283. Perkins, *Jesus as Teacher,* pp. 28-29.
284. In the following paragraphs I am indebted to the penetrating discussion in Borg, *Jesus,* pp. 81-91.

directly sanctioned by God. Living in accord with wisdom was a path of righteousness and blessing, while departing from it brought ruin and death. While some believed in rewards and punishments beyond the present life, there was no consensus on the matter. The great concerns of conventional wisdom in Jesus' day were family, wealth, honor, and religion, and this wisdom functioned by establishing social boundaries. Jews were distinguished from Gentiles, and also from Samaritans. More specific social distinctions existed between landowners and laborers, rich and poor, priests and laypersons, fathers and elder (or younger) sons, husbands and wives, and males and females generally. Those who followed the traditions were commended as righteous, and those who defied them were regarded as wicked. An underlying dynamic of this society is captured in Marcus Borg's phrase "the politics of holiness," wherein "to be holy meant to be separate from everything that would defile holiness."[285] The conventional wisdom of the culture had increasingly become structured around polar oppositions between clean and unclean, purity and defilement, sacred and profane, Jew and Gentile, righteous persons and sinners.

This "politics of holiness" was an intensification of a cultural trend that had begun after the restoration from exile. In the period of the Babylonian exile and return, Israel's survival as a people depended on maintaining a sense of separate identity, and this in turn required the Jews to accentuate the practices and beliefs that made them distinct. Moreover, the Jews had passed through a period of suffering and exile that the classical prophets attributed to God's anger, resulting especially from the people's adherence to foreign gods. Following the return from exile, many of the Jews were determined to be faithful to God and so to avoid another outpouring of divine judgment. As a small social group — and a conquered one at that, bereft of kingship and other national institutions — the Jews were in grave danger of assimilating into the surrounding cultures. Such has been the fate of most small social groups in history, and the culturally eclectic Hellenistic world would have made it quite easy for the Jews, if they had so wished, to blend in, intermarry with Gentiles, worship their gods and goddesses, and adopt Gentile customs. The Maccabean revolt of the second century B.C.E. was provoked in no small measure by the effort of the ruler, Antiochus Epiphanes IV, to force the Jews to adopt Hellenistic culture and religion. The quest for holiness was thus especially attractive for the Jews because both God and worldly prudence seemed to require it. It was the path of both religious fidelity and social survival. Thus "holiness" became the paradigm by which the Torah was interpreted. Interpreters of the Torah laid special emphasis on those portions of the law that spoke of the Jews' separateness from other peoples.

285. Borg, *Jesus*, p. 86.

The Pharisees, discussed above, were simply the most conspicuous instance of the drive toward holiness in this society. Their concern for strict tithing and for observing the food laws led them to limit contact with Gentiles as well as with nonobservant Jews. Some of the Pharisees may have believed that the nonobservant Jews had lost their standing as Jews, and had in effect turned themselves into Gentiles. To be faithful to the law as they understood it, the Pharisees had no choice but to practice a kind of social ostracism. While the Gospels contain references to the Pharisees as "hypocrites" (e.g., Matt. 23:13, 15, 23, 25, 27, 29), these should not be taken to mean that the Pharisees were not sincere in their beliefs and practices. What we know or surmise about the Pharisees from the various sources at our disposal would seem to indicate that they were passionately committed to fulfilling the letter of the ancient law. In fact, a point often overlooked is that the burden of Jesus' criticisms of the Jewish teachers in Matthew 23 is not that they are completely wrong but that they have failed to follow through on their own principles. "Do whatever they teach you and follow it; but do not do as they do, for they do not practice what they teach" (Matt. 23:3).[286] The point is that Jesus' disagreements with the Jewish leaders of his day — and disagreements there must have been, or else he would not have died as he did — were grounded in certain basic agreements. Jesus did not reject the Torah, but he interpreted it in a new way and presented a differing conception of holiness.

Jesus' novelty as a teacher appears in his critique of the key elements of the conventional wisdom of his day. In some subtle or overt fashion, he challenged the dominant ideas regarding family, wealth, honor, and religion. The family had tremendous importance in ancient Judaism, and indeed in almost all traditional societies. In a largely agricultural society, it was the primary economic unit. It was also the basis for an individual's identity, as each person was known as "the son (or daughter) of so-and-so." Yet many of Jesus' sayings challenged the idea of the family as an end in itself. At certain points in his teaching Jesus was ready to set the kingdom of God and its values in direct competition with those of the family.[287] Crossan even speaks of Jesus' "attack on the family."[288] One of his most radical sayings relates to the practice of burial, which was thought to be the most sacred of duties for a child to fulfill on behalf of parents. "To another he [i.e., Jesus] said, 'Follow me.' But he said, 'Lord, first let me go and bury my father.' But Jesus said to him, 'Let the dead bury their own

---

286. While the authenticity of the sayings in Matt. 23 is contested by scholars, it is not very plausible to imagine that the early Christians would have invented a saying in which Jesus says to "do whatever" the Pharisees say.

287. Borg, *Jesus*, p. 104.

288. Crossan, *Jesus*, p. 59.

dead; but as for you, go and proclaim the kingdom of God'" (Luke 9:59-60).[289] Some sayings attributed to Jesus seem to be disparaging toward his own family members (Luke 8:19-21; 11:27-28), and yet public criticism of one's family was not acceptable behavior within that society. Some other radical sayings concerning the family are found in Matthew: "Whoever loves father or mother more than me is not worthy of me; and whoever loves son or daughter more than me is not worthy of me; and whoever does not take up the cross and follow me is not worthy of me. Those who find their life will lose it, and those who lose their life for my sake will find it" (Matt. 10:37-39).

Such statements would have been even more scandalous and shocking in the first century than they are today. They presuppose a conflict between Jesus' followers and others, and seem to show disrespect for family members by insisting that loyalty to Jesus must come first. Most extraordinary of all, the words focus attention on Jesus himself, as Jacob Neusner has noted: "Here is a Torah-teacher who says in his own name what the Torah says in God's name." Jesus' form of address is distinctive, since "sages . . . say things in their own names, but without claiming to improve upon the Torah. The prophet, Moses, speaks not in his own name but in God's name, saying what God has told him to say. Jesus speaks not as a sage nor as a prophet."[290] The attributed sayings of Jesus raise many challenging questions of interpretation: What exactly is the kingdom of God, and what is the basis of its ethical claim? In what way does God's reign hold priority over other interests and loyalties? Does Jesus disparage or diminish the importance of human relationships if they are not somehow brought within the scope of God's reign? If the kingdom is God's kingdom, then is it Jesus' too? Or what relationship of Jesus to God is implied in Jesus' attributed words? Why does Jesus speak in the way that he does?

In Jesus' society, as in most, wealth and possessions were a major source of security and identity. Though the Jews of that era recognized that unrighteous people could have great wealth, the more fundamental idea was that great wealth was a sign of blessing from God. Yet Jesus regularly criticized wealth, and even is reported to have said that no one could be his disciple if he did not give up all his possessions (Luke 14:33). He told unfavorable stories about the pursuit of wealth, such as the so-called parable of the rich fool (Luke 12:16-21):

> The land of a rich man produced abundantly. And he thought to himself, "What should I do, for I have no place to store my crops?" Then he said, "I

289. See the discussion of Luke 9:59-60 in Sanders, *Jesus and Judaism,* pp. 252-55, and in Perrin, *Rediscovering,* p. 144.

290. Jacob Neusner, *A Rabbi Talks with Jesus: An Intermillennial, Interfaith Exchange* (New York: Doubleday, 1993), pp. 30-31.

will do this: I will pull down my barns and build larger ones, and there I will store all my grain and my goods. And I will say to my soul, 'Soul, you have ample goods laid up for many years; relax, eat, drink, be merry.'" But God said to him: "You fool! This very night your life is being demanded of you. And the things you have prepared, whose will they be?" So it is with those who store up treasures for themselves but are not rich toward God.

Jesus is said to have shocked his closest followers when he said: "How hard it will be for those who have wealth to enter the kingdom of God! . . . It is easier for a camel to go through the eye of a needle than for someone who is rich to enter the kingdom of God" (Mark 10:23, 25). It is not clear that Jesus opposed wealth in principle, and among his followers there may have been some rich persons, such as wealthy women (Luke 8:1-3) and Joseph of Arimathea (Mark 15:43). Yet clearly Jesus saw the possession of wealth as a major hindrance to his message concerning God's reign, and viewed greed as one of the passions that blinded people to God and spiritual realities.[291]

Another pivotal value of Jesus' day was honor. To some extent it was the product of birth, family, and wealth, but also it was regularly sustained by social recognition. Honor was not exactly the same thing as social status, since it referred to the regard or esteem in which one was to be held by others in light of one's status. A good deal of time and energy went into the effort to acquire, preserve, and display one's honor. Yet Jesus disparaged and even ridiculed the pursuit of honor, speaking against those who sought the places of honor at a banquet (Luke 14:7-11), the best seats in the synagogue (Matt. 23:6), or respectful greetings in the marketplace (Matt. 23:7). Jesus also spoke against religious practices that were motivated by a desire for social recognition (Matt. 6:1-6, 16-18). "Whenever you give alms, do not sound a trumpet before you" (Matt. 6:2). He even went so far as to claim that those who sought public recognition for their good deeds would have no recognition from God: "They love to stand and pray . . . so that they may be seen by others. Truly I tell you, they have received their reward. But whenever you pray, go into your room and shut the door and pray to your Father who is in secret; and your Father who sees in secret will reward you" (Matt. 6:5-6). Honor — the community's recognition of the individual — was a hindrance and a snare for Jesus' followers.[292]

Closely connected with honor was religion, and it might be regarded as the crowning aspect of conventional wisdom. The Jews regarded themselves as sons and daughters of Abraham and Sarah, and so their physical descent made them also heirs of the covenant and its promises. To the Israelites, wrote the

291. Borg, *Jesus*, pp. 104-5.
292. Borg, *Jesus*, p. 105.

apostle Paul, "belong the adoption, the glory, the covenants, the giving of the law, the worship, and the promises; to them belong the patriarchs, and from them . . . comes the Messiah" (Rom. 9:4-5). By accepting their spiritual heritage and obeying the commandments of the Torah, the Jews stood within the covenant and shared in its assurances of blessing by God and an intimate relationship with God. Yet many of Jesus' harshest sayings are directed against religious persons and religious practices. For Jesus, no one can count on his or her own religious practice as a basis for security with God. Penitence, or a humble recognition of one's unworthiness before God, was more important to Jesus than an outward conformity to the letter of the law. Consider the prayer that Jesus put on the lips of the Pharisee: "God, I thank you that I am not like other people: . . . I fast twice a week; I give a tenth of all my income" (Luke 18:11-12). This Pharisee does not seem to be a hypocrite in the usual sense, i.e., someone who said one thing and did another. Instead he is a model of what a faithful Jew should have been according to the strictest standards of the day. Yet Jesus' remarkable declaration was that the Pharisee did not go to his house "justified," but rather the tax collector who was too ashamed even to raise his eyes to heaven. The clear message is that no one can find security in religious practice, but only in the mercy of God.[293]

To understand Jesus' teaching, it is not enough to note where he differed from and critiqued his contemporaries. He was not a free-floating iconoclast who delighted in unmasking the follies of others but provided no alternative wisdom. On the contrary, the Gospel texts are rich in sayings and parables that delineate a way of life for Jesus' followers. One of the hallmarks of this way, as Marcus Borg has noted, is a call to *transformation*.[294] A purely outward or behavioral change was never enough for Jesus. His teaching again and again returns to the idea that people must change at their deepest level, or rather be changed, for them to live in a fashion that is pleasing to God. Jesus often spoke of "hearts" being either soft or hard, good or bad, pure or impure. The term "heart" here, in accord with its Hebrew background,[295] does not refer as in English to emotions only, but to the deepest aspects of the self. The "heart" represents the self in its innermost inclinations, where mind, affect, and will all coalesce into one. According to Jesus, the "heart" is where the problem resides: "This people honors me with their lips, / but their hearts are far from me" (Mark 7:6, quoting Isa. 29:13). Rather than actions making the person good or

293. Borg, *Jesus*, pp. 105-6.

294. Borg, *Jesus*, pp. 108-16.

295. See Friedrich Baumgärtel and Johannes Behm, "*kardia*, etc.," in *Theological Dictionary of the New Testament*, ed. Gerhard Kittel, 10 vols. (Grand Rapids: Eerdmans, 1964-74), 3:605-14.

bad, Jesus taught the reverse, that the actions of a person flowed from the "heart" or essential character. "Either make the tree good, and its fruit good; or make the tree bad, and its fruit bad; for the tree is known by its fruit" (Matt. 12:33). "A good tree cannot bear bad fruit, nor can a bad tree bear good fruit" (Matt. 7:18).

It is striking how often Jesus' teaching makes reference to death, and these references are usually in the context of a general call for the transformation of the self. The disciples must "deny themselves and take up their cross" (Mark 8:34). "Those who find their life will lose it, and those who lose their life for my sake will find it" (Matt. 10:39). In Mark both "drinking the cup" and "baptism" are images for the death that Jesus and his followers must undergo (Mark 10:38-40; cf. Luke 12:50). "Unless a grain of wheat falls into the earth and dies, it remains just a single grain; but if it dies, it bears much fruit" (John 12:24). In its positive aspect, Jesus' teaching offered the prospect of a transformed self and a transformed way of thinking and acting. Yet in its negative aspect, it required that the disciples renounce falsehood and leave behind their former selves and former lives. "Dying" is a metaphor that stresses the once-for-all and decisive nature of the transformation intended in Jesus' teaching, as Borg explains: "A hardened heart must in a sense die in order that a new heart may be created; it cannot change itself. 'Dying' is something that happens to the self as opposed to it being something that the self accomplishes."[296]

The death metaphor in Jesus' sayings shows that his teaching has a renunciatory and world-denying character. Yet this was not based on a dualistic understanding of the material or natural world. Jesus' sayings contain no hint that he negatively viewed the physical or material world and favored and commended the spiritual world instead. Rather he seems to have delighted in the natural world as God's creation, and he appealed to his hearers to "look at the birds of the air" and "consider the lilies of the field" (Matt. 6:26, 28). One must also bear in mind the ordinariness, the quotidian quality, of the parables and sayings. They reflect a careful and caring observation of daily life, and they suggest apt analogies between ordinary experience and spiritual realities. The parables and sayings of Jesus are not what one would expect from a man who was hostile or indifferent to the present life or felt himself an alien or stranger in it.

Jesus was not an ascetic in the usual sense, since he was reputed to enjoy food and drink and his opponents contrasted him unfavorably with John the Baptist in this respect (Matt. 11:16-19).[297] Though apparently Jesus never married,[298] his teaching does not reflect any opposition to sexuality as such. This is

296. Borg, *Jesus*, p. 113.
297. Borg, *Jesus*, p. 114.
298. William E. Phipps, *Was Jesus Married? The Distortion of Sexuality in the Chris-*

rather remarkable in that philosophical and religious movements of a world-denying character almost always involve some denigration of the body and of bodily appetites, and especially of sexuality. Such antisexual sentiment is usually accompanied by a denigration of women as spiritual hindrances to men or as agents of carnal temptation. Despite a brief reference to "eunuchs" who forsake marriage for the sake of God's kingdom (Matt. 19:12), Jesus' teaching is remarkable for its lack of antisexual sentiment. Jesus' followers were to renounce lust and a wandering eye (Matt. 5:27-30), just as they were to renounce covetousness and greed, but they were not in general called upon to abstain from sexual life. Dale Allison's recent book on Jesus contains an extended argument in favor of regarding Jesus as an "ascetic" in light of the fact that he asked some individuals to give away their money and goods, sent out itinerant preachers with less than the bare essentials for survival, and himself forsook work, family, and a stable home. The question hinges in part on the definition of the term "ascetic," and there is no question that Jesus' teaching involved a call to renunciation and was often very rigorous indeed.[299] My point is that Jesus' teaching — however one labels it — did not reflect any opposition to the material world as such, or to the body and to sexuality.

Jesus' teachings reflect a fresh observation of the social and natural worlds and the affairs of everyday life. "They have the ring of originality," writes C. H. Dodd. "They betray a mind whose processes were swift and direct, hitting the nail on the head without waste of words." In all of Jesus' teachings, there is a "sense for the concrete" and a "delight in imaginative picture-making."[300] The parables reflect a wide range of accurate observation, an eye for human affairs that was sympathetic and yet unsentimental. The parables depict human virtues — the affec-

---

tian Tradition (New York: Harper & Row, 1970), argued that Jesus may have been married as a youth and that his wife may have died before his ministry began. The most important argument is from the consideration that this was the normal pattern for Jewish males. Yet, as we have already noted, some of the Essenes did not marry, and there are traditions about some of the biblical prophets (Jer. 16:1-4) and later rabbis (e.g., Ben Azzai; *b. Yeb.* 63b) remaining unmarried. So there were exceptions to the practice of early marriage, and in any case it is not very sound to argue that a general custom must apply to the life of every individual within a society. See Meier, *A Marginal Jew*, 1:332-45.

299. See Allison, pp. 172-216. Allison defines "asceticism" as "the practice of the denial of the physical or psychological desires in order to attain a spiritual ideal or goal" (p. 172), and this description surely applies to Jesus' teaching. Yet such a definition is probably too broad to be useful, for almost all religious groups would thereby qualify as "ascetic." Vincent L. Wimbush, Richard Valantasis, and Elizabeth Clark all stress the difficulty in providing a useful cross-cultural definition of the term "asceticism," in Wimbush and Valantasis, eds., *Asceticism* (New York: Oxford University Press, 1995), pp. xix-xxxiii, 505-10.

300. C. H. Dodd, *The Founder of Christianity* (New York: Macmillan, 1970), pp. 37, 39.

tion of a father for his wayward son (Luke 15:11-32), the devotion of a shepherd to his flock (Luke 15:3-7), and the compassion of a passerby for a man robbed and left to die (Luke 10:29-37). At the same time, the parables also show the odd mixture in human motives — a man arises at midnight to help a friend, but only because the friend was making a pest of himself (Luke 11:5-8), and a dishonest servant about to be dismissed cuts a business deal that defrauds his master and yet still evokes the master's praise because of his shrewdness (Luke 16:1-9). The parables have a down-to-earth quality. To speak colloquially, they exhibit horse sense or "street smarts." They rest on the assumption that spiritual matters are not alien to worldly concerns, but can and should be understood on analogy with them. "The principles of human action," writes Dodd, "fall within a universal order . . . to be recognized at any level by those who have eyes to see and ears to hear. No circumstance of daily life is too trivial or too commonplace to serve as a window into the realm of ultimate values, and no truth too profound to find its analogue in common experience."[301]

One of the important yet neglected aspects of Jesus' teaching is the frequent presence of humor, paradox, wit, and irony.[302] Through most of the history of Christianity, the exalted view of Jesus held within the church resulted in a rather solemn and even sanctimonious image of him. The impression was certainly not that of a witty or entertaining individual. Yet there is no need to think that humor is necessarily a sign of frivolity, or that humor always seeks laughter as an end in itself. Within the Jewish tradition, even the most serious subjects have often been treated in humorous stories. As an oral teacher addressing himself to largely rural and illiterate audiences, Jesus' wit may have played a strategic role, so that the "twinkle in Jesus' eye" became "that most effective device for puncturing the pomposity of those grave authority figures."[303] Humor is often a sign of intellectual freedom, of detachment from fixed categories, and of the ability to view human affairs from multiple perspectives and so perceive the incongruities of life. These qualities were necessary for Jesus' followers to grasp the significance of the elusive reality he referred to as the kingdom of God.

The sense of humor is a highly individual phenomenon, and also closely tied to language, time, and place. So the sayings and parables that may have seemed humorous to Jesus' contemporaries may not be so to us, and vice

301. Dodd, *The Founder of Christianity*, p. 41.

302. One of the few studies of this subject is Jakob Jonsson, *Humour and Irony in the New Testament; Illuminated by Parallels in Talmud and Midrash* (Leiden: Brill, 1985).

303. Krister Stendahl, foreword to Jonsson, p. 6. Stendahl adds: "Perhaps there is a good deal of continuity between the Sages of the Synagogue and Woody Allen. . . . And even between Jesus and Woody Allen — although a student of the Western theological tradition must wonder where the humor went" (p. 6).

versa.[304] Yet it is still possible to note some statements that appear comic, ironic, or paradoxical. Some of Jesus' best-known statements are paradoxical word pictures, and occasionally the image evoked by the words borders on the absurd. A person blinded by an object that is stuck in his eye is hardly in a position to perform a delicate operation on another person's eye! "Or how can you say to your neighbor, 'Let me take the speck out of your eye,' while the log is in your own eye?" (Matt. 7:4). While God can change someone's hair color, humans cannot (at least in Jesus' day): "You cannot make one hair white or black" (Matt. 5:36). When blind people lead the blind, both fall into a pit (Matt. 15:14). Harsher in tone is the saying about the scrupulosity of the religious leaders: "You strain out a gnat but swallow a camel!" (Matt. 23:24).[305] Sometimes Jesus' paradoxes reveal some aspect of the kingdom of God: "Whoever wishes to be first among you must be slave of all" (Mark 10:44). The widow who had only two small coins to contribute to the Temple actually gave more than the wealthy with their large sums of money (Mark 12:41-44). Jonsson notes that these "paradoxes show that from the common point of view the life of the kingdom is in many ways contrary to the present aeon."[306]

Jesus was sometimes ironic, as in the saying at the time of his arrest: "Have you come out with swords and clubs to arrest me as though I were a bandit?" (Matt. 26:55). There is also an ironic saying associated with Jesus' visit to his hometown: "Doctor, cure yourself!" (Luke 4:23). At other times Jesus' irony was like that of Socrates, who posed questions that forced others to reassess their own opinions or question themselves and their values. This feature of Jesus' teaching becomes especially evident in the conflict stories regarding his final week in Jerusalem. When asked regarding the source of his authority, he responded to the question with another question: "Did the baptism of John come from heaven, or was it of human origin?" (Matt. 21:25). The refusal of his inter-

---

304. Some readers may have had the experience of going to a film or theater performance in a foreign country and finding that everyone else was laughing at things that were not funny and not laughing at things that were funny.

305. This saying may refer to the desire on the Sabbath day to avoid all killing (thus straining one's beverages before drinking them), since killing could be considered a form of work.

306. Jonsson, p. 176. Some other possibly humorous texts include the lamp (probably a Sabbath light) placed under a basket to be hidden (Matt. 5:15); the man who loses both coat *(himation)* and cloak *(chiton)* — and so is rendered naked (Matt. 5:40); giving children not bread but a stone, a serpent, or a scorpion to eat (Matt. 7:9-10; Luke 11:11-12); the gathering of grapes from thornbushes (Matt. 7:16); a house foolishly built on sand (perhaps in a dried-out riverbed; Matt. 7:26-27); looking in the Judean desert for a dandy dressed in fine clothes (Matt. 11:8); a person who started to build a house with no plan for it (Luke 14:28-30); a slave who sits to eat before the master does (Luke 17:7-10); a judge who is at the mercy of a pesky and persistent widow (Luke 18:1-8).

locutors to answer him showed that their minds were already made up. Likewise, the interchange regarding the "Son of David" (Matt. 22:41-46) has a Socratic flavor to it, since Jesus elicits a response from others but then from the response draws out a further and unanticipated question.

Perhaps the best-known and most celebrated aspect of Jesus' teaching was his use of parables.[307] Prior to Jesus the Hebrew literary tradition made frequent use of the *mashal*, a term that referred to a similitude or comparison and had a very wide range of meaning.[308] An example in the Hebrew Bible is found in the Song of the Vineyard, where Israel is compared to a vineyard and God to the keeper of the vineyard (Isa. 5:1-7). Although he took excellent care of the vine, it bore only worthless grapes. The story issues in God's call to "judge between me / and my vineyard" (v. 3). As this example shows, the genre of parable combines the qualities of narrative, metaphor, and brevity. The point of a parable is to tell, as concisely as possible, a story having a double meaning. One meaning is usually quite clear on the surface of the narration. Another, and presumably deeper meaning, lies hidden within the complexities of the narrative. The underlying meaning or meanings are a challenge for the recipient to consider and interpret the words. "Parables," as Crossan says, "are lures for interpretation."[309]

One of the debated points regarding the Gospel parables concerns the presence of allegory within some of the parables. In allegory there is a whole set of correspondences between elements in the story and certain persons or objects in actual life. Thus, to use the familiar parable of the prodigal son (Luke 15:11-32), one can attempt to identify the father, the runaway son, and the elder brother with certain persons or certain types of person. Since the pioneering study of the parables by Adolf Jülicher at the close of the nineteenth century,[310] there has been a tendency to interpret the Gospel parables as stories having a single, clearly defined point, and thus a single, clearly defined point of comparison. Any apparent allegory in the Gospel texts, on this view, comes from the later expansion and redaction of the original sayings of Jesus. More recently scholars are not quite so certain about this point, and today many accept that

---

307. On Jesus' parables see Bernard B. Scott, *Hear Then the Parable* (Minneapolis: Fortress, 1989); J. Dominic Crossan, "Parable," in *Anchor Bible Dictionary*, 5:146-52; Craig L. Blomberg, "The Parables of Jesus: Current Trends and Needs in Research," in *Studying the Historical Jesus*, pp. 213-54; and the previously mentioned standard works, Jeremias, *The Parables of Jesus*, and Dodd, *The Parables of the Kingdom*.

308. See David Stern, *Parables in Midrash* (Cambridge: Harvard University Press, 1991).

309. Crossan, "Parable," p. 147.

310. Adolf Jülicher, *Die Gleichnisreden Jesu im allgemeinen* (Freiburg: J. C. B. Mohr, 1899).

some of the parables as delivered by Jesus may have contained allegorical elements.[311]

The genre of parable or *mashal* in the Hebrew Bible tradition was broad enough to include many different kinds of comparisons, ranging from short pithy sentences to lengthier narratives and allegories. The New Testament parables are comparably varied in their form, as indicated within a single chapter, such as Mark 4. The section opens with "he began to teach them many things in parables" (v. 2) and concludes by saying that "with many such parables he spoke the word to them" (v. 33). Yet within these two framing statements are both narrative parables (the sower, vv. 3-8; the harvest time, vv. 26-29; the mustard seed, vv. 30-32) and brief aphoristic parables (lamp and bushel, v. 21; measure for measure, v. 24). Both types of parables include the warning: "Let anyone with ears to hear listen!" (vv. 9, 23). The most famous of Jesus' parables are the extended narratives, such as the prodigal son (Luke 15:11-32) and the good Samaritan (Luke 10:25-37). Since Jesus was an oral teacher, it is quite possible that the Gospel texts are in effect plot summaries of stories that took much longer for Jesus to tell his audiences.

Crossan, following Axel Olrik's work on oral storytelling, has identified some recurrent features in Jesus' parables. There is a "law of three" that appears in the path, the rocks, and the thistles of the parable of the sower (Mark 4:3-8), and also a "law of twins" whereby the first two servants in the parable of the talents (Luke 19:11-17) and the first two travelers in that of the good Samaritan (Luke 10:29-37) are in contrast to the third. The "law of contrasts," that is, of clearly polarized protagonists, appears in numerous parables: in the farmer and his enemy in the parable of the wheat and weeds (Matt. 13:24-30), in the rich man and Lazarus (Luke 16:19-31), in the Pharisee and the publican (Luke 18:10-13), in the former and latter guests of the parable of the marriage feast (Matt. 22:1-13), and in the wise and foolish bridesmaids (Matt. 25:1-13). An obvious feature of Jesus' parables is their normalcy — they speak of the realities of ordinary life in Galilee, of the weeds that spring up in a field along with the wheat, of a peasant woman who goes looking for a lost coin, of a rich farmer whose barns are filled with a bumper crop, and so forth.[312]

---

311. Blomberg, p. 235, based on David Stern's study of the Jewish *mashal*, notes that the typical pattern of the *mashal* was a division into two components — the *mashal* proper and the *nimshal*, an appended explanation that usually identifies or otherwise enables an identification of the main characters, objects, or events with God, Israel, historical events, etc. This may help to account for the parabolic explanations that occasionally occur in the Gospels (e.g., Matt. 13:3-8 with 13:18-23, and 13:24-30 with 13:36-43). "Such explanatory material fell well within the range of what Jewish interpreters expected the *mashal* to do, [and] ought not to be viewed as misrepresenting original intent" (p. 235).

312. Crossan, "Parable," pp. 147-50.

Together with their everyday quality, the parables of Jesus also point toward matters that are far from ordinary. Many of the parables relate to judgment. They are replete with dramatic images of crisis, reward, and retribution. The parables speak of the winnowing of wheat from chaff and the fire that burns up the chaff (Matt. 13:40-42), the owner of a vineyard who destroys his rebellious tenants (Matt. 21:33-44), and the household servant who is suddenly called to account for his stewardship (Matt. 24:45-51). There are maidens who awaken to find that their lamps have gone out (Matt. 25:1-13), people shut out of a banquet because they did not respond in time or came wearing inappropriate garb (Matt. 22:1-14), and a barren tree that is to be chopped down unless it bears fruit (Luke 13:6-9). Jesus' teaching is also filled with images of things that have lost their proper function. The foolish servant buries his money in the ground rather than investing it (Luke 19:11-27). Salt loses its taste and so must be thrown out (Matt. 5:13). A lamp shines and yet is hidden away under a basket so that its light cannot be seen (Matt. 5:14-16). Jesus judged that Israel had become unfruitful and was not as God had intended for it to be. The leaders of the people were "blind guides of the blind" (Matt. 15:13-14). They followed a policy of business as usual, unaware of the crisis and the opportunity facing them.[313]

Jesus' parables not only called for interpretation but also personal or existential response. Their insistent and challenging tone is one of their most distinctive features, as John Meier explains:

[Jesus'] parables (meshalim) served to tease the minds of his audience, throw them off balance, and challenge them to decide for or against his claim on their lives. The parables are not pretty Sunday-school stories. They are troubling riddles, meant to destroy any false sense of security and create a fierce feeling of urgency. Any moment may be too late: the hearer must stake all on Jesus' message now, no matter what the cost. For God is about to work his own kind of revolution: the poor will be exalted and the powerful dispossessed. This startling and disturbing program is at the heart of the parables. . . . It is a promise of radical reversal.[314]

The parables were linked with Jesus' proclamation of the kingdom of God: "The kingdom of heaven is like . . ." (Matt. 13:31, 33, 44, 45, 47). They called for a change of heart and a change of behavior in light of God's reign.

313. Borg, *Jesus*, pp. 156-58.
314. John Meier, "Reflections on Jesus-of-History Research Today," in *Jesus' Jewishness: Exploring the Place of Jesus in Early Judaism*, ed. James H. Charlesworth, The American Interfaith Institute (New York: Crossroad, 1991), p. 92.

The parables and sayings show that judgment and grace were both important themes within the teaching of Jesus. The primary thrust is to highlight the mercy and grace of God. God grants forgiveness to the penitent, and grants it apart from their attaining some level of spiritual or moral performance. Mercy is what God delights in. God is "long-suffering," or slow to condemn and reluctant to judge, and correspondingly quick to forgive and ready to receive sinners. When the prodigal son returns, the father comes running to meet him (Luke 15:20). In this respect Jesus' presentation of God is in accord with that of the Hebrew prophets. The book of Hosea presents God as profoundly ambivalent, both inclined to bring judgment on his erring people and reluctant to do so:

> How can I give you up, Ephraim?
>   How can I hand you over, O Israel? . . .
> My heart recoils within me;
>   my compassion grows warm and tender.
> I will not execute my fierce anger. (Hos. 11:8-9)[315]

Nonetheless, the God of Jesus' parables and sayings exercises judgment and does so decisively. One of the shibboleths of the Victorian era books on Jesus was the repudiation of the theme of judgment. Even a cursory study of the attributed sayings and parables of Jesus shows how lopsided this interpretation was, how much it represented a modernizing of Jesus' teaching to suit a later audience.

One of the striking features of Jesus' teaching is its frequent reference to, and commentary upon, the texts of the Hebrew Bible. Bruce Chilton and Craig Evans comment that "the sense of his teaching is often inaccessible unless its scriptural underpinnings are appreciated."[316] Some of the scriptural citations in the Gospels did not originate with Jesus himself but emerged in the transmission of the Gospel traditions. In an environment in which scriptural language and imagery were the common vehicles for religious reflection and discourse, references to the Bible would naturally appear in a presentation of Jesus' life and significance. The Gospel of Matthew is an especially important case where scriptural citations are frequently used to show that Jesus fulfills the

---

315. Abraham Heschel, in his classic study *The Prophets,* 2 vols. (New York: Harper & Row, 1962), shows how these individuals not only *saw* the world differently than others but *felt* differently as well (esp. 1:ix-xv, 3-26). They not only knew God intellectually but felt the feelings of God — including God's anger at sin and compassion for those who suffer. Jesus appears much like a Hebrew prophet when he sees the city of Jerusalem and weeps at the thought of the coming judgment (Luke 19:41-44).

316. Bruce Chilton and Craig A. Evans, "Jesus and Israel's Scriptures," in *Studying the Historical Jesus,* pp. 281-335, citing 281.

prophecies of the Hebrew Bible. Matthew has a formula for his scriptural citations: "This was to fulfill what had been spoken by the Lord through the prophet" (Matt. 2:15; cf. 1:22-23; 2:17-18, 23; 4:14-16; 8:17; 12:17-21; 13:35; 21:4-5; 27:9).[317] Nonetheless, it would be mistaken to conclude that Jesus himself never cited scripture in connection with his sayings and parables. There is wide agreement among New Testament scholars that the stringent sayings in the Gospels prohibiting divorce (Mark 10:11-12) are a departure from the general Jewish teaching on divorce and certainly go back to Jesus himself.[318] Yet these sayings attributed to Jesus are closely interwoven with scriptural citations that are also attributed to Jesus, and so there is good reason to think that Jesus on some occasions cited scripture to make his points. He may not have been a typical "Torah sage," as Marcus Borg rightly notes, but this does not mean that reference to scripture was not a part of his public teaching.[319]

Even where Jesus is not quoting the Hebrew scripture, the manner of his argumentation often shows an affinity to that of the rabbinical tradition. Certain principles of interpretation or midrash were common among the rabbis, and some of them are exemplified in Jesus' sayings. One must be careful about prematurely drawing conclusions, since the rabbinic principles seem only to have been formalized in the period of redefinition after 70 C.E. At the same time, it is probable that some of these principles were already in common use in Jesus' day. A number of "measures" (Heb. *middoth;* sg. *midda*) were later attributed to the first-century sage Hillel. According to *qal wa-chomer* (light and heavy), what is true or applicable in a "light" or less important instance is surely true in a "heavy" or more important case. As God cares for the birds, so he will also care for Jesus' followers (Matt. 6:26; Luke 12:24). If God clothes the grass of the field, he will also provide clothing for human beings (Matt. 6:30; Luke 12:28; cf. Matt. 7:11; Luke 11:13). According to *gezera shawa* (equivalent regulation), one passage may be explained by another if similar words or phrases are present. In Mark 11:17 Jesus is said to have quoted phrases from Isaiah 56:7 and Jeremiah 7:11. What connects these two passages is the word "house" that occurs in the quoted verse from Isaiah and in an unquoted part of the verse from Jeremiah.

According to *binyan 'ab mikkatub 'echad* (constructing a father from one [passage]), a general principle may be established from one key verse or phrase. Since God is not the God of the dead but of the living, "I am the God of Abraham," as spoken at the burning bush (Exod. 3:14-15), implies that Abraham is

---

317. See the discussion in Graham Stanton, "Matthew," in *It Is Written: Scripture Citing Scripture,* Essays in Honour of Barnabas Lindars, ed. D. A. Carson and H. G. M. Williamson (Cambridge: Cambridge University Press, 1988), pp. 205-19.

318. Meier, *A Marginal Jew,* 1.171-72. See the rabbinical discussion of divorce in *b. Gittin* 90a; *m. Gittin* 9:10.

319. Borg, *Jesus,* p. 98.

to be resurrected. From this one text one may infer that there is a general resurrection. According to *kelal uperat uperat ukelal* (general and particular, and particular and general), general interpretations can be inferred from specific statements in scripture, or specific interpretations can be inferred from general statements. Thus the commandment of love (Mark 12:28-34) is a general commandment that sums up all of the particular commandments. According to *dabar halamed me'inyano* (a word of instruction from its context), the meaning of a given passage must be clarified by its context. This rule is exemplified in Jesus' teaching on divorce (Matt. 19:3-8; Mark 10:2-9).[320]

Despite these points of contact with the Judaic tradition, Jesus' references to and reflections on the Hebrew scriptures differ from the common rabbinical approaches. As Chilton and Evans observe, "Jesus was not a rabbi in the sense of the mishnaic authorities, but his approach to Scripture was governed by his sense of fulfillment."[321] This brings us back, once again, to the overriding significance for Jesus of the kingdom of God. Even the sacred scriptures, whose authority Jesus does not seem to have challenged in principle, had to be viewed in a new light because of the eschatological fulfillment that was a part of Jesus' proclamation of the kingdom of God. "Today this scripture has been fulfilled in your hearing" (Luke 4:21). The sense of fulfillment becomes most obvious in what John A. T. Robinson referred to as Jesus' "challenging use" of scripture, where he does not so much argue over the correct interpretation of a passage, or use a text to prove a point, as pronounce a text as a challenge.[322] Usually such challenges are posed as interrogatives: "Have you not read?" (Mark 2:25; 12:10, 26; Matt. 12:3, 5; 19:4; 21:16, 42; 22:31; Luke 6:3), "What do you think?" (Matt. 22:42), or a simple "How?" (Mark 9:12; 12:35; Matt. 22:43; Luke 20:41). Often these questions are posed to the disciples as well as to Jesus' opponents, and this militates against reading them simply as a part of the early church's polemic against Pharisaic Judaism.[323] Yet these sayings do show how Jesus' sense of eschatological fulfillment was linked to the conflicts that characterized his ministry — a subject we will now consider in greater detail.

Career and Controversies

Having examined Jesus' works of wonder and the general character of his teachings, we turn now to what might be called Jesus' career. One thing known with

320. Chilton and Evans, "Jesus and Israel's Scriptures," pp. 287-96.
321. Chilton and Evans, "Jesus and Israel's Scriptures," p. 296.
322. John A. T. Robinson, "Did Jesus Have a Distinctive Use of Scripture?" in *Twelve More New Testament Studies* (London: SCM, 1984), pp. 35-43.
323. Chilton and Evans, "Jesus and Israel's Scriptures," pp. 309-10.

certainty is that he died by crucifixion at the hands of the Roman authorities, and it seems just as certain that he died under the charge of being "the king of the Jews."[324] Given the character of the actions already discussed — healing and exorcising — and the nature of his teachings — stressing God's love and acceptance for the unworthy — the outcome of Jesus' life is rather surprising, and one of the chief aims in interpreting it is to show how and why he died as he did.

The Gospels present Jesus as very popular and influential with the multitudes, and yet not winning favor with everyone. The "woes" he pronounced on the cities of Chorazin, Bethsaida, and Capernaum show that these cities did not respond to him in the way he had hoped or expected (Matt. 11:20-24). Also there are traditions that Jesus was rejected in his hometown of Nazareth (Mark 6:1-6). As mentioned earlier, Jesus does not seem to have gone out of his way to enter the larger urban areas, and this is rather surprising. His frequent travels from place to place and his willingness to face opposition indicate a strong sense of mission,[325] and this might well have led him directly to the cities where there was the greatest concentration of wealth, power, and influence. Yet it seems that Jesus did not reckon the effectiveness of his ministry as modern people might, in terms of winning over the greatest number of the most influential individuals. Instead Jesus spent his time with the same people he had known his entire life — village dwellers, craftsmen, tradesmen, farmers, and fishermen. His mode of life, according to the Gospels, was itinerant. Or, in the words of one of the more memorable utter-

324. It is highly unlikely that the tradition regarding Jesus as "the king of the Jews" originated with the early disciples. See the discussion in Nils Alstrup Dahl, *The Crucified Messiah and Other Essays* (Minneapolis: Augsburg, 1974), pp. 23-24, and especially Ernst Bammel, "The *Titulus*," in *Jesus and the Politics of His Day*, pp. 353-64.

325. By contrast Henry Cadbury suggested that "Jesus probably had no definite, unified, conscious purpose," that he was "much more of a vagabond or gipsy than many another in the land," and that "we can hardly make a picture of Jesus' life and that of his contemporaries that will be too casual for the facts" (Cadbury, pp. 141, 124). Cf. Mack, *A Myth of Innocence*, pp. 53-77, 353-57. Mack states: "Jesus' social critique, though pointed and sharp in particular cases of human event, did not include polemic against specific institutions. He did not name those who were at fault, nor did he suggest an alternative program to set things right. . . . He did not propose to do battle with Pharisees or synagogue leaders for the control or cleansing of a religious institution. He did not philosophize about the *polis*, how to legislate a better law, what to do about tyranny, or the chances of finding a perfect king. . . . He proposed no political program. He did not organize a church" (p. 64). Jesus' life is to be understood on analogy with the Cynics' "unconventional way of life" (p. 68). Yet some of Jesus' undisputed actions (e.g., the choice of the Twelve, the trip to Jerusalem at festival time, the action at the Temple) do not comport with the image of Jesus as an unreflective vagabond. Meyer, *The Aims of Jesus*, is a full-scale attempt to construct the possible purposes or intentions of Jesus' ministry.

ances: "Foxes have holes, and birds of the air have nests; but the Son of Man has nowhere to lay his head" (Luke 9:58).[326]

During Jesus' lifetime the core of the movement was centered on a person. Wherever Jesus was, there the movement was. Of the crowds of people positively attracted to Jesus, not everyone followed him literally in the sense that they left their homes and families and followed him from place to place. Most probably remained in their own communities as local sympathizers. No exact figure can be given for the number of such sympathizers Jesus may have won over before his death, but there probably were hundreds if not thousands. Among the sympathizers were Simon the Pharisee (Luke 7:36-50), Zacchaeus the tax collector (Luke 19:1-10), and Joseph of Arimathea, a member of the Sanhedrin (Mark 15:42-47). Yet there were others who followed Jesus on the road, and, as noted already, it was a remarkable thing for anyone in the rural Palestine of that day to leave behind home and family and take up an essentially rootless mode of life.[327] There are various indications in the Gospels that Jesus and his first followers were supported with food, temporary lodging, and financial donations from others (Matt. 10:9-13; Luke 8:1-3; cf. 1 Cor. 9:14). The Gospels sometimes depict Jesus or his disciples dining as guests in various houses (Mark 2:15-17; Luke 7:36-50; 11:37-44; 19:1-10). According to John 21:1-3, Jesus' disciples returned again to fishing right after his execution. Yet this may have been merely transitional. In Acts the apostles were immediately active in Jerusalem after Jesus' death, and there they had no visible means of support. Some followers were men and women of means who sold property for the benefit of the entire congregation (Acts 4:32-37).[328]

One of the interesting questions relates to the role of women in the early movement surrounding Jesus. Did Jesus have female followers who were as closely connected with him as were the male followers? On the one hand there were no women among the core group of the Twelve. If women had made a regular practice of physically following Jesus on the road, as the men did, this would have been quite scandalous in the eyes of that first-century society. In that day there were firm boundaries between men's and women's spheres. A man was not even to mention aloud the name of a respectable woman in a public place. If Jesus' women followers had been his usual traveling companions, and had spent the night in proximity with him, one would expect some echo of this directed as a criticism against Jesus in the Gospels. It is more likely, then, that the female disciples accompanied Jesus only on special occasions, such as

---

326. Sanders, *Historical Figure*, pp. 106-8.
327. Borg, *Jesus*, p. 128.
328. Sanders, *Historical Figure*, pp. 108-9.

pilgrimages, and that generally they played a more traditional role by providing food and lodging.[329]

On the other hand the Gospels contain indications that the female disciples of Jesus did not always conform to their traditional roles, and that Jesus in fact encouraged them to depart from these roles.[330] In the story of Mary and Martha (Luke 10:38-42), Martha has taken on the traditional female role of hostess, and she finds herself shorthanded because her sister Mary is listening to Jesus' teaching rather than helping with the household tasks. Mary has violated her accepted role or "job description" by sitting with the men. Yet in his response, Jesus affirms Mary's right to sit and learn at his feet, and he even commends Mary by saying that she has "chosen the better part, which will not be taken away from her" (Luke 10:42). This is all the more remarkable when one considers that later rabbinic teaching, as indicated by the Mishnah, often condemns those who taught Torah to women.[331] Kathleen Corley has argued that some of Jesus' early female followers may have been slandered as "prostitutes" because they were seen publicly with men and shared their meals with them. These were probably not peasant women, but upper-class women who had highly circumscribed social roles that did not allow for this kind of open association with men.[332] So the general conclusion would seem to be that Jesus' female followers were not treated just as the men were, and yet they were in some measure freed from some of the social constraints that would have applied within first-century Jewish society.

All four canonical Gospels and the Acts of the Apostles agree that there were twelve special disciples (collectively called "the Twelve"), but they do not agree on their names (see Matt. 10:1-4; Mark 3:13-19; Luke 6:12-16; and Acts 1:13). This may be because the number was a symbolic one, representing the restoration of the twelve tribes of Israel (Matt. 19:28), and the actual number of close disciples varied from time to time and from place to place during the ministry of Jesus. Another possibility is that the disciples had more than one name. ("Matthew," for instance, is sometimes called by the name of "Levi," and so it may have been with others.) John Meier draws some interesting conclu-

---

329. Sanders, *Historical Figure*, pp. 107-10.

330. For a discussion of the issues, see Elisabeth Schüssler Fiorenza, *In Memory of Her: A Feminist Theological Reconstruction of Christian Origins* (New York: Crossroad, 1983), esp. 118-54.

331. "R. Eliezer says: If any man gives his daughter a knowledge of the Law it is as though he taught her lechery" (*m. Sot.* 3.4). Yet there is a reference in *m. Ned.* 4.3 to one who "may teach Scripture to his sons and to his daughters."

332. Kathleen E. Corley, "Jesus' Table Practice: Dining with 'Tax Collectors and Sinners,' Including Women," in *Society of Biblical Literature Seminar Papers, 1993* (Atlanta: Scholars Press, 1993), pp. 444-59.

sions regarding the Twelve. First, he notes that the inclusion of Judas within the Twelve argues strongly for the historicity of this group during Jesus' ministry. If the whole idea of the Twelve were a later Christian invention, a projection back in time from twelve leaders in the early church, it is not plausible to think that Judas would have been included among their number. Second, the choice of the Twelve argues against an interpretation of Jesus' movement as sectarian. The number twelve signified the totality of Israel, not a separated sect, and his twelve "patriarchs" were "to be the exemplars and center of a renewed people of God in the endtime." Third, the fact that Jesus was not himself included in the Twelve argues that he stood over and against them, and that he was to play a distinctive role in the renewal of Israel.[333]

Three disciples seem to constitute an inner circle: Peter, James, and John. They alone are with Jesus in important moments, such as the transfiguration (Mark 9:2-8) and the prayer in Gethsemane (Mark 14:33). It becomes clear that Jesus had followers with differing degrees of responsibility and intimacy. There were "the Twelve," yet also the smaller circle of the three (Peter, James and John of Zebedee), and larger than this a much more numerous group of "disciples," and still larger a collection of sympathizers and well-wishers. Luke records that Jesus commissioned not only the Twelve for a preaching and healing mission (Luke 9:1-11), but also a larger group of seventy that went out and later reported success in exorcism (Luke 10:1-20). Visually, these groupings could be represented as a series of concentric circles. While Jesus proclaimed the gospel or "good news" of God's kingdom to large multitudes, it was only a smaller group that he called to follow after him in the stricter sense of the word.[334]

The role played by the twelve close disciples varies in the Gospel accounts. In the Gospel of Mark their role is largely negative, and they again and again fail to grasp the significance of Jesus' words and actions and person. Rather surprisingly, the miracle of the feeding of the five thousand does not bring insight to the spiritually dim-witted disciples: "They did not understand about the loaves, but their hearts were hardened" (Mark 6:52). Just as surprisingly, outsiders and even Gentiles like the Syro-Phoenician woman prove to be better models of faith than the closest disciples. It is also noteworthy that Jesus' own family members do not seem to have been followers. With the exception of certain sayings about Mary, most of the material in the Gospels casts them in a negative light. At one point his family members tried to seize him and take him away, fearing that he "has gone out of his mind" (Mark 3:21). Jesus, for his part, depreciates the importance of blood relation to himself when he says: "Who are my mother and my brothers? . . . Whoever does the will of God is my brother

333. Meier, "Reflections," pp. 90-91.
334. Sanders, *Historical Figure*, p. 123.

and sister and mother" (Mark 3:33, 35). Yet, after the resurrection, Jesus' mother and brothers joined the disciples in prayer (Acts 1:14), and one of Jesus' brothers, James, served as a leader of the early church in Jerusalem.[335]

What was it that made Jesus controversial? And why was he put to death? These two simple questions have evoked answers of enormous range, subtlety, and complexity among biblical scholars, historians, and theologians. Any response to them involves an interlocking set of judgments on Jesus' character, his possible alignment with or aloofness from the political and religious parties of his day, the defection of some of Jesus' own followers, the varying responses of the crowds, the policies of the Roman government, the relationship between Pontius Pilate and the high priestly clique, the attitudes within the differing religious groups in first-century Palestine, the legal procedures used by the Romans in governing their provinces, the customs of the Sanhedrin in judicial affairs, and the exercise of capital punishment in that time and place. The scholars' reconstructions of the issues are balanced as delicately as an artist's mobile: touch one piece and all the rest tremble in their places. Unfortunately there is just not enough information to provide an adequate social, religious, and political backdrop for understanding the Gospels' accounts of the controversies, trial, and death of Jesus. Even on so basic a matter as Roman legal procedure, far more is known of what happened in the city of Rome than in a provincial capital such as Jerusalem. With regard to the Sanhedrin, the later rabbinical statements regarding the way deliberations were conducted may or may not be an accurate reflection of the situation prior to 70 C.E. We cannot be certain.

In the last thirty or forty years, a few points of broad consensus have emerged regarding Jesus' controversies and death. First, almost all recent authors have recognized the inappropriateness of reading the Gospels as though Jesus were opposed in principle to something called "Judaism" and was put to death for this reason. This viewpoint, though common among Gentile Christians in the past and present, signally fails to recognize Jesus' Jewishness, his adherence to Jewish practices, and the wide disagreements on fundamental issues that existed among the subgroups within first-century Judaism. If Jesus engaged in disputes with other Jews on matters of Torah observance, this hardly proves that he opposed "Judaism." On the contrary, it proves just the reverse, namely, that he was within the circle of those who took legal or halakic observance seriously, and so, seriously debated it. Second, although the bulk of the Gospel narratives make frequent references to the Pharisees as Jesus' opponents, the Pharisees are conspicuous by their absence in the account of the arrest, trial, and death of Jesus. The Pharisees as a group played little or no role in

335. Sanders, *Historical Figure*, p. 123.

Jesus' death. Third, it is agreed that the final legal responsibility for Jesus' death lay with the Roman governor, Pontius Pilate. Jesus was executed as a perceived political threat and according to a Roman mode of punishment. He died under a placard bearing the words "the king of the Jews." Fourth, it is agreed that if any Jews were likely to have played an instrumental role in Jesus' arrest, trial under Pilate, and execution, it is likely to have been the high priest and his associates. The exact degree of involvement by the high priests and elders in the events leading up to Jesus' death continues to be debated. They have been variously regarded as the initiators of the proceedings against Jesus, as active collaborators with the Romans, as unwilling agents, or as passive spectators.[336] The issue of Jesus' trial and death will be treated later, after first discussing the earlier conflicts during his ministry.

The Gospels portray Jesus as being in conflict with some of the religious leaders of the Jews, and it may be helpful to make note of some of the specific conflicts that are mentioned. In the second and third chapters of the Gospel of Mark, there is a whole sequence of conflicts.[337] Jesus cured a paralytic with the words "your sins are forgiven," and this led the scribes to murmur that Jesus presumed to have the authority to forgive sins; they called it blasphemy. Jesus sensed their opposition but proceeded with the cure anyway (2:1-12). Jesus called a tax collector to follow as one of his disciples, and subsequently he dined with many other tax collectors. The scribes of the Pharisees complained about this to Jesus' disciples, and Jesus responded by defending his right to call sinners (2:13-17). People asked Jesus why his disciples did not fast in the way that the disciples of John the Baptist and the Pharisees were fasting. Jesus defended his disciples by saying that while the bridegroom was with them, the wedding guests should not fast (2:18-22). On a Sabbath day Jesus and his disciples were traveling through a grain field and, since the disciples were hungry, they began to pluck the heads of grain and eat them. When the Pharisees saw this and criticized them, he cited the example of David, who when he and his men were hungry ate the consecrated bread that was for the priests alone. Jesus also made two statements in defense of what had happened, that "the sabbath was made for humankind, and not humankind for the sabbath," and "the Son of Man is lord

---

336. Daniel J. Harrington, "The Jewishness of Jesus: Facing Some Problems," *Catholic Biblical Quarterly* 49 (1987): 1-13, esp. 12.

337. In what follows I am indebted to Sanders, *Historical Figure*, pp. 205-37, and *Jesus and Judaism*, pp. 174-97, but have also taken note of the discussion of the Pharisees in Jacob Neusner, *From Politics to Piety: The Emergence of Pharisaic Judaism* (Englewood Cliffs, N.J.: Prentice-Hall, 1973), pp. 67-80, and the critique of Sanders's positions in James D. G. Dunn, "Pharisees, Sinners, and Jesus," in *The Social World of Formative Christianity and Judaism*, pp. 264-89, and Bruce D. Chilton, "Jesus and the Repentance of E. P. Sanders," *Tyndale Bulletin* 39 (1988): 1-18.

even of the sabbath" (2:23-28). On another Sabbath day Jesus entered a synagogue where there was a man with a withered hand, and he asked those present whether it was legitimate to heal on the Sabbath day. They remained silent, and Jesus went ahead and healed the man, which led the Pharisees to go out and confer with the Herodians as to how to kill Jesus (3:1-6).

As Sanders has noted, these stories show a kind of progression in intensity. The conflict escalates in its severity. At first Jesus' opponents merely murmur their opposition to themselves, addressing neither Jesus, nor the disciples, nor the people at large. Next they complain to the disciples about Jesus. In the third and fourth stories they object to Jesus himself about his disciples. In the final story they move beyond complaint and objection and intend to kill Jesus. There is also an escalation in the number of Jesus' opponents. At first they are simply the "scribes" or legal experts, but soon they are "scribes of the Pharisees," that is, those who belonged to the Pharisaic party. Then they are unidentified, but perhaps Pharisees or the disciples of John. At the end they are Pharisees again, though they have consulted with the Herodians.[338]

To understand what is at stake in these stories of conflict, it is important to understand what is and is not being disputed regarding the Torah. Laws may be disputed in differing ways.[339] (1) One could argue that a certain law is wrong in itself and should be revoked or repealed. This is a very radical step, and although overt dissent and disobedience are common enough in modern history, it would have been much rarer in ancient times. Because of the Jewish view that the Torah was given by God, any assertion that the law was wrong would be tantamount to saying that God had made a mistake. (2) As an alternative, one could argue that a law is wrong and should be repealed, but should still be obeyed. (3) As a less radical step, a person may allege that there are certain mitigating circumstances that justify transgression on some occasions. (4) Yet another approach would be to interpret the law in such a way as in effect to change it. (A possible example might be the U.S. Supreme Court decision that "equal" schooling was not compatible with racially "separate" schooling.) (5) In some cases it may be possible to avoid or evade some laws without actually repealing them. (6) One may propose that the law be extended and criticize it for not going far enough. This is compatible with a continued adherence to the law in its present form. (7) Finally one may create a lot of supplementary rules and practices that govern precisely how laws are to be fulfilled. People who follow such supplemental rules may believe that those who do not are transgressing the law, and vice versa.

As we have seen already, first-century Judaism was rife with controversies

338. Sanders, *Historical Figure*, pp. 212-13.
339. Sanders, *Historical Figure*, pp. 206-7.

regarding the observance of the Torah, and yet these almost always fell into categories 3-7 above and not categories 1-2. Much of early Pharisaic Judaism and later rabbinic Judaism was devoted to the explication of supplemental rules (referred to as "the tradition of the elders" in Matt. 15:2), and the strictest groups, such as those in the Dead Sea community, regarded those who did not follow their particular interpretations of Sabbath, food, and other laws as flagrant transgressors. Yet, once one distinguishes the rejection of the law in principle from disagreements over the proper application of the law, Jesus basically appears as an observant Jew. Nowhere does he ride roughshod over the prescriptions of the Torah, or simply assert that they are not to be observed. If Jesus had done this, there would have been no basis for an argument with the Pharisees. Jesus would have been self-condemned.[340] Even when he healed a leper, Jesus is said to have told the leper to show himself to the priest, as prescribed in the Law of Moses (Matt. 8:4) — a detail not likely to have been invented by the early church. Jesus is said to have paid the required Temple tax, albeit reluctantly (Matt. 17:24-27). Moreover, the practice of the earliest Jewish Christians in the "Jerusalem church" under the leadership of James,[341] Peter, and John corroborates that Jesus did not advocate any fundamental break with Jewish law. These first followers of Jesus were pious adherents of Judaism, who observed circumcision, the Sabbath (on Saturday), the dietary laws, festivals and fasts, and other traditions. If Jesus had clearly broken with these Jewish practices, then it is quite unlikely that his earliest followers would have continued in them.[342] Peter's vision, as reported in Acts, confirms the point, for it takes a special revelation from God to convince Peter to begin associating with Gentiles. And when the heavenly voice tells him to "kill and eat," he objects by saying, "I have never eaten anything that is profane or unclean" (Acts 10:14; cf. 11:8). In other words, the leading disciple of Jesus kept kosher during the period following Jesus' death. The bald statement in the Gospel of Mark that Jesus "declared all foods clean" (Mark 7:19) must be taken, then, not as a report of Jesus' teaching per se, but as an interpretation of that teaching.[343]

340. The Palestinian Talmud contains the story of a certain Elisha ben Abujah who deliberately rode his horse in front of the Temple mount on a Day of Atonement that also happened to fall on a Sabbath. According to the story, a voice came forth from the Temple, saying: "Repent, children, except for Elisha ben Abujah, for he knew my power yet rebelled against me!" (*y. Hag.* 2.1). There is nothing even remotely comparable to this in the Gospels' portrayal of Jesus.

341. "James" is a modernization of the New Testament name "Jacob," and there are two important figures in the earliest church by the name of "Jacob" — (1) Jacob, son of Zebedee and brother of John, who was among the Twelve, and (2) Jacob, the brother (or some say kinsman) of Jesus. Here we refer to the second.

342. Maccoby, p. 35.

343. In the Epistle to the Galatians, Paul comes into conflict with Peter for not shar-

E. P. Sanders has stated that the whole picture of Jesus' conflict with the Pharisees in the Gospels is a retrojection or reading back into Jesus' lifetime of the later controversies between the church and synagogue toward the end of the first century. He asserts that there was no substantial conflict between Jesus and the Pharisees with regard to Sabbath, food, and purity laws, and finds the general picture of conflict in the Gospel accounts to be unrealistic and unhistorical.[344] Yet Jacob Neusner, in his detailed study on the Pharisees, has shown that "the central traits of Pharisaism concerned observance of dietary laws" and that "Pharisees furthermore ate only with other Pharisees, to be sure that the laws were appropriately observed." Thus the Pharisees were akin to the group known as *haberim* (associates), mentioned in rabbinical literature as a table-fellowship group. Aside from the invective in the Gospels, Neusner says, the basic picture of the Pharisees in the Gospels as concerned with ritual purity fits in with the rabbinical traditions about the Pharisees.[345] In light of their intense concern for ritual purity, it is ipso facto probable that Jesus would have come into conflict with them over matters of purity, and indeed it would be remarkable had there been no conflicts along these lines. According to the rabbinic traditions, the Pharisees had several disputes with the Sadducees over issues of purity, and so it would not be unexpected for them to have had similar disputes with Jesus.[346]

One of the most frequent and obvious points of controversy in the Gospels concerned Jesus' sharing of meals with "sinners." Who were these "sinners"? Some authors have tended to overemphasize the gap between the Pharisees and everyone else, and to portray the Pharisees as superbigots and

---

ing meals with Gentiles (Gal. 2:11-14). Yet one argument that Paul does not use is that Jesus abolished the dietary laws, and this militates against supposing that Jesus taught anything along these lines.

344. Sanders, *Jesus and Judaism*, pp. 264-67. "Pharisees did not organize themselves into groups to spend their Sabbaths in Galilean cornfields in the hope of catching someone transgressing" (p. 265; cf. 178, 199, 209). Paul Winter supports this position: "In historical reality Jesus was a Pharisee. His teaching was Pharisaic teaching. In the whole of the New Testament we are unable to find a single historically reliable instance of religious differences between Jesus and the members of the Pharisaic guild" (*On the Trial of Jesus* [Berlin and New York: Walter de Gruyter, 1961], p. 133, quoted in D. R. Catchpole, "The Problem of the Historicity of the Sanhedrin Trial," in *The Trial of Jesus*, Cambridge Studies in Honor of C. F. D. Moule, ed. Ernst Bammel, Studies in Biblical Theology 2/13 [Naperville, Ill.: Alec R. Allenson, 1970] p. 48).

345. Neusner, *From Politics to Piety*, p. 80.

346. James Dunn ("Pharisees, Sinners, and Jesus," esp. pp. 274-75, 282-83) sees Sanders's argument as a response to the traditional stereotype of Judaism as legalistic and Jesus as a kind of liberator from this legalism. Yet Sanders may have overreached in asserting that Jesus and the Pharisees had no disputes over ritual purity.

supersnoopers, ready to take offense at Jesus for associating with the common people. According to this account, the bulk of the populace or "people of the land" (Heb. *'am ha-aretz*) were cut off from God in the eyes of the Pharisees and other stricter Jews.[347] Sanders has offered a corrective to this viewpoint, pointing out that the Pharisees had in effect applied the stricter rules of ritual purity for the Temple priests to themselves in everyday life. They regarded the whole world as, in effect, a Temple. The question then was not moral worth but ritual purity. Not to observe these stricter rules of ritual purity was not the same thing as spurning God's law. Yet there were some whom the Pharisees and other stricter Jews regarded as "wicked" or "sinful." They were Jews who had no intention of observing God's law. They failed not through inadvertence or occasional lapses into ritual impurity, but through habitual inattention to the prescriptions of the Torah. Jesus incurred the wrath of the Pharisees, scribes, and other strict Jews by sharing meals with these people.

If we read the Gospels from a social-scientific perspective, it is not at all surprising that the controversies concerning Jesus should involve the issue of shared meals. Anthropologists, through cross-cultural study, have concluded that "in all societies both simple and complex, eating is the primary way of initiating and maintaining human relationships." For this reason "to know what, where, how, when, and with whom people eat is to know the character of their society."[348] In short, the rules for shared eating are a mirror image of the general rules for associating and socializing in a given society. Sharing food brings an individual into a certain economy or exchange that typically involves obligations to give, receive, and then repay after receiving. One often finds fine nuances of meaning attached to particular practices of eating. As Crossan points out, if beggars appear at one's front door, there is a difference between giving them some food to go, inviting them into one's kitchen for a meal, bringing them into the dining room for a meal with the family, or having them return on the weekend for a supper with a group of one's friends. These examples show a steady progression in the level of social intimacy.

From the Gospels, it seems that Jesus had the most intimate kinds of shared eating experiences with some of the most disreputable characters of his society. Is it any wonder that he raised both objections and eyebrows with his behavior? Yet, like his healings and his parables, this too communicated something regarding God's reign. Crossan explains that "the Kingdom of God as a process of open commensality, of a nondiscriminating table depicting in min-

---

347. As argued, for instance, in Jeremias, *New Testament Theology*, pp. 108-21, esp. 112.

348. Peter Farb and George Armelagos, *Consuming Passions: The Anthropology of Eating* (Boston: Houghton Mifflin, 1980), pp. 4, 211, cited in Crossan, *Jesus*, p. 68.

iature a nondiscriminating society, clashes fundamentally with honor and shame, those basic values of ancient Mediterranean culture and society."[349] When some Jews called other Jews "sinners" and refused to share meals with them, this created a partition within Israel that Jesus' table practice directly challenged. The breaking of this boundary between observant Jew and nonobservant Jew in Jesus' lifetime foreshadowed the overcoming of the still greater rift between Jews and Gentiles in the early church.[350]

Yet it was not only the act of associating with habitually nonobservant Jews that aroused opposition to Jesus. And it was not only the act of sharing meals with such nonobservant Jews, though everything we know or surmise about the Pharisees and other stricter Jews makes it likely that such shared meals would have provoked them to criticize Jesus. Above all else, it was Jesus' confident declarations of *divine forgiveness* for such nonobservant Jews that must have touched off a firestorm of controversy. "The promise of salvation to sinners," writes Sanders, "is the undeniably distinctive characteristic of Jesus' message."[351] The forgiveness that Jesus announced did not require the offering of the Temple sacrifices that were the prescribed means of atoning for sin.[352] Jesus proclaimed God's love to "sinners" *before* they repented. Sanders explains: "The novelty and offense of Jesus' message was that the wicked who heeded him would be included in the kingdom even though they did not repent as it was universally understood — that is, even though they did not make restitution, sacrifice, and turn to obedience to the law." Perhaps most shocking of all is that Jesus seemed to regard the association of "sinners" with himself as the functional equivalent of repentance. He even went so far as to suggest that such association with himself and participation in his group of followers was equivalent to admission into the kingdom of God. That, for clear-cut reasons, was "offensive to normal piety — not just to trivial,

---

349. Crossan, *Jesus*, p. 70.

350. Dunn, "Pharisees, Sinners, and Jesus," p. 283. David Noel Freedman makes an intriguing observation: "One thing [shown by] the reaction to Jesus' fellowship with sinners is that the opponents considered Jesus to be different from those he associated with, namely to be more like themselves (the opponents) — they grouped him with them, i.e., as a Pharisee, or like a Pharisee and expected him to maintain their standards — an important inference or induction. If they had considered him to be one of 'them,' i.e., outsiders, they would not have bothered or even noticed his associations" (letter to the author, August 5, 1999).

351. Sanders, *Jesus and Judaism*, p. 174.

352. Strictly speaking, the Temple sacrifices were to atone for inadvertent sins and not serious and deliberate violations of the Torah. For weighty transgressions there was no ritual or sacrifice, except the Day of Atonement (Yom Kippur) ritual for the entire nation. The point here is that Jesus' proclamation of forgiveness was not tied to either the regular Temple sacrifices or the Day of Atonement rituals.

externalistic super-piety."[353] So the scandal or offensiveness of Jesus has to be understood on a number of different levels. By openly associating with notoriously nonobservant Jews, Jesus cast a shadow across his own reputation. By sharing meals with these "sinners," he announced to the world that he did not abide by the stricter principles of Pharisees or *haberim*. By proclaiming divine forgiveness to these same Jews while they remained nonobservant, Jesus seemed to be setting aside the prescribed means of atonement or ritual purification set down in the Torah. By intimating that association with himself was equivalent to repentance, Jesus appeared to be setting himself altogether above the Torah and Temple alike. These were very serious matters indeed for Jews of the first century, and the issues came to a head when Jesus made his final and fateful journey to Jerusalem.

The Final Week

Why did Jesus make this journey? Did he do so in full recognition of his impending death? Did he not only foresee his own death, but actually intend it in some way? While Jesus remained in Galilee there was probably little or no danger to his life, but this was not the case once he arrived in Jerusalem at the time of the Passover festival. There may have been some 300,000 to 400,000 pilgrims in or around the city at this time,[354] in addition to the year-round population of about 40,000 to 60,000, and the chief concern of the Roman governor together with the Jewish high priest was to maintain public order in the potentially volatile situation of the festival — the most likely time for an attempted political strike of some kind. Albert Schweitzer surmised that Jesus went to Jerusalem believing that his mission was to bear the woes of the end time. He was to die "on behalf of the many," that is, in their stead. Perhaps one could say, on this account, that Jesus deliberately provoked the leaders to kill him.[355] His death was not merely the outcome but the purpose of the journey. Alternatively Marcus Borg suggests that Jesus' death was the outcome and not the purpose of going to Jerusalem.[356] In Luke Jesus identified himself with the succession of prophets sent to Jerusalem, and in bitter irony spoke the words: "It is impossible for a prophet to be killed outside of Jerusalem" (Luke 13:33). The Gospels

353. Sanders, *Jesus and Judaism*, pp. 207, 210; cf. 255. Meier agrees with Sanders on this general point (*A Marginal Jew*, 2:149-50).

354. This is Sanders's estimate (*Historical Figure*, p. 249). Josephus gives much larger numbers for attendance at the Passover, on the order of 2.5 to 3 million, but these figures are generally thought to be rather unrealistic (*Jewish War* 6.420-27; 2.280).

355. Schweitzer, *Quest*, pp. 387-92.

356. Borg, *Jesus*, p. 172.

contain repeated predictions of the sufferings that Jesus was to endure in Jerusalem, sayings regarding the suffering "Son of Man" (Matt. 17:9, 22-23; 20:17-19; Mark 9:31; 10:32-34; Luke 9:22, 44; 18:31-33). Although the authenticity of these, and other, "Son of Man" sayings is widely disputed, there is no reason to think that Jesus would not have been able to foresee some of the events that would transpire in Jerusalem. Especially if Jesus had already intended to take decisive action at the Temple mount at the time of the Passover festival, then certain consequences were bound to follow for Jesus.

Jerusalem was the most Jewish of cities in first-century Palestine, and was occupied by a garrison of Roman troops that received additional reinforcements at the time of the major festivals. At the season of the Passover, Roman troops arrived in the city from the west in a procession led by the Roman governor, and with all the trappings of Roman power. Jesus and his followers arrived from the east, perhaps even on the same day.[357] During his last week, there are five major scenes in the drama of Jesus' life. First, Jesus entered Jerusalem on a donkey, with people shouting acclamations. According to Matthew and Luke, they explicitly called him "Son of David" or "king" (Matt. 21:9; Luke 19:38). Second, Jesus went into the Temple, where he overturned the tables of the money changers and the seats of those who sold pigeons (Mark 11:15-19). The Gospel of Mark attributes to Jesus the words (partly based on Isa. 56:7 and Jer. 7:11): "'My house shall be called a house of prayer for all the nations[.]' / But you have made it a den of robbers" (Mark 11:17). Third, Jesus shared a final meal with his disciples, saying that he would not drink wine again until the day that he would "drink it new" with them in God's kingdom (Mark 14:22-25). Fourth, the guards belonging to the high priest arrested Jesus and took him before the high priest and his council. Although some witnesses accused him of threatening to destroy the Temple, their testimony was not consistent and so could not be used to condemn him. According to the Gospel of Mark, Jesus, in direct questioning by the high priest, admitted that he was both the "Messiah" and the "Son of God," and this led to a charge of blasphemy against him (Mark 14:43-64). Fifth, Jesus' captors sent him to Pilate, who interrogated him and then ordered him to be crucified under the charge of claiming to be "king of the Jews" (Mark 15).[358]

Both the entry into the city and the action at the Temple are probably to be understood as prophetic actions. The Hebrew prophets of earlier centuries not only delivered oracles from God, but also occasionally performed actions that carried symbolic significance. Thus we read in the Hebrew Bible that God commanded Jeremiah to break a pot and proclaim that Jerusalem would be de-

357. Borg, *Jesus*, pp. 173-74.
358. Sanders, *Historical Figure*, pp. 252-53.

stroyed (Jer. 19:1-13) and, on another occasion, to wear a yoke to indicate that Judah should submit to Babylon (Jer. 27–28). Isaiah and Ezekiel also performed symbolic actions (Isa. 20:3; Ezek. 4–5; 12:1-16; 24:15-24). Jesus' entrance into the city, riding on a donkey's colt, fulfilled the passage in Zechariah which spoke of a king of peace riding "on a colt, the foal of a donkey" (Zech. 9:9-10). Marcus Borg suggests that Jesus chose this particular symbolism to stress that his kingdom was a kingdom of peace and not of war.[359] An interesting feature of the final week is that certain actions are *not* recorded during this period: there are no reported healings or exorcisms. Instead the Gospel narratives highlight the prophetic and challenging teaching of Jesus to the multitudes.

Jesus' second prophetic action, which was even more provocative than the first, was done in the Temple area, a large flat platform of about thirty-five acres. This area included various courts and buildings, and the Temple itself. This was understood to be the dwelling place of God on earth. Public worship occurred in the courts surrounding the sanctuary. There were graded levels of holiness in this place: beginning with the Holy of Holies, where the high priest entered once each year on the Day of Atonement; the priests' court; the court reserved for male Israelites alone (where Gentiles were forbidden to enter on pain of death); and the court of the women. The Temple grounds also included a place where sacrificial animals could be purchased and pilgrims could exchange their image-bearing coins (needed to pay the Temple tax) for coins without images. In what Joseph Klausner called Jesus' "greatest public deed,"[360] he expelled the money changers and the sellers of sacrificial animals. This was a highly provocative action that must have caused a stir. Yet it clearly was not regarded by the onlookers as an attempt to take over the Temple area, for otherwise the Romans, whose garrison overlooked the Temple courts, would immediately have intervened. It was a symbolic act that made a powerful statement, but it did not change the way business was done in the Temple.[361] The force exerted was simply the personal authority of Jesus himself in confronting the crowd.[362]

E. P. Sanders has argued that Jesus' action should not be regarded as a "cleansing" of the Temple, or as a protest against the Temple priests and their alleged greed, abuse of power, or negligence in their duties. Instead it was a symbolic destruction of the Temple that prefigured a future eschatological intervention in which God would replace the existing Temple with a new one.[363] Sanders notes that this understanding of the action at the Temple ex-

359. Borg, *Jesus,* p. 174.

360. Joseph Klausner, *Jesus of Nazareth: His Life, Times, and Teaching,* trans. Herbert Danby (New York: Macmillan, 1953), p. 312.

361. Borg, *Jesus,* pp. 174-75.

362. Dodd, *The Founder of Christianity,* p. 145.

363. Meier seems to agree with Sanders that the Temple action "was probably not a

plains why the Temple came up as an issue during the Jewish trial of Jesus. The action at the Temple was the basis on which Jesus was taken into custody, though it was not ultimately the ground for Jesus' condemnation. So in a real sense, the action at the Temple triggered the series of events that led to Jesus' death.[364] While Sanders is right to emphasize the importance of the Temple action, the opposition to Jesus was based on a number of considerations that mutually reinforced one another, as noted already in the discussion of the controversies during the ministry in Galilee. It was not merely the action at the Temple that made Jesus a potential threat to public order. Moreover, Craig Evans has demonstrated that Jesus' action, in historical context, can appropriately be seen as a "cleansing" or a critique of the existing priestly leaders and their policies. The Judaic literature of the period is filled with attacks on the high priests for their greed, corruption, and oppressive policies toward the common people and even their fellow priests. The house of the high priest Annas was reputed to be especially corrupt. If Jesus' dramatic words and action were in fact an expression of indignation at the way business was done in the Temple precincts, then Jesus would not have been alone in his protest.[365]

If Jesus ever gave to his followers some explanation of how he viewed his approaching death, the most likely occasion would be the last opportunity that he had, namely, the Last Supper. The tradition regarding this final meal is especially well attested, since it is independently supported in Mark and the Gospel of John, in special traditions in Luke, and in an early formula that is preserved in Paul's first letter to the Corinthians. The variation in wording among these different accounts indicates that they are based on an actual event and not a self-conscious effort by early Christians to construct a last supper after the fact. One might expect there to be some harmonization of the divergent accounts if they were constructed after Jesus' death, without reliable traditions to support them.[366] The

---

call for reform but a prophecy that the present Temple would be destroyed" ("Reflections," 101).

364. Sanders, *Jesus and Judaism,* pp. 301-5, and *Historical Figure,* pp. 254-62. Crossan agrees with Sanders that it is likely that "what led immediately to Jesus' arrest and execution in Jerusalem at Passover was that act of symbolic destruction, in deed and word, against the Temple" (*Who Killed Jesus? Exposing the Roots of Anti-Semitism in the Gospel Story of the Death of Jesus* [San Francisco: Harper San Francisco, 1995], p. 65).

365. Craig A. Evans, "Jesus' Action in the Temple: Cleansing or Portent of Destruction?" *Catholic Biblical Quarterly* 51 (1989): 237-70; and Evans, "Jesus and the 'Cave of Robbers': Toward a Jewish Context for the Temple Action," *Bulletin for Biblical Research* 3 (1993): 93-110.

366. Crossan takes an opposing view that there was no "solemn, formal, and final institution by Jesus himself" of a ritual meal. Instead certain groups of followers ritualized the "open commensality" that had characterized Jesus during his ministry (*Jesus,* p. 130). See also Crossan's discussion of bread-and-fish meals (pp. 179-80).

meal took place either on 14 Nisan (the Gospel of John) or on 15 Nisan (synoptic Gospels). At the beginning and end of the meal, Jesus used bread and wine to represent tangibly his impending death, which he accepted as a part of God's will for bringing in the kingdom of God. Though most scholars feel that the original form of Jesus' words may be hidden behind these variations in form (that bear the influence of the later liturgical traditions of the church), the core sayings seem to be that "this is my body [or flesh]" and "this is the covenant [sealed] in my blood." This final meal, as Meier explains, "was a pledge that, despite the apparent failure of Jesus' mission to Israel, God would vindicate him even beyond death and bring him and his followers to the final banquet in the Kingdom."[367] By drinking from *one* cup, *his* cup, they were pledging themselves to hold their fellowship with Jesus even in death, and to await the renewal of that fellowship in the coming kingdom.

To what extent, or in what fashion, were the leaders of the Jewish people involved in Jesus' death? The issue is highly volatile, if not incendiary, since it ties directly into the tragic history of anti-Semitism whereby Gentile Christians regarded the Jewish people as collectively responsible for Jesus' death.[368] The notion of hereditary guilt became the pretext for unspeakable crimes against the Jewish people throughout the history of the Christian church. It is only within recent generations that a sizable number of Christians have become aware of the pervasive and virulent anti-Semitism that has existed within, and has often been fostered by, the church.[369] As early as the second century Gentile Christians came to see the actions of a ruling clique in Jerusalem as somehow representative of all Jews past and present.[370] Even earlier, while many New Testament texts were being written, from about 70 to 100 C.E., a struggle ensued between the Jesus movement and the larger Jewish community that disputed the claims of the earliest Christians. The question is: To what extent does this first-century conflict color the Gospels' presentation of Jesus' relation with the Jewish leaders, and especially the presentation of the events that led directly to Jesus' death?

Regarding an anti-Jewish bias in the earliest church, the evidence is mixed. On the one hand are numerous verses in the Gospel of John where those who oppose Jesus are simply designated as "the Jews," and such texts may con-

---

367. Meier, "Reflections," p. 103.

368. Binyamin Eliav, "Anti-Semitism," in *Encyclopedia Judaica* (Jerusalem: Macmillan/Keter Publishing, 1971), 3:87-160.

369. The encyclical *Nostra Aetate* (1965), in the Vatican II documents, contains an explicit repudiation of the notion of Jewish guilt for the death of Jesus (Austin Flannery, ed., *Vatican II Council: The Conciliar and Post-Conciliar Documents* [Northport, N.Y.: Costello Publishing, 1975], p. 741).

370. This becomes evident in the harsh tone of the mid-second-century work by Justin Martyr, *Dialogue with Trypho, A Jew*, in *The Ante-Nicene Fathers*, 1:194-272.

vey the unfortunate impression that Jesus and his first followers were not Jews themselves![371] Another text in Matthew has the people of Jerusalem call out for the release of Barabbas rather than Jesus, and then say regarding Jesus: "His blood be on us and on our children!" (Matt. 27:25). A text in the book of Revelation refers to some in the city of Smyrna, probably persecutors of the Christians there, as "a synagogue of Satan" (Rev. 2:9). On the other hand, one finds texts where Nicodemus and Joseph of Arimathea — said to be members of the Sanhedrin — are both singled out as respectable persons (Matt. 27:57-60; Mark 15:43; Luke 23:50-53; John 3:1; 19:38-42). Even Gamaliel, an outstanding Jewish sage of the era, comes across as neutral and not hostile toward the early followers of Jesus (Acts 5:33-40). At the culmination of Jesus' ministry in the Gospel of Mark, there is a scribe who is said to be "not far from the kingdom of God" (Mark 12:34). The Gospel of John speaks of certain Pharisees who were favorably disposed toward Jesus (John 9:16). Acts refers to a multitude of priests who turned to the faith (Acts 6:7). Even Caiaphas is described as a man with prophetic gifts (John 11:51), which is ironic since one might expect the Gospels to blacken his portrait as much as possible.[372] In light of these passages, it is not possible to make blanket assertions about a consistent anti-Judaic tendency in the New Testament. Some texts reflect the struggle of church and synagogue, and some do not. The reality behind the texts is too complex to fit into a single, easily defined category.

The question about the Jewish leaders and Jesus, despite its disturbing resonances with the later tortuous history of Jews and Christians, has to be answered in terms of historical sources and historical methods. By far the most thorough and wide-ranging examination of the arrest, trial, and execution of Jesus is the magisterial study of Raymond Brown in *The Death of the Messiah*.[373] Brown concludes that, despite the very early theologizing of the events connected with Jesus' death, the Gospel narratives are based on actual events. "It is inconceivable that they [i.e., the Twelve] showed no concern about what happened to Jesus after the arrest," writes Brown. While there is "no Christian claim that they were present during the legal proceedings against him, Jewish or Roman," he adds that "it is ab-

---

371. See especially the following verses: John 2:18-20; 5:10-18; 6:41, 52; 7:1, 13; 8:48, 52, 57; 9:18, 22; 10:31-33; 11:8; 18:36; 19:7, 12, 38; 20:19. Other texts in the Gospel of John speak of Jesus' followers as Jews and of a "division" among the Jews over Jesus, but the designation of Jesus' opponents simply as "Jews" is frequent.

372. Ernst Bammel, "The Trial before Pilate," in *Jesus and the Politics of His Day*, pp. 415-51, citing 449.

373. Raymond E. Brown, *The Death of the Messiah: From Gethsemane to the Grave*, 2 vols., Anchor Bible Reference Library, ed. David Noel Freedman (New York: Doubleday, 1994). Brown forthrightly discusses the questions of responsibility for Jesus' death, and anti-Judaism in the Gospel narratives, at 1:383-97.

surd to think that some information was not available to them about why Jesus was hanged on a cross."[374] The whole point of crucifixion, after all, was to *publicize* that certain crimes would be severely punished. Crossan disputes this, claiming that "Jesus' first followers knew almost nothing whatsoever about the details of his crucifixion, death, or burial." Into this void, according to Crossan, the early Christians brought new interpretations of Hebrew Bible texts to create a meaningful narrative of what happened to Jesus their leader. Thus the passion accounts are not "history remembered but prophecy historicized."[375]

As Brown has demonstrated in his massive work, the passion narratives in the Gospels are an interweaving of historical remembrance and theological reflection, an almost seamless garment of event and interpretation. It is often difficult to say where history ends and theology begins. Yet the texts are grounded in actual events. Given the working relationship that existed between the Roman governor and the high priest and his cohorts, it is unlikely that Jesus would have been executed apart from some collaboration of the Jewish leaders with the Romans. Josephus summarized the trial and death of Jesus by noting that "Pilate . . . hearing him [i.e., Jesus] accused by men of the highest standing among us . . . condemned him to be crucified."[376] Even Crossan, despite his general skepticism regarding the passion narratives, says that Josephus is not likely to have invented a tradition of Jewish responsibility for Jesus' death, and therefore he takes it "as historical that Jesus was executed by some conjunction of Jewish and Roman authority."[377] If the trial of Jesus had been a *purely* Roman affair, apart from any Jewish involvement, then this would imply that Jesus' conduct in religious affairs was offensive but that the trial bypassed all this. It would also lead to the implausible conclusion that Jesus was not involved in any indictable political activities but was nonetheless tried for such. On the other hand the known teachings and activities of Jesus do provide a coherent and logical prelude for a hearing before the Sanhedrin.[378]

There are a number of different reconstructions of the series of events constituting Jesus' arrest, trial, and condemnation.[379] One scenario is that a

374. Raymond Brown, *Death of the Messiah*, 1:14.

375. Crossan, *Jesus*, p. 145; highlighted in the original. Crossan presents at length his spirited dissent with Raymond Brown in *Who Killed Jesus?*

376. Josephus, *Antiquities* 18.63.

377. Crossan, *Who Killed Jesus?* p. 147.

378. Catchpole, p. 54.

379. See the following discussions: William Riley Wilson, *The Execution of Jesus: A Judicial, Literary, and Historical Investigation* (New York: Scribner, 1970); Bammel, *The Trial of Jesus*, including especially Catchpole, pp. 47-65; Bammel, "The Trial before Pilate," pp. 415-51; Richard A. Horsley, "The Death of Jesus," in *Studying the Historical Jesus*, pp. 395-422; Raymond Brown, *Death of the Messiah*, 1:237-877.

night trial was held before the Sanhedrin, presided over by Caiaphas the high priest (from 18 to 36 c.e.), and that this session lasted until dawn or else was followed by a brief session at dawn. This seems to be the general picture presented in Matthew and Mark. Another version of the events holds that the Sanhedrin held only an early morning session, as appears to be the case in the Gospel of Luke. A third account holds that an informal session with Jesus was held by some Jewish official, perhaps Annas, the father-in-law of Caiaphas, who had been high priest previously (6-15 c.e.), but that no formal trial took place before the Sanhedrin. This scenario is based on the Gospel of John. Paul Winter has argued in favor of the last option on the basis of the Mishnaic teaching on the trial procedures of the Sanhedrin. If either of the two other scenarios were true, then the Sanhedrin in trying Jesus would have been violating several of its stated rules (e.g., holding a trial at night, etc.).[380] Yet the problem is that the later rabbinical rules, written down about 200 c.e., may or may not have been in effect in the period prior to 70 c.e. Whether or not the meeting with Jewish leaders was a full-scale trial or simply an informal hearing, some accusation against Jesus must have come under consideration.[381]

One feature of the passion narrative that is reliably reported in the Gospels is Peter's cowardly denial of Jesus. This detail, though embarrassing, is noteworthy since it places one of the early disciples as an eyewitness during the first stages of Jesus' trial. Historians have debated whether or not the Jewish authorities needed to have recourse to Pilate for a death sentence to be executed. The various pieces of evidence are ambiguous, but it is more plausible than not that during this period the Sanhedrin no longer had the authority to enact a death sentence.[382] Pontius Pilate, who was prefect of Judea from 26 to 36 c.e., is described by some ancient sources as a ruthless ruler.[383] He would have been

380. Paul Winter, *On the Trial of Jesus,* 2nd ed. (Berlin and New York: Walter de Gruyter, 1974). Vis-à-vis the guidelines in the Mishnah, the trial as described in Mark violated five principles: (1) a night session, (2) a trial on a feast day, (3) the omission of the statutory second session, (4) meeting in the house of the high priest, and (5) a discrepancy between the understanding of "blasphemy" in the Gospel account and in *m. Sanh.* 7.5 (Catchpole, p. 58).

381. Meier, "Reflections," pp. 103-4.

382. John 18:31 implies that the Jewish leaders did not have the right to capital punishment. Some support for this is given in Josephus's treatment of the death of James, the brother or kinsman of Jesus and a leader in the early church (*Antiquities* 20.200-203), an event that aroused the ire of the Romans perhaps because it involved a capital sentence being executed without prior Roman approval.

383. Philo wrote of "the briberies, the insults, the robberies, the outrages and wanton injuries, the executions without trial constantly repeated, the ceaseless and supremely grievous cruelty" that marked Pilate's rule (*Embassy to Gaius* 302, quoted in Sanders, *Historical Figure,* p. 274). Josephus recounts an episode in which Pilate sought to bring Ro-

entirely uninterested in legal or theological disputes that divided Jews from one another. His only concern would have been with accusations that involved a threat to Roman rule. Hence Jesus was brought before Pilate on the charge that he had claimed to be "king of the Jews," which indicates that the Jewish interrogation and discussion had probably already touched on the issue of messiahship. Thus it was on the charge of kingship, understood no doubt in the sense of being a revolutionary, that Pilate tried and condemned Jesus. It is notable that Jesus alone was arrested and executed, and not his followers. This indicates that Jesus was not understood as a potential military threat to the Romans.[384]

Roman crucifixion was commonly preceded by scourging,[385] which apparently weakened Jesus to the point that he was no longer able to carry the crossbeam for the cross on which he died. (The upright stake probably remained in place at the site of the execution.) To aid Jesus the soldiers pressed into service a certain Simon from Cyrene (a province in North Africa). His sons, Alexander and Rufus, were well known as members of the early church (Mark 15:21). Just as with Peter's denial, this is a detail in the Gospel narrative that places an early member of the church as an eyewitness of the events of Jesus' last day. The crucifixion took place outside the walls of the Holy City, at a spot called "Golgotha" (Aramaic, "skull place"), possibly an abandoned quarry by the side of the road. Despite the traditional references to "Mount Calvary," the Gospels in fact say nothing about a hill. The best archaeological candidate for the site of Jesus' death is the Church of the Holy Sepulchre in Jerusalem. Despite some debates over the contours of the city walls in earlier times, it seems that the site of this church was

---

man military standards, bearing the emperor's image, into the Holy City, and he backed down before a multitude of protesters willing to face death (*Jewish War* 2.169-71; *Antiquities* 18.55-59). He also took money from the Temple fund to build an aqueduct into the city (*Jewish War* 2.175-76; *Antiquities* 18.60-62). Pilate was eventually dismissed from office because of his large-scale and ill-advised executions of political agitators (*Antiquities* 18.88-89). And the high priest Caiaphas, who had an extraordinarily long tenure in office that ended in the same year (36 c.e.) as Pilate's did (*Antiquities* 18.95), may have been a political partner to the Roman governor who fell from grace when Pilate did.

384. Against the viewpoint that Jesus was misunderstood by the Romans and died because they took him to be a potential revolutionary, Sanders writes (*Historical Figure*, p. 268): "The solitary execution of the leader shows that they feared that Jesus could rouse the mob, not that he had created a secret army. In other words, they understood Jesus and his followers very well."

385. The scourging that accompanied Roman crucifixion is noted by Philo (*Against Flaccus* 72, 84) and Josephus (*Antiquities* 12.256; *Jewish War* 2.306-8; 5:446-51). For a thoroughly documented study of the ancient practice of crucifixion, see Martin Hengel, *Crucifixion in the Ancient World and the Folly of the Message of the Cross* (Phildelphia: Fortress, 1977).

Paul Gaughin, *The Yellow Christ*
(Albright-Knox Art Gallery, Buffalo)

outside the walls early in the first century. The passion narrative does not say whether Jesus was tied to the cross or nailed to it, though nail marks are mentioned in the accounts of Jesus' resurrection, and a recent archaeological find of a crucified man indicates that he had been nailed to his cross.[386]

The horror and brutality associated with crucifixion may be difficult for us to visualize today. It was inflicted by the Romans on the lower classes, including slaves, violent criminals, and the unruly elements in the provinces, not least in Judea. Jesus' death by the method of crucifixion was not an indication of the heinousness of his crime, but rather a sign of his complete lack of social standing. This was how a slave, a nobody, was put to rest by the Romans. A chief reason for its use was its allegedly supreme efficacy as a deterrent. It was a form of state terrorism, intended to astonish and terrify the onlookers. Martin Hengel writes: "By the public display of a naked victim at a prominent place — at a crossroads, in the theatre, on high ground, at the place of his crime — crucifixion also represented his uttermost humiliation."[387] The cruelty of those who performed crucifixions is indicated in Josephus's description of the entertainment offered to the Roman soldiers at the end of the Jewish War in 70 C.E.: they competed with one another to find new and interesting positions in which to nail their victims to the wood.[388]

Jesus died relatively quickly, and Jewish law (Deut. 21:22-23) specified that the body not be left hanging overnight, all the more so when the Passover day (15 Nisan) coincided that year with a Sabbath day. An influential Jew, Joseph of Arimathea, interceded with Pilate to provide a burial, perhaps only temporarily, in a tomb that he owned nearby. The Galilean women who were said to be at the cross witnessed the preparation of the body for burial. The name of Mary Magdalene occurs in all the traditions about burial. With Friday coming to an end and the Sabbath day beginning at sunset (according to the Jewish reckoning of the week), the burial of Jesus took place in haste, and then those who deposited the body in the tomb hastened to their homes.[389]

The story of Jesus was at an end, or rather, was just beginning.

386. Meier, "Reflections," pp. 104-6. On the discovery of the corpse of the crucified man, see Charlesworth, *Jesus within Judaism*, pp. 122-23.

387. Hengel, *Crucifixion*, p. 87.

388. Josephus, *Jewish War* 5.447-51.

389. Meier, "Reflections," p. 106. Crossan holds that the disciples had no knowledge of what happened to Jesus' body: "By Easter Sunday morning, those who cared did not know where it was, and those who knew did not care" (*Jesus*, p. 158). He suggests further that the body was probably devoured by dogs — an idea that may be linked with his viewpoint regarding the resurrection (discussed in note 393). Yet now there is archaeological evidence that the body of a first-century victim of crucifixion, Jehochanan, received a proper burial, and so it is not true that crucifixion victims were never buried (Charlesworth, *Jesus within Judaism*, pp.

The Resurrection

The earliest Christians insisted that Jesus' death on the cross was not the end of his life, and that he reappeared to many of them, alive again. Their claim was not that he was resuscitated from death and simply returned again to the same kind of existence he had had prior to his crucifixion. Instead the resurrection narratives suggest that Jesus had passed into a new mode of existence. On the one hand he had a physical body, and in the Gospel of Luke he invited them to verify this for themselves with the words: "Touch me and see; for a ghost does not have flesh and bones as you see that I have" (Luke 24:39). Luke also states that Jesus ate a piece of fish in their presence (Luke 24:42-43; cf. John 21:13). On the other hand Jesus presents himself in the Gospels as victorious over death and therefore no longer existing in a mortal or perishable body. In the Gospel of John Jesus suddenly appears with the disciples in a room where the doors were shut and locked (John 20:19-20). In John, as in the Gospel of Luke, he shows them his hands and sides (John 20:20), presumably so that they could see the marks of his suffering and know that the one they saw was also the one who had died on the cross.

The narratives of Jesus' after-death appearances differ in their details. Matthew and Mark present the disciples as traveling to Galilee to see Jesus there (Matt. 28:7, 16; Mark 16:7), while in Luke they remain in the vicinity of Jerusalem (Luke 24:33-36, 50-53). There are also differences in the accounts of Jesus' ascension into heaven in Luke 24:50-53 and Acts 1:6-11, even though these were authored by the same person. In Matthew Jesus appears twice, once to Mary Magdalene and the other Mary (Matt. 28:9) and once to the surviving eleven disciples (Matt. 28:16-20; Judas had killed himself). Luke includes nothing about Jesus' appearance to the women (Luke 24:1-12), but rather tells of "two men in dazzling clothes" who announced to them that Jesus had risen from the dead. Luke then tells of Jesus showing himself to Cleopas and an unnamed disciple (Luke 24:13-35), and then to all the disciples, before whom he ate (Luke 24:36-49). According to Acts, Jesus was with the disciples appearing on and off over a period of forty days (Acts 1:3). Even earlier than the Gospels and Acts is Paul's discussion of the resurrection in 1 Corinthians, which may have been written in the early 50s. Here Paul claims that he is passing on what was "handed down" to him, a list of the appearances of the risen Lord: an ap-

---

122-23). Moreover, Mark 6:29 indicates that the disciples of John the Baptist were able to retrieve his body for burial as well. While it is a "peculiar circumstance" that Jesus' body should be turned over for burial to a nonrelative, i.e., Joseph of Arimathea, John 19:31 attributes this to the religious motive of insuring that the corpse did not remain on the cross during the Sabbath day (Pheme Perkins, "The Resurrection of Jesus of Nazareth, in *Studying the Historical Jesus,* pp. 423-42, esp. 431-32, 437).

pearance first to Cephas (i.e. Peter), then to the Twelve (not the Eleven), then to more than five hundred persons at one time, then to James (Jesus' brother or kinsman), then to "all the apostles" (apparently not only the Twelve), and then to Paul himself (1 Cor. 15:3-8).[390]

In 1 Corinthians Paul devotes considerable space to discussing the nature of Jesus' resurrection (1 Cor. 15), and seems to be steering a middle path between some who were denying the resurrection of the dead altogether and others who failed to understand that the resurrected body was something other than just a resuscitated corpse. It was a "spiritual body" (1 Cor. 15:44).[391] In Paul's letters the resurrection is a sign for the present age, perhaps the ultimate sign, of Jesus' vindication by God. In this event he triumphed over his enemies and "was declared to be Son of God with power . . . by resurrection from the dead" (Rom. 1:4). Paul also taught that the resurrection of Jesus was a sign that God would raise from the dead those who believe in Jesus. His resurrection was the "firstfruits" (1 Cor. 15:20, 23), which, as it were, pointed forward to a coming harvest.

In the modern period there has been a tendency among some scholars to interpret the resurrection language of the New Testament as referring to the experiences of the disciples rather than to the person and body of Jesus.[392] Such writers will say that the meaning of the resurrection is continuing hope in God, or a sense of divine presence, or joy in the face of tragedy, or some other experience that is religiously significant but not necessarily connected with the body of Jesus.[393] Here it is crucial to distinguish historical inquiry from theological

390. Sanders, *Historical Figure,* pp. 276-77.

391. This phrase "spiritual body" has evoked a good deal of discussion, as in the following: Robert H. Gundry, *Soma in Biblical Theology,* Society for New Testament Studies Monograph Series (Cambridge: Cambridge University Press, 1976), and Gundry, "The Essential Physicality of Jesus' Resurrection according to the New Testament," in *Jesus of Nazareth, Lord and Christ; Essays on the Historical Jesus and New Testament Christology,* ed. Joel B. Green and Max Turner (Grand Rapids: Eerdmans; Carlisle, U.K.: Paternoster Press, 1994), pp. 204-19; Murray J. Harris, *Raised Immortal: Resurrection and Immortality in the New Testament* (Grand Rapids: Eerdmans, 1983), and Harris, *From Grave to Glory: Resurrection in the New Testament* (Grand Rapids: Zondervan, 1990).

392. Marcus Borg is a clear instance of this trend: "The truth of the resurrection is not dependent upon an empty tomb or a vanished corpse. Rather, the truth of the resurrection is grounded in the experience of Christ as a living reality before his death" (*Jesus,* p. 189 n. 44).

393. Crossan writes that "the resurrection of Jesus means for me that the human empowerment that some people experienced in Lower Galilee . . . is now available to any person in any place at any time who finds God in and through that same Jesus. Empty tomb stories and physical appearance stories . . . are, for me, parables of resurrection, not the resurrection itself." Basically "resurrection" means "the continuing experience of God's

reflection. The historical question posed by the biblical texts is what the first Christians meant when they wrote narratives of postdeath appearances or used the term "resurrection" in reference to Jesus. Their entire way of speaking and acting indicates that they believed that Jesus, having died, was now actually alive again. The Acts of the Apostles contains an amusing reference to Porcius Festus (appointed procurator of Judea in 60 C.E.), who heard Paul defend himself before his accusers and did not really grasp the "points of disagreement" except for "a certain dead man, Jesus, whom Paul asserted to be alive" (Acts 25:19 NASB).

Among the early Christians, no one claimed to have seen Jesus at the time that he rose again and left the grave. What they claimed was that they had seen Jesus alive again after his death. Moreover, they also did not claim that the after-death appearances of Jesus were public events, seen by disciples and nondisciples alike. They were only for the eyes of the disciples, and so the basis for asserting that Jesus was alive a second time is the testimony of those who claimed to be eyewitnesses to this occurrence. This is why the resurrection of Jesus is a matter of faith.

Final Thoughts

The varied responses to, and interpretations of, Jesus belong properly to the study of the historical church rather than the historical Jesus. Yet there are two matters closely connected with the argument in this chapter that are worthy of comment: the significance of Jesus' eschatological language and the origin of Christology.

A striking feature of the most recent scholarship on Jesus is the appearance of two different paradigms: an eschatological or apocalyptic Jesus and a sapiential or wisdom-based Jesus. Needless to say, there are many differences

---

presence in and through Jesus" (*Who Killed Jesus?* p. 216). Crossan is to be commended for his forthrightness in stating what resurrection means for him, and yet it is almost certainly not what resurrection meant for the earliest Christians. Paul, for example, writes to the Corinthians that if the physical body of Jesus had not been raised, then "your faith is futile and you are still in your sins" (1 Cor. 15:17). Pheme Perkins states: "The resurrection kerygma found in the canonical texts would not have assumed its present shape without the belief that Jesus' body was no longer in the grave" ("Resurrection," p. 436). For further discussion see Gerald O'Collins, "Is the Resurrection an 'Historical Event'?" *Heythrop Journal* 8 (1967): 381-87; Pheme Perkins, *Resurrection: New Testament Witness and Contemporary Reflection* (Garden City, N.Y.: Doubleday, 1984); and the discussion on the resurrection between two leading Jesus scholars in Marcus J. Borg and N. T. Wright, *The Meaning of Jesus,* pp. 111-42.

in emphasis and nuance within these two broad paradigms, but most of the literature seems to be based on the assumption that Jesus was *either* a sage who gave instruction on how to live wisely and well in the present world *or* a prophet who announced the immediate ending of the present world. Marcus Borg expresses the contrast when he writes: "The difference between an apocalyptic eschatology and a sapiential eschatology is enormous; the latter involves no objective change in the world whatsoever."[394] It is presupposed here that Jesus could not have been both sapiential and eschatological, and that the two perspectives exclude one another as fire excludes water or darkness excludes light.

The Gospels contain plenty of sayings that present Jesus as a teacher of wisdom and also plenty that refer to a coming kingdom and some kind of cosmic transformation. The kingdom that Jesus envisaged is not like any age that has existed in the past, or any that is likely to arise apart from divine intervention. The Beatitudes (Matt. 5:3-11) point toward an aeon in which the meek will inherit the earth, those who hunger and thirst for righteousness will be satisfied, and the pure in heart will see God. In that day "the righteous will shine like the sun in the kingdom of their Father" (Matt. 13:43). Then "the last will be first, and the first will be last" (Matt. 20:16). In other words, the coming kingdom will not be the kind of world we now live in. On the other hand Jesus instructed his disciples on the proper use of their possessions, on marriage and divorce, on their relationships with one another, on living without anxiety, and so forth. There is not only a hope of a coming kingdom, but a wisdom of the kingdom that Jesus' followers were to embody in their everyday lives. One aspect of Jesus' parables and sayings is mundane, and the other is extramundane. Sometimes the tone of the teaching is almost worldly-wise, and at other times it verges on a full-blown apocalypticism. In both categories there are plenty of parables and sayings that scholars generally accept as authentic.

So why should scholars be at odds over Jesus as sapiential or as eschatological? Why not affirm that Jesus was both? Here, I believe, the primary objections to either a sapiential or an eschatological Jesus have not been textual or exegetical so much as philosophical. Schweitzer, as noted above, interpreted the eschatological language of the New Testament as an indication that Jesus expected the imminent or immediate end of the world. Beginning with Schweitzer, one of the major foci of discussion was whether an expectation of an imminent ending of the world was consistent with Jesus' specific ethical exhortations. In other words, if the world were ending in three months, would that spur you on to become a better person or a worse one? Does a firm expec-

---

394. Borg, "Reflections on a Discipline," in *Studying the Historical Jesus*, p. 20.

tation that life as we know it will soon be over encourage ethical exertion or moral lassitude? This is a very interesting psychological question that can be answered in contradictory ways. Martin Luther once declared that if the world were to end tomorrow, he would still plant a tree today. A fine sentiment, to be sure, but one wonders how many people would so act. For his part Schweitzer developed his notion of Jesus' teaching as an "interim ethic" that was intended for only a short period. Jesus could be quite rigorous and even perfectionistic in his moral instruction because his imperatives had to be obeyed for only a brief period. The commands were stamped with an expiration date.

The problem with this theory is that it makes far too much of a few isolated Gospel sayings that might hint at an immediate ending of the world and it ignores many more that hint that the world in its present order is going to be around for some time. Schweitzer took his starting point in a text where Jesus says to his disciples: "When they persecute you in one town, flee to the next; for truly I tell you, you will not have gone through all the towns of Israel before the Son of Man comes" (Matt. 10:23). This is one of a very few passages that might be taken to mean that Jesus expected the world to end within a few years or decades. Yet even this statement is ambiguous, and could simply be a way of saying: the task is great, and actually so great that you will always have more work to do; and so, if you are persecuted in one place, continue your work in another. There are many parables and sayings that present the kingdom of God as undergoing a process of growth and development through time. "The kingdom of heaven is like a mustard seed that someone took and sowed in his field; it is the smallest of all the seeds, but when it has grown it is the greatest of shrubs and becomes a tree, so that the birds of the air come and make nests in its branches" (Matt. 13:31-32). Here there is no Technicolor description of cosmic cataclysm but rather a description of gradual emergence. Jesus' simile is organic, suggesting that each new stage in the growth of the kingdom of God builds on that which preceded it. Jesus uses another organic simile in the same context in Matthew: "The kingdom of heaven is like yeast that a woman took and mixed in with three measures of flour until all of it was leavened" (Matt. 13:33). Yet another of the organic images is in Mark: "The kingdom of God is as if someone would scatter seed on the ground, and would sleep and rise night and day, and the seed would sprout and grow, he does not know how. The earth produces of itself, first the stalk, then the head, then the full grain in the head. But when the grain is ripe, at once he goes in with his sickle, because the harvest has come" (Mark 4:26-29). This parable in Mark adds something not in the parables of the mustard seed and yeast. There is not only gradual growth, but also a conclusion to the process, a time of harvest (cf. Matt. 13:23, 30). These parables militate against thinking that Jesus taught that the world was going to end immediately.

Jesus instructed his followers on how to live in the present world in the light of the world to come. His parables and sayings contain not only references to the kingdom's gradual growth and emergence, but also exhortations and imperatives that suggest the coming of the kingdom would be deferred. What Marcus Borg calls Jesus' "unconventional wisdom" was directed to people living in the present world — marrying and sometimes divorcing, setting up households, trying to make a living, suffering wrong and committing it, tempted by greed and lust, prone to distraction as well as devotion, and perhaps harassed and misunderstood for Jesus' sake. These teachings do not show the marks of what Schweitzer called an "interim ethic," if this means a teaching that was clearly limited to a brief span of time (e.g., don't leave your home — there's an air raid under way). Crossan has rightly emphasized the countercultural and inclusive community called into being by Jesus' ministry. Yet if Jesus was concerned with the formation of a new kind of human community, and planned and prepared for it with the call and instruction of his first followers, then this too is an argument against thinking that he believed that God was just about to intervene in history, abolish the present world, and start separating the sheep from the goats.

On strictly textual and exegetical grounds, rather than philosophical preconceptions, it seems to me that Jesus was both a sapiential and eschatological figure. He was an eschatological sage or sapiential prophet. He called his followers to a new way of living in the present time, and a transformed social order in their relations to one another. His teachings pointed forward to an ultimate transformation of the cosmos that might occur in the remote rather than the near future. In the end, the individual, society, and cosmos were all to be changed. I freely admit that one finds many conundrums in attempting to fit together the various aspects of Jesus' teaching. A critic might point out, for instance, that the *gradual growth* of the kingdom of God, suggested in the parables enumerated above, is not the same thing as the *deferred arrival* of an otherworldly or apocalyptic sort of kingdom. This is true. In the former case the kingdom is always advancing and emerging from what preceded, while in the latter it bears little relation to what preceded it and falls like a stone from heaven. Yet this objection does not undermine the position I am proposing. My point is simply that the sapiential and eschatological aspects of Jesus' teaching need somehow to be coordinated and not set against each other. How one does this remains an open question, susceptible to a number of answers.

The second matter I will address very briefly is the origin of Christology, or the early Christian images of Jesus. Sometimes this question is posed in terms of Jesus' view of himself and his role, or what is sometimes called his "self-understanding." My readers may have noticed that this chapter has used little or no "psychologizing" language regarding Jesus: "Jesus thought," "he intended," "feeling anger as he turned over the tables," "his compassion for the multitudes," and so on. As Henry Cadbury showed in his book *The Peril of Modernizing Jesus*, the nineteenth- and twentieth-century biographers of Jesus often erred in this respect. They engaged in wholesale psychologizing, and typically did so without first reconstructing any kind of social and historical background within which to understand Jesus. It is hardly surprising, then, that when they attempted to understand Jesus' inner life, they simply attributed to him the kinds of thoughts and feelings that they themselves might have had under similar circumstances. Undoubtedly the issue of Jesus' "self-understanding" is a legitimate question, and one that falls within the bounds of historical Jesus research. To understand any human being necessarily involves an assessment of his or her thoughts, feelings, and self-awareness. Some recent authors have done careful work on the issue of Jesus' self-understanding.[395] Furthermore, there are certain undisputed features of Jesus' life, such as his address to God as *Abba* (my dear Father), that could be a basis for claiming that Jesus had a distinctive sense of intimacy with God or "filial consciousness."[396] Yet, this said, there are plenty of pitfalls for anyone seeking to reconstruct the inner life of Jesus. One hopes for a surer route to firm conclusions regarding Christology.

Another common way of approaching the origin of Christology is through a study of the various titles attributed to Jesus in the New Testament and early Christian literature: "Son of God," "Son of Man," "Messiah," and so forth.[397] Generally the authors who write on this subject have sought to determine the first-century meanings of these various titles, and then to show whether there is a basis for affirming that Jesus applied any of these titles to himself. If Jesus had referred to himself as "Messiah" or "Lord" or with some other title, then the origin of Christology would lie within Jesus' own teaching. The problem with this approach, as E. P. Sanders points out, is that in first-century Judaism these titles may not have had fixed and unambiguous definitions that were understood alike by everyone. In this case, knowing the term that Jesus may have applied to himself, or that others applied to Jesus, does not

---

395. See James H. Charlesworth, "Jesus' Concept of God and His Self-Understanding," in *Jesus within Judaism,* pp. 131-64, and Ben Witherington III, *The Christology of Jesus* (Minneapolis: Fortress, 1990), esp. pp. 118-43, 215-33.

396. Joachim Jeremias, *The Prayers of Jesus* (Philadelphia: Fortress, 1967), pp. 11-65, esp. 57, 60, 62, argues that Jesus' address to God as *Abba* is unique to him, while this claim is disputed in Vermes, *Jesus the Jew,* pp. 210-13, and accepted in a qualified fashion in James D. G. Dunn, *Christology in the Making: A New Testament Inquiry into the Origins of the Doctrine of the Incarnation,* 2nd ed. (Grand Rapids: Eerdmans, 1996), pp. 26-28.

397. In addition to the works already cited by Witherington and Dunn, see also Martin Hengel, *The Son of God: The Origin of Christology and the History of Jewish-Hellenistic Religion* (London: SCM, 1976), and C. F. D. Moule, *The Origin of Christology* (Cambridge: Cambridge University Press, 1977).

tell us exactly what was meant by the term.[398] The phrase "Son of God," for instance, had a very wide range of meaning in Jesus' day. In one sense all the people of Israel were "sons [or daughters] of God," while in another sense the phrase could denote a special individual. To recount the most famous case of ambiguity, the phrase "Son of Man" has been subject to widely differing interpretations. Some scholars hold that the term refers to an exalted heavenly figure who will appear at the end of the world.[399] Barnabas Lindars argues that Jesus used the phrase not as a title but as a modest circumlocution, "a man like myself," and that it was the early church that turned the phrase into a title.[400] John Meier maintains that Jesus used "Son of Man" as "an enigmatic designation of himself" as the lowly and yet powerful servant of God's kingdom, and "may also have used the title to affirm his assurance of final triumph and vindication by God."[401] Other scholars are not convinced that Jesus ever used the phrase at all.[402] As with the issue of Jesus' self-understanding, there are many perplexities in approaching the issue of Christology by means of the early titles applied to Jesus.

My modest suggestion regarding the origin of Christology is simply this: The root of the early Christian images of Jesus lies not in any isolated statements or actions attributed to Jesus, such as titles he might have used for himself or references he made to God as his Father. Rather the origin of Christology lies in Jesus' entire mode of self-presentation, his whole way of acting and speaking. John Meier writes: "The crux of the problem lies in the paradox that, although Jesus rarely spoke directly about his own status, he implicitly made himself *the* pivotal figure in the final drama he was announcing and inaugurating. The Kingdom was somehow already present in his person and ministry, and on the last day he would be the criterion by which people would be judged."[403] Similarly E. P. Sanders observes: "Through him, Jesus held, God was acting directly and immediately, bypassing the agreed, biblically sanctioned ordinances, reaching out to the lost sheep of the house of Israel with no more me-

398. Sanders, *Historical Figure*, pp. 239-40.

399. Bultmann (*Jesus and the Word*, pp. 38-39, 49) held that Jesus did actually use the phrase, but possibly of some other figure still to come rather than of himself. Like Bultmann, Adela Yarbro Collins comments: "Jesus expected a radical transformation of the world and that this would involve the coming of a heavenly figure . . . [but] Jesus did not believe himself to be this figure" (in Ostling, p. 40).

400. Barnabas Lindars, "Re-enter the Apocalyptic Son of Man," *New Testament Studies* 22 (1976): 52-72, and *Jesus Son of Man* (Grand Rapids: Eerdmans, 1983).

401. Meier, "Reflections," pp. 100-101.

402. Norman Perrin argued that the term as applied to Jesus was simply a creation of early Christianity, in *A Modern Pilgrimage in New Testament Christology* (Philadelphia: Fortress, 1974), esp. pp. 65-66, 77-78.

403. Meier, "Reflections," p. 98.

diation than the words and deeds of one man — himself."[404] Jesus startled his contemporaries not because he somehow opposed the law in principle but because he implied that his own mission was what really counted. To cite Sanders again, the "most important point that can be made about Jesus' view of himself" is that "he regarded himself as having full authority to speak and act on behalf of God," and thus he might have thought of himself as God's "viceroy."[405] Jesus presented himself neither as a prophet who speaks in God's name — "thus says the Lord" — nor as a sage who speaks in the name of another teacher — "Rabbi Abba in the name of Samuel said." He had a very different way of presenting himself.[406] This modest suggestion — that the root of Christology lies in Jesus' entire self-presentation — is not without significance. For it implies that the divergent reactions to Jesus, ranging from shock and offense to skepticism, faith, and devotion, flow not from his incidental characteristics but from the central features of his life, teaching, and actions.[407]

404. Sanders, *Historical Figure*, pp. 236-37.

405. Sanders, *Historical Figure*, pp. 238, 242.

406. See Neusner, *Rabbi*, pp. 30-31, and Koester, *Introduction*, 2.78. A. Ginzberg was pointed in his criticism of Jesus' "I": "Israel cannot accept with religious enthusiasm, as the Word of God, the utterances of a man who speaks in his own name — not 'thus saith the Lord' but 'I say unto you.' This 'I' is in itself sufficient to drive Judaism away from the Gospels for ever" (*Ten Essays on Zionism and Judaism* [London, 1922], p. 232, quoted in Catchpole, p. 50).

407. In closing I wish to acknowledge the many helpful corrections and suggestions of David Noel Freedman, whose erudition in biblical studies spared me from numerous errors in this chapter. Robert Gundry also read the manuscript in its entirety and provided incisive commentary. My thanks are also due to my research assistant, Chris Crain, who helped by providing sources and checking the references to Josephus and the Mishnaic and Talmudic texts. All remaining errors of fact and interpretation remain my own.

Muhammad

DANIEL C. PETERSON

Overture

On the eve of the birth of Muhammad and the rise of Islam, in the seventh century of the common era, two great empires, the Byzantine and the Sassanid, faced each other — as they and their predecessors had for centuries — across an unstable border. That border ran from north to south across Mesopotamia but continued thereafter to separate the relatively fertile lands of the eastern Mediterranean coast and its immediate hinterlands from the vast and arid deserts of the Arabian Peninsula. Although the Byzantines exercised seemingly firm control over greater Syria and the Sinai to the west, Arabia had eluded control by either of the two rival states.

There may have been a vague awareness of other great cultures beyond the Byzantines and the Sassanids. Tang China was far away to the east, as were the kingdoms of India, Burma, Indonesia, and the empire of the Khmers. Even farther away was the mysterious island nation of Japan. Still, for the world between the Nile and the Oxus Rivers, only the "Romans" and the Persians really counted. Both empires were deeply ideological, verging on the theocratic. The Byzantine Empire, which controlled the Balkans up to the Danube, Anatolia, Syria, Egypt, and (to varying extents) Italy and North Africa from its great capital of Constantinople, was passionately Christian. The Byzantines' dominant

I should like to thank Professors David Noel Freedman and Michael McClymond for their comments on an earlier draft of this essay. I should also like to thank Alison V. P. Coutts for her vital computer expertise and my wife, Deborah, for her help at various stages.

language was Greek, although Latin continued to play an important role in the official documents of this continuation of the ancient Roman Empire.

The Sassanid Empire, to the east, had its base in the rich river lands of Iraq and extended eastward across modern-day Iran to Afghanistan and the banks of the Oxus River. It was equally passionate in its commitment to Mazdaism, or Zoroastrianism. Its language was Persian, an Indo-European tongue attested from Old Testament times whose greatest literary achievements were still in the future. The ideological loyalties of the two empires added fire to a rivalry that was, at its base, simply one of shared but indistinct and uncertain borders. The Persian rulers, however, confronted an ethnic and religious diversity within their domain that far exceeded the problems of their Byzantine rivals. Their Magian or Zoroastrian religion remained very much a matter for the ruling class, and there is little evidence that it ever became rooted among the Persian masses. Although they were officially Zoroastrian, their subjects included large numbers of Jews, Nestorian and Monophysite Christians, Manichaeans, Gnostics (Marcionites and proto-Mandaeans), and pagans. In fact, at least in late Sassanian Iraq, aggressive and successful Christian proselytizing became such a threat that apostates from Zoroastrianism were subject to capital punishment.[1] The Persians' diversity presented them with a real problem of social incoherence (which probably contributed, in the mid–seventh century, to the rather swift collapse of the Sassanid state before the armies of Islam) and, by rendering them somewhat insecure, heightened their religious aggressiveness.

Geopolitical conflict between the Persians and the "Romans" had been ongoing for many centuries, and it must have seemed to most contemporaries in what M. G. S. Hodgson has called the Nile-to-Oxus region that the two empires were permanent fixtures of the political scene. A third-century rabbi named Samuel predicted that the Roman and Persian Empires would remain until the advent of the Messiah, and little in the intervening centuries had suggested that he was wrong.[2] Indeed, the tendencies of the age were centralizing and urbanizing, and both the Sassanid and Byzantine states increasingly sought to govern their huge domains though a centralized bureaucracy based on political doctrines of absolute monarchy. Each sought economic mastery. Each sought to control the trade routes by which the products of East Asia, particularly silk, came to the West. The Byzantines wanted to reconquer Armenia and Mesopotamia, which their Roman predecessors had governed in the days of Trajan. The Persians, on the other hand, remembered the old days of Darius

1. Michael G. Morony, *Iraq after the Muslim Conquest* (Princeton: Princeton University Press, 1984), pp. 298-300.
2. Cited by Morony, pp. 326-27.

when they had owned Syria and Egypt, and dreamed of their return. The Byzantines and the Sassanids seemed strong, and growing stronger. But neither empire was as solid, by Muhammad's lifetime, as it appeared.

For one thing, the form of Christianity enforced by Byzantium in greater Syria and Egypt was unpopular among their peoples, who felt oppressed and alienated from imperial authority. "Adherence to completely incomprehensible dogmas, like the espousal of the Monophysite doctrine by great masses of people in the Orient and in Egypt," Max Weber observed, "was the expression of an anti-imperial and anti-Hellenic separatist nationalism. Similarly, the monophysitic Coptic church later preferred the Arabs to the Romans as overlords."[3]

Christendom was richly variegated then, as it is now. We in the West are perhaps inclined to see its history through the "mainstream" church. But much more was going on in Christian circles than merely the orderly working out of the creeds. In the philosophically sophisticated though not purely cerebral politics of the great ecumenical councils, schisms repeatedly arose among those who found themselves outvoted. In Judaism, too, the rather coolly rational spirit of the two fifth-century Talmuds, although it was and is immensely influential, should not be mistaken for the whole of the religion.[4] In both faiths the old apocalyptic imagination was still very much awake, and it testifies eloquently if indirectly of social dislocation and political dissatisfactions. The *Apocalypse of Peter*, for example, although it seems to have originated in Palestine early in the second century, was popular up to the eighth or ninth century in Egypt and perhaps elsewhere in the Near East.[5] But new works of quasi scripture were still being created as well. The *Apocalypse of Sedrach*, a Jewish text that underwent a later Christian redaction, may have been written as late as the fifth century, while the Hebrew *Apocalypse of Enoch*, or *3 Enoch*, seems to have originated in the fifth or sixth century in either Palestine or Babylonia. The *Vision of Ezra* may have been composed as late as the seventh century, during or after the lifetime of Muhammad, as were also the *Sibylline Oracles*, which seem to have originated mainly in Egypt, but also in Syria, Asia Minor, and elsewhere in the Near East. The *Revelation of Ezra*, a Christian work, was written sometime prior to the ninth century, while the *Greek Apocalypse of Ezra* may date somewhat later still. The *Apocalypse of Daniel* was probably written at the very beginning of the ninth century, in Palestine or perhaps Egypt.[6]

3. Max Weber, *The Sociology of Religion*, trans. Ephraim Fischoff (Boston: Beacon Press, 1993), pp. 70-71.

4. The final redaction of the Babylonian Talmud was completed around 540 C.E.

5. J. K. Elliott, *The Apocryphal New Testament* (Oxford: Clarendon, 1993).

6. Information on dating and provenance for these apocryphal materials has been drawn from James H. Charlesworth, ed., *The Old Testament Pseudepigrapha*, vol. 1, *Apocalyptic Literature and Testaments* (Garden City, N.Y.: Doubleday, 1983).

One of the great divisions in the Near East on the eve of Islam's advent, as today, was that between urban and rural areas. The socioeconomic distinctions that always exist between town and country were exacerbated by linguistic dissimilarity. In the eighth and seventh centuries B.C.E., the Assyrians had, by military conquest, spread a single high culture throughout the region. Its vehicle was the Aramaic language, which, owing to the social prestige of the new masters, gradually replaced the earlier languages and became the mother tongue of Syria and Iraq. It remained so, essentially, until the time of the Arab conquests. By means of the subsequent victories and colonial enterprises of the ardent Hellenizer Alexander the Great, however, Greek culture had been imposed upon the area, which thus entered the Hellenistic period. But it was the cities that absorbed Hellenism far more than the largely untouched countryside. The educated classes now frequently knew Greek, as well as the philosophy, science, and general ideals that it carried. But Aramaic was still the basic language of much of the Near East (including its Christian form, called Syriac), and would provide an excellent and easy bridge for transition to Arabic (a related Semitic language) following the rise of Islam. In Egypt it was Coptic, a form of the ancient Egyptian language that had adopted a modified Greek alphabet and some Greek vocabulary, that formed the daily speech of the hinterlands beyond Greek-speaking cities such as Alexandria. And the great church capitals of Alexandria, Rome, and Constantinople had Syriac-speaking counterparts in the episcopal sees and theological schools of such cities as Edessa and Antioch.

On the Sassanid side of the border, Khusraw I Anushirvan ("he of the immortal soul"), perhaps the greatest of the shahs, attempted to centralize power even more directly in the sixth century by taking it from the landowning gentry class, thus leaving them sullen and disaffected, and imported bedouin Arabs from Arabia for use in his army.[7] Both sides, in fact, had resorted to using bedouin mercenaries to patrol their borders in the far distant and very unpleasant areas along the Arabian and Iraqi frontiers. The Ghassanids, in and near Syria, and the Lakhmids in the vicinity of Iraq effectively formed client states for the Byzantines and Sassanids, respectively, protecting the interests of the two empires and occasionally providing soldiers for the imperial armies. In the

---

7. The centralization continued under his eventual successor, Khusraw II Parviz (d. 628), with very probably fatal consequences for the dynasty. (Muslim armies conquered Persia before the middle of the seventh century.) It was during this period, and as a result of this process, that the semiautonomous administrative structures built up by Babylonian Jewry were suppressed or destroyed. Khusraw I Anushirvan seems also to have presided over the writing down of the Avesta and the Zand, two scriptural documents of the Zoroastrian tradition — a conservative act that was probably designed to buttress the authority of Magian priests.

Sassanian realm, however, some Arabs became so powerful that they were able to interfere in the royal succession.

The partial Arabization of the Sassanid army would have consequences that no Persian military planner could possibly have foreseen at a time when the notion of a military threat from a disorganized rabble of camel nomads would surely have been dismissed as laughable. The alienation of powerful segments of their subject populations ultimately facilitated the lightning-paced Arab conquests that sharply reduced the Byzantine lands and eliminated the Sassanids altogether, not long after the death of Muhammad. During Muhammad's lifetime, in the early seventh century, the Sassanians and the Byzantines fought an extremely destructive war that at first seemed to achieve for the Persians what they had dreamed of: Syrian Antioch fell to them in 611, followed by the fall of the holy city of Jerusalem on May 5, 614. The patriarch of Jerusalem and the inhabitants of the city were taken captive, its churches were burned, and the sacred relic of the True Cross, upon which Christ had been crucified, was removed to the Sassanid capital amidst great ceremony. In 615 and again in 626 Persian forces seized the city of Chalcedon, famous for the ecumenical council that had been held there and strategically crucial because it lay across the strait from the Byzantine capital of Constantinople. Between 617 and 619 the Persians occupied Egypt, which had long been the granary of the Roman Empire and, in particular, of the capital.

But a new and resourceful leader, Heraclius, had come to the throne in Byzantium. In February of 628, as he was advancing on the Sassanid capital of Ctesiphon, the Persian generals and nobles overthrew and executed the shah and placed on the throne a new ruler who sued for peace. In March 630 Heraclius made a solemn pilgrimage to Jerusalem, bringing with him the True Cross. Thus the war ended in a decisive victory for Constantinople. But it proved to be a rather Pyrrhic one that left both empires financially, militarily, and politically exhausted. Islam arose and expanded in the relative vacuum of effective political power resulting from that war.

The Arabian *Jahiliyya*

The Arabian Peninsula, nearly a third the size of Europe, lay at the juncture of the two great empires. It was and is an arid land, sparsely populated because of its low rainfall and lack of water. (In some areas there may be no rainfall for a decade or more.) Vast lava fields occasionally come to surface, but the most picturesque feature of the region is its sand dunes, some of which rise higher than six hundred feet and are several miles in length. One particularly desolate region, the so-called Empty Quarter, is the size of France. Culture there and most everywhere else could not be agrarian. Rather it was bedouin based, resting on camel nomadism. (One nineteenth-century Orientalist famously described the Arabs as parasites on camels.) There were lesser herds of sheep and goats and some oases with wells, which permitted the cultivation of date palms.

On the north the peninsula bordered on the scattered territories in Mesopotamia and Syro-Palestine often referred to as the Fertile Crescent. Here migrant Arabs searching for better living conditions came into contact with the settled civilizations of the wider world, imbibing influences from them and occasionally influencing them as well. The Nabateans, for example, were Aramaicized Arabs who interacted with Rome from their famous capital of Petra until their territory was absorbed under the emperor Trajan in 105 C.E. and designated the provinces of Palaestina Tertia and Arabia. A common name among Nabatean rulers was Aretas, which appears also in 2 Corinthians 11:32. (This is simply a Hellenized form of the Arabic masculine name *Harith* or *Haritha,* from a root relating to the tilling of the soil.) In the first half of the third century C.E., at least two Arabs actually ruled the Roman Empire for brief periods. One, Elagabalus (218-22), had been the high priest of the sacred black stone of Syrian Emesa, and upon his accession to the imperial dignity he had the stone transported to Rome and enshrined within a temple there. The second, Philip, sat on the throne in 244 C.E., the year of Rome's millennial celebrations. Just after his death another Aramaicized Arab kingdom, Palmyra, arose, first as a Roman client state dominating the trade route between Damascus and Mesopotamia and then, briefly but famously, as an independent would-be empire under its rebel queen Zenobia.[8]

The great sixth-century Byzantine emperor Justinian appointed Harith, of the Monophysite Christian Arab tribe Banu Ghassan, king of the East and commander of the empire's Arab auxiliary forces. The fighting between the Byzantines and their predecessors the Romans, on the one hand, and the Parthians and Sassanids, on the other, had been going on for centuries and was fierce but desperately hopeless. Justinian, however, desired to focus his attention on the lands in Europe and North Africa that the empire had lost when the barbarians overran the imperial armies there in the fifth century.[9] He was more than happy to turn the conduct of the eastern wars over to Arab mercenaries. So, for that matter, were his Persian rivals. They, too, had more pressing concerns than the old and fruitless border wars of the Syrian and north Arabian

8. Her name in Arabic was Zaynab. She proclaimed her son Athenodorus — whose name in Greek denotes the "Gift of Athena" and probably reflects an underlying Arabic *Wahballat* ("Gift of Allat") — Caesar Augustus of the Near East.

9. Byzantium seems simply to have been unable to fight successfully on both fronts at once. See Maxime Rodinson, *Mohammed,* trans. Anne Carter (Harmondsworth: Penguin Books, 1971), p. 34, for the sixth century.

steppes, and consequently designated the Banu Lakhm tribe to do their fighting there for them.[10]

On the south and on the east, the peninsula's boundary was formed by the Indian Ocean and the Persian Gulf, while the Red Sea provided its perimeter to the west. The southwestern corner of the peninsula, the Yemen, was mountainous but relatively well supplied with water, which facilitated the rise of fairly advanced monarchical societies based on intensive terraced cultivation and irrigation. It produced a rich crop of incense, myrrh, and other perfumes and aromatic substances for sale to the Mediterranean basin, and was a major transit point for trade from India and East Africa. Pearls, ivory, silk, cotton, textiles, rice, pepper, slaves, monkeys, gold, and even ostrich plumes could be found in its markets and warehouses. Not surprisingly, Yemen's culture was quite distinct from that of the rest of Arabia. Its people did not call themselves Arabs, and they spoke a language that was distinct from but related to Arabic. Their rich temples and elaborate priesthood were without parallel elsewhere in Arabia.

Travel in the peninsula was difficult but not impossible, given the right combination of skills and a knowledge of the watering holes. Several trade routes crisscrossed the region, notable among them a course running from the ports of the Red Sea and the border outposts of Syria-Palestine and Transjordan, or even directly from Gaza and Damascus, down along the coast of the Red Sea to the Yemen. Dating to at least the time of Alexander the Great and his successors, and probably back to the time of the domestication of the camel, this route has in more recent years served the Hijaz railway.

Rome's commercial relationships with the East began in the days of its early empire, when its increasing hunger for luxuries turned its attention to the raw goods and exotics that could be had via the customs stations, first of the Parthians and then of the Sassanids. But the Arabian land route also grew in importance. Seafaring merchants who had mastered the monsoons brought goods from India and elsewhere to the Yemen, whence other entrepreneurs carried them overland. Not content to serve as transit points, however, the kingdoms of south Arabia also produced rich crops of frankincense and myrrh to feed the funeral pyres and the temple liturgies of the Mediterranean basin. With the massive influx of wealth that such trade brought, the Yemen earned its classical reputation as Arabia Felix, "Arabia the Blessed."[11]

---

10. It is not clear which appointment came first. The Lakhmids are said, at one point, to have massacred four hundred Christian nuns in honor of the goddess al-Uzza, and some have speculated that this outrage impelled Justinian to appoint Harith and the Ghassanids as his agents and policemen.

11. Classical authors by the time of Ptolemy (second century c.e.) had divided Ara-

For reasons easily grasped, Roman/Byzantine and Persian rulers were very interested in this route. The Sassanids wanted to control it for its profits; the Byzantines sought to control it in order to escape the tariff duties imposed on them by their hereditary enemies along the other trade route. The Romans had sent a large expedition into Arabia in 24 B.C.E., but it proved a disaster. In the middle of the fourth century C.E., their Byzantine successors sent a Christian bishop to the Yemen in an effort to counteract Persian political activity there by preaching the ideology of the Byzantine state, Christianity. Likewise, just across the narrow strait of today's Bab al-Mandab, the new Christian power of Abyssinia (Ethiopia) cast envious and greedy eyes on the riches of the Yemenis. Early in the sixth century the Byzantines encouraged their fellow Christians in Abyssinia to occupy Yemen as a way of heading off further Sassanid inroads.[12]

The remainder of the Arabian Peninsula, however, seemed far removed from the interests of the great powers. Bedouin culture is much less stratified than that of societies based on an agricultural surplus. There might be transient concentrations of wealth, perhaps, but no lasting class divisions. The herdsman or nomad cannot be exploited like the rooted peasant, who is, from the bedouin perspective, a slave to his fields and hence to others. The nomad has his pride, and he is, by definition, mobile. If the situation is not to his liking, he can simply strike his tent and move away.

Tribal organization was, and is today, based first on extended families and then, in ever larger circles, on conglomerations of groups known as "clans" and "tribes." At least in theory, the basis of these groupings was common kinship, based on descent — real or fictional — from a shared ancestor. Elaborate genealogies served both as an ideological prop for the system and, under early Islam, as tools for political analysis. (Muhammad's lieutenant and successor, Abu Bakr, was famous for his genealogical expertise.) Each group possessed a recognized pastureland in which to wander. There were limits and boundaries, but they were fluid and changed constantly in intertribal conflict. Each tribe was sovereign and was led by a chief, or *shaykh*, who was chosen partly on the basis of descent but partly also on the basis of proven valor and wisdom.

---

bia into perhaps four parts. They were somewhat familiar with Arabia Petraea (the area surrounding the spectacular rock-hewn city of Petra, in modern Jordan) and with the coastal regions. Of Arabia Felix and the much larger interior Arabia Deserta they had, at best, spotty and inaccurate notions. Solid treatments of the subject include G. W. Bowersock, *Roman Arabia* (Cambridge: Harvard University Press, 1983), and Fergus Millar, *The Roman Near East: 31 BC–AD 337* (Cambridge: Harvard University Press, 1993).

12. The Abyssinians were Monophysites while the Byzantines termed themselves "Orthodox," but that did not prevent them from regarding each other as Christians — nor from recognizing common political interests.

Under such circumstances, obviously, although lineage and group loyalties were intense, there could be no authoritarian political forms. Thus the political culture of Arabia — if there could truly be said to be one — was quite opposite that of the Sassanians. Indeed, there was really no Arabian concept of a "state" at all, except perhaps among the Lakhmids and Ghassanids to the north (who had come into contact with the settled regimes of Iran and the Mediterranean basin) and among the sedentary and quite distinct culture of Yemen to the south. The bedouin chief had no authority to coerce. He was, rather, obliged to entreat his followers by generosity and kindness and, no doubt, by leading them in directions that he could sense they had already chosen to travel. The very notion of kingship or even political authority was abhorrent to the nomads of Arabia. Bernard Lewis puts it well when he says that the Arabian ideal was "a maximum of freedom of action and a minimum of public authority."[13]

However, another factor in Arabian life needs to be taken into account, one far less well known and clearly understood: There existed, in Arabia, professional men of religion who came to their role by family inheritance and served as interpreters of customary law.[14] These were, in effect, holy families, certainly priestly families, and they were generally associated with a sacred enclave or sanctuary. In modern south Arabia this enclave is called a *hawta;* in ancient Arabia it was known as a *haram* — the term still used for the Meccan sanctuary of the Ka'ba, which is the sacred center of the Muslim world. In the Yemen, for example, the sanctuary of a god named Dhu Samawi was set within a sacred enclave which was apparently surrounded by boundary stones just like those in Mecca.[15] As the leading scholar of the subject has observed,

> In a society where war is the norm of existence, a neutral territory is a necessity for reasons religious, political, and economic. The ḥawṭah is such an area, often situated at a natural road junction, where tribes meet, perhaps an important market. A saint, it is often recorded, in his own lifetime will demar-

13. Bernard Lewis, *The Arabs in History,* rev. ed. (New York: Harper & Row, 1967), p. 35.

14. See R. B. Serjeant, "Ḥaram and Ḥawṭah, the Sacred Enclave in Arabia," in *Mélanges Taha Husain, publiés par Abdurrahman Badawi* (Cairo, 1962), pp. 41-58; and R. B. Serjeant, "The Saiyids of Ḥadramawt" (inaugural lecture at the School of Oriental and African Studies of the University of London, 1956). Both papers are now available in R. B. Serjeant, *Studies in Arabian History and Civilization* (London: Variorum Reprints, 1981). As Serjeant, "The Saiyids of Ḥadramawt," p. 6 n. 1, observes, the religious aristocracy of pre-Islamic Arabia seems, after the coming of Islam, to have distinguished itself in jurisprudence.

15. Serjeant, "Ḥaram and Ḥawṭah," p. 52. The name of the god seems to suggest astral worship, or something of the sort. It means, roughly, "he of the heavenly [things]."

cate a ḥawṭah with whitewashed pillars. After death his holiness and power are embodied in his tomb, now become a sanctuary, which his successor, known as Manṣab, and his posterity administer. The essential political factor herein is that the saint induces the tribes or [in Islamic times] sulṭāns to contract agreements with him to maintain the inviolability of the ḥawṭah and define penalties for its infringement. . . . The ḥawṭah and the Meccan ḥaram are institutions identical in essence.[16]

Early Muslims described the period before the rise of Islam in Arabia as the time of *Jahiliyya*, generally translated into English (and understood in modern Arabic) as the "Age of Ignorance."[17] The obvious point of the name — as was the point of the Enlightenment's rather misleading invention of the "Dark Ages" — was to heighten the contrast between the bad old days and the presumably better days that had followed.

The religious views of the pre-Islamic Arabians have been described as a kind of "tribal humanism."[18] There was, according to this reading, little faith in an afterlife and little real concern for the gods among the inhabitants of Arabia before the coming of Islam. Given no economic basis for a feudal or aristocratic society, Arabian life was egalitarian and unstratified, but everything was viewed in tribal terms. Group solidarity — what the later Arab social theorist Ibn Khaldun (d. 1406) labeled *asabiyya* — was the fundamental premise of bedouin life and its chief tool of survival. Fissiparous tendencies were limited, however, by the consideration that, if one struck out on one's own, one lost all claim to protection and support from one's kinsfolk and, in the absence of any kind of "government," could be attacked with impunity. On the other hand the threat of costly and debilitating blood feuds maintained a rough-and-ready intertribal peace. Vengeance was meted out by groups to groups, for the simple reason that the group was the basic unit of society rather than the individual, who had rights and obligations only as a member of his or her tribe or clan. As a poet named Durayd b. Simma put it, speaking of his own tribe,

---

16. Serjeant, "The Saiyids of Ḥaḍramawt," pp. 14-15.

17. Although it would probably be translated more accurately as the "Age of Barbarism." See the argument of Ignaz Goldziher, "What Is Meant by 'al-Jāhiliyya?" in Ignaz Goldziher, *Muslim Studies*, ed. S. M. Stern, trans. C. R. Barber and S. M. Stern (Albany: State University of New York Press, 1967), pp. 201-8.

18. The phrase is associated with W. Montgomery Watt, upon whose reconstruction of pre-Islamic Arabian social processes the following discussion is substantially dependent. For the phrase see W. Montgomery Watt, *Muhammad: Prophet and Statesman* (London: Oxford University Press, 1974), p. 51. For the social malaise of Mecca in the period just prior to the advent of Islam, see Watt, pp. 38, 43-55; Rodinson, pp. 65-66. On pp. 16-18 Rodinson echoes the notion of pre-Islamic Arabia as a rather irreligious place.

I am of Ghaziyya: if she be in error, then I will err;
And if Ghaziyya be guided right, I go right with her.[19]

The virtues most highly prized among the pre-Islamic Arabs included bravery in battle, patience in misfortune, persistence in revenge, protection of the weak, defiance of the strong, honor, and generosity. They were very much like the qualities that some scholars have identified as characteristic of "heroic" cultures such as Homeric Greece, pagan Scandinavia, and early Sumer.[20] In this context it is significant that the early Arabic term equivalent to the English "virtue" is *muruwwa*, or "manliness."[21] Much of the pre-Islamic Arabian moral ideal might be expressed in the vow that Tennyson ascribes to his Ulysses, "To strive, to seek, to find, and not to yield."

Revenge was an important element of that ideal. Here is one early Arab commenting on his kinsfolk who had refused to help him against the raiders who had stolen his camels:

For all their numbers, they are good for naught,
My people, against harm however light:
They pardon wrong by evildoers wrought,
Malice with lovingkindness they requite.[22]

The ancient Arabs were fond of the story of Shanfara of Azd, an ideal hero who, as a child, had been captured from his tribe and raised by the Banu Salaman. Years later, when he had grown up, he returned to his own tribe and vowed to extract vengeance from his onetime captors — a nice illustration of the power of blood kinship even over the ties of acquaintance and perhaps affection. He swore an oath that he would kill a hundred men of the Salaman. He was so successful that he managed to kill ninety-eight when he was caught in an ambush by his infuriated enemies. During the struggle that ensued, one

19. Cited by Reynold A. Nicholson, *A Literary History of the Arabs* (Cambridge: Cambridge University Press, 1969), p. 83. All of the translations of pre-Islamic poetry cited here are from Nicholson. The abbreviation "b." represents the Arabic word *ibn* (son [of]).

20. Following the classic statement of the idea in H. Munro Chadwick, *The Growth of Literature,* 3 vols. (Cambridge: Cambridge University Press, 1932-40), discussed most fully in vol. 1. See also Albert B. Lord, "Homer, Parry, and Huso," *American Journal of Archaeology* 52 (1948): 34-44; Samuel Noah Kramer, "New Light on the Early History of the Ancient Near East," *American Journal of Archaeology* 52 (1948): 156-64. In my opinion, accordingly, Nicholson is not far off when he labels Antara b. Shaddad, the dashing hero of a pre-Islamic Arabian romance, "the Bedouin Achilles." See Nicholson, p. 114.

21. Of course, the English word itself is derived from the Latin *vir,* or "man."

22. Nicholson, p. 92.

of his hands was severed by the stroke of a sword. Shanfara grabbed the severed hand with his other hand and threw it with such force into the face of one of his opponents that it killed the man. This brought him to within one victim of fulfilling his vow of vengeance. Unfortunately, though, the Banu Salaman killed him and left his body to rot in the desert. Sometime later, however, one of them was passing by the spot and saw Shanfara's skull lying on the sand, bleached out by the intense desert sun. He could not resist the temptation to kick it. It was a bad move. A splinter of bone from the skull went into his foot and, when the wound mortified, he died. Even after death Shanfara, the consummate Arabian hero in this regard, had completed his vow of revenge.[23]

Honor was another important pre-Islamic virtue. Even into the Islamic period, Arabs related the story of a Jewish Arab named al-Samawal b. Adiya, who owned a castle north of the agricultural oasis of Yathrib. According to this story, the great poet Imru al-Qays took refuge with al-Samawal while fleeing toward Syria from some of his many enemies. When he continued on his journey, he left five coats of mail, heirlooms of his family, with his host for safekeeping, intending to pick them up again on his return. But he never came back, for he died on the way home from an audience with the emperor in Constantinople. In the meantime the enemies of Imru al-Qays besieged al-Samawal in his fortified dwelling, demanding that he surrender the coats of mail he had promised to preserve for the poet. This he would not do. And when the besiegers captured his son, who had gone out of the castle to hunt, and threatened to kill him if his father did not yield up the armor, al-Samawal responded that they must do as they saw fit, for he could not in honor renege on his obligation to Imru al-Qays. At that, the enemies outside slew the boy and lifted the siege.[24]

Finally the pre-Islamic Arabs venerated the ideal of generosity. The model figure in this regard was a man named Hatim of Tayyi, who has served to illustrate the lavish generosity of the perfect Arab chieftain for many centuries.[25] To his wife, Mawiyya, he remarked:

The guest's slave am I, 'tis true, as long as he bides with me,
Although in my nature else no trait of the slave is shown.[26]

23. The story is told at Charles James Lyall, *Translations of Ancient Arabian Poetry* (New York: Columbia University Press, 1930), p. 83.
24. Nicholson, pp. 84-85, provides an easily accessible translation of the story from al-Isbahani's classical collection *Kitab al-Aghani*.
25. He is mentioned, for example, in Omar Khayyam's famous twelfth-century Persian poem, the *Rubaiyat*.
26. Nicholson, p. 87.

When Hatim's mother was pregnant with him, so the story goes, she had a dream in which she was asked whether she would prefer to bear a generous son or ten strong and brave warriors. She chose the first. When Hatim grew up, it became his custom to throw away his food if he could find nobody with whom to share it. Such prodigality irritated his father, who gave him a slave girl, a mare, and a foal and sent him out into the middle of nowhere to herd the family's three hundred camels, the core of their wealth. True to form, when it came time to eat Hatim looked desperately for someone with whom to share his food. Finally, just as he was about to cast it away, he saw three riders in the distance and went out to meet them. They asked him for something to eat, and he slaughtered three camels for them. The riders — who, as it happened, were a trio of well-known poets from diverse regions of the peninsula — protested that a drink of milk would have been enough for them and said that, at the most, he might have butchered merely a young she-camel for their refreshment. Hatim responded that he could tell that they came from various places, and that he had gone to such lengths in order to ensure that his reputation for generosity would be carried to their different homes. Obligingly they thereupon composed and recited verses in praise of his extravagance. But this only served, as Hatim saw it, to put him in their debt, and he insisted that they come forward and divide his camel herd among them. They did, and each left with ninety-nine camels. When Hatim's father heard what had been done, he was furious. But Hatim assured him — quite accurately, as it turned out — that his generosity had now assured for both of them everlasting fame and honor, seeing that it would be celebrated in poetry across Arabia and beyond forever. The camels were a good investment for such a return.[27]

Ancient Arabs made the same connection between expert horsemanship and the cluster of values associated with "chivalry" and "knighthood" — virtues such as heroism, nobility, and valor — that later peoples of western Europe made. Indeed, the Arabs used the same word, *furusiyya* (lit. "horsemanship"), for both.[28] "Knight-errantry, the riding forth on horseback in search of adventures, the rescue of captive maidens, the succour rendered everywhere to

27. The story is translated, again from the *Kitab al-Aghani*, at Nicholson, pp. 85-86. The father, by the way, was not mollified by Hatim's reasoning and disowned him, leaving him alone in the desert with his slave girl, his mare, and her foal.

28. It is very likely, in fact, that the western European notion derives from the Arabs, who occupied substantial portions of the Iberian Peninsula for nearly eight centuries and occasionally ruled other portions of southern Europe as well. The historical association of horsemanship with certain ideals is well attested in various European languages, where we speak, for example, of "chivalry," "caballeros," "cavalry," and a "cavalier attitude." Beyond the Romance languages, the same equation can be seen in the German *Ritter* (knight), cognate with the German verb *reiten*, "to ride."

women in adversity — these were essentially Arabian ideas, as was the very name of *chivalry,* the connection of honourable conduct with the horse-rider, the man of noble blood, the cavalier."[29]

Muhammad was a native of Mecca, a small oasis town dominated by an Arab tribe known as the Quraysh, who controlled its economy and politics and enjoyed immense religious prestige in connection with the local shrine known as the Ka'ba. This shrine was an object of pilgrimage venerated by people throughout Arabia. The ancient frankincense trail passed near or through Mecca, and caravans of all types constantly plied the route, which ensured at least a measure of acquaintance, on the part of the town's inhabitants, with cultures and religions beyond Arabia. It would seem that the residents of Mecca originally hired themselves out as guides or as guards for the caravans that moved through their territory — in the latter case, their "guardianship" may have been little more than the demanding of protection money — but that, somewhere in the sixth century C.E., they began actually to take control of the trade and to outfit their own caravans. This led to a rapid increase in wealth, and to the rise of class divisions within the formerly rather undifferentiated population of the town.

Especially in the years just prior to the revelation, when unprecedented wealth was flowing into Mecca, the leaders of the tribe of Quraysh saw themselves as having achieved just about all there was to be achieved. In the late sixth century both the Lakhmids and the Ghassanids had abruptly lost their official status as clients of, respectively, the Sassanids and the Byzantines.[30] No Arabian power now stood to rival the ambitions of the Quraysh. Their wealth was certainly to be enjoyed for its own sake, but it also enabled them to live out the ideal of Arab generosity in a way that perhaps had never been known before. By means of wealth a man could be powerful and could further strengthen his situation by arranging marriages with other families of wealth and status. Thus he could be a protector of the weak and a sought-after ally. On a daily basis he could be a lavish host and a giver of gifts, not because of some religious precept or out of hope for a transcendent reward in a life to come, but because of the praise it would bring him. Perhaps he could even hope for a kind of immortality in the words of some poet, who could be brought to praise him either out of honest admiration or, failing that, through a relatively modest transfer of wealth.

Poetry was the sole medium of literary expression among the Arabs of the pre-Islamic period. Indeed, since it took no space in a saddlebag and was easily portable, it was by far the most important artistic form developed by the bed-

29. Nicholson, p. 88.
30. On the Lakhmids and Ghassanids, see Rodinson, pp. 26-28.

ouin nomads. The earliest extant Arabian poems date from about 500 C.E., but, since the first poets of whom we know are consummate masters working within conventions that seem already set, there is good reason to believe that the poetic tradition extends backward considerably further. Many scholars think the earliest poetic or poetrylike compositions were created in *saj'*, a style of elevated prose in which the lines have no meter but their final words rhyme. This was also the rhetorical form in which the pre-Islamic Arabian seers or soothsayers known as *kahins* delivered their oracles.[31] (Significantly, perhaps, it is likewise the style of the Qur'an.) The pre-Islamic poet was thought to be a sort of wizard, in league with and inspired by the jinn or even the *shayatin* (satans). The jinn (sg. jinni), creatures that ancient Arabian thinking ranked above humans but below angels, could be either good or bad (hence the "satans") but tended to be mischievous and unreliable.

Poetry was immensely popular among the masses of Arabs, and not merely among an elite — which, in Arabia, was essentially nonexistent in any event. It is thus not surprising that among a people obsessed with words and in a culture that has been called "language intoxicated," the distinction between prophet and poet should have been so uncertain. And indeed, prophethood is not easy to distinguish from that ancient sense of the vocation of the poet, for the prophet is by definition someone who speaks the word of another, not himself. He or she is literally an "enthusiast," having the god or *theos* within, and can fittingly be described, at the moment of the reception of revelation, as "possessed."[32] In ancient Greece and Israel, as in pre-Islamic Arabia, prophet and poet were originally one.[33] In the Bible Moses, Miriam, and Deborah are all termed "prophets," and specific poetry is attributed to each of them. Indeed, most of the canonical prophets of the Bible delivered oracular speeches that are, by most standards, poetic, even if the larger parts of such books as Jeremiah and Ezekiel are written in prose.

A story from the early Islamic period will serve to illustrate the pre-Islamic passion for poetry, which survived into at least the early years of the new religion but was, as the story shows, clearly under attack. There was a great and often bitter rivalry between two poets named Jarir and Farazdaq, and each poet had an enthusiastic and multitudinous following. One day during the civil wars that rent the Islamic community after the death of Muhammad, the governor of Khurasan, who was marching forth with an army to do battle with a sect

---

31. Compare the Hebrew *kohen*, "priest."

32. G. van der Leeuw, *Phänomenologie der Religion*, 4th ed. (Tübingen: J. C. B. Mohr [Paul Siebeck], 1977), pp. 244-45; compare 457-63.

33. See the discussion of David Noel Freedman, "Pottery, Poetry, and Prophecy: An Essay on Biblical Poetry," *Journal of Biblical Literature* 96, no. 1 (1977): 5-26; also van der Leeuw, pp. 244-45, 250. Compare Plato, *Apology* 22.

of purist Muslim schismatics called the Azariqa, heard the noise of an upheaval in his camp. When he inquired about its cause, he learned that his soldiers had been arguing passionately about the respective merits of the two poets. They decided to submit the question to him for adjudication. The governor declined to enter the dispute, but suggested that they take their question to the Azariqa, who not only clung to the simple, fierce, and rather anarchic ways of the desert but retained a deep passion for poetry. Thus, on the following day, when the armies had faced off against one another and one of the Azariqa had stepped forward to issue the traditional challenge to single combat, a warrior in the governor's army accepted the challenge but demanded to know, first, whether Jarir or Farazdaq was the better poet. "God confound you!" cried the rebel champion. "Are you asking me about poetry instead of studying the Qur'ān and the law?" Nonetheless, the dissenting warrior proceeded to cite a verse by Jarir and to give judgment in that poet's favor.[34]

Poetry unified the Arabs. Across the peninsula it was composed in the same dialect, following the same rules of composition. This made it, in modern terms, a powerful public relations tool. A poet praised his tribe and vilified its rivals. If he was good, if his verses were memorable, his praise or his ridicule could stick to his subject for many years.

> When there appeared a poet in a family of the Arabs, the other tribes round about would gather together to that family and wish them joy of their good luck. Feasts would be got ready, the women of the tribe would join together in bands, playing upon lutes, as they were wont to do at bridals, and the men and boys would congratulate one another; for a poet was a defence to the honor of them all, a weapon to ward off insult from their good name, and a means of perpetuating their glorious deeds and of establishing their fame for ever. And they used not to wish one another joy but for three things — the birth of a boy, the coming to light of a poet, and the foaling of a noble mare.[35]

The early Islamic poets Jarir and Farazdaq figure in another story that will illustrate the power of poets and poetry — as well as the power that was thought to lie behind them — in ancient Arabia and that continued on for some years beyond the life of the Prophet. There was a rather well known poet known as "the Camel-Herd," a member of the tribe of Banu Numayr, who had been very vocal in his opinion that Farazdaq was a better poet than Jarir, despite the fact that Jarir had been known to praise the Banu Numayr while Farazdaq had sometimes attacked them in his verse. One day Jarir ran into the Camel-

---

34. Nicholson, p. 239, retells this story from the invaluable *Kitab al-Aghani.*
35. Ibn Rashiq, quoted in Lyall, p. 17.

Herd near the new city of Basra and an argument arose. The Camel-Herd, whose son Jandal had accompanied him, was riding a mule. Young and impatient, Jandal suddenly burst out, "Why are you stopping before this dog of the Banū Kulayb, as if you had anything to hope or to fear from him?" Saying so, he lashed the mule with his whip, and the surprised animal kicked Jarir, who was standing nearby. Picking up his cap, which had fallen to the ground, Jarir brushed it, put it back on his head, and said, in spontaneous verse,

> O Jandal! What will Numayr say of you
> When my dishonoring shaft has pierced your father?

Jarir was coldly furious. He returned to his home, performed the evening prayer, called for a lamp and some date wine, and then proceeded to plot his poetic revenge. An old woman in the house heard the sound of muttering coming from his room and, climbing the stairs to see what the problem was, discovered him crawling, naked, on his bed. She ran downstairs, shouting that he was "mad" (*majnun;* lit. "jinn-possessed") and describing to the others in the house what she had seen. But they seem to have been wiser about the ways of poets than she was. "Go away," they said. "We know what he is up to." By dawn the following morning, Jarir had composed a devastating eighty-verse satire of the Banu Numayr, and he signaled his triumphant satisfaction with a shout of *Allahu akbar!* (God is most great!). He immediately rode to meet the Camel-Herd and his friends, including Farazdaq himself. He said nothing to any of them, but proceeded directly to recite his poem. Farazdaq, the Camel-Herd, and their friends listened in horrified silence as the lethal satire unfolded.

Jarir closed his poem with an insult against the entire tribe ("Cast down your eyes for shame! For you are of Numayr — no peer of Ka'b nor even of Kilāb"), and the Camel-Herd, now agonizingly aware of the evil he had brought upon them all, hurried back to the camp of his tribesmen. "Saddle up!" he cried. "Saddle up! You cannot stay here any longer, for Jarīr has disgraced you all!" They left as soon as they could strike their tents, and they never forgave the Camel-Herd for the shame he had called down upon their heads. Centuries later his tribe still lamented what he had done, and in fact, his story and his shame are preserved to this day in the great Arabic poetic anthology known as the *Kitab al-Aghani,* or "Book of Songs."[36]

Although the view of pre-Islamic Arabia as a society dominated by a "tribal humanism" has much to recommend it, we should be careful not to ex-

36. The story is retold at Nicholson, pp. 245-46. The early Arabs often compared *hija'* (satire) to arrows. They believed in the intrinsic power of words to "cast a 'spell.'" The story of Balaam in Num. 22–24 may reflect similar notions.

aggerate its allegedly secular character. As Tor Andrae observes of Muhammad, "Every sentence of his discussions with his countrymen shows that they clung to the pagan gods and customs with a devout loyalty which possessed an unmistakably religious colouring."[37] For many years scholars have pointed to the striking lack of religious feeling in extant *jahili* poetry, and to the rarity of its allusions to the pagan deities of the peninsula, as evidence that the pre-Islamic Arabians were largely irreligious. This seems to me unjustified.

The ancient Arabian *qasida*, or ode, was not an organic whole, but rather something like a series of paintings by the same artist or, as the Arabs themselves liked to describe it, a necklace of pearls that differed in size and quality. Each line was a separate unit, a complete thought. The ancient Arabs did not employ the technique of enjambment, continuing a sentence on into a following line. This means that modern editors and scholars frequently disagree over the proper order of the lines in early poems, and it means, furthermore, that lines can easily disappear altogether. It is thus altogether possible — and, I would say, likely — that expressly pagan lines disappeared from these poems in the early and zealous days of Islam. One's suspicion that this must be so is strengthened when one considers the transmission history of the poems. They were orally composed and, for many years, orally transmitted. Although the oldest of the poems claim to date from the beginning of the sixth century, they were not reduced to writing and anthologized, in many cases, until the close of the eighth century. That allows abundant time for editing.[38]

And who preserved the poetry? As Islam spread with lightning speed beyond what was then the rather small world of Arabic speakers, into Mesopotamia and Syria and Persia and across North Africa, new converts to the faith found the language of their holy book, the Qur'an, formidably difficult. To help them, an array of commentators and lexicographers stepped forward with linguistic guidance. Quite predictably they turned to the great repository of Arabic, its poetry, for help in explaining difficult terms, just as modern dictionaries use illustrative sentences to clarify meanings and usage of terms under discussion. Thus, when the old patronage networks that had promoted poetic composition had broken down because of the religious revolution of Islam and the dispersion of Arabia's native sons from the peninsula to Iberia on the west

---

37. Tor Andrae, *Mohammed: The Man and His Faith,* trans. Theophil Menzel (New York: Harper & Row, 1960), p. 119; compare 120-21. See, too, the materials quoted by F. E. Peters, *Muhammad and the Origins of Islam* (Albany: State University of New York Press, 1994), pp. 172-73.

38. In fact, the great Egyptian scholar and writer Taha Husayn suggested, in his famous book *Fī al-shi'r al-jāhilī* (On Jāhilī Poetry), that the entire corpus of pre-Islamic poetry is a late fraud. However, I would judge that the consensus view is that, although he raised important issues, he went too far.

and the borders of India on the east, it was the religious scholars who preserved tag lines of the poetry for philological reasons. But these, of course, would be the most likely people of all to omit lines paying tribute to pagan deities or expressing explicitly polytheistic religiosity.

We should be wary of exaggerating the gulf between pre-Islamic and Islamic religiosity, large though it undoubtedly is. It is abundantly clear from the Qur'an, for example, that Muhammad felt no need to introduce Allah to his Arabian audience. Allah was already known to them.[39] Thus, for instance, when an early revelation given to him called on the people of Mecca to "worship the Lord of this House" — i.e., of the Ka'ba — no need was felt to explain who the "Lord of this House" *was*.[40] Still, Allah was what historians of religion have sometimes termed a *deus otiosus* — a deity so distant and transcendent that he was of little practical relevance to the lives of the people. Their attentions seem to have been focused more on his three purported daughters — Manat, Allat, and al-Uzza — and on the quasi-divine beings known collectively as the jinn, than on Allah.[41] (Both Tor Andrae and Bernard Lewis term pre-Islamic Arabian religion "polydaemonism.")[42] These deities and demigods lived in or were represented by trees, fountains, and most particularly certain sacred stones.[43]

39. The word *Allah* is cognate with the name of the old Semitic high god *El* and the biblical *Elohim*. It is not so much a name as a title, a contraction of the Arabic *al-illah* ("the god"), and is simply the Arabic equivalent for the English "God." As such, it is used by Arabic-speaking Jews and Christians as well as Muslims, and is the term employed in the Arabic Bible. It is derived from the same root as Hebrew *'lh* (= *'eloah*, the rare singular form of the very common plural [of majesty?] *Elohim*). The use of the definite article *al-* in the Arabic is equivalent to the Hebrew *ha-'eloah* or *ha-'elohim*, which would mean "the god" or, perhaps, "God himself." For a discussion of pre-Islamic attitudes toward Allah, see Peters, *Muhammad*, pp. 107-8, 117.

40. Qur'an 106:3. In citations from the Qur'an (hereafter Q), the number preceding the colon indicates the sura, or chapter; the number following the colon specifies the verse(s). All translations from the Qur'an are mine.

41. For a good brief summary, see Rodinson, pp. 16-17.

42. Andrae, *Mohammed*, p. 13; Lewis, p. 30. Our lack of clarity on the early Arabian religious situation is mirrored in the fundamental disagreements about it among Western Orientalists: Watt, p. 26, thinks pre-Islamic paganism was a polytheistic system that was moving in the direction of monotheism; Peters, *Muhammad*, p. 118, sees an "emerging henotheism"; Andrae, *Mohammed*, p. 16, says "the ancient paganism of Arabia may in general be regarded as an undeveloped polytheism, in which a development had just barely begun which would have gradually produced a pantheon consisting of a hierarchy of gods." Perhaps even more completely than the Deuteronomistic reform among the Hebrews, the Islamic "reform" of Arabian religion suppressed the evidence of earlier theological concepts.

43. For interesting information on ancient Semitic litholatry, see Andrae, *Mohammed*, pp. 13-14; Peters, *Muhammad*, pp. 12-13.

(Recall the Arabo-Roman emperor Elagabalus and his sacred stone from Emesa, in Syria.) The jinn, in particular, seem to have originated as personifications of natural forces — often malevolent, seldom better than puckishly indifferent to human interests. They sometimes had to be bought off, but they seem never to have made moral claims or propounded moral law. There were a few fixed shrines (of which the Meccan Ka'ba was the most important), but the sacred objects may often have been — as is appropriate to the life of nomadic peoples — portable, rather like the biblical ark of the covenant or the tabernacle of Moses. In any event, whatever the religious situation in Arabia on the eve of the rise of Islam may have been, early Muslims insisted that the peninsula had once been an important center for the worship of the true and only God, linked inextricably to the sacred history of the Bible itself.

According to Islamic tradition, when Abraham cast Hagar and her son Ishmael out of his presence, they were led southward to a distant and barren valley in the Arabian Peninsula, some forty camel-days distant from the land of Canaan.[44] This valley, fifty miles inland from the Red Sea, was called Becca. It lay along a great caravan route, often called the "frankincense trail," whose origins are enshrouded in the very ancient past but along whose length perfumes and incense and other goods were brought to the great templed cities of the eastern Mediterranean basin.

Becca was, perhaps even more than the rest of Arabia, an arid place, oppressively hot and dusty, and it was not long before Hagar and her son were in a desperate condition. Indeed, she feared that the boy was dying. As he lay in the sand, weakened by terrible thirst, she climbed up to a rock for a better view, to see if anybody was around to offer help. There was no one. Nearly hysterical, Hagar ran to another elevated location, but still could see nobody. Seven times she ran from the one place to the other, and then she sat down in despair. It was at this point, according to Arab tradition, that an angel spoke to her the words recorded in Genesis 21:17-19: "God heard the cry of the boy, and an angel of God called to Hagar from heaven and said to her, 'What troubles you, Hagar? Fear not, for God has heeded the cry of the boy where he is. Come, lift up the boy and hold him by the hand, for I will make a great nation of him.' Then God

---

44. The sources of Islamic tradition upon which this essay depends for its basic narration of Muhammad's life include the chronicle of al-Tabari and, preeminently, the *Sira* or biography of Ibn Hisham. The English translation of the former, by various scholars, is now virtually complete from the State University of New York Press. The latter is readily available in translation as A. Guillaume, *The Life of Muhammad: A Translation of Ibn Ishaq's "Sīrat Rasūl Allāh"* (Karachi: Oxford University Press, 1967). These sources and others have been conveniently blended, without scholarly comment or analysis, in Martin Lings, *Muhammad: His Life Based on the Earliest Sources* (New York: Inner Traditions International, 1983).

opened her eyes and she saw a well of water. She went and filled the skin with water, and let the boy drink."[45] The water gushed forth from the sand at Ishmael's heel, and he and his mother were saved. In the years that followed, the well became known as Zamzam and, because of the excellence and abundance of its water in parched Arabia, the valley of Becca emerged as a popular halt for the caravans that plied the ancient trail.

In fact, Abraham himself eventually came to visit his son at Becca where, according to the Qur'an, God showed him the precise location, adjacent to the well of Zamzam, where he and Ishmael were to build a sanctuary. The site had already been chosen by Adam, who had built an earlier shrine there that had subsequently been destroyed in the flood of Noah. God also gave the patriarch instructions on exactly how that sanctuary was to be constructed, as an earthly replica of a heavenly prototype.[46] It was built roughly as a cube — its name, Ka'ba, indicates its shape — with its four corners directed toward the four cardinal directions of the compass.[47] In its eastern corner is a meteoric stone that was brought to Abraham by an angel from a nearby hill. "It descended from Paradise whiter than milk," the Prophet would later teach his followers, "but the sins of the sons of Adam made it black." When the Ka'ba was completed, God again spoke to Abraham and told him to institute a regular pilgrimage to Becca and its shrine: "Behold, we provided for Abraham the place of the House, [saying] Do not associate anything with me, and sanctify my house to those who circumambulate it, or stand, or prostrate themselves. And proclaim the pil-

---

45. Gen. 21:17-19 JPS. Gen. 21:14, 21 seems to locate these events in "the wilderness of Beer-sheba," near "the wilderness of Paran," rather than in distant Arabia.

46. See Peters, *Muhammad*, pp. 4-6; Geo Widengren, *The Ascension of the Apostle and the Heavenly Book* (Uppsala and Wiesbaden: A.-B. Lundequistska Bokhandeln and Otto Harrassowitz, 1950), pp. 33, 33 n. 1; Geo Widengren, *Muḥammad, the Apostle of God, and His Ascension* (Uppsala and Wiesbaden: A.-B. Lundequistska Bokhandeln and Otto Harrassowitz, 1955), p. 97 n. 1. For cross-cultural perspectives on temples in general — phenomenologically, the Ka'ba is clearly an instance of the ancient temple type — and on the heavenly temple prototype, see various items by John M. Lundquist, including "Studies on the Temple in the Ancient Near East" (Ph.D. diss., University of Michigan, 1983); "The Common Temple Ideology of the Ancient Near East," in *The Temple in Antiquity*, ed. Truman G. Madsen (Provo, Utah: Brigham Young University Press, 1984), pp. 53-76; "What Is a Temple? A Preliminary Typology," in *The Quest for the Kingdom of God: Studies in Honor of George E. Mendenhall*, ed. H. B. Huffmon, F. A. Spina, and A. R. W. Green (Winona Lake, Ind.: Eisenbrauns, 1983), pp. 205-19; *The Temple: Meeting Place of Heaven and Earth* (New York: Thames & Hudson, 1993).

47. F. E. Peters, *Allah's Commonwealth: A History of Islam in the Near East, 600-1100 A.D.* (New York: Simon & Schuster, 1973), p. 44, says the Ka'ba was constructed in the second century C.E. However, since no archaeological excavation is permitted at the site, and since contemporary literary sources are utterly lacking, it is difficult to see how such a judgment can be made with any confidence.

The Ka'ba in modern Mecca, surrounded by pilgrims
(Nomachi photo; Aperture/Pacific Press Service)

grimage [*al-hajj*] among the people. They will come to you on foot and on every lean camel, coming from every deep mountain pass."[48] Included in the rituals of the pilgrimage would be a sevenfold run between Safa and Marwah, as the two locations were now called, commemorating Hagar's desperate search for help that resulted in the revelation of the spring of Zamzam.

When all was done, Abraham presented the Ka'ba to God and asked God's blessing on what had been accomplished in the once-barren and uninhabited area: "Our Lord, I have caused some of my posterity to dwell in a valley barren of cultivation at thy holy House, in order, O our Lord, that they

48. Q 22:26-27.

might establish ritual prayer. So incline the hearts of the people toward them and provision them with fruits so that they might give thanks."[49] And indeed, Becca did become a major center and object of pilgrimage that united all of the peoples of the Arabian Peninsula.[50] Furthermore, say the early Muslim authorities, in those first years it remained a center of pure monotheism and its intimate link with the family of Abraham was retained in the people's remembrance. Adjoining the northwest wall of the Ka'ba is a small enclosure, called the Hijr Ismail because the tombs of Ishmael and his mother Hagar are thought to lie beneath its paving stones. Islamic writers have connected Becca and its Ka'ba with the otherwise unidentified valley celebrated in Psalm 84:

> How lovely is Your dwelling-place,
>> O Lord of hosts.
> I long, I yearn for the courts of the Lord;
>> my body and soul shout for joy to the living God. . . .
> Happy are those who dwell in Your house;
>> they forever praise You.
> Happy is the man who finds refuge in You,
>> whose mind is on the [pilgrim] highways.
> They pass through the Valley of Baca,
>> regarding it as a place of springs,
>> as if the early rain had covered it with blessing. . . .
> Better one day in Your courts than a thousand [anywhere else];
>> I would rather stand at the threshold of God's house
>> than dwell in the tents of the wicked.[51]

But the worship at the shrine of Becca did not remain pure. As Ishmael's posterity multiplied, they were soon far too numerous to be accommodated in

49. Q 14:37. It is significant that the Qur'an never feels any need to argue for the association of Abraham with the Ka'ba. This suggests that the legend of its founding was probably widely known and accepted, even among the pagans.

50. In this regard, the legend may well reflect real history. Mircea Eliade observed correctly that "from its beginning Mecca was a ceremonial center around which a city progressively arose." See Mircea Eliade, *A History of Religious Ideas*, vol. 3, *From Muhammad to the Age of Reforms*, trans. Alf Hiltebeitel and Diane Apostolos-Cappadona (Chicago: University of Chicago Press, 1985), p. 64. For a theoretical and comparative perspective on analogous phenomena, largely in East Asia, see Paul Wheatley, *The Pivot of the Four Quarters: A Preliminary Enquiry into the Origins and Character of the Ancient Chinese City* (Chicago: Aldine, 1971). Scholars of Mesoamerican archaeology have occasionally debated whether the large but diffuse settlements of that region, which were clearly "ceremonial centers," could accurately be termed "cities" at all.

51. Ps. 84:2-3, 6-7, 11 JPS.

the valley of Becca, and many had to seek other places to dwell. Necessarily, too, given the aridity and sparse vegetation of Arabia, they had to remove themselves to considerable distances. Still, they wished to retain their connection to the sacred site in the valley established by their patriarchal ancestors. So, as they moved away, they carried with them stones from the sacred precinct of the Kaʿba shrine and performed rituals to honor those stones in their far-flung settlements. Gradually, though, the stones became idols, and the memory of the pure doctrine and ritual established by Abraham grew dim. Finally the apostasy became virtually complete as the idolaters returned for pilgrimage and placed the objects of their worship within the sacred shrine itself. A god named Hubal became the divine lord of the Kaʿba and the patron deity of the inhabitants. Moreover, through intrigue and confusion the location of the well of Zamzam was itself forgotten and the spring covered over, though by now the burgeoning population had located other water sources in the adjacent area, and the loss of the original spring — though symbolically significant — was not economically crucial.

Many long centuries passed. Even though God sent prophets to Arabia such as Hud, Salih, and Shuayb, the period from Abraham to Muhammad's call in the early seventh century c.e. was, on the whole, a time of complete pagan apostasy. But there were changes. By about 400 c.e. an Arabian tribe called the Quraysh had taken control of the settlement in the valley, now called Mecca, and had assumed guardianship of the Kaʿba sanctuary.[52] The custodianship of the sanctuary was entrusted now, if it had not already been, to a hereditary succession of guardians who functioned as a quasi priesthood. The ruler of the Quraysh collected a tax from the people of the valley, with which he was to feed pilgrims too poor to provide for themselves. Arabian tradition says it was at this time, too, that the tents of the keepers of the sanctuary began to be replaced by permanent dwellings. The lord of the Quraysh himself — at the beginning of the fifth century a man named Qusayy — resided in a relatively spacious building known as the House of Assembly. Customary law banned all violence from the immediate vicinity of the shrine, as well as from Mecca itself for a distance of several miles.

Thus, although its shrine was much more ancient, Mecca — in the sense of a real town with permanent residences and a secular economy — was less than two centuries old at Muhammad's birth. After all, it was not an inviting place. There was very little water, and not a blade of grass. Its soil was not especially good. It was suffocatingly hot and afflicted with swarms of irritating flies. For many long years only the holiness of the place drew the attention of the

---

52. Mecca appears in Greek materials of the second century c.e. as *Makoraba*, which may reflect an Old South Arabic or Ethiopic word denoting a sanctuary. The word *quraysh* means "shark," and probably derives from an ancient tribal totem.

Arabs. And, as that holiness must in some way be accounted for, perhaps the traditional story of Abraham's connection with the site will serve as well as any other explanation.

Qusayy's grandson, Hashim, appears in the historical traditions as a pivotal figure, and his clan, the Hashimites, has enjoyed considerable prestige in the Arabic and Islamic world ever since. It was he, says the tradition, who established the two great annual caravans from Mecca in the latter half of the fifth century — the Caravan of Winter, southward to the Yemen, and the Caravan of Summer to the northwestern portion of the Arabian Peninsula and beyond to Byzantine-ruled Palestine and Syria. The religious prestige of Mecca's Ka'ba was probably a major factor in the establishment of this trade, as the inviolability of the sanctuary was transferred to the caravans operating under its patronage.[53]

Both caravan journeys followed the ancient frankincense road, on which Mecca sat at about the midpoint between the Yemen to the south and the Byzantine depots in Gaza and Damascus to the north. Thus no caravans traveled the entire distance from the Mediterranean to the far corner of Arabia, and the Meccans, equipped with their unique knowledge of the landscape and its water sources, came to exercise virtually total control of the trade along the frankincense trail.[54] Whatever hopes the Byzantines and Sassanids had once entertained of dominating that trade were now quite obviously vain.

One of the first halts of the summer caravan to the northwest was in an agricultural oasis known as Yathrib, which lay a journey of eleven camel-days due north of Mecca. At one point the oasis had been dominated by Jews, and they were still an important and prosperous presence in the settlement.[55] But an Arabian tribe of south Arabian origin was now in control of Yathrib, though it had divided into two groups known as the Aws and the Khazraj. Hashim's younger brother, Muttalib, married a girl of the Khazraj, and she bore him a son. She and her boy continued to live in Yathrib for several years, until Muttalib convinced them that the son, who would come to be called Abd al-

---

53. See Serjeant, "Haram and Hawtah," pp. 54-55. Serjeant cites inscriptional evidence suggesting that caravans to the north and south, *Yaman wa-Sham* ("to Yemen and Syria"), were under way much earlier than the days of Hashim.

54. See Rodinson, pp. 35, 39-40. Peters, *Muhammad*, pp. 69-70, 72, 74, 75, 92-93, offers some cogent criticism of what he sees as exaggerations of the volume and importance of Meccan trade.

55. There were substantial Jewish populations in Yathrib and in all of the major oases to its north, which some have seen as evidence of a migration of Jews southward from Palestine. But it could just as easily indicate the radiation of Palestinian Jewish influence on preexisting Arab populations. Some legends have Moses and Aaron themselves coming to Arabia, with Aaron dying there and being buried on Mount Uhud. More typically the legends say the Jews fled to Arabia in the sixth century B.C.E. when the Babylonians destroyed the temple in Jerusalem.

Muttalib, ought to come and dwell with him in Mecca, eventually to take over the guardianship of the Ka'ba and the provisioning of the pilgrims as if he were a Meccan (which, in a sense, he was).

Abd al-Muttalib, who survived until roughly 580, did indeed become the master of the Ka'ba. During his time, and even into the days of Muhammad, the Ka'ba was probably a fairly humble structure, made of wood, unroofed, a little taller than a man's head, surrounded by crude mud huts, with its sacred meteoric stone embedded in one of its corners. Nevertheless, Abd al-Muttalib is said to have loved and reverenced the shrine so much that he sometimes spent the night in the Hijr Ismail adjacent to it. (It is said by the ancient Muslim authorities that he never prayed to Hubal, but rather to the true God, Allah — although modern scholars tend to mistrust this claim as too obviously apologetic in its intent.) During a period of sleeping there, he received instruction in a series of dreams that enabled him to rediscover and to reexcavate the well of Zamzam. Since he was already in charge of the Ka'ba and responsible for feeding and watering the pilgrims who came to it from across Arabia, it was only natural that he likewise assumed control of the waters of the holy spring.

His role as guardian of the sacred precinct established him as an important figure for all the tribes and clans of Arabia, who were united, if in little else, by their veneration of the Ka'ba and its meteoric stone. This required a certain diplomacy, and he was responsible to see that pilgrims from the entire peninsula, with their accompanying gods, felt welcome in the sanctuary and during the sacred seasons. Perhaps this was difficult for him, if his theology was really as distinct from the then-regnant Arabian religion as tradition says it was, or perhaps he had come to see Allah as symbolized, even if imperfectly, in the idols and gods of his kin.

Blessed as he was, though, Abd al-Muttalib was deficient, by Arabian standards, in one of the blessings most important to his people. He had only one son. However, God had just given him Zamzam, and no doubt encouraged by this striking sign of divine favor, he prayed for more sons, vowing that if he were given ten sons who grew to manhood, he would, when the appropriate time came, sacrifice one of them to God at the Ka'ba. (This story would certainly suggest that, even if he were a monotheist, Abd al-Muttalib's religion had not entirely escaped influence from the pagan practices surrounding him.) The blessing came. Nine more sons were born to him. Naturally delighted with them, Abd al-Muttalib was nonetheless a man of his word. By means of a traditional Arabian rite of arrow divination, he determined that the one chosen of God was none other than his youngest and favorite son, Abd Allah ("Servant of God").[56]

---

56. On Arabian arrow divination, see Toufic Fahd, *La divination arabe: études religieuses, sociologiques et folkloriques sur le milieu natif de l'Islam* (Leiden: Brill, 1966).

Abd al-Muttalib immediately headed with his son toward the place determined for the sacrifice, but, no doubt to his own relief, other members of the family intervened and prevented him from carrying out his vow. He agreed, instead, to go to a well-known wise woman in Yathrib to discover from her whether it was possible to find a way out of his vow in this matter, and if so, to determine what that way might be. When he and those with him had reached Yathrib, however, they found that the seeress had moved to Khaybar, a wealthy Jewish settlement in a fertile valley almost a hundred miles away. Finally they found her. Her advice was to place Abd Allah to one side and ten camels, the customary Arabian fine for the shedding of blood, to the other side, and then to cast lots between them, if necessary increasing the number of camels until the lot fell upon them rather than the young man. Abd Allah was finally delivered by the sacrifice of a hundred camels — a considerable ransom in the camel-based economy of bedouin Arabia.

Abd al-Muttalib was not alone in worshiping Allah apart from the received idols, if indeed he did so. There were others in pre-Islamic Arabia who held to a kind of monotheism. They seem to have believed, as Muslims now also do, that idolatry was an innovation in Arabia and at Abraham's sanctuary, an innovation that had illegitimately supplanted the worship of the one true God, Allah. These people, known as the *hunafa* (sg. *hanif*) — the term *hanif* might not inappropriately be rendered "generic monotheist" (as opposed to the "brand-name monotheists" of Christianity, Judaism, and later, Islam itself) — constituted nothing so specific and organized as a movement.[57] Rather they represented a tendency. They rejected the idols as a profanation and a pollution of the pure religion of God, as well as of the Ka'ba itself. The contact of the caravan traders with Christianity, Judaism, and Zoroastrianism during their travels had led some of them to wonder why Arabia had no comparable (and comparably sophisticated) revelation. These were people who sought a more demanding, and more intellectually satisfying, religion than that offered by Meccan paganism.

The surge in Meccan wealth in the generations immediately preceding Muhammad's call had evidently precipitated something of a social crisis. Meccan paganism was not sufficiently robust, not ethically demanding enough, to deal with the social strains created by the new class distinctions. The *hunafa* were appalled by what they viewed as the moral drift of Meccan society, which was undergoing a jarring transition from the heroic tribal ideals of a not-so-distant nomadic past to the not-yet-evolved ethics of a more individualistic mercantile lifestyle. And some of them were not particularly

---

57. For a discussion of the term and its etymological origins in Syriac, see Andrae, *Mohammed,* pp. 109-10. Rodinson, pp. 36-37, offers a useful discussion of the *hunafa.*

shy in expressing their opinions, which undoubtedly led to their being marginalized to the fringe of Mecca society. Yet, although they recognized the poverty of Arabian paganism and the superiority of the more developed religions they had encountered in their trading journeys, the *hunafa* seem to have been reluctant to take sides in the rivalry of the great Byzantine and Sassanid powers, which becoming Christian or Zoroastrian would have obliged them to do.[58]

Among them was a man named Waraqa b. Nawfal, a relative of Abd al-Muttalib (which does suggest that the notion of the latter's pre-Islamic monotheism need not be mere pious sanitizing). Waraqa had indeed become a Christian. Christianity was far from unknown to the pre-Islamic Arabs, and the inhabitants of the peninsula manifestly enjoyed some basic knowledge of the major biblical stories.[59] There were well-established Christian communities to the south, in Najran and in the Yemen, and the annual caravan to Syria had brought the Arabs into close contact with the venerable Christian culture of that region. In fact, the Ghassanids and the Lakhmids, the onetime Arab client tribes on the Byzantine-Sassanid frontier to the north, were themselves Christians of a sort. (The Lakhmids had converted late in the sixth century.) Additionally, there was a strong Jewish presence in the Lakhmid territories, including even a small rabbinical academy established there in 588 or soon thereafter, when Sassanian attempts to centralize and control Persian society disrupted the Jewish institutions that had existed for centuries elsewhere.[60]

It is even said that Christians occasionally came to the Ka'ba, to honor the sanctuary constructed by the prophet and patriarch Abraham, and that, in the ecumenical spirit of the place, they were made welcome.[61] In fact, an icon of the Virgin Mary and the infant Jesus had been painted on the inside wall of the Ka'ba, where it remained somewhat incongruously among the 360 idols that tradition says rested in or near the shrine. (It was probably this ecumenism, or syncretism, that made Mecca so little susceptible to the exclusivizing attractions of Christianity or Judaism. What was the icon, in the eyes of the Quraysh, but one more idol among very many?)

Waraqa seems to have been literate. And while it is almost certainly going too far to suggest that he was a student of the scriptures (let alone of "the-

---

58. In rather the same way, probably, as becoming a Marxist during the Cold War would have allied one with the Soviet Union.

59. See Rodinson, pp. 28-29.

60. See Morony, pp. 307, 309, 319-20, 322. The Jewish population in Iraq seems to have peaked early in the fifth century, and then, for various reasons, to have declined even as Jewish institutions were marginalized or demolished.

61. They had no problem in recognizing Allah as "the Lord of the House." Even today, *Allah* is the term for God employed in Arabic translations of the Bible.

ology"), Waraqa does seem to have known something of Jewish and Christian belief.[62] Among those beliefs, at least in the folk Christianity of the peninsula, was the notion that an Arabian prophet was soon to come. The Jews, naturally, expected that he would be an Arabian of Jewish descent, as all the earlier prophets had been Jews. The Christians, by contrast, had no such ethnically limiting notion.

It was into this environment, religiously complex and suffused with a sense of spiritual anticipation, that the Prophet of Islam would be born.

The Birth and Childhood of Muhammad

Now that Abd Allah had been spared, his father, Abd al-Muttalib, set about to find a wife for the boy. He chose a girl named Amina, who was destined to become the mother of the founder of Islam. As is appropriate for so important an event, the birth of Muhammad and the occurrences leading up to it have been surrounded by numerous legends and embellishments, some of which I will relate in the narrative that follows.

On the day appointed for the wedding, Abd al-Muttalib took the young man by the hand and set off with him. En route they encountered Qutayla, the sister of their Christian kinsman Waraqa b. Nawfal. She was standing at the entrance of her house as they passed by, and she was deeply smitten by the son of Abd al-Muttalib. He was, the sources agree, a strikingly handsome fellow, but that isn't what intrigued her. His face glowed with radiance. She offered herself to him on the spot. But he declined, informing her that he was on his way to his wedding, which had been arranged by his father and could not properly be delayed or avoided. (She very likely knew this already.)

After the marriage had taken place, Abd Allah stayed with his new wife in the house of her guardian for several days. One day, though, he needed to return to his own house to fetch something, and he again passed by Qutayla. This time, though, she did not offer herself to him, and he inquired as to why. She replied that the light that had been with him on that earlier day had left him. "Today," she said, "you cannot fulfill the need that I had for you." The marriage of Abd Allah and Amina took place in 569. It was in the next year, according to most traditional sources, that the birth of Muhammad occurred.[63]

---

62. There seems little if any trace, in the Judaism of the pre-Islamic Arabian Peninsula, of the ideas of the third–fifth century *amoraim* of Babylonia and Palestine, which eventually culminated in the Talmuds.

63. The year of Muhammad's birth is disputed, because the Arabs before Islam had no fixed annual dating system, but it must have been roughly 570 or 571 C.E.

It is necessary and appropriate here to offer a parenthetical word about the sources available to us for reconstructing the life of the Prophet of Islam. Even counting the New Testament Gospels, Muhammad is the only founder of a major world religion for whom we possess a detailed and complete biography. Unfortunately, no extant form of that biography was committed to writing until decades — probably 125 years — after his death, and what we have bears all the marks of hagiography and folklore.[64] Apparently, for his disciples as for the followers of the biblical prophets, "it was more important to preserve knowledge of the prophet's sayings than to recall a record of his life. The charisma was not important in itself; it mattered only in relation to the social and religious changes which the charismatic individual brought about."[65] Only relatively late did people somewhat removed from Muhammad in time begin to think seriously about gathering and writing down the scraps of biographical information that were circulating about him in the by-now far-flung Islamic empire. The one source for the Prophet's life that is generally accepted as reliable and authentic is the Qur'an itself, but unfortunately it is allusive, fragmentary, and often enigmatic, and its interpretation for biographical purposes is fraught with daunting difficulties. In the biographical sketch presented here, we shall rely on the traditional narratives, accompanying them with commentary but feeling free to omit such portions as seem obviously tendentious and folkloric — although even these will be discussed when they shed useful light.[66] If we were to restrict ourselves entirely to the undisputed facts of Muhammad's biography, we would run out of information after only a few pages. After his emigration to Medina, the chronology of his life steps onto more-or-less secure ground; prior to that, we are left essentially to guesswork.

Muhammad was born into a religiously aristocratic Meccan family, albeit into a faction of it that had fallen on hard economic times and had perhaps lost out in certain squabbles and conflicts with other factions. While his religious authority obviously did not derive solely from his family background — Qurayshi prophets were not an everyday event, after all — it is very doubtful that he would have been able to advance his prophetic claim so successfully had he not come from the lineage that he did.[67] In the Qur'an itself, the concept of a

64. See Peters, *Muhammad*, pp. 263-66.

65. Ronald E. Clements, "Max Weber, Charisma and Biblical Prophecy," in *Prophecy and Prophets: The Diversity of Issues in Contemporary Scholarship*, ed. Yehoshua Gitay (Atlanta: Scholars Press, 1997), p. 98.

66. Although the approach taken here is rather different from Montgomery Watt's, it still resembles his in the sense that "in the attempt to make a coherent story, [I] will give [the traditional sources] a more dogmatic form than is strictly justified" (Watt, p. 56).

67. Serjeant, "Ḥaram and Ḥawṭah," pp. 42, 53, 55; Serjeant, "The Saiyids of Ḥaḍramawt," pp. 6-7.

family or a kinship group that is uniquely endowed with spiritual power is explicitly present. "The Prophets were in all cases the lineal descendants of former Prophets," observes R. B. Serjeant. "To Muḥammad it is natural that spiritual qualities should reside exclusively in certain families and be inherited, just as trades were hereditary in other family groups."[68]

Muhammad's birth was, as it would turn out, by far the most important event of the year 570 in Arabia. But it was an eventful year in many ways, and things happened in the course of it that, in the short term, loomed far larger. At that period the Yemen was under the control of the Christian ruler of Abyssinia, or Ethiopia, known as the Negus.[69] The Abyssinian governor of the Yemen was a man named Abraha, who was determined to replace the purportedly Abrahamic but now clearly pagan shrine of Mecca with something overtly Christian. To this end he built a magnificent church in Sanʿa, intending that it supplant the Kaʿba as the chief object of Arabian pilgrimage. And it was truly a remarkable building. He constructed it, we are told, of marble taken from one of the ruined palaces of the ancient Queen of Sheba, and filled it with crosses made of gold and silver and pulpits made of ebony and inlaid ivory. But his ambitions for the building, quite freely proclaimed, irritated the Arabs of the Mecca region mightily, and one of them entered the church by night and deliberately defiled it.

Abraha was furious, and vowed to destroy the Kaʿba in revenge. Accordingly, he organized a large army and set off toward Mecca to carry out his plan. Accompanying the army was a large, armored elephant, in memory of which the year of Muhammad's birth has ever afterward been known as "The Year of the Elephant." Abraha's preliminary activities in the environs of Mecca went as he had planned, and so he summoned a representative of Mecca to his camp in order to give to him the ultimatum: Allow us to destroy the Kaʿba and there need be no shedding of blood. The chosen representative of Mecca was, not surprisingly, Abd al-Muttalib. When he entered the presence of Abraha, the Abyssinian vice-regent, no doubt attempting to strike a conciliatory posture, asked if there were any personal favor that he could render to the Meccan leader. Yes, replied Abd al-Muttalib. Two hundred of his camels had been seized by the Yemeni army, he ex-

---

68. Serjeant, "The Saiyids of Ḥaḍramawt," p. 7 n. 3. See, for example, Q 4:54 (where Serjeant correctly notes that *hikma,* or "wisdom," very likely connotes "the ability to arbitrate — a very important function of Saiyids"); 57:26; also 10:83. It is not difficult to see how Shiʿism, which earlier generations of Orientalists, misled by its relatively recent dominance in Persia as well as by their own racialist misconceptions, sometimes imagined to be an "Indo-European" reaction to "Semitic" Islam, could easily have arisen, with its veneration of the *ahl al-bayt,* the "people of the house," on completely Arabian soil.

69. There had been an earlier Abyssinian invasion of the Yemen in roughly 513 C.E., but it did not last.

plained, and he wanted them back. When Abraha expressed shocked disappointment that, at a time of such crisis, Abd al-Muttalib was thinking of his camels rather than of the religion that Abraha had come to destroy, the Qurayshi leader is supposed to have replied, "I am the lord of the camels, and the shrine likewise has a lord who will defend it." "He cannot defend it against me," asserted Abraha. "We shall see," responded Abd al-Muttalib. "But give me my camels." And Abraha did in fact order that the camels be returned.

Abd al-Muttalib went back to Mecca and the Quraysh, and advised them to withdraw to the hills that surround the town. He and his family and a few others then went to the Ka'ba and prayed for its deliverance, before they too retreated to the hills. The next morning Abraha and his troops prepared to enter Mecca and destroy its shrine. They led the richly caparisoned elephant before the soldiers. But rather than marching into the town, the elephant, which was facing Mecca, kneeled toward the Ka'ba (possibly, some demythologizing historians suggest, at the urging of an Arab guide who had been unwillingly pressed into service). No amount of prodding or torture could induce the animal to move, except in a direction away from the sacred valley and back toward the Yemen. Abraha should have taken the portent and gone home. But he repeatedly attempted to turn the army around. Suddenly the sky grew dark with birds, each one carrying a rock in its beak and one in each of its talons. The birds swooped over the Yemeni army, hurling the stones at it and killing many, and the army fled in disarray back in the direction from which it had first come. Abraha died soon after his arrival back in the Yemen.[70]

Abd Allah, the husband of Amina, was away from Mecca at the time. And in fact, he would never return, for he became ill and died in the home of his relatives in Yathrib while journeying back from a trading expedition to Syria and Palestine. His young wife was left a widow, and expecting a child. But it was to be no ordinary child. Muslim lore says a light shone forth from her womb so brightly that she was able to see the castles of Bostra in distant Syria. And a supernatural voice said to her, "You carry in your womb the lord of this people; and when he is born, say, 'I place him beneath the protection of the One, from the evil of every envier'; then name him Muhammad."

A few weeks later the boy was born. When Abd al-Muttalib was informed, he took his grandson in his arms and went with him to the sanctuary. He brought him into the Ka'ba itself, the holy house, and presented the infant to God, offering a prayer of thanks for the gift of this boy as a substitute for his dead son. It was customary among the families in the towns of Arabia to send their sons into the desert soon after birth, to be suckled by a bedouin wet nurse

70. Peters, *Allah's Commonwealth*, p. 28, is typical of Western scholars in ascribing the failure of Abraha's expedition to an outbreak of smallpox.

and to spend at least some portion of their childhood among the desert tribes. In fact, certain of the tribes seem almost to have advertised their services in this regard, and would come at regular intervals into the towns seeking babies to care for. Since Mecca had a reputation for epidemics and a high infant mortality rate, parents were eager to avail themselves of these services. But it was not only for health reasons that it was thought desirable to send a young son into the desert. The people of Mecca were themselves only a few generations removed from their nomadic past. Their "urbanism," such as it was, was of recent minting. It had only been in the days of Qusayy, at the beginning of the fifth century, that they had traded in their tents and begun to build permanent houses around Zamzam and the Ka'ba. And there still lingered, in their minds, the sense that the older way of life was the nobler. As previously noted, a nomad cannot be oppressed in the same way that a sedentary city dweller or an agriculturally rooted peasant can be, for he can simply move away. He is free. And, then as now, it was felt that the language of the bedouins was better, their diction and vocabulary richer. For pre-Islamic Arabia, living in its "heroic age," resembled the Greece of the Homeric period in its conception of the ideal hero as someone not merely equipped with courage and ability with weapons, but also endowed with eloquence and wisdom in council. And these attributes, it was thought, resided in their purity with the bedouins of the desert rather more than with their debased (if wealthier and more comfortable) cousins of the towns.[71] Sometimes the sons of the Quraysh would spend as many as eight years in the boarding school of the desert before they were allowed to return to their families at Mecca.

Amina, too, wanted her son to have the benefits of the desert. But she was at a disadvantage. Bedouin wet nurses did not expect direct payment for their services; to have demanded money for nursing and caring for a baby would have been considered a breach of good form. But they and their families certainly anticipated benefits from the people with whom they were, in the ancient Arabian view, cementing something very like a bond of kinship. Ultimately they expected an alliance with the boy, who would grow up as a quasi son and quasi brother to them. But that prospect was years away, and in the meantime they generally received some benefits from the father. Muhammad, however, had no father. And his economic outlook was not particularly bright. Abd Allah had died too early in his career to have amassed much wealth, and he left his

---

71. The idea survived for many years even after the rise of Islam. The famous fourteenth-century *Muqaddima* of Ibn Khaldun, which drew on the author's North African experience to elaborate a philosophy of history and historical process, places crucial emphasis on the perceived contrast between the toughness and discipline of the desert nomads, on the one hand, and the decadence of the urban dwellers, on the other.

son only five camels, a small flock of sheep and goats, and the services of one devoted slave girl. It was not much by the standards of the leading families of Mecca. Muhammad entered life, therefore, as the scion of a distinguished family, but poor — rather like a penniless aristocrat.

It took some time, therefore, for Amina to locate a bedouin woman named Halima who was willing to take Abd Allah's son. The traditional stories report, however, that economic benefits and the blessings of God immediately began to rest upon the foster parents, so that they not only never regretted their acceptance of the boy but eagerly sought to prolong his stay with them. His sojourn in the bedouin finishing school may also have benefited Muhammad's credentials as a future prophet. He is reported, much later, to have remarked that, like every prophet, he had been a shepherd.[72] But a far more spectacular sign of his preordained role has also been attributed to Muhammad's time in the desert:

One day, according to a story attributed to Halima, the future prophet and his foster brother were behind a tent, playing with some of the family's lambs. Suddenly the other boy came running to his parents, reporting with understandable alarm that two men, clothed in white, had come and laid Muhammad out on the ground. They had opened up his chest and, the boy continued, were stirring about in it. The two bedouins ran to see what was happening. They found Muhammad standing, apparently unharmed but very pale. He confirmed what his foster brother had said, but, though they searched diligently, Halima and her husband, Harith, could find no trace of the men nor any blood or wound on Muhammad that would confirm the story. Later on Muhammad is supposed to have supplied more details, telling of two men, dressed in white, who had come to him with a gold basin full of snow. When they split open his chest, they removed his heart and, opening it up, took out of it an ugly black clot which they threw away. Then they used the pure water of the melting snow to wash his heart and his breast, and restored him to his perfect physical condition.[73]

Mircea Eliade quite correctly notes that the cleansing of Muhammad's breast is reminiscent — indeed, events very like it are characteristic — of shamanic initiations around the world. And, since shamanic initiations also typically involve celestial ascents, this event should perhaps be connected with the ascension of Muhammad into the heavens that will be discussed below.[74]

---

72. Widengren, *Muhammad*, pp. 199-200, cites the parallels of Krishna, Cyrus, Faridun, and David.

73. There may be a reference to this event in Q 94:1-3. A similar story is told of Umayya b. Abi al-Salt. See Ignaz Goldziher, *Abhandlungen zur arabischen Philologie* (Leiden: Buchhandlung und Druckerei vormals E. J. Brill, 1869-99), 1:213.

74. Eliade, *History of Religious Ideas*, 3:63 n. 2; compare Andrae, *Mohammed*, p. 36. For a more complete discussion of shamanism in general, see Mircea Eliade, *Shamanism:*

Muhammad had remained perhaps three years with Halima and Harith in the desert. Not surprisingly, though, the experience with the two mysterious men unnerved the two bedouins, and they decided it was time to return their young charge to his mother. He lived with her in Mecca for another three years, and then he and Amina traveled to Yathrib to visit some of his relatives there. It was apparently an enjoyable time for the young boy, for he later recalled learning to swim in a pool that belonged to some of his Khazraj kin and being taught how to fly a kite. Unfortunately, though, his mother fell ill not far into the return journey; she died and was buried just outside of Yathrib. Later legends say the jinn themselves wept at the news of her death, so good a woman was she.

So his grandfather Abd al-Muttalib, who was eighty years old, took charge of Muhammad, the son of Abd Allah, his favorite. According to the traditional accounts, they were very close. Abd al-Muttalib would even take the young boy with him when he went to discuss important matters in the assembly with the most influential men of Mecca.

Still, Muhammad was now completely an orphan, and the situation of orphans in late sixth-century Mecca was even more undesirable than it normally would have been. Under the old unwritten code of nomadic values, clan or family chiefs were expected to care for the weaker members of their groups, for the widows and the orphans, and for the poor. "But at Mecca in a mad scramble for more wealth every man was looking after his own interests and disregarding the responsibilities formerly recognized. Muḥammad's guardians saw that he did not starve to death, but it was difficult for them to do more for him, especially as the fortunes of the clan of Hāshim seem to have been declining at this time. An orphan, with no able-bodied man to give special attention to his interests, had a poor start in a commercial career; and that was really the only career open to him."[75] Max Weber says "a distinctive concern with social reform is characteristic of Israelite prophets."[76] It would also become a characteristic of Muhammad and the Qur'an, and many have seen the impoverished widowhood of his mother and his own orphaned status as contributors to that reformist tendency.

For the hammer of fate was by no means done raining its blows upon the young boy. Two years after the death of his mother, his grandfather too died. While on his deathbed, Abd al-Muttalib entrusted Muhammad to his son Abu Talib, who was the full brother of Muhammad's father, Abd Allah. Abu Talib

---

Archaic Techniques of Ecstasy, trans. Willard R. Trask (Princeton: Princeton University Press, 1964).

75. Watt, p. 8.

76. Weber, p. 50. "This concern is all the more notable," he says, "because such a trait is lacking in Hindu prophecy of the same period."

treated the boy very kindly. But reversion into the family of Abd al-Muttalib and then of Abu Talib did not improve Muhammad's material prospects. For, although the family had considerable prestige, the grandfather's fortunes had declined a great deal in his later years, and Abu Talib too was poor. In fact, the entire clan of Hashim had seen its wealth and influence decline in the recent period, particularly when compared to the rival clan of Makhzum. So Muhammad spent many of the days of his youth pasturing sheep and goats on the hills around Mecca. No doubt the solitude helped him to develop a habit of reflection. But his uncle and surrogate father also took the boy on his commercial journeys. The importance of such expeditions, and of the opportunities they would have provided for an intelligent young man to observe varying cultures and religious traditions, would be difficult to overstate — although, as Montgomery Watt observes, while the journeys gave Muhammad experience, they did not give him the capital with which to profit from that experience commercially.[77]

Muhammad is said to have been *ummi*, which virtually all Muslims take to mean "illiterate."[78] The apologetic purpose of this is immediately apparent: an illiterate Muhammad renders the miraculous nature of the Qur'an more dramatically evident. The claim is an old one. The last neo-Babylonian ruler, Nabonidus, claimed to be a visionary and, as proof that his heavenly wisdom came through unmediated divine inspiration, also claimed to be ignorant of the art of writing.[79]

Western scholarship, on the other hand, has seen it as unlikely that a person deeply involved in the caravan trade would not be able, at least, to keep accounts and to reach a level of literacy that was not uncommon among the Meccans of Muhammad's day. But all agree that Muhammad was not a scholar of the Christian scriptures, and most probably had no direct acquaintance with them.[80] Arabian culture was an oral one, with little or no experience of book learning. (In this sense the word *ummi*, which derives from the Arabic term *umma*, or "community," may be lexically close, as it is etymologically analo-

---

77. Watt, p. 8.

78. Q 7:157.

79. See the discussion and references offered at Geo Widengren, *Religionsphänomenologie* (Berlin: Walter de Gruyter, 1969), pp. 547-48.

80. See, for example, Peters, *Muhammad*, pp. 141-42. Western Orientalists have frequently argued that the Qur'an betrays an incomplete or even inaccurate grasp of the character of the Bible, pointing to such things as the fact that Jesus is said to have "received" the Gospels as a revelation from God to him (as at Q 3:58; 5:46; 57:27), and that believers are advised that the Gospel should be "observed" as Jews observe the Torah (Q 5:66, 68). They have also pointed as an error to the Qur'an's apparent claim (at Q 48:29) that Muhammad and his followers are described in the Gospels.

gous, to the English word "lay" or "layman.")[81] Qur'an 21:150 features a quotation from the Psalms of the Hebrew Bible, but it is the only indubitable biblical quotation in the Qur'an.[82] Muhammad's enemies said he had foreign teachers.[83] It is more likely, if he can be said to have had any human sources at all (a proposition that orthodox Muslims would vigorously deny), that his contacts were with midrashic and apocryphal works, probably via oral transmission, than with the biblical text itself. There are several accounts of the birth and childhood of Jesus in the Qur'an, for instance, that have parallels in the so-called infancy narratives.[84] The Qur'an's account of the death of Jesus has parallels among both the Manichaeans and the Basilidean Gnostics.

Muhammad could have observed Christianity and Judaism at first hand during his own travels, or from speaking with caravans returning from Syria or Mesopotamia, or with those returning from trade by sea with Abyssinia/Ethiopia,[85] or from contacts with Arabian businessmen visiting the great markets of Mecca and elsewhere. Christianity had appeared in Arabia itself among some of the tribes, and Christians participated in the annual pilgrimage to Mecca.[86] Indeed, in Mecca itself there were not only captive Christians taken in raids, but immigrant Christian believers from among the Ghassanid clients of the Byzantines along the Syrian frontier. Jews were settled in Medina and the oases to the north.

One of his trips to Syria occurred when Muhammad was either nine or twelve. The caravan halted, as was customary, near Bostra, an important crossroads (adjacent to what is known today as the Jabal al-Druze) that was not only

---

81. "Lay," "layman," and "laity" all derive from the Greek *laïkos*, "of the *laos* or people." For a discussion of the term *ummi*, see A. J. Wensinck, "Muhammad und die Propheten," *Acta Orientalia* 2 (1924): 191-92. See also Peters, *Allah's Commonwealth*, pp. 50-51; Rodinson, p. 49.

82. The Qur'an does not appear to know the Psalms as a part of a larger entity, the Hebrew Bible (see Q 17:55). The reference in Q 7:40 to the camel and the eye of the needle does not appear to indicate direct knowledge of the New Testament. Nevertheless, the Qur'an knows, and relates at length and in detail, the story of the patriarch Joseph (Q 12), and speaks repeatedly of such biblical characters as Adam, Noah, Abraham, Moses, Mary, Joseph, Zacharia, and John the Baptist.

83. As at Q 16:103; 25:4ff.; 44:14. Q 16:103 certainly doesn't refute this claim.

84. E.g., Q 19:22ff.; 3:36; 5:110ff.

85. Contacts with Ethiopia are evident from Ethiopic loanwords in the Arabic of the period. See Theodor Nöldeke, "Neue Beiträge zur arabischen Sprachwissenschaft," *Beiträge und Neue Beiträge zur semitischen Sprachwissenschaft: Achtzehn Aufsätze und Studien* (Strassburg: n.p., 1904-10), p. 47. Andrae, *Mohammed*, pp. 38-39, argues against Muhammad's having been to Syria, but I am not convinced.

86. On the pilgrimage, see the evidence gathered in Christiaan Snouck Hurgronje, *Het Mekaansche Feest* (Leiden: E. J. Brill, 1880), pp. 28, 128, 159.

the capital of Roman Arabia but an ancient Christian center. It had come to be occupied by semisedentary ethnic Arabs, who formed what F. E. Peters calls a "bedouin suburb" around it.[87] Nearby was an anchorite's cell where a Christian hermit lived. The traditions suggest that the cell was occupied by one monk after another, in succession, always alone, each new inhabitant inheriting not only the cell but also certain cherished ancient writings. Included in these writings, say the accounts, was the prediction of a prophet to the Arabs.[88] Bahira, the current occupant of the cell, was acutely aware of the prophecy and apparently felt that its fulfillment was near.

On this particular occasion Bahira looked out from his cell and noticed something highly unusual. As the caravan approached, he saw a very small cloud that moved with the caravan to provide shade for one or two of its members. When they stopped to take cool shelter under a tree, the cloud stopped with them. Moreover, the tree itself lowered its branches in order to shade them more effectively. Bahira, quite naturally, was intrigued. Thus, for the very first time that any of the veteran caravanners could recall, the monk invited them to partake of a meal with him, insisting that all should come, of whatever rank. When they arrived, Bahira inspected each one eagerly. But he could see nobody who corresponded to what his studies had led him to expect. Muhammad, in fact, as the youngest, had been chosen to stay behind to watch the caravan's goods and supplies. The monk insisted that they fetch him, and they did.[89]

As soon as the anchorite saw the boy, he knew that he was the one. Everything about Muhammad corresponded with what had been predicted in his mysterious book. Bahira plied him, quite politely but eagerly, with many questions, which the young boy answered truthfully. The monk even asked to see his back, and there was the confirmatory seal of prophethood, a slightly raised oval mark (like the impress of a cupping glass) between his shoulder blades. He asked Abu Talib what their relationship was, and the older man said the boy was his son. No, the monk responded, that was impossible. The boy's father was dead. Abu Talib admitted that this was so, and that Muhammad was in fact his nephew. The encounter ended with Bahira warning Abu Talib against the machinations of the Jews, who, he said, if they knew the role that the boy was destined to play, would seek to do him harm. (Traditional Muslim accounts report that the Jews, too, were expecting the arrival of a prophet in Arabia — but

87. Peters, *Muhammad*, p. 71.

88. Peters, *Allah's Commonwealth*, p. 49, thinks Bahira's mysterious book was simply the Bible. This would accord with Muslim notions that — clearly in its original form, distortedly in the corrupt version available to us — the Bible predicts the advent of Muhammad.

89. The parallel to the story of the prophet Samuel, David, and the other sons of Jesse told in 1 Sam. 16:1-13 should be obvious.

that they also expected him, naturally enough, to come through a Jewish lineage. The thought of a non-Jewish prophet would not have pleased them, nor even seemed plausible.)

During Muhammad's youth, the Quraysh became involved tangentially in what, since it began in one of the months when fighting was supposed to be banned, came to be known in the annals of Arabia as "the sacrilegious war." It is possible that this messy conflict may have heightened the sense of discontent that many felt with the situation in Arabia. Most of the Meccan elite had participated in trading caravans to Syro-Palestine and had seen the rule of (Roman) law as it was administered in those relatively civilized areas of the Byzantine Empire. In Arabia, however, order was maintained, to the extent it was, by the blood feud. Shortly thereafter another incident occurred, which seems to show that the people of Mecca were beginning to move in the direction of a real system of justice, beyond merely the often rather amoral demands of tribal and clan loyalty. When a visiting Yemeni merchant was the object of the fraud of an Arab of the Meccan region, who was quite aware that the Yemeni had no local kin and hence no support, the merchant appealed to the sense of justice of the Meccans. And in fact, they responded, and obliged the would-be con man to pay what he owed. An oath-bound league was founded to deal with the situation, in which the young Muhammad participated. This incident can be read as an illustration that some notion of justice, transcending blind loyalty to kin, was beginning perhaps to root itself in the Meccan mind.

As Muhammad grew older, he had frequent opportunities to participate in Meccan caravans and thus to learn more about the surrounding world and perhaps about surrounding religious faiths. Apparently, too, his participation gave others an opportunity to learn about him, and his reputation began to increase. Later Muslims say that, well before the advent of Islam, he had been given the sobriquet al-Amin, or "the trustworthy one." Eventually Muhammad was invited to manage the goods of a merchant whose circumstances did not allow him to go with the caravan. Muhammad evidently did well with his assignment, and so other, similar opportunities began to come his way. One of them was to prove vitally significant, not only for the personal life of Muhammad but very likely too for his role as an Arabian prophet.

Khadija, the daughter of Khuwaylid of the Asad clan, was a cousin of the Christian Waraqa and his sister, Qutayla, who had attempted to attract the attention of Muhammad's father, Abd Allah. Khadija was also quite wealthy. Twice widowed, she had been obliged to hire men to handle her caravan trading. Now she turned to Muhammad, whom tradition makes out to be fifteen years her junior. She offered him the chance to travel with some of her merchandise to Syria and promised him twice the remuneration that she had ever paid before. Further, she granted him the assistance of a young manservant of hers named Maysara. Not surprisingly, Muhammad accepted the generous offer.

During this trip the story of Bahira essentially repeated itself. When the caravan reached its usual stopping place near Bostra, in the southern part of Syria, Muhammad sought shelter from the hot Levantine sun under a tree. A monk by the name of Nestor came out of his cell and asked Maysara the identity of the man who was enjoying the shade of the tree.[90] (It is hard to imagine that this is not the same monastic cell and the same tree as in the earlier story of Bahira. Perhaps the previous monk had died and been replaced by Nestor. Or perhaps this story is simply an ahistorical doublet of the first. Syrian monks are invoked on several occasions in the traditional histories to point to the imminent coming or the arrival of an Arabian prophet.) Maysara replied that Muhammad was of the Quraysh, the tribe that controlled the Ka'ba. Nestor replied that, in fact, Muhammad was a prophet. (Maysara later reported seeing a pair of angels shielding his master from the heat of the day, rather like the earlier cloud and tree of Bahira's story.) At his return, Khadija was much impressed by Muhammad's handling of her affairs. And she must have been impressed, too, by Maysara's indications of her business manager's unusual status with God and men. (Tradition says her cousin Waraqa encouraged her reflections on the matter by telling her that he had long awaited an Arabian prophet, and that the signs indicated that he had arrived.) So she proposed marriage to him.

Khadija was apparently still beautiful, and she was wealthy and of good character. Muhammad's distinguished biographer Montgomery Watt offers an unromantically realistic view of the situation: "In this world of unscrupulous business men, how was a poor orphan, however gifted, to make his way? The one possibility was to find a rich woman to marry him, so that he could, as it were, enter into a business partnership with her."[91] Muhammad accepted Khadija's offer. On his wedding day he freed the faithful slave girl, Baraka, that he had inherited from his father. As if in exchange, though, as a wedding gift, Khadija gave him a fifteen-year-old slave boy named Zayd, who would figure importantly in subsequent Islamic history.[92]

Watt's antiromanticism may not be entirely apt in the case of Muhammad and Khadija. They seem to have dwelt together in great happiness and contentment. While she lived, he never took another wife. His marriage to Khadija was of immeasurable significance to Muhammad. She became not only his wife, and not only his friend and confidante, but, especially as later events would show, his

90. The monk's name strongly suggests, if the story is historical at all, that he was a Nestorian Christian.
91. Watt, p. 10.
92. Watt, p. 35, thinks he was the first male convert to Islam.

moral support. Six children were born to the couple, including daughters named Zaynab, Ruqayya, Umm Kulthum, and Fatima, and a pair of sons.[93] But Muhammad was unlucky in the latter category, so very important to ancient Arabians. His eldest child was a son named Qasim, from which Muhammad gained the *kunya* name of Abu Qasim, or "father of Qasim," by which he is still sometimes called.[94] Unfortunately Qasim died before reaching his second birthday. And the sixth child of Muhammad and Khadija, also a son, died very young.

Muhammad's lack of male offspring — which would continue with his later wives as well — was to have serious implications for the future of Islam. When controversy surged over the question of succession, there was no male heir to the Prophet. The Shi'ites, who were to claim that the succession belonged by right to the closest male relative, could do no better than to point to Muhammad's cousin Ali as their candidate — which did not carry the day for them. Had there been a son, things might have turned out rather differently. There is also reason to believe that Muhammad himself, though he doted on children and loved his daughters, felt keenly his lack of sons. As part of its polemic against Meccan belief in the three goddess daughters of Allah, the Qur'an repeatedly asks Muhammad's opponents why, when they crave sons so much, they believe that God himself has only daughters.[95]

Muhammad did gain another "son" by adoption. He grew very fond of the slave boy Zayd, whom Khadija had given him on their wedding day. And the devotion was mutual. In fact, when Zayd and his family, from whom he had been separated years before in a raid, were finally reunited, Zayd chose to stay with Muhammad. Muhammad, the young slave said, was like both father and mother to him. This remark, and his preference for his master, provoked an outcry from his relatives, who decried his lack of loyalty to his own flesh and blood. But Muhammad silenced the furor by taking the group to the Ka'ba and, while standing in the Hijr Ismail, a place particularly potent for the taking of oaths, announcing that Zayd was his son and heir. So the former slave became known as "Zayd, son of Muhammad." Under the customary law of pre-Islamic Arabia, adopted kinship was every bit as real as literal blood kinship. (This would change, and Muhammad's relationship with Zayd would, in after years, lead to a very important principle of Islamic law effectively banning adoptions.) Unfortunately Zayd, too, predeceased his "father," dying during one of the Muslim raids late in the Prophet's career.

93. The number of children she bore to him would seem to cast doubt on the traditional claim that Khadija was forty at the time of her marriage to Muhammad.

94. The *kunya* is an Arabic surname or agnomen received by a mother or father at the birth, usually, of a first son. (Sometimes, however, it is purely honorific.) It contains the name of the son, preceded either by *Abu* (father) or *Umm* (mother).

95. Q 16:57; 37:149, 153; 52:39.

Muhammad's growing reputation as a man of probity and competence, and his marriage to the rich widow Khadija, lifted him from the obscurity of herding sheep and goats and made him one of the rising stars of the new Meccan generation. There is little reason to doubt the traditional claim that the people of Hashim and its allies viewed him as a hopeful augury for the future.

One story that the traditional narratives tell about Muhammad says much about his increasing stature and his reputation for wisdom: When Muhammad was about thirty-five years old, the leaders of the Quraysh, flush with increasing wealth, decided to rebuild the Ka'ba. At the time, the walls of the structure were slightly more than the height of a man. Furthermore, the shrine lacked a roof, which meant that locking its door did not greatly increase its security, and in fact, some of the sanctuary's treasure had recently been stolen. Besides, with all the money flowing into Mecca, the city fathers felt they really ought to do something for the holy shrine that was the chief glory of their town. Fortunately for dwellers in a place so barren of vegetation, a great deal of wood had just arrived at their figurative doorstep in the form of a Greek-owned merchant ship that had run aground and split apart on the Red Sea coast near Jiddah. Moreover, a skilled Coptic carpenter was in town.

The Meccans approached their task with deep religious awe — the story, if true, does not accord well with the claim, mentioned above, that the pre-Islamic Arabians were flippantly irreligious — realizing that repair of the Ka'ba meant, in the first instance, doing it some damage. The traditional accounts make much of the hesitancy and even fear with which they attempted to figure out a way to demolish its walls so that they could be rebuilt, and many horrifying portents are said to have accompanied their first faltering efforts.

When they had finally begun excavating, they found a piece of writing in one of the corners of the shrine, written in Syriac. They could not read it, but they kept it until a Jew was able to read it to them. "I am God," the note said, "the Lord of Becca [Mecca]. I created her on the day when I created the heavens and the earth, the day I formed the sun and the moon, and I placed round about her seven inviolable angels. She shall stand so long as her two hills stand, blessed with milk and water for her people."

In addition to the stones they had taken from the earlier structure, the Meccans gathered yet more in order to increase the height of the sanctuary's walls. Each clan worked separately. But then a crisis arose. Who would put the sacred black meteoric stone into its new place in the wall of the shrine? Which of the clans would be accorded that honor? It was one thing for all the clans to work on the walls, but only one person, representing one of the factions of the Quraysh, would be privileged to reinstall the stone. The controversy lasted for days and was on the verge of becoming violent when the oldest participant proposed a solution that all could accept. They would wait and see who would be the first person to enter the sanctuary. That person would be the arbiter.

Needless to say, the first man to enter the sanctuary was Muhammad, the thirty-five-year-old son of Abd Allah. He had just returned to Mecca following an absence, and was unaware of the conflict at the Ka'ba. Instantly, as he walked in, those within the sacred area recognized that he was precisely the man for the task. Muhammad had the men bring him a cloak. When they had fetched it, he spread it out on the ground, then picked up the sacred stone and placed it in the middle of the cloak. He next instructed each clan represented among them to take hold of the edge of the cloak and to lift it up, all together. They did so. When the cloak had been raised to the right level, Muhammad himself took the stone and secured it in its place with his own two hands. Then the reconstruction of the Ka'ba continued, and was completed without further discord. Muhammad's future role as the uniter of the Arabs had been clearly foreshadowed.

The Calling of a Prophet

W. Montgomery Watt suggests that, while the fifteen years after Muhammad's marriage to Khadija were good ones for the future prophet, they may also have been frustrating. Though he was able to marry his daughters to Meccans of moderate importance, every one of these husbands was a relative either of himself or of his wife. His mercantile career prospered in a modest way, but he was, on the whole, excluded from the inner circle of politics and commerce in the town. Perhaps, Watt suggests, he felt that his abilities were not being recognized. From his subsequent career we know that he had capacities as a leader and organizer that were far superior to those of any other among his townsmen. If he himself was aware of these, it must have deepened his dissatisfaction and perhaps made more acute his awareness of the flaws and injustices of Mecca's stratified society.[96]

Muhammad appears eventually to have found himself among the *hunafa*. It seems most likely, however, although Muslim apologetics would strenuously deny it, that he originally shared the religious beliefs of his environment. The name of his son, Abd Manaf, is manifestly a pagan one, and it is extraordinarily unlikely that later Muslim sources would have invented so embarrassing a detail.[97] His uncle Abu Lahab was a vociferous defender of paganism, even to the

---

96. Watt, pp. 12-13.

97. See the discussion in A. Sprenger, *Das Leben und die Lehre des Mohammed*, 2nd ed. (Berlin: Nicolaische Verlagsbuchhandlung, 1869), 1:200; Leone Caetani, *Annali dell' Islām* (Milan: Ulrico Hoepli, 1905), 1:172-73.

Black Stone
(Edinburgh Library)

point of becoming an enemy of Muhammad and Islam as the story went on. His other uncle and ersatz father, Abu Talib, never accepted Islam, although he was friendly to Muhammad and lived some years after Muhammad's prophetic call. And the Muslim historian Ibn al-Kalbi reports that Muhammad once bought a sheep as a sacrifice to the goddess al-Uzza. (Once again, an item no later Muslim writer would voluntarily connect with the Prophet.) Thus, says the Qur'an to Muhammad, God "found you astray and guided [you]."[98] "And thus we have revealed to you a spirit, to you who did not know what book or belief was."[99] Even after his revelations began, traces of his pagan environment can arguably be identified in Muhammad's thinking. Western Orientalists have even pointed to the mysterious oaths of the Qur'an, and especially to its use of *saj*, or rhymed prose — both of which were characteristic of the old Arab soothsayers of Muhammad's day and earlier.[100] At the most, however, these are side issues, and it is clear that, when he felt himself called by God, Muhammad's old ideas were driven out by the new revelation. Muhammad never saw himself as the continuation or fulfillment of old Arabian paganism; instead, and explic-

98. Q 93:7.
99. Q 42:52.
100. See Goldziher, *Abhandlungen zur arabischen Philologie*, 1:59ff.; al-Mas'udi, *Murūj al-dhahab wa-ma'adin al-jawhar* (Cairo: Al-maktaba al-tijariyya al-kubra, 1964-65), 3:381ff.

itly, he viewed himself as the continuation of Jewish and Christian revelation.[101]

Muhammad began the practice of withdrawing to a cave on Mount Hira, a few miles to the northeast of Mecca, where he apparently prayed and meditated, sometimes for several days and nights in a row.[102] It was a barren and monotonous place, perhaps therefore conducive to focused meditation. At some point in or near his fortieth year, Muhammad began to experience "true visions," which he said came to him while he was sleeping. They were, he said, "like the breaking of the light of dawn," and they made solitude become "dear" to him.

Serious Western scholars have long granted that something must really have happened to Muhammad to begin his prophetic career, something sudden and out of the ordinary; few if any, for many decades, have been willing to call him insincere — at least in his earliest years as a prophet — and they have insisted that his prophetic self-consciousness could not have been the result, merely, of a process of gradual evolution.[103] Opinions have been divided, however, on the later, Medinan revelations. Skeptical Orientalists, especially those of an earlier generation, have suspected that the paroxysms recorded in connection with the battle of Badr and the slandering of the Prophet's young wife, A'isha, could have been artificially self-induced. Even A'isha herself is recorded as saying, on one occasion, "Your Lord seems to have been very quick in fulfilling your prayers."

One night, toward the end of the month of Ramadan (probably of the year 610) while he was in his cave on the mountain, an angel appeared to him, commanding him to "read" or "recite." (Our distinction between the two terms was not particularly clear in ancient times; ancient people virtually always read

101. See, for example, Q 10:94.

102. Rodinson, p. 70, sees a parallel in earlier Christian practice. On the enigmatic word *tahannuth*, used in the sources to describe Muhammad's devotional activities in and near the cave, see Peters, *Muhammad*, pp. 128-30; M. J. Kister, "'Sha'bān Is My Month . . .': A Study of an Early Tradition," in *Studia Orientalia Memoriae D. H. Baneth Dedicata*, ed. J. Blau (Jerusalem: Magnes Press, 1979), pp. 34-37; reprinted as item XI in M. J. Kister, *Society and Religion from Jāhiliyya to Islam* (Aldershot: Variorum, 1990).

103. See Q 44:3ff.; 97:1; 2:185. Taking no stand on the ultimate source of Muhammad's revelations in this essay, I shall follow the rule enunciated by W. Montgomery Watt in his biographies of the Prophet. In citing the Qur'an, I shall neither write "God says" nor "Muhammad says," but "the Qur'an says." As evidence for Muhammad's early sincerity, Western scholars have pointed to such Qur'anic passages as 10:17, 21; 28:85ff.; 49:44; 75:16ff.; 7:203; 16:98; to the cogent imperatives of 79:2 and 96:1; and to the self-denunciation of 80:1ff. Biographers have noted Muhammad's unselfish dedication to what he must surely have believed to have been a divine cause, and to his patient endurance of hostility and humiliation.

aloud.) To the angel's command Muhammad responded that he was not a reader, or a reciter, and the angel choked him until he thought he would pass out. The angel then repeated the command, and Muhammad reiterated his refusal or his denial of his competency. The angel choked him a second time, and reiterated the command. Muhammad responded as before, and was choked as before. The angel released him, and then spoke words which, now canonized in the Qur'an,[104] are traditionally regarded by Muslims as the first revelation of God to the Prophet of Islam: "Recite [*iqra*] in the name of thy Lord, who created, created the human being from a bloodclot! Recite! And thy Lord is most gracious, who taught by the pen, taught the human being that which he did not know."[105] When the angel had declared these words, he departed and Muhammad was left to ponder them. He was immediately concerned that he might have become *majnun* — a word that today means "crazy" but that, etymologically and originally, signified possession by jinn (the state of the inspired pre-Islamic Arabian poet). In shock and fear Muhammad fled the cave. Halfway down the slope toward Mecca, however, he heard a voice from above him, saying, "O Muhammad! You are the messenger of God, and I am Gabriel." Muhammad looked up and saw the angel again, filling the entire horizon in every direction.

This is the traditional story. But some commentators, both medieval Muslims and Westerners among them, regard another, different Qur'anic passage as the first of the revelations received by Muhammad:

> O you wrapped up in a cloak,
> Arise and warn!
> And magnify your Lord!
> And purify your garments!
> And flee impurity!
> And do not give in order to receive more!
> But be patient for your Lord![106]

According to the stories associated with this passage, Muhammad had already completed his meditation on the mountain and was descending to-

---

104. The word *Qur'an*, which is unmistakably related to the Arabic verb *qara'a/yaqra'u* ("to read," "to recite"), was probably borrowed from the Syriac *qeryana* ("reading," "reader," "a lectionary" [*lectio*]). In the Syriac church the term referred to the scriptural lesson that was read in public worship, which has its obvious Islamic analogue in Muslim liturgical use of the Qur'an. Such use probably began very early. Within the Qur'an, the term *qur'an* frequently refers to individual passages of the revealed text.

105. Q 96:1-5.

106. Q 74:1-7.

Muhammad in Al-Aqsa Mosque
(Bibliotheque nationale, Paris)

ward his home when he heard a voice. Looking around, he could see nobody. Finally, though, he looked up into the sky, "and there he was, sitting upon the throne." It seems likely that this story tells of an anthropomorphic throne theophany — a vision of God in human form — that has been preserved by the scrupulous historians of the early Islamic tradition even though, given their own later, clearly antianthropomorphic theology, they find it rather awkward.[107] Such throne theophanies are commonplace in biblical and pseudepigraphical materials, and if this one is accepted as an accurate account (and there seems little motive for later Muslims to have invented so embarrassing a tale in connection with their prophet), it locates Muhammad squarely within the prophetic tradition of the earlier Near East.[108]

107. Anthropomorphic depictions of God appear throughout the Qur'an itself, as Rodinson, p. 235, notes: "Throned in infinite majesty, his limbs, movements and gestures were nevertheless described in anthropomorphic terms."

108. For a fuller discussion of this alternate call narrative, with references, see Daniel C. Peterson and Stephen D. Ricks, "The Throne Theophany/Prophetic Call of Muhammad," in *The Disciple as Scholar: Essays on Scripture and the Ancient World in Honor of Richard Lloyd Anderson,* ed. Stephen D. Ricks, Donald W. Parry, and Andrew H. Hedges (Provo, Utah: Foundation for Ancient Research and Mormon Studies, 2000), pp.

While Muhammad's prophetic career appears to have commenced with a vision, and while visions occasionally came to him thereafter, the overwhelming majority of his revelations seem to have been auditory, or even heard internally.[109] The agent of the revelation is variously identified: God gave the Qur'an to Muhammad.[110] The "Spirit" gave it to him.[111] The angel gave it to him.[112] In a late passage the angel Gabriel is specifically identified as having delivered the Qur'an to Muhammad.[113] Frequently when revelation came to him, he would undergo violent trembling, seeming attacks of fever, and severe chills. He suffered great pain, sometimes feeling as if he had been struck with a severe blow; heard loud noises; and even on very cold days sweat profusely.[114] The descriptions given in Qur'an 73:1 and 74:1 of his "wrapping up" in a mantle may refer to a preparation to receive divine revelation in the manner of the old Arabian *kahins*. His enemies repeatedly accused him of being "possessed" *(majnun)*, a "soothsayer" *(kahin)*, or a "magician" *(sahir)*. All were familiar figures on the Arabian scene, and he must indeed have resembled them in at least certain aspects if the accusations had, as they must have had, any force at all. In fact, the style of the Qur'an does resemble that of the pre-Islamic soothsayers.[115] Such descriptions of the mode of Muhammad's reception of revelation must be admitted as authentic on the grounds, once again, that no later Muslim would have invented these potentially embarrassing details. It is from such stories that the notion soon arose

---

323-37. See also Peters, *Allah's Commonwealth*, p. 54; Watt, p. 15; Widengren, *Muḥammad*, p. 126 n. 3.

109. Visionary experiences are alluded to at Q 8:43; 48:27; 53:1-18; and 81:22-23. Indeed, if Q 53:1-25 is read as a whole, it seems to contrast the certainty of Muhammad's belief in God — certain because he had *seen* him — with the Meccans' misplaced faith in the goddesses al-Lat and al-Uzza (whom they had *not* seen). (Contrast especially Q 53:12 with Q 53:19.) Q 53:10 and 81:19 seem to point to the primacy of auditory revelation.

110. Q 75:16ff.

111. Q 26:192ff.; 16:102; 42:52.

112. Q 16:2; 15:8; cf. 53:5ff.; 81:23ff.

113. Q 2:97. Peters, *Muhammad*, pp. 142-43, 148-50, is almost certainly correct in identifying God as the object of the early visions and noting that Gabriel was identified as the vehicle of the revelation only comparatively late.

114. Watt, p. 19: "Such accounts led some Western critics to suggest that he had epilepsy, but there are no real grounds for such a view. Epilepsy leads to physical and mental degeneration, and there are no signs of that in Muḥammad; on the contrary he was clearly in full possession of his faculties to the very end of his life."

115. David Noel Freedman, "Between God and Man: Prophets in Ancient Israel," in *Prophecy and Prophets*, p. 57, notes that the biblical prophets, too, shared claims and status with various types of diviners in other cultures, who can be considered their counterparts. See the references listed there.

that Muhammad was an epileptic.[116] In fact, some Western scholars have also adopted the idea, particularly in the nineteenth century, despite the fact that, as W. Montgomery Watt has observed, "there are no real grounds for such a view. Epilepsy leads to physical and mental degeneration, and there are no signs of that in Muḥammad; on the contrary he was clearly in full possession of his faculties to the very end of his life."[117] Moreover, even if it were true, it is not clear how epilepsy would explain Muhammad's career: epileptic seizures have not commonly resulted in the foundation of major world religions. When the revelations arrived, tradition says, those around Muhammad wrote them down on potsherds, palm fronds, scraps of leather, camel bones, or whatever material lay ready to hand.[118] There is no indication that Muhammad wrote any of his own oracles down. As with Jesus, the earliest writing of the teachings of the Prophet of Islam came from his followers and disciples.

The earliest themes of Muhammad's revelations are easily summarized. They include the benevolence and omnipotence of God, especially as it is manifest in nature; the proper human response to God's goodness, which is gratitude, submissive worship, and generosity to the poor, the widow, and the orphan; the imminence of the last judgment, both personal and cosmic; the rewards of paradise; the terrors and agonies of hell; and the prophetic call of Muhammad himself.[119] The earth and the heavens will pass away. The sky will be torn, the mountains will be moved, the moon and the stars will be extinguished. The dead will be raised, gathered, judged, and sent to either paradise or the flames. "The basic conviction of Mohammed's preaching, and the heart of his prophetic message, is the certainty that he alone, in the midst of a light-headed and thoughtless generation, sees the fateful event which awaits all of those who are now jesting and laughing so carelessly."[120]

It is important to note that the Arabic word *kafir*, before it took on the technical meaning in Islam of "unbeliever" or "infidel," carried the sense of "ingratitude." The Qur'an launched a frontal assault on the pride and arrogance, the heedlessness, of the Meccan elite who, on the basis of their financial power,

116. In, for instance, the Greek *Chronographia* of Theophanes the Confessor (d. 818 c.e.). See B. G. Niebuhr, ed., *Corpus Scriptorum Historiae Byzantinae* (Bonn: Weber, 1839), 1:512-13; or the English version of Harry Turtledove, trans., *The Chronicle of Theophanes* (Philadelphia: University of Pennsylvania Press, 1982), p. 35.

117. Watt, p. 19.

118. This may be an exaggeration designed to emphasize the simplicity of the early days of Islam.

119. Watt, pp. 23-34, offers a useful discussion of these themes and, particularly, of a plausible methodology for distinguishing earlier themes from subsequent ones.

120. Andrae, *Mohammed*, p. 53.

saw themselves not only as in control of the Arabian Peninsula but, in terms of their practical behavior at least, free from subservience to any higher power. In a striking phrase, Watt says they suffered from "the absence of a sense of creatureliness."[121] The very meaning of the term *Islam* is "submission [to the will of God]," and Muslim liturgical prayer, with its prostrations and its repeated touching of the forehead to the ground, is a striking physical representation of the creature's total surrender to the Creator, the monarch of the cosmos.

Perhaps surprisingly, the uniqueness of Allah and the utter nonexistence of other gods — the sine qua non of developed Islamic theology and, indeed, of Qur'anic doctrine itself — is apparently *not* a theme of the earliest revelations. Although the Qur'an eventually preaches a rigorous monotheism, it can be argued that, in their earliest phases, Muhammad and the Qur'an were only vaguely monotheistic, and that they were willing to recognize a number of other beings besides Allah as divine or at least archangelic.[122] But they were sharply subordinated to him and severely devalued:

> All that is upon the earth will perish,
> But the face of your Lord remains, majestic and noble.[123]

The diction of the revelations is elliptical and allusive rather than expository or explicit. The Qur'an often strikes non-Muslim readers as difficult because it refers to events and stories and peoples without explaining them. It offers no continuous narrative, but addresses "occasions" for which the context must be furnished from the outside.[124] It presumes that its audience already knows the things to which it refers. Only God's voice is heard in the revelations. Using the "royal We," he addresses Muhammad or, indirectly, either the Muslims or the people in general. The Qur'an is almost always timeless and without context. Indeed, the revelations come very close to poetry, with all of the obscurity that poetic style sometimes exhibits but without the geographical and everyday details that, for many readers, make the Bible come to life.[125]

As the revelations continued to come, however, they took on a more historical character. God was present in the processes of history no less —

---

121. Watt, p. 29.

122. I am persuaded by Watt, pp. 25-26, 60-66, that this was the Prophet's earliest position, and that it continued until roughly 615 c.e. and the obscure incident of the so-called "satanic verses." See, too, Rodinson, pp. 48, 97, 106-7; Peters, *Muhammad*, pp. 152-53, 160-62.

123. Q 55:26-27.

124. Peters, *Muhammad*, p. 2.

125. See Peters, *Muhammad*, p. 171, on the resemblance between the Qur'anic revelations and the poetry of ancient Arabia, and Muslim responses to it.

and perhaps in fact more — than in those of nature. Max Weber wrote of "the distinctively and eminently historical character of the theorizing of the Hebrew prophets, which stands in sharp contrast to the speculations concerning nature characteristic of the priesthoods of India and Babylonia."[126] The same interest in history is one of the distinctions between the prophets and the philosophers of the Mediterranean. Both the Abrahamic prophetic tradition and the Hellenizing philosophic and scientific tradition dealt with comprehensive life-orientational problems; Socrates and Plato were religious figures every bit as much as Amos and Isaiah. However, where the philosophers (especially those of late antiquity) found their inspiration in the rational harmonies of nature — in subjects such as mathematics, astronomy, and medicine — the prophets found it in the moral judgments of history.[127] Where the Abrahamic prophets saw God in historical events — for example, in the exodus from Egypt, at Sinai, and in the judgments imposed on Israel by the Assyrians and Babylonians — the philosophers saw historical events in the realm of "change and decay" or "coming-to-be and ceasing-to-be" as contingent and less than fully real.[128] For the prophets God was an "experienced challenge"; for the philosophers God was a matter of ontology — "a cosmic entity, as such not directly experienced, its very existence [needing] to be demonstrated."[129]

Max Weber defines a prophet as "a purely individual bearer of charisma, who by virtue of his mission proclaims a religious doctrine or divine commandment." The "decisive element distinguishing the prophet from the priest," Weber says, is his "personal call."[130] The notion of "charisma" is worth defining here. As Weber himself explained,

126. Weber, p. 22.

127. Clements, p. 103: "To a considerable extent, in the prophetic invective, the historical order was itself seen to be subject to moral judgement. In place of arbitrary and uncontrollable forces, history, with all its vicissitudes, was moralized."

128. Plato's doctrine of the Ideas or Forms makes this especially clear: triangularity is more real than any particular triangle in the physical world.

129. Marshall G. S. Hodgson, *The Venture of Islam: Conscience and History in a World Civilization*, vol. 1 (Chicago: University of Chicago Press, 1974), p. 425. Hodgson's general discussion of the prophetic and philosophical worldviews in Islam, on pp. 410-43, is nothing less than brilliant. His distinction between the two seems to me far more fundamental and important than that suggested in Weber, p. 53.

130. Weber, p. 46; cf. 54. Van der Leeuw, pp. 251-54, distinguishes the prophet from the preacher and the teacher by the diminution of the immediate presence of "Power" *(das Verblassen des Machtelementes)* in the message brought by the latter, and by a change in tense: in preachers and teachers, as opposed to prophets, God is not speaking — God has spoken.

The term "charisma" will be applied to a certain quality of an individual personality by virtue of which he is set apart from ordinary men and treated as endowed with supernatural, superhuman, or at least specifically exceptional powers or qualities. These are such as are not accessible to the ordinary person, but are regarded as of divine origin or as exemplary, and on the basis of them the individual concerned is treated as a leader. In primitive circumstances this peculiar deference is paid to prophets, to people with a reputation for therapeutic or legal wisdom, to leaders in the hunt, and heroes in war. . . . Charismatic authority is thus specifically outside the realm of everyday routine and the profane sphere.[131]

Clearly, under Max Weber's definition of prophethood, Muhammad is a textbook illustration of the class.[132] Weber goes on, however, to stress the opposition of the priestly character to the prophetic, asserting that prophets rarely emerge from the ranks of priests, whether brahmins or Levites. While the priest, he says, claims authority because of his place in a tradition, the prophet's claim is based on his charisma and on the personal revelation that he claims.[133] Weber allows that there have been a few possible exceptions where prophets have emerged from priesthoods, such as Zoroaster and Ezekiel, but he is in fact scarcely willing to acknowledge the latter as a prophet at all.[134]

David Noel Freedman's characterization of the biblical prophets is entirely consistent with Weber's: "From beginning to end, the stress in prophetic utterance is on the ethical dimension of biblical religion and how it affects the well-being of the nation and its individual members. Over against the cultic domain of the priests, the prophets stress the moral demands of the deity and the ethical requirements of the covenant."[135]

131. Weber, as cited by Clements, p. 93.

132. Plato distinguishes two distinct types of prophecy (*Phaedrus* 244). One is ecstatic prophecy *(mantikē entheos)*, while the other is a species of technique, the systematic study and interpretation of divine signs. (Plato gives, as an example of the latter, augury based on the flight of birds. We might add to that Babylonian liver omens and Chinese *feng shui*, the science of water and wind.) Muhammad is obviously a prophet of the first kind.

133. This may reflect Weber's Protestant background. He also distinguishes between prophets and magicians. Both exert their power on the basis of personal experience, but the magician lacks the definite revelations, the doctrines and/or commandments, of the prophet. (See p. 47.)

134. Weber, pp. 46-47, 51. An analogous denial occurs in Eduard Meyer, *Ursprung und Geschichte der Mormonen: Mit Excursen über die Anfänge des Islams und des Christentums* (Halle an der Saale: Neimeyer, 1912). In both cases the effective denial of Ezekiel's prophethood seems to me arbitrary, tendentious, and ad hoc. Jeremiah, too, was a priest, although he and Ezekiel evidently came from different clans.

135. Freedman, "Between God and Man," p. 68.

However, while Muhammad was clearly a prophet under Weber's definition of the term, and while he was very much in the style of the biblical prophets as described by Freedman, he cannot be neatly divorced from his origin in an aristocratic Arabian religious family. Indeed, he seems another counterexample to Weber's strong opposition of the priestly to the prophetic. For the religious families of ancient Arabia, from among whose ranks Muhammad emerged, fit very well Weber's definition of priesthood: "The crucial feature of the priesthood," he says, is "the specialization of a particular group of persons in the continuous operation of a cultic enterprise, permanently associated with particular norms, places, and times, and related to specific social groups."[136] This describes precisely the role and status of the ancient Arabian sanctuary guardians from among whom Muhammad emerged.

Weber likewise distinguishes prophets and reformers. While the prophet's message may contain a strong element of reform, he differs from the reformer by claiming a substantively new revelation and speaking on the basis of a divine injunction unique to him.[137] "Fundamentally," says one scholar, "Weber's notion of charisma is to be understood in connection with the qualitative difference of a relatively few outstanding individuals who are capable of initiating major social change." Thus, according to Weber, prophets tend to come from socially marginal and economically weak social strata, from groups that are alienated from the central structures of the society and hence have something considerable to gain from overturning them.[138]

Here too, though, the distinction may be too starkly drawn. "The thesis that the major prophets of the Hebrew Bible were drawn from socially marginal groups appears largely to have arisen in order to fit such figures into a recognizable pattern, rather than on the basis of substantive evidence." Indeed, Isaiah and Ezekiel seem to have arisen rather from the inner circles of government and sacerdotal authority, and their intent seems to have been rather a conservative one, to renew and reassert the authority of Israel's established religious and political institutions.[139] For that matter, Moses and Muhammad both, whatever the circumstances of their birth and lineage, indisputably married into prestigious families or clans, and both were helped in their careers by their newly acquired relatives. The same may be true of the early Mesopotamian

136. Weber, p. 30. Furthermore, Joseph Smith (whom Weber instances on p. 54 as a notable illustration of the prophetic type), although he manifestly did not emerge from a sacerdotal class, is also unmistakably "priestly" in the Weberian sense.

137. Weber, p. 54. Thus he contrasts Shankara, Ramanuja, Luther, Zwingli, Calvin, and Wesley, on the one hand, with such figures as Montanus, Mani, Joseph Smith, and Muhammad.

138. Clements, p. 95.

139. Clements, p. 100.

prophets at Mari, who apparently did not belong to marginalized social groups either. Indeed, again contrary to Weber's dichotomy, at least some of them seem to have held official status at Mari.[140]

Likewise, "Muḥammad did not so much create a new movement as revive and redirect currents that already existed among the Arabs of his time."[141] The ritual of Islam owes a great deal to the traditions not only of pre-Islamic Arabia but of the wider ancient Near East.[142] "It might be said that Muḥammad fitted into the system of law and custom into which he was born," and one well-informed scholar can speak plausibly of "the unbroken continuity of Arabian religion."[143] As we have seen, even the style of his revelations and the manner of his receiving them were reminiscent of the pre-Islamic Arabian *kahins,* or seers.[144] Muhammad did not claim originality; indeed, he expressly disavowed it. "Heresy," in Arabic, is denoted by the word *bidʿa* (innovation) and opposes *sunna* ("customary action" or "wont").[145] "I am not an innovator [*bidʿ*] among the messengers," Muhammad is commanded to tell his audience.[146] And the Qur'an re-

140. See Herbert B. Huffmon, "The Expansion of Prophecy in the Mari Archives: New Texts, New Readings, New Interpretations," in *Prophecy and Prophets,* pp. 7-22, with its abundant references.

141. Lewis, p. 48. Yet Andrae, *Mohammed,* pp. 74-77, argues persuasively against a simplistic view of Muhammad as a secular-style reformer.

142. Widengren, *Religionsphänomenologie,* pp. 564-65; F. E. Peters, *Children of Abraham: Judaism/Christianity/Islam* (Princeton: Princeton University Press, 1984), p. 128.

143. Serjeant, "Ḥaram and Ḥawṭah," pp. 51, 53; cf. 42. A willingness to recognize the *Arabian* character of Islam has modified the earlier desire to see it as derivative largely from early forms of Christianity and Judaism. As an example of that earlier view, see Andrae, *Mohammed,* pp. 11, 82, 87-92. Andrae sees heavy Syriac Christian influence giving way, in the latter years of the Prophet's life, to Jewish ideas. Such influences were undeniably present. (See, for example, Watt, p. 27; Widengren, *Religionsphänomenologie,* pp. 447-48.) The descriptions of paradise in Nestorian writings and in the Qur'an are, in some regards, strikingly similar. For instance, the wonderful maidens of paradise, the so-called *houris* (whose mention in the Qur'an has been mocked by Westerners), appear also in the sermons of Ephraim the Syrian. Christ is distinct from other prophets in the view of the Qur'an, which not only affirms his virgin birth and his miracles, but even seems to teach a form of *logos* doctrine in connection with him (as at Q 3:39; 4:171). Peters, *Muhammad,* pp. 127-28, briefly discusses evidence that the pre-Islamic Arabs had some knowledge, albeit indirect, of biblical lore. On the other hand, and this is crucial, the Qur'an's rejection of the divine sonship of Jesus of Nazareth, which is already apparent in the Meccan period of Muhammad's ministry (as at Q 43:57ff.), and its denial of his death and resurrection, starkly contradict Nestorian Christology. Whether or not the parallels to Christian belief compromise the truth or uniqueness of Islam is a theological issue, not a historical one.

144. Rodinson, pp. 81-82.

145. For sunna, see Q 4:26; 15:13; 17:77; 33:38, 62; 35:43; 40:85; 48:23.

146. Q 46:9. Religions naturally tend to be conservative. See Andrae, *Mohammed,* pp. 138-39.

peatedly exhorts believers to do good and to behave honorably, with the term used for "the good" or "the honorable" being *al-ma'ruf* (the known).[147] Muhammad saw himself as getting behind the divisions of Judaism and Christianity, back to the original *muslim* or "submitter," Abraham.[148] He was thus, in this and other senses, a conservative rather than a revolutionary. He was attempting to restore what had been before. He was getting back, as well, to the founder of the Ka'ba shrine in Mecca. It has, furthermore, been plausibly argued that Muhammad had, at least at the first, no thought of founding a new religion. He was to be a "warner" to the Arabs, since no previous prophet had been sent to the people of Arabia.[149]

None of this should be surprising. We should ever keep in mind the necessary, indeed unavoidable, dialectic between the prophet and the society and culture into which he was born.[150] "Every founding," says G. van der Leeuw, "must, to a certain extent, be a reformation. And that is actually the case. No 'man of God' builds his experience upon entirely new ground; all build further on the rubbish heap of earlier settlements. A reformer is also a kind of founder. . . . Just as the founder desires not to break up but to fulfill, so does the reformer wish to prove the new system that he is erecting to be the authentic ancient one, and to demonstrate the old, against which he struggles, to be falsely understood."[151] Muhammad was summoning his people back to their old worship of Allah, the one God of Abraham. His was, as he regarded it, the message of the former prophets, a restoration of the ancient, forgotten truth. His message was not a novelty; it was a new synthesis of ideas that had been present in Arabia for many decades at least.[152] Mont-

147. As at Q 2:178, 180, 228-29, 231-36, 240-41, 263; 3:104, 110, 114; 4:5, 8, 19, 25, 114; 7:157; 9:67, 71, 112; 22:41; 24:53; 31:15, 17; 33:6, 32; 47:21; 60:12; 65:2, 6.

148. Q 3:67. That is *muslim* with a lowercase *m*. Abraham's near sacrifice of his son (who is not named in the Qur'an) often figures in Islamic thinking as an illustration of his willingness to submit to the will of God. For a discussion of Abraham's role in Islam, see Rodinson, pp. 185-88.

149. See Q 51:50; 74:2; 79:45; 80:11; 88:21ff. on Muhammad as "warner"; see Q 6:157; 28:46; 32:3; 34:44; 36:6 on the absence of earlier Arabian prophets. For reasons that remain unclear, the Qur'anic prophets Hud and Salih — specifically identified as Arabian — go unnoticed in the latter passages.

150. As Clements, pp. 92, 99, reminds us to do with reference to the biblical prophets.

151. Van der Leeuw, p. 755. In this light Weber's model prophetic types all seem rather less distinct from the reformers than his somewhat schematic statement might suggest: The Montanist movement can easily be viewed as an attempt to return to the spiritual gifts (particularly prophecy) of the primitive church. Mani regarded himself as the latest in a series of prophets that included Jesus and the Buddha. Joseph Smith sought to restore pristine Christianity following a universal apostasy, and Muhammad believed he had received the pure religion of Adam, Abraham, and the prophets.

152. Rodinson, pp. 96, 98.

gomery Watt offers useful insight into the stories of ancient prophets that appear throughout the pages of the Qur'an:

> The stories give encouragement to Muḥammad and his followers in their troubles. They must sometimes have felt they were deserting their ancestors, especially when they were asked difficult questions about the present or future state of deceased pagans. The stories of the Old Testament prophets and others helped them to realize that, as themselves followers of a prophet, they had a distinguished spiritual ancestry. They also were members of a community with its roots deep in the past and, like most Arab tribes, able to boast of the excellence of its stock and the great merits of the forerunners.[153]

When he reached his house, the new prophet was terrified and upset. He asked his wife to cover him. When he was able to stammer out something of what had happened to him, Khadija attempted to comfort him as best she could. She then went to tell her cousin Waraqa. He was instantly supportive. "By Him in whose hand is Waraqa's soul," the now aged Christian said, "there has come to Muhammad the greatest Namus, even the one who used to come to Moses. Truly, Muhammad is the prophet of this people. Let him be assured." (The word *Namus* evidently reflects the Greek *nomos*, or "law," which Waraqa seems to have taken in the sense of the Torah as referring to divinely inspired scripture, and even to have personified as the angelic agent of the revelation itself.) But Muhammad was not left merely to human reassurances. Soon after the first revelation came a second: "By the pen and what they write, by the grace of your Lord you are not possessed [*majnun*]. And there shall be for you a reward which shall not be diminished, and truly you are of a great character."[154] The reception of the Qur'an must have been an awesome, intimidating, even terrifying experience. As a later revelation said, "Had We sent this Qur'an down upon a mountain, you would have seen it humbled and split asunder for fear of God."[155]

But then, troublingly, there was a lengthy interval during which no revelations came to the new prophet, and he was left once again to ponder and even to doubt, or at least to wonder whether or not he had done something to anger or displease God. At long last the word of the Lord again came to him: "By the brightness of dawn and by the nighttime when all is still, your Lord has not abandoned you nor does he hate you, and the last shall be better for you than the first, and your Lord will give to you so that you will be well pleased. Did he

---

153. Watt, p. 72.
154. Q 68:1-4.
155. Q 59:21.

not find you an orphan and give you shelter, and find you astray and guide you, and find you poor and make you rich? Therefore, as for the orphan, do not treat him harshly, and as for the beggar, do not turn him away, but as for the grace of your Lord, proclaim it!"[156] Muhammad accordingly began to speak to his closest kin of his revelations and of his experience with the angelic messenger.

There was still very little content to the new religion, but tradition says the angel Gabriel appeared to the Prophet shortly thereafter and, meeting him on one of the slopes above the town, taught him the ritual washing and gestures and recitations that were to accompany liturgical prayer among those who accepted Muhammad's inspiration. So Muhammad descended from the hill and taught the new practice to his wife and then to others. Such prayer became part of the procedure by which one entered into the Islamic faith. One was required to wash oneself, from head to foot, in order to be ritually pure, and to purify one's garments as well. Then one was required to testify that "There is no god but God, and Muhammad is the Messenger of God."

The first to embrace the new faith, as yet largely undeveloped in doctrine and practice, were, besides Khadija, Ali and Zayd and Muhammad's good friend Abu Bakr. Ali was but a boy, perhaps ten years old, and Zayd had little or no influence in Mecca. But Abu Bakr was a man of excellent reputation, three years older than Muhammad, a calm and steady man, and he used his influence without hesitation to spread the messages that were now coming through the Prophet.

We are told of miraculous signs that came to other Arabs at about this time, alerting them to the calling of the new prophet. Uthman b. Affan, who would later become the third caliph of Islam, was returning from a trading journey to Syria when he heard a voice in the desert calling out "Sleepers, awake! For verily Ahmad has come forth in Mecca." Uthman did not know what this meant, but the message occupied his mind, and when he had returned to Mecca he encountered another man who had just been asked by a monk of Bostra whether Ahmad had appeared among the people of the Ka'ba shrine. When the man inquired "Who is Ahmad?" the monk replied that he was the son of Abd Allah and the grandson of Abd al-Muttalib. "This is his month, in which he shall come forth," explained the monk, no doubt drawing on the same mysterious book that had told his fellow monks of Bostra so remarkably much about the coming of the messenger. "He is the last of the prophets." This was specific enough that both men were soon able to meet Muhammad — whose name comes from the same Semitic root *(hmd)*, connoting "praise," as does Ahmad — and to enter Islam. Muhammad himself claimed no miracles except the Qur'an, although Muslim tradition was quick to ascribe spectacular miracles to him.

156. Q 91.

DANIEL C. PETERSON

Rejection at Mecca

Muhammad waited for some time, perhaps three years, before beginning his public ministry, before openly summoning his Meccan neighbors to accept the imperious call of Allah for the submission *(islam)* of their wills to his, as expressed through his earthly messenger. Even before the commencement of the public ministry, however (it probably occurred about 613), a nucleus of believers began to gather about Muhammad. By 614, according to one careful estimate, thirty-nine people acknowledged his prophethood.[157] Both men and women were among them, but most were relatively young and, with low social status, relatively powerless in Meccan society. Slaves and freedmen were willing to listen to him, as were the younger sons and daughters of even some of the prominent families — those who stood to benefit rather less from the increasing wealth of their parents and of Mecca in general. Most of the free members of the Quraysh who accepted Islam in the earliest period were affiliated, on the other hand, with families that had been relegated, as less significant and influential, to the outskirts of Mecca.

The wealthy and influential citizens of Mecca largely held back from the new religion.[158] The ruling elite were too comfortable, too satisfied with the status quo, to feel any strong spur to change. (It is a phenomenon well known to proselytizing religions even today, and is apparent in the rise of Christianity too, where the well-rooted dwellers on the heath, the heathen, and the villagers [*pagani*] were far less willing to accept the new faith than the uprooted urban proletariat of Rome and the other cities of the empire.) Those who possessed wealth and honor saw little reason to change when Muhammad arrived with his message. And those whose satisfaction consisted in the very earthly achievements and possessions that Muhammad condemned could scarcely be expected to warm up easily to his preachments on the vanity of temporal things and the brevity of mortal life. "What is the life of this world," asked one of the Qur'anic revelations, "but amusement and play? But truly the abode of the hereafter, that indeed is life — if they only knew."[159] They wanted things to continue as they were; their satisfaction, their status, their very sense of meaningfulness depended on the stability of the values with which they had been raised. If they were not to live on in the praise of their descendants and successors, if the things they valued were to be devalued, what then could be the purpose of life? "There is nothing except the life of

157. Watt, p. 57.
158. See Q 19:73; 34:31ff.; 38:62ff.; 73:11; 80:1ff.; cf. 7:75; 11:27; 17:16; 26:111. See, too, Watt, pp. 36-39.
159. Q 29:64.

this world," the Qur'an quotes the infidels as saying, "and we will not be resurrected."[160]

At first there seemed no cause for concern. Maxime Rodinson observes that "the Qurayshites regarded the new group, which was gradually shedding its cloak of secrecy and emerging into the open, with amused tolerance, very much as Londoners today might watch a Salvation Army meeting on a street corner. They were harmless visionaries and there was no need to take them seriously. At the most, there was a certain contempt for the low social status of those involved."[161] Occasionally, though, there were confrontations. One day an infidel brought a decaying bone to Muhammad and demanded to know if he really claimed that God was going to bring such things back to life. To make his point he crumbled the bone in his hand and blew the dust of it into the Prophet's face. Muhammad waited until the man was finished with his little display and then replied that, yes, that was indeed what he believed. Someday, the Prophet told the disdainful Meccan, God would raise not only that bone but the man who had crumbled it and blown it into his face — and would then thrust that arrogant skeptic into the flames of hell. "Truly, those who do not yearn to meet Us, and are satisfied with the life of this world and pleased with it, and those who pay no heed to Our signs, the inferno is their abode, according to what they have merited."[162] But Muhammad's predictions of the end of the world did not seem plausible to many in his Meccan audience. The years went by, and the eschaton did not seem to be arriving.

The oligarchy of the Quraysh could hardly accept Muhammad's claim to prophethood without surrendering their privileges. What is more, acceptance of Muhammad as the messenger of God virtually entailed recognition of his right to political supremacy. For, if God commanded, who could legitimately resist? Montgomery Watt points out that those who resisted Muhammad most strenuously tended to be people of his own generation rather than their elders, for the obvious reason that he was a direct competitor with them for the control of Mecca.[163] Moreover — and this seems to have been an inflammatory issue from the start — if he were right, his preaching seemed to entail that their venerable polytheistic ancestors, the founders of their polity and the establishers of their traditions, were, at that very moment, burning in the flames of hell. That the Quraysh could not grant.[164]

160. Q 6:29.
161. Rodinson, p. 102. Others have noted that social contempt. See, for example, Andrae, *Mohammed*, pp. 122-23; Peters, *Muhammad*, pp. 167-69.
162. Q 10:7-8.
163. Watt, pp. 59, 74.
164. This issue is recognized by Peters, *Muhammad*, p. 169; Andrae, *Mohammed*, p. 116.

"Warn your nearest kinfolk," commanded an early revelation.[165] And Muhammad did so. Yet not a single one of Muhammad's four uncles accepted his message at the first. Abu Talib seems to have had no great interest in the subject, although he freely allowed his sons Jafar and Ali (the latter eventually to become the fourth and last of the "orthodox" caliphs, and the focus of veneration for the Shi'ite faction of Islam) to enter the new religion. Hamza would accept Islam a few years later, becoming a great warrior and ultimately a notable martyr for the faith. Abbas, in whose name the illustrious Abbasid dynasty of Baghdad would come to power somewhat more than a century later, seems to have been waiting to see which way the winds were blowing. As the likelihood of Muhammad's triumph became ever clearer with the passing years, Abbas's Islam became ever more open.[166] Abu Lahab, by contrast, remained an intractable enemy of the new faith, and openly said that his nephew was, if not a conscious fraud, at the very best a madman. An old story (very likely of Shi'ite tinge) tells of a gathering in which Muhammad invited the menfolk of his family to accept his message, and only the thirteen-year-old Ali was willing to speak up. Whereupon Muhammad pronounced the boy his executor and successor.

Muhammad no doubt wished to attract some influential men to his cause. To do so would clearly give prestige to the new faith, and would afford a measure of protection to its followers. A story is told of his eager attempt to win over one of the leaders of the Quraysh. While they were conversing, a blind man, a recent convert, happened to pass by. Recognizing Muhammad's voice, he implored the Prophet to recite to him some passage of the Qur'an. Muhammad, however, anxious lest he lose this relatively rare opportunity to have the respectful ear of one of the Meccan leaders, grew impatient with the blind man when he insisted on hearing a recitation. In the end the conversation went nowhere; the Meccan leader was deaf to the appeal of the divine message. But a stinging rebuke came to Muhammad: "He frowned," said a revelation referring to Muhammad, speaking first in the third person and then in the second, "and turned away because the blind man came to him. And what would teach you? Perhaps he would cleanse himself, or remember, and the reminder might profit him. But the self-sufficient one, to him you pay attention even though there is no blame upon you if he does not cleanse himself. And as for him who came to you earnestly and fearfully, to him you paid no attention."[167]

165. Q 26:214.
166. Peters, *Allah's Commonwealth*, p. 70 n. 34, is hardly alone in seeing Abbas's sympathetic role as a politically motivated retrojection. Watt, p. 200, thinks Abbas may actually have fought against Muhammad in his earlier days.
167. Q 80:1-10. Such changes of person are not uncommon in Semitic poetry (e.g., in the Psalms).

Muhammad's perhaps overly developed sense of the importance of the Meccan elite was not unique to him. They shared it. Why, asked the lords of the Quraysh, did the revelation not come to us? Why, if God were truly to speak to someone in Arabia, would he have chosen someone from Muhammad's declining clan rather than from one of the powerful and prestigious clans that had come to the fore in the previous generation or two? "Why are the angels not sent down to us," the Qur'an reports the Meccan leaders as demanding, "and why do we not see our Lord?" As R. B. Serjeant writes,

> The Meccan Saiyids constituted much of the opposition to Muḥammad himself. Expressing amazement that Muḥammad should claim revelation, al-Walīd ibn al-Mughīrah exclaims: "Is revelation given to Muḥammad while I am left, although I am the Ka'bīr of Quraish and their Saiyid, and Abū Mas'ūd 'Amr ibn 'Umar al-Thaqafī, the Saiyid of Thaqīf, is left [also], though we be the two great persons of the two cities [Mecca and Ṭā'if]?" The plain interpretation of al-Walīd's protest is that, as the spiritual head, the Saiyid, of Quraish, and the Ka'bīr or temporal ruler, he himself is the natural repository of that virtue of spiritual power and of revelation.[168]

"They are arrogant in their souls," comments the Qur'an of such men, "and they are immensely insolent."[169] One of the Meccan chiefs even saw Muhammad's prophethood as an ambitious, self-aggrandizing lie that attempted to regain his family's prestige by an unprecedented and underhanded shortcut. The proper way to vie for honor and status, in the chief's view, was through generosity and largesse, not by suddenly claiming to receive revelations from the one true God of heaven — a gambit with which, once the unique honor had been claimed, nobody else could really compete.

The leaders of the Quraysh wanted the verification of a miracle from Muhammad. Or so they claimed. (They were probably quite confident that he could not produce what they demanded.) They suggested that an angel come down in plain view to confirm the prophethood of their townsman. Or, they said, why did he not rise up to heaven? Such demands evidently made an impact on Muslim believers, who were eager to supply confirmatory miracles, even if Muhammad himself had not claimed them. Tradition attaches the stories of many miracles to Muhammad, such as the feeding of the family of Abd al-Muttalib with food that could not be diminished by their consumption of it. (It is impossible here not to detect echoes of the miracle of Elisha and the cruse of oil or, perhaps even more, of Jesus' feeding of the multitudes as recorded in

---

168. Serjeant, "The Saiyids of Ḥaḍramawt," p. 5.
169. Q 25:21.

the four Gospels.)[170] On one occasion several infidels are supposed to have approached the Prophet with the rather odd demand that he split the moon in half as a sign that he was truly God's prophet. When he did so, though, in plain view of all, they dismissed it as mere magic and refused to accept Islam despite their earlier promise that such a sign would settle the question for them.

In the first days of the revelation, the Muslims often went forth from the city in order to perform the ritual prayers away from the prying eyes of their disbelieving townspeople. Yet their attempts at seclusion did not always work. One day a group of Meccan pagans came upon them during their prayers and began to mock them, interrupting their devotions. The situation finally grew so intolerable that one of the believers grabbed the jawbone of a camel and smote a pagan with it, thus shedding the first blood in the short history of Islam. At this stage, though, God and his prophet did not approve of such responses. "Be patient with what they say," admonished a revelation, "and separate yourself from them pleasantly [*ahjurhum hajran jamilan*]."[171] "Deal gently with the infidels," said another, "grant them gentle respite."[172] Such pacifism would not last forever, but the Muslim community at this point was so small that no other practical course was open to them.

At this early stage there was little call for violence on the part of the rulers of the Quraysh, who surely did not yet perceive any kind of threat from this tiny movement of what must have seemed to them harmless eccentrics. As the disciples of Islam multiplied, however, it became ever clearer that the message of the new revelation was fundamentally hostile to the gods of the Meccans, to their way of life, to the traditions handed down to them from their ancestors, and, so it seemed at first, to the sanctuary that was the chief glory of their town. Fairly soon thereafter a delegation of them went to the Prophet's unbelieving uncle, Abu Talib, insisting that he put an end to his nephew's nonsense. At first he did nothing, perhaps hoping simply that Muhammad would outgrow this phase. But Muhammad did not, and the leaders of the Quraysh began to bring more and more pressure to bear on Abu Talib. Finally he went to Muhammad and asked him, as a member of the family with whom he had always maintained warm and close relations, to cease these activities that exposed his kin to potential harm. Muhammad, no disloyal relative but a man consumed with the conviction that he had been called by God, said he could not cease. The refusal — a clear offense against

---

170. See Matt. 14:13-21; Mark 6:32-44; Luke 9:10-17; John 6:1-15. The only miracle of Jesus recorded in all four Gospels, this story may have been known to Muhammad as well. Some have suggested that it finds an echo in the Qur'an at 5:112-15, although others relate that passage to the Last Supper or even to Peter's vision in Acts 10:9-18.

171. Q 73:10. There is, in the Arabic of this passage, a foreshadowing of the emigration of Muhammad and his community, the *hijra*, from Mecca to Medina.

172. Q 86:17.

traditional notions of filial piety — must have caused the Prophet some pain, for Muhammad rose to go with tears in his eyes. But his uncle called him back, saying, "O son of my brother, go and say whatever you will, for by God I will never forsake you for anything." Such was the strength of family loyalty.

And it was a strength with which the Prophet's opponents found it immensely difficult to contend. If Abu Talib granted protection to his nephew, the other clan chiefs would be very reluctant to attempt anything against Muhammad, for they did not want to open up a blood feud and were no doubt concerned that any violation of the rights of one chief would undercut the legitimacy and moral authority of them all. But they had to take action. Here, in the heart of Arabian paganism, a vocal and charismatic preacher was casting doubt on the very foundation of their religion — and he would not hesitate to do so, as well, among the pilgrims who came to Mecca from all over the peninsula. If he weakened their faith in the gods, would those pilgrims return? And if they did not, what would that mean for the economic future of the town? It was a situation rather like that of Paul in Ephesus, when he seemed to threaten the livelihood of that city's silversmiths by disparaging the goddess Artemis, for whose temple they manufactured profitable votive figurines.[173] At one point, seeing no other way short of violence to dissuade him from preaching further, the leaders of the Quraysh decided to offer Muhammad a lavish bribe as an inducement to silence. He refused it.

Still, if Muhammad himself was essentially untouchable, many of his followers were not. One prominent convert, a man of wealth named Arqam, had a large house in the center of Mecca, which he put at the disposal of the fledgling Muslim community. There the believers could meet to pray and recite the Qur'an and discuss the revelations without fear of being observed or molested by their hostile neighbors. But even those who could not be physically hurt could be mocked and harassed, or boycotted. Stories are told of unbelieving fathers torturing and attempting to starve their Muslim children into recanting their religion. No tribal rule protected an unfilial son or daughter against a father's authority.[174] Nor would any other tribe or clan intervene to spare someone who did not pertain to them. Accordingly, each kinship unit in Mecca dealt with its Muslims in whatever way it chose. There are many stories of imprisonment, beating, starvation, and thirst, and perhaps worst of all, of believers staked out on the ground under the scorching heat of the Arabian sun until they could be induced to repudiate their faith.

173. See Acts 19:21-41.

174. A similar situation has long been recognized in the law of the ancient classical world. See Henry Sumner Maine, *Ancient Law: Its Connection with the Early History of Society and Its Relation to Modern Ideas* [1861] (N.p.: Dorset Press, 1986).

Slaves were particularly vulnerable, for they had no one to protect them against their masters. One of them, a black Abyssinian named Bilal, was pinned to the ground by his master, with a large rock on his chest, and told that he would remain there until he either died or recanted — whichever came first. He was spared only because Abu Bakr, passing by, was horrified at this maltreatment of a fellow believer and bought Bilal's freedom. (This was not the first time he had manumitted a slave, and Abu Bakr would eventually spend his entire fortune in the service of Islam and the Muslims.) Some, it is said, died under torture. And others did indeed renounce their faith. If they were asked, "Are al-Lat and al-Uzza not your gods, along with Allah?" they would answer yes in order to be delivered from their agony. But their pain was so intense, relates Ibn Ishaq, that they would have acknowledged the deity of a passing dung beetle if doing so would have delivered them.[175]

On at least one occasion, though, the remorse of a persecutor led to a very significant conversion. Umar, who would later succeed Abu Bakr to become the second caliph of Islam, began his experience with the new faith as one of its most ardent and fiery opponents. His sister, Fatima, had already accepted Muhammad's prophethood but was afraid to tell Umar of her faith because of his violent character. Umar was a serious man who seems to have been genuinely devout in the manner of Arabian paganism and appears to have been angered by the divisions introduced into the Quraysh by this innovator Muhammad — whose followers still numbered probably fewer than a hundred but were increasing.[176] One day, when Umar was about twenty-six, he suddenly formed the resolution to go and kill the man who was responsible for all the problems that he saw afflicting his town and people. He was met en route, however, by a man who told him that he should first go to the people of his own house, to set them to rights. Umar had been kept in the dark, and was bewildered by this remark. When he was told that his sister and her husband were Muslims, he was furious.

He went hurriedly to the place where Fatima and her husband, as fortune would have it, were listening to a recitation of the Qur'an. When they heard his angry voice, Fatima took the manuscript of the revelation and hid it under her robe.[177] But it was too late. Umar had heard the sound of the recitation, and demanded to know what they had been saying. They tried to convince him that he had heard nothing, but he insisted that he had indeed heard them reciting, and

175. Translated at Guillaume, p. 145. Is there an implicit reference here to the scarab beetle, sacred to the ancient Egyptians?
176. So much, again, for the supposed irreligiousness of pagan Arabia.
177. Note that, in this story, at least a portion of the Qur'an had already been committed to writing during the lifetime of the Prophet — indeed, while he was still in Mecca. An argument has long raged as to when the Qur'an began to be written down.

that he knew they were secret Muslims. He assaulted his brother-in-law and, when Fatima came to his defense, struck her so violently that it broke the skin.[178] Yes, they said, they were Muslims. He could do with them what he wanted.

This sobered him. When he saw the blood of his sister, he was instantly remorseful. He asked if he could read the revelation that they had been sharing with one another before his entry. Fatima responded, rather daringly, that he could not, since his idolatry rendered him too impure to touch the document. But Umar was now thoroughly chastened, and when he had washed himself, she gave him the page containing the revelation. As he began to read, he was moved and transformed by the beauty and nobility of the words and immediately decided to embrace the religion of Islam. He went to the Prophet and made the formal profession of faith, and then went about openly summoning other Meccans to do as he had done. Indeed, true to his bold nature, he deliberately went to the most hostile among the Quraysh, proclaiming the truth of Muhammad's revelation.

Upon his conversion, Umar took to praying publicly at the Ka'ba, sometimes accompanied by Muhammad's redoubtable uncle Hamza and a company of other believers. The pagans of the Quraysh were not at all happy about this, but were reluctant to confront people of Umar and Hamza's forceful character. Since they could not simply stand by and appear to ratify Muslim use of the Ka'ba sanctuary, they chose instead to stay away — which can be seen, in retrospect, as one of the earliest of what would become a long series of Qurayshi surrenders and accommodations to the upstart new religion.

But the leaders of the Quraysh were not merely passive in the face of the growing threat. They decided about this time to launch an economic embargo and general ban against the entire clan of Hashim, Muhammad's clan, which was protecting Muhammad against persecution out of family loyalty, if not from religious conviction. (Muhammad's uncle Abu Lahab was an exception. He and his wife were bitter enemies to the Prophet.) Roughly forty of the Meccan elite composed a document pledging no intermarriages with the Hashimites and no commercial trafficking. The demand was that the Hashimites either pronounce Muhammad an outlaw — thus depriving him of any defense against persecution or even assassination — or convince him to yield up his claim of prophethood. Tradition says the text of the agreement was placed within the Ka'ba.

178. Though he was a man of undisputed integrity, Umar's temper was legendary. After his conversion, and during his tenure as caliph, he enforced Islamic law very sternly. Once when his own son was caught drinking wine, he punished him so severely that the young man cried out that he had killed him. "Then go," Umar is said to have replied, "and tell God how your father carries out his penalties!"

The interdiction lasted at least two years but, as often happens, seems to have had little of the desired impact. Indeed, it may actually have drawn attention to the claims of Muhammad and to have elicited for him a degree of sympathy. Certainly there was sympathy for many of the ordinary people of Hashim, since they had kinsfolk among the surrounding clans who did not enjoy seeing them suffer. When, finally, it was decided to lift the ineffective ban, someone went into the Ka'ba to fetch the document in which it had been decreed. And when he emerged, it was discovered that worms had eaten virtually all of the vellum on which the ban had been written, leaving only the opening words, "In thy name, O God!"

Not long after the lifting of the interdiction, however, in 619, two events dulled the joy Muhammad must have felt over surviving a serious challenge from the Quraysh. Khadija, his wife for a quarter of a century, his adviser, his first convert and his patroness, died. And not long — perhaps, indeed, only a few days — after Khadija's passing, Muhammad's protector and uncle Abu Talib died also, still a pagan and an unbeliever.

Abu Talib was succeeded as chief of the Banu Hashim by none other than Abu Lahab, the sworn enemy, as tradition represents him, of the Prophet. Actually he may at first not have been as hostile to Muhammad as he is commonly depicted. Some sources represent him as having been moved by the troubles of his nephew, and as having promised him that he would take care of him as Abu Talib had done. But he soon changed his mind. Some of Muhammad's enemies sought out Abu Lahab and reminded him that, in the view of the Prophet, both Abd al-Muttalib and Abu Talib, despite their loyal protection, were even now suffering the flaming torments of hell because they had died pagans. When Muhammad confirmed to Abu Lahab that this was indeed so, his uncle was horrified and deeply offended at the brazen lack of filial piety that such an attitude disclosed.

Abu Lahab continued to do his family duty by Muhammad, but only perfunctorily, and the Prophet now found himself subject to ill-treatment as he had never before experienced it. Much of the persecution was petty and mean-spirited. Someone threw a sheep's uterus at him. Another cast a piece of offal into his cooking pot. Abu Lahab did nothing to deal with such acts.

The leaders of the Quraysh sought also to discredit Muhammad by casting doubt on the validity of his claim to revelation. The early biographies tell of a delegation sent to Yathrib to consult the Jews resident there about Muhammad, as they were surely greater experts on prophets and how to deal with them than were the pagans of Mecca. The Jews, say the accounts, supplied three diagnostic questions to put to Muhammad. If he could answer the questions, they said, he was a genuine prophet of God. If he could not, he was a fraud.

They were to ask him, first, about some young men who left their people in ancient times. He should be able to tell them about these young men and their wonderful story. Second, they were to ask Muhammad about a traveler who had reached the ends of the earth, both to the east and to the west. Third, they were to request that he tell them about the Spirit, and exactly what it is.

After a lengthy and rather embarrassing silence, the Prophet was enabled by revelation to answer the questions: First, the Qur'an recounted a fascinating but somewhat unclear tale about a group of men sleeping in a cave.[179] This story is generally connected by scholars, both medieval and modern, with the very old legend concerning the third century c.e. "seven sleepers of Ephesus," although at least one scholar has suggested that it rests on dim memories of the community at ancient Qumran, near the Dead Sea.[180] The second story was that of Dhu al-Qarnayn, "he of the two horns," who is often connected with the widely traveled hero of the old romance about Alexander the Great.[181] In answer to the third question, about the nature of the Spirit, the Qur'anic revelation said simply that the Spirit exceeds the understanding of humankind.[182] Still, although the Prophet had answered the questions well, neither the Jews who had formulated them nor the people of the Quraysh who actually posed them converted to Islam.

Eventually the stress in Mecca grew so severe that the Prophet began to cast about for some way of escape, some sanctuary or refuge where he and his followers could practice Islam without resistance or persecution. One promising place was Christian Abyssinia, with which the Arabs had long had relatively close contact.

The *Hijra*

About eighty Muslims, not counting small children, had fled to the court of the Negus in Abyssinia, probably in or near 615. They did not go all at once but, fearing that the Meccan leadership would attempt to stop their emigration, left secretly in small groups. There they received a friendly reception from the Ethiopian Christians.

When the heads of the Quraysh noticed their departure, however, Mecca sent an embassy to the Abyssinian court to attempt to bring them back. The

179. Q 18:9-25.

180. Hugh Nibley, "Qumran and the Companions of the Cave," *Revue de Qumran* 5, no. 2 (April 1965): 177-98; reprinted as "Qumran and the Companions of the Cave: The Haunted Wilderness," in Hugh Nibley, *Old Testament and Related Studies* (Salt Lake City: Deseret Book and the Foundation for Ancient Research and Mormon Studies, 1986), pp. 253-84.

181. Q 18:93-99.

182. Q 17:85.

question naturally arises why the Meccan rulers would do such a thing, and why it would matter to them if some of those who were causing problems in their town were to leave. The answer probably has something to do with trade. Mecca and Abyssinia had commercial relations, and perhaps the Quraysh feared an attempt on the part of Muhammad to interfere with their livelihood and divert it toward his own followers. (Subsequent events show him doing precisely that, elsewhere.) It may be that Muhammad was attempting to open up an alternative trade route, beyond the reach of Meccan authority.

The Meccans brought with them gifts for the Negus and his retainers, to induce them to listen. The Negus, however, refused to send the Muslims back to Mecca without first granting them a hearing. This was precisely what the Meccans had sought to prevent, for they were aware that the religious views of the Muslims might well find a more sympathetic hearing among the Ethiopic Christians than would their own pagan and polytheistic objections to Islam. Although Mecca had good commercial relations with Abyssinia, there remained an ideological gulf between them — the gap between a morally serious monotheism and, as it must have seemed to the Abyssinians, a rather lax heathenism.

When all were assembled, the Negus inquired about the new religious views that had caused this breach among the inhabitants of Mecca. A Muslim spokesman stepped forward and, confirming the worst fears of the Qurayshi leadership, told of how, before the revelation, they had been an ignorant, idol-worshiping people, among whom the rich and powerful oppressed the poor and the weak. But now, the Muslim speaker said, God had sent a messenger to them who had summoned them to recognize the one true God, to renounce idolatry and the shedding of blood, to speak the truth and fulfill promises. The speech could not have been better calculated to impress the Negus and his Christian entourage. And when the monarch asked if they could provide for him a sample of the revelation that their prophet had brought to them, they responded with a brilliantly chosen passage from the recently received chapter of "Mary":

> And mention in the book Mary, when she withdrew from her people in a place to the east and veiled herself from them. So we sent to her Our Spirit, which appeared to her in the likeness of a perfect man. She said, "I take refuge from you in the Merciful One, if you are God-fearing." He said, "I am none other than a messenger of your Lord, to give unto you a pure son." She said, "How shall I have a son, when no man has touched me and I have not been unchaste?" He said, "Thus it shall be. Your Lord has said, 'It is easy for Me, that We make him a sign to the people and a mercy from Us, and it is a matter decreed.'"[183]

183. Q 19:16-21.

The Negus was delighted when the interpreters had rendered the Arabic of the Qur'an into his language. This was, he said weeping, the very same doctrine that Jesus had brought, and he was certain that it came from the same source. No, he would not give the Muslims back to their pagan pursuers.

But the Meccans were themselves not without ability, and they soon thought of a way to sow strife between the Abyssinian Christians and the Arabian Muslims, who had won their favor by seeming to believe the same things about Jesus and Mary. For the Muslims denied the deity of Christ and regarded him merely as a servant of God — a great servant, to be sure, and a prophet, but not essentially different from any other mortal and still divided from God by the unbridgeable gulf that separates divinity from humanity.

The next morning, when the Negus questioned them, at the prodding of the Quraysh, about the nature of Jesus, the Muslims were troubled at the potentially dangerous trap that had been set for them. Finally they elected to tell the Ethiopian monarch the truth, that they believed Jesus to have been a virgin-born prophet, but a human. Perhaps to their surprise, and certainly to the astonishment of the Meccan delegation, the Negus agreed with them and again promised them his protection. However, when the Abyssinian people heard of the apparent apostasy of their ruler from Christian orthodoxy, strife arose, and the Negus was obliged for the sake of domestic peace and the stability of his throne to disassociate himself from the Qur'anic position on the status of Jesus — though he privately remained a believing Muslim to the day of his death.

There are some things about this story that do not ring true. It is scarcely plausible, for instance, that the Negus of Abyssinia would publicly repudiate perhaps the central tenet of his Christian faith on the basis of so little as the traditional narratives recount. Moreover, something led him to distance himself from the Muslim position, and it may be that the second day of questioning did not go as well as the traditional accounts say. He might have seen in the Muslims a belief indisputably far closer to his own than the pagan polytheism of the Meccan elite but might still have found their Christology defective and unacceptable, so that he chose a middle course of dismissing the Meccan delegation and allowing the Muslims to remain.

Meanwhile, with the death of Abu Talib and the succession of the hostile Abu Lahab to the leadership of the Banu Hashim, Muhammad's situation in Mecca had materially worsened. Besides, the death of his beloved wife, Khadija, had perhaps weakened his emotional tie to the town. He began to cast around for a place to which he and his followers could go for refuge. He first looked at the mountain town of Ta'if, the stronghold of the people of Thaqif, the guardians of the shrine of the goddess al-Lat. But his visit to Ta'if proved to be humiliating and nearly disastrous, as he had to withdraw from the town under a hail of stones from the unwelcoming pagans.

It may also have been during this time — the years 617 and 619 are often suggested — that one of the most famous events of the Prophet's life occurred, at least according to the traditional accounts. This was his famous *mir'aj,* or "Night Journey." Among the principal objections raised by the people of Mecca against Muhammad was what Mircea Eliade has termed his "existential banality."[184] He was simply an ordinary person, and it seemed wildly implausible that the God of the universe had somehow singled him out for special attention. (This would very likely be a powerful objection to *any* prophet, in any time.) The Qur'an preserves some of their reasoning: "What's with this 'messenger'? He eats food and walks about in the marketplace. Why hasn't an angel been sent down to him, to be a warner with him? Or a treasure bestowed upon him? Or why does he not have a garden from which he can eat?"[185] "What the sceptical citizens here demand of the Prophet," observes Geo Widengren, "is nothing else than that he should be capable of bringing forth the Garden of Paradise."[186] The Meccans' somewhat enigmatic mention of the "garden" may also be connected with the idea of a *haram* or *hawta* sanctuary, which was often associated, in its turn, with a *hima,* a sacred grove or garden enclosure.[187] Possession of such an enclosure was expected of sacred families.

> We shall not believe in you until you cause a spring to burst forth for us
> from the earth,
> Or until you have a garden of dates and grapes and cause rivers to burst
> forth abundantly in their midst,
> Or until you cause the sky to fall upon us in pieces, as you have pretended
> it will, or you bring God and the angels before us,
> Or until you have a gilded house or you mount up into the sky. And we
> will not believe in your mounting up until you cause to come down
> upon us a book that we can read.[188]

Those who disbelieve say, "Why is the Qur'an not sent down to him all at once?" Thus, that your heart might be built up by it, and We recite it to you gradually.[189]

184. Eliade, *History of Religious Ideas,* 3:69.
185. Q 25:7-8.
186. Widengren, *Muhammad,* p. 99.
187. See Andrae, *Mohammed,* pp. 14-15. The two concepts are not mutually exclusive. See Donald W. Parry, "Garden of Eden: Prototype Sanctuary," in *Temples of the Ancient World: Ritual and Symbolism,* ed. Donald W. Parry (Salt Lake City: Deseret Book and the Foundation for Ancient Research and Mormon Studies, 1994), pp. 126-51.
188. Q 17:90-93.
189. Q 25:32

Muhammad astride Buraq, being led by the angel Gabriel
(Bibliotheque nationale, Paris)

The Qur'an advises Muhammad to respond to such complaints with a simple declaration: "Say, 'Glory to my Lord, am I anything but a mortal human being and a messenger?'"[190] But Islamic tradition did not long remain content with this response.

Muhammad was being asked to confirm the authenticity of his prophethood by ascending to heaven and there receiving a holy book, in one instant of time. In this he was to conform to a model illustrated by many still-extant legends — at least some of which must have been known to his Meccan audience or they would not have made the demand — regarding Enoch, Moses, Daniel, Mani, and many other messengers who had risen to heaven, met God, and received from his right hand a book of scripture containing the revelation they were to proclaim.[191] Both rabbinic and apocalyptic Judaism knew the idea, as did the Samaritans and the Gnostics.[192] The Mandaeans believed in heavenly books existing before the

190. Q 17:93. Compare Q 6:35; 15:14-15.

191. Even David can perhaps be added here (1 Chron. 28:19), with Ezekiel (Ezek. 2:9–3:2). A classic treatment of the concept of the heavenly book is that of Johannes Pedersen, in his review of *Ursprung und Geschichte der Mormonen,* by Eduard Meyer, *Der Islam* 5 (1914): 113-15.

192. See Helmer Ringgren, *The Faith of Qumran: Theology of the Dead Sea Scrolls,* trans. Emilie T. Sander, expanded ed. (New York: Crossroad, 1995), pp. 54-55.

creation of the earth, of which their savior figure brings transcripts to human-kind.[193] It seems to go back at least to the legendary Mesopotamian king Emmenduraki, and to draw on a royal ideology in which the concepts of ruler and prophet were united (just as they would be again in the person of Muham-mad).[194] Geo Widengren argues convincingly that Muhammad's title of *rasul* ("messenger" or "sent one") is a time-honored designation, earlier belonging to royalty, given to those in the ancient Near East who were thought, following a ce-lestial ascent, to have been "sent down" from heaven with a message.[195]

One night Muhammad was sleeping at the home of kinsfolk. But he awoke in the middle of the night and made his way down to the Ka'ba, where he seems to have enjoyed spending the midnight hours in meditation and reflec-tion. Then he grew sleepy again, and eventually lay down to rest in the enclo-sure known as the Hijr. Sometime during the night, however, he was awakened by the angel Gabriel, who led him to the gate of the Ka'ba precinct, where a strange animal was waiting for him. It was Buraq, a white and winged beast, something of a cross between a mule and an ass in appearance, each of whose

193. Widengren, *Religionsphänomenologie*, pp. 549-50.

194. Widengren, *Religionsphänomenologie*, pp. 483-500, 550, 553, 555 n. 36, 583-85, offers a good general discussion of the motif of celestial ascent, with many references. Also Widengren, *Ascension of the Apostle*, pp. 9, 9 n. 1, 10, 16-17, 20, 33 n. 3; Widengren, *Muḥammad*, pp. 52, 199, 202. Widengren has noted many parallels to the concept of the heavenly book in ancient Mesopotamian "Tablets of Destiny," by which, at the festival sea-son of New Year, the gods determine the fate of the cosmos and all that is in it for the next year. "Few religious ideas in the Ancient Near East have played a more important role than the notion of the Heavenly Tablets, or the Heavenly Book . . . [and] the oft-recurring thought that the Heavenly Book is handed over at the ascension in an interview with a heavenly being, or several heavenly beings, mostly gods (a god)." See Widengren, *Ascension of the Apostle*, p. 7. Compare Widengren, *Religionsphänomenologie*, pp. 546-47; Widen-gren, *Muḥammad*, pp. 199, 204; Kister, "'Sha'bān Is My Month . . . ,'" pp. 15-37. Obvious similarities can be identified between Moses' ascent of Mount Sinai and the old Mesopotamian idea, and the notion that persisted in Judaism in such texts as *1 Enoch*, *2 Enoch*, and the *Testaments of the Twelve Patriarchs*. It existed among the Mandaeans and the Persians, and in Islamic sectarian movements even after the death of Muhammad. See Widengren, *Ascension of the Apostle*, pp. 10, 22-24, 26 n. 1, 27, 35, 42-43, 46, 58, 68, 72, 74-75, 84-85; Widengren, *Muḥammad*, pp. 29-30, 80-95. Dan. 10:21 may reflect a belief in the heavenly book.

195. Widengren, *Religionsphänomenologie*, pp. 505-6; Widengren, *Ascension of the Apostle*, pp. 19-21, 31-33, 47, 58, also adduces Moses and Ezekiel as parallels; Widengren, *Muḥammad*, cites a Syriac parallel to the title *rasul*. In some versions of the story, Muham-mad (like Paul in 2 Cor. 12:1-5) is given secret knowledge, which later becomes important in the claims of the Shi'ite imams to esoteric wisdom. See Widengren, *Muḥammad*, pp. 106-7; Alan F. Segal, *Paul the Convert: The Apostolate and Apostasy of Saul the Pharisee* (New Haven: Yale University Press, 1990), pp. 34-71.

strides took him to the horizon. By means of this miraculous steed Muhammad made his way northward, accompanied by the angel Gabriel, past Yathrib to the holy city of Jerusalem. There, on the temple mount, he met a number of the ancient prophets, including Abraham, Moses, and Jesus, whom, as their imam, he led in prayer.

From the temple mount Muhammad then ascended through the seven heavens, each inhabited and supervised by a prophet from earlier times, and eventually entered into the presence of God himself.[196] It was directly from God — in this vision — that Muhammad received the commandment to lead the Muslims in five prayers daily. (The Qur'an itself knows only three — morning, noon, and night.) Actually, God first imposed on Muhammad a requirement of fifty daily prayers. But when Muhammad began his descent through the heavens to the surface of the earth, he encountered Moses once again. That great ancient prophet asked Muhammad how many prayers God had commanded. When the Arabian prophet replied "fifty," Moses told him to return to God and ask the burden to be lifted. Muhammad did so, and God removed ten prayers from the daily quota. But Moses remained unsatisfied, and continued to advise Muhammad to return until the number was reduced to five. Even that was too much, Moses declared, but Muhammad was embarrassed to bother God further and said he would petition for no more reductions.[197]

Soon after Gabriel and Muhammad had descended to Jerusalem, they returned to Mecca by the same route they had come, passing above several caravans that were returning to Mecca by the much slower means of earthly camels. The Prophet arrived back at his relatives' home before the dawn. But immediately prior to sunrise, he woke his kin and told them that, while he had prayed the evening prayer with them the night before and now stood in their midst in the valley of Mecca, during the night he had been to Jerusalem for prayer. One tradition says the journey was instantaneous: the jar that Muhammad had upset in his departure was still spilling its contents when he returned.

His relatives begged him to say nothing of this experience to the unbelieving Meccans, lest it give them unprecedentedly good reason to mock him. But Muhammad insisted. And the response was precisely as might have been

196. Peters, *Muhammad*, pp. 144-47, furnishes a good, brief discussion of the *mi'raj*. Widengren, *Muhammad*, pp. 96-114, offers a much longer treatment, with comparative material. The anthropomorphism of the accounts is striking. See Widengren, *Ascension of the Apostle*, pp. 22 n. 1, 81, 108.

197. Judaism, too, knew only three daily prayers, as did Nestorian Christianity (from which the Arabic *salat*, usually translated "prayer," may have been borrowed). It may be significant, though, that Magian or Zoroastrian prayers were to be said five times a day — at dawn, noon, midafternoon, sunset, and midnight. See Morony, p. 292; Peters, *Muhammad*, pp. 164-66; Watt, p. 100.

expected. Still, when Muhammad was able to describe the caravans he had overflown in great detail and predict their time of arrival in the valley, some came to believe him. To the public he told only of his journey to the holy city of Jerusalem. To his inner circle, however, he spoke of his ascension through the heavens to the presence of God. The account may have been pivotal then, as it certainly has been in the centuries since, in establishing, in the minds of his disciples, Muhammad's "personal and private access" to God — the basis of his claim to authority, as it was for the prophets of the Bible.[198] "Glory be to Him," says the Qur'an, "who took His servant by night from the holy shrine [*al-masjid al-haram*][199] to the furthest shrine [*al-masjid al-aqsa*],[200] the precincts of which We have blessed, in order to show him some of our signs. For He is hearing, seeing."[201] The Qur'anic evidence for Muhammad's ascension is ambiguous at best. While Qur'an 17:1 and perhaps 17:60 allude to a journey to "the furthest shrine" *(al-masjid al-aqsa)*, scholars debate whether that phrase alludes to a location in Jerusalem (where the Al-Aqsa Mosque — in Arabic, *al-masjid al-aqsa* — stands today) or to a heavenly sanctuary. But the story attached itself to him early, and its roots in antiquity are very deep.

Muhammad clearly understood and accepted the notion of a heavenly book, and he always saw himself as producing a book on earth to represent the heavenly original.[202] In his view the revelations of the Qur'an, like the Torah *(tawrat)* and the Gospel *(injil)* before it, were "recitations" or "readings" from the very words of God, which were written in the "Mother of the Book" *(umm al-kitab)* and kept on a closely guarded tablet *(lawh mahfuz)* in the divine presence.[203] As noted, it was communicated orally to Muhammad, piece by piece, in an Arabic version.[204] Not all of the heavenly book was given to him, but only a portion.[205] Thus the Qur'an did not exhaust it. Other revelations to the "people of the book" *(ahl al-kitab)* — not, be it noted, the "people of the *books*" — were derived from it and were thus, at least originally, consistent with it and confirmed by it. (Unfortunately the Jews and the Christians had corrupted the rev-

---

198. The phrase, originally intended to characterize the Hebrew prophets, is from Freedman, "Between God and Man," p. 57.

199. Presumably the precincts of the Ka'ba in Mecca.

200. This is sometimes thought to refer to the temple mount in Jerusalem (hence the al-Aqsa Mosque there, which was built decades after Muhammad's death), but may refer to a heavenly sanctuary.

201. Q 17:1.

202. See the discussion and references at Widengren, *Religionsphänomenologie*, pp. 568-69; Widengren, *Muhammad*, pp. 115-19.

203. Q 80:13ff.; 56:79; 85:21ff.; 93:3ff.

204. See Q 12:1; 13:37; 20:113; 26:192ff.; 41:3; 44:58; and esp. 91:44.

205. Q 90:78; 4:164.

elations they had received.) Islamic tradition soon assimilated Muhammad to the ancient model of a single, complete reception of a heavenly book during an ascension into the presence of God. Somehow, it was felt, the Prophet had received the Qur'an all at once; it had been brought down to earth on the night of the first revelation. That night, probably the twenty-sixth of Ramadan, was later described as "the Night of Power" or "the Night of Destiny" *(laylat al-qadr).*

> We have indeed revealed it in the Night of Destiny.
> And what will make you understand what the Night of Destiny is?
> The Night of Destiny is better than a thousand months.
> By God's leave, the angels and the Spirit come down in it on every kind of
>   errand.
> Peace it is, until the rising of the dawn.[206]

Meanwhile two hundred miles north, in Yathrib, there was also strife, but of a rather distinct kind. Yathrib was a very different place from Mecca. Situated on a high plain partially covered by lava, it was an agricultural oasis of perhaps more than twenty square miles, whereas Mecca was a commercial town. For several miles around it the land was intensively cultivated. The settlement was especially famous for its date palms. More importantly, Yathrib was far less urbanized than Mecca; its residents still lived in various fortified compounds scattered about the oasis. Its two main Arab tribes, Aws and Khazraj, could not get along. A bloody quarrel had broken out between a man of Aws and a man of Khazraj, and, as often happened, others of the tribes had become involved along with their allies from the three local Arab-Jewish tribes — Jewish in religion, deeply Arabian in culture — of Qurayza, Nadir, and Qaynuqa (who may actually have been the first inhabitants of the oasis). Four indecisive but deadly battles had served only to make the situation worse, and to give more reasons for the seeking of revenge. Moreover, although Aws and Khazraj maintained alliances with the various Jewish groupings in the settlement, even those relations were not always cordial, as the traditional accounts indicate and as subsequent events seem unmistakably to confirm. The Jews, though Arabized (if not natively Arabian), remained both monotheistic and, probably as a consequence, rather aloof from the pagans of Yathrib. They were conscious of being the chosen people of God through whom the prophets had come and through whom, presumably, any future divine message would also be delivered.

No real peace had arrived, even following the fourth battle, and the people of Yathrib lived together uneasily, in constant expectation of further vio-

---

206. Q 97. For another account of the "Night of Destiny," see Peters, *Muhammad,* pp. 203-7, 215-18.

lence. In fact, several unexplained murders had recently disturbed the residents. Without any central authority to enforce order, even the slightest provocation could easily lead to civil war, and the ancient Arabian practice of the blood feud, which maintained a rough order in the vast spaces of the desert, posed a huge risk in a relatively densely settled oasis. In the midst of these century-old difficulties, the leaders of Aws had once determined even to send a delegation to Mecca to ask for Qurayshi help against Khazraj. To others, though, it was becoming apparent that Yathrib needed a ruler with a strong hand, someone who could stand above the endless tribal bickering and dispel the chaos that had plagued them for so long. In fact, there was a man in the oasis, one Abd Allah b. Ubayy, whose stature and reputation for fairness had already led many, including himself, to see him as a possible king of Yathrib. But opinion had not yet coalesced sufficiently to permit his assumption of such a role.

The people of Khazraj may have recalled that they were linked by ties of kinship to Muhammad. (Every Arab was acutely aware of genealogical links several generations back. One's lineage, in fact, was a substantial component of one's name.) The Prophet had spent time in Yathrib with his relatives. His mother was buried nearby, his father was buried there, and he had probably visited at least a few times in subsequent years as he participated in the caravans to Syria. In 620 six men of Khazraj accepted Islam upon meeting the Prophet while away from Yathrib. The next summer, in 621, five of them came to Mecca on the pilgrimage, accompanied by seven others, including two members of the rival tribe of Aws. At Aqaba, a place not far from Mecca, these twelve men — the number is perhaps significant, and perhaps suspicious — pledged their allegiance to Muhammad in what is often known as the First Pledge of Aqaba. Included in the pledge were promises to refrain from the worship of any being other than the one God, to forgo theft, infanticide, slander, and fornication. More relevant to the political scene at Yathrib, they promised obedience to Muhammad — a promise that would have ramifications that they could probably never have foreseen in their wildest imaginings.

In the next year twelve men, perhaps representing a larger group totaling seventy-five,[207] again made a pledge to Muhammad, known as the Second Pledge of Aqaba. (A number of secret meetings seem to have occurred between the two pledges and continued thereafter, as the terms of Muhammad's emigration to Yathrib were settled. The Prophet did not want to repeat his mistake at

207. David Noel Freedman reminds me in a personal communication that, just as the number twelve is biblical, the number seventy-five may derive from the story of those who went down to Egypt with Jacob. He observes that the round number is seventy (Gen. 46:24-27), but that the number seventy-two also appears and that seventy-five is found as well, especially in the Septuagint (also Gen. 46:24-27) and in the account given by Stephen at Acts 7:14.

Ta'if.) But this time, the sources say, the pledge of obedience included an obligation to fight on behalf of Islam. Henceforward, because it contained no mention of warfare, the First Pledge began to be known and continued to be used as "the pledge of the women." It is unlikely that those making the pledge envisioned an attack on Mecca, or even the necessity of defending their own city against Meccan attack; one is entitled to doubt that they would have entered into the pledge had they seen the immediate consequences it was to drag down on their heads. They probably intended merely to extend to Muhammad and his followers — who would, by forsaking homes and families in Mecca, be leaving their tribal ties behind — the protections typically afforded by a tribe to its members. The Meccan Muslims were, in a sense, being adopted.

At this point, in 622, the Prophet began to encourage his followers to emigrate to Yathrib — in small groups and without fanfare, as had earlier been done in the emigrations to Abyssinia. As before, the leaders of the Quraysh attempted to stop the emigrants, and stories are told of some being held prisoner in Mecca in order to prevent their going. As with the emigration to Abyssinia, the Meccan leaders may have sensed a threat to their trade supremacy. And they were right. But, over the months of July, August, and September, almost all the Muslims who wanted to leave Mecca managed to do so. One of those most eager to leave was Abu Bakr. But the Prophet asked him to wait, hinting that, once the others had gotten safely away, he himself would accompany Abu Bakr to Yathrib. Perhaps the Prophet wanted to remain behind in order to encourage waverers.

The increasingly desperate leaders of the Quraysh finally came up with a plan that, although dramatic, they must have felt would pose few risks to them and was almost certain to be successful. Each clan was asked to nominate a representative, and the men chosen were to come together and, at the very same instant, plunge a dagger into Muhammad. The theory was that, with each clan of the Quraysh guilty in the death of Muhammad, the Banu Hashim would realize that they were far too weak to enter into a blood feud with everybody else in Mecca, and would thus be unable to seek revenge and obliged to accept blood money. And the plan called for this to be generously offered. The cost would be relatively cheap for ridding the community of an obnoxious and persistent troublemaker.

Somehow forewarned — traditional sources say the angel Gabriel came to the Prophet and informed him of what was afoot — Muhammad told Abu Bakr that, at last, the time had arrived for them to emigrate together to Yathrib. And, since virtually all the other believers had already left, the time was indeed appropriate. However, Muhammad asked Ali to remain behind to settle outstanding economic obligations. But Ali also served another important function at this crucial moment of Muhammad's life. Giving him the cloak in which he often slept, the Prophet advised Ali to wrap himself in it and to sleep on Muhammad's bed, assuring him that he would not be hurt. Then the Prophet slipped away, eluding the conspirators, who had been keeping his house under guard to make sure he did not escape.

As time passed, the would-be assassins grew ill at ease, but one of them managed to catch a glimpse inside the Prophet's home and assured them that Muhammad was asleep on his bed. The extra time this bought for the Prophet and Abu Bakr was very useful for their successful escape. (Ali did, in fact, eventually arrive quite safely in Yathrib, only a few days after Muhammad and Abu Bakr. Although the Qurayshi assassins were undoubtedly quite angry at the way they had been tricked, their conspiratorial covenant covered only the killing of the Prophet.) Meanwhile, to throw their expected pursuers off the scent, Muhammad and his friend Abu Bakr headed south rather than northward toward Yathrib. They took refuge for several days in a mountain cave.

Incensed at Muhammad's escape, the leaders of the Quraysh offered the handsome reward of a hundred camels for whoever found him. All the routes northward were combed carefully for any sign of the fugitive. But as the hours went by and he was not found, some began to think that maybe he was hiding in one of the caves near Mecca, and they began to look in all directions around the city, not merely on the roads to the north. This was a real danger for the Prophet, for the bedouin trackers of the desert are legendarily effective. On the third day Muhammad and Abu Bakr heard birds cooing and fluttering at the entrance to their cavern hideout, and then, not long thereafter, they heard men's voices, faint at first but drawing ever nearer. Oddly, though, the men paused outside the cave, loudly discussing their options and concluding that there was no need to search it. Finally they left. What had prevented their entry into the cave, in which they would certainly have found the Prophet? When they were safely gone, Muhammad and Abu Bakr made their way to the mouth of the cave where, the traditional narratives say, they found an acacia tree taller than a man. Although it had not been there that morning, it now covered the entrance of the cave almost entirely. Moreover, a spider had spun its web between the tree and the cave wall, signaling to the Meccan searchers, quite falsely, that a great deal of time had elapsed since anybody had passed that way. And a pair of rock doves had built their nest at the entrance to the cave.

Having eluded the Meccans thus far, Abu Bakr and Muhammad now continued their journey to Yathrib with the help of a bedouin guide who knew all the least-traveled paths. First they went farther away from Mecca toward the west, and then somewhat to the south, reaching the shore of the Red Sea. From there they followed the coastal road to the northwest for several days. Finally they headed toward Yathrib. They arrived at an oasis outside the town proper on Monday, September 27, 622. There they stayed for a few days, until on Friday they actually went into the settlement.

Naturally, everybody in Yathrib wanted the honor of hosting the Prophet, this new dignitary. They cried out for him to sit his camel down here, or over there. But Muhammad wisely let his camel have free rein, and told them that her movements were under the control of God. Finally the camel turned into a large walled enclosure that was used for the drying of dates and, at one end, as a burial ground. There she settled to the earth, and Muhammad announced that this spot, the very place where she sat down, would be his dwelling place. The Prophet bought the site, and he soon decreed that the enclosure be transformed into a mosque, a place for Muslims to meet for worship and other purposes.[208] In the work of construction, the Prophet labored along with all the rest. The few palms that stood within the walls of the courtyard were hewn down, and their trunks were used as columns to support a roof of palm branches at the northern end. Most of the mosque was left open to the sky. Bricks were used for most of the construction, although stones were placed on either side of the prayer niche, or mihrab, that occupied the middle of the northern wall and marked the direction of Jerusalem.

Now that Islam could manifest itself openly in Yathrib, believers routinely performed the five daily ritual prayers in the mosque as a congregation. People would judge the times of the day by checking the position of the sun in the sky and, when they felt it was the appropriate time for prayer, go to the mosque. In a relatively simple society like that of seventh-century Arabia, this was probably the customary mode of telling time. But it was too imprecise for managing congregational worship, and, rather like the need for a unified authority to settle disputes in Yathrib, Muslims soon realized that a single authority should determine the times of liturgical prayer in the mosque and announce the times to the worshipers dispersed throughout Yathrib and its environs. Some suggested using a horn, like the shofar of the Jews. The Prophet settled, for a time, on following the lead of certain eastern Christians: he had a wooden clapper made, a *naqus*. But this device was never used, for, shortly thereafter, a Khazrajite named Abd Allah b. Zayd, a man who had been present at the Second Pledge of Aqaba, related a dream to the Prophet in which he had been told that the best way to summon believers to prayer was by crying out "Allahu akbar" (God is most great). This was to be repeated four times, followed by a twofold repetition of each of the following phrases: "I testify that there is no god but God"; "I testify that Muhammad is the messenger of God"; "Come unto prayer"; "Come

208. Rodinson, pp. 149-50, explains the Syriac origin of the word (Arabic *masjid*), and describes the structure.

unto salvation"; "God is most great." The call to prayer was to be closed, then, with one final declaration that "There is no god but God."

Muhammad responded that this was indeed a true vision — it is noteworthy that he was not averse to recognizing divine inspiration in others — and he appointed the Abyssinian former slave Bilal, who had a strong voice, to be the first muezzin, or caller to prayer, in the history of Islam. Thereafter, at the appropriate times, Bilal would climb to the roof of the tallest house in the vicinity of the mosque and issue the call to prayer. From this rather humble beginning has come the romantic call of the minaret, one of the most characteristic and lovely aspects of daily life throughout the world of Islam.

Yathrib is not well known to most Westerners, despite its crucially important role in the life of the Prophet. Why? Because it soon lost its name. Instead of Yathrib, the oasis settlement began to be known as *madinat al-nabi,* "the city of the Prophet," or even simply as *al-madina,* "The City." And it is under this name, Medina, that it is universally known today.[209]

The year of the *hijra,* rather than the birth year of Muhammad or the year of the commencement of his revelations, marks the beginning of the Muslim calendar.[210] This may seem strange, but it is really quite appropriate. For the move of Muhammad from Mecca to his new home placed Islam and its message, as well as the Prophet himself, on an entirely new plane. From being merely a messenger, a rather lonely voice crying in the wilderness, Muhammad became a prophet-statesman, the founder of a political order and eventually of an empire that would change the history of the world. And Islam took on a political dimension that it has never abandoned in all the centuries that have passed since then.

The people who had made the *hijra,* or emigration, with Muhammad to Yathrib came almost immediately to be known as the "Emigrants" or *muhajirun.* The natives of Medina who had converted to Islam were called the *ansar,* or "Helpers."[211] One of the first things Muhammad did upon establishing himself in Medina was to work out a covenant between the Helpers, the Emigrants, and the other monotheists of the town, the Jews, which has been

209. This is the standard account. However, Rodinson, p. 139, may be correct in contending that the name *Medina* antedates Muhammad's arrival.

210. One cannot, however, determine a year in the Islamic calendar simply by subtracting 622 from the common era date. Islamic years are lunar, and hence are incongruent with the modified solar year of the Gregorian calendar. The year of the *hijra* was not actually selected as the starting point of the Muslim era until half a decade after the death of Muhammad, during the caliphate of Umar, in 637.

211. It may be significant that, as Serjeant, "Ḥaram and Ḥawṭah," p. 45, observes, the term *ansar* is used in modern-day Arabia for the tribes supporting a *hawta,* or sacred enclave.

known ever since — with a certain rough appropriateness — as the Constitution of Medina.[212] The notion was to link them together in a community, while allowing for the religious differences between the two faiths of Islam and Judaism and granting each a position of legal equality. They were to be allies against the polytheists, and promised that they would enter into no separate peace or alliance with pagans. (This provision would be important in subsequent events.) They were to defend each other against wrongs. In a marked departure from the tribal ethics of pre-Islamic Arabia, Muslims were to defend a Jew against injustice, even if that injustice had been committed by a fellow Muslim, and Jews were to take the part of an injured Muslim against a Jewish wrongdoer. Although the Jews were not required to recognize him as a prophet, Muhammad was to be the arbiter in disputed matters.

Muhammad was constructing a new Arabian community, an *umma*, in which the social bond was not blood but a shared faith, or at least a shared allegiance to him.[213] Political authority was a foreign concept to the pre-Islamic Arabs, but personal obligation and religious authority were not, and it was only on such a basis that any organization other than a kin group could be constructed in Arabia.[214] And in fact, it is very likely that "the ummah in the sense of a confederation round a religious nucleus was a pattern well established long before Muḥammad."[215] In any event, the Islamic *umma* became a kind of "supertribe," supplementing but not supplanting the social usages of its pagan, blood-based predecessors. It maintained pre-Islamic practices in such areas as property, marriage, and intratribal (i.e., intra-Muslim) relations, and it saw its relationships with non-Muslim Arabs, even with those related by blood, in much the way that members of one pre-Islamic kin group had seen their interactions with those of another: they were fair game for raiding and plundering.

---

212. Actually, as R. B. Serjeant has persuasively argued, the so-called Constitution is probably a composite document, composed on various occasions over time rather than at a single point. But the ramifications of this are beyond the scope of the present paper. See R. B. Serjeant, "The 'Constitution of Medina,'" *Islamic Quarterly* 8 (1964): 3-16; R. B. Serjeant, "The *Sunnah Jāmiʿah*, Pacts with the Ya<u>th</u>rib Jews, and the *taḥrīm* of Ya<u>th</u>rib: Analysis and Translation of the Documents Comprised in the So-called 'Constitution of Medina,'" *Bulletin of the School of Oriental and African Studies* 41 (1978): 1-42. Both articles are conveniently reprinted in Serjeant, *Studies in Arabian History and Civilisation.* For a good brief discussion of the document as we have it, see Peters, *Muhammad,* pp. 198-202.

213. See Watt, pp. 106-7.

214. Personal obligation, rather than political/institutional loyalties, continued to be an important element in the construction of Islamic polities for many centuries, as shown, for example, in Roy P. Mottahedeh's study of the Buyids in the tenth and eleventh centuries, *Loyalty and Leadership in an Early Islamic Society* (Princeton: Princeton University Press, 1980). It is still characteristic of the Near East in many ways.

215. Serjeant, "Ḥaram and Ḥawṭah," p. 49.

A new Islamic community is precisely what Muhammad had set out to create in the first place; one of the recurring themes of the Qur'an is that revelation engenders communities. Additionally, the fact that Islam built a polity so early in its existence has had fundamental ramifications for its character to the present day. Where Christianity had three centuries in which to develop its own character before assuming political rule, Islam had existed for only a few years and was still in its initial stages of development. Accordingly, notions such as the separation of "church" and "state," which had a difficult enough time evolving within Christendom, have had virtually no soil from which to grow in Islam. For Christians who seek the ideal model there is Christ, who held no political office. Thus a Christian can follow Christ without attempting to implement Christianity via the state. The ideal Islamic paradigm, however, is Muhammad, who ruled a state for nearly half his prophetic ministry and received numerous revelations instructing him how to do it.

Given his new status as a ruler, Muhammad's role changed dramatically from what it had been in Mecca. From being a voice crying in the wilderness, he grew into a prophet and statesman. The change is clearly manifest in the revelations he received, and the distinction between Meccan and Medinan suras in the Qur'an is the fundamental chronological device for dating the revelations even today. Where the earlier, Meccan revelations tended to be short, composed of terse and powerfully poetic verses on apocalyptic themes, the later, Medinan revelations were much longer and dealt with legal, organizational, and sociopolitical issues as much as purely "religious" ones. Where the basic theology of Islam was in place by the time of the *hijra,* it was only in Medina that the details of Islamic cultic practice — in such matters as prayer, fasting, almsgiving, and pilgrimage — were revealed.

As part of the development of his new Islamic community in Medina, Muhammad appears to have established a *haram,* a sacred enclave, in his new residence to rival that of his hometown, Mecca.[216] Several years after his arrival there, he is said to have sent Ka'b b. Malik out to mark the points of the boundary of the *haram* about the settlement; some traditions relate that an area of twelve miles surrounding Medina was declared a *hima,* or inviolate pasture — perhaps this was a partial response to the Meccans' demand for a sacred and miraculous "garden" — and that, just as in Mecca, severe penalties were decreed for homicide committed within the *haram.* "Each prophet has a *haram,*" Mu-

---

216. Several decades later, having lost control (temporarily, as it turned out) of the sacred cities of Mecca and Medina, the Umayyad caliph Abd al-Malik did precisely the same thing: he established a *haram* — the word is still used for the area — around his new Dome of the Rock in Jerusalem, which is clearly designed for Meccan-style circumambulation centered on a sacred rock. On this, see Serjeant, "Ḥaram and Ḥawṭah," p. 56.

hammad is supposed to have said, "and Medina is my *ḥaram*." Or, according to another tradition, "Mecca was Abraham's *ḥaram,* and Medina is my *ḥaram*." True to ancient Arabian tradition, Muhammad, scion of a holy family and now the lord of a sacred sanctuary in Medina, was the person, as the Constitution of Medina repeatedly stipulates, to whom disputes were to be referred for adjudication.[217] Like the biblical Samuel before him, he was seer, judge, and priest. He also established a market, something of a "free trade zone," which may have been connected with his sacred precinct, just as the two were connected in the commercial shrine town from which he had come.[218]

Muhammad's domestic routine in Medina was constrained by his obligations as the head of a community. A stone bench along one of the sides of the mosque was reserved for those who, newly arrived in Medina, had no place to live and no way to support themselves. Accordingly, they became known as "the people of the bench." The mosque was attached to the Prophet's house, and so he apparently felt himself responsible for these people, who had come to the town because they had heard reports of his prophethood and had accepted his message. He would often share his family's food with them, and apparently also called on those who lived in the immediate neighborhood of the mosque to do likewise. "The food of one person is enough for two," he used to say, "the food of two is enough for four, and the food of four is enough for eight." Yet his problems and challenges were far from over. The Qur'an speaks repeatedly of the various groups in Medina. Two of them were very much like the cast of characters in Mecca. There were the believers, who accepted the revelation of God, and the infidels, who rejected it.

> This is the book in which there is no doubt, a guidance to the God-
> fearing,
> Who believe in the unseen, who pray, who expend from that with which
> we have blessed them,
> And who believe in that which has been sent down upon you and that
> which was sent before you, and who are certain of the life to come.
> These are truly guided by their Lord, and these are they who will prosper.
> As for the infidels, it is all the same to them whether you warn them or
> you don't warn them: They will not believe.
> God has sealed their hearts and their hearing, and a veil covers their sight,
> and a great punishment awaits them.[219]

217. See the discussion of Serjeant, "Ḥaram and Ḥawṭah," pp. 50-51; compare Serjeant, "The Saiyids of Ḥaḍramawt," p. 15.
218. The phrase is from Peters, *Muhammad,* pp. 197-98.
219. Q 2:2-7.

Besides the monotheistic Muslims and Jews, however, and the still-considerable number of people who simply had no interest and no faith in the new revelation, another group of Medinans confronted Muhammad with a challenge he had not been required to face in Mecca. These were the people the Qur'an labels with the unflattering title of "hypocrites" *(munafiqun)*.

> And among the people there are those who say, "We believe in God and in the Last Day," but they are not believers.
>
> They attempt to deceive God and those who believe, but they deceive only themselves and do not realize it.
>
> In their hearts is a disease, and God has increased their disease, and theirs is a painful punishment for the lies they tell.
>
> If it is said to them, "Do not spread corruption in the earth," they reply, "Why, we only want to do what is right!"
>
> But they are the spreaders of corruption, although they do not realize it.
>
> And if it is said to them, "Believe as the people believe!" they reply, "Shall we believe as the simpletons believe?" But they are the simpletons, though they don't know it.
>
> When they meet those who believe, they say, "We believe." But when they are alone with their satans, they say, "We are with you. We were only mocking."
>
> God will mock *them*. . . .
>
> These are they who have purchased error in exchange for guidance. But their commerce profits them nothing, and they will not be guided.[220]

In Mecca there had been no worldly inducement to feign acceptance of Islam. Conversion there brought disdain, ostracism, persecution, harassment, and occasionally torture and death. In the new climate of Medina, though, where the Prophet was the ruler of the community, insincere people could see outward profession of Islam as a route to social advancement, or at least as a means of preserving their earlier status or maintaining space in which to maneuver for advantage. Much as with Christianity in an earlier time, particularly following Constantine's legal establishment of the church, the rapid expansion of Islam and its power now ensured that the Islamic community would never again be totally free — if it ever had been — of hypocrites with an eye open to worldly gain rather than the will of God.

The arch-hypocrite of the traditional sources is the Khazrajite named Abd Allah b. Ubayy, whom we have already met. He had valid reason to feel injured by the coming of Muhammad to Medina. As we have seen, amidst all the

220. Q 2:8-16.

strife and bloodshed and the yearning for a strong central authority that eventually led to the summoning of Muhammad, Ibn Ubayy had been poised to become the ruler, if not the king, of the city. But Muhammad now filled the void into which Ibn Ubayy had been set to step. The Khazrajite seems to have decided from an early time to wait patiently, trying not to oppose the Prophet in any obvious way, even professing support for him, but endeavoring at the same moment to avoid giving any real support. Muhammad apparently understood this, and treated Ibn Ubayy, on the whole, with gentleness and sympathy throughout the man's life.

Attempting to unite the believers and to deal with the practical problem of how to sustain the Emigrants from Mecca, who had left their property and kinship networks behind to come to Medina, Muhammad created new relationships between them and the Helpers. Each Helper was assigned an Emigrant as a brother, for whom he was to have special, essentially kinlike responsibilities. Not wanting to create jealousies, the Prophet wisely exempted himself from this system, announcing rather that Ali — his cousin and son-in-law, and one of the earliest converts to Islam — was his brother. In the meantime he was entering into other important personal alliances as well. A'isha was the daughter of Muhammad's close friend and lieutenant Abu Bakr, and one of the first children to be born and raised a Muslim. Thus she knew only an Islamic home life, and she had grown up expecting the Prophet as a daily visitor to the home of her father. Gradually there grew in Muhammad the sense that A'isha was to be his wife, and he and Abu Bakr eventually signed a marriage contract making her so. A'isha herself was not present at the signing of the contract. She first learned about her marriage on a day when she was outside, playing with a few of her friends. Her mother came and took her by the hand, leading her inside. From now on, her mother told her, her friends must come to her house to play with her, since it was no longer appropriate for her, as a married woman, to be seen by everybody outside.

A'isha's betrothal to the Prophet took place when she was still living in Mecca and was only six years old, young even by the standards of ancient pagan Arabia. Her actual wedding to Muhammad occurred in Medina, in 623, when she was nine. She was too young, perhaps, to comprehend fully the significance of the event. In after years, at any rate, she recalled that, just before she and her family were supposed to leave their house for the ceremony, she had wandered off into the courtyard to play with a friend who had happened by. When the adults came to find her and prepare her for the wedding, she was playing on a seesaw with her hair flying in the breeze. And she was still a very young girl after her marriage to the Prophet. Her friends continued to visit her at her new home, where they would play with their dolls. But when the Prophet sometimes dropped in, the intimidated little girls would leave, and he had to go after them

541

on occasion to bring them back for his wife to play with. Indeed, sometimes Muhammad himself joined in their play. A'isha would become, after Khadija, Muhammad's favorite wife, and in the years following the death of the Prophet, one of the major sources for information about his life, opinions, and practices. For, because of her youth when she married him, she outlived him for many years, and was one of the last intimate links to their prophet for the Muslims of the first generations after his passing. She always felt insecure, though, about her status in the affections of her husband, and required continual reassurance, especially when, as she apparently often did, she thought about his feelings for his departed first wife, Khadija, who had supported him during some of his greatest trials and disappointments.

As Muhammad's personal relationships changed, so too did the relationship of his religion to its Jewish precursor. Most ancient Semitic peoples prayed in a particular direction. Eastern Christians and others prayed to the east, in the direction of the rising sun. Jews and the earliest Muslims prayed toward Jerusalem.[221] Traditional sources say the first Muslim thought of praying toward Mecca rather than Jerusalem came to a chief of the Yathribi Khazraj by the name of Bara' even before the time of the *hijra*. He is said to have reasoned, as he and a number of his townspeople were making their way toward Mecca to meet the Prophet, that since Muhammad, the holy Ka'ba shrine, and the place of the revelation of the Qur'an were there, it was wrong that they turn their backs toward so holy a place in order to pray toward a city in far-off Palestine whose association with prophets lay in the distant past. So he began for a brief period to pray toward Mecca, although his companions continued to follow what they correctly believed to be, at the time, the practice of the Prophet. But God vindicated Bara'. In the month of Shaban in 624, Muhammad received a revelation whose importance can hardly be overstated, altering the direction of prayer from facing Jerusalem to facing Mecca. He received it in a mosque belonging to the clan of Bara'. "The simpletons among the people will say, 'What has turned them from the prayer-orientation [*qibla*] that they were used to?' Say: 'To God belong both east and west.' He guides whomever He will to a straight path. . . . We see the turning of your face to the sky. Now we shall turn you to a *qibla* that will please you. Turn your face in the direction of the sacrosanct mosque. Wherever you are, turn your faces in that direction."[222] At the same time, a clan chief named Sa'd b. Mu'adh, a powerful rival of the "hypocrite" Ibn Ubayy — who had close ties to the local Jews — emerged as the leader of Muhammad's Medinan followers and a powerful ally to the Prophet. (Sa'd's harsh decision in the later case of the Banu Qurayza, a lethal one to be dis-

---

221. See, for instance, 1 Kings 8:44 and Dan. 6:10.
222. Q 2:142, 144.

cussed below, may suggest ethnic or religious hostility.) Montgomery Watt sees practical political considerations entering into the change, as well as revelation.[223] So the Muslims built a mihrab, a marker for the *qibla,* or direction of prayer, into the south wall of the mosque at Medina, facing Mecca and directly opposite the former mihrab on the north wall, which had indicated the direction of Jerusalem. At roughly the same time, the monthlong Ramadan fast replaced the ten-day Jewish fast connected with the Day of Atonement, which the Muslims had observed as Ashura.[224] By these moves Islam made clear that it was not merely a strange sect of Judaism or Christianity. It was an independent, new, Arabian revelation.

Strife with Mecca

Not very long after his arrival in Medina, Muhammad received a revelation with fateful consequences for the subsequent history of Arabia and the world. "Permission is granted to those against whom war is being conducted, because they have been wronged. And truly God is able to grant them victory — those who have been unjustly expelled from their homes simply because they declare, 'Our Lord is God.'"[225] Muhammad had been facing a serious problem. His followers, who had fled Mecca with him, were now confronted with the necessity of earning a living in an agricultural settlement. But most of them had no agricultural experience at all (since Mecca was virtually without vegetation), and certainly no expertise in the cultivation of dates, and the arable land was in any event already divided up among the local population. Thus they had little choice but to hire themselves out to the Medinan Muslims and the Jews as day laborers. The work of drawing water from wells and tending date palms was demeaning and irregular. But the revelation offered a way out, consistent with the ethic of Arabia and with their own quite justifiable sense of having been wronged.[226]

In the fall and winter the caravans of Quraysh were generally directed to the south, particularly to the Yemen and, beyond that, to Abyssinia. But in the spring and early months of summer the caravans from Mecca went mostly northward, toward Syria, which meant they were potentially quite vulnerable to a hostile and highly motivated force operating out of Medina. The Muslims grasped this very

223. Watt, pp. 113-14.
224. Watt, pp. 99, 114.
225. Q 22:39-40.
226. Watt, pp. 105-7, attempts to justify early Muslim raids within the ethical worldview of ancient Arabia.

quickly, and soon set about establishing alliances with the various bedouin tribes dwelling along the Red Sea coast where the trade routes ran. For their part the leaders of the Quraysh were not unaware of the threat they faced. But they must have been quite surprised when one of the first Muslim raids on their caravan traffic took place near Nakhla, a place between Mecca and Ta'if on the southern road to the Yemen. And their surprise was greatly magnified, beyond doubt, by the timing of the raid. Muhammad had sent one of his cousins along with eight other Muslims to spy on a caravan returning from the south, perhaps to find out how well guarded it would be. It was the month of Rajab, one of the four sacred months of the Arabian calendar in which fighting was prohibited.

The Prophet's instructions to the supposed reconnaissance party — sealed until the group was well away from Medina so as to avoid the intelligence leaks that seem to have spoiled earlier attempts — told them to proceed to Nakhla and attack the caravan. The letter did not mention the sacred months. When they found themselves, unobserved, looking over a small and vulnerable Meccan party bringing leather and raisins and other commodities from the Yemen, the temptation to attack the enemy was irresistible. But were the old Arabian taboos still in effect? By revelation God had authorized them, as aggrieved victims, to make war on those who had oppressed and robbed them, who were now profiting from and enjoying the property that the Emigrants had been forced to abandon. Could they wait for the attack? It was the last day of Rajab; in the morning the inviolable month would be past. But by that time the caravan would be within the sacred precinct surrounding Mecca. So they decided to attack, and their attack was quick and very successful. A fifth of the spoils were set aside for the Prophet, and the rest was divided among the members of the raiding party.[227] But their reception was at best cool when they returned to Medina. "I did not order you to fight in the sacred month," Muhammad told them, refusing to accept his designated portion of the booty. The Muslims and the Jews in Medina were unhappy with them for their violation of the taboo, and the Quraysh in Mecca set about zealously to turn the episode into a public relations nightmare for the Prophet, who, they said, was guilty of sacrilege. But then came a revelation from God: "They ask you about fighting in the sacrosanct month. Say: 'Fighting therein is a serious offense. But barring men from the way of God and disbelief in him and in the sacrosanct mosque and driving his people from it are more serious with God. And persecution is more serious than killing.'"[228]

---

227. This may be significant, in regard to Muhammad's perceived status. In modern-day Arabia as well, the lord of a *hawta* or *haram* shrine enclave extracts from its people the *khums* tax — a "fifth," as its name indicates. See Serjeant, "Ḥaram and Ḥawṭah," p. 44. Arabian chieftains generally took a fourth, as Rodinson, p. 225, observes.

228. Q 2:217.

Muhammad said this revelation confirmed the customary ban on fighting in the sacred months — another indication of the truly Arabian character of the new religion — but also clearly justified an exception in the case of the Nakhla raid. He therefore accepted the fifth of the booty that the raiding party had allotted to him and, no doubt, greatly relieved the minds of the Muslim warriors, who feared that they had committed a sin and, perhaps worse, a blunder. Western students of Islam, however, have struggled with the morality of Muhammad's resort to offensive warfare. Tor Andrae, for example, calls it simple "banditry."[229] Maxime Rodinson labels it "brigandage."[230]

A much more serious battle took place in 624. A heavily laden Meccan caravan was returning from Syria, near the Red Sea shore. The sources say it included a thousand camels. Muhammad sent a party out to gather intelligence on the whereabouts, the numbers, and the armaments of the caravan. They apparently returned a glowing report, because Muhammad soon had a force of three hundred men eager to seize the caravan's wealth. Only a third of them were *muhajirun;* the rest were native Medinans.

The martial and martyr spirit that had taken root in Islam is illustrated poignantly by the story of a fifteen-year-old named Umayr, who stole along with the expeditionary force. When Muhammad assembled the warriors, he noticed Umayr, who, hoping perhaps to attain a martyr's death in conflict with the infidels, had been trying as hard as he could to look inconspicuous. Telling him that he was too young for warfare, Muhammad ordered Umayr to return home. But the boy wept so much that the Prophet relented and allowed him to come. "He was so young," the boy's cousin later recalled, "that I had to fasten the straps of his sword belt for him."

The Prophet and his forces headed for Badr, a point on the coast route between Mecca and Syria. Muhammad sent a pair of observers ahead to discover what they could of the Meccan caravan's movements. But the caravan leader, Abu Sufyan, got word of the movements of the spies instead, and when he saw date stones in the dung left by their camels, he knew they were from Medina. Accordingly, he attempted to take evasive action and sent ahead to Mecca for reinforcements to guard the caravan. Eventually Abu Sufyan and the caravan did make their way safely home, evading the booty-seeking Medinans and leaving them to a battle over theology rather than spoils. Seeing now no threat to the caravan, the army that was still en route from Mecca desired to turn back. There seemed no purpose to any confrontation with Muhammad. But their leader, Abu Jahl, mocked them as cowards and urged them on.

229. Andrae, *Mohammed,* p. 140.
230. Rodinson, p. 162.

The Muslim army hurried to reach the wells at Badr before the Meccans could get to them. At the first well they came to, Muhammad ordered his men to halt. But one of his fighters, a member of the Medinan tribe of Khazraj, came to him and asked, "O Messenger of God, this place that we are at now — Has God revealed it to you, so that we should neither move forward nor retreat from it, or is it a matter of opinion and military strategy?" Muhammad, who again showed here his willingness to learn from others and to adapt, replied that it was merely a matter of his own opinion. "This is not the place to stop," the Khazrajite then said. "Lead us further, O Messenger of God, until we come to the large well that is near the enemy. Let us then stop there and plug up the wells that are beyond it, and make a cistern for ourselves. Then we will fight the enemy, and all of the water will be ours to drink, and they will have none." The Prophet instantly agreed.[231] The Muslims stopped up the other wells, built a cistern, and filled their individual water containers. They now held a vastly important advantage over the Meccan army in the harsh desert environment. For the army's camels and men would be in desperate need of water, and the force from Medina controlled every available source.

On March 15, 624, the battle of Badr irretrievably altered the relations between the rising Islamic state in Medina and the pagan resistance headquartered at Mecca. When the forces of the Quraysh, needing the waters of Badr, began to advance toward the Muslims, they seemed few against the vast background of the Arabian desert. But they outnumbered Muhammad and his men, and the Prophet withdrew to his tent to pray for divine help against them. When he emerged, he was able to tell Abu Bakr that no less a personage than Gabriel himself was on hand, armed for war and ready to assist the Muslims. A revelation received following the battle reminded Muhammad that "You implored your Lord for assistance, and he answered you: 'I will assist you with a thousand angels, rank upon rank.'"[232] The revelation even recounted the words of God to the angelic hosts: "I am with you. Fortify those who believe. I will cast terror into the hearts of the infidels, so you strike above their necks and strike off from them all their fingertips."[233] To his men the Prophet declared that the soul of any man killed that day while advancing against the enemy (retreating was another matter) would go immediately into the paradise of God. The early sources relate that young Umayr, when he heard of the Prophet's promise, was eating a handful of Medinan dates. "Wonder of wonders!" he cried out, tossing

---

231. For the incident and a slightly different alternate translation, see Guillaume, pp. 296-97.

232. Q 8:9.

233. Q 8:12.

the dates to the ground and grabbing for his sword. "Is there nothing between me and my entry into paradise but that these men kill me?"

The battle commenced, as was the custom in ancient Arabia, with a series of single combats. The three chosen Muslim warriors, who included Muhammad's uncle Hamza and his cousin Ali, dispatched their three pagan opponents, but one of them, another relative of the Prophet named Ubayda, was himself fatally wounded. When he was carried back to the camp of the Muslims, his leg severed, he asked, "Am I not a martyr, O Messenger of God?" "Indeed, you are," the Prophet replied. A Khazrajite named Awf had actually been the first Muslim to accept the challenge of single combat, but Muhammad had restrained him. At this point, still standing beside the Prophet, he turned to Muhammad and asked, "O Messenger of God, what is it that causes the Lord to laugh with joy at his servant?" Muhammad responded that it was when such a servant plunged without armor into the midst of the enemy. At this, Awf removed the coat of mail that he was wearing. Meanwhile the Prophet reached down to the ground and brought up a handful of pebbles. Shouting "Defaced be those faces!" he flung them at the Quraysh and gave the order to charge.[234] "You did not throw when you threw," a revelation to the Prophet commented after the battle, "rather it was God who threw."[235]

Awf was among the first to die. Later, veterans of the battle recalled that they had all felt the presence of angels during the fighting. Even the Meccans are supposed to have sensed something extraordinary, although they felt it not as joy but as terror. A few even claimed to have caught glimpses of the angelic host. A pair from a neighboring Arab tribe, not affiliated with either of the warring factions but watching, vulturelike, to see if any booty was to be had, stood at the top of a nearby hill to await the outcome. Suddenly a cloud rushed past them, filled with the loud neighing of stallions. One of the men instantly dropped dead of fright. A believer, in hot pursuit of one of the Meccans, was astonished to see the man's head severed from his body with nobody visibly near enough to have struck the blow. Yet others reported fleeting glimpses of angelic horses whose feet never touched the sand, ridden by supernatural beings in white turbans. (Only one, Gabriel, wore a yellow turban to indicate his archangelic status.)

When the fighting was over, between fifty and seventy of the Meccans were dead, including Abu Jahl. A number of prisoners were taken, and, true to form, Umar favored executing them all. Muhammad contented himself, though, with demanding ransoms for the prisoners. He ordered the execution of two men, both of whom knew something of Jewish and Persian lore and had

---

234. Widengren, *Ascension of the Apostle*, p. 28 n. 4, points to the analogous use of "battle magic" by Moses (Exod. 17:9-13) and Joshua (Josh. 8:18).

235. Q 8:17.

mocked him with difficult questions. When one of them rather plaintively asked, "But who will take care of my sons, Muhammad?" the Prophet responded tersely, "Hell!" Only fourteen Muslims died at the battle of Badr. Among them was the fifteen-year-old Umayr, so young and so eager for martyrdom.

The bodies of the slain Meccans were thrown, at the Prophet's order, into a pit. Among them was the father of one of the Muslims. The son's face was sorrowful as his father's body was dragged toward the common grave. But when the Prophet noticed his sorrowing look and expressed compassion, the son quickly regained his composure. It was not, he said, that he questioned the Prophet's choice of a burial place for his infidel father. It was only that he had once known his father to be a man of wise counsel and virtue, and that he was sad to see his father die a pagan despite such qualities.

Muhammad's position was now immeasurably strengthened. His unexpected defeat of a much larger force, sent from the great commercial power of Mecca, taught others to look on him with a new respect. In the minds of the Muslims, Badr was and is the great deliverance of God's people, comparable to the escape of the children of Israel from the armies of Pharaoh at the Red Sea. The ransoms paid into Muhammad's coffers for the release of prisoners gave him new leverage among his followers and with his rivals in Medina.

The momentum of the growth of Islam began to pick up substantially at around this time, and the success at Badr was certainly no hindrance to that. The story of Salman will serve to illustrate the appeal of Islam beyond its initial Arab audience. Salman was born a Zoroastrian in Persia, but he had converted to Christianity as a young man and gone to Syria and then to Iraq, associating himself always with Christian bishops and other wise Christian saints. As might have been predicted, Muslim tradition says that the last of these, speaking from his deathbed, told Salman that the time had come for a new prophet to appear and to restore in Arabia the true religion of ancient Abraham. Much like the monks of Bostra, he told Salman of the signs that would confirm the identity of the new prophet, including the seal of prophecy that would be found between his shoulders. The prophet, said the dying saint, would be forced to leave his home, but would make his way to a place of palm trees, situated between two lava flows. The place in question was none other than Yathrib, or Medina. Salman, the eager religious seeker, now determined to make his way to Arabia, to find this prophet of whom he had been told. He paid some Arabian caravan merchants to take him back with them to their native country, but they treacherously sold him into slavery. Eventually, though still a slave, he arrived in Yathrib and knew at once that this was the place he sought. Within a very short time of Muhammad's entry into the town, Salman had managed to meet him, and it took very little to convince the Persian slave that this was indeed the prophet for whom he had yearned.

On the other side, the death of many of the Meccan elite at Badr left Abu Sufyan the leading man of the Quraysh by default. And he was not inclined at this stage to compromise. In this he was supported by his wife Hind, who had lost several relatives at Badr, including her brother, her uncle, and her father — the latter two killed by Hamza, Muhammad's formidable uncle. Hind vowed that when the Quraysh finally defeated the Muslims, she would personally eat Hamza's liver raw from his body. In the meantime, despite the Muslim victory, the rich treasure of the caravan that had been the original Muslim target arrived safely at Mecca, and the leadership of the city unanimously resolved that all the profits from that caravan would be devoted to raising an invincible army to crush the upstarts in Medina. This time, too, following an ancient Arabian custom, the women would accompany the men of the army to urge them on and encourage them to acts of heroism. (And to provide tangible evidence, no doubt, of what another defeat would immediately cost them — their women.)

Muhammad decided that he needed to consolidate his position in Medina, and to eliminate potentially threatening weaknesses. He took action almost immediately against Asma bt. Marwan, a poetess whose verses had satirized and attacked him.[236] A Muslim member of her clan who had failed to join the fight at Badr demonstrated his loyalty to the Prophet by running her through with a sword at night, while she slept with her children. A month later another poet, the centenarian Abu Afak, met the same fate during his sleep for the same offense.

Muhammad was very concerned about the power of poets. The reason was not necessarily that he shared the ancient Arabian notion of poets as inspired by the jinn (*majnun*, which, as noted, has come to mean simple insanity in modern Arabic), although he very likely did. Rather he recognized the immense practical power that a poet possessed. For poets, in early Arabia, were very much like today's advertising executives or public relations consultants. To have one in one's tribe, praising the virtues and achievements of one's tribe in memorable lines that would be repeated, if they found audience appeal, from one end of Arabia to another, was a great blessing and asset. But to have a poet in a rival tribe satirizing one's tribe or clan in memorable and repeatable verses was a curse like no other, and was deemed an injury as serious as, if not more serious than, a defeat in literal battle. For a successful poet was not merely one enemy. As his verses began to be adopted and repeated by others, he became many foes.

The Quraysh knew the power of poets. The tale is told of the poet al-A'sha, who once set out to visit Muhammad at Medina in order to recite an ode

---

236. The abbreviation "bt." represents the Arabic word *bint* (daughter [of]), the feminine equivalent of *ibn* (son [of]).

that he had composed in the Prophet's honor. When the Quraysh heard of his intention, they were terrified, and they instantly set out to intercept him on his way. When he acknowledged that he was going to Medina to accept Islam, the Meccans pointed out that Muhammad's doctrine would prohibit certain things of which he was very fond. Al-A'sha asked for specifics. "Fornication," responded Abu Sufyan, the spokesman for the Qurayshi delegation. Al-A'sha replied that that would be no loss since, although he had not forsaken fornication, it had (presumably because of his advanced age) forsaken him. When mention of Islamic prohibitions against gambling, usury, and wine also failed to move him, Abu Sufyan offered the old poet a hundred camels if he would return to his home in Yamama and simply await the outcome of the struggle between the Quraysh and Muhammad. Al-A'sha accepted the offer, and Abu Sufyan turned to his associates. "O Quraysh!" he cried. "This is al-A'sha, and, by God, if he becomes a follower of Muhammad, he will inflame the Arabs against you with his poetry. So collect a hundred camels for him!"

Muhammad's own fear of the power of poets is apparent again in the story of Ka'b b. al-Ashraf, a poet of the Jewish Banu al-Nadir, who composed verses satirizing the Prophet and his associates and summoning the Quraysh to take revenge for their defeat at Badr. It finally became intolerable for Muhammad, and he is said to have prayed, "O Lord, deliver me from the son of al-Ashraf however you choose, on account of the evil he declares and the poems he recites." Then, turning to those present, he said, "Who is for me against the son of al-Ashraf? For he has injured me greatly."[237] Five Muslims volunteered. But, as they thought about how they might gain access to Ka'b and kill him, they began to realize that some form of deception would be necessary if they were to be successful and not become involved in a dangerous pitched battle with the entirety of the Banu Nadir, for Ka'b had taken up his residence in their fortified stronghold and could not be easily reached.

They were troubled in conscience, for they wanted to carry out the Prophet's apparent desires, but they saw no way to do it except through a kind of treachery, and they knew that Muhammad hated treachery and lying. However, he assured them that they could do or say whatever they needed to in order to accomplish their mission, for, he said, deception was legitimate as a strat-

---

237. The words are not unlike those attributed to Henry II ("Who will rid me of this turbulent priest?"), which led, whether by design or not, to the death of Saint Thomas à Becket. Note that Ka'b's poetry was supposed to have done Muhammad real injury. The mentality here is a great distance from our common notion that "sticks and stones may break my bones, but words can never hurt me." Names, words, were thought to have their own intrinsic and potentially dangerous power. The modern case of the Anglo-Indian writer Salman Rushdie has its roots, in a certain sense, in the case of Ka'b b. al-Ashraf and other poets who were targets of Muhammad's wrath.

agem of war, and since Ka'b's poetic attacks on him were acts of war, lying was legitimate here.[238] And indeed, in September 624, despite the warnings of the girl he had with him in bed, Ka'b was eventually lured from his fortress under false pretenses and killed. His triumphant assassins returned to the Prophet and laid Ka'b's head at his feet.

W. Montgomery Watt attempts to put the episode, a horrible act by modern standards, into perspective:

> In the gentler or (should we say?) less virile age in which we live men look askance at such conduct, particularly in a religious leader. But in Muḥammad's age and country it was quite normal. Men had no claims upon you on the basis of common humanity. Members of your tribe and of allied tribes, and those protected by your tribe, had very definite claims; but outside this circle no one had any claim at all. That is to say, in the case of a stranger or enemy there was no reason why you should not kill him if you felt inclined. . . . A man like Ka'b ibn-al-Ashraf was a clear enemy of the Islamic community, and so there was no obligation to consider him in any way. . . . So far were the Muslims who killed him from having any qualms about it that one of them, describing the return from the deed, wrote that they returned "five honourable men, steady and true, and God was the sixth with us."[239]

The Jews of the Banu Nadir were, naturally, both incensed and terrified at what had been done to one of them and at the seemingly underhanded way in which the act had been carried out. A delegation of their leaders went to the Prophet, complaining that one of them had been treacherously murdered — in their view, without cause. However, Muhammad did not apologize or acknowledge that they had a grievance. Rather he noted that Ka'b's execution — for so he viewed it — was entirely justified. "If he had remained as others of the same opinion are," the Prophet said, knowing full well that the opinion of him among the Nadir leaders was probably indistinguishable from that of their late poet, "he would not have been killed by stratagem. But he injured us and composed poetry against us, and none of you shall do this or he too shall be killed."

The Qur'an warned believers against the designs of those in Medina who appeared to be friends but were, in reality, enemies.

> Oh you who believe! Do not take outsiders as your close friends. They will not fail to corrupt you. They desire your ruin. Hatred has already appeared from their mouths; what their breasts conceal is still worse. . . . You are those

---

238. Again, the Arabian understanding of poetry as a real weapon is apparent.
239. Watt, pp. 128-29.

who love them, but they do not love you although you believe in the entirety of the Book. When they meet you, they say "We believe." But when they are alone, they gnaw their fingers against you for rage. Say, "Die in your rage! God knows what is in your hearts." If any good thing touches you, it grieves them. But if some evil strikes you, they rejoice at it. Still, if you are patient and devout, their scheming will not harm you in the slightest. Truly, God encompasses what they do.[240]

Troubles between the Muslims and the Jews of the Banu Qaynuqa came to a head over a trivial incident that occurred in the marketplace of Medina. A Muslim woman who had come to do business there was grossly insulted by one of the Jewish goldsmiths. A Medinan convert who was nearby came to her assistance, and in the struggle that followed, the goldsmith was killed.[241] At that the surrounding Jews attacked and killed the Muslim man who had aided his sister in the faith. True to Arabian custom, his family then demanded vengeance, stirring up hostile feelings among the so-called Helpers against the Jews. Even at this tense moment, though, the situation could have been resolved under the provisions of the so-called Constitution of Medina, had the parties resorted to arbitration as that document specified. Instead the Qaynuqa withdrew into their strongholds, which were fortified and stocked with provisions, and appealed to Ibn Ubayy and others of their former allies, the Khazraj, to come to their defense.

In the end, it was no good. After more than two weeks of blockade, the Jews surrendered. Some sources record that Muhammad wanted to execute them all, but that Ibn Ubayy passionately confronted him and, in a scarcely veiled threat, warned him that human events go in cycles. The Qaynuqa were ultimately obliged to migrate toward Syria, leaving their property behind. The Meccan Emigrants now moved into their deserted houses and, abandoning their work as day laborers, resumed their more accustomed activity as merchants. The Qaynuqa had probably been the weakest of the Jewish tribes in Medina, but they had been supporters and allies of Ibn Ubayy, who still saw himself as Muhammad's rival for temporal power in the oasis, and their removal benefited Muhammad immensely.

Other things in Muhammad's life were also going well. When Fatima, the youngest of his daughters, was about twenty years old, the Prophet married her to his cousin Ali. This bound Ali even more closely to the Prophet, who was now his father-in-law. Earlier Uthman b. Affan, who was to precede Ali as the third successor to Muhammad, had married Fatima's older sister Ruqayya.

---

240. Q 3:118-20.
241. Watt, p. 130, doubts the traditional story of the goldsmith's insult.

During the fasting month of Ramadan, just before the first anniversary of the Muslim victory in the battle of Badr, Fatima gave birth to a son, the Prophet's grandson, who would receive the name of al-Hasan, "the beautiful."

At the end of the month, though, Muhammad received word that a force of three thousand men was marching forth from Mecca against him. The sources say that seven hundred of the men bore armor and two hundred rode on horseback. It was, by the standards of early Arabia, a formidable army. In the week of preparation left to them, the Medinans concentrated on bringing all the people and animals in from the outlying areas of the settlement. Then they could only wait to see what the precise intention or plan of the Meccans might be. It soon became evident. The army came up the western caravan route, near the Red Sea coast. Then they turned inland and passed within about five miles of Medina before continuing on to its northeast. There, in an area of cultivated land in the plain at the base of Mount Uhud, which looks down upon Medina from the north, they came to a halt. The Prophet's scouts were able to confirm the predicted numbers and strength of the Meccan army, which included allies from Thaqif and Kinana and other groups. Worse, they reported that the large number of men and animals were devouring the pasture and consuming the crops to the north of the city, which had not yet been harvested. In a region where cultivable land and pasture were rare and where alternative food sources were very distant, this was serious news indeed. Even without striking a blow, the Meccans represented a serious threat to Medina. Moreover, the scouts said, there were no signs that the Meccans were in any particular hurry. With an abundance of Medinan pastureland and food, they could remain where they were indefinitely.

Nonetheless, Muhammad was at first inclined simply to wait his enemies out. He held a council with the leaders of the town and asked their advice. Ibn Ubayy, too, counseled restraint. Medina, he said, was like a virgin that had never been violated. No enemy had ever entered her without suffering defeat and severe losses. On the other hand, he declared, the Medinans had never gone out from her against an enemy without themselves suffering severe casualties. Eventually, Ibn Ubayy predicted, the Meccans would return home in frustration, having accomplished nothing. Others, both Emigrants and Helpers, agreed with Ibn Ubayy and supported Muhammad in his initial decision. If they simply remained within their fortifications, the cavalry of the Quraysh would be useless.

But the younger men were not satisfied. Hotheaded, perhaps, they did not want the Meccans to feel that the armies of Islam were too weak, or that they feared them. What is more, the argument went, to leave the Meccans unpunished despite their theft of Medinan crops and pasturage would be to encourage them to repeat such actions in the future, and would embolden the

Meccans' bedouin allies to further depredations. Better to act now than to face worse situations in the days to come. Had the Prophet forgotten the experience of Badr, where he had inflicted a terrible defeat upon Quraysh with an army only a fraction of theirs in size? Now he was stronger. Why fear the godless forces of the enemies of Islam? One of the older men in the assembly then arose and spoke more personally. During the previous night, he reported, his son, who had been among the few Muslims killed at Badr, had appeared to him in a dream, standing in immortal beauty among the gardens of paradise. His son had confirmed to him that everything they had been told of paradise and the life to come was true, and had invited him to join him and the other martyrs there. Finally Malik b. Sinan stood, pointing out that there were really only two outcomes that could follow a Muslim attack upon the Meccan army: If the Muslims triumphed, that would be good. But if the Muslims were defeated, their dead would enter instantly into paradise, and that too was good. So there was really nothing to be lost either way. It soon became apparent that a majority of the assembly desired to take military action. Muhammad decided to attack.

The attitude of the Muslim army is clearly illustrated by the stories of two men who sought Muhammad out at the close of the meeting. One told of a dream he had experienced, rather like the one just recounted. In it he had been promised martyrdom and paradise, and he was eager to go to war. Muhammad confirmed his interpretation of the dream, and the man, a widower with a son and seven daughters, immediately went home to make arrangements for the maintenance of his daughters after his anticipated death. His son, too, was eagerly preparing for battle, but the father forbade him, requiring him to stay home to look after the unmarried girls. Another man, named Hanzala, told the Prophet that he was eager to fight, but that he was set to be married that day and did not want to postpone the wedding. Muhammad advised him to go ahead with the wedding and to spend the night in Medina. He could join the Muslim forces on the following day; no military action was likely to occur before then anyway. (That night, following their wedding, Hanzala's wife would have a dream in which she saw him standing at the entrance to paradise. A door opened for him, and he passed through it, whereupon the door closed on him and he was lost to her view. The next morning, although she begged him to stay with her and not to go out to battle, and although they both understood perfectly well what her dream portended, Hanzala could not be dissuaded from joining the Muslim forces on the plain before Mount Uhud.) There were still those, perhaps a majority among the older and wiser Medinans, who felt that Muhammad's first inclination had been the correct one. And perhaps certain others who had voiced a desire for battle were now reconsidering what they had said in the enthusiasm of a mass assembly. Give the decision back to the Prophet, some said. You have forced him to go against his first judgment, and it is he who communicates with God. But when the Prophet emerged from his house clad in armor, he informed them that prophets do not remove their armor once they have put it on, before they have gone forth against their enemies. Muhammad could probably not afford to give further evidence of indecision. His course was now fixed. He mounted his horse, slung his bow over his shoulder, and took a spear in his hand. Nobody else among his force, which numbered approximately one thousand, was mounted.

The Prophet gathered with his warriors at a place called Shaykhayn, which was located approximately halfway between Medina and Uhud. There he surveyed the men at his disposal. Among his soldiers Muhammad noticed eight boys who were, he felt, too young to participate in combat, and he ordered them to go home. Two, however, claiming and demonstrating great prowess in archery and wrestling, convinced him that they should be allowed to stay.

In the predawn hours of the next morning, when the Prophet ordered the Muslim army to be prepared to continue on to Uhud, Ibn Ubayy, who had evidently spent the previous evening discussing the situation with some of those who, like himself, were not entirely convinced of Muhammad's inspiration, instead took three hundred men — roughly 30 percent of the already grossly outnumbered Muslim force — and returned to Medina. As he explained it, Muhammad had refused to take his advice, but had instead listened to young men, zealots without sound judgment, and he could see no reason why he and those who followed him should lose their lives in a quixotic and foolish effort such as this.

Though weakened, the army from Medina nonetheless moved toward the Meccan force under the cover of early-morning darkness. No doubt aided by their superior knowledge of the local geography, they were able to position themselves between Mount Uhud and the Meccans — which gave them the considerable advantage of being uphill from their enemies. There they performed the morning prayer, simultaneously facing Mecca and their Meccan foe.

Muhammad placed a company of his finest archers on an elevation somewhat to the left of the main body of his fighters, with orders that they were to maintain their position there whatever seemed to be happening on the battlefield. They were not to leave their assigned location even if the Muslims appeared to be losing the struggle, and they were certainly not to evacuate it for the sake of grabbing booty if the battle seemed to be won. Their vitally important task was to protect the Muslim army against the highly mobile cavalry of its Meccan opponents, for which the Prophet had no equivalent force, and especially to keep the cavalry from coming in and attacking the Medinans from the rear.

When the sun rose over the plain of Uhud, the Meccans were already drawn up in a battle line. The Medinans watched in fury as men and horses trampled their rich barley and corn crops underfoot. The holy family known as the Banu Abd al-Dar, the "sons of the slave of the House," bore the standard of the Ka'ba and the Meccan *haram*.[242] On the right wing Khalid b. al-Walid (who, ironically, would later become one of the greatest generals of the Arab conquests, "the sword of Islam") commanded a hundred men on horseback; on the left Ikrima b. Abi Jahl controlled an equivalent number. In the center Abu Sufyan bore overall command. It was he who gave the order to advance.

After an exchange of speeches and verbal abuse, however, it was the Muslims who began the actual combat, sending a flight of arrows into Khalid's cavalry. There followed a series of single combats, in which the Muslims — notable among them Ali and the Prophet's uncle Hamza — were very successful. A major setback to the Muslim forces came early in the battle, however, when an Ethiopian slave, an expert javelin thrower who had been promised his freedom if he killed Hamza, succeeded in slaying that fearsome warrior with a single long-distance strike. The newlywed Hanzala, who fought heroically, also fell early on, fulfilling the portentous dream of his young wife.

On the whole, however, the Muslim forces continued to advance against their Meccan enemies, and when it became apparent that they were likely to lose, the pagans began to flee in disarray. The opening in their ranks left the Meccan camp undefended, and, true to the nature of ancient Arabian warfare, a rush to take plunder now began. Muslim discipline itself collapsed at the very moment of triumph. Most significantly, a sizable body of the archers Muhammad had placed on the hill overlooking the battle, commanding them not to leave their post, now abandoned their position in a headlong rush for booty. The battle, they felt, was over, and they did not intend to be left out of the spoils.

The Meccan general Khalid, giving a foretaste of the military talent he would later display in the great Arab conquests that followed the death of the Prophet, immediately sensed what had happened and grasped his opportunity. Gathering his cavalry, who until now had scarcely been a factor in the battle, he charged the hill where a very small group of archers had remained faithful to Muhammad's assignment. He and his men killed them, every one. Then he attacked the main Muslim forces from their unprotected rear. Ikrima, the other cavalry commander, brought his troops into the same position as well, and together the two units of horsemen did great damage to the largely defenseless Muslims. The momentum of the battle had changed swiftly and lethally. As the Muslims turned to face the Meccan cavalry, the demoralized pagans who had been retreating before them now wheeled about and, renewed in spirit, attacked again. The struggle began slowly to move up the slopes of Mount Uhud,

242. Serjeant, "Ḥaram and Ḥawṭah," p. 54.

toward the place where Muhammad himself had taken his position. Some of the Muslims now fled for their lives.

The great concern of the Muslims who remained more or less lucid during these terrible moments suddenly became the safety of the Messenger of God, toward whom the fighting was swiftly moving. He and those immediately around him were defending themselves with volleys of arrows, greatly advantaged by their location on the slope where the cavalry of the Quraysh were unable to reach them, but they could not hold the seemingly inexorable Meccan attack off forever. For one thing, their supply of arrows was finite. Moreover, as the fighting came ever closer, archery became almost useless. Nonetheless, the Prophet and his little band of defenders, which included two women, fought fiercely. In the struggle Muhammad himself was nearly killed when a sword blow glanced off the side of his helmet, drove a portion of it into the flesh of his cheek, and knocked him briefly unconscious. Several among his bodyguard died. The Prophet's standard-bearer was cut down only a few feet from where the Messenger of God stood. The rumor now began to spread throughout the two armies that Muhammad himself, the hope of the Muslims and the bane of the pagan Quraysh, was dead.

And once again the indiscipline that characterized much early Arabian warfare came into play. The pagans could see that the battle had gone their way. They had regained their honor after the humiliating defeat at Badr. Now, hearing that the Prophet was dead, they relaxed their effort. And for those in close proximity to Muhammad and his guard, there seemed no further purpose in risking one's life against people who fought like dragons.

Only about twenty-two of the Meccan force had lost their lives, compared to approximately sixty-five slain among the Muslims. The pagans could not fail to take satisfaction in the ratio. But, try though they might, they could not find the body of Muhammad, whom they were certain they had killed. Still, there was reason enough for celebration, and some of it was conducted in a way that showed with painful clarity how little distance separated some of the Meccan pagans from sheer barbarism. Hind, the wife of Abu Sufyan, had made a vow to eat raw the liver of Hamza, the Prophet's uncle, because of the damage he had inflicted on her family at the earlier battle of Badr. This she now did, at least in a token portion. Not content with that, however, she mutilated him, cutting off his nose and his ears and other pieces of his flesh and making them into ornaments, and leading the women of Quraysh in doing similar things to others among the Muslim dead. Indeed, some of the Meccan men joined in such behavior, until the disgust and outrage of their bedouin allies shamed them into stopping it. Afterward, furious at learning what had been done to Hamza and other Muslim casualties, Muhammad vowed that he would mutilate thirty Meccans at the next opportunity. But a revelation soon advised him against such action, and he never fulfilled his vow.

Indeed, he subsequently forbade his followers to mutilate the bodies of the dead, and taught them to show particular respect to the human face, for it was created, he said, in the image of God himself.

Abu Sufyan, perhaps by now suspecting that Muhammad was not dead after all, was nevertheless determined to make plain what he regarded as the lesson of the day. He rode to a point on the slope of the mountain, near the spot where Muhammad had last been sighted, and cried out, "War goes by turns, and this is a day in exchange for a day. Exalt yourself, O Hubal!" he said, addressing one of the pagan deities. "Make your religion prevail!" But Muhammad would not concede the last word to his pagan adversary. Instead, he ordered Umar to stand at the edge of a cliff above Abu Sufyan and to call out, "God is Most High, supreme in his majesty. We are not equal: Our dead are in paradise; yours are in Hell." Abu Sufyan, who knew that Umar could be trusted, now took the opportunity to settle the question once and for all. Was Muhammad dead? Umar replied that he was not, and that he was even now listening to their conversation.

Finally the pagans withdrew from the field, and the Muslims were greatly relieved to see them returning to Mecca rather than following up their advantage against the severely damaged and rather demoralized believers by attacking Medina. The Meccans knew better, perhaps, than to launch a difficult siege against the Medinans in their fortified settlements, which could only serve to unite the Jews and the faction of Ibn Ubayy with the Muslims in shared resentment. Their cavalry would be of no use in such a siege, and their infantry, on which the burden of the campaign would fall, had not performed especially well during the battle just concluded.

In a show of strength and perhaps bravado, the Prophet instantly ordered a force of Muslims, under his own leadership (though he himself was suffering badly from a sword blow to his shoulder), to follow the Meccan force as it returned homeward. That a show was intended is demonstrated by the fact that Muhammad, far from pursuing his enemies in stealth, went to great lengths to have his army observed. Indeed, he sought to deceive the pagans into overestimating his strength. At their first encampment out of Medina, at the Prophet's direction, the Muslims scattered themselves out over a wide area and then, gathering large quantities of wood, lit a fire for each man in the pursuing force (who reportedly numbered more than five hundred). It was a militarily risky move but, as psychological warfare, it was extremely effective. If the Quraysh and their allies had entertained any thoughts of returning to Medina and finishing off the wounded Muslim state — and the sources suggest that such notions were indeed under consideration — the deliberately misleading impression that Muhammad's stratagem gave to them, that there were hundreds of eager Muslim warriors hot on their trail, strangled the idea in its infancy. They could not even be sure that they had won.

And in fact, it is not clear in retrospect that Uhud was a Meccan victory, though it is generally described as such. Obviously it was a serious psychological blow to the Muslims. If Badr had been a sign of God's miraculous intervention and of his care for the new community, how was Uhud to be interpreted? But the Meccans had sought to eliminate Muhammad, and they had failed. Where once they had controlled much of Arabia, they had now managed at best to even the score of dead against the upstart Prophet.

In the next couple of months the Prophet would find himself obliged to take further military action in order to stave off attacks from those who, following the apparent setback at Uhud, thought to take advantage of what they thought would be Muslim weakness. When the Banu Asad b. Khuzayma tribe, allies of the Quraysh based in Najd, began preparations for a raid on Medina, Muhammad dispatched a small but well-equipped force to raid them first. The resulting battle was militarily inconclusive but highly effective politically. The tribesmen scattered, and the Muslim warriors returned home with camels and other plunder. At about the same time, the Prophet decreed the assassination of a chief of the Banu Lihyan, who was also planning an attack on the oasis of Medina. Again the attack fulfilled its purpose; no Lihyanite raid occurred.

Muhammad's departure from Medina created more than merely military risks, however. Back in the city, Ibn Ubayy was speaking with anyone who would listen about the foolishness of Muhammad's going out against the Meccans to battle. The results of the fighting had simply confirmed, in Ibn Ubayy's view, that he had been right to take his fighters and return to the city. And he was not alone. The sources suggest that many of the Medinan Jews, chafing under the chieftainship of this parvenu non-Hebrew claimant to prophecy, saw evidence of Muhammad's merely human status in his military defeat at Uhud. The Qur'an responded to such talk in a verse that would prove important for the day, some years in the future, when Muhammad really would depart from the scene and his followers would be obliged to carry on without him. "Muhammad," the revelation declared, "is nothing but a messenger. Many messengers have passed away before him. So if he were to die or were killed, would you turn upon your heels? Whoever turns upon his heels does not hurt God a bit, and God will reward the thankful."[243]

The Muslims, too, responded to the insinuations of Ibn Ubayy, who found his status in the town further reduced rather than enhanced by his conduct. Where his importance in pre-Muslim Medinan society had once secured him a privileged place in the mosque, he was now barred from it.

More serious social dislocations were about to follow, however. Sometime after Uhud, Muhammad was invited to a dinner hosted by the Jewish

---

243. Q 3:144.

tribe called the Banu Nadir in their fortified settlement somewhat to the south of the main part of the Medinan oasis. But while he was waiting to be ushered in to the meal, the angel Gabriel came to him and warned him that the Jews were in fact planning to kill him, and that he must return home immediately. Nobody else saw the angel, and Muhammad left his associates there with neither explanation nor word of any kind. When he did not return, his companions also left. Muhammad then sent to the Banu Nadir a messenger, who not only recounted to them in precise detail the character of their plot but announced to them the fateful decree of the Prophet: They had ten days to leave the vicinity of Medina. Any member of their tribe found in the area thereafter would be decapitated.

Ibn Ubayy, though weaker than ever — indeed, perhaps *because* he felt himself weaker than ever, and bound to grow weaker still if his fellow critics of Muhammad were exiled — sent word to the Banu Nadir to stay, while others convinced them that their allies among the bedouin, and their fellow Jews, the Banu Qurayza, would stand by them. So the Jews determined to stay, and announced their determination to the Prophet, who regarded it as a declaration of rebellion and war. In little time at all, he and his followers were besieging the Jews in their fortresses, with arrows and stones passing back and forth until sunset. To the dismay of the besieged Banu Nadir, however, their expected reinforcements did not arrive. Ibn Ubayy, to the further diminution of his credibility, was unable to deliver any support whatever. After ten days or so, the Jews saw that their position was hopeless. After some negotiation, they finally agreed to leave their land in Medina, taking with them all that they could load on camelback except their weapons and their armor. A revelation preserved in the Qur'an commented on these events and predicted the outcome:

> Have you not observed the hypocrites, saying to their brothers among the people of the Book who disbelieve, "If you are exiled, we will go into exile with you, and we will not obey anyone in your affair. And if you are attacked, we will help you." But God bears witness that they are lying. If they are exiled, they will never go into exile with them, and if they are attacked, they will not help them. And if they do help them, they will [eventually] turn their backs, and then they will not be helped. Truly, you are stronger than they are, owing to the terror in their breasts from God. That is because they are a people who do not comprehend. They will not fight you, except in fortified villages or from behind walls. Their hostility among themselves is strong. You think them united, but their hearts are divided. That is because they are a people who do not think.[244]

244. Q 59:11-14.

It was disunity, both between the Jews and their pagan allies and among the Jews themselves, that made Muhammad's successful siege of them possible. Then the revelation made a very unflattering comparison of the Jews' purported allies to the devil, and predicted the ultimate end of both groups: "Like Satan, when he says to a human being 'Disbelieve!' And when he does disbelieve, he says 'I have nothing to do with you. I fear God, the lord of the worlds.' The final end of both of them will be the inferno, dwelling in it forever. That is the reward of those who do wrong."[245]

The proximate factor in the surrender of the Banu Nadir was Muhammad's order to begin felling the date palm trees that were their pride and the chief source of their wealth. It is possible that they still held out hope of someday returning to their position within Medina; certainly the Quraysh were still promising to eradicate Islam and the rule of Muhammad, hateful both to the Meccan pagans and many of the Medinan Jews, and the defeat at Uhud made it plausible that they might succeed. Thus they probably still expected to return after a shorter or longer period to the enjoyment of their lands and their trees. But if those trees were felled, it would take many years to replace them even if their most optimistic anticipations came true.

So the Banu Nadir left Medina. They went out in a blaze of glory and wealth, dressed in their finest jewels and accompanied by the sound of timbrels and fifes. Some went all the way to Jericho in Palestine, or to the north in Syria, but many settled on lands they owned at the oasis of Khaybar. Meanwhile their land and their weapons and their armor and whatever else they had been obliged to leave behind as uncarryable by their camels fell to the Prophet Muhammad, who used it to supply the poor and the destitute among his followers — particularly the Emigrants, who had fled Mecca and whose economic situation in Medina continued to be precarious even at this point.

Not long after the beginning of 626, Muhammad's daughter Fatima, married to Ali, gave birth to a second son. The baby was given the name of al-Husayn, a diminutive form of the name al-Hasan, which had already been bestowed on his older brother.

Mecca: The Beginning (of the End)

The Jews of the Banu Nadir, who had been exiled from Medina and had mostly settled in the oasis of Khaybar, were not resigned to the loss of their lands and their date palms. Near the commencement of 627, some of their leaders are said to have gone secretly to Mecca to urge the Quraysh to settle the thorny problem

245. Q 59:16-17.

of Muhammad once and for all. They entered into oaths together, within the sacred Ka'ba, swearing that they would be allies for the destruction of the Prophet and his new religion. The Jews agreed to stir up the bedouin nomads of the Najd region, many of whom had grievances, real or imagined, against the inhabitants of Medina (or, at least, were aggrieved by the relative wealth of the settlement when contrasted with their own lean and difficult lives). The assistance of others was to be secured by bribes, or by the promise of spoils. The Banu Ghatafan, for instance, were offered half the annual Khaybar date harvest if they assisted the conspirators. The warriors of the Quraysh and their allies marched along the western or coastal road toward Medina, the same route they had taken on their way to the triumph at Uhud. The Jews and their motley group of allies and mercenaries, on the other hand, would come in against Medina from the deserts to the east. All totaled, there were ten thousand men in this new force — more than three times the number of those in the victorious battle of Uhud. It was late March 627, and surely the end of Muhammad and Islam was at hand.

But the Prophet received advance warning of the attack from sympathetic sources in Mecca, which gave him a week — but only a week — to prepare for the onslaught. As he had prior to the battle of Uhud, Muhammad summoned a council to discuss a course of action. Many suggestions were offered, but the one of Salman the Persian gained acceptance. Drawing on his experiences in Persia, he suggested that a trench would be an effective barrier against cavalry attack. The trench did not have to encircle the settlement, for large rocky areas to the northwest would serve as barrier enough if they could be connected, and there were several areas of fortified settlements that could be similarly tied together. At one end of the trench lay a hill from which Muslim archers would have an effective vantage point to fire on the attackers. Supplied by the Jewish Banu Qurayza with digging implements and date baskets for carrying away the dirt, the Muslims began to excavate a ditch that would be sufficiently deep and sufficiently wide to stymie the cavalry of Quraysh. Each faction of the community was assigned a certain portion of the trench to construct. The Prophet himself worked with his disciples, amidst chanting and singing. Traditional narratives relate miracles from this time, when the workers on the trench were unable to do their usual work and the normal economic and domestic activities of the settlement were in abeyance. Many of the workers, including the Prophet himself, were frequently unable to get enough to eat, especially as they were exerting themselves in unaccustomed and urgent physical labor. So God multiplied their food in remarkable ways, feeding many workers from meager rations that would normally have sufficed for only a few.

When the Meccan force and its allies from Najd arrived in the vicinity of Medina, they were dismayed to discover that the settlement's crops had already been harvested, perhaps intentionally early. This meant that their camels would have only the scarce local bushes to eat, which would soon be depleted, and that their horses would have to survive on such fodder as they had brought with them. Such constraints were crucial, as they would limit the time the attackers would be able to maintain a siege. The two separate armies, which had first pitched separate camps, now joined together and launched their advance toward the Muslim capital.

They must have been quite encouraged when they first saw the Muslim camp, at the end of March 627, not barricaded up within the settlement but lying directly in front of them outside the town. With their vast numerical superiority, it would be quick work to take care of the upstart Muhammad and his followers. It was only as they drew nearer that they saw a trench in the ground, lined with Muslim archers on the far side. This was an innovation for which they had not reckoned. Furthermore, the slope was in the favor of the Muslims, for the edge of the trench on their side was higher than that on the side of the Meccans, giving the Muslim archers considerable advantage.

But the attackers, too, had their stratagems. The traditional accounts relate that a man named Huyay, a leader of the exiled Banu Nadir who had encouraged this latest Meccan attempt to extirpate Muhammad and his followers, went to the dignitaries of the Quraysh with a plan. He would approach his fellow Jews, the Banu Qurayza, who were still part of the Medinan community, in an attempt to persuade them to renege on their covenant obligations to Muhammad. Thus a new battlefront would be opened at the enemy's rear, much like the literal second front that Khalid's cavalry had been able to open up behind the Muslims in the Meccan victory at Uhud.

At first the Banu Qurayza rejected Huyay's blandishments. But as he sketched for them the overwhelming strength of the Meccan and allied forces, as he stressed the determination of the Quraysh (this time) to end the nuisance of Muhammad's movement forever — and Huyay's powers of persuasion were near legendary — their resistance weakened. After all, Muhammad had made their life much more difficult. He was a newcomer to the settlement, but he had supplanted the old leaders and turned their traditional arrangements upside down, besides challenging their religious beliefs. Finally they agreed to withdraw from their agreement with the Prophet.

As expected, this created new problems for Muhammad and his warriors, who were now required to dispatch men from the front line at the trench in order to maintain a defensive garrison back in the previously secure center of the settlement. Rumors began to circulate, in fact, that the Quraysh and their allies were planning to sneak a thousand men each night into the fortresses of the Banu Qurayza, in preparation for a massive assault on the very homes of the Muslims and to carry off their wives and children. Though such an attack never materialized, the rumors themselves were undoubtedly demoralizing. A revelation received subsequent to the battle of the trench spoke of the mood that prevailed, and more than hints at discord among the ranks of Medina's defenders:

> Behold, they came upon you from above you and from below you, and behold, eyes were dimmed and hearts leaped to throats and you had second thoughts about God.
>
> In that situation, the believers were tested and were terribly shaken.
>
> And behold, the hypocrites, in whose hearts is a disease, say, "God and his messenger promised us nothing more than vain hopes!"
>
> And behold, a faction among them said, "O people of Yathrib! You cannot stand. So retreat!" And a group of them sought leave from the Prophet, saying, "Our houses lie exposed." But they were not exposed. They simply wanted to flee.
>
> And if they had been entered upon from the sides of [the city] and they had been incited to sedition, they would have done it, and they wouldn't have hesitated for a moment.
>
> Yet they had already covenanted with God not to turn their backs, and a covenant with God is something that must be answered for.[246]

Since the guard at the trench still had to be maintained both day and night, but now with reduced manpower, the hours of watch were increased and, with them, the fatigue of the Muslim defenders. To make things worse, the weather was unusually cold. And Khalid and Ikrima — who, as before, were commanding the Meccan cavalry — were constantly searching for weakness or any signs of carelessness along the trench. Once, indeed, when there was a momentary lack of defenders at one point on the line, several Meccan horsemen had been able, briefly, though ultimately with the loss of two of them, to cross the trench, thus demonstrating the possibility of breaching the Muslim defenses if conditions were suitable.

So tense was the situation that, for the first time in the history of Islam, the canonical daily prayers were neglected by the Muslim community as a whole. When the time for the noon prayer came, the Muslims simply could not relax their vigilance in order to perform it. When some of them came to the Prophet in concern about the issue, he replied that he, too, had been unable to pray. Only after sunset, when the advent of darkness had forced the attackers to return to their camp, could the believers resume their regular worship. And Muhammad led his disciples in four sets of prayers, to compensate for those they had missed.

246. Q 33:10-15.

Faithful believers knew that such tests and trials were to be expected. They had always beset the path of those who sought to do the will of God. "Do you think that you will enter paradise without there coming to you the like of what happened to those who passed away before you? Misfortunes and adversities afflicted them, and they were shaken so much that the messenger of God and those who believed with him said, 'When is the victory of God?' Ah, truly the victory of God is near."[247]

But if things were difficult for the Muslim defenders of Medina, they were probably not significantly better — and may have been much worse — for the pagans of the besieging army. They too felt the cold. If the Muslims were hungry, they certainly were as well. Feed for their animals was growing scarce. Some of their valued horses were dying, from hunger as well as from arrows. The mercenaries among them must have begun to wonder if even the promised booty would be adequate compensation for their wretchedness, and whether, indeed, it would ever materialize. At one point Muhammad worked out a secret deal whereby a powerful faction of the Meccans' bedouin allies agreed to withdraw from the standoff in exchange for a third of the Medinan date harvest, but the Prophet's lieutenants, after ascertaining that he was acting out of compassion for his people rather than from divine commandment, rejected the arrangement.

But the Meccan-led coalition was beginning to unravel of its own accord, without bribes. One of the bedouin leaders came to Muhammad by night and professed his belief in Islam, putting himself at the Prophet's disposal. Muhammad knew instantly how to use him. He told the man to return to his camp and to commence sowing discord among the factions, for, he said, "war is deception."

Before long the Quraysh and the Medinan Jewish Banu Qurayza were deeply distrustful of one another's resolve and virtually at one another's throats. It was at this time that a fierce storm from the east hit the area, first dropping a torrential rain on the two armies and then rising to the force of a hurricane. The weather had been cold before, but now it was worse. However, the invaders got the brunt of the storm. While the camp of the Muslims was at least partially sheltered, that of the pagans was exposed on the open plain; no warming fire could be maintained, nor could any sheltering tent stand before the blast. It was too much. Wet, cold, hungry, with their horses dying, concerned about apparent treachery on the part of their allies, frustrated at the lack of any momentum or any realistic chance of ending the battle — casualties for the encounter totaled five or six for the defenders and three among the invaders; most of the time was spent exchanging versified insults and shooting ar-

247. Q 2:214.

rows at one another from a safe remove — the leaders of the Quraysh decided to abandon the field. The battle was over. And finished, too, were any real hopes of a Meccan victory. They had thrown as much power against Medina as they were capable of fielding, and they had failed. Never again would the Quraysh be able to mount a serious threat to Muhammad or the religion of Islam. The Qur'an memorialized this triumph for all time to come, within the Muslim community: "O you who believe! Remember the grace of God upon you, when armies came upon you. So we sent against them a wind and armies that you did not see. And God observes all that you do. . . . And God repelled those who disbelieved, in their fury. They gained nothing. And God is sufficient for the believers in battle. And God is powerful and mighty."[248]

The doubt and despondency that had, for a time, afflicted the Muslim fighters was now gone, as the Qur'an recalled: "'This is what God and his messenger promised us, and God and his messenger told the truth.' And it only increased their faith and their submissiveness [to God and his messenger]."[249] But Muhammad did not spend much time basking in his triumph. Just after the noon prayer the angel Gabriel visited him, dressed elaborately in gold and silver brocade. He was surprised to see that Muhammad had laid down his weapons, and commanded the Prophet to take them up again and go with him against the treacherous Banu Qurayza. The siege of the last remaining tribe of Medinan Jews lasted nearly a month. Finally the Banu Qurayza sent to Muhammad, asking if he would permit one of their old tribal allies, now a Muslim, to come out to their fortified dwellings to consult with them. The man, Abu Lubaba, went, and soon found his feelings softened, against his will, by the obvious distress of his former friends. When the men asked him if he felt they should submit to the Prophet, he instantly replied that they should, but then indicated by pointing to his throat that such submission would mean certain death. As soon as he had done so, he felt guilty for having possibly prolonged their resistance, and he spent many days thereafter in penance for his double-mindedness.

But the Banu Qurayza failed to heed his warning. On the following day the Jews opened the gates of their fortresses and submitted to Muhammad. The Muslims immediately separated the men from the women and children, leading the men out of the tribe's dwellings with their hands bound behind their backs. Their armor and weapons were gathered together with their garments and all their other possessions. Their grape and date wine was poured out onto the ground. The Banu Qurayza had, in the past, been allies of the clans of Aws. These now sent a deputation to the Prophet, requesting that he treat their former allies with the same degree of clemency with which he had earlier treated

---

248. Q 33:9, 25.
249. Q 33:22.

the Banu Qaynuqa, the former allies of their rivals, the Khazraj. On the face of it, it seemed a reasonable request. Muhammad responded by asking whether Aws would be content if it were one of their own who pronounced sentence on the treacherous Banu Qurayza. They responded that they would. So the Prophet had one of their chiefs, a man named Sa'd b. Muadh, brought out to perform the office. As he came, his fellow clansmen reminded him to treat the Jews well. After all, they informed him, the whole purpose for which judgment had been granted to Aws was to see that the Banu Qurayza were treated leniently.

Sa'd had been wounded during the battle of the trench, and though he was still alive, his wound was not mending. (It ultimately proved fatal.) Perhaps he was in ill temper. Certainly he had never been inclined toward leniency. With the rather fiery Umar, for instance, he had opposed sparing the prisoners at Badr. And those freed prisoners had lived on to kill Muslims again at Uhud, and yet again at the trench. Moreover, it might have been noted, this most recent threat to the Muslims and their leader had come about largely through the machinations of the exiled Banu Nadir. If the Muslims did not intend to face threat after threat from the same unrepentant enemies, perhaps it was time to make the repetition of their threat impossible while they were, as these enemies were now, wholly in Muslim power. Severe punishment would further serve to deter future treachery.

After receiving promises from all the Muslims present that they would indeed abide by his judgment, Sa'd decreed the execution of the men of Banu Qurayza, the enslaving of their women and children, and the division of their property among the Muslims.[250] "You have judged," said the Prophet, "with the judgment of God from above the seven heavens."[251]

The women and children were then removed from the area of their own dwellings and taken into the main part of Medina. The men remained in the camp, where the narratives recount that they recited from the Torah and exhorted one another to be of good courage and to endure their fates with patience and resignation. The next morning Muhammad ordered several large trenches dug in the marketplace. The mature men and youth of the Banu Qurayza were then taken to these trenches in small groups, and made to sit down beside them until Ali and Zubayr and some of the more vigorous Mus-

250. Some of the women and children were later ransomed by their fellow Jews, the exiled Banu Nadir in Khaybar. They perhaps felt some responsibility for the catastrophe that had come upon Banu Qurayza, for it was one of their chieftains who had lured the Banu Qurayza to their fatal decision to go against their covenant with Muhammad.

251. Perhaps with some apologetic intent, the late English scholar Martin Lings notes, correctly, that Sa'd's judgment accords with that of the law of Moses as recorded in Deut. 20:10-14. See Lings, p. 232 n. 1.

lims were able to behead them with a sword stroke and push their bodies into the waiting mass graves. The bloody process continued into the evening, and had to be concluded by the light of torches. Traditional estimates place the number executed at between six hundred and nine hundred.

The Qur'an later recalled this episode as an example of God's grace toward the faithful: "And he brought down from their castles those among the people of the book [*ahl al-kitab*] who assisted them, and he cast terror into their hearts. Some of them you killed, and some you imprisoned. And he caused you to inherit their lands, their dwellings, and their goods, and a land you had not trod. Truly, God is all powerful."[252]

A rather touching story is told of an aged Jew named Zabir, who had once spared the life of a Khazrajite named Thabit b. Qays. Thabit now sought to return the favor, and interceded with Muhammad on Zabir's behalf. The Prophet granted the request, but Zabir, when presented with the gift of life, responded that he could see little point in survival without his wife and children. At Thabit's request, the Prophet now granted Zabir the freedom of his family. But, Zabir said, they could scarcely be expected to survive without their possessions. So, once again at the behest of Thabit, Muhammad allowed Zabir to regain his possessions, excepting his weapons and his armor. Even so, though, Zabir could see no purpose or sweetness in continuing to live when his people were either dead or enslaved, and he begged Thabit, for the sake of the favor that he had once done him, to allow him to join the rest of his people quickly. When Thabit realized that Zabir was fully serious, he escorted him to the side of one of the trenches, where Zabir's head was cut off by one of the Muslim executioners. Thabit did insist, however, on the freeing of Zabir's widow and her children, and on the restoration of their property to them.

Despite the horror of the destruction of the Banu Qurayza, the French Jewish Orientalist Maxime Rodinson is probably correct in his judgment that Muhammad's actions were not driven by any particular prejudice against Jews.[253] Contrary to repeated claims, for example, he did not attempt altogether to cleanse the region of its Jewish population. The Qur'an's criticisms of the Jews are no harsher, really, than those of the New Testament: they had received the law and the words of the prophets, but they had not obeyed. "The likeness of those upon whom the Torah was imposed and then did not obey it is as the likeness of a donkey bearing books."[254] Still, it is clear that Muhammad did not hesitate to act against the Jews with remarkable harshness, and that he did not regret his actions afterward. Not very long after the destruction of the

252. Q 33:26-27.
253. Rodinson, p. 158.
254. Q 62:5.

Banu Qurayza, Saʿd b. Muadh, who had decreed their fate, lay on his deathbed. The Prophet came to him, held his head gently, and prayed: "O Lord, truly Saʿd has striven in the path, full of faith in your messenger and leaving nothing undone that he was supposed to do. Therefore, take unto yourself his spirit in the very best way that you take the spirits of your creatures." Within a couple of hours, Saʿd was dead. (His death, we are told, shook the very throne of God.) When the mourners were carrying him to his grave, they marveled at how light he was, particularly since he had been well known to be a very large man. Muhammad explained that angels had borne him, along with the earthly pall-bearers.

Muhammad had, indeed, largely ended the civil strife that had plagued Yathrib, or Medina, for so many years, and that had occasioned his own invitation to the settlement as an arbitrator. Where once there had been division, now there were unity and strength, built solidly on an ideology shared by perhaps the large majority of the residents of the oasis. Where once Yathrib had been vulnerable to intrigue and even to outside attack because of its disunity, Medina could now project its strength far across the Arabian desert. But Muhammad had ended the city's disputes in a way that its leaders and original inhabitants probably did not envision and that some of them clearly did not approve of. He had thoroughly displaced them. Indeed, he had expelled two of the town's once powerful and wealthy Jewish tribes, and had essentially exterminated the third. He had drawn down upon the city the hostility of much of the central Arabian Peninsula, where, not so long ago, nobody had given Yathrib a moment's thought.

Ibn Ubayy, in particular, was still willing to voice these objections. He had sought the leadership of Yathrib earlier, and Muhammad's arrival in the settlement had thwarted his ambitions. He had hoped to become something like a king — a role without precedent in the oasis, but which Muhammad was now filling to perfection. He would have attempted to unify the town, but probably without the foreign ambitions and complications in which the Prophet and his new religion had embroiled it. Muhammad was aware of Ibn Ubayy's scarcely concealed sentiments. Umar suggested that the man be decapitated as a traitor, but the Prophet refused the suggestion, declining to let it be said that Muhammad killed his own companions. But as Ibn Ubayy's murmuring continued, his son, Abd Allah, a very zealous Muslim, grew concerned that the Prophet would eventually find such behavior intolerable and would suspend his scruples and order him killed. So Abd Allah went to Muhammad with an interesting, and to our sensibilities quite unexpected, proposal. If, he said, the Prophet intended to kill Ibn Ubayy, his father, he hoped the assignment would be given to him. For he was, he continued, filled with an unusually strong feeling of duty toward his father, and he feared that, if the order to kill Ibn Ubayy were given to anyone else, he would feel himself irresistibly obliged to avenge the death of his father. Thus he would eventually have to kill the assassin and, having murdered a believer for the sake of an infidel, would go to hell. Therefore, in order to save his own soul, he sought the assignment of murdering his father. Muhammad declined his offer, saying rather that Ibn Ubayy should be treated with gentleness and his companionship enjoyed.

One night in March 628, Muhammad had a dream in which he saw himself, his head shaved like that of a pilgrim, entering the Ka'ba in Mecca, holding its key in his hand. The next day, having related the dream to some of his associates, he invited them to perform the *umra*, or "lesser pilgrimage," with him. Without hesitation they assented, and it was not long before they were under way with seventy camels to be sacrificed and then distributed to the poor in Mecca. Muhammad went bareheaded, wearing the traditional pilgrim's two-piece garb of unstitched cloth, one portion over his shoulders and the other about his waist.

The Prophet's decision to perform the pilgrimage was a dramatic indication of the truly Arabian character of Islam, and was perhaps intended as a signal to the Meccans that their interests would not really be harmed by the new religion. He was no longer campaigning against them, but was seeking to convert them. Still, the Quraysh were naturally alarmed when they heard of the departure of over a thousand Muslims from Medina in the direction of Mecca. As the hereditary guardians of the Ka'ba, they could scarcely block pilgrims from entering the sanctuary, for the shrine had traditionally been open to all. If they were to act in such a manner, they would, in the eyes of many Arabs, not merely Muslims, call into serious question their right to custodianship of the sacred quarter. On the other hand, to allow their archenemy to enter their city and to worship at their shrine without opposition was virtually unthinkable. Additionally, Muslim veneration of the ancient site would obviously mean that the Ka'ba, venerated by Arabs throughout the peninsula, would play a role in Islam. Heretofore that had been, at the least, unclear. But now it would perhaps tend to lessen the resistance of other Arabs to accepting the prophethood of Muhammad and the religion he taught. Meeting in assembly, the leaders of the Quraysh decided that he and his followers could not be permitted to enter the city. But how to keep him out without damaging their own status?

In the meantime Muhammad and the Muslims were drawing ever nearer. When they reached a place known as Hudaybiyya, near the edge of the sacred precincts of Mecca, the Prophet's camel suddenly stopped, knelt, and refused to advance any farther. For Muhammad this was a divine sign. (He had not forgotten the miraculous behavior of the elephant many years before, during Abraha's siege of Mecca.) There was little or no drinkable water at the site, but the traditional accounts tell of a miracle by which fresh water gushed forth in huge amounts for men and animals. Emissaries from the Quraysh now came out from Mecca to ascertain the precise numbers and intentions of the Muslims. Entering the Muslim camp, one of them informed the Prophet that the leaders of the city were determined that he would not enter, and had vowed to fight to the death to prevent it. Muhammad gave a conciliatory reply, offering the people of Mecca time to prepare and to clear the way for his approach, saying that the Muslims had come with no intention of fighting, although they would indeed fight those who stood in their way. Muhammad decided to send his own emissary into Mecca, and he chose Uthman b. Affan, a pious believer whose extensive kinship ties within the city would surely protect him from harm.

While Uthman was in Mecca, a kind of revelation descended on the Prophet — different from those that typically constituted the Qur'an, though, in that he remained conscious and alert to his surroundings while receiving it. The revelation directed Muhammad to have his followers pledge their allegiance to him, one by one. So he seated himself at the foot of an acacia tree while all but one of those present — the exception being one of the "hypocrites," who tried to hide himself — came forward and pledged themselves ready to obey whatever the Prophet had in mind. (He had given them no specific idea as to what was to claim their obedience.) Having thus secured the absolute obedience of his followers (of which, in any event, he could not have entertained much doubt, so frequently had it been illustrated), and with the significant refusal of his camel to advance well in mind, Muhammad was disposed to accept any reasonable offer the leaders of Mecca might proffer.

It was at this point, in fact, that they sent a trio of representatives out to him, in hopes of concluding some sort of treaty. The negotiations went well, for, as is shown in what happened at the conclusion of the discussions, Muhammad proved easy to please. When they had finally reached a mutually acceptable agreement, Muhammad asked Ali, who was serving as scribe, to record the terms of the treaty. He was to begin with the typical Muslim invocation, "In the name of God, the Merciful [*al-rahman*], the Compassionate." But the Quraysh spokesman objected, saying he did not know who or what *al-rahman* was. Rather, he insisted, Ali should write the traditional invocation, "In thy name, O God." This was met with a chorus of animated protests from the Muslims in attendance. But Muhammad directed Ali to accept the Meccan suggestion. Almost immediately thereafter, the Meccans again objected to the language Muhammad wanted to use. When he dictated to Ali "These are the terms of the treaty between Muhammad, the messenger of God, and Suhayl b. Amr," Suhayl erupted. If, he said, the Meccans knew Muhammad to be what he claimed, namely, the messenger of God, they would hardly bar him from the Ka'ba, nor would they have warred against him. Ali should write "Muhammad b. Abd Allah," and nothing more. But Ali had already written "Muhammad, the messenger of God," and when Muhammad asked him to cross the words out, he said he could not in conscience do it. So Muhammad had him point to the words with his finger — there is an unmistakable trace here of the traditional Muslim emphasis on Muhammad's illiteracy as a means of heightening the miracle of the Qur'an — and the Prophet himself crossed them out. Ali then willingly wrote in their place what Suhayl had demanded.

The agreement called for both the Muslims and the Meccans to refrain from fighting for the space of a decade. The Prophet undertook to return to the Quraysh any person who fled to him for refuge or as a convert without having obtained leave from parent, guardian, or master, but anyone fleeing from Medina back to Mecca would be allowed to stay there. Muhammad and his followers would not be permitted to perform the pilgrimage that year, but the Quraysh promised to vacate the city during the coming year for three days, during which Muhammad and the other Muslims would be permitted to come and worship in the sanctuary. Muhammad's followers — very loud among them the impulsive Umar — were horrified at the terms of the agreement. They had come to perform the pilgrimage, and were now obliged to return home to Medina having, in their view, accomplished nothing. What is more, the requirement that Muhammad return runaways while the Quraysh were under no such obligation was manifestly one-sided. (It probably reflected the Prophet's serene confidence in the superior appeal of Islam.) And, to make matters worse, while they yet sat there disappointed at Hudaybiyya, a young Muslim — the son of Suhayl himself, whom Suhayl had imprisoned because of his conversion — had, at this very time, just escaped from Mecca. He entered the Muslim camp to the great joy of his elder brother, who had come from Medina with the Prophet. But, true to the terms of the just-concluded agreement, Muhammad ordered him returned to Mecca.

When the Meccan envoys left the camp, the Prophet ordered his followers to sacrifice their camels as if they had actually completed the pilgrimage, and to shave their heads in pilgrim fashion. During the return journey a revelation descended on Muhammad, giving the view of the truce of Hudaybiyya that has, ever since, been that of believing Muslims around the world. It is recorded, now, in a chapter of the Qur'an known as *Surat al-fath,* "The Chapter of the Victory":

Truly, we have granted unto you a manifest victory. . . .

He it was who sent peace [*al-sakina*] down upon you in the hearts of the believers, that they might increase in faith upon their faith, for to God belong the armies of the heavens and the earth, and God is knowing, wise.

That he might admit the believers, men and women, to gardens beneath which rivers flow, to dwell in them forever, that he might expiate their sins. And that, with God, is a great victory. . . .

Truly, those who pledge their allegiance to you pledge their allegiance to God. The hand of God is over their hands [as they make their pledge], so that anyone who violates his covenant violates it against himself and anyone who fulfills what he has sworn to God, God will grant him great reward. . . .

God was pleased with the believers when they pledged their allegiance to you beneath the tree. He knew what was in their hearts, and he sent peace [*al-sakina*] down upon them, and he rewarded them with imminent victory.[255]

It was, the revelation said, because of believers living quietly and perhaps unknown in Mecca who might have been harmed by battle that God had held the Muslims back from asserting by force their right to perform the pilgrimage. But ultimate triumph would be theirs: "God truly fulfilled the vision for his messenger. You will enter the inviolable mosque, if God wills, safely, with your heads shaved or your hair cut short, fearing nothing. For he knows what you do not know and, besides that, has granted you imminent victory."[256]

Even with such revelatory assurance, however, many of the Muslims must have wondered precisely wherein the victory of Hudaybiyya consisted. Perhaps it was related to the fact that, for the first time, the leadership of the Quraysh had been obliged to negotiate with Muhammad as at least an equal, and as, in effect, a head of state. But there is another plausible angle from which to regard this question. Under the truce agreement it was now possible for people from Mecca and Medina to meet and to speak with one another. This meant that Islam's missionary message could now be conveyed far more freely, even into the heart of hostile Meccan paganism. And there is reason to believe that this had its predictable effect. The early accounts suggest that the number of Muslims doubled over the next two years.

During this period, say the traditional sources, the Prophet dictated letters to the Chosroes, the shah of Persia, the Byzantine emperor Heraclius, the Ethiopian Negus, and the governors of Syria and Egypt, summoning them to accept the religion of Islam. Modern historians have doubted, however, that Muhammad's ambitions for Islam extended beyond the boundaries of the Arabian world, and they have universally dismissed the letters as figments of the imaginations of traditional historians, born of a desire to make of the Prophet a world-historical figure who was recognized as such and was already playing that role during his lifetime. According to the old stories, the shah, when he had

255. Q 48:1, 4-5, 10, 18. The relationship between the *sakina* and the Jewish concept of the *Shekinah* demands further investigation. A good place to begin is Ignaz Goldziher, "La notion de la sakīna chez les Mohamétans," in Ignaz Goldziher, *Gesammelte Schriften*, ed. Joseph DeSomogyi (Hildesheim: Georg Olms Verlagsbuchhandlung, 1969), 3:296-308.
256. Q 48:27.

read Muhammad's epistle, tore it to pieces. "Even so, Lord," said the Prophet, when the Persian king's reaction was related to him, "tear his kingdom from him." Also at this time, not long after the return of the would-be pilgrims from Hudaybiyya, early narratives say a Jewish sorcerer attempted to assassinate Muhammad by means of a magical spell involving knots tied in some clippings from the Prophet's hair, which were attached to a sprig from a palm tree and thrown into a well. The Prophet soon began to feel weak, as well as to sense that his memory was playing disorienting tricks on him. The curse was overcome by the recitation of two brief, recently revealed Qur'anic suras over the well in question. These two passages now form the last chapters of the Qur'an in its standard edition.

The peace with his enemies in Mecca now enabled Muhammad to turn his focus from the south to the north. Initially he concentrated on the oasis of Khaybar, where many of the exiled Banu Nadir had settled. It can scarcely have surprised him that they were deeply hostile to him, seething over their expulsion from Medina, and their hostility had expressed itself in concrete and threatening ways. It is quite probable, for instance, that the attempt by the Jewish sorcerer on the life of the Prophet, just alluded to, was sponsored by those in the oasis. And Khaybari encouragement had goaded the Quraysh into the abortive siege of Medina that had foundered on the edge of Salman's trench. Thus there was good reason for paying attention to the embittered exiles in Khaybar. Moreover, an attack on Khaybar promised rich reward in the form of spoils. Nobody in Medina could forget the Banu Nadir's splashy show of wealth as they marched out of the settlement into exile. And Khaybar itself was famed for its palm groves and its corn.

Unfortunately though, Khaybar also possessed a well-justified reputation for impregnability. And Muhammad was obliged to set off against the oasis with a relatively small force, because the Qur'an forbade him to take with him the desert bedouin who had failed to accompany him during his attempt to make the lesser pilgrimage.[257] The divine revelation consistently called into question the depth of conversion even of those bedouin who professed to have accepted Islam: "The Arabs [i.e., the bedouin] say, 'We believe.' Say, 'You do not believe, but say, "We have submitted [or accepted Islam, *aslamna*]," for belief has not entered your hearts. But if you obey God and his messenger, God will not belittle any of your deeds. Truly, God is forgiving and compassionate.'"[258]

257. Q 48:15-16.
258. Q 49:14. Such comments, and the fact that Islam was actually born in the mercantile environment of an Arabian town — the Qur'an consistently uses commercial metaphors — exposes as essentially nonsense the frequently heard claim that Islam is a religion of the open deserts, a rigorous bedouin monotheism born of the simplicity of sand, endless sky, and a solitary, overwhelming, omnipresent sun.

Since that earlier expedition had promised no booty, the bedouin had shown no interest in it — thus making their motives clear for all to see. As punishment, they were to have no share in the potential spoils of wealthy Khaybar.

When the two forces were finally mustered for engagement, the warriors of Khaybar and their allies numbered fourteen thousand — against which the attacking army from Medina could claim only sixteen hundred, or just over a tenth as many. But the smallness of the Muslim force did make it easier to conceal preparations for the expedition, which were aided by the widespread perception that the canny Muhammad could not really be contemplating an attack against such overwhelming odds. When Muhammad and his army were very close to Khaybar, he obtained the services of a guide and marched his troops — during the night, in complete silence — into the position he desired. It was very dark; the moon had already set. Reports indicate that no birds stirred, no animals sounded the alarm, and nothing moved in Khaybar, so stealthy was the approach of the Medinan force. Even when the sun rose and the time had come for the dawn prayer, it was conducted in virtual silence. Only when the agricultural workers of the oasis came out in the morning with their tools did they notice the Muslim army that had managed to interpose itself between Khaybar and its bedouin allies of the tribe of Ghatafan. In terror, they hastily retreated into their fortified dwellings.

Despite the threat, though, the leadership of the oasis was still confident of its ability to resist. Their numbers were far greater than those of the enemy. More importantly, they felt that their seven fortified strongholds here were more impressive than those they had been obliged to abandon in Medina. Thus, although some warned against it, the council of Khaybar chose not to form a unified battlefront, but rather to rely on the individual strength of its fortresses. In practice this meant that, when the Muslims attacked a fortress, its garrison was on its own. Its Khaybari allies did not come forth to break the siege, which might have changed the outcome of the struggle dramatically, but stayed behind their own walls, complacently attending to their own defenses. Muhammad was thus able to follow a policy of dividing and conquering his opponents, one fortress at a time, and their great numerical advantage was largely neutralized by their own strategic incompetence. Although the strategy of taking the fortified Jews on, one stronghold at a time, undoubtedly tested the patience and endurance of the Muslim forces, the army from Medina had the great advantage of ideologically based unity. "Truly," the Qur'an had declared, "God loves those who fight in his path in order of battle as if they were a firmly compacted building."[259]

The various campaigns to overcome the fortresses of Khaybar were taxing. The defenders of the strongholds showered arrows down on the Muslims

259. Q 61:4.

who were besieging them, wounding many. At first the Medinans seemed to make little headway. But then, during the sixth night of their siege, they caught a spy in their camp who, upon promises that cooperation would save his life, agreed to help them out with information. He was able to tell them which of the fortresses were richest, and which housed caches of valuable weapons. Very importantly, he told them of siege engines that had been used during local civil discords in the past. (Once again, disunity would prove the undoing of the Banu Nadir.) The next day the Muslims took their first fortress. It yielded an engine for casting stones and two devices that would allow men to approach the walls beneath a roof that protected them against arrows. Thereafter the fortresses began to fall one after another. Meanwhile the bedouin allies of Khaybar, the Ghatafan, who had not only promised to come to the aid of the Jews of the oasis but had actually set forth, rather mysteriously returned home to their own families. The Muslim accounts say that this occurred because of a supernatural voice that came to them during the night. In any event, the expected reinforcements from the outside, which could have come in behind the Muslims and caught them from the rear, never arrived.

Meanwhile the siege continued, with the Prophet's son-in-law, Ali, distinguishing himself in the fighting and as the Muslim standard-bearer. The strongest of the Khaybari fortresses was the citadel of Zubayr, which sat high up on a rocky eminence with sheer cliff walls on three sides and a very steep approach to its gate on the fourth. Three days of siege had accomplished nothing, when a Jew from one of the other fortresses came to the Muslims with an offer. If they would spare him, his family, and his property, he would tell them the secret of the citadel of Zubayr. Muhammad, who well knew that war involved stratagem as well as heroism, quickly agreed. The man informed them of a subterranean stream that fed the citadel. The people within had cut steps down to it, protected from the outside, so that they could get water. And, since water was by far the most pressing need for any settlement under siege, they could, having taken care of that need, withstand attack indefinitely. But the Jewish informant showed the Muslims how they could dam the stream and cut off the flow of water to the defenders of the citadel. Since they had been supremely sure of their water supply, the defenders had never troubled themselves to keep a reserve. The effect was not long in coming. Forced by thirst to emerge from behind their walls, the warriors of the citadel of Zubayr were defeated in fierce fighting.

The last of the fortresses to put up real resistance was known as Qamus. Although it held out for two weeks, it too eventually fell, the Prophet granting the promise to its leaders that, if they left Khaybar and abandoned all their wealth, their lives would be spared. However, he reserved the right to annul that agreement if it were found that they had attempted to conceal any of their possessions. Unfortunately the leaders attempted to do just that. But the Muslims were not taken in. This was one of the richest of the Jewish clans, and one that had flaunted its wealth when it had withdrawn from Medina some years before. Nobody, therefore, was willing to accept its protestations that it had turned over all of its considerable possessions when in fact there was remarkably little brought forward. It took little time to find the hidden treasure, and the leader of the clan and one of his relatives paid with their lives for this attempt to deceive the Muslims and their prophet. The two fortresses that had remained defiant with Qamus now surrendered on the same terms that it had been granted. But they and their surviving fellow Jews now begged the Prophet to allow them to remain in the oasis. They were, they noted, experts in the agricultural work that was the settlement's chief source of wealth; who else would take care of the palm trees and the other crops? Muhammad saw the logic of their appeal and agreed to let them stay, demanding that they pay him an annual rent amounting to half the produce of the town and reserving the right to expel them in the future should he deem it wise to do so or regard them as rebellious.

Hearing what had happened, the Jews of the adjacent oasis of Fadak — smaller than Khaybar but still quite wealthy — hastened to submit to the Prophet on the same conditions, fearing that they would eventually be compelled anyway to submit to such terms or worse, and at the cost of many of their lives. Since it had not been won as booty in fighting, Fadak became the personal property of Muhammad (which, it should be noted, he generally used to help his poorer followers). The Prophet's triumph was marred somewhat by an attempt to assassinate him not long after the surrender terms had been settled, via a poisoned lamb that was served to him by one of the Jewish women. She had lost her father, her uncle, and her husband in the fighting, and was understandably bitter. Although the Prophet, it is said, instantly discerned the poison via supernatural gifts and spat it from his mouth, one of the other Muslims died from the lamb. Nonetheless, after questioning the woman, Muhammad pardoned her.

Mecca Submits

Finally the time drew near when, according to the terms of the truce at Hudaybiyya, Muhammad and his followers were to be allowed to enter Mecca to perform the rituals of the lesser pilgrimage. When the two thousand Muslims reached the edge of the sacred precincts of Mecca in March 629, the Quraysh withdrew, as they had promised, to the tops of the hills that surrounded the town, leaving the hollow of the valley where Mecca and its shrine lay open to the Prophet and those accompanying him. Muhammad came mounted on his favorite camel, while the others either rode or walked. They came with heads bare and dressed in white robes, in the traditional manner of Meccan pilgrims. Not hesitating anywhere else in the town, the Muslims went directly to the sacred enclosure of the Kaʿba. Muhammad, who had been absent from his native town for seven years, rode to the building's southeastern corner and there touched the black stone with the staff that he carried. Having done so, he circled the Kaʿba seven times and then traveled seven times back and forth between the hill known as Safa and another hill called Marwa. Closing that part of the ritual at the latter hill, he sacrificed a camel and had his head shaved.

Thus far Muhammad had complied with the traditional requirements of the lesser pilgrimage. Now he wished to enter the Kaʿba. But the leaders of the Quraysh, aware that such entry was not part of the traditional observances, had kept the key with them and informed a Muslim emissary sent to fetch it that yielding up the key was not among their treaty obligations. Muhammad was obliged, therefore, to forgo entering the shrine that year. But he did direct Bilal to climb onto the roof of the Kaʿba and intone the noon call to prayer. For the very first time the Muslim profession of faith, "I testify that there is no god but God; I testify that Muhammad is the messenger of God," rang out openly, loudly, and defiantly through the streets and the valley of Mecca. Hudaybiyya, it must now have been clear, had indeed been a victory.

Upon his return from the pilgrimage, Muhammad again turned his attention northward. He sent a delegation up to the Syrian border, summoning one of the Arab tribes there to accept Islam. The delegation was assaulted, and only one of them returned alive. The Prophet then sent a messenger to Bostra, the Byzantine headquarters. But the messenger was intercepted and murdered by a chief of the Byzantines' Christian Arab allies, the Ghassanids. Determined to punish the Ghassanids, Muhammad organized an army of roughly three thousand men and dispatched them under the leadership of his adoptive son, Zayd. The Prophet told the troops that if Zayd were killed, a man named Jaʿfar was to assume his place. And if Jaʿfar, in his turn, were slain, one Abd Allah b. Rawaha was to take charge of the expedition. Finally, if all three were killed or incapacitated, the troops were to choose themselves a leader.

According to the ancient accounts, Abd Allah was determined to find martyrdom for himself during this expedition, and his desire would prove to have consequences for more than just himself. When the Muslim force reached the borders of Syria, intelligence came to them of a much larger enemy army than they were prepared to meet. (Some said there were as many as a hundred thousand troops in the Byzantine-Arab force — which was doubtless a wild exaggeration. Still, there were more in the opposing army than the Muslims had envisioned.) Zayd decided to stop and hold a council. Many of those who expressed themselves counseled that, in the light of rather dramatically changed circumstances, they should send to the Prophet for further guidance. He might choose to call them back to Medina. Otherwise he would surely send them reinforcements. But Abd Allah was against either option. They should attack, he insisted. For either way, they would win. If they were victorious, it would be a magnificent triumph for the army of God. If, however, they were killed, they would go directly to paradise as martyrs and enjoy the delights of the heavenly garden. There was simply no bad option.

Abd Allah's opinion prevailed. So the Muslim army continued marching to the north, up to the region near the south end of the Dead Sea in Palestine. There they caught their first glimpse of the Byzantine forces and their Arab allies, who not only outnumbered them but represented a far more sophisticated fighting force than anything Muslims had yet confronted. Zayd gave the order to withdraw to the south, toward a place called Mu'ta that he deemed advantageous. The enemy pursued. Then, suddenly, Zayd ordered his men to stop their retreat and to attack. Zayd himself carried the white battle standard of his army against the foe. In the ensuing struggle, first Zayd was killed, then Ja'far took up the standard until he died, and finally Abd Allah took it and led a charge in which he was granted his dream of martyrdom. In the end Khalid b. al-Walid, the same Khalid who had led important Qurayshi cavalry units at Uhud and the battle of the trench but had now become a Muslim, took command of the beleaguered Muslim force. Amidst the chaos of battle, he was able to regroup his army and to drive the Byzantines and their allies back at least sufficiently to allow a safe Muslim retreat. It was Khalid's first commanding role as a Muslim, but it would not be his last. He would go on to win glory and fame in the Arab conquests after the death of the Prophet. And, although Mu'ta was an undeniable defeat for Muhammad's warriors, Khalid's role in saving the Muslim army from even greater disaster was memorialized thereafter by his bearing the title "the sword of Islam." The early Arabic sources say that only five other Muslims lost their lives that day, besides the three appointed leaders of the expedition.[260]

The loss of his much-loved "son" Zayd was difficult for Muhammad, and the traditional narratives, which claim that he saw the whole battle in vision as it unfolded, represent him as weeping uncontrollably at the death. Had he lived, Zayd might have succeeded Muhammad as the leader of the Islamic community.[261] The Prophet was comforted that very night, however, by a vision of Zayd and the other martyrs of Mu'ta in the gardens of paradise. But Muhammad's personal loss was not the only concern that arose from the defeat. Emboldened by the events at Mu'ta, some of the northern Arabs decided to chal-

260. The casualty figures are a bit suspicious. Why, in so large a battle, would all of the Muslim commanders perish while the losses among the ordinary soldiers were so low?
261. This is the suggestion of Watt, p. 157.

lenge the nascent Islamic state to their south, whose obviously growing ambitions were undoubtedly and quite understandably beginning to worry them. Many were finding the Prophet's movement very alluring. The momentum was on his side, and Muhammad had consistently demonstrated that he was a highly effective enemy. (The Quraysh, powerful though they were, had been thwarted by him at every turn.) At the same time, though, he had shown himself to be a generous and reliable ally, as well as an increasingly powerful one. For those who could tell which way the wind was blowing, Islam was clearly the party of the future. Thus purely secular motives — political and, in a sense, economic — made alliances with the Muslim state or even professions of Islamic faith increasingly attractive. Many of the tribes around Medina now hastened to line up with its ruler. But of course, the religious appeal of Islam was also a major factor. The doctrines of Muhammad offered meaning and purpose, and consolation in times of trial and loss, and they lacked both the ethnic exclusivism of Judaism, at least as the Arabs knew it, and the complex doctrines (trinitarian, christological, and others) of Christianity. But it would probably be folly, in any given case, to attempt to separate secular from spiritual appeal with absolute finality. In the Arabia of the seventh century, as indeed at any other time and place, human motives were inextricably mixed. Those who did not yet feel the allure of Islam, however, found Muhammad's increasing power a menace. Only a month after the death of Zayd, word reached the Prophet that Arab tribesmen were gathering on the Syrian border for a march to the south. In response Muhammad sent first one military unit and then another as a reinforcement toward Syria. The quick military response seems to have intimidated the tribesmen, and they dispersed with little fighting.

In the south, meanwhile, an event took place that was to have fatal and final consequences for the rule of the pagan Quraysh in Mecca. Not long after the successful expedition to Syria, fighting broke out in and around the sacred precincts of the city between allies of the Quraysh and allies of Medina. The Quraysh are said to have supplied weapons to their allies, and one or two of them even joined in the fighting. (They did so during the night, hoping that the darkness would protect their identity — which indicates that they very likely knew the political risk to which their actions were exposing them.) The tribe affiliated with Muhammad lost no time in sending a delegation to the Prophet, informing him of the wrongs they had suffered and calling on him to come to their aid. He declared that he would indeed. The Prophet was very angry at what had happened, and he regarded the fighting, and most particularly the surreptitious participation of the Quraysh in it, as a breach of the truce of Hudaybiyya. But there can be little doubt, too, that he recognized this as an opportunity. He was stronger than ever before, and he perhaps saw it as time to put an end to pagan rule in Mecca once and for all. When the Meccan leadership, suddenly aware of the potentially disastrous consequences of the incident, dispatched Abu Sufyan to Medina to attempt to ward off a breach of the truce, Muhammad treated him with deliberate coolness.

In fact, it is difficult not to feel some pity for the once proud lord of the Quraysh, even at the remove of centuries, as he tried to find some sympathetic or even listening ear among the Muslims. Rebuffed by the Prophet, Abu Sufyan went to visit his daughter, Umm Habiba, who, by now widowed of her first husband, had become one of Muhammad's wives. They had not seen each other for fifteen years, but he naturally hoped the ties of father to daughter would still incline her to listen to him and perhaps intervene on his behalf with the Prophet. But her reaction, too, was disdainful. As Abu Sufyan was about to sit down, she hastily (and quite literally) pulled the rug out from under him and folded it up. Addressing her in affectionate terms, the unsuspecting father asked if she had done so because it was too good for him, or because he was too good for such a rug. "It is the Prophet's rug," she explained. Her father, an impure idolater, was unworthy to sit on it. How, she demanded, could he, a lord of the Quraysh, bring himself to worship stones, mere idols that have power neither to see nor to hear? Why had he not accepted Islam? Shocked by her lack of daughterly respect, perhaps, Abu Sufyan was also astonished at her demand that he abandon the religion of his ancestors. "Am I," he asked, "to abandon that which my ancestors worshiped in order to follow the religion of Muhammad?"[262] But that is precisely what his daughter demanded of him. And, sensing that no help was to be gained from her, Abu Sufyan moved on. He went to Abu Bakr, but to no avail. He spoke with others he had once known in Mecca. They could offer him nothing. Finally he went to Ali, who was unmoved. In desperation the Meccan chief turned to Ali's wife, Fatima, the daughter of the Prophet, and to her son Hasan, who was sitting on the floor at her feet, and begged them to intervene. They would not. He repeated his imploring of Ali, made one last appeal to Muhammad himself, and then returned home to Mecca, having accomplished nothing and filled with foreboding about the future.

Muhammad immediately began to signal to those closest to him that he intended to march on Mecca, because the Quraysh had broken their agreement. But preparations were to be kept secret, and the leadership of the enemy were to be kept as much as possible in the dark about his intentions. Indeed, even after the expedition had set forth, only a very few of the warriors had any certain idea against whom they were marching. At one point, when rumors were flying and the men were agonizing with curiosity, Ka'b b. Malik got up the nerve to approach the Prophet and attempt to get an answer to the question everybody was asking. Hesitant to pose the question directly, he instead recited a poem he had

262. Once again we see an indication of a rather passionate pagan religiosity.

just composed, according to which the men were now reduced to drawing their swords and asking them if they knew against which enemy they would be used. The Prophet smiled, but answered nothing. When the army was finally assembled, it is said to have numbered something on the order of ten thousand. No Muslim who was capable of fighting was left behind. There were seven hundred "Emigrants," including three hundred on horseback. Four thousand of the Yathribi "Helpers" formed another portion of the army, including five hundred cavalry. The rest were the tribal allies of Medina, including many who joined the army as it passed by. Nine hundred mounted warriors from the Banu Sulaym added greatly to the strength of the Muslim expedition.

Arriving at Mecca, Muhammad used a trick he had employed before, when following the Quraysh after the battle of Uhud. He ordered his men to spread out and to light, each one, an individual campfire. Thus, when the Quraysh's spies surveyed the Muslim army that night, they saw ten thousand fires burning, and their hearts sank. Again Abu Sufyan was dispatched to see if talking could accomplish anything. When he was ushered into the Prophet's tent, Abu Sufyan began to rebuke him, faulting Muhammad for coming against his native city, his relatives, with such an assortment of men, some of them kin of the residents of Mecca and some of them unrelated and unknown. But Muhammad would have none of it. The conflict was not his responsibility, he said. It was the Quraysh who had broken the truce of Hudaybiyya and polluted the sacred enclosure by aiding and even participating in the violence against his allies, the Banu Ka'b. Abu Sufyan responded, not unreasonably, by suggesting that Muhammad's enmity ought to be concentrated instead on the primary perpetrators of the violence. After all, he pointed out, the Hawazin were the guilty party, and besides, they were even fiercer enemies of the Prophet than the Quraysh and not his relatives. In words that must have chilled the Meccan leader, Muhammad responded that he hoped, indeed, to punish the Hawazin — by conquering Mecca, establishing Islam as the religion of the city, and then going after them from a position of strength in the headquarters of their old ally. He thereupon turned to Abu Sufyan and his two fellow emissaries and ordered them to bear testimony of the unity of God and his own prophethood. Abu Sufyan's two companions immediately professed their faith in Islam by bearing the desired testimony. By contrast, the Qurayshi chief declared only that there was no god but God — in itself, a not insignificant concession for a pagan Arab — but could not bring himself to declare that Muhammad was the messenger of God. When he was told to make the second profession of faith, he asked for a temporary reprieve and was allowed to spend the night in the Muslim camp. He was awakened very early the next morning by the call to dawn prayer. Demanding to know what it meant, he was told that it was the first of five daily prayers, which struck him as excessive. But he was impressed that Muhammad had been able to persuade his people to perform frequent rituals. And he was even more impressed when he witnessed how deferential the normally rather anarchic Arabs were to their prophet-leader. Finally, pressed by his hosts, he asked to be taken to Muhammad, where he bore record of his conviction, not only that there was no god but God, but that Muhammad was God's messenger. In a very real sense, now that its leader had accepted Islam, Meccan paganism was dead. Muhammad's uncle Abbas, feeling compassion for his friend, kinsman, and former leader, now drew the Prophet aside and asked him to grant to Abu Sufyan some gesture that would help him preserve his honor and status after his surrender to Islam. Muhammad, who showed repeatedly throughout his life that he could be magnanimous in triumph, agreed without hesitation. He told the Qurayshi delegation to return to Mecca and tell the people there that, during the Muslim entry into the city, whoever had entered the dwelling of Abu Sufyan would be safe, as well as those who locked themselves within their own doors and those who sought sanctuary in the inner precincts of the Ka'ba.

The Medinan force prepared for its entry into the city. Muhammad divided the army into four parts. The central column of the expedition, in which Muhammad himself rode, was divided in two, while Zubayr led the column on the left and Khalid b. al-Walid — who, just two years before, had blocked the Muslims from approaching Mecca — commanded the column on the right. The four units now divided, with Khalid to enter the city from below and the three other groups coming down to the city from three passes in the hills surrounding. There was little resistance. Three of the Qurayshi chieftains, including Khalid's old cavalry colleague Ikrima, had gathered together a force of Meccans and bedouin allies, and when they saw Khalid's division approaching the city, they came down from the hills to attack it. It was an uneven battle, however, and the Muslims repulsed them — killing about thirty while losing only two — and continued into the city. Ikrima and one of his fellow leaders fled to the coast on horseback; the third leader, a man named Suhayl, escaped to his house and, now complying with the terms Muhammad had laid down to Abu Sufyan, locked himself behind his door.

When the Prophet entered the city, he went directly to the southeastern corner of the Ka'ba, where the black stone is mounted in the wall of the structure, and, as he had done the previous year during the lesser pilgrimage, touched the stone with his staff. As he did so, he exclaimed, "Allahu akbar! Allahu akbar!" meaning "God is most great!" repeated twice. Those standing nearest him repeated it, and then all of those in the shrine picked it up until Muhammad motioned with his hand and bade them be silent. Then he circumambulated the Ka'ba seven times, mounted. Following his circumambulation, he turned his attention to the idols that stood in a circle around the shrine. Tradition has it that there were 360 of them, which, if true, would seem to suggest an astronomical or calendrical association. He recited a verse from the Qur'an: "Truth has come," he declared, "and falsehood has vanished away. Indeed, falsehood vanishes by nature."[263] Then he destroyed each of the surrounding idols. (The traditional accounts say he simply pointed his staff at each of them, one after another, and they fell over.) He decreed that the idols be burned, and that Hubal, the largest of them, be smashed into pieces. Additionally, every home possessing a domestic idol or figurine was to see that it was destroyed. He prayed at the so-called "station of Abraham" and then proceeded to the well of Zamzam, where he took a drink. Following this, Muhammad entered the Ka'ba itself. Inside, all the walls of the building had been adorned with paintings of pagan deities. These he ordered Uthman to destroy, with the exception of a painting of an old man who was said to be Abraham and that of a painting of the Virgin Mary and the infant Jesus, an icon, over which he placed his hand in a gesture of protection.

By this time many of the Meccans who had taken refuge in the Ka'ba and in their homes were gathered near the shrine, waiting to see what their new lord would do and say. Muhammad turned to them and spoke to them the words attributed by the Qur'an to the patriarch Joseph when, in forgiveness, he addressed his treacherous brothers, who had come to him in Egypt in hopes of temporal salvation and had belatedly recognized him for who he really was. "Truly," he declared, "I say as my brother Joseph said: 'There shall be no blame upon you today. God, the most merciful of those who show mercy, will forgive you.'"[264] The *harams* of Mecca and Medina were now coalesced under one lord, Muhammad.[265]

And he was indeed clement — quite contrary to the image by which he has been stigmatized in the West, of bloodthirstiness and cruelty. Perhaps only four people were executed as part of the Muslim seizure of Mecca, and these were, characteristically, poets and people who had satirized the Prophet. The actual leaders of the Quraysh were not only spared, but were treated with extreme generosity. When he was done in the city, Muhammad withdrew to the hill of Safa, very near to Mecca, and received the submission (*islam*) of hundreds of Meccans who came to profess their acceptance of his God and his prophetic authority. Among these was Hind, Abu Sufyan's wife, who had tasted of the liver of the Prophet's uncle Hamza at the battle of Uhud, and whose hatred of Islam and the Prophet had been implacable. Fearing for her life, she came before him wearing a veil and professed her submission before she identified her-

---

263. Q 17:81.
264. Q 12:92.
265. Serjeant, "Haram and Hawtah," pp. 55-56. Even today, Mecca and Medina are referred to as *al-Haramayn*, "the two sanctuaries."

self. Muhammad welcomed her. He also pardoned Ikrima in absentia, at the behest of that warrior's wife.

The conquest of Mecca, though it dealt a crippling blow to Arabian paganism, had not yet eliminated it completely. No sooner was the situation in Mecca under control, in January 630, than Muhammad sent Khalid with a small detachment to Nakhla, where the principal shrine of the important pre-Islamic goddess al-Uzza was located. The guardian of the temple, say the Muslim accounts, learning of the approach of the victorious Muslims under their intimidating commander, girded the statue of the goddess with his sword and bade her defend herself. She did not, and Khalid demolished her shrine. But the Hawazin, the former allies of the Quraysh who had been centrally involved in the difficulties that led to Muhammad's attack on Mecca, were a far more dangerous enemy, and they remained. Indeed, Abu Sufyan's claim seems to have been accurate, that they were even more hostile to Muhammad than the Quraysh. Probably they saw the weakness and then the defeat of their old rival, Mecca, as an opportunity to seize control of its dominance in trade and to claim its religious prestige for themselves.

About two weeks after the occupation of Mecca by its new Muslim overlords, word came to Muhammad that Hawazin, mobilizing to the north of Ta'if, a town less than a hundred kilometers to the east-southeast of Mecca, had managed to put together an army of approximately twenty thousand warriors bent on attacking him in his new possession. Ta'if was the stronghold of the Thaqif tribe and was centered on a *haram* dedicated to the goddess al-Lat, which rivaled the sanctuary in Mecca.[266] The Prophet decided not to wait for them, but to go out on the offensive. He took with him the entire army with which he had come against Mecca, but which was now augmented with an additional two thousand men from the Quraysh of the city. Most of them were newly converted Muslims, but even a few of those who had not yet accepted Islam came out to fight in defense of their hometown and families.

When the two armies joined in battle, it was in a valley called Hunayn. The Hawazin launched a furious attack and, at the first, seemed to sweep the Muslim forces away. Indeed, many turned and fled. Muhammad, however, made a stand with a few of his closest associates and called for the others to cease their flight and to turn and stand with him. In the chaos and the noise, his voice could scarcely be heard. Gradually though, the tide of battle turned, and the warriors of Hawazin were themselves forced to flee, some to the oasis of Nakhla and some to the walled city of Ta'if. Muslim casualties had been heavy at the first, but in the rout with which the battle culminated they had inflicted heavy losses on their enemy while taking relatively few of their own. They captured many Hawazin women and children, for these had been just behind the

---

266. Serjeant, "Haram and Hawtah," p. 52.

enemy lines, and they took large numbers of livestock as well as four thousand ounces of silver that they found among the spoils.

The Prophet pursued the enemy all the way to Ta'if, where he besieged them behind their fortifications. But Ta'if was admirably equipped to withstand such a siege, and it had a year's supply of provisions within its walls. Moreover, the men of the city demonstrated that their reputation as expert bowmen was well deserved, and they made the besieging army pay dearly whenever it let down its guard. After nearly a month, Muhammad concluded that little was to be gained by prolonging the siege, and he lifted it. As the Muslim army was pulling away, some of his followers appealed to him to pronounce a curse upon the city and its recalcitrant residents. He made no other response than to lift his hands in the attitude of prayer and to ask God to guide the people of Ta'if and to lead them to him and the acceptance of Islam.

The battle at Hunayn was yet another great and remarkable victory for Muhammad and Islam, and a revelation commemorated it not long thereafter:

Truly, God has helped you on many battlefields, and on the day of Hunayn, when you were so pleased with your numbers but they availed you nothing, and the earth, for all its spaciousness, constrained you and you turned to flee.

But God caused his serenity [*sakinatuhu*] to descend upon his messenger and upon the believers, and he caused armies that you could not see to descend, and he punished those who disbelieve — that being the reward of the unbelievers.[267]

With the battle now behind them, members of Muhammad's army were eager, in the typical fashion of ancient Arabia, to divide up the booty. Muhammad stalled on the division of the spoils, however, for, as had been made clear by his raising of the siege against Ta'if, he had decided to treat his opponents there with leniency and to see if he could thereby win their hearts to Islam without further fighting. But the one-fifth portion of the spoils that came to him under Islamic practice was another thing altogether. The same Qur'anic revelation that had commented on the battle of Hunayn had also given him guidance on what to do with the alms that came his way — and these spoils were, he considered, to be used in precisely the same manner. "Alms are for the poor," the revelation explained, "and for the needy, and for those who collect them, and for those whose hearts are to be reconciled, for those in bondage and those in debt, and in the path of God, and for the wayfarer — an obligation from God, God being knowing and wise."[268]

267. Q 9:25-26.
268. Q 9:60.

Among "those whose hearts are to be reconciled," the Prophet clearly considered his recent allies of the Quraysh. So he treated them with remarkable generosity. To Abu Sufyan he gave a hundred camels. And when Abu Sufyan asked if his two sons, Yazid and the future caliph and founder of the Umayyad dynasty Muawiya, could not expect something as well, Muhammad gave to each of them a further one hundred camels.

The sources depict Muhammad returning to his adopted home in Medina from his victory at Hunayn and his conquest of Mecca in a reflective mood, as well he might have been. He told some of his followers that they were returning now from the lesser jihad to the greater jihad. Puzzled as to how he could be talking about any greater "holy war" than the one they had just concluded by their triumph over the capital city of Arabian paganism, they asked him what he meant. The greater jihad, the Prophet replied, alluding to the primary meaning of the word, which is not literally "war" but "struggle," is the struggle with one's own soul.

Arabia under Muhammad

The momentum continued to run in favor of Muhammad and his religion, as is shown in the conversion to Islam of Ka'b b. al-Zuhayr, one of the leading poets of the day. He had spent most of his life among the desert Arabs of Ghatafan, the allies of the Jews of Khaybar, and had therefore not entered Islam previously. Indeed, he had mocked the revelations of Muhammad and satirized the Prophet himself. But the conquest of Mecca helped him change his mind, and one day he appeared in the mosque at Medina, approached the Prophet, and took him by the hand. "O messenger of God," he said, "if Ka'b b. al-Zuhayr were to come to you, repentant, a Muslim, asking you to grant him immunity, would you receive him if I were to bring him to you?" Muhammad answered, quite in character, that he would. At that, Ka'b identified himself. One of the nearby Muslims instantly stood up and offered to decapitate the poet, but the Prophet forbade him. Ka'b, he pointed out, had repented, and was no longer an enemy of Islam but instead a brother Muslim.

Muhammad once again turned his attention to the north, toward Syria, and began to gather a huge army for a campaign against the Byzantines. His decision seems to have been precipitated by rumors — essentially baseless, as it turned out — of plans for a massive Byzantine offensive against the rising Muslim threat in Medina. But he may also have felt the need to channel the energies of his followers into outward aggression, since the time-honored Arab practice of raiding one another was no longer permitted among Muslims. Certainly the weakness of the Byzantines, who had just concluded their long war with the

Persians, invited such attack, although the Prophet's primary goal was probably more to influence the Christian Arabs of northern Arabia and Syria than to confront the Byzantine Empire directly.

Muhammad made no attempt at covert activity this time; the summons for troops was sent out to Mecca and the tribal allies of the Muslims throughout Arabia. Not everybody was enthusiastic about the opportunity. It was one thing to fight desert bedouins, but quite another (as Mu'ta had clearly illustrated) to confront the professional soldiers of Constantinople, the successor state to imperial Rome. Additionally, the weather in the fall of 630 was unusually hot. Arabia, always dry, was in the grip of a drought. And it was harvest season. Still, an army of thirty thousand men, a third of them mounted, gathered to obey the command of the Prophet of God.

When they were ready, Muhammad came out to their encampment to take personal command. According to the traditional sources, he had asked his son-in-law, Ali, to stay behind and care for his wives and family. Some of the dissidents — the "hypocrites," who were still present in Medina even after the Prophet's long string of triumphs — began to spread disruptive tales that Ali had been left behind because Muhammad didn't like him and couldn't endure his presence. Ali, a legendarily heroic warrior who was probably already distressed at being left out of a great and important expedition, was now thoroughly upset. He donned his armor, grabbed his weapons, and set out in pursuit of Muhammad. When he caught up with him, he told him the kinds of rumors and murmuring he was being subjected to, and implored the Prophet to let him join the army. Muhammad denied the motives the "hypocrites" were imputing to him, but he also denied Ali's request. "Return," he ordered him, "and represent me among my family and yours. Aren't you satisfied, Ali, that you should be to me as Aaron was to Moses (except that, after me, there is to be no prophet)?" The story is, frankly, a bit suspicious. It seems too clearly to be constructing a basis for the succession of Ali as caliph after the death of Muhammad — the position of the Shi'ites — particularly in its careful formulation of an authoritative role for Ali that nonetheless closes the door on future claims of revelation or prophethood.

The Muslim army eventually reached a spring called Tabuk, located roughly midway between Medina and Jerusalem, and remained there for nearly three weeks. By the end of this period, it had become clear that the rumors of a Byzantine offensive against the Muslims were untrue, and perhaps the heat and drought had also become simply too oppressive. Whatever the precise motive, the Prophet took the main body of the Muslim force back to Medina, having engaged in no military action. But he did not return without results. During his stay at Tabuk, Muhammad entered into a truce agreement with some of the Jews and Christians who lived at the head of the Gulf of Aqaba (also known today, on some maps, as the Gulf of Eilat) and down its eastern coast. The Islamic state guaranteed them protection in exchange for an annual tribute, and thus greatly expanded the effective range of its rule. He also sent Khalid and a cavalry force of 420 to seize control of a stronghold called Dumat al-Jandal, located northeast of Tabuk along the road between Medina and Iraq and Syria.

When the Prophet had arrived back in Medina, he was visited by a delegation from the besieged city of Ta'if, offering to accept Islam and seeking a guarantee of safety for their families, their animals, and their lands. Although the Muslim forces outside their fortified town had made no progress on gaining entry into Ta'if, they had managed to make life very difficult indeed for its residents. Ironically, the leader of the forces opposing Muhammad at the nearly disastrous battle of Hunayn, a very effective fighter named Malik b. Awf, had since converted to Islam, and now made the life of the Banu Thaqif quite unpleasant. By the time of their delegation to the Prophet, they were surrounded not only by the besieging armies of the Muslims but by numerous communities that had accepted the religion of Islam and saw it as their duty to intercept any caravans bound for or leaving Ta'if and to seize any livestock sent out to graze on the city's pasturelands. Malik's men had furthermore promised to execute any Thaqifi they captured, unless he foreswore polytheism and entered Islam.

Muhammad readily accepted his erstwhile enemies into the Islamic community and, by that very act, granted them and their lands and goods protected status under the authority of the Medinan state. That did not, however, exhaust their requests. Could they retain their idol of the goddess al-Lat for three years? No, the Prophet replied, they could not. And he likewise refused their requests for a respite of two years, or just one year, or even one month. But he did grant that they would not be required to destroy their venerable idol with their own hands, and he sent one of his disciples, accompanied by Abu Sufyan, to take care of that duty. When they asked to be excused from the requirement of five daily prayers, he refused that, too, commenting that a religion that required no regular daily prayers was without value.

The residents of Ta'if were not alone in sensing that the tide had turned irrevocably against the old paganism, and that Muhammad and his Medinan state were the future of Arabia. The ninth year of the *hijra* is frequently labeled "the year of delegations" in the traditional sources. Emissaries came from various quarters of the Arabian Peninsula, pledging fealty to the Prophet and often renouncing polytheism and accepting Islam. In exchange Muhammad pledged the treaty protection of his new government, on condition that they receive his representatives well and remit their taxes to Medina. Needless to say, there was some reason to question whether all these conversions were entirely sincere or totally motivated by spiritual conviction, but Muhammad was happy to accept pledges of support and loyalty no matter their motivation, if they were kept.

Christians and Jews were also to receive the Prophet's protection, and would not be forced to convert to the new religion. On the other hand they were asked to pay a slightly higher tax. Adherents of Judaism and Christianity received protected status alongside those of Islam itself, all of them being considered "peoples of the Book." When a delegation from the Christians of Najran, to the south, came to Medina with hopes of a treaty covenant with Muhammad, the Prophet permitted them to pray in the mosque there, although their prayer was directed not to Mecca, which lay almost due south of Medina, but toward the east, the direction of sunrise. They spent considerable time in theological discussion with Muhammad, disputing with him the nature of Jesus, whether he was the Son of God or merely, much like every other human being, one of God's creatures. In the end they agreed to disagree, and the Prophet granted them his protection and that of his Islamic community for their churches and all that they owned.

Muhammad's tolerance of these Christians was fully consistent with the revelations he had received, in which God spoke to him and said:

> Truly we revealed the Torah, in which was guidance and light and by which the prophets and the rabbis and the learned scholars judged. . . .
>
> And we sent Jesus, the son of Mary, in their footsteps, confirming the Torah that had come before him, and we gave him the Gospel, in which was guidance and light, confirming the Torah that had come before him — a guidance and an admonition to the God-fearing.
>
> Let the people of the Gospel judge according to that which God has revealed in it. And whoever does not judge according to what God has revealed, they are transgressors.
>
> And we revealed the Book to you in truth, confirming the book that came before it. . . . To each one of you we have given a law and a path, and, had God willed it, he would have made you one people. But in order to test you according to what he has given you [he has not done so]. So compete with one another in good works. The return of all of you is unto God. Then he will inform you about that in which you have disagreed.[269]

The same tolerance did not, however, apply to paganism, which was not accepted as a religion of "the Book" or of revelation, but rather as an evil instance of rebellion and apostasy against God. When the time of the greater pilgrimage next approached, Muhammad let it be known that pagans would be permitted to participate in the ancient rites only one more season, and would then be banned from the precincts of the Kaʿba. Furthermore, nobody would

---

269. Q 5:44, 46-48.

be allowed to circumambulate the Ka'ba naked after that year, as some pagans occasionally did. Pagans would be given a grace period of four months to repent, but after that there was no guarantee of protection. Indeed, a war was effectively declared against any idolaters holding out beyond that period, and they were promised that, when the four months had expired, unless they could point to some special preexisting treaty with the Prophet, they would be taken captive or killed wherever they were found.[270]

Muhammad had now reached a respectably advanced age, by Arabian standards. If he was not precisely old, he was nonetheless clearly no longer young. Yet he had not been fortunate in his posterity. Among all of his wives, only Khadija had thus far borne children to the Prophet. And when another child did come, it arrived via his beloved Coptic Christian concubine, Mariya. Having received a vision of the angel Gabriel during the night of the baby's birth, in which Gabriel addressed the Prophet as "father of Ibrahim," Muhammad gave to his new son the Arabic form of the name of the great biblical patriarch, the father of the monotheistic tradition. Muhammad loved the boy dearly, visiting him almost daily and often taking his midday rest with the baby.

Unfortunately the little boy was not destined to live. Muhammad was with the child as he died and, when the struggle was over, took Ibrahim in his arms and wept deeply. Earlier he had forbidden Muslims to engage in overly dramatic displays of grief or affliction, and some now questioned him about what they thought must be a double standard. But Muhammad responded that it was not sorrow that he forbade, nor the expression of sorrow, but exaggerated shows and even counterfeits of such emotion. Then he addressed his dead son: "O Ibrahim, if it were not that the promise of reunion is certain, and that this is a path that all must walk, and that the last of us shall catch up with the first, truly we would grieve for you with a greater sorrow still." Yet later, after the little boy had been buried, the Prophet sprinkled some water on the grave and tenderly smoothed the surface of the earth that covered his son's body. "It does no harm," he said, "and it does no good, but it does give some relief to the soul of an afflicted person."

Abu Bakr was delegated to direct the hajj in 631, but the Prophet announced that he would personally lead the next great Meccan pilgrimage. Multitudes came to Medina from all over Arabia, including many of the desert bed-

---

270. It may well be significant that (as is noted in Lings, p. 323 n. 1) this revelation, which appears in the Qur'an as the *Surat al-tawba*, "the chapter of repentance," is the only one of the 114 chapters in the sacred book of the Muslims that does not begin with the words *Bismi Allah al-rahman al-rahim* (typically rendered "In the name of God, the Merciful, the Compassionate"). The absence of that formula certainly serves to heighten the sternness of the warning declared in the chapter.

ouin, eager to participate in the venerable rituals of the hajj under the personal tutelage of the Lord's messenger himself. Probably few if any suspected that it would be their only opportunity to do so. This would be the first year (at least since the ancient days of Abraham and his first descendants) when all the participants in the rites would be monotheists. When Muhammad left Medina, he not only took all of his wives with him but, so the accounts say, thirty thousand Muslim pilgrims.

What the Prophet did and said during this, the only full pilgrimage that he led, has become the pattern for all the world's Muslims during every hajj of every year throughout the nearly fourteen centuries that have elapsed since. In the course of it he delivered a great sermon that has been treasured ever since. "Hear me, O people," he cried out, "for I do not know whether I shall meet with you in this place after this year." He advised the Muslims to treat one another with justice and kindness, and instructed them on some of the commandments and prohibitions of the religion into which very many of them had only recently entered. "I have left among you something which, if you adhere closely to it, will keep you from all error — a clear guide, the book of God and the word of his prophet." Then he recited to them the last revelation that he would ever receive: "Today, those who disbelieve have despaired of prevailing against your religion, so don't fear them but fear me. Today I have perfected for you your religion and have completed my grace upon you, and have chosen Islam [submission] for you as your religion."[271] The Prophet ended his sermon with the question, "O people, have I faithfully delivered my message to you?" When the people answered yes, he raised his index finger and prayed, "O God, bear witness!"[272]

The journey back to Medina was slightly marred by some discord and murmuring concerning the Prophet's son-in-law, Ali. Muhammad was much distressed by it. "Am I not," he exclaimed to one of the complainers, "nearer to the faithful than their own souls?" When the man acknowledged that, yes, he was, Muhammad informed him that whoever was close to him would be close to Ali. Somewhat later in the journey, when the returning pilgrims had stopped to rest at a place called Ghadir al-Khumm, he assembled them and repeated what he had said to the man. Then he took Ali's hand in his and prayed, "O God, be the friend of whoever is his friend, and be the enemy of anyone who is his enemy!" The murmuring stopped, but the echoes of that declaration and prayer at Ghadir al-Khumm have resounded through the centuries. Shi'ite

271. Q 5:3.

272. Muhammad's question is reminiscent of the concern expressed by the apostle Paul in Acts 20:17-38, when, in Miletus, he took solemn leave of the elders of the church at Ephesus. Compare Ezek. 33:1-9; also Samuel's farewell speeches in 1 Sam. 8 and 12.

Muslims are convinced that Muhammad intended Ali to succeed him, and that the Prophet explicitly announced it there at Ghadir al-Khumm.

But the dispute between Sunnis and Shi'ites over the authority to lead the community as the successor of the Messenger properly belongs to the period after the Prophet's death. In the meantime there were rivals to Muhammad's own authority. If paganism was no longer a serious threat, perhaps the very success of Muhammad's prophethood was now inspiring yet another challenge. The Banu Tamim now claimed a prophetess, one Sajah, while the Banu Asad had a prophet by the name of Tulayha and the Yemen could boast of a prophet named Aswad b. Ka'b. None of these threats proved to be major. The Yemeni, for example, was soon assassinated by his disaffected followers, and Tulayha, defeated by Khalid, would accept Islam and yield up any pretense of prophethood. Not long after he returned from the Meccan pilgrimage, Muhammad received a letter from a man of the territory of Yamama addressed to "Muhammad the messenger of God" from "Musaylima the messenger of God." This Musaylima — his name was actually Maslama, but has come down to modern times transformed by Muslim hostility into an Arabic diminutive — claimed to be a prophet of his people, the Banu Hanifa, just as Muhammad was a prophet of and to the Quraysh, and he offered to share authority with Muhammad and to divide the land with him. Musaylima too was the lord of a *haram*.[273] He preached in the name of a deity he called Rahman — a name that also appears frequently in the Qur'an after a certain point (with the meaning, applied to Allah, of "Merciful" or "Compassionate") and that seems to have perplexed its Meccan audience.[274] He evidently possessed a written revelation in rhymed prose, rather like the Qur'an, and if Geo Widengren is correct, his claim of the title of "Messenger," or *rasul*, may indicate that he, too, claimed an ascension into heaven and a reading of the heavenly book.[275] Some have suggested that he actually proclaimed himself a prophet before Muhammad's own call. Muhammad responded with a note "from Muhammad the messenger of God to Musaylima the liar." Musaylima would eventually perish by a javelin thrown by the same man who had killed Hamza at the battle of Uhud.

Muhammad seems not to have lost much sleep over any of these rival claimants. His sights were set elsewhere. At the end of May 632 he announced a campaign against the Arab tribes of Syria, the Byzantine clients or mercenaries who had fought alongside the imperial army at the tragic battle of Mu'ta. He

273. Serjeant, "Haram and Hawtah," pp. 48, 52; Serjeant, "The Saiyids of Hadramawt," p. 15.

274. See Peters, *Muhammad*, pp. 48-49, 156-59.

275. Widengren, *Muhammad*, pp. 15-17, 135.

appointed as commander of an army numbering three thousand a young man named Usama, the son of his adoptive son, Zayd, who had died at Mu'ta.

But Muhammad would not live to see his army avenge that earlier defeat. He began to experience serious headaches and, the sources say, to express presentiments of his approaching death. Soon he was weak and feverish, unable to lead the prayers in the mosque except from a seated position. Seeing how ill he was, and knowing that he wished to be cared for in the dwelling of his beloved A'isha, the other wives waived their rights to his companionship and ceded him to her. But he was unable to walk to her home without the aid of his uncle Abbas and his son-in-law Ali. Eventually he was too weak to lead the prayers even sitting, so he designated Abu Bakr to lead the prayers in his absence. (Adherents of Sunni Islam cite this as evidence that Muhammad wanted his dear old friend and loyal supporter to succeed him, instead of Ali.) Lying on A'isha's lap, Muhammad suffered great pain.

But then, early in the morning of June 8, 632, his fever broke. He decided to attend the dawn prayer at the mosque, and the people were overjoyed to see him. Abu Bakr, who had been poised to commence the prayer, moved to withdraw in favor of Muhammad, but the Prophet, who was still feeling very weak, directed him to proceed as imam, or prayer leader, while he himself offered the prayer sitting at Abu Bakr's right. It was a false recovery. Muhammad returned to A'isha's and went downhill rapidly. She held his head while he lost consciousness. Just before he died, he spoke softly, and the report has circulated ever since that he told of being shown his place in paradise, and of being offered the choice of entering the garden or remaining on the earth.[276] His choice was clear. When A'isha realized that he was dead, she placed his head gently on a pillow and, with the other wives who had gathered when they realized that his passing was near, began her lament for her dead husband, the messenger of God.

Usama's army, although ordered to Syria, had waited just outside the city for news of the Prophet's health, and they had been greatly encouraged when they had heard of his apparent recovery. Now, with the dreadful news of his death, they returned home. Umar, who had been with the army, went to the mosque, where he assured the assembled and bewildered Muslims that Muhammad was not really dead, but that his spirit had simply left his body — as it had during his ascent into heaven — and that it would return and the Prophet would revive. While he was speaking, Abu Bakr, who had also been out of town, likewise returned. He went directly to the home of his daughter, A'isha, to see the situation for himself. Tenderly he uncovered Muhammad's face, looked at him, and then bent over to kiss him. "Dearer than my father and my mother,"

276. I think it worth noting that this choice is a common motif in modern accounts of so-called "near death experiences," or NDEs.

he murmured, "you have tasted that death which God decreed for you. Never again shall death befall you." Then, covering the Prophet's face again, he made his way to the front of the mosque, where Umar, almost hysterically attempting to suppress his own doubts and anxieties as well as those of his audience, was still holding forth. "Gently, Umar!" he said. Still the younger man continued to shout his reassurances, but the people turned to hear what Abu Bakr had to say. First, he praised God in the traditional Muslim manner. Then he said, "O people, whoever worships Muhammad — truly, Muhammad is dead. And whoever worships God — truly, God lives and does not die." Thereupon he reminded them of the Qur'anic verse that had been revealed immediately following the battle of Uhud, in which the Prophet had been wounded and could easily have been killed: "Muhammad is nothing but a messenger. Messengers have passed away before him. If he were to die or was killed, would you turn back upon your heels? Whoever turns back upon his heels will not harm God in the least, and God will reward the grateful."[277] This brought Umar to his senses, and he afterward recalled that it was only then that he realized that the Prophet was really dead. He fell to the ground, and his legs were too weak to support him. Muhammad was buried beneath the floor of A'isha's house, in the very spot where he died.

Reflections

When the Prophet died, he left a political vacuum in Arabia. Out of the chaos that followed over the next few days, his loyal lieutenant Abu Bakr emerged as the caliph or vicar of the Messenger of God. But the selection of the older man left Muhammad's kinsman Ali feeling that he had been slighted, and his legitimate right to rule usurped. He withdrew for several years from active participation in the affairs of the Muslim community, while there coalesced around him a group of sympathizers who came to be known as the "faction of Ali," the *shi'at Ali*, or, as the West knows them, the Shi'ites. When Abu Bakr died after only two years, he named Umar to succeed him, and when Umar was assassinated, he was, in his turn, succeeded by Uthman b. Affan. Uthman too met a violent end, which left the caliphate open, at last, to Ali. But Ali never really had time to savor his vindication; he himself eventually fell to an assassin and, in what surely must rank as one of the supreme ironies of history, left the rising empire to the descendants of the Prophet's old enemies, the Quraysh. Less than three decades after Muhammad's death, the Ummayads, the descendants of Abu Sufyan, ruled the empire from Damascus. The strongest leader of that house was Mu'awiya, the son of Abu

277. Q 3:144.

The Prophet's mosque as it appears in contemporary Medina
(Nomachi photo; Aperture/Pacific Press Service)

Sufyan and of Hind, who had torn out and eaten the liver of Muhammad's uncle Hamza following the battle of Uhud. And when they were overthrown a century later, it was by another faction of the Quraysh, the posterity of Muhammad's ever prudent uncle Abbas, who continued to rule from their new capital of Baghdad until the Mongols destroyed them in the middle of the thirteenth century.

It was a vast empire. The Qur'an had elevated the status of the Arabs and impelled them to the remarkable conquests of the seventh and subsequent few centuries that took them into Spain and over to India. "A century after an obscure camel-driver named Muḥammad had begun collecting a few poor Meccans round him in his house, his successors were ruling from the banks of the Loire to beyond the Indus, from Poitiers to Samarkand."[278] And once there, the appealing simplicity of Islam, aided by its power as a tool of social advancement and the prestige of its association with the rulers, slowly transformed the region from Morocco to India into the Islamic world that we know today.

As Muhammad's revelations arrived, at least some of them had been written down and all of them had been committed to memory by various of the faithful Muslims.[279] (In a culture centered on the memorization and recitation

278. Rodinson, p. 295.
279. Widengren, *Religionsphänomenologie*, pp. 567-71, sees evidence for a very early

of vast quantities of poetry, this was no serious challenge.) Now that Muhammad was no longer on the scene to receive new guidance through divine directive and to interpret what had already been received, and especially now that Muslim rule of a huge territory confronted them daily with unprecedented questions and demanded the instruction of new converts, it became vitally important to establish a reliable and complete text of the revelations so that the community could look to them with confidence. The final gathering of the Qur'an probably occurred under Uthman just after 650, or roughly two decades following the Prophet's death.

The creation of a canon commences when revelation is thought to have come to a halt, and in turn the concept of a canon reinforces the notion that revelation has ceased.[280] And the writing down of a revelation, and eventually its establishment as "canon," inevitably and by definition indicates and strengthens a conservative tendency in a developing religious tradition.[281] As Max Weber noted, "a religious community arises in connection with a prophetic movement as a result of routinization *(Veralltäglichung)*, i.e., as a result of the process whereby either the prophet himself or his disciples secure the permanence of his preaching and the congregation's distribution of grace, hence ensuring the economic existence of the enterprise and those who man it, and thereby monopolizing as well the privileges reserved for those charged with religious functions."[282] On the basis of his study of the biblical prophets in the light of Weber's sociological insights, Ronald E. Clements says that "charismatic authority tended to remain a relatively infrequently experienced and ideal type of authority. On the other hand . . . written records of the major charismatic heroes tended to be utilized in support of more long-lasting patterns of authority vested in institutions. The ideal of divine charisma was appealed to in support of institutions which might otherwise remain weak and insecure."[283]

---

commitment of the Qur'an to writing, and argues that this grew out of a general Near Eastern equation of God's word with written scripture.

280. See the discussion of Widengren, *Religionsphänomenologie,* pp. 591-93.

281. See Widengren, *Religionsphänomenologie,* pp. 571-72. Widengren points to the often observed preference of religious groups for archaic or archaizing language — which, in the Catholic Church, led for many centuries to a privileging of Latin and the Vulgate Bible, corresponding to ancient Egyptian cultivation of hieroglyphs long after they had ceased to be generally used. Modern-day Muslims everywhere read the Qur'an in its original Arabic, while Jews still recite prayers and scriptures in Hebrew even if they do not understand the language. The Samaritans still write the Pentateuch in a modified form of preexilic Hebrew script, which also occurs in the Dead Sea Scrolls (notably in the paleo-Hebrew Leviticus Scroll from Cave 11).

282. Weber, pp. 60-61.

283. Clements, p. 94.

Charismatic authority needed to be transformed, by the nature of its own unstable character, into a variety of forms of more traditional authority. The spoken word of the original prophet needed to become the meticulously preserved written word of the prophetic book. . . . The unique and transitory situation which the original prophet had encountered had to be set in a perspective that made it possible for the more enduring and practical needs of the community that respected him to be met. . . .[284]

From this point of view, the replacement of the unpredictable voice of prophecy with the more manageable one of scholarship and bureaucratic precedent was a good thing. Certainly it was so for the intellectuals and the politicians, to whom it opened up whole new avenues of advancement.[285] For the divine word had now to be interpreted, debated, and judiciously applied. The essential task of theologians, as G. van der Leeuw notes, is to speak systematically or connectedly about the acts of God. Their obligation is to bring the revelation they have received to bear upon the history of their community, to deal with heresy and innovation, and to respond to the intellectual currents in which they find themselves and their tradition floating.[286]

"Theology," writes F. E. Peters, "discourse about God according to the principles of reason, was the invention of a people without benefit of revelation."[287] Peters is referring to the Greeks, and his statement is not quite as true, perhaps, as he intended it, for the Greeks were not without claimants to revelation (including Socrates and his *daimon*). Still, theology tames prophecy, manages it, and most often, worships at its tomb. At Delphi official interpreters stood near the oracle of Apollo to make sense of the enraptured statements of the prophetess. Plutarch called them *theologians,* and felt that they did not do justice to the oracle's pronouncements.[288] Muhammad might have felt much the same about his own interpreters.

But the Prophet was by no means eclipsed within Islam. He could not

---

284. Clements, p. 104.

285. Patricia Crone and Martin Hinds, *God's Caliph: Religious Authority in the First Centuries of Islam* (Cambridge: Cambridge University Press, 1986), show persuasively how the jurists and the theologians stripped the caliphate of any claim to genuinely religious (as opposed to political) authority, and did so with such astonishing effectiveness that it has been virtually forgotten that the caliphs ever asserted such a claim. Ringgren, pp. 173-74, briefly discusses the replacement of prophets by lawyers in postexilic Judaism, which, although celebrated by the lawyers, did not altogether destroy the hope that prophecy would return.

286. See van der Leeuw, pp. 761-62.

287. Peters, *Children of Abraham,* p. 156.

288. Plutarch, *On the Cessation of the Oracles* 15.417f.

have been. For Muhammad's personal life shows up, from time to time, in the pages of the Qur'an, where even rather ordinary domestic situations are now memorialized forever in Islamic scripture. There was the time, for example, when Muhammad took a Coptic Christian slave girl named Mariya as his concubine. His other wives became extremely and overtly jealous of her when he began to spend a great deal of time with her. In response he moved her farther away, but then continued to visit her both by day and by night, now taking even more time away from the other wives because of the increased distance he had to travel to reach her. Retaliating, several of his wives began to make his life thoroughly miserable, and he finally swore that he would visit the beautiful Copt, Mariya, no longer.

Amidst these very personal unpleasantnesses came a revelation now known as Surat al-Tahrim, "The Chapter of Prohibition": "O Prophet!" it begins. "Why have you prohibited that which God has made lawful to you? You seek to please your wives. But God is forgiving and compassionate."[289] Then the revelation turns to address the wives: "It may be, if he divorced you all, that his Lord would give him better wives than you in exchange — submissive, believing, devout, repentant, worshipful, given to fasting, previously married or virgins."[290] The revelation closes with a contrast between two pairs of women from sacred history. The wife of Noah and the wife of Lot betrayed their husbands, and both accordingly were condemned to the flames of hell. By contrast the Qur'an points to the wife of Pharaoh, who, it says, listened to and received the message of the prophet Moses, and also to Mary, the daughter of Imran, who preserved her chastity and became the virgin mother of Jesus, the Messiah.[291]

Muhammad thereupon avoided his wives for the next month. At the end of it, though, he went first to A'isha and recited to her a new Qur'anic revelation:

> O Prophet! Say to your wives, "If you desire the life of this world and its adornment, come! I will provide for you and will set you free in a pleasant manner.

289. Q 66:3.
290. Q 66:5.
291. See Q 66:10-12. Western scholars of Islam have often pointed to the information mentioned here about "Mary, the daughter of Imran," as evidence that Muhammad had confused Mary, the mother of Jesus, with Miriam, the daughter of Amiram and the sister of Moses and Aaron. Both names would occur in Arabic as Maryam. According to early Christian tradition, the father of the Virgin Mary was named Joachim. See, for example, the second-century *Protevangelium of James* 1–5, conveniently available in J. K. Elliott, *The Apocryphal New Testament: A Collection of Apocryphal Christian Literature in an English Translation* (Oxford: Clarendon, 1993), pp. 57-59.

"But if you desire God and his messenger and the abode of the hereafter, God has prepared a great reward for those among you who do good."

O women of the Prophet! Whoever among you commits manifest uncleanness, her punishment will be doubled. That is an easy thing for God.

And whoever among you is obedient to God and his messenger and works righteousness, we shall grant her reward twice, and we have prepared a noble sustenance for her.

O women of the Prophet! Do not be like one of the [other] women, if you fear God. Do not be [too] compliant in your speech, so that one with a diseased heart desires [you], but speak honorably.

And remain in your houses, and do not ornament yourselves ostentatiously in the manner of the time of ignorance [al-jahiliyya]. Establish prayer and give alms, and obey God and his messenger. God only wants to remove abomination far from you, O people of the house [ahl al-bayt], and to purify you.[292]

When the choice was presented to her, A'isha did not hesitate to choose God and his messenger over divorce and a generous settlement. The other wives, too, in their turn, repented and pledged their fidelity to Muhammad anew.

The personal life of the Prophet also became a source of legal and theological precedent for the rising Muslim community. One day, for instance, Muhammad went to the house of his adopted son Zayd to speak with him. Zayd, however, was not at home, and the door was opened by his wife, Zaynab. She was roughly forty years old but was still, as most of the accounts agree, a woman of remarkable beauty.[293] It was as if she and the Prophet had never previously laid eyes on one another. Instantly Muhammad knew that he was in love with her and that she was in love with him. He hurriedly turned and walked away, but Zaynab heard him say to himself, "Glory be to the Most High God! Glory be to the One who disposes men's hearts!" When Zayd returned home, his wife told him of her strange encounter with the Prophet. Zayd instantly divined what was going on and went to Muhammad, offering to yield up his wife to the Prophet if the Prophet so desired. "Keep your wife," the Prophet responded, "and fear God." Muhammad was very much opposed to divorce, saying that, of all legal things, it was the most hateful in the sight of God. But Zayd returned the following day with the same offer. Again Muhammad refused the proposal, but Zayd now divorced Zaynab, making her thereby available to marry the Prophet.

292. Q 33:28-33.
293. Watt, p. 158, rather unchivalrously observes that the story of Muhammad's enchantment with Zaynab's beauty does not occur in the earliest source, and points out that she was quite old by ancient Arabian standards.

But not really. Marrying her was still not an option open to Muhammad, for two quite different reasons. First of all, he already had four wives, and four was the maximum number permitted under Qur'anic revelation.[294] Furthermore, the Qur'an forbade men to marry the wives of their sons, and Arabian tradition considered adoptive sonship to be just as real as literal genetic descent. However, a revelation came to Muhammad several months later that solved the problem for him:

> Lo, you say to him whom God and you have favored [i.e., Zayd], "Keep your wife, and fear God." And you hide in your soul what God has made manifest, and you fear the people. But God is more deserving of fear. So when Zayd divorced her, we gave her in marriage to you so that there would not be a restriction for the believers regarding the wives of their adopted sons if they have divorced them. And God's command is to be carried out.
>
> There is no restriction for the Prophet in what God has stipulated for him . . .
>
> Muhammad is not the father of a single one of your men, but he is the messenger of God and the seal of the prophets. And God knows all things.[295]

When Muhammad emerged from the revelatory state, he said to those nearby, "Who will go to Zaynab, and tell her of the good news that God has given her to me in marriage?" He had been granted an exception to the limit of four wives, to marry Zaynab. The implications of the revelation went far beyond the personal circumstances of these two Arabians, however. In effect it undercut the entire notion of adoption in all of subsequent Islamic history. The revealed dictum that "Muhammad is not the father of a single one of your men" meant that Zayd, despite Muhammad's formal adoption of him, was not to be considered Muhammad's son. In the future, Muslims concluded, adopted sons should continue to be named after their literal fathers, and not after their adoptive ones. Thus, although Zayd had been known for nearly four decades as Zayd b. Muhammad, his name now reverted to Zayd b. Haritha, after his biological father. Practically speaking, adoption was no longer a viable or desirable option.

Another incident from Muhammad's personal life that proved important for subsequent Muslim religious practice involved an onyx necklace that belonged to his beloved wife A'isha. One day while traveling with the Prophet during a military expedition, A'isha's necklace somehow came loose and fell from her neck, although she did not notice that it was missing for some time. The necklace was very precious to her because it had been given to her on her

294. Q 4:3.
295. Q 33:37-38, 40.

wedding day. The place where the travelers had stopped was a waterless one, and the intention had been to rest there for only a few moments. Now, however, in deference to his wife and her distress at the loss of her necklace, the Prophet announced that they would camp there until the next morning. It did not take long before the reason for their prolonged stay became general knowledge throughout the army, and needless to say, more than a few of the men were highly indignant that they were being required to stay in an unpleasant place, without water, for the sake of a necklace and a young woman's apparent carelessness. Some of the soldiers, confident that they would soon be arriving at a well-watered campsite, had taken no special care to conserve their personal water supplies, and now they were in somewhat uncomfortable straits. Abu Bakr, A'isha's father, was extremely embarrassed.

But embarrassment and discomfort were not the only problems. Without water, the Muslims would not be able to pray the dawn prayer, for they would be unable to make the required ritual ablutions. In answer to this problem, though, in the hours just before the dawn, God spoke to his prophet, revealing what has been called "the verse of earth-purification." If you are traveling, the Qur'an now informs believers, "and you do not find water, take good sand [or dirt] for yourself and with it rub your faces and your hands."[296] As to the necklace, when day had broken and further searching had still not found the missing object, the expedition prepared to set out. But when A'isha's camel rose from the spot where it had been kneeling, there was the necklace.

However, that piece of jewelry was destined to play yet another important role in the development of Islamic practice and law. Later during the same journey, A'isha lost her necklace again. She was already seated in her howdah, the canopied and enclosed seat that was to be placed on her camel, with her curtains closed, and the order to commence the day's travel had already been given, when she suddenly realized that, once more, her necklace had slipped from her. Without saying a word to anyone — she was still quite young, only fourteen[297] — she slipped from the howdah to find the missing ornament. When the men came to place the howdah on the camel, they apparently did not notice that it was even lighter than normal. (A'isha was very small even for her age.) When A'isha returned from a successful search for the necklace, the camp was deserted. The caravan had proceeded on its way, never imagining that the

296. Q 4:43.
297. At almost precisely this time, and indeed, in connection with the event being narrated here, A'isha's maidservant told Muhammad that the one complaint she could think of against her mistress was that she was just a young girl. When she was kneading dough, she explained, and having an errand elsewhere, she asked A'isha to watch it, the girl would sometimes fall asleep. And then her pet lamb would come and devour the undefended dough.

Prophet's wife was not in the howdah where she belonged. There was nothing for her to do except to sit down in the abandoned campsite and wait for a search party to return for her when she was missed. In the heat of the Arabian day, however, she fell asleep.

When she awoke, a young man by the name of Safwan b. Mu'attal was standing over her. He had fallen behind the main body of the expedition for some reason or other, and had not spent the night with them in the camp. While attempting to catch up with them, he had noticed a young girl asleep, all alone in the wilderness, and when he investigated had recognized her as the wife of Muhammad. (The veil had only recently been imposed on the wives of the Prophet, so he knew what she looked like.) A'isha immediately drew her veil over her face. Safwan naturally offered her a ride on his camel as he sought to overtake the other Muslims. He led the camel on foot. Meanwhile the main expedition did not notice her absence for a surprisingly long time. Even after they had arrived at the next halt and had placed her howdah on the ground, they were not surprised that she did not emerge from it. The warmth of such an enclosure and the rhythmic, monotonous motions of the supporting camel were quite likely to put its occupant to sleep, and nobody — certainly no other man — would have dreamed of invading the privacy of one of the wives of the Prophet in order to check on her, even had they suspected something amiss. So everyone was surprised when, toward the end of their rest, A'isha came riding into their midst on a camel led by the young Safwan.

But that was far from the end of the story. Suspicions soon began to circulate among the travelers, and then, upon their return to Medina, throughout the Muslim community, that something untoward had occurred between the Prophet's teenage wife and Safwan. Before long, although presumably not everyone believed them, they were on every tongue. Only A'isha herself seemed to be ignorant of the circulating rumors, although she eventually became aware of a certain coolness and distance on the part of her husband, the Prophet. Naturally, Ibn Ubayy and the others known in the traditional Muslim accounts as the "hypocrites" were among the most vocal and insistent in the matter. But Ali too believed A'isha guilty of misbehavior in the case, and the rift that his suspicions created between them had fateful consequences for the Islamic empire in the years after Muhammad's death. Disputes about A'isha's chastity, between those who doubted it and those who sought to defend her honor, eventually threatened even to become violent.

When A'isha finally realized what was being said about her, she was horrified. And she was deeply distressed to hear that her husband, Muhammad, was asking questions about her and seeking to make up his mind whether or not to believe in her fidelity to him. He eventually came to the conclusion that he could trust her, but the community at large remained divided on the issue, and it was easy to dismiss Muhammad's confidence in A'isha as nothing more than the wishful thinking of a doting husband. But after a month of doubts and anguish, a revelation on the subject finally came to Muhammad assuring him of her innocence.

> Truly, those who brought forth the lie are a party among you. Do not think it an evil to you, but rather a good to you. Every man among them will receive what he earned of sin, and he among them who took the lead in it will receive a great punishment.
>
> Why, when they heard it, did the believers — both men and women — not think good within themselves, and say, "This is a manifest lie"?
>
> Why did they not bring forward four witnesses? So, since they have not brought forward such witnesses, these people, in the view of God, are the liars.
>
> Had it not been for the favor and mercy of God upon you in this world and the next, there would have come upon you a grievous punishment for that which you rushed into here.
>
> When you took it upon your tongues and said something with your mouths about which you had no knowledge, you thought it a small thing, but with God it was an enormity.
>
> And when you heard it, why did you not say, "We have no business speaking of this. Glory be to Thee! This is a monstrous slander"?
>
> God admonishes you that you never repeat such conduct, if you are believers.[298]

Thus, in the future, allegations of adultery against a woman were to be supported by the testimony of four witnesses (which makes such accusations virtually impossible to prove). Moreover, the penalty for those who brought false accusations against chaste and honorable women was that they be scourged. The sentence was actually carried out against some of the most outspoken bearers of the rumor, but, perhaps for political reasons, the "hypocrites" (along with Ali, of course) escaped earthly punishment. A'isha, in the meantime, was not only fully vindicated in the minds of the faithful, but was astonished, unimportant as she thought herself, to figure in a revelation from the throne of God.

Muhammad's importance as a guide to Muslim belief and practice is, however, by no means limited to his appearances in the holy book. As Islam spread, it encountered new situations and questions for which the Qur'an provided no direct answer. Devout Muslims, therefore, earnestly sought for whatever guidance they could find. And they found it in the life of the Prophet, or at

298. Q 24:11-17.

least in accounts of his life and actions and sayings that were compiled to meet their needs. If anyone had ever understood the principles of Islam and their proper application, it was felt, that person would be the Prophet, through whom they were revealed. Thus Muhammad himself became a kind of revelation of the divine will, and narrations of his deeds, of what he said, of what he approved and disapproved were eagerly sought for by jurists and theologians — and in many cases perhaps created by them. (In the matter of these narratives — called hadith — as in economics, demand seems to have called forth supply.) Muhammad's primary distinction lies in his being the conduit through whom the divine message came that is contained in the Qur'an. But the Muslim profession of faith, the *shahada* or "testimony," quite aptly refers both to God and to the Prophet: "I testify that there is no god but God, and that Muhammad is the Messenger of God."

F. E. Peters compares Muhammad's sunna, his paradigmatic behavior and commentary, and the consensus of the *umma*, or community, that also went into forming the overall Islamic sunna, with the "tradition" of the Mishnah in Judaism.[299] Ronald Clements sees the shaping and choosing of the prophetic literature in the Hebrew Bible as reflecting "a work of interpretation and routinization that endeavored to make the insights and messages of the great prophets applicable to the ongoing needs of a larger world of followers."[300] In other words, there was a dynamic relationship between the community and the sacred traditions upon which it was built. Each shaped the other. Much the same could be said of the legacy of the Prophet of Islam. G. van der Leeuw makes the point (and, with the aid of G. K. Chesterton, makes it wittily) that a scripture means everything or nothing without the help of a living interpretive community. In Islam, that community has built its interpretation largely upon the hadith.[301]

Max Weber identified two types of prophets. One, the "exemplary prophet," is someone "who, by his personal example, demonstrates the way to

299. Peters, *Children of Abraham*, p. 89.

300. Clements, p. 105.

301. Van der Leeuw, pp. 501-2. Van der Leeuw writes of "the terrible problem of *interpretation*" (emphasis in original, here and below). "What does the Bible say? Everything and nothing. 'When will people understand that it is useless for a man to read his Bible unless he also reads everybody else's Bible? A printer reads a Bible for misprints. A Mormon reads his Bible and finds polygamy; a Christian Scientist reads his and finds we have no arms and legs.' The Bible must be *interpreted*. But how, and by what authority? A not inconsiderable portion of the most important questions that have agitated Christendom in the course of its history have their origin in these difficulties. In Islam, moreover, it was precisely the same." I have taken the original English of the Chesterton passage that van der Leeuw cites from G. K. Chesterton, *The Innocence of Father Brown* (Harmondsworth: Penguin Books, 1950), p. 226.

religious salvation." "The preaching of this type of prophet," writes Weber, "says nothing about a divine mission or an ethical duty of obedience, but rather directs itself to the self-interest of those who crave salvation, recommending to them the same path as he himself traversed." The paradigmatic exemplary prophet, according to Weber, is the Buddha, and Weber sees the phenomenon as especially characteristic of India — although he will admit that it has also manifested itself in China (e.g., in Lao Tzu) and in the Near East. The other type of prophet, the "ethical prophet," is to be found, in Weber's view, only in the Near East, and he finds especially clear illustration of it in the lives of Zoroaster and Muhammad. In this understanding of prophecy the prophet is a messenger, "an instrument for the proclamation of a god and his will, be this a concrete command or an abstract norm. Preaching as one who has received a commission from god, he demands obedience as an ethical duty." Such prophecy was absent from East Asia and the Indian subcontinent, says Weber, because of the "absence," in those places and their cultures, "of a personal, transcendental, and ethical god." In the Near East, by contrast, the concept of such a god was present because it had grown out of the real-world notion of "an all-powerful mundane king with his rational bureaucratic regime."[302] The Muhammad of the Qur'an is clearly a case of the "ethical prophet." But the Muhammad depicted and remembered in the vast, canonical hadith collections is not so easily distinguished from Weber's "exemplary prophet."

Muhammad himself might not have been altogether surprised or dismayed by the role he assumed in later Islam. He was made deeply conscious, by the revelations he received, of the gap that separated him from ordinary men. The later revelations, in fact, spoke not merely of obedience to God, but of deference to "God and his messenger." Others were not to address him by name in the normal, everyday way. Unlike him, they were limited to four wives. His wives, however many there might be, bore the title "mothers of the believers," and they were never to marry another after him. If one of the believers sought their intercession, that person was to speak with them from behind a curtain:

> It is not for any male or female believer, if God and his messenger have decided a matter, to have any option in the matter. And whoever rebels against God and his messenger has clearly erred. . . .
> O you who believe! Do not enter the houses of the Prophet unless permis-

---

302. Weber, pp. 55-56. However, since India and certainly China also enjoyed such earthly kings and their courts, it is not clear that Weber's comments on the Near East possess much real explanatory power.

sion is granted to you — for a meal, not waiting for it, but when you are invited, enter. And when you have eaten, disperse, without seeking familiar conversation. Such behavior annoys the Prophet. He hesitates to send you away, but God does not hesitate to tell you the truth. And when you ask his wives for anything, ask them from behind a curtain. That is purer for your hearts and for their hearts. Nor should you annoy the messenger of God, nor marry his wives after him. Indeed, such a thing, with God, would be a terrible wrong.[303]

And the believers, too, treated him as their superior. When an unbeliever, at one point, engaged him in earnest conversation and, as was sometimes done, took hold of his beard while addressing him, a Muslim bystander offered to remove the man's hand with a sword if he did not let go of the Prophet's beard. That same unbeliever later reported to Quraysh that he had never seen anyone who could claim such complete loyalty and veneration from his followers as could Muhammad. They vied with one another, he said, in their eagerness to fulfill his every wish. When he spoke, they were quiet and reverent in his presence, and they lowered their eyes while speaking with him, as if to look him straight in the face were to commit a kind of sacrilege. In fact, he said, perhaps exaggerating, they even fought for the water that he discarded after his ritual ablutions.[304]

The believers' veneration of Muhammad sought to attribute to him all possible perfections. Although, for example, he never claimed to have performed any miracle other than the supreme feat of bringing the Qur'an, Muslim tradition soon ascribed to him a wide variety of miracles. "This," writes David Noel Freedman of miracle working among the biblical prophets,

> was a distinctive aspect of prophetic behavior in certain cases only, and it is not clear whether it was regarded as important for a prophet to demonstrate such powers, or whether these were more or less incidental and associated with certain charismatic personalities. Thus, miracles are clearly and strongly associated with prophets such as Moses, Samuel, and especially Elijah and Elisha, as well as with Isaiah among the so-called writing prophets; however, there are many prophets with little or no such connection, for example, Jeremiah, Amos, Hosea, and Micah. . . . Certainly they were not obligatory, and

303. Q 33:36, 53.

304. Perhaps he was not exaggerating. Abu Sufyan is said to have witnessed the same thing on the morning of his conversion, when the Muslims were about to enter Mecca. It was perhaps one of the factors in his conversion, for he sensed that such devotion could not easily be explained away and might indeed be evidence of a supernatural agency at work.

such miracles seem to be attached to unusual charismatic individuals who were also prophets, but not necessarily to the role or office of prophet.[305]

But it was precisely such prophets as Moses and Samuel and Elijah and Elisha who were likely to live on in the folklore of the Arabian Jews and their pagan neighbors, and it is such figures who appear in the pages of the Qur'an. (By contrast, Jeremiah, Amos, Hosea, and Micah are virtually if not completely invisible in the Muslim tradition.) And they served as the models against which the story of Muhammad would be judged, both by Muslims and by the Christians and Jews whom they sought to convince.

For many centuries and still today, Muhammad has been and is the ideal model of masculine beauty, the paradigm of pure spirituality. For the Muslim mystics known as the *Sufis*, Muhammad or the "Light of Muhammad" is the first creation of God. His birthday is celebrated annually with lights and delicious desserts, and he is praised in poems and folk songs across the Islamic world.[306]

Speaking in regard to ancient Israel, David Noel Freedman mentions, besides the prophet's primary role as a messenger of and a spokesman for God, his role as an intercessor with God on behalf of his people. This is not the case — or, at least, not expressly so — with every biblical prophet. In fact, as Freedman points out, Jeremiah mentions two prophetic intercessors, Moses and Samuel, with the explicit admission that such a role has been divinely denied to him.[307] Freedman is willing to add to this very short list the names of Amos and, less confidently, Abraham.[308]

---

305. Freedman, "Between God and Man," p. 62. "With Ezekiel, strange things happen to the prophet and he has extraordinary extra-sensory experiences, but these are hardly in the same category with the popular healing and feeding miracles associated with Moses and the period of the Exodus-wanderings or with Elijah and Elisha at a later time." As Freedman notes on p. 57, biblical prophets were both "foretellers and forthtellers." So was Muhammad, but the emphasis must clearly be overwhelmingly on the latter role.

306. Excellent discussions of this subject and of the general subject of this section include Annemarie Schimmel, *And Muhammad Is His Messenger: The Veneration of the Prophet in Islamic Piety* (Chapel Hill and London: University of North Carolina Press, 1985); Tor Andrae, *Die Person Muhammads in Lehre und Glaube seiner Gemeinde* (Stockholm: P. A. Vorstedt og söner, 1918); Rodinson, pp. 302-11.

307. Jer. 15:1.

308. Freedman, "Between God and Man," pp. 70-71. For Moses' intercessory role, see the story of the Golden Calf as recorded in Exod. 32. For Samuel see 1 Sam. 15:10-34 — where he is actually unsuccessful in his attempt to mediate between God and Saul. Amos's intercession is described in Amos 7:1-6, while Abraham appears as a mediator or intercessor in Gen. 18:16-33; 20:7, 17. For general remarks on the figure of the mediator, see van der Leeuw, pp. 764-67.

Is Muhammad an intercessor? Emphatically yes, and his intercession is eagerly sought, for it is thought to extend even beyond the gates of death. One of the most offensive aspects of Muhammad's preaching, in the minds of his pagan hearers, was its condemnation of their venerated ancestors to everlasting torment in the flames of hell. But Muhammad played no favorites in the matter. The story is related that, soon after his conquest of Mecca, the Prophet was seen lying prostrate on an unkept grave, weeping. When Umar asked him the cause of his sorrow, Muhammad explained that this was the grave of his mother. He had, he said, sought from God the privilege of visiting his mother's grave before he died, and that had been granted. But his request that she be forgiven for her pagan polytheism had been denied. Later, though, the tradition arose that, because of the Prophet's intercession, God in his mercy had miraculously permitted both Muhammad's mother and his father a brief revivification from the grave so that their son might preach Islam to them and, thus, save their souls.[309]

The Qur'an would not seem, at first glance, to offer much support for such a notion. But there is no underestimating the ingenuity of lawyers and theologians. When Muhammad's dear and supportive uncle Abu Talib lay on his deathbed, Muhammad went to him and implored him to accept Islam before it was too late. But two of the Prophet's most implacable enemies had already visited the old man and convinced him that it would be terribly wrong to abandon the faith of his ancestors, and his dying words to Muhammad were "I hold to the faith of Abd al-Muttalib." When he finally died, still a pagan, it is said that the Prophet locked himself in his house for several days, praying for Abu Talib's soul. But then the angel Gabriel came to him, bringing a revelation that reads, in part:

> It is not for the Prophet and those who believe to seek forgiveness for polytheists, even if they are close kin, after it has become clear to them that they are people of hell [i.e., after they have died?].
>
> Abraham would not have prayed for his father except for a promise that he had made to him. But when it became clear to him that he was an enemy to God, he dissociated himself from him. Truly, Abraham was compassionate, kind.[310]

This would seem definitively to close off the hope of postmortem salvation for idolaters and unbelievers. But the theologians argued, from an early time, that the revealed declaration that "It is not for the Prophet and those who believe to seek forgiveness for polytheists" really means "It is not for the Prophet and

---

309. Andrae, *Mohammed*, pp. 36-37, relates the stories and supplies the references.
310. Q 9:113-14.

thóse who believe to seek forgiveness for polytheists except insofar as God grants him permission to do so."[311]

Western skeptics have been disturbed by what seems like apparent cruelty on the part of Muhammad. We have tried to set such acts as the extermination of Banu Qurayza and the assassinations of various poets in the context of their time. But it should also be noted that the traditional accounts portray a man who was, on most occasions, very far from cruel. He was an entirely human prophet. At one point the sources depict him pulling up the hem of his robe and running a footrace with his young wife A'isha. He was also tender toward children. He adored his grandchildren, including Hasan and Husayn, whom his daughter Fatima frequently brought to see him. We read of him performing the canonical prayers, the five daily prostrations, with one or the other of the boys climbing on his back. And his granddaughter Umama would come with her mother, his daughter Zaynab, to visit. A few times the Prophet took the little girl with him to the mosque, where he would recite from the Qur'an while she sat on his shoulders.

All accounts agree that Muhammad was a man of what we would today call unusual charisma. He was a marvelous conversationalist, who could make anyone feel that all his attention and time were reserved for just that individual. When he shook hands, he was never the first to release his grip. Perhaps his abilities as a listener gave him what seemed to his contemporaries to be uncanny discernment. Some, like his uncle Abbas, are said to have been astonished at his supernatural ability to know of private thoughts and confidential acts. Muhammad was notably kindhearted toward animals. The traditional sources about his life tell, for example, of an incident when one of his disciples brought a baby bird into camp, and suddenly one of the baby's parents hurled itself at the hands of the man. The bystanders were surprised at the adult bird's behavior, but Muhammad asked them what else they were to expect, seeing that the man had seized the bird's baby. He used the occasion to teach his disciples about the mercy of God, which, he said, far exceeded even the self-sacrificing mercy demonstrated by the older bird. And he directed his followers to put the young bird gently back in its nest. On another occasion, during the final march against Mecca, the Prophet saw a mother dog lying beside the road nursing her newborn pups. Concerned lest the passing army disturb her or some member of the army feel disposed to molest her, he set one of his followers beside her as a guard until the entire army of ten thousand had moved on. At yet another time, the Prophet rebuked a man for mistreating a donkey.

And what of his appetites for women and food? For many years anti-Muslim polemics have delighted in portraying Muhammad as a lustful de-

---

311. Andrae, *Mohammed,* pp. 39-40; compare Schimmel, pp. 81-104.

bauchee. And it is true that, although he certainly fasted and prayed and encouraged abstinence from unlawful pleasures and even from lawful pleasures at certain times, Muhammad was not an ascetic, nor did he encourage asceticism in others. While, he said, he loved the "coolness" that came to him in prayer — an interesting word, and no doubt a significant one in the extreme heat that often afflicts Arabia — Muhammad is also said to have declared, without any sense of embarrassment or impropriety, his love for perfume and women.[312] *La rahbaniyya fi al-Islam,* he announced: "There is no monasticism in Islam."

He zealously sought to wean his formerly-pagan followers from some of their rather depraved former practices, but he intended also to guard against the opposite extreme. One early convert to Islam, a certain Uthman b. Ma'zun (who is not to be confused with Uthman b. Affan, the man who would succeed Muhammad as the third caliph), was deeply inclined toward self-denial and ascetic behavior, and had been so since before his acceptance of Islam. Once he had moved to Medina, his ascetic impulse grew so strong that he even sought the Prophet's permission to make himself a eunuch, and then to spend the remainder of his life as a wandering mendicant. Muhammad refused his request. "Do you not have a fair example in me?" the Prophet asked. "And I go in to women, and I eat meat, and I fast, and I break my fast. Whoever makes men eunuchs or makes himself a eunuch is not of my community." On another occasion Muhammad again addressed Uthman, who, it would seem, had not fully abandoned his desire to go beyond normal Islamic observance in his zeal for the next world: "Do you not have in me an example?" the Prophet again demanded. Uthman enthusiastically agreed that indeed he did, and asked to know what might be wrong that provoked such a question. "You fast every day," Muhammad responded, "and you keep a prayer vigil every night." Yes, Uthman replied, perhaps not yet understanding what the problem might be, since Muhammad had often commended the virtues of fasting and of prayer in the watches of the night. "Do not do so," said the Prophet. "For, truly, your eyes have their rights over you, and your body has its rights, and your family have their rights. So pray, and sleep, and fast, and break your fast." While Muham-

---

312. Muhammad seems to have been quite sensitive to odors of any kind, both pleasant and unpleasant. He was especially offended by bad breath. (Although he is also said to have commented that the breath of those who were fasting is sweet like the breezes of paradise.) He discouraged Muslims from eating foods that were excessively flavored with onion or garlic, particularly before going to the mosque for prayer. His wife A'isha recalled that the very first thing he did whenever he returned to his house was to seek a "tooth-stick," made from green palm wood, that he used for oral hygiene. His followers always made sure that such a stick was available for him during journeys as well. His use of the tooth-stick became a precedent for his "companions" and for subsequent generations of Muslims, who also followed his practice of rinsing his mouth after every meal.

mad was no ascetic, he was also, by the frank and earthy standards of his time and culture, no lustful epicure.

How should non-Muslims view Muhammad? There are few Western scholars today, if any, who doubt that the Prophet of Islam was honest and was genuinely convinced that his revelations came from a source outside himself that he identified with God or with Gabriel. Even the French Marxist Maxime Rodinson is more than willing to grant Muhammad's sincerity, although he is firmly convinced that the Prophet was hallucinating and that the Qur'an was a product of Muhammad's unconscious mind.[313] A touching story from the period immediately following the Khaybar campaign illustrates the Prophet's honesty. After the successful siege, one of the pieces of plunder that was taken was a camel's skin full of jewels and ornaments. Before the booty was divided, Muhammad took a pearl necklace from this treasure to A'isha. But he could not sleep that night because of his acute awareness that, in removing an item from the spoils before they were divided, he had taken more than he was legitimately entitled to take. However, in the morning when he asked A'isha to return the necklace, he learned that she had already given the pearls to the poor. As Tor Andrae writes, "The frankness with which this error is acknowledged does credit both to Mohammed and to the Moslem tradition."[314]

Muhammad remains, today, a challenge for interpretation, a complex but commanding figure — much as he was for his own contemporaries.

313. Rodinson, pp. 75-81, 218-20, 300.
314. Andrae, *Mohammed,* p. 162.

Prophet or Loss?
Reassessing Max Weber's
Theory of Religious Leadership

MICHAEL J. McCLYMOND

Questions about Founders

A mention of religious founders as a scholarly topic is likely to raise some academic eyebrows. The use of the term "founder" might seem to suggest that a handful of exalted figures set the course of religious history and carry the masses along with them, like Pied Pipers of the spiritual realm. The word itself is reminiscent of the now discredited great man theory of history (note the gender-exclusive language) as propounded in the nineteenth century by G. W. F. Hegel and popularized by Thomas Carlyle. According to this viewpoint, it is only select individuals — men of destiny — who have given decisive impetus to world history and initiated the crucial changes.[1] Yet recent historical scholarship exhibits a very different sensibility and outlook. In the latter part of the twentieth century, a broad thrust toward social history in the various humanistic disciplines accented the local, the concrete, the idiosyncratic, and the popular, and correspondingly de-emphasized the universal, the abstract, the norma-

1. Thomas Carlyle states his thesis as follows: "For, as I take it, Universal History, the history of what man has accomplished in this world, is at bottom the History of the Great Men who have worked here. They were the leaders of men, these great ones; the modellers, patterns, and in a wide sense creators, of whatsoever the general mass of men contrived to do or to attain" (*On Heroes, Hero-Worship, and the Heroic in History*, ed. Michael K. Goldberg [Berkeley: University of California Press, 1993], p. 3).

tive, and the elite. Since by definition the major religious founders are of general significance and not only of local import, a discussion of religious founders would appear to highlight elite rather than popular religion.

The term "founder" carries the connotation of building an edifice from the ground up, and it may be worthwhile to note some of the associations evoked by the related words "founder," "founding," and "foundation." The mental image is of a person who sets in place the lowest part of a building while others erect a structure on top of it. The activity of the founder is both chronologically and logically prior to that of everyone else. If there is no foundation, the work of building cannot be carried on. If there is a foundation, then others may carry on the work of building in the fashion that seems fit to them, but only along the lines laid down by the founder. The foundation may be small or large, rectangular or circular or irregular, deep delved and reliable or shaky and shoddy. Yet none of the later builders will ever be able to replace or supplant the foundation on which they build. However careful or careless they may be, they cannot make a good foundation bad or a bad foundation good. For better or for worse, those who come after are all dependent on the founder. Thus the hallmark of the idea of a founder is an asymmetrical relationship between the original founder and the subsequent followers: they depend on the founder, but the founder does not depend on them.

One of the objections to the concept of religious founders, as already noted, is that it may come across as elitist or authoritarian. Who is there to tell me, the critic intones, what I should believe or practice? The religious sensibility of our age, at least in the so-called developed nations, is marked by the idea that religion is what each individual chooses for himself or herself, and is not a matter of what is passed down by tradition or culture. The sociologist Edward Shils refers to this idea paradoxically as the "antitraditional tradition" of the modern West, according to which it is better for each person to break with established customs and do something novel than just to continue in the given pattern.[2] The extreme limit of this line of thinking appears in Robert Bellah's sociological study of life in the United States, *Habits of the Heart* (1985), which includes an interview with a nurse named Sheila who insisted that her religion might be termed "Sheilaism" — an individually invented faith containing only beliefs and practices that were congenial to her. "Just my own little voice," as she commented.[3] The founder of Sheilaism was evidently Sheila, and each person who shares this outlook becomes in effect his or her own religious founder. Moses, Buddha, Jesus, and the other towering figures of history vanish across a distant horizon, and an omnipotent individual fills the foreground.

---

2. Edward Shils, *Tradition* (Chicago: University of Chicago Press, 1981), esp. pp. 235-39.
3. Robert N. Bellah et al., *Habits of the Heart: Individualism and Commitment in American Life* (Berkeley: University of California Press, 1985), pp. 220-21, 235.

If Sheilaism seems too radical as a general interpretation of contemporary culture, then one might consider Peter Berger's argument in *The Heretical Imperative* that modernity, by emphasizing religious *choice*, has turned all modern people into "heretics" — a Greek word that originally had the connotation of "one who chooses [his own beliefs]."[4] A young man living in Pakistan today has almost certainly heard something regarding Buddhism, Christianity, and other faiths, and if he has on-line computer access, he can go on the World Wide Web to learn more, and decide whether to pursue his religious investigation or continue in the Islamic tradition that he has been taught. Even if he does not invent his own individual religion in the manner of Sheilaism, he nonetheless has access to knowledge regarding many different traditions and the prospect of personal contact with those who practice these traditions, and therefore he faces a religious choice that many of his Pakistani predecessors did not have. Thus today's milieu in many respects serves to highlight the role of the individual in fashioning religious beliefs and practices, rather than the historical founders who established a pattern for others to follow.

To return to the earlier image of the foundation and the builders, one notes the asymmetry in which the builders depend on the founder but the founder does not depend on anyone else. This image may need to be revised in a number of ways. What if our hypothetical founder did not accomplish his or her task alone, but required assistance in laying the groundwork? In this case the founder would no longer remain in splendid isolation, but would be one person among others, obliged to the others for their aid and complicit with them in a common endeavor. Mutuality, rather than solitariness, would characterize the first and foundational phase of building as well as the later period of expansion and completion. Thus we would no longer have an individual founder so much as a foundational generation or cohort. While one person might still be largely responsible for initiating the process of building, there would be some degree of collaboration from the ground up.

Alternatively the initial image of the independent founder could be reconstrued in another way. What if the building process were in fact a rebuilding rather than a first construction at a new site? This is not too difficult to visualize. Many of us either live in or have visited some very old cities, such as Jerusalem, and often the architectural history there is so complex that it is hard to make a definitive statement as to when a particular building was founded. There may be a series of founders and foundings, and the relative priority or significance of each is a matter of debate. The way one construes the history of a particular building may ultimately depend on architectural taste. One person

---

4. Peter L. Berger, *The Heretical Imperative: Contemporary Possibilities of Religious Affirmation* (Garden City, N.Y.: Anchor Books, 1979), pp. 26-31, esp. 28.

might regard the Gothic arches added to the ancient basilica a deformation or corruption of the intended design, while another might consider them a clever updating or even a splendid completion of the original.

There is yet another way to modify the typical image of the foundation and founder, and this is the most radical of all. What if the whole notion of a building that rests on a foundation were inaccurate, and the building itself supported the foundation as much as the foundation supported the building? In this case we would have to jettison the mental image of a building and search for a different physical analogy. Taking a cue from a contemporary movement in philosophy known as nonfoundationalism or antifoundationalism, we could perhaps suggest an appropriate analogy in a net, in which each part is tied to and supports every other part but no part can properly be said to be the basis or foundation for all the rest. Philosophical nonfoundationalists insist that human knowledge is like this. Rejecting Descartes's search for indubitable first principles as the foundation of all human knowledge, they assert that our beliefs are reciprocally related so that every individual belief is in some sense both a foundation for beliefs and a construction founded on beliefs outside of itself.[5] When we adapt and apply this concept to the topic of religious founders, the conclusion would be that there are, properly speaking, no founders at all. Religious founders engender religious communities, but communities also engender founders. In this case there would be reciprocal causality rather than a one-way relationship of founder as cause to community as effect.

Certain themes in the preceding chapters would suggest a need to rethink the notion of the religious founder in some of the ways just indicated, that is, construing the founder as a collaborator, as a rebuilder, or as somehow dependent on the very community that is thought to derive from the founder. From the preceding discussions of Moses, Buddha, Confucius, Jesus, and Muhammad, it should be evident that our knowledge of religious founders is mediated by historical communities that have shaped and reshaped the images of the founders in accordance with their own concerns. Gu Jiegang comments, as quoted above: "Each era has its own Confucius, and moreover, each era has various disparate types of Confucius."[6] The same could be said regarding Moses, Buddha, Jesus, and Muhammad.[7] This does not mean, however, that we should

---

5. Nonfoundationalism is based in part on the groundbreaking work of Harvard philosopher Willard V. O. Quine, and is briefly presented in John E. Thiel, *Nonfoundationalism* (Minneapolis: Fortress, 1994).

6. Quoted in Mark Csikszentmihalyi, "Confucius," p. 235.

7. An excellent study of the changing historical images of Jesus in Christendom is provided by Jaroslav Pelikan, *Jesus through the Centuries: His Place in the History of Culture* (New Haven and London: Yale University Press, 1985). Pelikan discusses some eighteen

succumb to skepticism and accept any and all portrayals of a given religious founder as equal in historical value to all other portrayals. The nature and value of the historical sources available to us vary significantly from case to case.

Arguably the documents relating to Jesus and Muhammad, for instance, provide the basis for more reliable and detailed life histories than is the case with either the buddha or Confucius. In the case of the buddha, as Richard Cohen notes, the written sources derive from a period many generations removed from the time of the buddha's life, during which the early Buddhist community had already divided into competing parties that maintained their separateness by appeal to divergent accounts of the buddha's life. Yet even here it may still be possible to glean some basic biographical information regarding the buddha. Or so some scholars of Buddhism say. It is not a question of abandoning one's historical judgment, but rather of making judgments carefully and then acknowledging frankly those areas in which it is difficult to make any judgment at all. Once we recognize the degree to which the narratives of the founders are constructed by the religious communities devoted to their memory, it is no longer possible to read these narratives in a naive or uncritical fashion. Hence the following discussion will attend to both the more-or-less canonical versions of the founders' lives and these lives as Ehrlich, Cohen, Csikszentmihalyi, Peterson, and I have critically reconstructed them.

More than any other author in this volume, Richard Cohen has expressed doubts about the entire project of designating certain historical individuals as religious founders, placing them in a comparative context, and then seeking to understand them using broad-gauged categories, such as Max Weber's notion of "the prophet." Specifically Cohen voices reservations about interpreting Buddhism as "a great personality religion . . . that originated in, and centers around, the person, life, and experience of a single individual."[8] There is an important point here. The older literature by phenomenologists of religion tended to dwell on the irreducibly individual and unique experience of particular figures. Gerardus van der Leeuw, for instance, described "the founder" as an individual who "appeared at some turning-point of time and 'established' some specific experience of [sacred] Power." The founder is "a *witness* to revelation: he has seen, or has heard, something. . . . Then he speaks of his experience." "Whenever this initiating experience possesses special intensity," he adds, "so that it arouses many subsequent experiences . . . then we speak of a 'foundation of religion.'"[9] For van

different images of Jesus, e.g., "The Rabbi," "The Cosmic Christ," "The Monk Who Rules the World," "The Bridegroom of the Soul," "The Teacher of Common Sense," "The Poet of the Spirit," etc.

8. Richard S. Cohen, "Shakyamuni: Buddhism's Founder in Ten Acts," p. 132.

9. Gerardus van der Leeuw, *Religion in Essence and Manifestation*, 2 vols. (New York: Harper & Row, 1951), 2:650-51.

der Leeuw the intense religious experience of the founder had a certain contagiousness. The original experience of the founder evoked a corresponding and comparable (though secondary and derivative) experience among the followers.

The discussion above should indicate what objections might be directed against this sort of "personality religion." It isolates the founder from the historical and cultural contexts, and intimates that there is a simple unilinear relation of the founder to the followers. Moreover, it appeals to a rather vague notion of "experience" as something that subsists in its own right apart from rituals, myths, doctrines, ethics, and the social order, and then is somehow ineffably transmitted from the founder to the religious community — a kind of spiritual blood transfusion accomplished without the use of needles or containers! None of this fits in with a historically and culturally sensitive reading of the lives of the founders and their relations to the religious communities. The intellectual background to the phenomenologists of religion, including Rudolf Otto and Gerardus van der Leeuw, lies in the thought of Friedrich Schleiermacher, who characteristically held that the human experience of the divine was independent of cognitive, moral, and institutional factors, and so could not be interpreted in their terms. Some recent philosophers of religion have judged Schleiermacher's idea of religious experience to be incoherent, since it denies that religious experience has any cognitive status while it simultaneously uses rational argument to express and explicate this experience.[10] All religious experience is *embodied* experience. Hence the experience of a founder or of a religious community cannot be grasped apart from the particulars of the historical and cultural contexts of the individual or community.

The issue of "personality religion" can be approached from a different angle, that is, by asking to what extent a particular religious tradition is tied to the personhood or identity of the purported founder. One might draw distinctions among the major religions at this point. Christianity would seem to qualify as a personality religion in a sense that Islam is not. In general Islam conceives of Muhammad's role as that of a human mediator of revelation. The message is a "sending down" (Arabic, *tanzil*), and through Muhammad

---

10. See Wayne Proudfoot, *Religious Experience* (Berkeley: University of California Press, 1985), pp. xi-xix, 1-40. Compare the analogous arguments in Steven Katz, ed., *Mysticism and Religious Traditions* (New York: Oxford University Press, 1983), which stress that mystical experience is not to be understood as somehow detached from or unconditioned by cultural and historical factors. Responses to Proudfoot, and especially his critique of Schleiermacher, may be found in reviews of *Religious Experience:* Grace Jantzen, *Journal of Theological Studies* 38 (1987): 593-95; Carl Raschke, *Journal of the American Academy of Religion* 55 (1987): 620-22; Charley D. Hardwick, *Theological Studies* 48 (1987): 352-54; and William J. Wainwright, *Faith and Philosophy* 5 (1988): 208-13.

the word of Allah comes to others. Yet the Islamic tradition emphatically denies that the Qur'an is the word of Muhammad, and so the message of Islam is to that extent detached from the person of Muhammad.[11] Yet Christianity, at least in its traditional or orthodox varieties, has stressed the ontological uniqueness of Jesus, the "only-begotten Son" of the Father. Christian thinkers have insisted that salvation itself depends on the affirmation that Jesus, and he alone, is both divine and human. So within Christianity one finds an elaborate and even elephantine body of theological reflection on the "divine and human natures," "hypostatic union," "two wills" of Christ, and so forth. Perhaps the Buddhist discussions of the *trikaya* (triple body) of the buddha are to some extent a parallel development. In any case, it should be clear that the five religions treated in this book do not conceive of their founders' roles in identical fashion. While each religious community conceives its founder — Moses, Buddha, Confucius, Jesus, and Muhammad — as a mediator of knowledge and/or salvation, the nature of that mediation differs significantly among the religions. When knowledge or salvation cannot in principle be distinguished or separated from the mediator who conveys it, as is the case in traditional Christianity, then there may be grounds for speaking of a "personality religion" in that specific sense.

Having noted the possible pitfalls in a discussion of religious founders, have we any compelling reason to continue the discussion and press ahead with the inquiry? An affirmative answer to this question implies the viability of comparative studies of religions. While criticizing the notion of the religious founder, Richard Cohen also acknowledges what is potentially valuable in the comparative approach exemplified by Max Weber: "We gain a greater ability to generalize across cultures through the Weberian type. Perhaps we even gain the ability to specify general laws about the foundation and formation of religions. But the price we pay is the reduction of cultural specificity and native context. Is the gain worth the loss?"[12] This is our line of inquiry: prophet or loss? In pragmatic terms the concept of the religious founder is vindicated to the extent that it enables the scholar of religion to "generalize across cultures" and to become aware of certain features in the life of an individual founder that might pass unnoticed if the person in question were not examined within a broader and comparative context. If in the end the com-

11. This is not to deny the high esteem in which Muhammad is held by Muslims, and the veneration that is accorded to him. See Annemarie Schimmel, *And Muhammad Is His Messenger: The Veneration of the Prophet in Islamic Piety* (Chapel Hill and London: University of North Carolina Press, 1985).

12. Cohen, p. 136. As will be noted below, Weber in fact did not attempt to specify "general laws" that governed society, and his approach highlighted the specificity and particularity of diverse cultures (see pp. 621-22, 625-26).

parative study of religious founders were merely to replicate what is already known from the study of founders singly and separately, what would be the point of comparison? Jonathan Z. Smith argues that comparison is an inescapable feature of intellectual analysis: "Whether revealed in the logical grouping of classes, in poetic similes, in mimesis, or other like activities — comparison, the bringing together of two or more objects for the purpose of noting either similarity or dissimilarity, is the omnipresent substructure of human thought."[13] With respect to religious founders, Joachim Wach has asserted: "There are striking parallels and similarities in the biographies of the great founders of religion. These resemblances cannot be accounted for merely by pointing out parallel developments in the literary 'style' of the respective traditions."[14]

What follows may be read as an investigation of Wach's basic claim, and is to be judged by its outcome — the fruitfulness of a comparative model of religious founders for understanding the dynamics of religious change in particular historical contexts. An appropriate starting point is the impressive theory of religious leadership developed by the great German sociologist Max Weber (1864-1920) in his major work *Economy and Society* (1922), to which we will now turn.

Max Weber on Religious Leadership

It is striking to see how twentieth-century scholars have all but ignored the topic of religious leadership. While Moses, Buddha, Confucius, Jesus, and Muhammad are of crucial significance in religious history, there are few studies of the founders that approach their subject with any theoretical perspective on the processes of religious leadership, and fewer still that treat their subject in a comparative perspective. In her article on "Leadership" for the *Encyclopedia of Religion*, Gillian Lindt laments:

> The concept of religious leadership . . . has advanced little beyond the pioneering studies of Max Weber and Joachim Wach. While we know a great deal about individual religious leaders and have accumulated a reservoir of case studies of such leaders, we know far less about the phenomenon of lead-

13. Jonathan Z. Smith, *Map Is Not Territory* (Leiden: Brill, 1978), pp. 240-41. J. Z. Smith and a number of other scholars have sought to vindicate the comparative method in Kimberley C. Patton and Benjamin C. Ray, eds., *A Magic Still Dwells: Comparative Religion in the Postmodern Age* (Berkeley: University of California Press, 1999).

14. Joachim Wach, "Types of Religious Authority," in *Sociology of Religion* (Chicago: University of Chicago Press, 1944), p. 341.

ership. Indeed, what is lacking at present is a generally acknowledged concept of religious leadership. Scholars working in different religious traditions use diverse modes of theorizing and analysis and do so in pursuit of differing and largely unrelated questions.[15]

Given Lindt's comments, and in light of the time that has passed since Weber's *Economy and Society* (1922), one can easily see why there is need for a fresh consideration of this subject.[16]

Weber's *Economy and Society,* which includes the book-length essay on *The Sociology of Religion,* may be regarded as the first strictly empirical examination of the structure and normative order of societies in world-historical depth. He developed a general typology of religious leadership as well as a perspective on domination and the bases of legitimation in differing types of leadership. Despite his stress on religious ideas and moral values as causative factors in the historical development of societies, Weber did not by any means ignore the concomitant role of economic conditions and physical environment. This breadth of outlook makes his social analysis rich and multifarious, and adds multiple dimensions to his treatment of religious leadership. Weber employed a theory of ideal types, yet did not think that these types implied that there were rigid laws or rules of development in society. Instead he was concerned with identifying the distinguishing features of particular social phenomena (following the German *Verstehen* tradition). Finding discrepancies between an ideal type and the actual course of events did not render the ideal useless, but indeed this is just what the type was designed to do. It was a critical and heuristic device to reveal what adheres to and what departs from expectations. Thus Weber's discussion of religious types such as the prophet, priest, and so on, was not an attempt to specify a set of cross-

15. Gillian Lindt, "Leadership," in *Encyclopedia of Religion,* ed. Mircea Eliade et al., 18 vols. (New York: Macmillan; London: Collier Macmillan, 1986), 8:485-90. In the subsequent paragraphs on Weber's model of religious leadership, I am indebted to Lindt's article.

16. Weber's great work exists in English translation as *Economy and Society: An Outline of Interpretive Sociology,* ed. Guenther Roth and Claus Wittich, 3 vols. (New York: Bedminster Press, 1968). The most important section of *Economy and Society* for the present discussion is the "Religionssoziologie," separately published in English as *The Sociology of Religion,* trans. Ephraim Fischoff (Boston: Beacon Press, 1963). Also worthy of mention is Joachim Wach, *Einführung in die Religionssoziologie* (1931), translated into English by the author as *Sociology of Religion* (Chicago: University of Chicago Press, 1944). Wach (pp. 331-74) builds on Weber's theory of religious leadership (pp. 20-31, 46-59, 60-79; cf. xxxiii-xlv) and never really breaks new ground, though he expands the typology of leadership to include "founder," "reformer," "prophet," "seer," "magician," "diviner," "saint," "priest," and *"religiosus."* See also van der Leeuw, 2:650-67, which discusses and compares the "founder," "reformer," "teacher," "philosopher," "theologian," "example," and "mediator."

cultural laws of development that might threaten the singularity or uniqueness of particular phenomena.[17]

Weber isolated features peculiar to three types of leaders — magicians,
prophets, and priests — through a comparison with one another as well as with
the subsidiary leadership roles of lawgivers, teachers, and mystagogues. Priests
may be distinguished from magicians in that priests are "functionaries of a regularly organized and permanent enterprise concerned with influencing the
gods," while magicians are engaged with "individual and occasional efforts."[18]
Priests are actively associated with some explicit social organization by which
they are employed, while magicians are typically self-employed. Moreover,
priests exert influence by virtue of professional expertise in fixed doctrine and
by vocational qualification, whereas magicians exert influence by virtue of personal gifts made manifest in miracles. The processes for entering these leadership roles differ: priests undergo intellectual training and discipline while magicians prepare themselves through a nonintellectual "awakening." Weber
himself recognized that these contrasts between priest and magician are fluid
and by no means unequivocal in empirical observation. The defining feature of
a priesthood is "the specialization of a particular group of persons in the continuous operation of a cultic enterprise permanently associated with particular
norms, places, and times and related to specific social groups."

Over and against the category of the priest, Weber defines the prophet as
"a purely individual bearer of charisma who by virtue of his mission proclaims
a religious doctrine or divine commandment."[19] For Weber it is this personal
call that decisively distinguishes the prophet from the priest. While the priest
claims authority by virtue of service in a sacred tradition, the prophet's claim is
based on personal revelation and what Weber calls "charisma." It is no accident
that priestly classes seldom, if ever, produce prophets. Closely related to the preceding is Weber's depiction of the prophet as an agent of change who takes personal responsibility for breaking with the established normative order, declaring this break to be morally legitimate and influencing others to follow his or
her example in breaking away. Unlike the magician, the prophet claims definite
revelations, and the core of the prophet's mission is doctrine or commandment
rather than magic.[20] Once again Weber acknowledges that these distinctions

17. I am indebted to Professor Brad Starr of California State University, Fullerton,
for these general points regarding Max Weber.

18. Weber, *The Sociology of Religion*, p. 28.

19. Weber, *The Sociology of Religion*, p. 46.

20. One of Weber's less central categories of religious leader is the mystagogue, who
is like the prophet in demanding a break with the established order yet legitimates that
break not in ethical or moral terms, as the prophet does, but rather in magical terms (*The
Sociology of Religion*, pp. 54-55).

are rather fluid in practice. Another distinguishing feature of the prophet in contrast to both the priest and the magician is the prophet's lack of remuneration.

Central to Weber's understanding of the prophet is the distinction between two subtypes, the ethical prophet and the exemplary prophet. The former preaches as one who has received a commission from God and demands obedience as an ethical duty. Muhammad and Zarathustra are examples of the ethical prophet. The exemplary prophet provides a personal example for others to emulate as they seek for salvation. The buddha is an example.

Weber was concerned with religious followers as well as religious leaders. For a prophecy is successful only if the prophet wins permanent helpers and co-workers. A distinctive mark of the prophet is the presence of personal devotees who, in contrast to those of the priest, are not organized into guilds or official hierarchies. In addition to these most active coworkers, there is a widening circle of followers who support the prophet in various ways and expect to attain salvation through the prophet's mission. These followers may engage in intermittent action or associate themselves continuously in a congregation. The latter sort of community does not arise in connection with every type of prophecy, but is generally the result of routinization — i.e., a process that secures the permanence of the prophet's teaching and the congregation's role as recipient and distributor of grace.

Since as a rule both the ethical prophet and the exemplary prophet are themselves laypersons (nonpriestly), the prophet's social influence depends in large part on the social roles of the lay followers. All prophets make use of the prestige of their prophetic charisma to gain support among the laity. This is because the sacredness of the tradition, as guarded by the priests, stands against the radically new revelation announced by the prophet. Depending on the success of the propaganda by each side, at least three different outcomes are possible in the power struggle between the prophet and the priests: the priesthood may overcome the prophet, the prophet may overcome and displace the priesthood, or the two may reach an understanding and arrive at some kind of compromise.

Weber's notion of religious leadership is intimately tied to his understanding that leaders of any and all sorts need to establish a claim to legitimacy. In the case of priests it is easy to see how this is done through an appeal to inviolate and time-honored tradition. In the case of magicians (or mystagogues) the miracles themselves are the only argument offered or needed. In the case of the prophet announcing a break with the established order, the question of legitimacy is obviously more complicated. Weber's notion of "charisma" is his response to this problem of prophetic legitimacy. He defines the term as "a certain quality of an individual personality by virtue of which he is considered extraordinary and treated as endowed with supernatural, superhuman, or at least specifically exceptional powers or qualities. These . . . are regarded as of divine origin or as exemplary and on the basis of them the individual concerned is treated as a 'leader.'"[21]

What matters is how the individual leader is regarded by those subject to the leader, how "charisma" evokes a response of veneration or obedience or trust. The charismatic leader's legitimacy to speak and to act is thus not derived from the followers' consent, or from custom or law, but from a transcendent realm. Yet, if the community founded by the charismatic leader is to endure through time and become permanent, then it becomes necessary for the character of the original charismatic authority to change radically. Here we encounter Weber's celebrated notion of "the routinization of the charismatic." What begins in prophetic charisma typically ends in a priestly tradition.

Weber recognized that the process of leadership transfer from the charismatically endowed leader to his or her successors is inherently unstable. How this problem is resolved — if it is ever resolved! — depends on many factors. In some cases the charismatic leader simply chooses a successor. Alternatively there may be a search for a new leader, using criteria that will fit that person for the position of authority (as in the search for a new Dalai Lama). Supernatural guidance may be sought through the use of lots or other means of divination. The new leader may be chosen by the old leader's intimate companions, with or without a ratification of the choice by the religious community at large. Leaders may arise by dynastic succession or through ritual means. In this last case the leader's charisma becomes disassociated from particular individuals, is objectified, and becomes instead a charisma of office — a transferable entity that may be passed from person to person. An example is the transmission of priestly charisma by anointing, consecration, or the laying on of hands.

While Weber's model of the religious founder as "prophet" has much to commend it, and Weber was about as knowledgeable of world history and social theory as anyone in the early twentieth century could possibly have been, there are a number of salient points of criticism. In Weber's conflict-driven model of religious founders, the prophet is an individual characterized by a charisma that sets him or her apart from others. The prophet's message is a call for a break with the existing cultural and religious traditions, and this inevitably brings about opposition from the priests whom Weber regarded as the guardians of the status quo. The discussion will turn to four salient themes in the lives of religious founders — reaffirmation, radicalization, ritualization, and responsiveness — that may call for a revision in Weber's theory of religious leadership.

21. Weber, *The Sociology of Religion*, pp. 66-67.

My critique of Weber is based on a recognition of his enduring value for the various branches of social science. Talcott Parsons, who was a leader in American sociology through much of the twentieth century, described *The Sociology of Religion* as "*the* most crucial contribution of our century to the comparative and evolutionary understanding of the relations between religion and society, and even of society and culture generally."[22] This statement alone is a remarkable testimonial to Weber's influence and importance. Unfortunately the early reception of Weber's ideas in English-speaking countries was shaped by the vagaries of the translation process. So long as most American scholars were acquainted only with the 1930 translation of *The Protestant Ethic and the Spirit of Capitalism,*[23] and remained unfamiliar with the vast text of *Economy and Society,* it was easy for them to misinterpret Weber as an "idealist" who held to the simplistic notion that people's ideas determine their economic behavior and most other elements of their social existence. Only a narrow aspect of his multidimensional theorizing was adequately grasped.[24]

In fact Weber grounded his approach to each sociological theme within a whole set of interactive concepts such as the symbolic construction of the world as a meaningful totality, rationality (a modern, Western development) as compared with rationalization (a process in all societies), theodicy as a re-

---

22. Talcott Parsons, "Introduction," in *The Sociology of Religion,* p. lxxvii.

23. Max Weber, *The Protestant Ethic and the Spirit of Capitalism* (London: George Allen and Unwin, 1930).

24. Weber's treatment of the Protestant ethic and the rise of capitalism has elicited a vast bibliography in multiple languages. A few of the book-length contributions to the discussion are as follows, in order of appearance: Hector Monteith Robertson, *Aspects of the Rise of Economic Individualism: A Critique of Max Weber and His School* (Cambridge: Cambridge University Press, 1935); Philippe Besnard, *Protestantisme et capitalisme; la controverse post-weberienne* (Paris: A. Colin, 1970); Ettore Passerin d'Entrèves, *L'incidenza del protestantesimo sulle transformazioni culturali . . .* (Torino: G. Giappichelli, 1972); Robert W. Green, *Protestantism, Capitalism, and Social Science: The Weber Thesis Controversy,* 2nd ed. (Lexington, MA: Heath, 1973); Hisao Otsuka, *Max Weber on the Spirit of Capitalism* (Tokyo: Institute of Developing Economics, 1976); Gordon Marshall, *In Search of the Spirit of Capitalism: An Essay on Max Weber's Protestant Ethic Thesis* (New York: Columbia University Press, 1982); Gianfranco Poggi, *Calvinism and the Capitalist Spirit: Max Weber's Protestant Ethic* (London: Macmillan, 1983); Hartmut Lehmann, Guenther Roth, eds., *Weber's Protestant Ethic: Origins, Evidence, Contexts* (Cambridge: Cambridge University Press, 1993); Kurt Samuelsson, *Religion and Economic Action: The Protestant Ethic, the Rise of Capitalism, and the Abuses of Scholarship* (Toronto: University of Toronto, 1993); Annette Disselkamp, *L'ethique protestante de Max Weber* (Paris: Presses Universitaires de France, 1994); Michael H. Lessnoff, *The Spirit of Capitalism and the Protestant Ethic: An Enquiry into the Weber Thesis* (Brookfield, VT: E. Elgar, 1994); Richard F. Hamilton, *Max Weber's Protestant Ethic* (Madrid: Centro de Estudios Avanzados en Ciencias Sociales, 1995).

sponse to suffering and evil, asceticism versus mysticism, and other-worldly versus this-worldly forms of ethical action. Weber further inflected each theme in his writing according to the particulars of specific cultures — ancient Near Eastern, medieval or modern European, Indian, Chinese, and so forth. The result was a richness of interpretation in *Economy and Society* that is probably unequalled in twentieth-century social science. Even in that phase of his work strictly concerned with economics, Weber's contribution may equal or exceed that of Karl Marx, although Weber is usually given much less credit.

Yet some of the liabilities of Weber's theory of social and religious change were noted even by his translator and advocate, Talcott Parsons, who wrote:

> We have seen . . . how gradual, cumulative, and interrelated changes can be; yet Weber seemed unable to conceive that major evolutionary steps could take place by gradual process. Such prophetic breaks as he describes have probably occurred, but he seems to have a theoretical bias toward highlighting them, to the neglect of the possibility of more gradual and cumulative processes of change.[25]

In Weber's favor it might be added that he at least took seriously the entire phenomenon of *change* within society, culture, and religion, and attempted to give an account of it sociologically. As often noted, Weber in this respect differs from Emile Durkheim, who was more concerned with analyzing society within a given place and time than with identifying and characterizing the dynamics of social change. Yet Weber's "sharp emphasis on the importance of the prophetic *break*," as Parsons calls it, will be one of the main points treated within the following critique.

First Theme: Reaffirmation

To a remarkable degree, the five founders we have examined here all began their work with a reaffirmation of the existing traditions. The idea of the prophet as presented by Weber strongly underscored the way the charisma of the prophet set him apart from others and especially from the priestly authorities. Tradition, for Weber, stands against charisma. Yet in all five cases, there are important elements of continuity between the prophet and the existing traditions. While Weber did not sharply distinguish the religious "founder" from the religious "renewer," he reserved the term "prophet" for a person who brought a "substantially new revelation." This revelation was based on "a special divine

25. Parsons, "Introduction," in *The Sociology of Religion,* p. lxxv.

injunction," and Weber adds that "all ethical prophets . . . were necessarily skeptical of the priestly enterprise."[26] Thus the accent falls decidedly on the prophet's discontinuity with the traditions of his time and place.[27]

The figures treated in the preceding chapters all emerge against the backdrop of some movement that precedes and anticipates them: Moses and the "Kenites" (e.g., Jethro), Buddha and the *shramana* movement, Confucius and the *ju*, Jesus and the eschatological movements of Second Temple Judaism (e.g., the Qumran community), and Muhammad and the *hunafa*. When Moses in the book of Exodus comes to the children of Israel, he comes with the message of the "God of Abraham, Isaac, and Jacob" (Exod. 3:6, 15, 16). This is not only an identification of Moses' God with the God worshiped by the patriarchs, but even represents a kind of religious genealogy that situates Moses, and the Israelites, in a lineage of God's true worshipers. As Daniel Peterson's chapter on Muhammad makes clear, Islam from its earliest days rested on an analogous idea of a monotheistic lineage.[28]

A different sort of reaffirmation occurs with respect to the theme of covenant *(běrît)*. As Ehrlich notes: "Israel's entry into a covenantal relationship with God is based on the model of ancient Near Eastern treaty texts. What this implies is that the relationship between God and Israel was conceived of in legally binding terms taken from the world of ancient Israel."[29]

26. Weber, *The Sociology of Religion,* pp. 46, 54, 66.

27. What is here termed "reaffirmation" has certain affinities with the concept of "revitalization" as described in an influential essay by Anthony F. C. Wallace, "Revitalization Movements," *American Anthropologist* 58 (1956): 264-81, reprinted in William A. Lessa and Evon Z. Vogt, eds., *Reader in Comparative Religion: An Anthropological Approach* (New York: Harper & Row, 1979), pp. 421-29. Wallace defines "a revitalization movement" as "a deliberate, organized, conscious effort by members of society to construct a more satisfying culture" (p. 422), and he contrasts such deliberate efforts with the more gradual processes of general cultural change. Wallace asserts that Christianity, Islam, and probably Buddhism originated in "revitalization movements" (p. 423), and explains his concept with reference to an organismic model of a living being under stress that has to adapt itself in order to survive and thrive.

28. Gerardus van der Leeuw noted the close connection between religious foundation and religious reformation: "Every foundation must, to a certain extent, be at the same time a reformation. . . . No 'man of God' ever erects his experience on quite new ground, but all build afresh on the ruins of previous settlements. A reformer is thus a kind of founder, and we employ the narrower designation whenever the historic emphasis falls on the transformation of what had already been given. . . . From these considerations it follows that the most important founders were also more or less influential reformers; Zarathustra, Buddha, Mohammed, Jesus — but also Ramanuja, St. Paul, St. Francis, Ignatius Loyola, Wesley and Pusey — were founders whose labours had reforming value" (*Religion in Essence and Manifestation,* 2:655).

29. Carl S. Ehrlich, "Moses, Torah, and Judaism," p. 88.

Specifically the analogy for Israel's relation with God may have been based on the Hittite suzerain/vassal treaties from the Bronze Age (1550-1200 B.C.E.), although other, more recent studies have suggested a parallel with the much later vassal treaties of the Assyrian king Esarhaddon (681-669 B.C.E.). There were two different kinds of treaties in the ancient Near East. Those between equals, known as "parity treaties," spoke in terms of a "brotherhood" between the partners and were founded on a notion of reciprocity. "Suzerain"/"vassal" treaties, in distinction, used paternal language to express the unequal relationship between the partners to the treaty. The overlord or king was addressed as father while the vassal was addressed as son. Just as every child has only one father, so too the vassal owed allegiance to only one suzerain. This sort of treaty tended to emphasize the obligations of the vassal to the suzerain. The paradox, as Ehrlich notes, is that the freedom won by the Israelites was a freedom to serve their God.[30] Thus it is clear that the canonical traditions regarding Moses in the book of Exodus ground his activity in the existing religious and political contexts (i.e., pre-Mosaic monolatry and ancient Near Eastern suzerain-vassal treaties).

Turning to the theme of religious reaffirmation in South Asia, the buddha transmits many of the key cosmological conceptions of Hinduism, especially the principle of karma and transmigration (or many lives). Perhaps one could say that the first three of the Four Noble Truths were already taught within Hinduism, or at least that they accorded with what emerged in later centuries in India as Hinduism. The Fourth Noble Truth, which expounds the Eightfold Aryan Path — a specifically Buddhist approach to overcoming ignorance, greed, and lust — is not exactly replicated within Hinduism. Yet Cohen could almost be describing Hinduism when he writes: "Buddhist theodicy, the religious explanation for how the world got to be the sorry place it is, begins with the fact of suffering. The First Noble Truth is *duḥkha,* a term that connotes suffering, unsatisfactoriness, disease, unacceptability, imperfection. Ultimately, for Buddhism, *duḥkha* is not a fact about the world, but rather a fact about living beings' (mis)apprehensions thereof. Beings cause their own suffering."[31] Given the way that early Buddhism carries over from its Indic context the themes of karma and rebirth and suffering and ignorance, it is surprising to see that a number of seemingly small differences make for large deviations in the long run. With the buddha, just as with other founders, the basic teachings were modeled on well-established cultural forms. The fourfold form of the Four Noble Truths, as some scholars have noted, is reminiscent of the medical custom in India whereby physicians would first identify the disease in a diagnosis and then state the necessary cure to be applied.

30. Ehrlich, p. 89n.201.
31. Cohen, p. 155.

The work of the buddha is related to the Indic context in yet another way. Richard Cohen notes that "Buddhist renunciants were certainly not the only renunciants to wander the byways of fifth, fourth, or third century B.C.E. India."[32] Cohen acknowledges that we are unable today to reconstruct the social history of India in the time of Shakyamuni. Yet one can say without fear of contradiction that this was a time of "critical transformation" in the Gangetic plain. People dissatisfied with the religious and ideological status quo left behind their home and families to become *shramanas* (lit. "strivers"). They may have been dissatisfied with the priest-centered traditions of the day and had concerns that Vedas and rituals could not address, as Cohen explains: "One can speak of a '*shramanic* movement' of the late fifth century. This movement was comprised of men who exerted themselves in the practice of austerities toward the realization of truth, and who often defined themselves in opposition to the established religious order of the brahmins, Vedas, and sacrifices. Thus an Indian grammarian presents the construction *shramana*-and-*brahmana,* ascetic-and-priest, as an example of ceaseless animosity, on a par with cat-and-mouse or snake-and-mongoose."[33] In this case one might speak less of a reaffirmation of tradition than a challenge to tradition. Yet the buddha's teachings may well have incorporated themes that were, so to speak, in the air in his day.

Confucius exhibits a self-conscious archaizing tendency, perhaps more clear-cut than any of the other four. The concern for intellectual lineage becomes an important feature of Confucian traditions. Confucius gives credit to the texts and individuals that have instructed him, and his followers do the same. Confucius described himself as a follower of the old ways, of *ju.* He is a cultural conservative. His political traditionalism becomes evident through his lifelong conflict with the members of the Ji clan, whom he saw as usurping the rightful power of the dukes of Lu.[34] Confucius's affirmation of existing customs is evidenced by his faithful service in such minor offices as Foodstuffs Scribe and Scribe in the Field. As he says regarding the former office: "It is just a matter of keeping the supply numbers correct."[35] Rather than breaking radically with the existing social mores, Confucius cleaves to them with surprising tenacity — an irony in the life of one whom later generations regarded as an initiator of cultural and religious change. Confucius's ambition to appropriate and understand the cultural traditions of his day appears in an intriguing episode in the *Historical Record* in which Confucius was practicing a tune on the zither and his music teacher prompted him to go on to another piece. Confu-

---

32. Cohen, p. 187.
33. Cohen, pp. 187-88.
34. Csikszentmihalyi, p. 238.
35. Confucius, cited in Csikszentmihalyi, p. 241.

cius refused because he sought to master not only the melody, but also the technique, and finally the intention of the music. Finally the teacher said Confucius had mastered the technique, and could move on. Confucius replied: "But I have not yet grasped how he was as a man."[36]

Just as Moses was preceded by the patriarchs, the buddha by the *shramanas,* and Confucius by the *ju,* Jesus was anticipated in many respects by John the Baptist, who is named no fewer than eighty times within the canonical Gospels. "Some key elements of John's preaching and praxis," writes Meier, "flowed into Jesus' ministry like so much baptismal water."[37] Although the four New Testament Gospels present John in somewhat different ways, they all proceed from the assumption that Jesus' ministry and the beginning of the Gospel message lie in John and his preaching. And John himself, with his "leather belt," garment of "camel's hair," and diet of "locusts and wild honey" (Mark 1:6),[38] was so much a reminder of the earlier prophet Elijah that a tradition arose that he was none other than Elijah raised from the grave (Mark 9:13; Luke 1:17; cf. Mal. 4:5-6). To say that Jesus' ministry took its point of departure in the activity of John the Baptist is thus an affirmation of continuity between the traditions of the Israelite prophets and the new traditions that began with Jesus.

Another element of reaffirmation is found in the role of the Hebrew scriptures in the message and ministry of Jesus. One of the striking features of Jesus' teaching, as noted above, is its frequent reference to and commentary on the texts of the Hebrew Bible. He argues his case, at least in part, on the basis of the written scriptures. Chilton and Evans go so far as to say that "the sense of his teaching is often inaccessible unless its scriptural underpinnings are appreciated."[39] So it is not really a case of a new message supplanting the old, but rather of a new interpretation of some very old and already very well known traditions of the Torah. In the Sermon on the Mount Jesus signals his new interpretations of the old traditions by the frequent repetition of the phrase "you have heard it said . . . but I say to you" (Matt. 5:21-22, 27-28, 33-34, 38-39). Perhaps the most startling expression of Jesus' reaffirmation of the tradition is the statement regarding the absolutely binding and irrevocable character of the written Torah: "Do not think that I have come to abolish the law or the proph-

---

36. Csikszenmihalyi, p. 245.

37. John P. Meier, *A Marginal Jew: Rethinking the Historical Jesus,* 2 vols. to date, Anchor Bible Reference Library, ed. David Noel Freedman (New York: Doubleday, 1991-), 2:7.

38. All biblical quotations in this chapter come from the New Revised Standard Version.

39. Bruce Chilton and Craig A. Evans, "Jesus and Israel's Scriptures," in *Studying the Historical Jesus: Evaluations of the State of Current Research,* ed. Bruce Chilton and Craig A. Evans (Leiden: Brill, 1994), p. 281.

ets; I have come not to abolish but to fulfill. For truly I tell you, until heaven and earth pass away, not one letter, not one stroke of a letter, will pass from the law until all is accomplished. Therefore, whoever breaks one of the least of these commandments, and teaches others to do the same, will be called least in the kingdom of heaven; but whoever does them and teaches them will be called great in the kingdom of heaven" (Matt. 5:17-19). Moreover, Jesus' way of using the Hebrew scriptures parallels that of other Torah scribes of his day, as explained in chapter 4 above. Not only does Jesus appeal to the scriptures, but he does so using many of the same interpretive or midrashic techniques that are well known from other Judaic sources.[40]

Regarding Muhammad and the birth of Islam, Daniel Peterson writes: "We should be wary of exaggerating the gulf between pre-Islamic and Islamic religiosity, large though it undoubtedly is. It is abundantly clear from the Qur'an, for example, that Muhammad felt no need to introduce Allah to his Arabian audience. Allah was already known to them."[41] While Muhammad broke with polytheism, the all-important Ka'ba shrine and pilgrimage traditions are retained, though with new meanings attached — a point to be taken up below under the theme of ritualization. Peterson describes the *hunafa* of pre-Islamic Arabia as persons who "held to a kind of monotheism" and "seem to have believed, as Muslims now also do, that idolatry was an innovation in Arabia and at Abraham's sanctuary, an innovation that had illegitimately supplanted the worship of the one true God, Allah." While the *hunafa* (sg. *hanif*) were not an organized movement, they represented a definite tendency within sixth-century Arabia.[42] Peterson intimates that the *hunafa* may have looked for a monotheistic revelation that was comparable to that which was first given to the Jews and to the Christians who dwelt outside of Arabia. "The contact of the caravan traders with Christianity, Judaism, and Zoroastrianism during their travels had led some of them to wonder why Arabia had no comparable (and comparably sophisticated) revelation. These were people who sought a more demanding, and more intellectually satisfying, religion than that offered by Meccan paganism."[43]

The *hunafa* not only advocated monotheism, but also a distinct ethical

---

40. Michael J. McClymond, "Jesus," pp. 423-24.

41. Daniel C. Peterson, "Muhammad," p. 475. The curious episode of the "satanic verses" might be an indication that Muhammad was not clear at the beginning on his stance toward the existing religious traditions. As Peterson points out, although pre-Islamic Arabs affirmed Allah as a single supreme deity, their day-to-day religious life was more directly shaped by the purported daughters of Allah: Manat, Allat, and al-Uzza (Peterson, p. 475).

42. Peterson, p. 483.

43. Peterson, p. 483.

tradition. To cite Peterson again: "The *hunafa* were appalled by what they viewed as the moral drift of Meccan society, which was undergoing a jarring transition from the heroic tribal ideals of a not-so-distant nomadic past to the not-yet-evolved ethics of a more individualistic mercantile lifestyle."[44] Muhammad affirmed important elements of the ethics of the *hunafa*, including the need to protect the innocent and not simply seek for personal advancement. As has often been said, the hardships of Muhammad's earlier life may have some role in sharpening his awareness of the wrongfulness of the mercantilistic ethic. Peterson writes that "the impoverished widowhood of his mother and his own orphaned status" may have been "contributors to that reformist tendency" that he exhibited.[45]

Muhammad's reaffirmation of existing traditions may be seen in the role Arabian tribal distinctions had for him and for early Islam. Daniel Peterson writes: "While his [Muhammad's] religious authority obviously did not derive solely from his family background — Qurayshi prophets were not an everyday event, after all — it is very doubtful that he would have been able to advance his prophetic claim so successfully had he not come from the lineage that he did. In the Qur'an itself, the concept of a family or a kinship group that is uniquely endowed with spiritual power is explicitly present." R. B. Serjeant noted that "the Prophets were in all cases the lineal descendants of former Prophets," and so "to Muḥammad it is natural that spiritual qualities should reside exclusively in certain families and be inherited, just as trades were hereditary in other family groups."[46] Very early in the history of Islam, the principle of dynastic succession becomes a disputed issue, and the conflict ultimately brings about a division between Sunni and Shia traditions. (The Shi'ites claimed that the succession rightly belonged to the closest male relative, and so their focus lay on Muhammad's cousin and son-in-law Ali, while the Sunnis denied this.)

The idea of a dynastic succession of leadership within the Prophet's family stands in tension with an idea of a community in which national, tribal, and familial distinctions take second place before the unity of all before Allah. The conflict between the two ideas becomes concretely embodied in the caliphate, and ultimately is resolved *against* the hereditary principle for the majority of Muslims — Sunnis — while the minority continue to hold to the hereditary principle — Shia. While Muhammad started within Arabian tribalism, his teaching on the *umma* as a single community without spiritual divisions overturned this tribalism — at least for the majority of Muslims. In terms of the categories used here, one might say that the radicalization implicit in the new Is-

---

44. Peterson, p. 483.
45. Peterson, p. 491.
46. Peterson, pp. 486-87.

lamic teaching was ultimately stronger than the reaffirmation of the preexisting traditions of tribalism. Peterson writes that "Muhammad was constructing a new Arabian community, an *umma,* in which the social bond was not blood but a shared faith, or at least a shared allegiance to him," and in time the *umma* became a kind of "supertribe," supplementing but not supplanting the customs of its blood-based predecessors. It maintained pre-Islamic practices in such areas as property and marriage relations, and used the intratribal model to understand intra-Islamic relations.[47]

There are other important elements of continuity or reaffirmation in the life and work of Muhammad. Peterson underscores the role of poetry as a primary cultural product of the Arabian tribes, and one could view the Qur'an in cultural terms as an expression of this valuation of verbal artistry. Peterson writes: "Poetry unified the Arabs. Across the peninsula it was composed in the same dialect, following the same rules of composition. This made it, in modern terms, a powerful public relations tool. A poet praised his tribe and vilified its rivals. If he was good, if his verses were memorable, his praise or his ridicule could stick to his subject for many years."[48] Muhammad's reaffirmation of the pilgrimage traditions of pre-Islamic Arabia was truly critical for the development of Islam. In laying the foundation for a world community of faith, Muhammad shifted the Arabian pilgrimage onto a vastly greater stage. Mecca continued to be a pilgrimage center but with visitors from around the globe — a development that might have astonished Muhammad's Arabian contemporaries, could they have foreseen it.

The basic themes of the Qur'an were already well established in Judaism or in Christianity or in both: the benevolence and omnipotence of God; the proper human response to God's goodness, which is gratitude, submissive worship, and generosity to the poor, the widow, and the orphan; the imminence of the last judgment, both personal and cosmic; the rewards of paradise and the terrors of hell; and the prophet's divine call. At first blush the most striking thing is how *unoriginal* the teaching of Islam sounds compared with Muhammad's monotheistic predecessors. Peterson quotes Bernard Lewis as follows: "Muhammad did not so much create a new movement as revive and redirect currents that already existed among the Arabs of his time."[49] Moreover, as Widengren argued, the rituals of Islam owed much not only to the traditions of pre-Islamic Arabia but also to those of the wider ancient Near East. Even the rhyming style of his revelations, and his manner of receiving them, were remi-

---

47. Peterson, p. 537.
48. Peterson, p. 472.
49. Bernard Lewis, *The Arabs in History,* rev. ed. (New York: Harper & Row, 1967), p. 48, cited in Peterson, p. 510.

niscent of the pre-Islamic Arabian *kahins,* or seers.[50] Muhammad in fact disclaimed originality.[51] In the Qur'an Muhammad is commanded to tell his audience: "I am not an innovator among the messengers" (46:9). The only thing new, in Muhammad's view, seems to be that he was the "warner" sent to the Arabs, who had not previously had such a figure appear among them.

Second Theme: Radicalization

Weber's prophets seem to be rather lonely figures. They emerge from the fringes of society. Their "charisma" is conferred from above. They are not understood or appreciated by the people at large. They suffer rejection. They appeal in the first instance to individuals who are as socially marginalized as themselves. They may even suffer death because of their message and their actions, and their followers long remain a despised and misunderstood minority. While Weber's image of the founder carries an element of truth, there is much that it leaves out. Almost forty years ago Peter Berger wrote an article that challenged the notion that agents of religious change are social outsiders and hence uninterpretable in terms of the existing cultural categories. Instead Berger insists that the prophet may be an insider who is gradually driven out toward the social or ideological periphery: "Charisma may, indeed, be characteristic of socially marginal individuals, coming into a society in the role of strangers, perhaps even legitimating their authority by virtue of this strangeness. But charisma may also be a trait of individuals located at the center of the institutional fabric in question, a power of 'radicalization' from within rather than of challenge from without."[52] Radicalization is, so to speak, the obverse or flip side of reaffirmation. A simple reaffirmation of existing traditions would not likely result in the sort of profound and pervasive social changes that one associates with the major religious founders. On the other hand, as Berger intimates, a person who arrives on the scene as a complete alien — straight from Mars, one might say — will probably never win a sizable following or leave behind any significant religious legacy.

In the process of radicalization, an individual of charisma affirms the existing tradition in general terms and yet begins to transform it by accentuating certain elements within it. Berger's model helps account for both the continuity

50. Peterson, p. 510.

51. The word "heresy" in Arabic is denoted by the word *bid'a,* meaning "innovation," and is opposed to the notion of *sunna,* or tradition.

52. Peter Berger, "Charisma and Religious Innovation: The Social Location of Israelite Prophecy," *American Sociological Review* 28 (1963): 950.

and discontinuity one finds in the career of the religious founder. Often the full scope of radicalization is not apparent at the beginning of a new tradition. The New Testament Gospels, for instance, record a number of positive and mutually respectful encounters between Jesus and individual Gentiles, and these episodes might be construed within the bounds of existing Jewish traditions regarding "righteous Gentiles" whose lives were pleasing to God despite their non-Jewishness. Moreover, it is difficult to find very much in the four Gospels suggesting that Jew and Gentile were later to be placed on a common footing in a new community. Jesus sends out his disciples on their preaching mission with the instruction: "Go nowhere among the Gentiles, and enter no town of the Samaritans, but go rather to the lost sheep of the house of Israel" (Matt. 10:5-6). Yet there was an implicit radicalism in Jesus' teachings on such topics as forgiveness and the kingdom of God, and this sowed the seeds for the apostle Paul's assertion of the Gentiles' place alongside of Jewish Christians. It was up to the earliest Christians to struggle with divergent interpretations of Jesus' intentions on this point (Acts 15). This sort of radicalization may be observed in the narratives regarding other religious founders as well.

The preceding discussion of religious reaffirmation called attention to a number of continuities between the ancient Near Eastern culture and the traditions associated with Moses. Yet there are elements of discontinuity as well, which might be explained by an appeal to the principle of radicalization. A familiar idea in the ancient Near East was that each people had its own gods and goddesses — tutelary or protective deities, as commonly imagined — and that as the nations contended with one another, so did their gods. Military victory over a rival group would generally include the invasion of their temples, followed by the removal of their idols to a new locale, or alternatively, the destruction or desecration of these images as a sign of the superiority of the victors and their gods. There are ancient Near Eastern accounts of captured idols being tied to a chariot and then dragged through the dirt. The narratives of conflict in the book of Exodus contain much that is familiar in this cultural context, and yet also some new and unfamiliar ideas.

The strife between Moses and Pharaoh, or Israelite and Egyptian, provides a scenario in which the character of the God of Abraham, Isaac, and Jacob becomes publicly known among the nations. The Lord speaks through Moses to Pharaoh in the following words: "For this time I will send all my plagues upon you yourself, and upon your officials, and upon your people, so that you may know that there is no one like me in all the earth. . . . But this is why I have let you live: to show you my power, and to make my name resound through all the earth" (Exod. 9:14, 16). Yahweh executes judgment on the gods of the Egyptians (Exod. 12:12), as well as on Pharaoh and the Egyptian people. Ehrlich points out that the Nile River was "the very lifeblood of the land, and one of its deities, Hapi, was the deified Nile inundation," and so the plague turning the Nile to blood was an attack on Egypt at its core. John Currid and Nahum Sarna have both noted the strong anti-Egyptian polemic in the account of the plagues.[53] The conflict of peoples and deities is nothing new in the ancient Near East, yet what is rather novel is the notion that one God has final and ultimate supremacy over all others.

Yahweh, the God of Abraham, Isaac, and Jacob, is Pharaoh's own master whether or not Pharaoh chooses to accept this fact. The Egyptian belief that the Pharaoh is himself divine in some sense makes the situation all the more poignant. An obvious reason Pharaoh cannot accept the demands of Moses' God is that Moses' people are mere slaves, and evidently their deity had not proven himself powerful enough to take very good care of them up to that point! Ehrlich writes: "The Hebrew Bible is a work that constantly subverts convention, in part because it is the legacy of a people that was itself a Johnny-come-lately on the world stage, and a very insignificant one at that. Thus there are any number of tales that end with the triumph of the one whom we would least expect."[54] The Exodus tradition, by asserting the supremacy of Israel's God over the deities of the Egyptians, laid the foundation for the later emergence of a full monotheism within Judaism. According to strict monotheism, not only is there only one God who has supreme power, but also only one God who is ultimately real or true or existent. One might see monotheism in this sense as a radicalization of what is implicit in the traditions regarding Moses and the conflict with the Egyptians.

The preceding comments rest on a straightforward reading of the biblical narratives. In light of modern critical studies of the Hebrew Bible, Ehrlich comments: "Recent scholarship on the history of the religion of ancient Israel has overwhelmingly come to the conclusion that the concept of monotheism was not introduced into a polytheistic world at one fell swoop. On the contrary, monotheism stood at the end of a long line of development from polytheism through henotheism and monolatry."[55] Some scholars speak of the earlier stages of Israelite religion as henotheistic (i.e., asserting that only one God is rightly worshiped) rather than monotheistic (i.e., asserting that only one God exists). One might interpret this process of development as a kind of radicalization. A purely monotheistic tradition did not exist at the outset, but very gradually, by fits and starts, monotheism began to displace both henotheism and polytheism.

Biblical law represents a radicalization of the principle that human life is

53. Ehrlich, p. 74.
54. Ehrlich, p. 48.
55. Ehrlich, pp. 69-70.

to be protected. While the Code of Hammurabi is justly praised for the balance and moderation it applied to the administration of justice in the ancient Near East, the laws attributed to Moses were far more sweeping in their implications. Ehrlich explains:

> In general ancient Near Eastern law, capital punishment was more often than not reserved not for crimes against humanity but for crimes against property. Although murder could be punished by death in ancient Near Eastern law, this was generally the case only when a member of the upper class had been murdered. Crimes against people of lower classes were not punished as harshly. This can be contrasted with the situation in the Hebrew Bible, in which crimes against property were not capital offenses, with the exception of cultic property and objects under the ban.[56]

The entire tradition regarding human rights in Western jurisprudence owes much to the concerns expressed in the Pentateuch for socially marginal persons — slaves, women, children, foreigners, and the poor.

The buddha's teaching, or Dharma, is at least in part a radicalization of Indic or Hindu ideas that antedated him. As noted above, one of the striking things about the Dharma is its conservatism. It preserves the basic cosmological notions of Hinduism regarding many lives, reincarnation, and the principle of karma. One of the departures of early Buddhism from Hinduism is the notion that a person can progress to ultimate salvation or liberation (Sanskrit, *moksha*) through a single lifetime of disciplined effort. Buddhist teaching presents the arhat as an individual who has already attained the goal of salvation, and has become a "never-returner" who will not be reborn again subsequent to his or her death. While this idea is not altogether unparalleled within Hinduism (which speaks of the *jivanmukhti* in much the way that Buddhism does of the arhat),[57] the notion of a final liberation after a single human life span of effort is not particularly characteristic of Hindu thinking. Buddhist teaching is a sort of distillate that concentrates certain aspects of Hinduism but leaves behind many more. This becomes clear when one considers the overriding importance of priestly ritual and caste distinctions within Hinduism, and the failure of the Buddhist Dharma to reinforce these principles. The buddha's followers are not told to observe caste distinctions, nor to seek spiritual liberation by means of sacrifices or rituals. Indeed, there are texts that speak of reliance on ritual and sacrifice as an impediment to spiritual progress.

An interesting instance of radicalization in early Buddhism pertains to

---

56. Ehrlich, p. 92.
57. Sanjukta Gupta, "Jivanmukti," in *The Encyclopedia of Religion*, 8:92-94.

the role of compassion on the part of those seeking liberation. All beings seeking liberation must free themselves of greed, lust, and hatred, but what of their attitude toward others who might or might not be following the same path? Is it enough to strive for one's own liberation without taking notice of those who are still stuck on the wheel of rebirth? The compassion of the buddha — who attained liberation but then freely chose to remain on in human form, defer his entrance into nirvana, and so instruct many others — became the foundation and inspiration for the ideal of the bodhisattva, who followed a similar path of liberation and compassion.

Cohen explains the points of contrast between the arhat and the bodhisattva: "Indeed, from the little glimpses we have had of the bodhisattva path, we can see just how different the arhat ideal is from the bodhisattva. The arhat seeks nirvana, which he must necessarily accomplish alone; the bodhisattva seeks *bodhi*, awakening, for the sake of living beings. . . . The arhat strives for the quickest possible liberation; the bodhisattva's liberation is deferred to the almost infinite future." The differences can be so great that *The Questions of Upali Sutra* states that "a pure precept observed by disciples [striving for arhatship] may be a great breach of discipline for bodhisattvas, while a pure precept observed by bodhisattvas may be a great breach of discipline for disciples."[58] It would be simplistic to assert that the arhat came first and then the bodhisattva, first self-reliant practice among Buddhists and then compassion toward others. The complex developments of early Buddhism, combined with the paucity of dated materials, make it impossible to establish any sort of trajectory or chronology of the earlier period.[59] Yet it may be safe to say that the early traditions regarding the buddha's compassionate life contained elements whose fuller implications were drawn out over the course of centuries.

Confucius has often been conceived as one who helped turn Chinese culture toward a self-consciously bookish or scholastic mind-set. Indeed, the Chinese master would on the surface seem to be the least "radical" of any of the five founding figures. While Csikszentmihalyi lends some support to the traditional image, he also uncovers another side of Confucius that is "prophetic" in its critique of established authorities. Csikszentmihalyi explains that "many central claims of the traditions collectively known as Confucianism, such as Confucius's conscious distancing from and traditionalist critique of the status quo,

58. Cohen, p. 218.
59. As with other historical issues vis-à-vis early Buddhism, it may be possible to establish a correlation or elective affinity between various elements of the tradition but not a strict cause-and-effect relationship. The narratives regarding the buddha's compassion might have arisen prior to the emergence of the bodhisattva ideal and been an inspiration for this ideal, or else the bodhisattva ideal may itself have led to the emergence of new and increasingly compassionate narratives regarding the buddha.

might even be read as critical of bureaucratic authority." Confucius in some respects appears as a Weberian prophet in the traditions of the *Spring and Autumn* and the apocryphal books. Yet Weber's outlook on Confucius was limited because he "accepted the self-identification that late imperial scholar-officials made with Confucius . . . and saw a Confucius whose authority derived from official position."[60]

Another element to be considered in Confucius's biography is that he made a circuit of the various Chinese states, and yet was not utilized by the rulers. Thus he "was willing to put good government into effect in any state whose ruler was willing to accept his counsel. Confucius's loyalty was neither to his family's home state of Song nor to his birthplace in Lu, but rather to the principles behind the program he tried to set up."[61] This observation shows the error in thinking of Confucius as a sort of patronage hound, subservient or even obsequious toward any nobleman willing to entertain him. According to the *Analects,* Confucius taught that an official salary is secondary both to the virtue of benevolence (4.5) and to reverently attending to official affairs (15.38). The gentleman, he says, must not be "ashamed of ugly clothes and nasty food," and so "in matters of food does not seek satiety, and in matters of residence does not seek security."[62] These statements are reminiscent of a theme running throughout the Hebrew Bible: the false prophet is motivated by money or other rewards, while the true prophet delivers God's message apart from any monetary compensation and even in the face of opposition.[63] In one sense Confucius was not even a "teacher," since he had no fixed payment for his instruction.[64] Rather he was more like Weber's prophet who propagates ideas for their own sake and "not for fees."[65] Thus Confucius called the rulers of his day to govern not according to their own desires but according to principle. He promulgated the radical idea that government could be good only if rulers were good, and that rulers were good only to the extent that they conformed their will to the will of heaven.

Confucius's radicalism — if one can call it such — found embodiment in his community of disciples. In the *Analects* there is no stronger bond than that

---

60. Csikszentmihalyi, p. 304.

61. Csikszentmihalyi, p. 241.

62. Csikszentmihalyi, p. 268.

63. See Amos 7:10-15, where Amos's prophecy arouses the opposition of the high priest, Amaziah, and Amos is told: "O seer, go, flee away to the land of Judah, earn your bread there, and prophesy there" — the implication being that he was making his living by prophesying. Amos replies that "I am no prophet, nor a prophet's son; but . . . a dresser of sycamore trees, and the LORD took me . . . [and] said to me, 'Go, prophesy to my people Israel.'"

64. Csikszentmihalyi, p. 268.

65. Weber, *The Sociology of Religion*, p. 48.

between a father and a son, and it appears that Confucius acted *in loco parentis* for his disciples once they left home to join him. The fact that the parents of disciples ask Confucius for financial aid shows that he did to some extent take on financial responsibility for his disciples, or else act as custodian for the wealth of the entire group.[66] Religious radicalism generally has a social analogue — the "school of the prophets" in the Hebrew Bible, the early *sangha* surrounding the buddha, the disciples of Jesus, the "companions" of the Prophet Muhammad, and so on. Even Confucius, who seems less radical than the other four founders, gives birth to a community of disciples with a countercultural flavor. They were linked by fictive kinship relations of Confucius as father and disciples as sons.

God's love for and acceptance of sinners is a theme in the Hebrew Bible, and yet this is radicalized by Jesus. Like John the Baptist, Jesus proclaimed a message concerning "the kingdom of God." Yet, unlike John, Jesus laid emphasis not on a future coming for judgment but rather on a call to participate in the kingdom here and now. The kingdom announced by Jesus was inclusive of those whom his contemporaries termed the "tax collectors and sinners" (Luke 7:34), and found expression in the meals that Jesus and his disciples shared with outsiders to the fledgling movement. Likewise, Jesus did not coin the idea that Israel's God is king over the cosmos and over history. Yet he radicalizes the kingdom by stressing its immanence, and by presenting his own ministry of miracles as a sign of its arrival. Israelite tradition insisted that God was a "father" to the nation, but Jesus radicalizes this idea in teaching his followers to pray to God using the most intimate appellative, *Abba* — a practice that is highly unusual if not unparalleled in first-century Judaism.

The Jews of the first century were well acquainted with a God characterized by both mercy and justice. Yet the teaching of Jesus is that God's action contradicts customary morality (Luke 16:1-9) and religious values (Luke 18:9-14), and does not conform to the usual idea of just desert (Matt. 20:1-16). Love is not bounded by any sort of human expectations, but rather exceeds all that might be expected (Luke 15:11-32). The parables of Jesus contain a characteristic element of surprise. They begin within the framework of customary idea but then conclude with a twist in the plotline and an affirmation of unconventional wisdom. Imagine a farmer who does nothing during the growing season, allowing the weeds to sprout up with the crops (Mark 13:30), or a rich man who invites hooligans and street people to be the guests at his lavish feast (Matt. 22:10), or a father running down the street to greet the return of a wastrel son who had already taken away his inheritance money and squandered it (Luke 15:20). Jesus' teaching stresses the mystery and majesty of the divine mercy.

66. Csikszentmihalyi, pp. 269-70.

The earlier discussion, inspired by Marcus Borg, showed the novelty of Jesus' critique of the key elements of the conventional wisdom of the day. In surprising and even shocking ways, he subverted the dominant ideas regarding family, wealth, honor, and religion. Often Jesus was ready to set the kingdom of God and its values in direct competition with those of the family. "Whoever loves father or mother more than me is not worthy of me" (Matt. 10:37). "To another he [i.e., Jesus] said, 'Follow me.' But he said, 'Lord, first let me go and bury my father.' But Jesus said to him, 'Let the dead bury their own dead'" (Luke 9:59-60). Jesus seemed to make statements that were disparaging of his own family members (Luke 8:19-21; 11:27-28). He criticized the pursuit of wealth and condemned those who sought after honor (or honorable titles and seats of honor). He even condemned religious devotion as a thing that could serve as a pretext for sinful pride and self-righteousness, in the parable of the Pharisee and the sinner (Luke 18:9-14) and in the Sermon on the Mount (Matt. 6:1-18).

This last theme in Jesus' teaching — a religious critique of religion itself — is in certain respects a radicalization of the teachings of the Hebrew prophets. The book of Isaiah includes an astonishing oracle in which God tells his people to cease presenting offerings at the Temple:

> Trample my courts no more;
> bringing offerings is futile;
> incense is an abomination to me. . . .
> I cannot endure solemn assemblies with iniquity. (Isa. 1:12-13)

These words set the Temple rituals over and against the peoples' misdeeds, and the remedy is not found in priestly ceremonies but rather in moral reformation:

> Seek justice,
> rescue the oppressed,
> defend the orphan,
> plead for the widow. (Isa. 1:17)

The Sermon on the Mount further radicalizes the prophetic critique of religious formalism, since Jesus teaches that one's motive in acting (e.g., seeking human or else divine approval) is just as important as the act itself in assessing its religious worth. A kind of introspective conscience takes its origin here, and is developed further in Paul, Augustine, monasticism, Pietists, Jansenists, the Puritans, and others in the history of Christian spirituality.[67]

---

67. See the discussion and critique of this in Krister Stendahl, "The Apostle Paul

The most far-reaching radicalization in Jesus' teaching relates to Jesus' own role and identity. As noted above, the shock and offense of Jesus' contemporaries derived in no small measure from the way Jesus presumed to have full authority to speak and act on God's behalf. He treated the relationship of the "lost sheep" of Israel to himself as more important than their relationship to Torah and to temple. While earlier prophets and holy persons claimed to speak God's message, Jesus went so far as to claim that the kingdom of God was already present in his person and ministry, and that on the last day he himself would serve as the criterion by which people would be judged by God.

The life of Muhammad, no less than that of Moses, Buddha, Confucius, and Jesus, illustrates the principle of radicalization. Daniel Peterson notes that there is evidence — notwithstanding the claims of some Muslim apologists — that Muhammad in his earlier life shared the religious beliefs and customs of his pagan environment. The name of his son Abd Manaf is "manifestly a pagan one," and it is unlikely that later Muslim sources would have invented such an embarrassing detail. His uncle Abu Lahab remained a vociferous defender of paganism until the end, while his other uncle and ersatz father, Abu Talib, never accepted Islam though he remained friendly to Muhammad during the earlier years following his prophetic call. Muslim historian Ibn al-Kalbi reports that Muhammad once bought a sheep as a sacrifice to the goddess al-Uzza — another detail that would not have been invented by a later Muslim writer.[68] The Qur'an says regarding Muhammad that God "found you astray and guided [you]" (93:7).

Nonetheless, Muhammad did not see himself as a defender of the older paganism, and neither did he understand his own teaching as a fulfillment or continuation of paganism. Instead he viewed himself as a continuator or repristinator of the Jewish and Christian revelation.[69] When he at last gained control of Mecca, Muhammad kept the Kaaba stone in its place and then systematically destroyed the 360 idols that were traditionally said to have stood in a circle around the shrine.[70] While the one and supreme God, Allah, was not unknown prior to Muhammad's appearance, Muhammad's claims on behalf of Allah increasingly involved a disparagement of all other deities. Regarding the Qur'an, Peterson comments: "Perhaps surprisingly, the uniqueness of Allah and the utter nonexistence of other gods — the sine qua non of developed Islamic theology and, indeed, of Qur'anic doctrine itself — is apparently *not* a

---

and the Introspective Conscience of the West," in *Paul among Jews and Gentiles, and Other Essays* (Philadelphia: Fortress, 1976), pp. 78-96.

68. Peterson, p. 500.
69. Peterson, pp. 500-501.
70. Peterson, pp. 583-84.

theme of the earliest revelations. Although the Qur'an eventually preaches a rigorous monotheism, it can be argued that, in their earliest phases, Muhammad and the Qur'an were only vaguely monotheistic, and that they were willing to recognize a number of other beings besides Allah as divine or at least archangelic."[71] Peterson cites the authority of Watt for this conclusion, and it nicely underscores the principle of radicalization. The enigmatic "Satanic verses" episode could be yet another indication that Muhammad's radical monotheism emerged only gradually in the course of his prophetic career.

Third Theme: Ritualization

One of the weaknesses in Weber's treatment of religious founders relates to the place of cultus or ritual in the life of new or emergent communities. In general Weber's prophet is an individual who provides moral instruction for his followers and an ethical program for the society at large. While this is certainly a part of the picture that one sees with each of the five founders examined in this volume, it is nonetheless incomplete. The preceding chapters have indicated already that the processes of religious change do not by any means bypass the ritual dimension. Weber hypothesized that the prophet would necessarily come into conflict with the so-called priests, and by construing the prophet in this fashion Weber gave the impression that priestly ritual was largely concerned with the maintenance of the status quo. The impetus toward religious change arose from ethical teaching, while the existing order — and resistance to change — found its basis in ritual practice. The priests or ritual specialists were the counterrevolutionaries of the religious realm. They were committed to keeping things as they were. Some theoretical studies have proposed that ritual is a way of creating a perfect, changeless, and self-contained world that is safe from the confusions and contradictions inherent in ordinary life. This general interpretation of ritual might support Weber's dualism of religious change through the prophet's activity versus religious stasis as supported by ritual practice.

Yet Weber's model of religious founders does not adequately account for the ways in which ritual can in fact be a reaction or protest against the status quo. A given ritual can either uphold or challenge tradition. Perhaps a loose analogy to recent events will illustrate the point. Those who are acquainted with the social movements of the 1960s may recall how the civil rights and antiwar movements reacted against "the Establishment," and yet quickly developed their own conventionalized and highly predictable modes of speaking and acting. The student strikes and sit-ins followed a set pattern, and were accompa-

71. Peterson, p. 506.

nied with regular songs ("We Shall Overcome") and chants ("Hey, Hey, LBJ / How many kids did you kill today?"). This is an instance of ritual, after a fashion, used to subvert rather than support the existing structures.[72] In effect, the protesters were priests of an alternate social order. One set of rituals displaced another. To generalize, one might say that human nature abhors a ritual vacuum. Where one ritual disappears, another is bound to appear in its place. Contrary to what might be suggested by Weber's model, there is no transition from a ritualized sort of religion to a purely ethical form and then to a new or secondary ritualization. Ritual practices continue through each successive stage of religious change. So, in fact, what is here termed ritualization might just as readily be referred to as re-ritualization, since the process unfolds endlessly.

Ehrlich notes the tendency of modern Reform Judaism to de-emphasize the ritual traditions associated with Moses and to highlight the ethical traditions. Beginning in nineteenth-century Germany (Weber's intellectual backdrop too), the leaders of Reform Judaism "stressed . . . Judaism's nature as an ethical monotheism. The laws and customs . . . were a secondary expression of the prophetic and moral insights to be gleaned from the text. For these reformers, Moses the lawgiver became Moses the prophet." Although Reform Judaism in recent years has tended to conform more closely to traditional practice, "its basic theology is still based on individual choice and the nonbinding nature of the law."[73]

Yet Ehrlich's treatment of Jewish festivals shows the importance of ritualization in the traditional narratives regarding Moses. The three ancient pilgrimage festivals that are still celebrated in Judaism — Passover; the Feast of Weeks, which is also known as Pentecost or Shavuot; and the Feast of Booths, also Tabernacles or Sukkot — arose out of a kind of re-ritualization of Canaanite practices, as Ehrlich explains:

> All three have had their original cause for celebration assimilated to the story of the exodus. In this manner Passover became associated with the rescue of the Israelites from Egypt. Shavuot, whose origins are to be sought in the festival of the barley harvest, was reinterpreted to commemorate the giving of the commandments on Mount Sinai. Sukkot, named after the huts in which the Canaanite farmers would sleep during the frenzied last harvest before the on-

72. See the discussion in Evan M. Zuesse, "Ritual," in *The Encyclopedia of Religion*, 12:405-22. Zuesse claims that "all rituals may be divided into those whose purpose is to maintain distinctions within a divine order and those whose purpose is to bridge divisions and effect transformations, renewing that order when it is threatened by internal or external change" (p. 414). The former, termed "confirmatory rituals," are concerned with upholding order, while "transformatory rituals" may seek to challenge order.

73. Ehrlich, p. 118.

set of the winter rains, became a commemoration of the desert wanderings of the Israelites. The agricultural huts were reinterpreted as symbolic of the temporary shelters in which the Israelites are supposed to have slept during their forty years in the desert.[74]

The Jewish festivals here have a twofold aspect, related both to reaffirmation and to ritualization. On the one hand the rituals are a continuation of pre-Mosaic Canaanite traditions, and on the other a re-ritualization based on the Israelites' new historical experiences and/or traditions regarding their past.

In the case of the buddha, the paucity of firm historical data from the founder's own time period makes it difficult to say which rituals might be traced back to the actual time of Gotama and which should rather be attributed to subsequent developments. Some later Buddhist practices may derive from the buddha's own life span, such as the monk's retreat during the monsoon season followed by begging during the remainder of the year. Yet it is hard to refer to such practices as "rituals." The verbal act of the threefold refuge — "I take refuge in the buddha, in the Dharma (i.e., teaching), and in the *sangha* (i.e., monastic community)" — fits the bill as a ritual practice, and yet it is not clear when and how this first arose. The familiar Buddhist rituals of veneration toward the buddha, e.g., laying food or flowers before an image, are likely to have emerged long after the life of the founder. So, for Buddhism, only tentative assertions can be made regarding a process of ritualization that occurred in connection with the founder and his activity. If ritualization is an established feature in the founding of new religious movements in general, then one might guess that such is likely to have occurred in the earliest phases of Buddhism too.

Confucius showed a scrupulous concern for the proper performance of the existing rituals. Indeed, one of the aims of Csikszentmihalyi's chapter is to recover the ritualizing Confucius that has been all but eclipsed in Western scholarship by the ethicizing Confucius. The *Historical Record* recounts the objections against Confucius's followers made by an adviser to the ruler of Qi: "Now, Master Kong makes demeanor and dress so intricate, accumulating rituals for ascending and descending and formalized rules for when to hasten and walk with open arms. It would be impossible to understand his teachings over several generations — a single lifetime is insufficient to master his rites!"[75] Sima Qian made it clear that "his ritual expertise acted as the magnet that attracted students to him," while Robert Eno goes so far as to say that in Confucius's teaching "all elements of the syllabus were directed toward the end of

74. Ehrlich, p. 76.
75. Csikszentmihalyi, p. 266.

ritualizing every aspect of speech and conduct."[76] For Confucius, *ritual* propriety was an indication of *moral* fitness for exercising authority as a ruler. Consequently the Weberian split between morality (connected with the prophet) and ritual (associated with the priests) breaks down when applied to Confucius.

Csikszentmihalyi describes a system of ritual exchange that characterized Confucius's relation with others. "The currency that Confucius recognized was not gold or copper coin, but instead one that derived its value from its use in the context of ritual sacrifice." The Confucius of the *Analects* accepted meat from the nobility he served and from those who sought his counsel. He said: "I have never failed to instruct a person who freely presented me with a bundle of dried meat" (*Analects* 7.7).[77] This use of sacrificial meats as a medium of exchange was a rejection of an exchange based on salary, luxury items, or sex. Confucius would accept certain gifts that were not meat, but preferred meat because it was the ritually correct form of exchange for his services. The gift might have high monetary value: "Even if it was a carriage and horses, if it was not sacrificial meat he did not make a ritual bow" (10.23).[78] There were some gifts so inappropriate as to be unworthy of acceptance, e.g., the gift of female entertainers made by the people of Qi.

Max Weber thought of Confucius as an academic and not a prophet, and so, in Csikszentmihalyi's words, "Weber overlooked the genuinely religious dimensions of the fifth century B.C.E. master-disciple group headed by Confucius, specifically its recourse to the immanent order of *tian* (heaven) and the reflection of that order in the ritual system."[79] While modern thinkers generally take ritual to be an aspect of culture, for Confucius it had a great deal to do with heaven. People in ritual act according to established roles, which play out in society in terms of a set of hierarchies of superior and inferior — ruler and subject, father and son, elder brother and younger brother, husband and wife.

Csikszentmihalyi cites the recent scholarship by Asano Yuichi, which lays stress on those very features that tend to be omitted from the common Western image of Confucius — his special knowledge concerning ritual, the exceptional virtue shown by portents on his physical body, and the transmission of these qualities to Confucius from heaven above. There is a "magical dimension of the sage's ability" which "derived from his special connection with heaven." The transformative power of the gentleman is like wind blowing over the grass (*Analects* 12.19), or the command of the Pole Star over the others in the night

---

76. Csikszentmihalyi, p. 266.
77. Csikszentmihalyi, p. 267.
78. Csikszentmihalyi, p. 267.
79. Csikszentmihalyi, p. 298.

sky (2.1). The disciple Zigong uses supernatural metaphors to describe the influence of Confucius, who is said to be like the moon, sun, and sky (19.23-25).[80]

Ritualization is a theme that pertains to Jesus no less than to the other founders. Two ritual practices that are all but universal throughout the history of Christianity — baptism and eucharist (also known as communion, or the Lord's Supper) — derive from the lifetime of Jesus himself.[81] The "baptism of repentance for the forgiveness of sins" (Mark 1:4) as practiced by John the Baptist was conferred also by Jesus' closest followers and perhaps even by Jesus himself.[82] The background to John the Baptist and his practice of baptizing is unclear, and the issue is disputed. Some have theorized that John the Baptist was a member of a community like the Qumran sect which practiced frequent purifications through a ritual bath (Heb. *mikva*). Others have proposed a plausible yet still unproven hypothesis that the Jewish proselyte baptism which was practiced after the first century C.E. — whereby a Gentile convert marked the transition into the Jewish community with a ritual plunge into water — actually antedated the appearance of John the Baptist and served as the model for John's practice. If this is correct, then it gives a new twist to John's message and ministry, which is in effect a declaration to the Jews of his day that they were as Gentiles in God's sight and needed cleansing to prepare themselves for "the Coming One" (Matt. 3:7-12).

In general the practices of proselyte baptism provide a better analogy for the water rituals of John the Baptist and Jesus' disciples than do the lustrations practiced by the temple priests and the Qumran sectaries. The priestly and Qumran washings were repeated again and again, whenever there was ceremonial uncleanness, while both proselyte and early Christian baptisms were once-for-all events that brought initiation into a new community. However one interprets the washings or baptisms at Qumran, by John the Baptist, and among Jesus' followers, this is a fascinating case of ritualiza-

---

80. Csikszentmihalyi, p. 297.

81. A few groups generally considered Christian have broken with one or more of the rituals of baptism and eucharist, e.g., the Quakers and the Salvation Army. Yet they represent a tiny minority. Conversely it should be noted that Roman Catholicism has affirmed not fewer but rather more than two rituals (or sacraments) that were instituted by Jesus himself. The traditional view, as expressed at the Council of Trent (1545-62), is that Jesus inaugurated the seven sacraments of baptism, eucharist, confirmation, ordination, marriage, penance (or reconciliation), and last rites (or extreme unction, or anointing of the sick). Contemporary Catholic scholars generally see the latter five sacraments as developments that took their origin subsequent to the time of Jesus.

82. John 4:1-2 is somewhat ambiguous, but seems to suggest that the first baptisms that occurred among Jesus' followers were a mark of affiliation with Jesus, and yet that it was Jesus' disciples rather than Jesus himself who baptized.

tion and re-ritualization whereby the action of washing with water had new meanings attached to it. What had been at first an action mandated only for temple priests became, in time, a sign of repentance among lay or nonpriestly Jews, and eventually a mark of affiliation to the nascent Christian movement for Jews and Gentiles alike. The ritual of baptism became essential to initiation among Jesus' followers: a baptized person was a Christian, and an unbaptized person was not.

Like the practice of baptism, the last supper of Jesus with his disciples provides an instance of re-ritualization where a familiar action has a new and unfamiliar meaning attached to it. If we presume (with most but not all scholars) that the Last Supper occurred in the context of the Jewish Passover celebration, then Jesus' words and actions are a dramatic transformation of the existing ritual. Whereas the disciples might have expected a simple blessing pronounced upon the bread and wine, instead they hear the words "Take; this is my body" and "This is my blood of the covenant, which is poured out for many" (Mark 14:22-24). One can only surmise the reaction such words and actions might have evoked in their original context. The significance of the Passover meal is irrevocably altered for the early Christians through its connection with Jesus' imminent suffering and death. As baptism in time becomes the defining mark of Christian initiation, the ritual of remembrance with bread and wine becomes the mark of Christian participation. A Christian is one who "communicates" by partaking in the eucharistic meal.

The life of Muhammad contains a number of incidents related to ritual. The shift in the direction of prayer (Arabic, *qibla*) from Jerusalem to Mecca is a clear instance of ritualization, or rather re-ritualization. Traditional sources attribute this change to a certain Arab chief, Bara, who even before the *hijra* reasoned that, as he and a number of townspeople were making their way toward Mecca to meet the Prophet, it would be wrong to turn their backs on so holy a place and pray toward a city in distant Palestine. Jerusalem's connection to the prophets and prophethood lay in the remote past, while Mecca's was contemporary. Bara's practice of bowing toward Mecca was not followed by the others, but a revelation that came to Muhammad in 624 altered the direction of prayer (Qur'an 2:142).

Another ritual change occurred as the Muslims replaced the fast connected with the Jewish Day of Atonement, called Ashura, with a monthlong fast during the month of Ramadan.[83] As Peterson points out, ritualization may be one of the most decisive ways the movement led by Muhammad marked itself out as distinct from what preceded it: "By these moves Islam made clear that it was not merely a strange sect of Judaism or Christianity. It was an independent,

83. Mahmound M. Ayoub, "'Ashura," in *The Encyclopedia of Religion*, 1:462-63.

new, Arabian revelation."[84] Yet another important ritual is the tradition regarding washing before prayer. The sources indicate that an angel appeared to the Prophet and taught him the ritual washing and gestures and recitations that were to accompany liturgical prayer. He taught this practice to his wife Khadija, and then to the other earliest followers, Ali, Zayd, and Abu Bakr.[85] Lastly one notes the place of ritual within the whole sequence of events, as recounted by Peterson, wherein Muhammad entered and in effect "cleansed" the shrine in Mecca — touching the Ka'ba, declaring *Allahu akbar* ("God is supreme"), then circumambulating the Ka'ba seven times, destroying the images, and drinking from the well of Zamzam. Many of these actions by the Prophet soon came to be regarded as exemplary, and Muslims who make the pilgrimage to Mecca imitate many of Muhammad's actions.

Before leaving the topic of ritualization, it is worth noting the role of sacred space in the emerging traditions regarding the five founders, with the possible exception of Confucius. At the burning bush Yahweh announces to Moses that the people of Israel will return to worship at the very same spot. Mount Sinai becomes both a place of public worship and the site where God reveals the commandments. In the later development of the Judaic tradition, Yahweh is said to have "chosen" not only the children of Israel as his covenant people but also "Mount Zion" as the specific location for the temple. This space is sacred, set apart from all other places. In Buddhism Bodh Gaya — the site of the Buddha's enlightenment — is a sacred locale and place of pilgrimage for multitudes. The relics of the buddha, such as the sacred tooth in Sri Lanka, are carefully preserved, cared for, housed, venerated, and celebrated in ritual practices. For Christians the regions of Galilee and Jerusalem have been pilgrimage sites throughout the centuries. There is Mecca in Islam, as well as other less prominent sites, such as the Al-Aqsa mosque and the Dome of the Rock in Jerusalem. Many of these sites mark the place of important events in the lives of the religious founders.

Fourth Theme: Responsiveness

Max Weber, as already indicated, stressed the way that the prophet's "charisma" evokes a response of trust and obedience on the part of followers. There is not only an extraordinary individual, but there is also a community that recognizes and responds to the individual perceived as extraordinary. Weber writes: "It is recognition on the part of those subject to authority which is decisive for the

84. Peterson, p. 543.
85. Peterson, p. 513.

validity of charisma. This is freely given . . . and consists in devotion to the corresponding revelation . . . or absolute trust in the leader."[86] It is worth pausing over and reflecting on the words "absolute trust." Does this phrase actually correspond to the founders' historical situations, so far as we are able to reconstruct them? Were there not some halfhearted, skeptical, or ambivalent persons — a doubting Thomas or two or three — who accompanied each of the religious founders and may have been numbered among the closest disciples? What sorts of interactions occurred between the religious founder and the first followers? If "absolute trust" is not an accurate description of these interactions, then what would be?

Weber's notion of prophetic charisma finds its correlative in the "absolute trust" of the followers. Yet this is a rather limited model for understanding the leader-follower relationship. Taken at face value, Weber's idea of charisma might suggest that the founder is an individual who retires to the desert, mountain, or forest, and then — perhaps after arduous self-discipline and reflection — returns with a new teaching. The message is already a finished product. The questions posed to the founder result in a further elaboration of the message, yet not in any substantive changes in the message. The general picture just sketched is clearly at variance with the content of the preceding chapters on Moses, Buddha, Confucius, Jesus, and Muhammad. It is important to note how much of the teaching of the five founders is given in dialogical form. What story would there be of Moses' life apart from Aaron's collaboration — not to mention Pharaoh's opposition? What would become of the buddha's teaching apart from Ananda's queries and gentle prodding? What of Jesus without Peter, James, and John; or Confucius without Duke Ding of Lu or Zigong; or Muhammad without Khadija, Ali, or Abu Bakr? According to the Hebrew Bible, Moses was at a loss in governing Israel until Jethro, his father-in-law, told him that he needed to delegate some authority to others (Exod. 18). This story typifies the improvised quality of the lives of religious founders.

Perhaps in some sense one can say, with Weber, that the teaching of the prophet, like charisma itself, was conferred or given extrinsically. Yet, if so, then it was given to the founders in the context of the give-and-take of their encounters with disciples, well-wishers, doubters, and opponents. The major religious founders were characterized by their *responsiveness* to new situations. Thus one really cannot understand these figures apart from the specific situations in which they interact with other people and confront new and unanticipated circumstances. It may be helpful to distinguish different sorts of response, such as a response to disciples as contrasted with a response to adversaries. The

---

86. Max Weber, *On Charisma and Institution Building*, ed. S. N. Eisenstadt (Chicago: University of Chicago Press, 1968 [1922]), p. 49.

claim here is that the five founders came up with creative ways of responding to disciples and detractors alike. Their actions and teachings often had an improvised and ad hoc character. Homer's *Odyssey* describes its hero, Odysseus, with the Greek word *polytropos,* meaning "shifty," "versatile," or "wily" — a characterization borne out in many adventures and clever ruses and narrow escapes from danger. One might say that each of the five founders was "polytropic" in this sense.

To be sure, Weber's model of religious leadership includes the prophet's encounter with his followers — charisma — and the encounter with outsiders — conflict. Charisma and conflict are the two themes that characterize the prophet's relationship with his contemporaries. Yet this bifurcation between charisma and conflict smooths over the complex and untidy situations that can and do occur. It is not always a case of a small cadre of true believers over and against a hostile mob. Typically conflicts arise between leader and followers, including (but not limited to) defections within the inner ranks. Disputes often break out between disciples, sometimes resulting in different parties during the lifetime of the religious founder. The most significant conflict does not have to be between the founder and the followers on the one side and everyone else on the other. Furthermore, the charisma of the prophet may, to some degree, be recognized by a larger public without carrying the same meaning for them as for the circle of disciples. Those who are not fully convinced of the prophet's message, or divine commission, may still wish to form a strategic alliance with the prophet and his followers. The life of Muhammad provides numerous illustrations of this phenomenon.

In the case of Moses there are shifting situations that emerge in the course of his prophetic career. Pharaoh does not listen, so Moses is given one new sign after another. The people grumble, so Moses is instructed to do certain things to lessen their grumblings and to provide for their needs. The episode with Jethro portrays Moses as overburdened with judicial duties. He listens to Jethro's advice and establishes a kind of appellate court system. Here is a clear instance of adaptation according to pragmatic considerations rather than simply according to divine dictates.

One may also consider the dialogical form of the teaching ascribed to Confucius in the *Analects.* Csikszentmihalyi notes the frequent repetition of the phrase *zi yue,* "the Master said," which stresses that the words were given as advice to disciples and princes.[87] Thus the appropriate context for interpreting Confucius's sayings is this interaction of master with disciples, and not the Chinese educational and civil examination system, which subsequently adopted these sayings and the texts that contain them. Max Weber thought of charisma

---

87. Csikszentmihalyi, p. 243.

not as something that Confucius had, but rather as something intrinsic to the whole Chinese bureaucracy.[88] Despite Csikszentmihalyi's critique of Weber's interpretation, at this point it can be seen as indirect affirmation of the strong connection of master and disciples. If Confucius possessed "charisma" in Weber's sense, then it was not a private spiritual achievement but rather a charisma directed toward the ethical instruction and cultivation of others. In the common Western image of Confucius, he is the one who has stamped his impress on the people. They "did not see Confucius as a character in the tableau, but rather credited him with its design."[89] Perhaps Confucius's responsiveness to differing persons and situations is one reason for this image of him.

Consistently the New Testament Gospels present Jesus as a teacher engaged in spirited repartee with those around him. The Gospel of Luke even portrays Jesus' childhood as an anticipation of his adult life. At age twelve he is in the temple "sitting among the teachers, listening to them and asking them questions" (Luke 2:46). The Jesus of the Gospels sometimes allows his disciples to pose questions that he is already prepared to address: "One of his disciples said to him, 'Lord, teach us to pray, as John taught his disciples.' He said to them, 'When you pray, say: Father, hallowed be your name. . . .'" (Luke 11:1-4). On other occasions he does not wait for his disciples to raise an issue, but takes the initiative himself: "Now when Jesus came into the district of Caesarea Philippi, he asked his disciples, 'Who do people say that the Son of Man is?'" (Matt. 16:13). On still other occasions he becomes embroiled in debates over the interpretation of the Torah, relating to the tax owed to Caesar (Matt. 22:15-22), the resurrection of the dead (Matt. 22:23-33), the "greatest commandment" in the law (Matt. 22:34-40), and the identity of the Messiah as the "son of David" (Matt. 22:42-46). He plies not only his disciples but also his opponents with questions (e.g., Matt. 21:28-32).

In general Jesus comes across as mercurial, unpredictable, and uncontained. In the pages of the Gospels he encounters a wide cast of characters — a tax gatherer, leper, Gentile, member of the Sanhedrin, Pharisee, demoniac, prostitute, beggar, paralytic, rich man, child, and so forth — and his responses are as varied as the persons he encounters. One is struck by Jesus' gentleness with the social outsiders and misfits he might well have snubbed, and his bluntness with the social and religious leaders whom he indicts for their hypocrisy, greed, pride, and lack of compassion. He is a responsive leader, but not one who curries favor with the powerful. The instructions Jesus gives his disciples suggest that they too must be discerning in their responses to others. He conveys a vivid warning: "See, I am sending you out like sheep into the midst of wolves" (Matt. 10:16). When they go out to preach, they too are to ad-

88. Csikszentmihalyi, p. 298.
89. Csikszentmihalyi, p. 233.

just their actions according to the responses they evoke. If rejected by a house or a town, they are to "shake off the dust" from their feet in protest (Matt. 10:14). When opposed, they need not stick around: "When they persecute you in one town, flee to the next" (Matt. 10:23). Not everyone will be either able or willing to accept the disciples' message, and so there is a further warning: "Do not give what is holy to dogs; and do not throw your pearls before swine, or they will trample them under foot and turn and maul you" (Matt. 7:6).

Peterson's chapter on Muhammad demonstrates that many of the specific revelations now enshrined in the Qur'an were first given in response to specific situations. Muhammad for his part was very adaptable to changing situations. One might consider, for instance, the Prophet's adoptive son, Zayd, and his wife Zaynab. Muhammad came to love Zaynab and yet could not marry her, since he already had four wives — the maximum allowed under the existing Qur'anic revelation — and the revelation did not allow men to marry the former wives of their sons. This situation brought on the new revelation in Surah 33:37-40 that allowed Muhammad to marry the now divorced wife of Zayd, and it included the sweeping principle that "Muhammad is not the father of a single one of your men, but he is the messenger of God." Muhammad was given an exception to the limit of four wives. Although Zayd had been known for almost forty years as Zayd b. Muhammad, now his name reverted to that of his biological father, Zayd b. Haritha. As Peterson explains, this episode had a major impact on subsequent Islamic history by effectively undercutting the legitimacy of adoption.[90] Another intriguing episode, involving one of the Prophet's wives, occurred when A'isha lost her necklace and those accompanying Muhammad went searching for it and got stuck in the desert without any water to perform the mandatory washings prior to their regular prayers. Muhammad received a revelation that they could "wash" for prayer in either sand or dirt, and so fulfill their obligation to pray (Qur'an 4:43).

Frequently Muhammad demonstrated his shrewdness, and this should temper any impression of him as an otherworldly character. Even so important an event as the *hijra* of 615 — the starting point of the Islamic calendar — was a strategic move. The complex military and political maneuvering of the final years of Muhammad's life also shows how responsive he was to the changing circumstances among the Arabs. He escaped from Mecca by having Ali impersonate him by wrapping up in his cloak and pretending to be sleeping in his bed. In fleeing Mecca Muhammad and Abu Bakr threw off their pursuers by heading south, away from the direction of their destination in Yathrib/Medina. There they remained hidden for several days in a mountain cave.[91] Upon Mu-

90. Peterson, pp. 600-601.
91. Peterson, pp. 533-34.

hammad's arrival in Medina, site of a sizable Jewish population, he came to the shrewd decision to break with tradition, as Peterson explains: "In a marked departure from the tribal ethics of pre-Islamic Arabia, Muslims were to defend a Jew against injustice, even if that injustice had been committed by a fellow Muslim, and Jews were to take the part of an injured Muslim against a Jewish wrongdoer. Although the Jews were not required to recognize him as a prophet, Muhammad was to be the arbiter in disputed matters."[92] Muhammad was constructing a new Arabian community, an *umma*, in which the social bond was not blood but a shared faith, or at least a shared allegiance to him.[93] Perhaps the whole development of the *umma* can be viewed as a strategic response to the specific historical situation of the Prophet. In tracing the career of Muhammad one is struck at how often his revelations and innovations are evoked by the particular circumstances that he encountered.

Some aspects of Muhammad's leadership are disturbing to consider, or at least to most non-Muslims. He sanctioned the use of trickery to capture and kill the poet Ka'b b. al-Ashraf, an outspoken opponent of the early Muslims.[94] At the battle of Uhud, an opponent of the Muslims fulfilled a vow to eat raw the liver of Hamza, the Prophet's uncle, and then proceeded to mutilate the body by cutting off the nose and ears and other pieces of flesh. Muhammad's response was a vow to mutilate thirty Meccans at the next opportunity. Yet a revelation advised him against doing so, and he never fulfilled the vow.[95] One episode involved a mass execution of some six hundred to nine hundred apparently unarmed men, who were beheaded with a sword stroke and then pushed into a mass grave. This was done by order of the Prophet.[96]

Often Muhammad was adroit in battle, as when he had his army scatter over a wide terrain during the night, gather large quantities of wood, and build campfires for each individual soldier — so as to deceive his enemies into thinking that his army was larger than it really was.[97] To get the Banu Nadir to surrender and leave their fortresses, Muhammad began felling the date trees that were the source of their wealth, and which would take many years to replace.[98] To counter a massive force of ten thousand soldiers in league with Mecca, Muhammad convened a council for military advice and decided to follow the suggestion of Salman the Persian that they build a trench to protect themselves

92. Peterson, p. 537.
93. Peterson, p. 537.
94. Peterson, pp. 550-51.
95. Peterson, p. 557.
96. Peterson, pp. 567-68.
97. Peterson, pp. 558 and 582.
98. Peterson, p. 561.

against attack by cavalry.[99] A Jew from Zubayr said that if the Prophet would spare him and his family and property, he would tell them how to break into the citadel that protected his people. Muhammad, "who well knew that war involved stratagem as well as heroism," agreed.[100] In short, Muhammad appears as a responsive and adaptable leader, always ready to vary his strategy in reaction to shifting circumstances.

Conclusions

The foregoing discussion of five founders and four themes — reaffirmation, radicalization, ritualization, and responsiveness — has reevaluated Max Weber's theory of religious leadership, and has laid the groundwork for a revised picture of the religious founder. The general outlines of this critique should now be clear enough. Weber's theory hinges on the individual prophet who is characterized by a charisma that sets that person apart from others. The prophet's message is a call for a break with the existing cultural and religious traditions, and evokes opposition from the priests, whom Weber regarded as the guardians of the status quo. Weber conceived of the prophet as a rather lonely figure whose message derived from unusual or even unique spiritual experiences.

A first objection is that the religious founders examined in these chapters commonly began their work with a *reaffirmation* of the existing traditions. At first glance they were rather conservative. The process of innovation was gradual and perhaps even imperceptible at the beginning. The changes that eventually resulted in a new religious tradition, distinct from what preceded it, typically came about by a process of *radicalization* from within. Some element within the inherited tradition was accentuated while other elements were deemphasized. Thus the founder did not achieve success by convincing his followers that he was the recipient of a radically new message that was discontinuous with what preceded it. Rather the founder won support by persuading others that the prevailing interpretation of the inherited tradition was erroneous.

A key element in this transformation from within is *ritualization*. Weber started by presuming a sharp contrast between the "prophetic" or "ethical" dimension of religion and the "priestly" or "ritual" aspect. Yet when one scrutinizes the work of the religious founders, one discovers that they not only brought to their followers new maxims or imperatives, but new rituals as well (e.g., the Last Supper, bowing toward Mecca, etc.). In fact, the process of ritual-

99. Peterson, p. 562.
100. Peterson, p. 576.

ization typically takes the form of re-ritualization, that is, the replacement of one set of rituals with another. The earliest followers of Muhammad begin by bowing toward Jerusalem when saying their prayers, but within a matter of years the direction of prayer (Arabic, *qibla*) is set toward Mecca.

A final aspect of the founders' lives that Weber tended to shortchange is their *responsiveness* to community and context. The chapters on Moses, Buddha, Confucius, Jesus, and Muhammad show that we ought not think of the founders as retiring into the desert, forest, or mountain, and then returning from solitude with their mission and message in finished form. Instead there is generally a kind of creative improvisation that characterized the founder and his relationship to the community of followers. A religious founder is more like the leader of a jazz quartet than the conductor of a chamber orchestra. Without any sheet music for guidance, and with only a general set of chord changes, the jazz musician guides the quartet through these changes and yet is open to moving in new and unanticipated directions. Often there is an interesting interplay between the leader and other musicians. In an ensemble of experienced performers the bassist might decide to add an entirely new riff in the middle of the song, and the trumpeter and pianist will follow along before the musicians all finally return to the original set of changes.

So it is with the major religious founders. The teachings attributed to Moses, Buddha, Confucius, Jesus, and Muhammad in the canonical sources are rendered in *dialogical* form, and it would be gratuitous to imagine that the interlocutors and the situations in these dialogues were all invented at a later stage. More plausible is the assumption that the teachings and practices of the religious founders evolved over the years as new issues emerged and new questions were posed. So, in a manner of speaking, one could say that Moses and Confucius and the others were shaped by their respective communities just as the communities were shaped by the founders.

To return to the initial image, a founder is generally conceived as one who sets in place the lowest part of a building, while others erect a structure on top of it. Many others may carry on the work of building, but only on top of the foundation already laid down. Whatever the shape and character of the foundation, none of the later builders will ever supplant the foundation on which they build. Their relationship to the founder is asymmetrical: they depend on the founder, but the founder does not depend on them. In light of the discussion here, this picture is accurate only if it is modified to stress the founder's dependence on a preceding culture and tradition and on the work of many other persons. The founder, as noted earlier, should be conceived not in lonely isolation, but as a *collaborator* with others and as a *rebuilder* upon the work of others. In light of our contemporary understanding of the five founders — Moses, Buddha, Confucius, Jesus, and Muhammad — it is less plausible than in Max

Weber's day to imagine the religious founder as a more-or-less isolated individual who acts with grim yet lonely determination to lay down a foundation for others to build upon.

One of the possible implications of this reappraisal of Weber for the general study of religion would be an application of a revised model of religious founders to other historical or contemporary movements. Whether one is examining a twelfth-century monastic order, a nineteenth-century leader such as Bahaullah, or a contemporary leader of a new religious movement, one might expect to find not only the phenomena that Weber described under the categories of prophet, priests, and charisma, but also what has here been termed reaffirmation, radicalization, ritualization, and responsiveness.

In a comparative study of this sort it is appropriate to say a word regarding contrasts. Comparative religion is also contrastive — if it is true to its sources. The differences between the founders and their teachings are legion. Nirvana is not the same as heaven — a state of individual selves in communion with God. *Shariah* or Islamic law is not in any sense equivalent to the law of Moses. The stress on family relations in Confucianism is not paralleled in any of the other four traditions considered here. The place of Jesus within Christianity is not like that of Moses within Judaism or Muhammad within Islam. The list of differences could go on and on. Jonathan Z. Smith, who has written much on comparisons between religions, has commented: "For, as practiced by scholarship, comparison has been chiefly an affair of the recollection of similarity. . . . The issue of difference has been all but forgotten."[101] The limited aim of this book has been to examine Moses, Buddha, Confucius, Jesus, and Muhammad with respect to one selected theme, namely, their identity and activity as religious founders. The discovery of certain common themes among the five figures is consistent with the recognition of disparity and difference as well.

One is puzzled by the now fashionable notion that all religions are the same, when the initial impression conveyed in a study of world religions is that of disparity or even incommensurability. Even on so weighty a matter as the legitimacy or illegitimacy of violence, the major faith traditions seem to be saying different things, although almost all of these traditions include elements that favor a policy of nonviolence.[102] Yet a Muslim's reasons for choosing nonviolence may be different from those of a Jew, Christian, Buddhist, or Confucian, not to mention a Hindu, Baha'i, traditional religionist, or secular person. To

101. Jonathan Z. Smith, *Imagining Religion: From Babylon to Jonestown* (Chicago and London: University of Chicago Press, 1982), p. 21. The first sentence is highlighted in the original.

102. See David Noel Freedman and Michael J. McClymond, "Religious Traditions, Violence, and Nonviolence," in *Encyclopedia of Violence, Peace, and Conflict,* ed. Lester Kurtz and Jennifer Turpin, 3 vols. (San Diego and London: Academic Press, 1999), 3:229-39.

misunderstand this is to misunderstand a religion as it is experienced and practiced by its adherents. Some well-intentioned scholars and laypersons have insisted that the comparative study of religions must begin by presuming some kind of ontological unity among the major faith traditions. Yet this is a metaphysical or theological presupposition, and it runs the risk of distorting one's perspective and limiting one's capacity for thorough empirical study of the differing religions. A more academically sound procedure is to begin from the observed differences of the religions — a veritable cacophony of sounds! — and only cautiously and tentatively address the question of what kind of unity, if any, may exist between the major religious traditions. R. C. Zaehner, who held the chair in Eastern Religions and Ethics at Oxford, in a book that ought to be better known than it is, suggested a model of "concordant discord" among the religions.[103] The present work may serve as a specimen of "concordant discord" that stresses a number of formal concordances or similarities among five major religious founders, and in so doing provides a new cross-cultural and interreligious model for understanding the dynamics of religious change.[104]

103. R. C. Zaehner, *Concordant Discord: The Interdependence of Faiths*, The Gifford Lectures, 1967-69 (Oxford: Clarendon, 1970).

104. Thanks are due to four individuals who read an earlier draft of this conclusion and provided corrections and comments: David Noel Freedman of UC San Diego, Ninian Smart of UC Santa Barbara, Brad Starr of California State University, Fullerton, and Carl Ehrlich of York University. All remaining errors of fact and interpretation are my own.

Final Thoughts: Responses to
McClymond's "Prophet or Loss?"

Final Thoughts of Carl S. Ehrlich

Michael McClymond has both delivered a powerful critique of Max Weber's theory of religious leadership and proposed an important new theoretical model of religious leadership. In essence, McClymond's major criticism of Weber's work is the latter's system of classification, whereby the religious founders become identified as innovative prophets standing over against the entrenched orthodoxy of the priesthood. This is justifiably attacked as an oversimplification of the evidence. In his defense, it could, however, be argued that Weber was the victim of his own success in presenting an original paradigm of leadership.

Weber stood in a German academic tradition that was on the one hand concerned with the classification of human and natural phenomena into neat categories, and on the other was influenced in its reconstruction of ancient Israel's religious history by the liberal Protestant scholarly tradition that reached its apex in the careers of the source-critic Julius Wellhausen and the form-critic Hermann Gunkel. It is often the weakness of systems of classification that they are forced to tailor their analyses of the evidence to fit their preconceived theoretical frameworks. McClymond makes a very strong case for the inapplicability of much of Weber's theory of religious leadership to the five leaders discussed in this book, based as the latter's theory is upon the presupposition that the founder was a prophet who opposed and was opposed by the priesthood. On the other hand, as McClymond admits, the categories into which Weber divided the types of religious leaders, i.e. priests, prophets, magicians, lawgivers, teachers, and mystagogues, were conceived as fluid categories by Weber. Nonetheless, as Weber's treatment of Moses makes clear,[1] his assignment of a leader to one of these categories greatly influenced his overall treatment of the leader.

In fairness to Weber, it should be noted that what distinguishes McClymond's approach from Weber's is not an essential disagreement about the fluidity of roles assigned to religious founders, but their respective methodologies, indicative as they are of their time and place of proposal. Whereas Weber was more interested in defining the specific social context of the founder, or — in the words of his contemporary Hermann Gunkel — the *Sitz-im-Leben,* the founder/leader's "life setting," McClymond is more concerned with the narrative development of the accounts of founders' lives and actions. Thus one can characterize McClymond's methodology and analysis as postmodern and essentially processual.

Weber established and formulated his analysis of religious leadership according to a more or less rigid systematization of the roles that the leader could assume. In his posthumous book *Ancient Judaism,* Weber presented Moses as a prophet who introduced the worship of a new God to the Israelites and cemented the relationship between the people and their God through the imposition of a covenant or *berith,*[2] but who nonetheless was "a hierocratic and popular leader."[3] However, in light of the conclusions of his contemporaneous scholarly colleagues, the legalistic tradition of Judaism was divorced from Israel's prophetic heritage. Hence, while Moses did in Weber's view introduce basic religious and ethical teachings, the expansion of these into the legalism that Wellhausen, a major influence on Weber in his reconstruction of the history of ancient Israel, associated with late biblical Judaism was not connected with Moses according to Weber. In his opinion, Moses introduced the worship of the previously unknown Midianite God YHWH into Israel and established basic guidelines for his divine service, which included setting in place an ongoing oracular structure presided over by the Levites.[4] These ritual guidelines were the extent of the *berith* that Moses introduced.[5] Later tradition was to expand quite greatly on the Moses of history, turning him for instance into a "therapeutic miracle worker" in the account of the brazen serpent Nehushtan (Num. 21:6-9; 2 Kings 18:4).[6] Hence, Weber took a developmental approach to under-

1. See Max Weber, *Ancient Judaism,* trans. from the German and ed. Hans H. Gerth and Don Martindale (Glencoe, IL: The Free Press, 1952).

2. Weber, *Ancient Judaism,* p. 118.

3. Weber, *Ancient Judaism,* p. 372.

4. Weber, *Ancient Judaism,* pp. 241, 263.

5. Weber, *Ancient Judaism,* p. 126.

6. Weber, *Ancient Judaism,* pp. 159(-61, 174-75).

standing the character of Moses. While one can quibble about the details of his reconstruction of the Moses of history vs. the Moses of legend, his approach to the subject is one that lies within the purview of critical investigations of the biblical traditions.

In his analysis of religious leadership, one can deduce that McClymond takes a more holistic approach in analyzing Moses and his leadership roles. Since his examination of Moses is based on the biblical text as a whole, he is able to include aspects of the Moses tradition in his analysis of leadership that Weber had to dismiss as later legend. McClymond's Moses is, of necessity, both more multi-faceted and more limited in scope than Weber's. For McClymond, Moses is the Moses of the whole Hebrew Bible. Hence, he is able to include many passages and traditions concerning Moses that Weber would not have attributed to Moses. Yet, by limiting himself to a holistic reading of the biblical text, McClymond is not able to include the Moses picture as it developed within postbiblical Judaism. In addition, by taking the biblical narrative at face value for the sake of argument, McClymond combines into one model of Mosaic leadership traditions that span close to a millennium of development and encompass the religious viewpoints of various communities.

Weber, on the other hand, was acutely aware that the Moses tradition was an evolving one that is not framed solely by the parameters of the biblical text. Therefore, he was able to include both biblical and extra-/postbiblical sources in his discussion of the evolving picture of Moses. Since Moses is someone whose role is for the most part a reflection of the evolving Jewish community, Weber was able to employ Moses as a foil reflective of evolving Judaism, even though Moses was by no means the central focus of Weber's analysis of "ancient Judaism."

In light of my chapter on Moses in this volume, it should be evident that I do not view the search for a historical Moses as one likely to yield tangible results. Hence, I have attempted to present Moses as a conglomeration of differing images reflecting the ideology, theology, and needs of an evolving faith community. It could be argued that all six of Weber's categories of religious leadership can be identified in the person of Moses, although not all appear in the biblical account. As Weber, however, recognized, the Hebrew Bible represents just one moment in the development of the Moses traditions. Nonetheless, Weber limited his interpretation of Moses on the basis of his understanding of the historical prophet who lay behind all later legendary accretions. Weber was quite correct in his understanding of Moses as the archetypal prophet. Yet, when one approaches the Moses traditions from a more holistic perspective than Weber's, one can identify all six of Weber's types of religious leadership.

Although implicit in the text, Deuteronomy 34:10 provides a fitting epithet to Moses as *prophet* when it claims that "Never again did there arise in Israel a prophet like Moses." His status as a *magician* is exemplified in a number of accounts, such as those in which the outcome of battle relies on Moses keeping his hands raised or the stories of striking water from the rock (Exod. 17; Num. 20). Since there was a priestly house that claimed descent from Moses (Judg. 18:30), it can be assumed that there was a tradition according to which Moses was a *priest*. Significantly, Moses was the one who ordained the first priests in Israel (Lev. 8). Hence, priestly succession and ritual were based on Mosaic authority. Moses as *lawgiver* is as central to the Torah as he is to Judaism as a whole. Although Moses instructs the people throughout the latter four books of the Pentateuch, it was Rabbinic Judaism that transformed Moses into Moshe Rabbenu, "Moses our Rabbi," i.e., Moses as *teacher* par excellence. And finally, in the *Zohar*, the classic work of the medieval Jewish mystical tradition known as Kabbalah, Moses functions very clearly as a *mystagogue*. In Jewish memory, therefore, Moses is much more than the founding prophet that Weber proposed.

What about McClymond's four R's (reaffirmation, radicalization, ritualization, and responsiveness)? Are they applicable to the Moses traditions? Again, it must be stated that the Moses whom McClymond is dealing with is different from Weber's Moses. He is not Weber's reconstructed historical Moses, but the Moses of the whole Hebrew biblical narrative. It is this Moses, who most likely is a legendary patchwork, who is the object of McClymond's attention and whose story he attempts to fit into his type-pattern of religious founders. McClymond is undoubtedly correct in his claim that the Hebrew Bible does not view Moses as the creator of "something completely different." The Bible is very careful to situate him within the context of a longer narrative that begins at the creation of the world and includes the formation of the people of Israel. Moses initiates a new chapter in the people's history and in their relationship with the divine, but it is the ancestral God who commissions him (Exod. 3:15). In this manner Moses reaffirms the religious traditions of the Israelites. Rabbinic Judaism extended this theme to read many of the laws given at Mount Sinai back into the earlier history of the people. This *reaffirmation* then allows Moses to initiate a new chapter in the people's saga by bringing them into a new covenant with their God. Although there had been previous covenants between God and individuals such as Noah and Abraham, according to the biblical narrative this Sinaitic covenant was a *radicalization* of the previous concept. The ensuing *ritualization* of the people forms the core of the Mosaic covenant and belies Weber's juxtaposition of the priest and the prophet. Ritual is absolutely central to the image of Moses the biblical prophet. The sundering of ritual from revelation in Weber's thought can be considered a function of his intellectual milieu. Indeed, for the later development of Judaism it is to the authority of

Moses that all ritual innovations are attributed.[7] Finally, the "improvisational quality" that McClymond finds "in the lives of religious founders" is amply documented in the traditions concerning Moses, whose pattern of leadership appears quite ad hoc at times. Situations arise and are dealt with in consultation with God, a famous example of which is the question of female rights of inheritance in the case of the daughters of Zelophehad (Num. 27:1-11; 36:1-12). This communal dialogue with the divine as mediated by Moses becomes the pattern for the development of later Jewish ritual change and innovation. As time went by, the authority for change passed from priests and prophets to rabbis. In all these cases, the *responsiveness* of both the founder and the traditions deriving from his authority is the operative dynamic principle.

Ultimately, the story of the founder, at least in the case of Moses, is the story of the tradition and community based on the founder. Thus one may posit a symbiotic relationship between the founder, who derives his (posthumous) significance from the traditions and reinterpretations of his character by his latter-day adherents, and the community that derives its religious justification from its image of the authority of the founder. While one may question whether McClymond's model of foundational religious leadership would have applied to the hypothetical Moses of history, there is no doubt that it advances our understanding of the dynamic regulating the Moses of tradition and — perhaps more importantly and directly — the development and self-understanding of the religious tradition itself.

Final Thoughts of Richard S. Cohen

An introduction to Buddhist doctrine written in fifteenth-century Tibet by the monk mKhas-grub-rje (pronounced, Kay-troob-jay) opens with an overview of various Buddhist positions on how and when Shakyamuni became an awakened one, a buddha.[8] This Tibetan scholar writes that Buddhists belonging to the Hinayanist Vehicle of Disciples believe that Shakyamuni was a human being who gained complete awakening while sitting under a tree in Bodh Gaya at the age of thirty-five. The Mahayanists, by contrast, are not as interested in *when* Shakyamuni gained awakening, as they are in *where* the transformation happened. The bodhisattva's final existence took place in a high heaven called

---

7. The change from a Temple-centered community to a synagogue-centered one in the early Rabbinic period can be considered a form of what McClymond has termed "re-ritualization."

8. See F. D. Lessing and A. Wayman, trans., *Introduction to the Buddhist Tantric Systems* (Delhi: Motilal Banarsidass, 1983), pp. 17-39.

Akanishtha, where countless buddhas from every direction congregated around him and conferred an initiation with great light. Following this consecration, the bodhisattva experienced the final ultimate realizations that transmuted him into a god above all other gods. Indeed, Shakyamuni's spiritual body resides perpetually in Akanishtha heaven, in permanent bliss, while it sends down magical emanations to one hundred myriad worlds that put on the play of human buddhahood. Finally, mKhas-grub-rje's treatise presents the doctrine of Tantric Buddhism, a special branch of the Mahayana accepted by mKhas-grub-rje himself. According to Tantric Buddhism, bodhisattvas are usually ignorant of the actual mechanism by which buddhahood is attained until just before they attain it. Shakyamuni was no exception. When the bodhisattva entered what he thought would be his final trance as a mere human, his mistake was soon corrected. Buddhas from every direction gathered around him, snapping their fingers and saying, "You cannot become a complete buddha by this trance alone." The buddhas then instructed the bodhisattva in secret practices that lead to the ultimate state. These practices include sexual intercourse, which requires the assistance of a knowledgeable partner. The buddhas thus summoned a goddess named Tilottama, whose adamantine vagina helped convey the bodhisattva to the brink of buddhahood. Finally, at dawn, the buddhas bestowed the highest initiation on the bodhisattva and he awakened as Shakyamuni buddha.

How did Shakyamuni become a buddha? How did he gain that special power without which he would have been incapable of founding a new religion? Was he a man when he did it? Or was he a god? Was he a celibate ascetic? Or did he participate in the erotic arts? Did he reach his goal through his own effort and insight? Or was ritual consecration by other buddhas a critical moment in the process? Did Shakyamuni become a buddha in the fifth century B.C.E.? Or did he become a buddha in time out of time? Has he been a buddha on earth only once? Or is he a buddha in one hundred myriad worlds simultaneously?

What really happened? Indeed, is not this last question the first legitimate question to ask in a book on founders? Should we not begin by acknowledging that Shakyamuni buddha was a man? You and I both might reflect upon the common thread of our own biographies, from birth, through school, to family, work, and finally death. Can we understand how Shakyamuni, the man, was unlike us until we first know how much he was just like us? How can we appropriate Shakyamuni's accomplishments as a religious founder, and thereby compare him to other founders, if we do not get to the bare bone facts of his life on earth? Indeed, it is easy to see why one would *not* cite mKhas-grub-rje's Tantric doctrines when writing the history of Shakyamuni's awakening. mKhas-grub-rje's view is thoroughly that of an insider; it builds myth upon myth; it represents local, historically situated doctrines as universal norms and absolute truths. Instead, should not a scholar follow the example of H. W. Schumann, whose *The Historical Buddha* promises its readers the life of "a demythologized person." In Schumann's volume, the buddha is not "a holy man floating in the air, so to speak, but a worldly-wise organizer who knew how to exploit political situations with tactical skill."[9]

Of course, I ask these questions tongue in cheek. When invited to contribute a chapter to *The Rivers of Paradise* I agreed precisely because it offered the opportunity to revisit the issue of religious founders apart from pieties, scholarly and religious. I wanted to ask: What is uncommon about the commonsense expectation that the demythologized biography of a man should serve as the basis for understanding his accomplishments as a founder? My own reading, both in the history of Buddhism and the theory of religion, has suggested to me that it is neither self-evident nor a universal tenet that the examination of biographical facts must be the first place to look when studying the life of a religious founder. Though I did not discuss mKhas-grub-rje in the chapter itself, for me the important question is not: How does mKhas-grub-rje's text fall short as a source for recovering Shakyamuni's actions as founder? But rather: How does a reading of mKhas-grub-rje's representation of Shakyamuni as founder enable us to modulate the very idea of *founder*?

Let us leave mKhas-grub-rje aside, for my chapter in *The Rivers of Paradise* also takes its structure from a complex doctrine of embodied buddhahood. But I am no Buddhist. I did not present Shakyamuni as the performer of ten necessary acts because *that* Shakyamuni is *my* Shakyamuni. Rather, I adopted that model because I wanted to test the strategic practices of scholars. My allegiances here are divided. On the one hand, the inspiration for *The Rivers of Paradise* is Hans Küng's statement: "There can be no peace among the nations unless there is peace among the religions." This is a call for scholars to take public responsibility for their representations of religion. On the other hand, I agree in full with Russell McCutcheon's prescription for how scholars of religion should play the role of public intellectual: "In our analysis of the manner in which humans represent the world and their place in it . . . we are equipped to scrutinize the ideological sleight of hand that leads to a seemingly perfect fit between the model constructed and sanctioned by the society or group in question, on the one hand, and reality, on the other."[10] My representation of Shakyamuni attempts to mediate these two claims. Peace among the nations may be impossible without peace among the religions, but peace has its price. War gives way to

---

9. H. W. Schumann, *The Historical Buddha,* trans. M. O'C. Walshe (London: Arkana, 1989), p. ix.

10. Russell McCutcheon, "A Default of Critical Intelligence? The Scholar of Religion as Public Intellectual," *Journal of the American Academy of Religion* 65 (1997): 454.

peace through either conquest or compromise. My concern is that peace among the religions may be won through an "ideological sleight of hand" in which conquest masquerades as compromise.

Let me put the matter plainly. My representation of Shakyamuni as the performer of ten necessary acts was inspired by Jonathan Z. Smith's *Drudgery Divine,* which describes a "Protestant hegemony" governing the study of Christian history.[11] According to Smith, insofar as scholars of early Christianity "imagine a 'pristine' early Christianity centered in Paul and subjected to later processes of 'corruption'" their work is "almost always apologetic."[12] This conception of Christian history, characterized by Smith as an "old Reformation myth," is given voice by John Calvin, among others: "You know," Calvin wrote in 1539 to Jacopo Sadoleto, a Catholic Cardinal, "not only that our (i.e., the Protestants') agreement with antiquity is far closer than yours, but that all we have attempted has been to renew that ancient form of the Church which, at first sullied and distorted by illiterate men of indifferent character, was afterwards flagitiously mangled and almost destroyed by the Roman Pontiff and his faction."[13] When Smith speaks of a "Protestant hegemony" he is claiming, in brief, that the terms of this debate were not buried with Calvin and Sadoleto. Calvin's conception of an unsullied ancient Church informs academic practice to this day to such a degree that the bulk of scholarship on early Christianity is now, for Smith, "an affair of mythic conception and a ritual practice."[14]

Smith's observations helped shape my contribution to *The Rivers of Paradise,* for in my view the same hegemony holds sway over the general practice of comparison within the study of religion. Scholars who compare religious founders can be interrogated, to see whether they are apologists promoting Protestant-inspired myths and practicing Protestant-inspired rituals. Scholarly formulae, such as the equation between the demythologized buddha and the historical buddha, can be interrogated, to see whether they are Protestant-inspired, building myth upon myth and presenting historically situated doctrines as universal norms and absolute truths. In short, I saw this volume's interest in founders as one more attempt to authorize Protestant sensibilities as universal. I wanted to see whether I could represent the buddha as founder in a way that thwarted this hegemony of the Protestant gaze. But I was not exclusively critical in my agenda. I also wanted to see how a distinctly non-Protestant

11. Jonathan Z. Smith, *Drudgery Divine* (Chicago: University of Chicago Press, 1990), p. 143.

12. Smith, p. 143.

13. John Calvin and Jacopo Sadoleto, *A Reformation Debate: Sadoleto's Letter to the Genevans and Calvin's Reply* (New York: Harper & Row, 1966), p. 62.

14. Smith, p. 143.

representation of a religious founder might inflect the category *founder* so that it could be useful in a global context.

It was in this light that I was nonplused to read Michael McClymond's conclusion to the book, "Prophet or Loss?" Before I take issue with McClymond's words, let me express my gratitude to him. The editor at Eerdmans was concerned that allowing each author to express his own final thoughts would detract from McClymond's own conclusion, but McClymond convinced him that a dynamic plurality of voices was preferable to a static but conclusive conclusion. In fact, McClymond's final essay is fair in many of its details. McClymond cites Jonathan Z. Smith to make the point that "comparison is an inescapable feature of intellectual analysis."[15] Not only do I agree, but I would even extend this point further by citing David Chidester's insight that "the discovery of religion arose out of the practice of comparison itself."[16] Again, when McClymond proposes that one can find the themes of reaffirmation, radicalization, ritualization, and responsiveness running through Shakyamuni's life, I would agree, albeit with the proviso that we should speak in terms of *representations* of Shakyamuni's life. And I would even concur that these themes can serve as a basis for comparing representations of Shakyamuni to representations of Moses and representations of Muhammad, representations of Jesus and representations of Confucius.

However, there are two points at which I take issue with McClymond's final thoughts, which is why they do not speak for me as a contributor to *The Rivers of Paradise*. The first point responds to the question: What are we looking for when we investigate religious founders? The second point responds to the question: What are we finding when we find religion?

What are we looking for when we investigate religious founders? "Prophet or Loss?" suggests that we are looking for individuals who, standing in their own respective streams of tradition, work to divert those streams until new self-sustaining channels are formed. Religious founders *reaffirm* the validity of certain existing religious doctrines and practices, but also *radicalize* those beliefs and practices, by emphasizing some and de-emphasizing others; they use a process of *ritualization* to establish a social basis for the dissemination of their teachings; and they are *responsive* to their followers', and detractors', needs and interests. Thus, the religious founders for whom we seek are not "more or less isolated individual[s] who [act] with grim yet lonely determination to lay down a foundation for others to build upon,"[17] as Weber would have it. Rather,

15. McClymond, "Prophet or Loss?" p. 620.

16. David Chidester, *Savage Systems* (Charlottesville and London: The University of Virginia Press, 1996), p. 17.

17. McClymond, "Prophet or Loss?" p. 657.

they are bebop masters of the spirit, who collaborate in playing out gloriously new expressions of religious truth. Who could say this does not improve on Weber? McClymond's four R's offer a more nuanced understanding of how religious founders operate than that presented by Weber, but these four R's do not address my concerns as a contributor to this volume because they do not go far enough. The four R's "save the appearances" of Weber's model, while I would critique that model in a thoroughgoing manner. What is the global value of a volume such as this if it does not historicize and globalize the epistemological space carved out by the term *founder* itself?

One can see McClymond's conservatism, for example, in his commentary on Gu Jiegang's commentary on Confucius. Gu Jiegang writes, "Each era has its own Confucius, and moreover, each era has various disparate types of Confucius."[18] I have no broader context within which to assess Gu Jiegang's remark, but it would seem that he is raising an important problem vis-à-vis the ability to study Confucius as a singular individual. One can draw (at least) two distinct implications from Gu Jiegang's words: Either he is suggesting that scholars should search for the *real* Confucius by compiling a phenomenological survey of representations of Confucius; or he is saying that Confucius, the man, serves an ideological function within his eponymous tradition. McClymond is clearly sympathetic to the first implication. His footnote, for instance, approvingly cites Jaroslav Pelikan's *Jesus through the Centuries* as offering eighteen different images of Jesus keyed to the historical development of a Christian society. Each age may have its own Jesus, but behind all stands the true Jesus of Nazareth. And while McClymond accepts the first implication of Gu Jiegang's words, he explicitly cautions against the second: "We should [not] succumb to skepticism, and accept any and all portrayals of a given religious founder as equal in historical value to all other portrayals." Historical value, in this passage, is measured by fidelity to "what really happened," or at least what we can know of what really happened, that is, the positive facts. Behind representations of historical reality stands that reality itself. It would seem, for McClymond, that our job in a book like *The Rivers of Paradise* is to seek out that reality as best we can, for only thus will we have the surest basis for a positive comparison of religious founders, and the most accurate evidence for a general model of religious foundation.

We should not succumb to skepticism, but not for the reason McClymond supposes. We should not succumb because "what really happened" is neither a necessary nor sufficient basis for the investigation of religious founders. When we compare religious founders, *what* is being compared? Why do we consider Confucius, Shakyamuni, Moses, Jesus, and Muhammad to be found-

18. McClymond, "Prophet or Loss?" p. 616.

ers at all? What is the genesis of this category, founder? What is its genealogy? As a constructive process, comparison is constitutive of the study of religion. Indeed, Chidester even suggests that the category "religion" itself is a product of comparative analysis. But comparison is an act of attention that focuses the mind and arranges information, two actions that are always guided by intellect and taste. Thus comparison in the study of religion is not unlike comparison in the choosing of mangos. To find the right mango, you have to know what to look for: size, shape, feel, and smell. Of course, there is no one right mango. To make a sour chutney, look for small, green, immature mangos; to make a sweet chutney, you want fruit that is large and ripe.

On this analogy, it is wrong to claim, as McClymond does, that "by definition the major religious founders are of general significance and not only of local import,"[19] however reasonable this might sound. The phrase "by definition" is an instance of what McCutcheon calls an "ideological sleight of hand that leads to a seemingly perfect fit between the model . . . and reality." To whose definition does McClymond refer? What interests are camouflaged by the association of universality with "definition" and the simultaneous diminution of the local through the rhetorical "not only"? The well-known cliché, "all politics is local," has a lesser-known corollary, "all religion is local, for all religion is political" or, more broadly, social. The expectation that Moses, buddha, and the rest have an abstractly translocal significance that can be brought out through a direct comparison of their precise deeds and words is itself a local expectation, one enveloped within what Smith has called "Protestant hegemony."

In short, if we are going to acknowledge that the act of comparison is central to scholarly analysis of religion, we are going to have to acknowledge as well that the terms of comparison are historically determined. Functionally this means that we cannot compare these figures as founders until we articulate what we mean by founder, and why we have chosen one conception of founder over another. Confucians have various conceptions of Confucius, but do they also have various conceptions of Confucius as founder? Do Muslims and Jews differ in this regard? Certainly Buddhists do. McClymond's titular pun "Prophet or Loss" is fun, even light-hearted, but it harbors a dark truth that I think stands at the center of the study of founders as McClymond describes it: To pose the question "Prophet or Loss?" is to have lost already, for implicit in this question is the expectation that one is lost without a Weberian prophet.

This brings me to my second point: What are we finding when we find religion? For Weber the prophet is "a purely individual bearer of charisma, who by virtue of his mission proclaims a religious doctrine or divine com-

19. McClymond, "Prophet or Loss?" p. 614.

mandment."[20] Again, McClymond's four R's nuance the singularity of the prophet, and emphasize his involvement in a variety of social relations. But the four R's do not touch the prophet's core distinction: Prophets proclaim religious doctrines or divine commandments. In fact, McClymond's four R's do not directly address the specifically religious dimension of founders at all. I would imagine that reaffirmation, radicalization, ritualization, and responsiveness are as critical for the development of competitive corporations as they are for founding new religions. Did not Bill Gates reaffirm, radicalize, ritualize, and respond when he copied the Apple Macintosh computer's graphical user interface and launched the Windows revolution? The four R's do not tell us what distinguishes Bill Gates from Muhammad, Jesus, Confucius, Moses, and Shakyamuni as *religious* founders. Let me suggest that McClymond does not explore this point because he does not differ from Weber here, and so it goes without saying: religious founders are *religious* because they proclaim religious doctrines or divine commandments. Religion, principally, is a matter of doctrinal truths; actions are religious insofar as they are reflect and refract those truths.

In this, McClymond fits well within the mainstream. I could cite a raft of authorities to elaborate this point, but let me use the words of Talal Asad, who in a recent interview says: "Belief has become a purely inner, private state of mind, detached from everyday practices. But although it is in this sense 'internal,' belief has also become the object of systematic discourse, such that the system of statements about belief is now held to constitute the essence of 'religion.'"[21] Again, to expand upon a point I made above, the equation of religion with belief dates to the Reformation, born of a Protestant desire to recover the essence of Christianity at its origin, in the Spirit as revealed by the Word, Jesus Christ. The words of John Calvin illustrate this point: "There is nothing of Christ, then, in him who does not hold the elementary principle, that it is God alone who enlightens our minds to perceive His truth, who by His Spirit seals it on our hearts, and by His sure attestation to it confirms our conscience."[22] For Calvin individual religiosity is known through individual belief engraved on the heart by a transhistorical source. Just as we should challenge the apologetic underpinnings of scholarship that presupposes the historicity of an unsullied ancient Church, and just as we should be skeptical of attempts to recover the activities of founders exclusively in terms of bio-

---

20. Max Weber, *The Sociology of Religion,* trans. E. Fischoff (Boston: Beacon Press, 1964), p. 46.

21. Talal Asad, "Modern Power and the Reconfiguration of Religious Traditions," *Stanford Electronic Humanities Review* 5/1 (1996): http://www.stanford.edu/group/SHR/5-1/text/asad.html.

22. Calvin and Sadoleto, p. 79.

graphical data, so we should be on guard against appeals to religion that take their start from words like conscience, belief, insight, realization, experience, and faith.

Let me conclude these final thoughts by restating that although I have been critical of *The Rivers of Paradise* as described by McClymond, a project such as this does have its value insofar as it provides an opportunity to interrogate and modulate terms and ideas that have been fundamental to the conception of religion. I have already suggested that the notion of founder must be shorn from its Protestant moorings. The same is true of religion. At the very least, a comparative work like *The Rivers of Paradise* should take a creative look at how religion is *not* essentially a matter of belief. We must reject all expectations that the Spirit as known to personal, private experience is necessarily central to the religions we compare. Only thus can we take seriously mKhas-grub-rje's representation of Shakyamuni becoming a buddha through ritual consecration and sexual intercourse. Certainly mKhas-grub-rje's doctrine deserves as much respect as that of Jesus' Resurrection or Moses' encounter with a bush that burns but is not consumed. Again, only if we are willing to look beyond Weber's association of founders with doctrines and commandments can we understand the profound ways in which Shakyamuni's role as founder has been associated with his body as a source of relics. To cite the *sutra On Commissioning Buddha Images*: "The blessed one showed relics belonging to previous buddhas and [his own] bodily remains, because each and every single minute atom produces a marvelous heap of merit." This representation of buddhahood offers an understanding of Shakyamuni's religiosity that differs radically from the one given him by Weber. What happens to Shakyamuni's status as founder if we conceive of him not as a teacher of truths but as a provider of relics, not as a speaker of wisdom but as a source of mundane and supermundane power? Does this make Shakyamuni any less religious? Does it make him any less a founder? Of course not! But it does force us to reconsider the constrictions and constructions, assumptions and anticipations, faiths and heresies that circumscribe all representation of men as religious founders.

Final Thoughts of Mark Csikszentmihalyi

In his concluding essay, Michael J. McClymond attempts two very interesting things. First, he attempts to revive Weber's project of comparing religious founders by appealing not so much to the possibility of finding universals among them, but instead by emphasizing the appreciation of particulars that may come from such a comparative study. Second, he defines four themes in the lives of religious founders, themes that at times read less like common characteristics than axes along which one may compare these founders. Ending with Zaehner's idea of "concordant discord," this new model of religious leadership attempts to find common threads without disturbing the particularities of distinct religious traditions.

This is a very thought-provoking piece, and deserves more careful discussion than it will be receiving here. What I would like to do is address a particular problem that the examples of Confucius and some other Asian religious founders introduce to the project of comparing such figures, both within and across cultures. As I have tried to show with respect to Confucius, there is no standard "life" of the founder that is not to some extent constructed by later members of various traditions associated with him. This observation could be stated with even less qualification about Laozi (Lao Tzu), the figure most often identified with the founding of China's other major indigenous religion. This raises the question: If there are common themes in the biographies of religious founders, are these commonalities the product of similarities between their lives, of common concerns among the interpretive communities through which the stories of their lives have been mediated, or perhaps of the way that modern scholars of religion are receiving the stories?

Let us begin with the idea that social institutions involved in the retrospective construction of religious biographies might create or emphasize common traits in those biographies. Scholars have often divided Chinese religion into the *sanjiao,* or "Three Teachings" of Confucianism, Taoism, and Buddhism. While different groups transmitted the biographies of the founders of these traditions, shared characteristics of the process of transmission may have resulted in a common spin given to the descriptions of their lives. The earliest extant biographies of both Laozi and Confucius come from the pen of Sima Qian at the end of the second century B.C.E., and while there are myriad differences between his descriptions of these two figures, there are also some surprising connections. Both accounts emphasize their methods of spiritual training and their intent to implement their particular *dao* or way. Both describe them as serving in official capacities: Laozi in charge of Zhou records and Confucius in minor state offices. More interestingly yet, the early record attributes to both an expertise in ritual and maintains that Confucius traveled to learn about it from Laozi.[23] The first extant description of Buddha in Chinese describes his spiritual training in Taoist terms, a regimen that allowed him to perfect his *dao.*[24] There is no question that

23. These biographies are in ch. 63 of the *Shiji.* For a discussion of the story of the encounters between Laozi and Confucius see A. C. Graham, "The Origins of the Legend of Lao Tan," in *Studies in Chinese Philosophy* (Albany: State University of New York Press, 1990), 111-24.

24. It also mentions the possibility that the buddha was really Laozi (*HouHanshu* 20b.1082).

when these initial biographies were written, their subjects were consciously being described in terms of one and other.

The reason for similarities such as these are impossible to determine, however, given that both the lives of the founders and the portraits drawn of them are subject to similar cultural parameters. While it is impossible to know to what degree these biographies simply transmitted accurate biographical information and to what degree they altered or created new details, there are some shared features that suit the didactic lessons of biography rather well. An example is the fact that the first descriptions of Confucius and the buddha both emphasize they were impervious to corruption by gifts of beautiful women. The Han dynasty memorial that includes a brief reference to the temptation of the buddha by "Heavenly spirits" uses his example to chastise the debauched emperor. Similarly Sima Qian's biographical treatment of Confucius concludes with these words: "From the emperor through the lower officials. . . . All rely on the words of Confucius to rectify their standards, and so one may say that he was the ultimate sage."[25] Both these accounts use the founders as instructive examples of behavior with which to contrast that of the ruler, and thereby emphasize the quality of self-restraint that rulers should emulate. In these cases, it is certainly tempting to hypothesize that the presence of identical features in some biographies of these Chinese religious founders might stem more from a common didactic interest on the part of those transmitting the biographies.

In a discussion of religious founders across cultures, of course, this comparison of the treatment of founders in one culture may only serve as an analogy. It would be odd to expect stock features of Chinese biography, such as the auspicious portents before birth and the signs of precociousness in areas of later achievement, to appear in biographies written outside the cultural context. At the same time, it is not unreasonable to expect that if there are features that the *religions* selected as deserving attention in a volume like this share, then these features might result in common patterns in the hagiographical accounts those religions generate. This is especially the case once a particular tradition becomes aware of standards in the portrayal of founders in other cultures. In the treatment of Confucius in this volume, the Buddhist aspects of Confucius after the arrival of Buddhism in the Six Dynasties and the Christian overtones in Qing dynasty interpretations of the Sage show that this was the case for China.

Finally, it is worth asking whether there are institutional features of the contemporary study of religion that might systematically affect the portrayal of religious founders. One could rephrase this question by generalizing about those creating the portrayal, asking what Bourdieu's *homo academicus* would

25. *Shiji* 47.1947.

want to see as it invents the characteristics of Dubuisson's *homo religiosus*. Here again, I would like to look to the Chinese examples I have used to illustrate a related but slightly different issue.

In China, those who have emphasized common traits among founders of religions have most often been those involved in promoting the compatibility of these traditions. Indeed, as in the legend of the face-to-face meeting between Confucius and Laozi, the notion of the commonalities between religious founders in Asia has often elided into concrete historical claims of connections between them. The earliest description of the buddha in Chinese, cited above, raises the possibility that he was simply Laozi after he left China for points west. This claim was understandably the subject of heated historical debate, as was the Japanese Heian and Kamakura doctrine of *honji suijaku* that involved the identification of Shinto deities as early manifestations of buddhas.[26] Even within traditions, writers have explained the "inspiration" of particular leaders by the example of a founder as the historical reappearance of a cosmic principle. So it was that Celestial Masters *(tianshi)* Taoists understood Laozi, the buddha, and later foundational members of their own tradition to simply be embodiments of the *dao* in human history.[27] Tendai Buddhists explained differences between sects as the result of "expediencies" used by the buddha that allowed the coexistence of competing doctrines without absolutely denying the truth-value of any of them. In Asia, such historical claims have had a dual function. On one hand, they allowed for a certain amount of jockeying for position between traditions based on the historical primacy of their founding, the relative karmic level of their shared founder, or the contrasting degrees of enlightenment of the audience that received their key teachings. On the other hand, the acknowledgment that the differences between them were of degree and not of kind ultimately meant that these traditions belonged to the same species.

The project of finding commonalities between religious founders has something in common with such projects. Manifestations of an "ideal founder" are avatars of a single archetype — one Hero, just possessed of a thousand faces. As with the early use of the term by Calixtus, promoting syncretism by underlining religious commonalities was often an attempt to reduce the conflict between different groups. One assumption behind many influences on the formation of the field of religious studies, from Ecumenism to Theosophy, has

26. The identification of the buddha as Laozi is treated in Livia Kohn's *Laughing at the Dao: Debates among Buddhists and Taoists in Medieval China* (Princeton: Princeton University Press, 1995). The evolution of the Buddhist-Shinto rapprochement is detailed in Joseph M. Kitagawa, *Religion in Japanese History* (New York: Columbia University Press, 1966), pp. 46-85.

27. Stephen R. Bokenkamp, *Early Daoist Scriptures* (Berkely: University of California Press, 1997), p. 158.

been an essential similarity and hence commensurability between some or all religions. This assumption had something in common with the ahistorical claims of contact between East Asian religious founders outlined above: that differences between religious traditions are not differences in kind.

This is in no way to diminish the goals of such enterprises, but rather to attempt to scrutinize contemporary biographers of religious founders in the same way it seems so easy to do with "traditional" sources. An absolute constructivist position might predict that a contemporary reexamination of religious founders would differ from Weber in ways that mirror the ways that ideas of what constitutes religion have changed since Weber. To the extent that we have seen this happening throughout history (and to the extent that our seeing is not totally dictated by own needs) some version of this position must be true. To borrow the premise of a myriad of contemporary jokes: If Muhammad, Buddha, and Christ were all sitting at a bar, can we say that they have something in common? Well, we can say with certainty that we put them together at the same imagined bar.

Probably much of what I have said will seem obvious to those who have had occasion to reflect on method in comparing religion. It is worth asking why such concerns about the project of comparing religious founders are strongest in the articles in this volume that treat buddha and Confucius. Is this because these cultures have room for the notion that the teachings of particular sages or the *dharmas* of particular buddhas may not apply to all times or all cultures? Is it because it is more acceptable to suggest the constructedness of these religious founders? If, as Richard Cohen has suggested, there are multiple buddhas, and, as I have tried to point out, different communities have constructed different Confuciuses, then the step of singling out the particular figures in this volume as "religious founders" has to some extent affected the possible outcomes of such a comparative project. While the magnitude of this effect is a matter that needs exploration, these considerations should at least demonstrate that the study of religious founders must focus on both biography and biographer.

Final Thoughts of Daniel C. Peterson

It is deeply unfashionable these days to hold to anything like "the now discredited great man theory of history," as Professor McClymond terms it.[28] Nonetheless, I'm reluctant to let that theory go altogether. Muhammad is one of the prime examples cited in Thomas Carlyle's famous *On Heroes, Hero-Worship and the Heroic in History* (1841), the book that most famously gave explicit voice to the theory. Indeed, Muhammad was the subject of the second in the se-

---

28. McClymond, "Prophet or Loss?" p. 613.

ries of six 1840 lectures that resulted in the book — and the first real historical character discussed. (Carlyle devoted his first lecture to the Norse god Odin, whom he took to have been a high-achieving mortal man who evolved into a deity as the memory of his mortal career faded.) Michael Hart's relatively recent attempt to list the most influential personalities in human history goes so far as to rank Muhammad first.[29]

It scarcely needs saying that lists of "most influential persons" are highly subjective. (In Hart's catalog, for example, while Muhammad is first, Jesus comes in third after Sir Isaac Newton.) Yet I think that Hart's ranking of Muhammad, while it is eminently debatable, is also entirely plausible. Despite his many disadvantages — among them poverty, social marginality, geographical and cultural isolation, poor education, and lack of contact with any important, established political center — it is arguable that, as Hart contends, Muhammad was "the only man in history who was supremely successful on both the religious and secular levels."[30] And Hart is surely correct in observing that,

> Of many important historical events, one might say that they were inevitable and would have occurred even without the particular political leader who guided them. For example, the South American colonies would probably have won their independence from Spain even if Simón Bolívar had never lived. But this cannot be said of the Arab conquests. Nothing similar had occurred before Muhammad, and there is no reason to believe that the conquests would have been achieved without him.[31]

In the study of Islam, the late Marshall G. S. Hodgson contended persuasively against any scheme of historical periodization that focuses too much on prominent individuals, and particularly on rulers.[32] Such individuals, he noted, often come and go without really having much impact on the way life is lived or society is organized. Although they are easily visible, and although they have often preened themselves on their importance, monarchs and government ministers can seldom be categorized among the most fundamental forces of history; relatively impersonal technological advances and economic phenomena (e.g., the stirrup, new configurations of nautical sails, the printing press, gunpowder, the influx of New World gold into Europe after Columbus) have often had far

29. See Michael H. Hart, *The 100: A Ranking of the Most Influential Persons in History* (New York: Hart Publishing, 1978).

30. Hart, p. 33.

31. Hart, pp. 39-40.

32. Notably in Marshall G. S. Hodgson, *The Venture of Islam: Conscience and History in a World Civilization*, vol. 1: *The Classical Age of Islam* (Chicago and London: University of Chicago Press, 1974).

greater impact. Accordingly, Hodgson was concerned to identify and analyze what he called "circumstances of hominid natural and cultural ecology." Yet even he noted that

> such ecological circumstances merely set the limits of what is possible. Within those limits, the personal vision has its opportunity. For when habitual, routine thinking will no longer work, it is the man or woman with imagination who will produce the new alternatives. At this point, the concerned conscience can come into play. It may or may not prove adequate to the challenge. But in either case, it is such personal vision that is the most human part of human history.[33]

Clearly, in our post-Darwinian age, we are more inclined than Carlyle and many early historians to recognize continuities-in-evolution, process, and less inclined, perhaps, to think in terms of seemingly unchanging Aristotelian essences or substances. But we should be wary, it seems to me, of overcorrection. And we should realize that even evolutionary theory itself is now having to reckon with such notions as "punctuated equilibrium," wherein long periods of stasis are suddenly invaded by unlooked-for change. What is manifestly needed is a dialectical approach to the role of individuals in history, one that recognizes both their originality and their conventionality, their culture-boundedness but also their power as agents of change.

In this respect, Professor McClymond's proposal to reexamine Weber's theory of religious leadership in its aspects of reaffirmation, radicalization, ritualization, and responsiveness seems to me both right and promising.

With regard to reaffirmation, I tried in my essay to illustrate the strong elements of continuity between Muhammad and the traditions of pre-Islamic Arabia. I completely agree with McClymond that there can be no firm or final distinction between the religious founder and the religious reformer. The two terms are not synonymous, but they do significantly overlap. Muhammad, for instance, would have been horrified at the thought that what he brought was something new.[34] In his view, he was simply restoring the religion of Adam, Abraham, Moses, and Jesus.

And yet, Muhammad's mission manifests an unmistakable radicalizing aspect as well, whether he recognized it or not. Had he simply taught the "old

33. Hodgson, *The Venture of Islam*, 1:26.

34. By and large, antiquity did not value originality. For example, Plotinus, the effective founder of the philosophical movement we call Neoplatonism (his teacher Ammonius Saccas, the other candidate for the role of "founder," wrote nothing by which we can evaluate his role), would have been offended at the prefix *neo-*. He believed he was merely expounding Platonism.

time religion" — whether Arabian polytheism or even some form of Judeo-Christianity — had there not been substantial discontinuity between Muhammad and the traditions he received, he would merit, at most, a footnote in human history. One might think here of certain writers known for their remarkably fresh and novel use of language (e.g., James Joyce and Gerard Manley Hopkins). If there had been no continuity between their language and that of their audience, there would have been no communication whatever. They would soon have been forgotten, if not institutionalized. If the continuity had been total, they would have been forgotten just the same, because there would have been nothing new and memorable about them. But the potential range of allowable/required discontinuity is almost infinitely varied. In the matter of religious history, this is the spectrum along which, with no clear line of demarcation, reform blends into prophetic revolution.

One of the areas of greatest weakness in Weber's theory involves what McClymond calls "ritualization." As Professor Csikszentmihalyi observes, "Weber overlooked the genuinely religious dimensions of the fifth century B.C.E. master-disciple group headed by Confucius, specifically its recourse to the immanent order of *tian* ('Heaven') and the reflection of that order in the ritual system."[35] "While modern thinkers generally take ritual to be an aspect of culture," McClymond comments, "for Confucius it had a great deal to do with Heaven."[36] Perhaps because he was surrounded in northern Europe by a Protestantism that emphasized preaching and moral instruction, and by a Reform Judaism in the process of dispensing with ancient practices, Weber was culturally ill-equipped to recognize the centrality of ritual in various religions.[37]

Surely, as I attempt to show in my essay on Muhammad, Weber's insistence on an essential opposition between priests and prophets is overdone. Muhammad himself seems to have come from what can without too much injustice be termed a priestly line. And the rituals that he inherited and repristinated at the Ka'ba, and that he made central in every way to the religion of Islam, indisputably represent a regularly organized and permanent enterprise associated with a particular place — in Weber's view, the hallmarks of priestliness.

In fact, the Ka'ba and its attendant rituals appear to have their roots in very ancient Semitic notions, and, at least as Muhammad's disciples understood them, to reflect the order of heaven. Traditionally, Muslims have claimed

35. Csikszentmihalyi, "Confucius," p. 298.
36. McClymond, "Prophet or Loss?" p. 646.
37. The pendulum may now be swinging back. John W. Welch, *Illuminating the Sermon at the Temple and Sermon on the Mount* (Provo: Foundation for Ancient Research and Mormon Studies, 1999), even argues for a connection with ritual in the case of that seemingly most purely ethical of exhortations, the Sermon on the Mount.

that God built the original Kaʻba in the days of Adam on the model of the divine residence above. Worshipers in the earthly Kaʻba are thought to be engaged in the same activity as the angels on the celestial plane.[38] Islam has been a notable creator of sacred spaces, not only in the Kaʻba itself but in thousands of ordinary mosques, where visitors' shoes must be removed as they enter in upon holy ground.[39] Non-Muslims — "Gentiles," as it were — are barred from the Kaʻba and, indeed, from the city of Mecca altogether, but also from certain other mosques (such as Sayyidna Husayn in Cairo).

Finally, we come to consider what Professor McClymond has called "responsiveness." "Taken at face value," McClymond writes, "Weber's idea of charisma might suggest that the founder is an individual who retires to the desert, mountain, or forest, and then — perhaps after arduous self-discipline and reflection — returns with a new teaching. The message is already a finished product." But this idea is incorrect. It sounds much more like Nietzsche's fictionalized Zarathustra than it does any of the historical founders discussed in this book. "It is important," McClymond points out, "to note how much of the teaching of the five founders is given in dialogical form."[40]

This is certainly crucial in considering the career of Muhammad. As I have tried to show, many of the revelations of the Qurʾan, if not indeed all of them, can be correlated with events in his life to which they respond. The Qurʾanic revelation did not arrive all at once. It was dictated over the span of nearly a quarter of a century. Moreover, we must consider the so-called *hadith*, the reports of Muhammad's *ad hoc* sayings and actions and replies to questions, which are firmly tied to specific stories, incidents, challenges, issues, and crises, and which form the basis of much of Islamic law. Officially, the canonical *hadith* collections rank below the Qurʾan as a source of Islamic doctrine and practice. In actual fact, however, given the frequent opacity of the Qurʾanic oracles, the *hadith* often play a primary role in settling disputed questions and establishing consensus.

38. For a good, brief summary statement on the ancient and heavenly counterparts to the Kaʻba, see Gaye Strathearn and Brian M. Hauglid, "The Great Mosque and Its Kaʻba as an Islamic Temple Complex in Light of Lundquist's Typology of Ancient Near Eastern Temples," in *The Temple in Time and Eternity*, ed. Donald W. Parry and Stephen D. Ricks (Provo: Foundation for Ancient Research and Mormon Studies, 1999), pp. 275-302 (especially 285-88). Compare Helmer Ringgren, *The Faith of Qumran: Theology of the Dead Sea Scrolls*, expanded ed., trans. Emilie T. Sander, ed. James H. Charlesworth (New York: Crossroad, 1995), pp. 217, 228, which says that, among those who produced the Dead Sea Scrolls, the liturgy of the Temple or of Qumran itself was thought to have its precise counterpart in a heavenly Temple, and that the angels who led the worship in heaven were also expected to participate in the ceremonies of their earthly community.

39. Compare Exodus 3:5.

40. McClymond, "Prophet or Loss?" p. 650.

Professor McClymond writes that, "in a manner of speaking, one could say that Moses and Confucius and the others were shaped by their respective communities just as the communities were shaped by the founders."[41] This is certainly true of Muhammad, but not only with respect to the *hadith*. As McClymond says in another context, "Once we recognize the degree to which the narratives of the founders are constructed by the religious communities devoted to their memory, it is no longer possible to read these narratives in a naive or uncritical fashion."[42]

Some years ago, Patricia Crone and Michael Cook published a radically revisionist account of the origins of Islam. Although their theory has not, so far as I can see, carried the day, they sounded an important alarm that cannot be lightly ignored. "Virtually all accounts of the early development of Islam," they noted,

> take it as axiomatic that it is possible to elicit at least the outlines of the process from the Islamic sources. It is however well-known that these sources are not demonstrably early. There is no hard evidence for the existence of the Koran in any form before the last decade of the seventh century, and the tradition which places this rather opaque revelation in its historical context is not attested before the middle of the eighth. The historicity of the Islamic tradition is thus to some degree problematic: while there are no cogent internal grounds for rejecting it, there are equally no cogent external grounds for accepting it. In the circumstances it is not unreasonable to proceed in the usual fashion by presenting a sensibly edited version of the tradition as historical fact.

This verdict is a comfort to me, because such is the approach that I have taken in this book. However, Crone and Cook go on to remark,

> But equally, it makes some sense to regard the tradition as without determinate historical content, and to insist that what purport to be accounts of religious events in the seventh century are utilisable only for the study of religious ideas in the eighth.[43]

41. McClymond, "Prophet or Loss?" p. 656.
42. McClymond, "Prophet or Loss?" p. 617.
43. Patricia Crone and Michael Cook, *Hagarism: The Making of the Islamic World* (Cambridge: Cambridge University Press, 1980), p. 3. "The only way out of the dilemma," they suggest, "is thus to step outside the Islamic tradition altogether and start again." They recommend reconstructing early Islamic history and belief on the basis of early discussions of Islam in seventh-century Christian documents from the Near East (chiefly in Syriac). Here, unfortunately, I grow nervous. I offer a personal observation, from within my

The simple fact is that even the ancient documents through which we see Muhammad today already represent interpretative portraits of him, shaped by a century or two of reflection and by the theological and political conflicts that ravaged the Islamic community after his death. Just as his message was molded by his interaction with the believers and unbelievers of his day, so too was it molded and filtered by the interactions of the next few generations of Muslim disciples with what they had inherited from him. A dialectical approach is necessary. In crucial ways, it is inevitable and unavoidable.

Neither the "great man theory of history" nor Weber's concept of religious leadership is altogether wrong, in my view. Both, however, are in substantial need of balancing perspective. Thus, I see a proper response to this complex question as, in Professor McClymond's terms, both reaffirming and radicalizing. Beyond that, although I'm not sure how or whether we academics should be in the business of ritualization, I surely hope that this discussion will prove a useful part of an ongoing, expanding, mutually responsive dialogue.

---

own religious tradition: A colleague, a Latter-day Saint or "Mormon" who specializes in the history of early Egyptian Christianity, once remarked, after reading several "outsider" accounts of Mormonism, that he despaired of ever really understanding, say, Ophite Gnosticism. Some of the authors whose work he had been reading were admittedly hostile, but many were making a real effort to "get it right." If, he asked, they could so fundamentally misapprehend a modern faith represented by accessible living adherents and by intact texts in a major and fully understood modern tongue, what were the chances of his ever really understanding a long-dead faith through fragmentary texts in an only partially understood language? Similarly, I cannot bring myself to rely wholeheartedly on even seventh-century documents about Islam, if they were written by hostile outsiders who didn't know Arabic. How far can we really trust the early Christian heresiographers, even in intra-Christian matters?

Contributors

Richard S. Cohen is Assistant Professor of South Asian Religious Literatures at the University of California, San Diego. He was educated at the University of Michigan and took his Ph.D. there in 1995. His research focuses upon the social history of Indian Buddhism, especially as found in the fifth-century C.E. Buddhist monasteries located at Ajanta. His articles can be found in *History of Religions, Journal of the American Academy of Religion,* and *Indo-Iranian Journal.* Currently he is researching and writing a book-length study of ancient Indian Buddhism as a modern artifact, tentatively entitled *Beyond Enlightenment.*

After earning an AB in East Asian Languages and Literatures at Harvard and a Ph.D. in Asian Languages at Stanford, **Mark Csikszentmihalyi** joined the Department of Religion at Davidson College. He currently teaches in the Religious Studies Program and the East Asian Languages and Literature Department at the University of Wisconsin at Madison. He is co-editor of *Religious and Philosophical Aspects of the Laozi* (SUNY Press) and is completing a manuscript called *Material Virtues: Ethics and Natural Philosophy in Early China.* He is editor of the Texts and Translations series published by the American Academy of Religion, a member of the editorial board of Early China, and part of the Research Group on Newly Excavated Manuscripts at Tokyo University.

Carl S. Ehrlich received his BA (1976) in Judaic Studies from the University of Massachusetts at Amherst and his MA (1984) and Ph.D. (1991) in Near Eastern Languages and Civilizations from Harvard University. He is currently an Associate Professor of Hebrew Bible in the Division of Humanities at York University (Toronto). He has also taught at Oberlin College and Vassar College, as well as at the Hochschule für Jüdische Studien (Heidelberg), the Kirchliche Hochschule (Wuppertal), and the Humboldt University (Berlin) in Germany. Professor Ehrlich has authored *The Philistines in Transition: A History from ca. 1000-730 B.C.E.* (1996), in addition to numerous articles in the *Journal of Biblical Literature,* the *Zeitschrift des deutschen Palästina-Vereins, European Judaism, Trumah, Foi et vie,* the *Anchor Bible Dictionary,* the *Oxford Companion to the Bible,* and others. He is co-director of the Tell es-Safi/Gath Archaeological Project and lives in Toronto with his wife, Rabbi Michal Shekel, and their two sons. He is an opera fanatic and a die-hard Red Sox fan.

David Noel Freedman holds graduate degrees from Princeton Theological Seminary (M.Div.) and Johns Hopkins University (Ph.D.). He has held faculty positions and endowed chairs at Western Theological Seminary in Pittsburgh/Pittsburgh Theological Seminary (1948-64), San Francisco Theological Seminary (1964-71), the University of Michigan (1971-92), and the University of California, San Diego (1985-). He was also a professor at Graduate Theological Union (1964-71) and a visiting professor at numerous institutions. Dr. Freedman is a prolific author and editor. He is the author of nine books and co-author of another sixteen books, as well as the author of several hundred articles. He is the editor of the Anchor Bible Project, the Eerdmans Critical Commentary series, and the Bible in Its World series (Eerdmans), as well as many other volumes. Dr. Freedman has also served as editor of the *Journal of Biblical Literature,* the *Bulletin of the American Schools of Oriental Research,* and *Biblical Archaeologist.*

Michael J. McClymond was educated at Northwestern University (B.A. in Chemistry), Yale University (M.Div.), and the University of Chicago (M.A. in Religion, Ph.D. in Theology). He is Assistant Professor of American Religion at Saint Louis University, having previously taught at Wheaton College (Illinois), Westmont College, and the University of California, San Diego. His book, *Encounters with God: An Approach to the Theology of Jonathan Edwards* (Oxford, 1998), received the Brewer Prize (for best first book in the history of Christianity) from the American Society of Church History. His articles and reviews have appeared in *The Journal of Religion, Journal of the American Academy of Religion, Religious Studies Review, Church History, Scottish Journal of Theology, Theology Today, Theological Studies, Journal of the History of Modern Theology,* and other periodicals. He has recently received grants from the John Templeton Foundation and The Louisville Institute. When not engaged in scholarship, he plays rhythm and lead guitar in "The Unlikely Blues Band," a six-member combo that performs regularly in the St. Louis area.

CONTRIBUTORS

Following studies in classics, philosophy, and Near Eastern history in the United States, Israel, and Egypt, **Daniel C. Peterson** earned a doctorate in Arabic and Persian at UCLA. Author of numerous books and papers on both Islamic and Mormon subjects, Peterson is associate professor of Islamic studies and Arabic at Brigham Young University in Utah, edits the Islamic Translation Series, and directs the Center for the Preservation of Ancient Religious Texts (CPART). Recent works include the book *Abraham Divided: An LDS Perspective on the Middle East* and articles on such topics as "'Ye are Gods': Psalm 82 and John 10 as Witnesses to the Divine Nature of Humankind," "The Throne Theophany/Prophetic Call of Muhammad," "Al-Kirmani on the Divine *Tawhid*," "Nephi and His Asherah: A Note on 1 Nephi 11:8-23," "Hamid al-Din al-Kirmani on Creation," "Neoplatonism and the Medieval Mediterranean Magical Traditions," and "Does the Qur'an Teach Creation *Ex Nihilo*?"

Index